Nations under God

Nations under God

HOW CHURCHES USE MORAL AUTHORITY TO
INFLUENCE POLICY

Anna Grzymała-Busse

PRINCETON UNIVERSITY PRESS

Princeton and Oxford

Copyright © 2015 by Princeton University Press
Published by Princeton University Press, 41 William Street, Princeton, New
Jersey 08540
In the United Kingdom: Princeton University Press, 6 Oxford Street, Woodstock,
Oxfordshire OX20 1TW
press.princeton.edu

Jacket photograph: The Lord Mayor of Dublin greets the Cardinal Legate at the
City Gates, 1932, from *The 31st International Eucharistic Congress Pictorial
Record* (Veritas, 1933). Image courtesy of the General Research Division,
The New York Public Library, Astor, Lenox and Tilden Foundations.

Library of Congress Cataloging-in-Publication Data

Grzymała-Busse, Anna Maria, 1970–
    Nations under God : how churches use moral authority to influence policy /
Anna Grzymała-Busse.
        pages cm
    Includes bibliographical references and index.
    ISBN 978-0-691-16475-5 (hardback)—ISBN 978-0-691-16476-2
(paperback) 1. Christianity and politics. 2. Church and state. 3. Democracy—
Religious aspects—Christianity. 4. Nationalism—Religious aspects—
Christianity. I. Title.
    BR115.P7G79 2015
    261.7—dc23
                                                                2014037857

British Library Cataloging-in-Publication Data is available
This book has been composed in Sabon LT Std
Printed on acid-free paper. ∞
Printed in the United States of America

10 9 8 7 6 5 4 3 2 1

For Casimir and Julian

Contents

Figures

Tables

Acknowledgments

I HAVE BEEN VERY LUCKY in writing this book. I am extremely grateful for the careful readings and thoughtful comments I received at workshops and presentations at Arizona State University, University of Chicago, University of California–Los Angeles, Columbia University, European University Institute, University of Florida, Florida International University, Georgetown University, George Washington University, University of Illinois, Harvard University, the Juan March Institute, Northwestern University, Princeton University, University of Toronto, Woodrow Wilson International Center for Scholars, and Yale University.

Margaret Levi and Kathy Thelen organized a fantastic book workshop at Brown University; along with Yelena Biberman, Sigrun Kahl, Rick Locke, Nazar Mammedov, and Jim Morone they carefully read the manuscript and provided invaluable engagement and criticism. As anyone who knows her can attest, Margaret is a wonderful mentor, editor, and thinker. I am so grateful for all her support and advice over the years. Peter Hall and Kathy gave me very wise advice exactly when I needed it. Many thanks go to Dario Gaggio, Timothy Heaton, Ignacio Sanchez-Cuenca, Andrew Muldoon, and Carolyn Warner for their readings and the comments, suggestions, and critiques of many aspects of the argument. And finally, Dan Slater and Monika Nalepa lent me their considerable wisdom in the final stages of this project.

At Michigan, I am very grateful for colleagues and friends who have enriched and improved not only my work. Bill Clark, Allen Hicken, Pauline Jones Luong, Rob Mickey, and Geneviève Zubrzycki all read the manuscript and made an enormous difference both in their comments and in their friendship. Pauline kindly agreed to organize a conference on "Religion, Identity, and Politics" with me at Michigan in 2013—and always provided a sounding board and wise advice. Bill taught me a great deal about religion, formal theory, and the importance of asset mobility. My colleague and neighbor Ron Inglehart generously shared World Values Survey data. Conversations with Jenna Bednar, Skip Lupia, and Scott Page were singularly inspiring. I presented parts of this project at the Center for Political Studies, the Research in Political Science Workshop, and at the Weiser Center for Emerging Democracies (WCED) at the University of Michigan; one could hardly hope for lovelier set of colleagues or a better home audience. WCED and its fantastic staff, led by Marysia Ostafin, made it possible to write this book while directing an academic center.

I am especially grateful to Dustin Gamza, David T. Smith, Seth Wolin, and Hanlin Yang for their excellent research assistance, and to Timm Betz for his work on the formal model. Dawn Hall and Alexa Stevenson read and edited much of the book and made it far more readable. A special thanks goes to Mathias-Philippe Badin for his artwork.

At Princeton University Press, my thanks go to Eric Crahan, for expertly guiding the project and answering my many questions, and to Eric Henney and Mark Bellis, for preparing the manuscript for publication.

This book could not have been written without the love, patience, and constant distraction of my family. I am grateful to my parents and brothers for their love and for inspiring a lifelong interest in religion. My husband, Josh Berke, is a constant source of love, intellectual rigor, and a steady stream of inside jokes. Our oldest son, Conrad, began to read the manuscript in its first draft, but it had too few pictures and not enough swords. Our younger sons, Casimir and Julian, were born while I was working on this book and grew up with it; and so it is dedicated to them.

Nations under God

CHAPTER 1

Introduction

THE PUZZLES OF RELIGIOUS INFLUENCE ON POLITICS

IN LATE 1988, A GROUP of Catholic bishops met privately with communist officials in a Polish parliamentary commission. Their purpose: to discuss a legislative proposal that would outlaw abortion.

Abortion was legal in communist-era Poland, but the regime was beginning to crumble, and the communist government hoped the proposal would divide its resurgent opposition. For the church, eliminating abortion was not a new priority, but an especially timely one—the hierarchy was keenly aware that public attention was elsewhere, focused on possible regime change and the Round Table negotiations between the opposition and the communist regime. And so, over the next few months, bishops and church lawyers drafted a bill that would unconditionally ban abortion in all circumstances and impose jail sentences on both patients and doctors for violation of the law. Parliamentary discussion of the proposed legislation began in May 1989, only a month before the communists were swept from power. Despite widespread public opposition (59% of Poles opposed the restrictions), the church bill remained the unquestioned basis for all subsequent debate in the democratic parliament, and for the final abortion law of January 1993.[1]

The procedure was now limited to cases in which the mother's life was threatened, testing indicated severe and irreversible damage to the fetus, or the pregnancy was due to rape or incest. The law also required a consensus of doctors that one of the conditions had been met, and doctors commonly disagreed upon what constituted a threat to the mother's life or severe and irreversible damage to the fetus. What's more, in 1991 the National Association of Physicians forbade its members from performing the procedure, making the required consensus virtually unattainable. As a result of this law, the number of *legal* abortions performed annually in Poland fell a thousandfold, from over 100,000 in 1988, to only 312 a decade later. The official abortion rate plunged from 18% to 0.07% of all

---

[1] Gowin 1995, 104ff.

pregnancies. And today, despite legal challenges and unfavorable rulings by the European Court of Human Rights—in Polish cases involving the denial of abortion to a woman facing blindness as a result of pregnancy, and a fourteen-year-old victim of rape—the law remains unchanged. The Roman Catholic Church had effectively banned abortion in democratic Poland.

Churches[2] embody the sacred and the divine, but their interests and influence extend well beyond the spiritual realm. Many countries are "nations under God," where churches are powerful political actors, shaping policy and transforming lives in the process. This book explores how and why some churches gained such enormous political power—and why others did not. It argues that churches ironically gain their greatest political advantage when they can appear to be above petty politics—exerting their influence in secret meetings and the back rooms of parliament rather than through public pressure or partisanship. A church's ability to enter these quiet corridors of power depends on its historical record of defending the nation—and thus gaining moral authority within society and among politicians.

Church influence on policy varies widely from country to country. In some democracies, churches have succeeded in couching political debates in religious terms, vetting government appointments, and influencing legislation in domains ranging from education to abortion to the drafting of constitutions. In Poland, the Roman Catholic Church has achieved most of its policy goals, including the effective ban on abortion. The church is a major political figure. Priests have blessed soccer games—and they helped ensure Poland's entry into the European Union in 2004.

But in other countries, religious representatives have been roundly ignored—or even castigated, by politicians and commentators alike, for even voicing their concerns. When in 2010 the Canadian Cardinal Marc Ouellet expressed his opposition to abortion (a stance the Roman Catholic Church has consistently advocated for decades) the public reaction in Canada was furious, with physicians declaring themselves "blue with rage" and one columnist wishing the Cardinal a "long and painful death."[3] Ouellet's public comments—condemning the legality of abortion and indicating disapproval of government funding to clinics performing the procedure—were rejected as a wildly inappropriate attempt to influence state affairs.

---

[2] Since the focus of this book is on organized religion in predominantly Christian democracies, I refer to these denominations and organizations as "churches." References to a "church" further mean its elites: the religious leaders, such as bishops, pastors, spokesmen, etc., rather than the vast masses of the faithful, whose views are considerably more nuanced and diverse than the hierarchy's. Allies and proxy organizations are also identified separately.

[3] Gagnon 2010.

Surprisingly, stark differences in the extent of religious influence persist across countries that are otherwise similar in patterns of religious belonging, belief, and attendance. For example, Ireland and Italy are both "Catholic societies," with close to 90% of the population identifying as Catholic. Yet the Roman Catholic Church in Ireland influenced the public debate and the eventual laws concerning abortion, divorce, and education far more (and for far longer) than it did in Italy, where the church has been markedly less influential, at times struggling against a tide of political opposition and popular indifference. Similarly, while the Roman Catholic Church in newly democratic Poland heavily influenced policy, the church in—equally Catholic—newly democratic Croatia failed to limit abortion (much less abolish it), forestall civil unions for gays, restrict stem cell research, or constrain divorce. If anything, religiosity in Croatia *increased* over the 1990s, with rates of "firm believers" doubling from around 40% in 1989 to nearly 80% in 2004;[4] yet religious influence on policy actually *decreased*, with many politicians openly opposing the enacting of church preferences.

We also see disparities in church influence in more diverse religious settings. Both the United States and Canada have relatively high rates of belief and attendance, especially when compared to other developed democracies (96% of Americans and 90% of Canadians believe in God, and 49% and 36%, respectively, attend church more than once a month). Both are over two-thirds Christian, with a large Roman Catholic minority. Yet the degree to which religion has influenced policy differs dramatically. In the United States, religion has become a central political cleavage,[5] and conservative Catholic and Protestant religious groups made considerable inroads toward their policy goals, especially in curtailing access to abortion, contraception and sex education, and stem cell research.[6] In Canada, in contrast, public policy debates are rarely framed in religious terms, even when the policies in question have moral overtones and stand in clear opposition to religious doctrines. Despite the efforts of the Catholic Church and conservative Christian groups, abortion, for example, was not restricted and did not become a dominant political issue, at either the elite or popular levels. Table 1.1 summarizes some of these differences in influence.

Just as curiously, churches' influence upon democratic politics often occurs despite broad opposition from the public. As Table 1.2 shows, in all the countries mentioned above, over two-thirds of survey respondents

[4] Jerolimov and Zrinščak 2006, 282.

[5] Layman and Carmines 1998.

[6] In contrast, the mainstream Protestant churches not only lost members but also were unable to either resolve their internal conflicts over issues such as gay rights or mobilize effectively in their pro-choice stances in the 1970s and 1980s.

TABLE 1.1.
Church Influence on Policy Outcomes

	Ireland	Italy	Poland	Croatia	USA	Canada
Abortion?[1]	Yes	No	Yes	No	Yes	No
Divorce?	No[2]	No	No	No	No	No
Religion in schools?[3]	Yes	Yes	Yes	Yes	No	Yes
Stem cell research?	Yes	Yes	Yes	No	Yes	No
Same-sex marriage?	Yes	Yes	Yes	Yes	Yes	No

Church Influence on Policy Debates

	Ireland	Italy	Poland	Croatia	USA	Canada
Abortion?	Yes	No	Yes	No	Yes	No
Divorce?	Yes	No	No	No	No	No
Religion in schools?	Yes	Yes	Yes	Yes	Yes	No
Stem cell research	Yes	Yes	No	Yes	Yes	No
Same-sex marriage?	No	No	Yes	No	Yes	No
Summary Score	8	5	7	4	7	1

Note: Influence on policy outcomes is coded as a yes if changes to policy were compatible with church teachings and justified by the legislator as having a Christian character
or compatible with church teachings. Influence on debates is coded as a yes if churches
were protagonists in the national debate, first to frame the issue in religious terms, and
national legislators then adopted the language.
[1] Abortion is defined as "unrestricted" if abortion is available freely up to twelve weeks
of pregnancy.
[2] Divorce was unconstitutional in Ireland, and this provision was upheld by a 1986
referendum, but it was legalized in 1995 with support of governing party.
[3] Either the state funds religious schools, or mandatory religion/ ethics classes are
taught in public schools.

reject church influence on voting, and over half reject influence on politics
more broadly. Figure 1.1 shows that this opposition is widely shared:
majorities in all the polled countries, observant and not, oppose religious
influence on politics. Across a larger set of democracies surveyed, an average of 72% of survey respondents oppose church influence on politics, 78% oppose church influence on voting, and 72% oppose church
influence on government.[7] They do so even where the church is highly

[7] 2005 World Values Survey and 2003 International Social Survey Programme data,
$n = 44$ and $n = 28$, respectively. Standard deviations are 9, 5.4, and 8.1, respectively.

TABLE 1.2.
OPPOSITION TO RELIGIOUS INFLUENCE ON POLITICS

	Ireland	Italy	Poland	Croatia	USA	Canada
% surveyed: religious leaders should *not* influence government	72%	70%	78%	79%	50%	71%
% surveyed: religious leaders should not influence votes	78%	70%	83%	84%	71%	78%

World Values Surveys, Ireland (1999), Italy (2005), Canada (2006), United States (2005), Poland (2005), Croatia (1999). The question was not asked in the 6th wave of WVS, 2008-2011.

influential among individuals:[8] in Ireland, where 93% of the population declares itself to be Catholic and over half attends Mass once a month or more, over 79% of poll respondents do not want the church to influence government, and 82% do not want the church to influence votes.

Even very pious Christian electorates are unlikely to demand religious influence on politics. First, Christianity itself views the sacred and the profane as two distinct domains. Jesus commanded Christians to "render to Caesar the things that are Caesar's, and to God the things that are God's."[9] Second, individual experiences and priorities often conflict with religious tenets: Catholics and Evangelicals still get divorced (and at rates as high or higher than other Americans). As a result, the democratic societies examined here reject church influence on governments, voting, and policy, even when they are religious. Yet churches continue to shape politics even where vast popular majorities oppose such influence.

The odd outcome is that on the one hand, popular religious observance, faith, and belonging *do* in fact correlate with the influence of religion on politics, as we will see; on the other, this religiosity does not create a popular *demand* for religious influence on governments, voting, or policy. In other words, religion and religious influence on politics go

---

[8] An average 50% of respondents wanted the church to have less influence on politics throughout the 1990s and 2000s in Poland, and 78% respondents did not wish the church to be politically active (CBOS. 2007. *Komunikat z Badań*. Warsaw, March 2007). In the United States, 70% of respondents do not want churches to endorse political candidates (Pew Forum on Religion and Public Life 2002). Majorities believe it is wrong for churches to speak out on politics (51%) and for clergymen to address politics from the pulpit (68%) (Pew Forum on Religion and Public Life 2000).

[9] Mark 12:17.

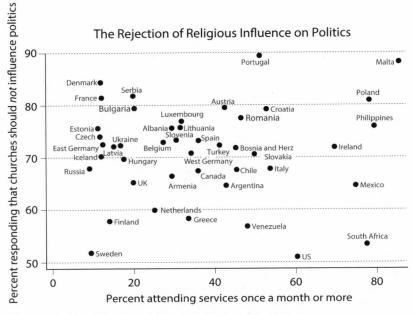

Figure 1.1. The Rejection of Religious Influence on Politics

hand in hand—but not because voters insist upon (or even desire) such influence.

The missing links between religion and religious influence on politics are the churches themselves—churches that serve not just as communities of faith, but as political advocates and actors. Many churches hold strong doctrinal commitments, and their leaders perceive an obligation to ensure that public policy reflects respect for God's order. Divine agendas aside, churches want to ensure their own survival; apart from the obvious benefits of preferential tax and legal status, influencing policy is a way of disseminating and enshrining their religious values, fending off both secularization and potential competitors. Without the active politicking and involvement of the churches, we would be unlikely to see either the legislation of theological preferences into policy, or the broader prominence of religion in politics.

There is nothing new about churches attempting to manipulate public policy. Popes crowned the emperors of the Holy Roman Empire, and Cardinals Richelieu and Wolsey served as advisors to kings in seventeenth-century France and in sixteenth-century England, respectively. With its enormous landholdings and an effective monopoly on education, the Roman Catholic Church in medieval Europe was a singularly powerful political and economic player (and has been accordingly analyzed as such[10]). Whether legitimating monarchs, shaping public morality, exerting control over the welfare state, or simply securing favorable standing under the law, religious groups have a long history of intervention in politics.

Yet in the modern era, churches face considerable constraints on their political activity. Even in predominantly Christian countries, church and state are conceptually two distinct realms, separated by constitutions, legal precedent, and informal norms. Legal and institutional firewalls stymie even powerful churches with pews full of loyal adherents. In most modern democracies, clerics no longer hold secular office, and churches have no formal representation in most legislatures, governments, or administrative bodies. As a result, religious bodies seldom have direct access to policy making. Yet some organized religions continue to exercise considerable influence despite these impediments, while others are left to press their faces against the glass.

Since they cannot directly legislate, churches rely on secular proxies and intermediaries, and specifically, political parties. Churches often trade electoral mobilization on behalf of these secular political actors for subsequent policy concessions. Accordingly, a prominent set of explanations emphasizes the alliances between religious groups and political parties as the critical channel of church influence. These accounts examine electoral coalitions with political parties, asking when churches ally with parties and the policy consequences of these partnerships.[11]

Yet coalitions with particular political parties can be as fraught and unreliable as reliance on public support, as we will see. Political parties and partisan representatives have interests of their own—and these are often much more diverse than (and contradictory to) the interests of churches. Contemporary public opinion, as already noted, is against overt church interference in politics, making attempts to mobilize voters a risky business. Finally, reaching out to the electorate necessitates persuasion and reframing of religious perspectives—and the compromises necessary to gain a broader electorate undermine the churches' own theological commitments, the very ones that led them to press for policy change in the first place. Rather than asking why churches ally with particular parties, perhaps we should ask why churches ally with parties at all.

Explaining Church Influence

We thus face a set of interlocking puzzles: (a) the differences in the influence of organized religion on politics, (b) the peculiar ability of religious

---

[10] See Ekelund et al. 1996.
[11] Castles 1994; Gill 1998; Warner 2000; Htun 2003.

efforts to overcome widespread popular opposition, and (c) the mechanisms of this influence in the face of formal strictures and firewalls.

To answer these questions, this book argues that the most influential churches do not rely on pressure at the ballot box or on partisan coalitions. Instead, these churches gain direct *institutional access*, essentially sharing sovereignty with secular governments. Such access comprises helping to write constitutions and everyday legislation, having direct input into policy making and policy enforcement, vetting secular state officials, and even running entire swaths of government—typically welfare institutions such as hospitals, schools, reformatory institutions, and so on. The channels of institutional access may vary considerably. Besides actively participating in policy discussions and formulating legislative bills (special episcopal commissions, for example, formulated both the abortion law in Poland and school policy in Ireland), church officials have influenced personnel and organizational decisions within ministries (as was the case in Poland and Ireland) and taken part in national negotiations during regime transitions (as was the case in Poland and Lithuania). Institutional access gives churches tremendous political power, while obviating the need to appease an intermediary, whether a partisan ally or their own congregation.

If institutional access is valuable, it is also hard to come by. Not only do substantial legal and institutional impediments block church involvement in state affairs, but secular governments are also loath to share sovereignty, and few politicians willingly give away authority. Still, some churches *do* gain such access. How are they able to do so, and what separates them from the churches that do not?

The roots of present power are buried in the past, and to explain a church's contemporary policy influence, we must look to the historical role of that church in society. Conflicts between the "nation" and its secular opponents gave some churches the opportunity to act as defenders of national identity and cohesion. Where the church shielded the nation, patriotism became inseparable from religious loyalty. In the course of these fierce struggles (and even bloody battles) national and religious identities thus melded, forging a powerful form of religious nationalism.

In turn, the more nation and religion fused as a popular identity, the more churches gained *moral authority* in politics: the identification of the church with national interest, rather than with interests that are purely theological. Fusion is a societal identity; moral authority is a political resource. All churches wield authority over religious matters and morality— where religious and national identity are fused, such churches also gain a particular, *political*, moral authority: a voice in policy debates and a reputation as defenders of broad societal interests, above secular partisanship and petty politicking. Churches with such high moral authority are seen as impartial, trusted, and credible representatives of the *nation*, allowing them to mobilize society beyond purely religious observance and pronouncements. This trust placed in a church does not equate demand for church influence on politics, but it indicates widespread identification of the church with the common good. For example, several Polish bishops acted as both mediators and national representatives during the Round Table negotiations in 1989, and their participation was widely accepted (and sought) by the communist party and by its democratic opposition.

Where, then, do we find the historical origins of this religious nationalism and subsequent moral authority? Churches responded to past national conflicts very differently: the Roman Catholic Church protected national identity and anti-communist dissidents alike in twentieth-century Poland, even as it had opposed national aspirations and democracy in nineteenth-century Italy. As a result, some churches have become far more closely identified with the nation than others. On the one end of the spectrum we have Poland or Ireland, where national identity and religious denomination fused as the Catholic Church sided with the nation against foreign-imposed regimes, whether communist (in Poland) or colonial (in Ireland). On the other end we find countries such as the Czech Republic or France, where national identity consists partly of *rejection* of a religion, as a result of the church siding with a discredited ancien régime, whether the Habsburg Empire or an absolutist monarchy. The United States lies closer to the "fused" end of the spectrum, but with a caveat. On the one hand, American national rhetoric is suffused with religion, such as the "Judeo-Christian ethic"—the postwar articulation of a generally held (if shifting) consensus that to be American is to be religious. The majority of Americans see atheism as foreign, and welcome religion as a source of moral values important in public policy and as a critical personal characteristic of their political representatives (a candidate's atheism would make over 60% of Americans less likely to vote for him or her).[12] On the other hand, American religious diversity means that no one religion can claim credibly to speak for the nation—or present a coherent set of policy demands. Influence on policy then necessitates the formation of alliances among denominations, vulnerable to internal theological differences and subject to the vagaries of political coalitions.

These different levels of fusion then foster corresponding levels of moral authority, which gives churches indirect and direct influence over policy. First, the more religious and national identities fuse, and the greater churches' moral authority, the more *all* politicians are wary of offending organized religion. Given their standing as trusted guardians of the national interest, churches can portray opposition as anti-patriotic. As a result, few politicians dare to criticize the church for fear of condemnation from the pulpit and backlash at the ballot box. Anxiously anticipating the churches' reaction, many politicians will formulate policy with

---

[12] Pew Forum on Religion and Public Life 2008.

church preferences in mind, even without any active politicking by the churches themselves. For their part, churches try to frame policy domains they consider important as moral issues—not merely as matters of doctrinal significance, but as crucial underpinnings of national moral character. When religious and national identities are fused, such framing resonates with the public—and even more so with anxious politicians.[13] As a result, once the churches frame issues as moral imperatives, they can indirectly influence policy outcomes—regardless of which political party or secular politician is in power.

At lower levels of moral authority, there are fewer costs to offending religious sensibilities. The looser the alignment between nation and religion, the harder it is for churches to frame policy as a moral or religious issue, and the less likely it is that any attempts at such framing will resonate with the broader public. Churches are unable to rely upon the anticipatory anxiety of politicians, and politicians have greater freedom to pursue anti-clerical constituencies and agendas, without the fear of being painted by the church as enemies of national identity, and incurring the resultant electoral backlash. When moral authority is low, indirect influence is both unlikely and unreliable.[14]

Churches can also *directly* invest their moral authority, for instance by explicitly endorsing a particular political candidate or party. Here, they have to be careful; moral authority rests on the notion that churches represent *national* interests and identity, and churches are at their most influential when they appear above partisanship and petty politics. Electioneering and coalitions with political parties are explicitly (and publicly) partisan affairs, undermining that authority and soiling the churches' reputations. Churches may still obtain policy concessions by campaigning for parties, but because these alliances are explicitly partisan, churches pay a higher price in moral authority, and their influence then rests on the allied party's status. Such reliance on specific parties or politicians is thus costly. It is also risky: churches may campaign on behalf of parties that go on to lose elections.

Churches can instead obtain institutional access to policy making if their moral authority is great enough, and the political situation grave enough. Such access takes a variety of forms: joint commissions, vetting

---

[13] Most research on framing effects focuses on the effects on the public (see Chong and Druckman 2007), but they also apply to uncertain politicians facing powerful societal actors, especially in new, volatile, or unstable democracies.

[14] Where national and religious identities oppose each other, as in the Czech Republic, politicians have little to fear from offending a weak church and pursue their own policy preferences, knowing that offending religious authorities carries few costs. Churches become marginal political players and either do not get involved in politics or fail to attract coalition partners.

of bureaucrats and ministers, policy and legislative consultations, and sharing control over state sectors. This access is usually non-partisan (for example, taking over education), and/or covert (for example, government consultations with church officials). What church influence cannot be, if moral authority is to be preserved, is both partisan (or self-interested) *and* overt.

As a result, institutional access is more palatable to the public, either because it appears to be concerned with national rather than partisan priorities or because most people are unaware of it altogether. Churches retain their reputation as unbiased moral arbiters—and preserve their moral authority, a resource they can then use in the future. In exchange, churches keep societal peace. They defuse potentially explosive political situations, keeping the incumbents in power not by endorsing their politics, but by advocating social quiescence in the name of national stability. Because it is non-partisan, institutional access is also less susceptible to shifting fortunes of political parties. Churches can thus exact not only short-term concessions but also long-term influence over institutions and joint policy making.

It is easy to see why institutional access is so attractive to churches. For their part, all else being equal, secular politicians would prefer coalitions, since sharing sovereignty via institutional access grants the churches not only specific policy concessions but also the authority and ability to gain others. Institutional access tends to multiply in a process familiar to anyone who has seen a bureaucracy burgeon and spill over into policy areas. But for the politicians who grant it, institutional access is often seen as the only way to ensure their survival. It is not a key to securing greater power, but to holding on to power at all.

The case of Poland illustrates how churches can gain access to secular institutions. Under late communism and during the regime transition in Poland, *both* the communist regime and the democratic opposition saw the Roman Catholic Church's moral authority in its role as a national representative as critical to maintaining social stability. The church exploited first the desperation of a threatened communist regime and later the instability of a fledgling democracy to take advantage of a joint state-church parliamentary commission, to formulate policy proposals, to veto government officials, and to subsequently obtain significant policy concessions. Much of this direct (and critical) access was covert; neither the church nor governments called attention to it. The gravest threat of destabilizing social conflict came immediately after the regime transition in 1989, precisely the moment when entire swaths of policies were being reevaluated and reformulated. If they were to preserve the new democratic order, vulnerable politicians felt they had no choice but to accede to church demands—even when the church prioritized its interpretation of natural law over the principles of democratic rule.[15] The fusion of national and religious identities empowered churches not just as moral authorities but also as guarantors of social peace. Church officials could urge patience or nonviolence on moral grounds, and in the interest of preserving national stability. Sharing sovereignty was a small price for the secular actors to pay.

In short, the fusion of national and religious identities on the societal level is a form of religious nationalism that gives rise to and fortifies a church's moral authority—and when that authority is great enough, it becomes a potent political resource that can be parlayed into institutional access, or shared control of the state. Churches with lower moral authority do not have that option and either rely on coalitions or have no influence at all. Figure 1.2 summarizes the relationship between fusion, moral authority, and institutional access.

Once we shift our focus away from popular religiosity to church moral authority, we resolve the puzzle of influence without popular demand. Religiosity, and the fusion of religious and national identities, is necessary for churches to exercise policy influence; popular demand for such influence is not, given mechanisms of influence—like institutional access—that bypass popular involvement entirely. Depending upon the historical roots of national identities, and the role of a church in shaping these identities, the same church can either exercise massive influence on policy or fail to obtain any footholds. We can now also explain differences in political influence among churches as reflecting the differences in the levels of their moral authority and thus the channels of influence available to them.

Focusing on moral authority also explains changes over time, as moral authority is brittle, and can erode. It is a valuable political asset for churches, but one that must be carefully tended and invested. To sustain their moral authority, churches must act as national representatives and as moral agents, in non-partisan and principled ways, respectively. Anything that smacks of partisan politics, church self-interest, or representing narrow interests belies churches' claim to act as *national* representatives. Similarly, defying moral standards set for the faithful through criminal, unethical, or impious behavior has the same effect, undermining the claim of *moral* authority. If churches fail to live up to these standards (which they themselves set out), they lose their moral authority.

This is not to suggest that moral authority is all powerful; even in countries where national and religious identities are strongly fused, individual behavior is frequently at odds with church teaching, and private individual preferences may be still more so. Both Irish and Polish commentators have noted their compatriots' ability to believe one thing and

---

[15] Gowin 1995.

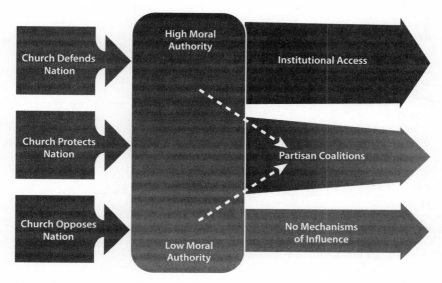

Figure 1.2. Summary of the Argument

Churches that defended the nation against a hostile regime or colonial aggression gain high moral authority. Churches that protected or aided national identity, without necessarily defending it against an alien aggressor, can also gain moral authority. Finally, churches that opposed the nation gain low moral authority. These levels of moral authority then translate into strategies of policy influence: churches with high moral authority gain institutional access, but can also enter partisan coalitions, as indicated by the white dotted lines. Churches that opposed the nation cannot gain institutional access, and generally have low influence: but they, too, can enter partisan coalitions under specific circumstances, indicated by the white dotted lines.

Note that partisan coalitions are an option for churches at most levels of moral authority, depending on how badly the secular political actors need church support and how durable the church's moral authority is.

do another, honed by decades, if not centuries, of living with the strictures of the Catholic Church. What fusion does is to make religion powerful *politically*, in spite of individual disapproval or inconsistent behavior, by reinforcing churches' reputation as national representatives.

Examining Influence in Practice: Countries and Cases

To answer how churches in some countries are able to influence policy, I compare countries that are as similar as possible, eliminate some important confounding factors, and carefully trace the causal processes. First,

TABLE 1.3.
RELIGIOUS PROFILES

	Ireland	Italy	Poland	Croatia	USA	Canada
Belief: % believing in God.	96%	94%	97%	93%	96%	90%
Belonging: % belonging to a religious denomination.	91%	82%	95%	88%	79%	69%
Attendance: % attending services more than once a month	70%–50%[1]	54%	75%	53%	49%	36%
Pluralism: % Catholic	93%	88%	96%	91%	24%	43%

Data on popular attitudes, beliefs, and participation come from the most recent available World Values Surveys, Ireland (1999), Italy (2005), Canada (2006), United States (2005), Poland (2005), Croatia (1999). The CIA Factbook is the source for prevalence of Catholicism.
[1] *The first figure is for the 1990s; the latter for 2010. Church attendance has dropped significantly in the late 1990s.*

three paired comparisons help to unlock the puzzles of religious influence on politics: Ireland and Italy, Poland and Croatia, and the United States and Canada. Second, a formal model demonstrates the logic of church influence on politics, and the conditions under which we see various mechanisms of influence. Third, regression analyses show how countries beyond the six examined in depth demonstrate similar correlations between national identity and church influence. The model and the regressions help to translate the argument about the importance of fusion and moral authority into the language of logic and statistics, and are fully discussed in the Appendix. While references to their results appear throughout, the argument relies chiefly on the paired comparisons, and it is the discussion of these comparisons that makes up the majority of the book.

The paired countries are similar in their rates of religious belonging, belief, attendance, and diversity (as seen in Table 1.3). Importantly, all countries analyzed are ones where church and state have been historically separated, and where churches compete with other groups for policy influence. The argument presented here was not intended to apply to theocracies, or to cases where the formation of the nation-state never allowed for a distinction between religion and politics.

Despite their similarities, these countries vary considerably in the influence that religious authorities have had over policy debates and their eventual outcomes. Each paired study seeks to examine why and how religious and secular actors chose and carried out their particular strategies given the available options, and each of these pairings illustrates a facet of the complex relationships between national-religious fusion, church moral authority, and the channels of policy influence. Chapter 3 presents the starkest comparison: Ireland and Italy. In these established and similarly very Catholic democracies, the role the Catholic Church played in the creation of the nation-state differed dramatically—the Irish church defended the nation in the face of colonial rule, while the Italian one objected to the very founding of Italy. As a result, the Irish and Italian churches had different levels of moral authority and became archetypes of influence via institutional access and influence via partisan coalition, respectively. Poland and Croatia, in contrast, both developed high levels of fusion and moral authority under the communist system, an autocratic regime hostile to religion. Once communism fell, however, these Roman Catholic churches invested their moral authority very differently, and wound up poles apart. The Polish church emerged triumphant and more powerful than ever, while the Croatian church was dragged into a costly and unreliable partisan coalition. This pairing, examined in Chapter 4, further emphasizes the importance of careful stewardship of moral authority on the part of churches and shows how both moral authority, and institutional access itself, can be acquired under autocracy. The final paired comparison, of the United States and Canada, demonstrates how fusion develops (or fails to develop) in religiously diverse societies. Religious pluralism can foster a particular type of diffuse fusion—of nation to religion per se, rather than to any one denomination. In the United States, abstract myths of the religious character of the nation took the place of a particular church in fusing nation to a broad religious sensibility—while in Canada, no such myth took root (with one critical provincial exception). As Chapter 5 argues, the United States can be described as a case of fusion without denominational monopoly, while Canada is a religious oligopoly without fusion (similar to Germany, where two robust religious traditions have precluded an easy identification of nation with a single religion).

Thus these are not randomly chosen cases,[16] but rather ones that maximize the variation within the analytical and geographic boundaries of Western Christianity. These pairings are matched by religiosity, regime type, and economic development, meaning that we cannot simply attribute differences in policy influence or degree of fusion to these factors in these cases. As Table 1.4 shows, relevant aspects of societal and political context are also unlikely to explain the variation. Ethnic diversity is

[16] Fearon and Laitin 2008; Freedman 2008.

TABLE 1.4.
THE SOCIETAL AND POLITICAL CONTEXT

	Ireland	Italy	Poland	Croatia	USA	Canada
Ethnic fractionalization[1]	0.12	0.11	0.12	0.19[2]	0.69	0.67
Religious fractionalization[3]	0.16	0.30	0.17	0.21[4]	0.82	0.70
Church-state regime[5]	Formal separation, informal privilege	Partial establishment: Lateran Pacts	Formal separation, informal privilege	Formal separation, informal privilege	Formal separation	Formal separation[6]
Separation of church and state[7]	4	4	4	4	1	2
State funding of churches[8]	"The state guarantees not to endow any religion" (Art 44, Sec 2), but religious schools publicly funded	0.8% of income tax designated for supporting churches, religious teachers paid by state, exemption from property taxes	Church Fund[9] until 2014: then 0.5% of income tax to support churches, religious teachers paid by state	Some clerical salaries, pensions and health care. Religious teachers paid by state.	"Congress shall make no law respecting an establishment of religion"	Clergy receive tax reductions and minor privileges. Six of ten provinces fund religious schools and pay teachers' salaries.
Federal/unitary	Unitary	Unitary	Unitary	Unitary	Federal	Federal

National referenda	To amend constitution (and to pass bills, but these have not been held.)	To abrogate a law, or to amend constitution	On important matters touching all citizens. Three held after 1989: two in 1996 regarding privatization and government funding and in 1997, the constitution.	On issues within the purview of parliament, or on issues the President considers important for independence, unity, and existence of Republic. Three held: independence in 1991, EU accession in 2013, and gay marriage in 2013.[10]	¾ of states ratify national constitutional amendments. In 25 states, bills can be repealed by referendum, 17 states allow citizen initiated constitutional amendments	Rarely used, three held so far: prohibition (1898), conscription (1942), division of powers (1992)
Political Institutions	PR-STV/ Parliament	PR-SMD/ Parliament	PR/ Parliament	PR/ Parliament	SMD/Presidential	SMD/Parliament

1. Alesina et al, 2002 and Montalvo and Reynal-Querol 2005. Fractionalization indices measure the probability that two randomly selected individuals do not belong to the same group. Higher numbers are interpreted as indicating more diverse societies.

2. Measured in 2003–7, down from 0.37 in 1991, when the Wars of Yugoslav Succession broke out. Nauro Campos, Ahmad Saleh, and Vitaliy Kuzeyev, "Dynamic Ethnic Fractionalization and Economic Growth," mimeo, October 2009.

3. Alesina et al 2002, Campos, Saleh, and Kuzeyev 2009.

4. Measured in 2003–7, down from 0.445 in 1991. See Campos, Saleh, and Kuzeyev 2009.

5. Minkenberg 2003; Kabl 2010.

6. More precisely, state non-interference in religion. The Queen of England is Head of State and Head of Church of England and Defender of Faith in Canada, but Jonathan Fox and the RAS project classify Canada and the United States as having full separation of church and state. Fox 2008.

7. Fox 2008, 48, 114, chap. 6; Minkenberg 2003. Lower values indicate greater separation.

8. US Department of State, 2012. "International Religious Freedom Report for 2012," available at http://www.state.gov/j/drl/rls/irf/religiousfreedom/index.htm#wrapper.

9. The Church Fund was established in 1950 by the communist government to compensate the church for the confiscation of church land holdings. It paid for priests' pensions, to maintain church buildings, and so on.

10. A 50% quorum requirement was dropped in 2012.

similar across the paired comparisons; religious diversity differs, but if proponents of the argument that religious competition makes for stronger, more active churches are right, we should see *more* religious influence in Italy and Croatia than in Ireland and Poland, respectively, while in fact we see quite the opposite. State funding of churches, and broader church-state relations[17] are likewise not responsible for religious influence on politics in these cases; while Catholicism was not formally disestablished as the state church in Italy until 1984, and remains partially established, with special privileges accruing to both clergy and the institution, formal separation between church and state prevails elsewhere. Further, as we will see, the churches themselves have influenced the writing of constitutions and other legal aspects of the church-state relationship, making it difficult to argue that these aspects are the *source* of that influence. The formal legal codification of the church-state relationship is often at odds with reality. In the United States, the strict separation of church and state should make it especially difficult for religious groups to influence policy, and yet the level of religious political influence in the United States is quite high. And while it would be convenient to pin differences in access to channels of policy influence on different forms of governance, proportional representation and parliamentary regimes are found in countries with high and with low levels of religious influence on politics.

These specific pairings also minimize the possibility that a set of previously existing conditions could be responsible for *both* national-religious fusion/subsequent church moral authority *and* religious influence upon policy outcomes. As noted earlier, these pairings make it plain that neither piety nor denominational affiliation explains differences in the level of church influence. The European cases all underwent conversion to Christianity over a thousand years ago, meaning that the denominational framework was in place prior to differences in belief and participation and the foundation of national myths. "Europe" and "Christianity" are not proxies for the role of the churches in shaping policy; the paired countries share these characteristics, so something else must thus be responsible for the (very different) channels and outcomes of church involvement in politics. At the same time, comparison of post-communist and established democracies reveals how differences in regime and historical context affect the opportunities for church influence; for example, the Roman Catholic Church's role in the newly independent Ireland of the early 1920s—before the Vatican II reforms spelled out greater ecumenism and respect for secular institutions—differed greatly from its role in Poland in the aftermath of the communist collapse in 1989.

Furthermore, while the Roman Catholic Church is an important policy actor in these cases, it alone is not responsible for religious influence on pol-

---

[17] Kahl 2014; Minkenberg 2003 and 2013.

icy. It is true that until the twentieth century, the Roman Catholic Church viewed natural law as taking priority over secular law, and actively entered the political arena—supporting certain monarchs and states, fomenting religious wars, and so on—while many Protestant churches deliberately isolated themselves from politics on doctrinal grounds.[18] Yet as American history shows, Protestant churches can also be active political players. Moreover, we find divergent levels of influence among primarily Catholic countries, from Poland, to Italy, to France. These Catholic churches share a formally identical doctrine and a centralized organizational hierarchy that culminates in the Vatican—and the Pope. Nonetheless, the same political actor, the Roman Catholic Church, has had very different levels of impact, both across countries and across policy areas.[19] These policy domains—education, divorce, abortion, stem cell research, and same-sex marriage—are elaborated further in the next chapter. They illustrate how church tactics have varied over time and from place to place—and how church influence on politics is not simply a result of popular piety or religious doctrine, but of a conscious exercise of formidable power.

Implications

This story of fusion, moral authority, and how they open the doors to corridors of secular power recasts several prevailing understandings of religion and politics.

First, scholars have focused on partisan coalitions as the key vehicle for translating church preferences into policy. Yet as we will see, such

[18] The Protestant Reformation did not have the same effect everywhere, and even where it did, no clear consequences followed for policy influence. The Reformation had little impact in Italy, Spain, Poland, and Ireland, yet their subsequent levels of the influence of religion on politics vary.

[19] In all the cases examined, the Catholic churches share theological commitments, many initially developed in the nineteenth century, that support traditional morality: an opposition to abortion or to stem cell research as ending life, a concern with the content of education, an opposition to divorce and to same-sex marriage as negating the true meaning of family (and its role as a basic unit of society). The vehemence with which the church pursued these commitments varies across the countries to some degree, but the biggest changes occurred over time. In the nineteenth century, the Roman Catholic Church simply assumed that natural law trumped civil legislation, and further assumed that it would be the ultimate authority on morality: "the churches could not conceive that civil law could differ from moral law, still less contradict it. They considered themselves guardians of moral law; it was up to legislators to build it into the rule of law which was imposed on everyone" (Rémond 1999, 71). The church has softened this position, especially after the reforms of Vatican II in the 1960s, in that it fully recognizes secular authority and repeatedly asserts that its goal is not the establishment of religion. Nonetheless, in all the cases discussed here, the church not only shares a set of moral preferences but also a willingness to defend them, passionately and vociferously.

alliances are often ineffective and costly. Better options exist for some churches, and those that are able to avail themselves of institutional access are more influential, and for far longer. This quiet access to the state is not the churches' goal alone; business interests, trade unions, and other organizations have all sought it.[20] But in contrast to these interest groups and lobbies, churches gain access and shape policy against the wishes of their own adherents.

Second, an exciting body of research in economics, political science, and sociology has given us new insights into the role of religious competition in creating vibrant religious landscapes. This literature on the "political economy of religion"[21] argues that religious competition unfettered by state regulation, such as the one found in the United States, is the source of religious vigor and religious influence, and religious monopolies are inherently weak—the etiolated creations of state subsidies and fiats.[22] Yet the fusion of national and religious identities can support vibrant religious marketplaces and also sustain powerful religious monopolies, often in the face of state *opposition*.

We thus need a richer account of how nations, states, and religions interact. For example, political economy accounts view the state as a regulator of religious markets that privileges certain religions over others. "State regulation" is inevitably measured as the state support *for* a given church, but not as the *active repression* of denominations. Yet state repression can make national martyrs out of religious bodies—and subsequently powerful political actors. More fundamentally, we simply should not take for granted the "nation-state" as a coherent entity; the political entity may oppose the national aspirations of the people, as communist states were accused of doing.[23] Religion can then protect the nation, defend national interests against a hostile state—and provide resonance to subsequent political claims by religious authorities.

Finally, an august scholarship has mined the histories of nations, and analyzed forces, ranging from the homogenizing effects of "high culture," to notions of "invented tradition" and "ethno-symbolism" that help to create powerful and durable "idioms of nationhood."[24] Yet with a few notable exceptions,[25] this tradition has tended to neglect religion as a source and cement of national identities. This book partly remedies this oversight by focusing on one particular aspect of national identity—the

---

[20] Culpepper 2011; Hacker and Pierson 2010.

[21] Stark and Finke 2000; Gill 1998; Gill 2001; Clark 2010.

[22] Yet, as Olson 2002 points out, it is not clear what level of competition would engender pluralism and vibrancy.

[23] Grzymala-Busse and Jones Luong 2003.

[24] Breuilly 1982; Gellner 1983; Hobsbawm 1990; Smith 1998; Brubaker 1992 and 2004.

[25] Hastings 1997; Smith 2003; Juergensmeyer 2008.

fusion of religion and nation—and how religious nationalism gives the churches such a powerful hand in shaping policy. If scholars of religion have focused on the *social* aspects of religiosity, its diversity, and its ebbs and flows, this book instead examines the *political* manifestations of religion. It explains how churches obtain moral authority and how they can continue to influence politics and retain adherents despite unpopular policies. The key to answering these questions lies in the fusion of national and religious identities and the moral authority it grants the churches.

CHAPTER 2

Weapons of the Meek

HOW CHURCHES INFLUENCE POLICY[1]

> Patriotism and religion are the only two motives in the
> world which can permanently direct the whole of a body
> politic to one end.
>
> —Alexis de Tocqueville, *Democracy in America*, 1831

FOR ALL THEIR CONCERN with the sacred and the divine, churches have
long been adept players at secular politics.[2] Their arsenal of tactics is vast
and includes everything from prayer vigils and mass marches to explicit
politicking on behalf of allied politicians and political parties. Religious
bodies have participated in government commissions, advised individual
politicians—and even, in the case of the Roman Catholic Church, threatened to excommunicate supporters of policies (like abortion) they deem
"sinful." Clergy have used their pulpits to openly denounce specific laws
and the political actors who supported and passed them. In the nineteenth century and in the early twentieth, members of the clergy ran for
office, headed political parties (as Don Luigi Sturzo did in Italy), and
even governed (as the notorious Monsignor Jozef Tiso did in interwar
Slovakia). Churches have used a wealth and breadth of means in search
of political power. What is less clear is how effective these strategies are,
and under what circumstances.

This chapter develops the core argument of this book: that the historical fusion of national and religious identities gives churches moral
authority, a powerful if brittle resource that allows them to influence
political discourse and policy. If plentiful enough, moral authority even
lets churches share secular sovereignty through direct access to state in-

---

[1] With apologies to James C. Scott and Scott 1985.

[2] I assume here that churches care about policy, both on theological and political
grounds (policies may either be sinful or undermine the church's societal standing). For
Catholic churches especially, the desire to influence policy is both exogenous to involvement
in national politics and constant, given the uniform doctrinal interpretations imposed by
the Vatican hierarchy on national churches.

stitutions. I trace how national and religious identities fuse, how churches gain and sustain moral authority, how they channel this authority into policy influence, and why they target the policy domains they do.

How National and Religious Identities Fuse

Religion and nation often go hand in hand. In Irish, *pobal* means both "church" and "people,"[3] and scholars and historians have long noted that both before and after Ireland's independence, "to be Irish was to be Catholic. These were two seamlessly intermeshed identities."[4] In Poland, the more laconic expression "Polak = Katolik" has served as shorthand for the assumption that being Catholic is an obvious and expected aspect of national identity. And in the United States, a "civil religion" has made sacred secular symbols such as national documents, flags, and holidays—while politicians regularly invoke America's "Judeo-Christian tradition" to justify policy as in the national interest.[5] While religious and national identities remain conceptually distinct,[6] such differences are often lost in practice.

The fusion of religious and national identities is a culmination of a process of historical interpretation: the careful tending of national and religious identity at home, in schools, and if possible, in the public conversation. It is a product of favorably homogenous demographics and historical political opportunities. Fusion relies on the notion that a religion stands on the same side as the nation, that when oppression threatened the nation in the past, religion protected national representatives and safeguarded national identity. The "hedge priests" who secretly taught Irish children when the British forbade education by Catholics in the eighteenth century and the Polish clergy who opened their churches to serve as shelters and distribution points for the anti-communist opposition in the twentieth, each contributed to the myth of the heroic church standing up to defend the nation physically and spiritually, even if the reality was far more complex.[7]

[3] Inglis 1998, 42.
[4] Dillon 2007, 240.
[5] Bellah 1967; Moore 2004.
[6] Rogers Brubaker cautions that the admixture of religious and nationalist rhetoric does not mean a full fusion: "languages of religion and nation, like all forms of language, can be intertwined pervasively. But even when the languages are intertwined, the fundamental ontologies and structures of justification differ" (Brubaker 2012, 17). Leah Greenfeld argues that religion and nationalism are not only contradictory concepts, but that religion has become subservient to, and an instrument of, nationalism (Greenfeld 1996).
[7] Thus, for example, it is true that Catholic schools were forbidden in Ireland by the Penal Laws from 1723 to 1782. But these laws chiefly targeted formal Catholic education,

The fusion of national and religious identities is conceptually and empirically distinct from religiosity, whether defined as religious observance, affiliation, or belief.[8] Societies may be deeply religious but fragmented denominationally, so that no church can claim to be a national representative. Moreover, national and religious identities may be experienced as fused even when individual actions and preferences vary. Religious tenets—by their very nature general and absolute—frequently conflict with how many practicing believers act in their private life.[9] As a result, voters have complex private preferences when it comes to religion, and may keep their "real" preferences hidden, for fear of religious ostracism. Fusion is also distinct from the state establishment of churches (or the constitutional separation of church and state); fusion is an identity, an ideological concept, while establishment is a formal state endorsement, an institutional decision.

Constructed by historical interpretation and underpinned by demography, fusion can be a durable "idiom of nationhood," a way of understanding both national identity and national interests.[10] When "religion supplies the myths, metaphors, and symbols that are central to the discursive or iconic representation of the nation"[11] national identity and religion can become so intertwined that "the sense of belonging to the group and confession are fused and the moral issues of the group's history tend to be coded

---

and hedge teachers were even included in the formal census. Still, a powerful historical memory arose of the persecuted Catholic priest secretly teaching, and the "hunted headmaster" sought by bloodhounds who nonetheless "fed to his eager pupils the forbidden fruit of the tree of knowledge" remained a powerful one (McManus 2005 [1921], 461).

[8] See Barker 2009, Layman 1997; Eisenstein 2006; Jelen and Wilcox 2002; Beatty and Walter 1984. *Belief* is an internalized and personal adherence to the doctrine and to the sacred: the personal level and kind of faith, acceptance of church doctrine, and relationship to the deity, the sacred, and religious teachings. Commitment, or *participation*, is activity within the church(es): attending services, evangelizing, meeting with other church members. In many ways, this is a measure of the intensity of religiosity, or the degree to which the believer is willing to sacrifice time and effort in the name of religion. Belonging, or *affiliation*, is a much weaker connection to a religion than participation: in many cases, it is simply self-identification, or a nominal membership. Even though this may be the weakest indicator, it "traditionally has been the only religious variable in studies of political behavior" (Layman 1997, 289). For more on measuring religiosity, see chapter 2 in Leege and Kellstedt 1993.

[9] Further, religious people can be found across the political spectrum, and both Left and Right have used and repackaged religious concepts. Political similarities also cross the religious divide: the European Catholic and Marxist Left both reject pragmatism, both are convinced contemporary society is based on exploitation and injustice that has to be addressed through revolutionary means, and both are committed to political action: "not to defend men as they are, but man as he could be" (Berger 1977, 38).

[10] Brubaker 1992; 2004.

[11] Brubaker 2012, 9.

in religious language."[12] In this "collective imaginary,"[13] religion demarcates the nation, establishes collective norms, and binds society together.

This striking melding of national and religious identities in several countries led several scholars to argue that religious influence on politics and the persistence of religious monopolies are explained by this fusion *tout court*.[14] If national and religious identities are the one and the same, then "heresy becomes a national definition of treachery, and the all-inclusive and automatic inheritance of baptism becomes an all-inclusive inheritance in the holy spirit of the nation and the sacred emblems."[15] Straying away from the true religion is treason, and disloyalty to the nation a grave sin.

As a result, in this view, churches can easily and permanently influence public policy, as politicians scramble to fulfill their obligations to "the nation." Churches inevitably "pass judgment on political realities,"[16] and church support (or acquiescence) is highly sought by politicians; it is, after all, cheaper to rule through ideological legitimation than through patronage or coercion. The more intense and prevalent the religious nationalism, more the churches can manipulate politicians and sway outcomes. Politicians worry about offending religious constituencies, especially where adherents are loyal to a centralized and cohesive church that can easily mobilize its faithful.[17] Opposing religious authorities can be electorally costly and politically deadly. In turn, dominant churches predictably try to influence politics and society; in the language of the political economy of religion, "to the degree that a religious firm achieves a monopoly, it will seek to exert its influence over other institutions and thus society will be sacralized."[18]

It is true that where religion and nation fuse, the payoffs of church support are redoubled, as are the costs of its opposition. Yet this chapter argues for a more nuanced view of the fusion of nation with religion and its consequences, a view in which such religious nationalism is not absolute or binary and exists instead on a spectrum, with correspondingly

[12] Charles Taylor 2007, 458. See also Hastings 1997 and Smith 2003 and 2008. While some scholars in this tradition have emphasized the role of hostile neighbors or religious frontiers in fostering religious nationalism (Barker 2009, 35; Rieffer 2003, 226), I argue a threat alone is not sufficient: we need an account of the *supply* of religious rhetoric and symbols, in the form of an active and trusted church. The broader debate about the general timing and causes of religious nationalism is beautifully captured in Gorski and Türkmen-Dervişoğlu 2013.

[13] Hall and Lamont 2013.

[14] Burleigh 2007; Stark 1999; Stark and Iannaccone 1994.

[15] Martin 2005, 131.

[16] Gill 1998, 2.

[17] Fink 2008.

[18] Stark and Finke 2002, 37.

more complex effects on organized religion's influence on policy. The first and most obvious point is that the fusion of national and religious identities is not equally powerful everywhere. Poland and Ireland are not unique or idiosyncratic; national and religious identities have fused in other countries as well, such as Malta, the Philippines, Croatia, Lithuania, or arguably the United States, where a more diffuse "Judeo-Christian" identity arose. The degree of fusion, however, varies widely, and the mere existence of fusion does not guarantee influence. In other words, if religious nationalism has been defined as "fusion of nationalism and religion such that they are inseparable,"[19] I argue here that nation and religion fuse to differing degrees, and often in distinct ways. And even within any one country, some people view religion as far more central to national identity than others. These differences "in the precise settlement between national and religious worldviews"[20] are a starting point for considering the consequences of religious nationalism for policy.

A second point is that fusion is not static; its intensity and its content can change as the political context does, sometimes dramatically. The best of partners can make the worst of enemies; thus, the Guelphs in 1840s Italy "fused religious ideals with national sentiment."[21] But their position did not survive Pius IX's condemnation of the new Italian state thirty years later. In an extraordinary case, national identity in Québec changed over the course of from a religious to a territorial one over the course of a decade, the 1960s, as the state wrested enormous powers from the Catholic Church. Third, fusion is not hegemonic, but challenged and questioned. Even where the core of the identity and its empirical referents remain, the nature of fusion is complex and contested. For example, in Spain powerful anti-clerical traditions fought the equation of nation and religion. Even in Poland, anti-clerical parties arose in the interwar period and in the 2010s. Finally, fusion is not necessarily a product of centuries of history; the idea of "Pole = Catholic," for example, is a relatively recent construct that is decades (rather than centuries) old.

How do we know fusion when we see it? We observe religious hymns, symbols, and icons that reference the nation—and national anthems, symbols, and icons reference religion. Historical myths explicitly refer to religion, and a popular consensus equates national and religious identities; opinion polls show that for many Americans, it is important to be Christian to be "truly American," for example. Where religious and national identities have fused, political arguments can be justified in religious terms, and religious authorities use the national interest to pro-

[19] Rieffer 2003, 225.
[20] Eastwood and Prevalakis 2010, 105.
[21] Donovan 2003, 99.

mote and justify their policy demands. Religious values become national norms, and religious symbols and practices enter secular politics. Some specific examples include the hanging of the cross in the Polish or Québécois parliaments, the inclusion of God in the Pledge of Allegiance in the 1950s in the United States, or the veneration of the American flag, with specific rituals regarding its display, disposal, and even folding.

To measure the extent of fusion, I use three indicators: first, if fusion is a popular identity, how many people actually share it? Here, I rely on the percentage of public opinion poll respondents who claim that it is necessary to identify with a given religion to be a member of a given nationality (using the 2003 International Social Survey Programme). Second, I look at the historical role of churches in the rise of the nation-state and how that record is reified and received, and third, the degree to which we observe mutual references between religion and nation in national symbols and narratives. Table 2.1 summarizes how the countries under consideration score on each of these dimensions and includes a comparison with two self-avowedly secular countries that are not analyzed in the book: the Czech Republic and France.

What is striking, and what we will explore more deeply in the chapters devoted to the paired comparisons, is that countries with higher levels of fusion also show higher levels of religious influence on policy—the United States, Poland, and Ireland all score relatively highly on both measures. Canada and Italy show less fusion, and less policy influence, and anchoring the lower end of the spectrum, the Czech Republic and France show that where there is minimal fusion, the churches have very little influence on policy. (Unfortunately, Croatia was not included in the ISSP survey.)

For us to identify fusion (or any other historical legacy), it must be clear and sustained; that is, we need to identify a consistent and empirically demonstrable set of conditions, actors, resources, institutions, attitudes, or relationships and their persistence over time. For historical fusion to influence contemporary events, it must be transmitted over time. If fusion persists despite political, cultural, or economic upheaval, for example, we can be more certain that it exerts an independent influence beyond the circumstances that gave rise to it. These standards—clarity, consistency, and transmission—are quite demanding.[22] At the same time, they do not imply that powerful historical legacies must be long-standing; as we will see, fusion often developed and solidified over decades rather than centuries.

---

[22] These standards mean that we overlook relevant legacies such as the effects of long-ago cultural conflicts or subtle changes. However, since the fusion of religious and national identities is hypothesized to have such powerful effects, a false negative (Type II error) is preferable to a false positive (Type I error).

TABLE 2.1.
SUMMARY INDICATORS OF FUSION OF RELIGION AND NATION

	Perceived fusion[1]	Historical beliefs about the role of churches
Ireland	58%	Roman Catholic Church as protector of Irish nation in the nineteenth century, pro-independence and anti-colonial.
Italy	52%	Opposed united Italian nation-state, anti-communist bulwark, ally of Democrazia Cristiana, implicated in the DC party-state.
Poland	75%	Protector of Polish nation during partitions and loss of independence, shelter for anti-communist opposition.
Croatia	n/a	Protector of Croat nation, argued for greater Croat autonomy in the federation, pro-independence after 1990, allied with HDZ even though critical of 1991–95 war.
US	66%	Religion itself critical to American political identity. Invention of "Judeo-Christian" tradition, veneration of state symbols, piety expected of politicians.
Canada	54%	Roman Catholic Church played critical role in maintaining Québécois identity until the 1960s as explicitly Francophone and anti-Protestant Canadian. Anglican Church established until mid-nineteenth century, did not develop the same moral authority.
Czech Republic	29%	Roman Catholic Church opposed Czech nation, associated with Habsburg rule against pro-independence ambitions of Protestant nobles, neutral under communism.
France	18%	Opposed 1789 nation-state ambitions, associated with reactionary forces, never regained pre-1789 public position.

[1] *Poll respondents answering that it is important or very important to be [dominant religion] in order to be [respondent's nationality] in 2003. Data from International Social Survey Programme. The full range runs from 13% (Netherlands) to 84% (Philippines), for a mean 43% of and a standard deviation of 19.6%.*

The Rise of Fusion

The fusion of national and religious identities has its roots in the process of building nations and states, and specifically, in the conflict between national aspirations and the stifling of these ambitions by hostile political actors. These enemies of the nation can be an alien, repressive state (as in the communist regimes of Poland or Croatia) or a colonial or imperial power (as in Ireland).[23] The more secular authorities tried to repress societal protest and thwart national aspirations, and the more churches stood in defense of these, the greater the opportunity for the fusion of nation and religion.

Historically, formation of *states* has been a secular process, often at odds with dominant churches. Both states and churches attempted to create hierarchies of control and to enforce rules over individual behavior—and unsurprisingly, their claims often competed. For one thing, some churches believe they are empowered to rule by God, and that their various dictates are divinely mandated, while the very concept of a secular bureaucratic state "rests on the idea that power and source of power reside in nature and are manipulable, rather than residing in an autonomous supernatural."[24]

In contrast, the building of *nations* can be suffused with religious meaning, and easily incorporates the active participation of religious authorities. Unlike states, nations do not rely on secular administration or authority. Religious bodies can build national identity by infusing the nation with religious significance and by physically protecting important national symbols and representatives. National myths can also serve to fuel religious belief and participation, especially when national sovereignty is threatened. Some religious thinkers themselves, trying to square the circle of national and religious fusion in multiethnic societies, have defined the "nation" as the organic community to be protected under a religious umbrella, and the "state" as the administrative framework that is distinct from both the nation and its religious allegiances and identities.[25]

Over time, three distinct patterns of relations between religion, nation, and state have emerged. In the first, churches could *protect* national identity against a hostile state, where that administrative state and an existing national community opposed each other (for example, in cases of colonial domination, such as pre-independence Ireland, or the foreign imposition of a regime on an existing nation, as in communist-era Poland). Churches could offer this protection through informal education, by providing space for opponents for the hostile state to gather, and by imbuing religious symbols with national meaning. Religiosity allowed the churches to gain secular authority in society—and when national identity is threatened, this shared belonging becomes all the more important, and

---

[23] Repressive rule, colonial or otherwise, is not enough to result in the fusion of national and religious identities or moral authority for the churches, as the history of Latin America shows. The churches still have to explicitly side with "the people."

[24] Thomas 1989, 150.

[25] Porter-Szücs 2011, 333.

this authority all the more compelling. In short, "major national communities or else national sub-communities have experienced alien and external rule, and have found their major resource and identity in an historic faith."[26]

In a second pattern, the churches could help to *build* the nation-state. Where the state arose before any national identity coalesced, religion provided one basis for a coherent identity for the fledgling nation-state. A religious national myth can take shape: "one nation, under God." Rather than religious symbols taking on national meaning, national symbols took on a religious resonance. The nation need not be identified with a particular denomination for the myth to function, and the myth itself becomes a powerful unifying force, particularly in diverse societies with many separate immigrant histories and populations. Thus in the United States, churches and religious communities became a fundamental unit of social organization,[27] and some of the most profound social and political conflict of the early republic occurred between denominations.[28] A nonsectarian "American creed" or "civil religion" eventually celebrated democracy and infused it with religious meaning.[29] No one denomination or church became a dominant source of national identity. Instead, religion itself became a useful trope in uniting the nation.

The third pattern is one in which churches *opposed* the merging of the nation with the state, while the state acted to build and to unify the nation. For example, the papacy (and most of the local Catholic hierarchy), explicitly and vigorously battled the liberal creation of the modern nation-state in Italy, Spain, France, and the Czech Lands. The Roman Catholic Church opposed the liberal nationalist revolutions of the nineteenth century,[30] going as far as to threaten to excommunicate voters in newly united Italy, and defending the claims of the Habsburg Empire against Czech aspirations of independent nationhood. The nation-state and the Roman Catholic Church in these countries subsequently had an uneasy relationship. Where the churches had historically opposed the aspirations of a nascent nation, they subsequently met with widespread skepticism and suspicion regarding their motives. Deeply held private religious beliefs coexist with sometimes equally strong (and incompatible) secular political identities.

The result is a spectrum of religious nationalism: from the fusion of national identity with a particular denomination, to a diffuse national cohesion brought about by religious principles and rhetoric, to skepticism

---

[26] Martin 1991, 469.
[27] Atran 2002.
[28] Carwardine 2007, 178.
[29] Lipset 1963; Bellah 1967; Berger 1967.
[30] Burleigh 2007, 134.

about the role of the churches in society, all the way to the rejection of religious organizations as sources of political authority or national identity. The common concept of the "nation-state" obscures the frequent historical conflict *between* the nation and state, and the opportunities this conflict creates for religious authorities.

Sustaining Fusion

How is fusion sustained in the face of inevitable upheaval, the shifting of national borders, and even war? Several mechanisms help to insulate fusion from the forces of change, and to transmit it from one generation to the next. One is education. For example, the Roman Catholic Church formally controlled education in Ireland for most of the nineteenth through twenty-first centuries—providing teachers, vetting the curriculum, and setting the educational standards, teaching generation after generation of Irish children that the church was critical to both individual and national salvation. Controlling education is certainly one way to generate widespread identities and norms with which church attempts to influence politics will resonate. It is no coincidence that churches and their secular opponents have fought for centuries over formal and informal education, and the right to inculcate their own values in the public.[31] These shared values in turn confer identity, prescribe behavioral norms, and proscribe boundaries between religious and secular domains.[32] In communist Poland, where the government and its educational policy were resolutely secular, the church turned to a network of catechism classes held outside of school hours and relied as well on the informal transmission of norms relating to Polish national identity. These counter-narratives to the official version of Polish history were disseminated through family stories, reminiscences, and later via unofficial "Flying Universities," where anti-communist historians and sociologists lectured gatherings of students and activists. Indoctrination within the family is especially powerful, despite—or even because of—considerable repression from the state, and such transmission was a powerful source of post-communist political identities.[33]

Another mechanism that reproduces and sustains religious-national fusion is comparison, both to the past and to comparable contemporary actors. Where churches claimed to act "in defense of the nation," society could compare church behavior to counterfactuals—what churches *could* have done—and to counterparts—what churches *were* doing in

---

[31] Lipset and Rokkan 1967.
[32] Wildavsky 1987.
[33] Darden forthcoming; Darden and Grzymala-Busse 2006; Wittenberg 2006.

other countries. For example, the Polish Catholic Church's legitimacy as a protector of the nation was further solidified in the communist era, when it could have accepted the blandishments of the communist regime. Instead, the church offered sanctuary to the opposition and thus gained considerable standing in the eyes of the public—especially when compared to its Hungarian counterpart, which did not oppose the communist government as vociferously.[34] This legitimation enabled the church to frame their political preferences as matters of national concern and argue that dissent was tantamount to a lack of patriotism.[35] Polish bishops dismissed opposition to their proposed ban on abortion in 1989 by noting "with sorrow" that such views were "against not only the law of God, but well-understood national interest."[36] In contrast, such comparisons and counterfactuals did no favors to the Roman Catholic Church in Québec, long the mainstay of French-Canadian identity. There, the church gradually began to be seen as *hampering* national ambitions; by the 1960s, compared to other Canadian provinces, Québec remained underdeveloped and poorly educated. The church was increasingly blamed for mediocre outcomes in the educational system under its authority and for doing little to stem the corruption associated with the Maurice Duplessis government—a regime that worked hand in hand with the church.

The third mechanism by which fusion perseveres is the conscious adoption of national rhetoric in ostensibly religious contexts. For example, some religious authorities have explicitly included national symbols in their liturgy: creating national shrines and sponsoring pilgrimages to them, displaying the sacred relics of monarchs, holding religious celebrations on national holidays, and even designating national holidays as religious ones. In enormous, nationwide celebrations such as the Great Novena in Poland (1956–65) and its conscious duplication in Croatia (1975–84), venerated religious icons visited every parish, and masses for the nation were celebrated in every church. The result of this kind of piggybacking and reification of national and religious identity is that it becomes increasingly difficult to envisage oneself as X but not Y—Polish but not Catholic or, conversely, French but not secular.

Together, these mechanisms illustrate that fusion is a process of closing off alternatives. Even if a society begins with a choice of many equally feasible identities, as history marches on some of these will be privi-

---

[34] Wittenberg 2006.

[35] Note that these comparisons are not necessarily based on performance per se, but on the *appropriateness* of a given regime or institution for the nation, given its perceived historical and cultural standing.

[36] *Pismo Okólne*, hereafter *PO*, May 19, 1989.

leged, and the conversion costs greatly increase.[37] When these mechanisms are present—education, favorable comparison, religious reification of national-religious identity—fusion is durable. It persists in the face of external attack, and it is difficult for secular authorities to eradicate, whether these authorities come in the form of a laicizing government or colonial or imperial powers. In fact, governmental attempts to eradicate the fusion of national and religious identities often have the paradoxical effect of strengthening that fusion considerably.

Fusion is so robust for several reasons. First, religious identities (and more precisely religious practice) are unique in their ability to offer supernatural rewards—and punishments. Promises of salvation and nirvana and fears of damnation or exclusion may "enable religious organizations to exert on their members pressure unimaginable in most secular organizations."[38] Precisely because the stakes are so high, religion can withstand the sort of secular onslaught that eradicates other communal identities and associations; religious organizations are much harder to repress than unions, newspapers, political groups, or student organizations.[39] Religious passion is not just intense, but distinct. As one analyst put it, "people do not get shot for preferring a Volvo to a Ford. Men in white sheets do not burn crosses in front of the houses of people who switch brands."[40]

Second, the clergy's standing in society demands they defend both their faith and their community. They are seen as having little to lose, and it is expected that their concerns and motivations be spiritual ones, making inaction or passivity in the face of perceived injustice costly to their reputation. This is perhaps why, under communism, the more public the local clergy's anti-communist protest, the greater their subsequent authority and legitimacy.[41] And once a domestic national movement is under the protection of the church, attempting to eradicate that movement means crossing over into this sphere of the sacred—a move even Stalin was reluctant to make.

---

[37] These two mechanisms are compatible with Weber's trichotomy: comparison and identity acquisition can underlie charismatic, traditional, or bureaucratic-rational legitimacy. They further allow for different thresholds of legitimation across individuals (who may have different standards for comparison), and across institutions (legitimation of a church versus of a state may have different standards). Finally, these two mechanisms help to explain *selection* among competing authorities. Some will gain greater legitimacy than others, based on how they compare to the alternatives or how much they can represent salient identities (which themselves had gained earlier legitimation), such as the nation.

[38] Wald, Silverman, and Fridy 2005, 132.

[39] Sahliyeh 1990, 13.

[40] Bruce 2002, 180.

[41] Wittenberg 2006.

These distinctive characteristics—its promise of divine reward and the commitment of its clergy—make religion a potentially potent reinforcer of national identities, even if classical theorists of nationalism, such as Gellner, Anderson, and Hobsbawm, have tended to instead emphasize material factors and viewed nationalism as part of broader modernizing and secularizing processes.[42] Religious monopolies thrive because they are a part of national identity, and benefit from the same reinforcing forces of education, informal norms, and in-group boundary maintenance.[43] Dissenters face a double bind, faced with the prospect of betraying the nation if they reject the religion.

Religion and nationalism thus form an easy partnership. Religion strengthens national identities in countries with dominant religions,[44] thanks to its own ideological affinity (doctrine), association with entrenched institutions (clerical hierarchies and places of worship), and emphasis on collective ritual.[45] Religious observance can be a surrogate for political activity when oppression makes other options unavailable.[46] As a result, ostensibly secular identities often have significant religious components,[47] and the degree of religious practice and the level of national pride are closely correlated.[48] Nationalism may be "wanton" in that it cohabits with various political ideologies (in the felicitous phrasing of Valerie Bunce),[49] but it also happily weds religion.

This marriage of religious and national identities may be difficult for outsiders to tear asunder. Like all relationships, however, it is susceptible to its own *internal* failings—the partners themselves changing in incompatible ways or behaving badly.

First, religiosity is a prerequisite for fusion, as Figure 2.1 shows.[50] Without those full pews and masses of faithful, churches have a hard time convincing politicians or society that they represent broad national

[42] Gellner 1983; Anderson 1991; Hobsbawm 1990; Greenfeld 1996. Greenfeld in particular argues that religion is instrumental in fostering nationalism, but is now subservient to nationalism and used mainly as a tool for the promotion of nationalist goals. Yet, as this study argues, religion can also use nationalist rhetoric to achieve its own policy goals. See also the discussion in Gorski and Türkmen-Dervişoğlu 2013, 194.

[43] Breuilly 1982; Ramet 1998; Martin 2005.

[44] Voicu 2011.

[45] Mitchell 2006.

[46] Kunovich 2006; Enloe 1980. For a classic analysis, see Kubik 1994.

[47] Mitchell 2006; Trejo 2009.

[48] Soper and Fetzer 2011, 12.

[49] Bunce 2005, 412.

[50] There are of course exceptions: Greece shows high levels of religious nationalism, but low regular religious attendance (Barker 2009, 138), as does Russia. In Christian Orthodox countries in general, high levels of fusion between national and religious identities do not translate into broader policy influence: Orthodox churches are institutionally and finan-

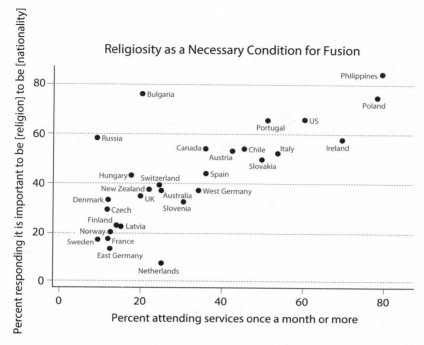

Figure 2.1. Religiosity as a Necessary Condition for Fusion

interests. If only 10% of the electorate is religious, the church can hardly claim to speak for the nation. For the same reason, churches that enjoy monopoly or near-monopoly status within society have an easier time claiming the mantle of moral authorities. (Intense and uniform religiosity also makes coherent the "sacred canopy," or the widely shared religious beliefs within which political and social life takes place.[51]) A decrease in belief (or, though this is less likely, new religious loyalties) thus undermines the equation of national and religious identities.[52] In Québec during the Quiet Revolution, secularization went hand in hand with a national reawakening and economic modernization, devastating the earlier fusion of religious and national identities.

Second, if national or communal identities change, the national myth and its religious underpinnings are also called into question. Such change

---

cially closely linked to the state, and their policy demands center on eliminating competitors and ensuring their financial survival.

[51] Berger 1967; Jelen 2002, 197.

[52] Critically, while religiosity is necessary for fusion, the converse is not true: fusion may sustain the political manifestations of religiosity, but not necessarily private belief or participation.

can be the result of new transnational identities and opportunities (for example, free travel and the free movement of labor within the European Union), an influx of new immigrants, or other shifts in population. Conversely, as a result of violent population shifts, the Catholic Church became a monopolist in postwar Poland and post-communist Croatia. Ethnic homogeneity, no matter how brutal its roots, does wonders for national unity—and thus for the potential for fusion.

In sum, fusion is a powerful social identity bolstered by religious monopoly, high religiosity, ethnic homogeneity, and a favorable historical record that is memorialized and reified through conscious church efforts in education and ritual. Yet because fusion operates at the level of societal identities, it can be undermined by demographic change, whether through secularization, a transformation of national identities, or a redefinition of the very community identified with the religion.

Fusion further means that individuals may disagree with the church's teachings—and its actions—yet remain loyal to the faith itself, so integral is it to their social identity. As a result, objections to church political activity can coexist with high religiosity; in Poland, even when the church's political activity in the early 1990s led to its lowest popularity rankings ever, church attendance did not decrease. Further afield, in the Philippines, high levels of religiosity and fusion (99% of poll respondents believe in God, 80% attend church frequently, and 84% agree that it is necessary to be Catholic to be truly Philippine) coexist with almost equally high disapproval rates of church involvement in politics.[53] This dynamic is most pronounced in Catholic churches, but it surfaces in Protestant denominations as well.[54] To a limited extent, fusion is self-sustaining— where fusion is high, individual disapproval is unlikely to affect religiosity, and where religiosity is intact, fusion is likely to persist. Churches can enter the political arena and find that their claims resonate with a society that views them as national representatives and with secular politicians for whom the line between offending religious sensibilities and national insult is blurred. Politicians and secular elites are anxious about opposing a powerful societal actor and incurring popular backlash as a result, and instead seek church support to smooth the path of governance.

Investing Moral Authority

The fusion of religion and nation as a popular identity reinforces churches' moral authority and transforms it into a specifically *political* force. Such

---

[53] Seventy-six percent of poll respondents opposed church influence on politics, and over 65% opposed church influence on governments and on votes.

[54] Hertzke 1988, 147.

moral authority relies on the widespread perception that churches are principled representatives and loyal defenders of society as a whole: the "nation," rather than narrower regional, partisan, or sectarian interests.[55] Once churches successfully establish such a reputation, they have to fulfill the moral and political standards they have set out for themselves, and they are subject to constant public evaluation, in the eyes of the public and the ruling elites.

This *political* moral authority is not the only authority churches wield, of course; they embody a particular view of the divine, and pious men and women faithfully observe religious tenets in everything from the wording of prayers, to what foods can be eaten and when, to how children are raised. Churches are an authority on life and death, and many otherwise secular societies rely on religious ritual to mark certain milestones. Even in very secular Norway, where only 3% attend church regularly, over 80% of children are baptized, and most weddings and funerals are held in churches.[56] When backed and reinforced by the fusion of national and religious identities, however, the moral authority of churches is no longer limited to theology or to ritual but allows them to embody the national interest and enter the political arena.

Evidence of such moral authority comes from a variety of sources: historical memoirs and participant accounts, newspaper editorials, parliamentary debates and statements, and the participation of churches in national rites and celebrations. In contemporary societies, we also have public opinion data regarding the degree of popular confidence in churches, summarized in Figure 2.2. These public opinion data are rough indicators at best,[57] but they show that the Irish, Polish, and American churches have enjoyed more popular trust on average than the Italian, Croatian, or Canadian ones. The Irish-Italian divergence is unusually striking: the Irish church fell from grace after the pedophilia and abuse scandals of the 1990s, while at the same time, as the Italian church withdrew from its partisan coalition, confidence and trust in it grew.

[55] Churches are not the only societal actors with such moral authority; armed forces in many countries, and courts in others, are also widely and equally trusted as behaving in the nation's interests. Similarly, there are cases of churches that temporarily gained moral authority without fusion, as in the period of late communism in East Germany, where the Lutheran churches protected the anti-regime protesters. Without religious nationalism, however, this moral authority was evanescent, and did not translate into church influence on post-communist politics.

[56] "Church Should Be a Place to Come to during Life's Greatest Events," http://www.kirken.no/english/news.cfm?artid=6605, accessed October 17, 2013.

[57] Available public opinion polls do not tap directly the perception that the churches are either moral agents or representatives of national interest, and not every country is compared at every point in time.

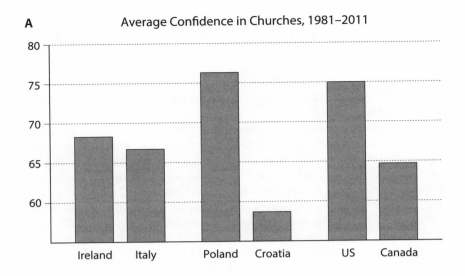

A   Average Confidence in Churches, 1981–2011

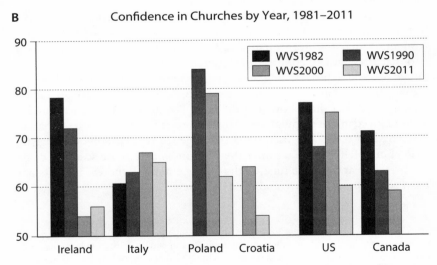

B   Confidence in Churches by Year, 1981–2011

Figure 2.2. Contemporary Moral Authority of Churches: Percentage of Respondents Reporting Confidence in Churches

Data: World Values Surveys, Question: "How much confidence do you have in churches?" "A great deal of confidence" and "quite a lot of confidence" are reported together. Note that there are no 1982 data for Poland, and no 1982 or 1990 data for Croatia, which is also reflected in the averages.

Because it relies on the perception that the churches are national representatives and righteous defenders of the common good, the political moral authority that results from fusion is a brittle resource. If fusion helps to set the initial levels of this authority, subsequent church actions can either sustain or undermine it.[58] Once they establish moral authority, churches must tread carefully. Violating their own codes of morality makes churches into hypocrites, and their immoral behavior costs them their authority, as it did in Ireland.[59] Pursuing narrowly self-interested, parochial, or local interests also risks dissipating this valuable capital.[60] Elsewhere, actors expected to act impartially have been punished for acting instrumentally: for example, judges who are seen by the public as acting strategically lose legitimacy.[61] Tying itself closely to a particular government or subnational group, rather than the organic nation, makes suspect a church's claims of national protection. For example, in Latin America, those churches that allied themselves with right-wing regimes had little moral authority left once these regimes fell.[62] Openly supporting or mobilizing voters on behalf of political parties can also have a perverse effect for the churches; they are no longer national representatives, but partisan ones, and by using their political power, they lose it (as in Italy or Croatia). In short, moral authority can be squandered by failing to live up to standards the churches set for themselves, the standards by which they were judged worthy of authority in the first place.

Ironically, moral authority, and how it is used, reinforced or dissipated, depends on secularization, or a growing distinction between the sacred and the secular. Secularization processes comprise both cultural and social change, a popular disenchantment and a differentiation of institutional

---

[58] In other words, if fusion determines the intercept values—the initial levels of moral authority—further church actions determine the slope—both whether moral authority is retained or lost, and the rate of that loss.

[59] In a more pluralistic religious setting, where no one religion is fused with national identity, and no one church claims a monopoly on moral authority, churches as a whole are more buffered. Thus American churches can suffer individual losses in moral authority, as the Catholic Church did in the early 2000s, but churches as a group can absorb them without a significant drop in moral authority for churches *overall*.

[60] Religious authorities may also overreach; advocates of morality policy often seek an absolute vindication of their values and will not be satisfied with marginal reductions in sin. Accordingly, they will continue to press for stringent policies long after any large policy changes are possible (Meier 2001, 31). Politicians may then lash back against impossible demands—or claim that budgetary or other constraints prevent them from fully implementing church demands. Obvious state privileges may similarly backfire (Casanova 1994, 214–15).

[61] Staton 2010.

[62] Gill 1998.

spheres, respectively.[63] Tectonic processes, not an angry deity, are now held responsible for earthquakes. Churches can no longer assert primacy over secular governments. God no longer appoints kings. These processes do not imply a decrease in belief,[64] and the resulting distinctions are politically contested and often unstable.[65] However, since the sacred and the secular now appear as different realms, churches have to actively endeavor to influence secular policy. And since religion is in a distinct sphere, churches pay a higher price in popular opinion for overt and undue influence on politics.

Thus the dilemma is that to remain politically successful, churches have to maintain the appearance of being above the political fray. As Tony Gill posits, when a hegemonic religious group is not tied to any secular political actor, its bargaining power grows. In contrast, once tainted by partisanship, "religious leaders who have always been *visibly* supportive of one political faction will have a difficult time convincing politicians of the rival faction and of the citizenry that they have switched sides."[66] One implication is that political action that is perceived to protect the nation may be acceptable, but partisan politics are not. For example, the Polish Catholic Church was widely lauded for mobilizing Poles to vote out the communist party in the historic 1989 elections, but lost a great deal of trust once it favored specific parties in the 1991 elections and thus *divided* the nation. Once a church dirties its hands with partisan, regional, or sectoral politics, its claims of representing the interests of the nation become less credible, and it is on this very claim that their political moral authority rests. Narrow and explicitly political alliances may even lead some of the faithful to abandon the church, appalled by its politicking. Further, they can fragment the churches themselves, as open controversy over church strategies splits the faithful and clergy alike. Such possibilities are profoundly worrying and costly to churches, which, after all, are not simply driven by policy concerns—they are also "soul maximizers," keen to increase the number of adherents and their commitment to the divine.

[63] Parsons 1977; Bell 1977; Casanova 1994; Berger 1999; Sommerville 1998; Martin 2005; Taylor 2007. For an illuminating review of the concept of secularization and the debates it generated, see Swatos and Christiano 1999.

[64] Bell 1977, 427.

[65] As Elizabeth Shakman Hurd has argued, "'Religion' and 'politics' are not well defined and stable sub-categories with their origins in the European Enlightenment, as is commonly assumed. They are deeply contested categories. It is misleading to assume that secularist divisions between religion and politics are stable and universal. . . . Secularist distinctions between religion and politics are hard won and always temporary. Political scientists have stumbled in the attempt to theorize the return of religion because their concept of authority fails to recognize the politics involved in defining, enforcing, and contesting authoritative conceptualizations of the secular" (Hurd 2007, 660–61).

[66] Gill 2008, 54, emphasis mine.

Secular political actors such as autocratic rulers or democratic political parties (or, as in the case of communist regimes, autocratic political parties) may seek and rely upon church support to maintain social peace, to lower the costs of governance, and to hold onto office or gain votes. There are three ways churches can invest their moral authority to directly benefit politicians. First, they can stabilize mass politics; in critical moments of regime crisis or societal unrest, a church with high moral authority can keep societal peace by urging patience and nonviolence in the name of national unity. As a result, secular political actors turn to such churches to prevent a crisis from escalating (and the incumbents from losing office), and to ensure political stability. Whether it means avoiding bloodshed, preserving a favorable regime, or defending fragile new governments, churches may choose to keep the peace in order to protect the nation—and their own interests.

Second, churches can mobilize support for secular politicians and specific government policies more directly, by collecting signatures, fundraising, registering voters, and campaigning on behalf of particular political parties or politicians. As mentioned earlier—and as we will see in the paired case studies in subsequent chapters—this can be a costly tactic. However, in the short term, it can also be an effective one.

A third way churches help politicians is by resolving uncertainty around the policies themselves. Especially in very religious societies, legislators are uncertain—and anxious—about voters' private preferences when it comes to "sin" policies, such as pornography, divorce, and contraception. Voters' private behavior may contradict their religious commitments, and public surveys are not much help, as they often provide conflicting information. For example, large majorities of Americans support both a woman's right to choose and restrictions on abortion. Churches can thus provide an "informational subsidy" to politicians, helping them to decode which policies are likely to be deemed acceptable.[67] Churches can resolve uncertainty within society as well: if they have high moral authority, they can persuade and credibly frame issues for the public in some instances.[68]

Of course, the fact that churches *can* help politicians hardly means that they will—or should. Moral authority gives churches the ability to ensure social peace, to mobilize the faithful, and to reassure politicians and society, yet it is only worthwhile for churches to invest their authority on

---

[67] Hall and Deardorff 2006. As a result, policymakers' ideal policies do not reflect the public's; they are likely to be more conservative and rely more on moral authorities such as churches than on perceptions of public preferences (Meier 2001, 23). Broockman and Skovron (2013) find that both liberal and conservative politicians overestimate the conservatism of their constituents, and that this bias is impervious to the effects of electoral selection.

[68] Lupia and McCubbins 1998; Druckman 2001.

behalf of any politician if they obtain significant concessions—and they still must worry that this hard-won resource will erode if they appear unacceptably sullied by partisan politics.

Influencing Policy: Coalitions and Institutional Access

Religious organizations do not legislate directly and rarely have direct political representation. A healthy flock of the faithful is a powerful asset, and churches can always try to mobilize that flock and pressure politicians through mailings, signatures, referenda, and public demonstrations. Yet churches must steer a careful course; popular majorities oppose church interference in politics. Reaching out to gain broader support beyond the faithful can backfire, not just by making the church appear politicized, but also because the genial rhetoric of compromise required to secure this broader support may undermine theological commitments. Churches run the risk of not only losing the policy debate but also of further eroding their moral authority. Relying on plebiscites or referenda is equally problematic. Only supremely confident churches can count on referenda producing the desired result—and as we will see, in both Ireland and Italy, churches that mobilized the faithful in referenda often lost. Churches were most effective in referenda when public opinion already reflected church preferences—and when threshold requirements were low, so that the actions of the mobilized faithful were the decisive force.

Instead of directly mobilizing fickle electorates, then, churches may rely on secular proxies, such as ruling parties or regime incumbents formally charged with policy making and implementation. In contemporary democracies, these critical actors are chiefly political parties; accordingly, much of the existing scholarship on religious influence in politics emphasizes the role of these parties, and how they represent and channel voter preferences, form alliances, and propose and pass policy.

Churches may thus simply rely on political parties to represent and channel popular demand for policies already favored by the churches and religious voters. They can direct the faithful in general terms to support political actors with preferences that align with the churches'—or merely count on the faithful to translate their doctrinal convictions into voting decisions. For example, much has been made of the increasing loyalty of Protestant Evangelical voters to the Republican Party in the United States. By becoming party activists and candidates, these religious voters have changed the platforms and image of the Republican Party drastically in the years since 1980.[69]

[69] Coffey 2007; Conger 2010; Conger and Green 2002; Guth, Kellstedt, and Smidt 2010.

One potential source of such electoral demand for policies congruent with religion is insecurity—material, economic, psychological, and political. Such insecurity increases religiosity by leading individuals to seek comfort and security in the church.[70] In this set of explanations, religion and economic development (or more precisely, the security of the welfare state) effectively act as substitutes for one another.[71] Lower economic development should correlate with higher participation and belief, and in turn, religious belief and participation lead to demand for religious influence over policy, and for policies consistent with religious teachings. Given religion's traditional concern with morality, such constituencies should be especially receptive to religious incursion into public policy domains framed as "moral" issues.[72] Political parties then loyally represent religious constituencies demanding church influence.

One implication is that economic development will be negatively correlated to religious influence on politics, as wealthy countries escape the insecurity that leads to religiosity and thus popular demand for policies that reflect religious preferences. Another is that countries undergoing massive transitions and upheavals, such as those after the collapse of communism in East Central Europe, ought to "turn to religion," and by extension be more accepting of increased influence of religion on politics. In both predictions, insecurity breeds popular religiosity, and religiosity in turn leads to religious influence on politics—via channels these explanations leave relatively vague.

Yet economic development does *not* in fact correlate with religious influence on policy, either in the paired cases or more broadly (see the Appendix). What's more, the insecurity that followed the fall of (secular!) communism in East Central Europe has not resulted in an increase in religious observance or belief. Economic and social insecurity can prompt individuals to seek comfort and reassurance in religious practice, but they do not translate into a societal consensus on the desirability of religious influence on politics. A fundamental problem here is that structural conditions are held responsible for behavior—yet even when these structural conditions change, behavior does not.

For churches, relying on popular demand is problematic for three further reasons. First, even very religious voters are pragmatic and tend to care first and foremost about their pocketbooks. Accordingly, it is secular factors—such as socioeconomic status, attitudes toward the economy, and security issues—rather than moral or religious stances, that most

[70] Norris and Inglehart 2004.
[71] Scheve and Stasavage 2006; De La O and Rodden 2008. For results conditional on religious doctrine, see Jordan 2014.
[72] Mooney 2001, 16.

convincingly explain the behavior of religious voters.[73] Even when religious factors play a greater role in voter decisions (as they have in the United States since 1988), they are still not the priority for most voters.[74] Political parties may bundle economic and moral policies,[75] but religious voters do not always respond by prioritizing moral over economic policies.

Second, political parties often have other programmatic priorities. Even conservative parties rarely faithfully translate the traditional moral stances of religiously conservative voters into legislation.[76] And even when churches instigate popular referenda, they lose more often than not, even in very religious countries.[77] Nor do politicians simply follow the preferences of religious constituencies, even if they are an overwhelming majority. Such preferences do not suffice; voter attitudes change, but policies often do not. For example, in Italy and in Croatia disapproval of abortion grew over the 1990s and 2000s, yet no new restrictions appeared.[78] In Ireland, in contrast, attitudes toward abortion liberalized considerably from 1980 to 2010, yet no party moved to liberalize access to abortion, seen as the third rail of Irish politics.[79] Increasing acceptance

---

[73] Bartels 2006; Burden 2004; Claassen and Povtak 2010; Gelman, Lax, and Phillips 2008; Hillygus and Shields 2005.

[74] Kohut et al. 2000, 87.

[75] Roemer 2001, Gill and Lundsgaarde 2004.

[76] Abramowitz 1995; Bartels 2006; Bartels 2008; Brooks and Manza 2004; Campbell 2007; Layman 1997.

[77] Thus, in Ireland, the Roman Catholic Church "won" the abortion referendum of 1983 and the divorce referendum of 1986, but "lost" the 1992, 1996, and 2002 referenda on the same issues. In Italy, the church lost the 1974 divorce and the 1981 abortion referenda, but succeeded in invalidating the 2005 stem cell referendum. (Such a mixed record, of course, calls into question the value of the informational subsidy the churches can provide, if they cannot gauge their own support accurately.) The Croatian church supported (but at an arm's length) the successful 2013 referendum that established marriage in the Constitution as purely heterosexual. In Poland, the church actively avoided instigating or participating referenda on issues such as abortion.

[78] The percentage of Italian respondents who rejected abortion as "never" or "almost never" justified increased from 33% in 1990 to 50% in 2010, while the percentage of those who found it acceptable in most to all circumstances dropped from 25% in 1981 to 16% in 2010. In Croatia, 26% rejected abortion as unjustifiable in 1996, and over 50% did in 1999 and 2010 (World Values Surveys, "When Is Abortion Justifiable," with 1 as "never" and 10 as "always," responses 1 and 2 reported).

[79] The share of Irish respondents who rejected abortion dropped from 84% in 1981 to 55% by 2011 (World Values Surveys, "When Is Abortion Justifiable," with 1 as "never" and 10 as "always," responses 1 and 2 reported). Only 3% of Irish respondents found abortion justifiable in 1982—but 12% did in 2011 (World Values Surveys, "When Is Abortion Justifiable," with 1 as "never" and 10 as "always," responses 9 and 10 reported). Support for divorce also grew enormously: from 12% of poll respondents finding it justifiable in 1981 to 35% in 2011.

of abortion in the United States also did not bring about corresponding policy change.[80]

Third, even in very religious societies, public opinion can tilt away from church views, as with stances toward same-sex marriage and homosexuality. Here, conservative churches simply could not articulate their objections in a way that would overcome secular cultural change. As Cardinal Timothy Dolan of New York conceded, the Catholic Church was "outmarketed" on the issue of same-sex marriage by its proponents.[81] Around 10% of respondents in the countries examined accepted homosexuality in the early 1980s—but over next two to three decades, acceptance rose spectacularly in the United States and in Ireland, as Figure 2.3 shows.[82] (In contrast, Poland and Croatia show lower, and more stable, rates of acceptance. This is typical of post-communist countries, where an average of 8% of poll respondents in post-communist countries agree that homosexuality is justifiable, compared to 30% elsewhere.[83] The lack of tolerance of homosexuality in post-communist countries is widespread, and irrespective of religious affiliation.) In short, relying on voter preferences is a very tenuous path for churches to obtaining their policy preferences.

If voter preferences are unlikely to lead to substantial policy influence, churches can instead form more direct *coalitions* with political parties or incumbents and exchange policy concessions for church support of given parties. Such coalitions, as salient and seemingly common as they are,

---

[80] Fifty percent of American respondents rejected abortion in 1982 but only 30% did by 2011 (World Values Surveys, "When Is Abortion Justifiable," with 1 as "never" and 10 as "always," responses 1 and 2 reported). In both the United States and Canada, the percentage of respondents who found it acceptable in "most" to "all" circumstances close to doubled, to around 29% by 2011. Support for divorce also grew in the United States (25% in 1982 to 44% in 2011) and in Canada (16% in 1982 to 42% in Canada) (World Values Surveys, "When Is Abortion Justifiable," with 1 as "never" and 10 as "always," responses 9 and 10 reported).

[81] "Cardinal Timothy Dolan: Catholics 'Outmarketed' on Gay Marriage," *Associated Press*, November 29, 2013, see also http://abcnews.go.com/US/wireStory/dolan-catholics -outmarketed-gay-marriage-21050764, accessed December 2, 2013.

[82] In Ireland and the United States, acceptance of homosexuality rose from 10% and 7% in 1980–82 to 36% and 37% by 2010–11, respectively.

[83] The gap here is considerably deeper than on similar issues: 18% of post-communist respondents find abortion justifiable while 22% of other respondents do. 23% of post-communist respondents find divorce justifiable and 37% do in other European and Anglo democracies. Views on these three issues are closely correlated (views that abortion and gay marriage are justifiable correlate at 0.83, $p = 0.000$, and divorce and gay marriage correlate at 0.88, $p = 0.000$. Divorce and abortion are also strongly correlated, at 0.88, $p = 0.000$, WVS 6th wave (2010–14) data for Europe, United States, Australia, and New Zealand). See also http://themonkeycage.org/2012/05/17/support-for-gay-marriage-in-europe-and-the-us/.

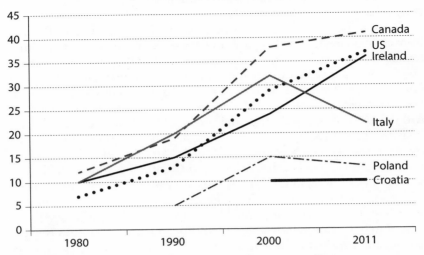

Figure 2.3. Changes in Rates of Acceptance of Homosexuality
Data: World Values Surveys, including the 6th wave (2010–11). Question: Is
Homosexuality Justifiable? Scale ranges from 1 (never justifiable) to 10 (always
justifiable.) Table reports answers 7–10.

have been a powerful explanation of church influence on politics.[84] In
these accounts, churches effectively mobilize the faithful to support political parties during electoral campaigns, and in exchange obtain desired
policy concessions from the government parties they helped bring into
office. Churches pursue alliances with those parties that are most likely
to translate preferences into policy, and do so at the lowest cost to the
churches. Parties, in turn, pursue various alliances depending upon their
need for electoral support, their ideology, and benefits they are likely to
gain.[85] For example, the center-right Christian Democratic Party (Democrazia Cristiana, DC) relied on the support of the Roman Catholic Church to
keep them in power for nearly five decades after World War II in Italy, and
the church is said to have obtained significant policy concessions as a result.[86]

[84] Warner 2000; Donovan 2003.

[85] Warner 2000, 12. These calculations can be quite complex: churches and sympathetic
political parties exchange policy concessions for electoral support based on asset specificity
(can churches get the same good elsewhere?), transaction costs (would it be less costly for
churches to supply their own politicians?), market uncertainty (how stable and popular an
ally is the party?), and core competencies (what are both the parties and the churches good
at doing?) (Warner 2000).

[86] Hanley 1994; Kalyvas 1996; Warner 2000; Donovan 2003.

In another version of this explanation, secular and religious actors contract *over time*. Where the churches protected the democratic opposition under a previous authoritarian regime, new democratic incumbents incurred a "debts of gratitude" to their religious sponsors.[87] Once in power, democratic parties pay back these debts and reward churches with policy concessions for years of rhetorical and physical protection of their nascent party as democratic dissidents.[88] Simply put, earlier alliances translate into contemporary policy influence. Where the churches were either neutral or on the side of authoritarian governments, we would expect little church influence on politics once democratic governments are in power.[89]

Yet as prominent as they are, such alliances between parties and churches face three potential difficulties. First, the partisan partners for organized religions are not as obvious as one might suppose. As Stathis Kalyvas noted, "the presence of large Catholic populations in a country is analytically and empirically insufficient for predicting the emergence of a common Catholic identity in politics, even less the formation of a political party."[90] Christian Democratic parties might seem "natural" candidates for a church alliance, but in fact these parties have had a historically uneasy relationship with churches, preferring to assert their autonomy and pursue broad, cross-class coalitions. Voter support for Christian Democratic parties in any given country is not tied to either the policy influence of the churches or to popular religiosity.[91] That is not to say that Christian Democratic parties never ally with churches; for example, in the years immediately after World War II, the Italian Christian Democratic Party formed a close alliance with the Catholic Church. But Christian Democratic parties also succeed where there is no Christianity, as in the Czech Republic—an avowedly secular country with a weak Catholic Church. At the other extreme is Poland, where *high* levels of popular religiosity have not translated into support for either Christian Democratic or clerical parties. And of course, even if a church can find a political partner, that party may simply not get elected.

Second, such agreements are difficult to enforce. Concessions made between *political parties* have staying power; in parliamentary regimes, when such parties form governmental coalitions with one another, their survival in office is a function of their joint efforts. If one party withdraws its support, the government falls, and all parties face the arduous process of new elections or forming a new coalition government. Promises made to churches, on the other hand, can be forgotten with fewer consequences

---

[87] Htun 2003, 134.
[88] Htun 2003, 102; Castles 1994; Gill 1998.
[89] Juergensmeyer 1993.
[90] Kalyvas 1996, 10.
[91] Grzymala-Busse 2013.

for the party. Once churches mobilize their support on behalf of parties, there is little to keep the party from reneging; it may well decide that it can find other means of mobilizing voters in the future. In short, churches have fewer instruments than political parties with which to enforce coalitions.[92] The Italian Christian Democratic Party, for example, moved to a strategy of clientelism and patronage in the 1950s and 1960s so that it could reach the electorate without the church's mediation, opting to deliver pork to voters rather than rely on church mobilization. For its part, the church eventually began to pressure individual parliamentarians, a more laborious and inefficient strategy. Political gratitude is notoriously short-lived and fragile, and it is not clear why coalitions with a church should be any more robust. Once church protection is no longer needed, there is no need to heed church preferences.

Third, and above all, partisan coalitions erode churches' moral authority—the very authority that makes them attractive to political parties in the first place. Party alliances are overt and, naturally, partisan affairs, and churches are easily accused of being more concerned with narrow political (and self-) interests than with saving the souls of the nation and pursuing the public good. Choosing to support an existing autocratic regime can be costly—as the churches that supported the 1976–83 military regime in Argentina and the Vichy collaborationists in wartime France discovered—but supporting dissidents does not translate into automatic policy influence once they are in power.

In short, coalitions with political parties can clearly achieve policy concessions—but these concessions come at a high price, when they come at all. Not surprisingly, then, when we examine the broader universe of Christian democracies, coalitions do not appear to be a particularly effective way to influence politics. Figure 2.4 shows the relationship of coalitions to policy influence, conditional on the fusion of religious and national identities; the 95% confidence interval (marked by dotted lines) always includes 0, and so we can be reasonably sure that even with repeated sampling, coalitions are not associated with significant policy influence. (The full analysis is in the Appendix.)

What, then, is a politically ambitious church to do? Rather than relying on fickle electorates or less-than-reliable partisan alliances, churches understandably prefer to have direct input into policy making—in effect, to share sovereignty with secular politicians. This *institutional access* includes the formulation of legislative bills; participation in government and parliamentary committees; vetting state officials; and controlling im-

---

[92] Unlike churches, political parties can also use formal agreements, portfolio allocations, investiture votes, cabinet power sharing, and parliamentary questions to monitor and enforce coalition agreements. See Strøm et al. 2010, 522.

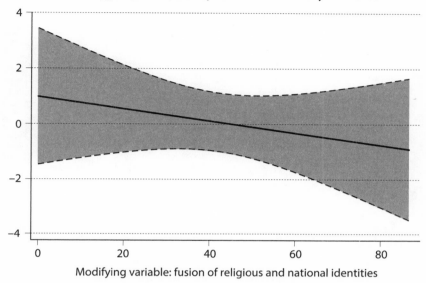

Figure 2.4. The Marginal Impact of Partisan Coalitions on Policy Influence

portant state sectors, such as education, the welfare system, and health care. The key advantage of institutional access is that it does not diminish moral authority by conflicting with church's image as concerned broadly with nation and the greater good—the public activities involved, such as ministering to the sick, are hardly partisan, and the specific (and more narrowly political) policy pressure is covert, taking place behind the closed doors of ministries and high offices, with personal meetings rather than public demonstrations or exhortations. Moreover, as Figure 2.5 indicates, it correlates with policy influence (the full analysis is in the Appendix). This time, the confidence interval crosses 0 at about 30% of fusion. At higher levels of fusion, institutional access appears strongly and positively correlated to policy influence.

If they obtain institutional access, churches can directly shape policy and yet retain moral authority, making such access a far more attractive option than the alternatives.[93] If partisan alliances are highly visible and negotiated on a policy-by-policy basis, institutional access is more covert

[93] If we assume churches prefer to influence policy at minimum cost, their ranked preferences are having their preferences legislated without participation in politics, followed by directly participating in policy making, exchanging electoral support for policy concessions through partisan coalitions, and lastly, no influence.

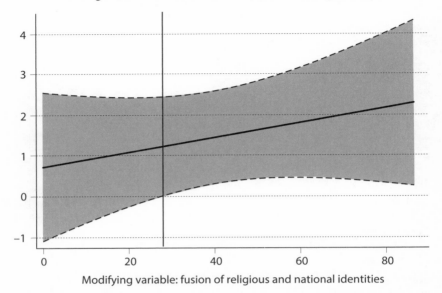

Figure 2.5. The Marginal Impact of Institutional Access on Policy Influence

and durable (controlling education, for example, allows the church to inculcate generations of citizens with religious values and a specific national identity). The result is that churches can retain influence and adherents even as they (covertly) advocate highly unpopular policies, and even as ever-growing majorities denounce church influence on politics. Such access may be long-lasting and often persists despite the transformation of a political regime from a communist autocracy to post-communist democracy. In Poland, for example, a joint commission established by the communist regime with the church still meets regularly, nearly seventy years later. Not surprisingly, churches would prefer to obtain institutional access.

What do secular politicians obtain in return? In coalitions, political parties receive direct support from the church: the churches' organizational capacity to organize and mobilize voters, public pronouncements, voter education, and even financing.[94] In exchange for granting churches institutional access, secular politicians instead receive more diffuse support for the status quo, such as public pronouncements praising democracy and national sovereignty, reassuring meetings with societal leaders, and symbolic legitimation in homilies and sermons that counsel patience in light of

[94] Warner 2000.

economic or other difficulties—but these will all endorse "democracy" or "independence" and general national interests, rather than specific politicians or parties. They are unlikely to mobilize votes or provide funding. Individual politicians or parties will benefit less in the short term than they would from a coalition—unless the entire system is about to collapse. Moreover, precisely because it may involve sharing sovereignty, secular politicians would prefer not to grant institutional access, even when they trust the churches to represent national interests. Not surprisingly, then, politicians prefer entering coalitions to sharing sovereignty.

Yet if their survival depends on the support of a powerful church, politicians will readily grant institutional access; for example, if they stand to lose office because the very regime or nation-state they have created is about to collapse, taking them along with it. In short, the less secure the secular incumbents, the more assistance the church can provide.[95] Situations like these are no time to quibble, and for this reason, institutional access is often granted to churches in foundational moments: after a regime collapse, upon gaining state independence, when building a brand-new democracy, and during critical elections (where the vote determines the future of the regime, not merely the future incumbent). Institutional access is made palatable to politicians when a fragile secular state needs extensive support—and may not itself have the capacity to staff and oversee certain sectors, such as education. This is the story of the new Irish Free State handing over education and welfare policy to the church in the 1920s—and of the British Crown entrusting the same sectors to the church in Québec after 1840 and the expulsion of the Liberal elites. As a result, churches can gain enormous policy influence during times of upheaval and instability, such as regime transitions—precisely when institutional and policy frameworks can be most easily and radically transformed. Decisive church action means regime or government survival is ensured, while the church's new gains ensure long-term influence without imperiling its moral authority.[96]

Churches may also obtain institutional access in times when the survival they ensure is quite literal—when their high moral authority can prevent fratricidal conflict. This was the case in communist Poland,

[95] Tony Gill argues that the more secure the tenure of politicians, the lower the bargaining power of religious actors—and the more competition there is among secular rivals, the greater the power of religious groups (Gill 2008, 53). The argument here does not rely on competition as the only source of incumbent insecurity, and it builds on Gill by specifying when the bargaining power of the religious groups is increased independently of secular competition and the conditions under which particular channels of influence are adopted.

[96] At *extremely* high levels of moral authority, churches could afford the inevitable depreciation of moral authority that comes with partisan coalitions—but as we will see, such situations require several other conditions that rarely occur in political life.

where both after the protests of 1956 and the enormous mobilization of 1980–81 the church gained not only policy concessions but also greater authority over its assets, continued contacts with high-ranking communist officials, and policy input through several joint committees.[97] In exchange, the church calmed a furious populace and prevented violence and bloodshed by advocating a return to order in the name of national peace and survival. Highly respected churches can thus resolve dramatic national crises, and the fact that the secular actor may not survive without church involvement makes the price of institutional access worth paying. Even if such crises occur rarely, and institutional access emerges only periodically, these crises are an enormous opportunity for churches to gain influence—without surrendering precious moral authority. Thus institutional access depends on the churches' high moral authority, and upon secular politicians' extreme need for such diffuse and costly support.

Subsequently, institutional access acts as an insurance policy for the incumbent: as a channel of communication with a powerful political actor and as way to give the church a stake in the incumbent's survival and establish joint responsibility. If the church's moral authority drops, or if the incumbents find a substitute source of support, they can move to close off institutional access to policy making. Yet even then, the earlier institutional influence of the churches leads state officials and bureaucrats loyal to the church to resist, necessitates the reversal of informal policies (and the constituencies they created), the writing and passing of new legislation, and overcoming the objections of at least some citizens educated and cared for by the church. Institutional access weaves the churches into the fabric of the state and policy making, and unraveling this influence is not straightforward.

At lower levels of moral authority—too low for institutional access to be a viable option—the churches' options are more constrained. Even if specific constituencies might trust them, they are not trusted as broadly, and not as *national* representatives. They are thus unable to address such major, widespread social crises, and secular actors are accordingly unwilling to pay the price of institutional access. Churches may still expend moral authority to influence policy, but policy gains will depend

---

[97] For example, as strikes and societal protests culminated in the rise of the opposition trade union Solidarity in Poland in the fall of 1980, Cardinal Stefan Wyszyński reminded the anxious communist party and society alike that "the first condition for order and social peace is the recognition of God in our Fatherland and the abandonment of any form of forcible secularization of children and youth, any form of secularization of society. The Church has to be given freedom and respect for its rights" before it could help to calm down the situation (*PO*, September 8, 1980). The communist party attempted to only broadcast those parts of the Cardinal's speech that referred to the need for order, and not those that referred to the need for respecting the church and its religious efforts.

on narrower coalitions with allied political parties, whose commitment is unreliable. These gains come at a steep price, as public and partisan politicking erodes what moral authority churches possess.[98] They start off with less and obtain their goals at a higher cost.

In short, where national and religious identities have fused, churches have the moral authority to enter politics as national representatives. Where a single religion strongly fuses with society, the church's high moral authority translates into institutional access. Where a single religion is more tenuously identified with the nation, and moral authority is lower, the result is often a costly partisan coalition. Where the nation identifies with many religions, or the *idea* of religion, moral authority is diffused among many denominations, and partisan coalitions are the likely channel of influence, but they will be less costly to any individual denomination, since individual responsibility is blurred.[99] Finally, where multiple religions exist but without any consensus on a religiously inflected national identity, the moral authority of individual churches is minimal—as is their policy influence.

This argument is captured in a formal model summarized in Figure 2.6, which clarifies the conditions under which churches obtain different forms of policy influence (the full model and the equilibria are in the Appendix). Secular incumbents in need of support offer either institutional access (A) or a coalition (X) to the churches,[100] depending on how badly they need church backing (the lower the p is, the less secure they are in office) and how high and durable the church's moral authority is ($\delta_A M_{t-1}$ and $\delta_X M_{t-1}$ denote how much moral authority the churches retain after obtaining access and entering a coalition, respectively). The churches decide to accept or reject these offers, depending on the policy gains they can make (A or X) and the level and resilience of their moral authority.

The logic is that governments offer *institutional access* to churches with high political moral authority and when the secular incumbents badly need church support to govern (as was the case in post-1989 Poland,

[98] Such churches can become "tragically dependent" on partisan coalitions, influencing policy but losing moral authority in the process, becoming even more dependent on partisan coalitions—to whom they can offer less and less.

[99] This is akin to the clarity of responsibility and accountability in parliamentary coalition governments: voters have a harder time identifying the responsibility of individual parties for policy outcomes in coalition governments with multiple parties. See Powell and Whitten 1993, or Powell 2000.

[100] While the model makes a stark distinction between offering coalitions or access, in practice governments have offered both; for example, the Lateran Pacts were included in the Italian Constitution, giving the church some access to education even as it formed a coalition with the ruling Christian Democratic party. (See Chapter 4.) That said, if a church accepts both a coalition and institutional access, it will pay the price it would if it only accepted a coalition, since the coalition is the public face of cooperation and influence.

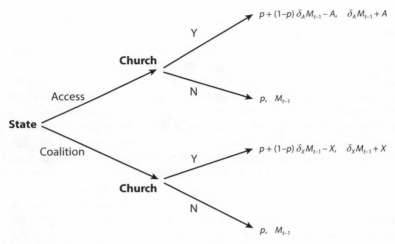

Figure 2.6. A Model of Church Influence on Politics
M: moral authority of church.
X: coalition offer made by secular state to church, concession made by state.
A: institutional access given by a secular state to church, concession made by state.
p: probability of secular actor remaining in office *without* church support.
M_{t-1}: church moral authority inherited from the past.
δ_X and δ_A: retention rate of M for church if it enters into coalition or obtains institutional access, respectively.

independent Ireland, or nineteenth-century Québec). Governments will offer *coalitions* to churches with lower levels of moral authority when they need church support (as in postwar Italy) and/or when the moral authority of the church is not going to be compromised too much from accepting a coalition (as was the case in the United States). Churches with higher moral authority may also enter a coalition when they are convinced their moral authority is particularly resilient, as the Croatian church did after 1989 when it inadvertently entered a partisan alliance. Where the secular incumbent does not need the churches' moral authority to retain office, no offer is made, as in Anglophone Canada.

If this argument captures the logic common to church influence on policy, what should we look for in the paired studies that follow? First, the fusion of popular national and religious identities should correspond to a political moral authority in society—a widespread recognition that churches represent the national interest and defend the common good. In turn, strategies of influence should reflect levels of church moral authority. Second, churches with high moral authority act to calm down society and stabilize governments—meeting with societal representatives, exhorting society to avoid violence and bloodshed (in the name of the nation), and declaring that national interest is tied to the newly independent or democratic state. In exchange, during and after these moments churches with high moral authority gain institutional access: formal representation in national legislative bodies, joint episcopal-parliamentary commissions, running a ministry or a ministerial sector funded from the state budget, repeated consultations during formal policy making, or vetting powers over national appointments. Because institutional access tends to be hidden, evidence is often obscure; it includes sharing authority in specific sectors,[101] records of church-state meetings, and authorship of legislation. One test of the power of moral authority to influence policy occurs when the church has a policy preference that runs counter to public opinion, and yet still gets its way.

Churches with lower moral authority, who cannot speak to society in the name of the nation, will be unable to obtain such systematic access. They will enter coalitions, mobilizing particular constituencies on behalf of parties that need their support. The critical characteristic of such a coalition is that church representatives will explicitly advocate voting for a specific party during elections—and the party will grant policy concessions to the church. We will see such politicking erode moral authority, making the churches less attractive as partners over time. Moral authority may also crumble when churches do not live up to representing the nation in other ways—as we will see, the pedophilia scandals in the Catholic Church hurt its standing in Ireland because the church there had established itself as the moral guardian of the nation, to whom the care and education of children had been entrusted.

Areas of Policy Influence and Its Determinants

Where might churches choose to exercise their policy influence? The answer is a question as much of political calculation as of religious doctrine. Churches are selective in which issues to emphasize; across the cases examined here, for example, divorce has garnered far less church effort than either abortion or same-sex marriage. Out of the pool of potential issues, which is defined by their relevance to doctrine, churches are likely to pick those issues that (a) are most salient, given their current interpretations

---

[101] Churches controlled some state sectors such as education or the welfare state before the modern state arose, as in older European democracies. To count as institutional access here, the state has to explicitly hand over or expand existing sectors, rather than simply continue the status quo.

of doctrine and its priorities, and (b) offer the greatest political leverage at the lowest cost to the greatest number of adherents. In one version of this argument, a Polish bishop argued that "abortion is a question of preventing murder: divorce does not kill. So although divorce touches many more people, abortion remains our priority."[102] Same-sex marriage and abortion are such attractive targets for churches because relatively few of their faithful are likely to consider them, while assisted reproductive technologies and divorce are daily experiences for many people inside and outside of the church, and battling IVF or condemning divorce alienates these faithful.[103]

I chose to examine education, divorce, abortion, embryonic research technologies (including both stem cell research and assisted reproduction), and same-sex marriage for three reasons. First, the choice of these issues does not predetermine the relationship between national identity, channels of church influence, and the levels of that influence. Second, Christian churches have explicitly focused on these. Contemporary churches have devoted attention less consistently to other potential "morality policies" such as capital punishment, poverty, pornography, prostitution, alcohol and drug prohibitions, and organized crime,[104] or to other issues viewed as consistent with Christian doctrine, such as environmental laws, social justice, poverty, immigrant rights, and so on. Instead, many Christian churches concentrate on preserving what they view as a natural and traditional family structure and see these areas as directly affecting the family. Since religion is sustained by community norms[105] and the family is a critical unit of Catholic social thought, for example, the issues of marriage, divorce, and abortion fundamentally define communal boundaries. Yet despite this shared concern, the churches' success in obtaining their policy preferences has differed over time and across countries.

Third, this variation has occurred despite consistency in Roman Catholic Church teachings across the countries examined, and in four out of the six cases considered, the Catholic Church is the critical player. The Catholic Church has consistently opposed divorce, abortion, stem cell research, and same-sex marriage, even if its political mobilization against

---

[102] Archbishop Wojciech Polak, May 29, 2012, interview, Warsaw.

[103] The sheer numbers are instructive; for example, less than 5% of the American population identifies as gay, lesbian, or bisexual, and abortion ends roughly 20% of all pregnancies in the United States (but only half the population can undergo the procedure). In contrast, divorce affects close to 40% of American marriages, religious or otherwise, and infertility affects an estimated 20–30% of all couples at least once in their lives (Guttmacher Institute 2014, Kreider and Ellis 2011).

[104] American and Canadian churches have focused on issues such as temperance and civil rights, see Chapter 5.

[105] Martin 2005, 84.

these phenomena (and success in obtaining policy preference) has varied. It took on an explicitly *political* stance in defending what it sees as the natural order, focusing on morality issues that are traditionally the domain of conservative political parties. Protestant churches, and alliances among churches (such as the Evangelical-Catholic coalition in the United States, unthinkable fifty years ago but now the mainstay of religious support for conservative Republican candidates) have tended to be similarly idiosyncratic, more concerned with abortion than bioethics, and with same-sex marriage than with divorce. Even where Evangelical and Catholic doctrines are united in condemning divorce, this has not resulted in a concerted effort to abolish it. As we will see, these were conscious political decisions rather than doctrinal mandates.

Of course, church efforts to influence policy have not been limited to these domains; in the United States alone, churches have mobilized to end slavery, promote temperance, ensure civil rights, end nuclear armament, change immigration laws, and reduce poverty.[106] In Ireland, the church worried about dance halls—and in Poland, about alcoholism—in ways that are not mirrored in the other cases. Churches respond to specific problems in their societies, but as important as these are, they cannot easily be compared across countries. For that reason, they are not examined in this study.

In short, these five issues are where we would expect the greatest contemporary efforts by churches—yet we see enormous differences in influence across similarly religious countries, and over time. To impose a rough chronology, churches emphasized education and divorce in the nineteenth century, abortion and religion in public schools in the twentieth, and stem cell research and same-sex marriage in the twenty-first (they are discussed in this order in the country chapters). There are important exceptions to this periodization: abortion continues to be a major cleavage in the United States and Poland, for example. But for the most part, this time frame means the churches encountered these controversies with different levels of moral authority, and with different secular actors. To maximize comparability, therefore, I focus on postwar policy influence. Italy and Ireland are chiefly examined in the twentieth century, after gaining independence.

---

[106] The concerns of the Catholic Church have been especially broad: José Casanova identifies a strengthening of democratic politics (calling for good governance and just elections), a more general mobilization for human rights and social justice, and the defense of a natural divine order that rests on traditional notions of gender and marriage and precludes abortion (Casanova 1996; Casanova 2001). These first two "public Catholicisms" focus on civil society rather than on the state or political parties (Cassanova 1996, 367). The church did so even after Vatican II disavowed integralism, the nineteenth-century stream of Catholic political thought that sought a "reconquest of society and . . . rejected the notion that any spheres of life lay beyond the reach of religious regulation" (Berger 1977, 32).

Poland and Croatia are investigated after 1945—from the imposition of communism until its collapse and the rocky rise of national independence and democracy. I also focus on the last five decades of American and Canadian history, which includes the end of the Catholic hegemony in Québec and the unprecedented appropriation of religious language by the Right in the United States.[107]

Two indices summarize church policy influence in these domains.[108] First, as a measure of the churches' framing of political and policy debates, I examine whether (a) the churches were the protagonists in the public debate over the issue, (b) whether churches first framed the issue in religious terms, using phrasing such as "sanctity of marriage," "the culture of life," appeals to the "Christian character" of the nation, or to "natural law," and (c) whether secular politicians then adopted the same language.[109] Political debates in countries where religious and national identities are fused more easily become framed in terms of fundamental religious and moral principles, with churches as the key protagonists in public debates. Public policy becomes a "morality issue," where the debates focus on first principles, the issues are portrayed as one of fundamental ethical principles, and at least one side uses moral arguments in advancing its case.[110] Familiar examples in the United States are those of abortion, stem cell research, and the teaching of evolution.

The impact of religion on policy *outcomes* also varies enormously. As an indicator of churches' efficacy in achieving policy gains, I measure whether the restrictions or changes to policy in each domain were (a) compatible with church teachings, and (b) justified by the politicians passing them as having a Christian character. These measures thus attempt to avoid the possibility of an accidental coincidence between the

---

[107] The summary ratings for institutional access, coalitions, and policy influence used in the statistical analyses are all confined to 1945–2014. See the Appendix.

[108] Measures of state regulation and support of religion (see Chaves and Cann 1992) do not indicate either the *source* of a close state-church relationship or its broader policy implications. Other indices measure state recognition of denominations, clergy appointments and salary payments by the state, the collection of taxes by the state on behalf of the parties, and outright state subsidies to churches. These show the extent to which the state may support church organizations but says little about how effective churches are in influencing policy rhetoric or outcomes. Similarly, indices of the separation of religion and state (SRAS, see Fox 2006) measure both state support and state restrictions on religion but tell us little about informal policy influence, or the legitimacy of religious demands in the eyes of the public and political elites. They may also be misleading for our purposes: the United States is the only country that scores a perfect separation of church and state (Fox 2006; Fox 2008), yet its policy making is significantly influenced by religious mobilization.

[109] Private lobbying, of course, can be extremely powerful and reflect very different motives from public announcements. However, it is difficult to capture and does not reflect attempts to set the public agenda or reframe policy issues.

[110] Mooney 2001; Meier 1994.

preferences of secular and religious authorities. As noted earlier, churches can influence policy indirectly—when anxious politicians anticipate church objections and restrict policies accordingly, and directly—when politicians exchange policy concessions for church support. The Appendix specifies these codings.

Two kinds of measures assess the fusion of religious and national identities, each with its advantages and limitations. First, if fusion means that religious and political identities have become conflated over time, it is necessary to examine these identities. We would expect to see political arguments justified in religious terms, and religious authorities successfully use the nation as both a religious category and a justification for incursion of religion into politics. Observable aspects include a popular and elite consensus that equates national and religious identities; historical and national myths that explicitly refer to religion; and mutual references between religion and nation in songs, symbols, and icons. The ethnographic and historiographic literature provides a wealth of data on these aspects of fusion and their development over time, even if considerable care has to be exercised assessing the extent of fusion.[111]

More difficult to assess is either the comparability or representativeness of these measures, so I supplement these analyses with data from the International Social Survey Programme's 2003 survey, which explicitly asked respondents how important a particular faith (Christianity in the case of multi-denominational countries such as the United States and Canada, Catholicism in predominantly Catholic cases such as Ireland) was to national identity (V15, ISSP 2003).[112] This survey captures only a snapshot of identity politics at one point in time, the 2000s, but it allows us to compare fusion across many more countries.

No single source of data can fully show how churches influence public policy—or the role of moral authority in the success of church efforts. Many of the channels of influence are informal and occur outside of the public eye; some, such as a phone call to a politician, are simply lost to scholars.[113] I therefore use a variety of data sources, including historical and contemporary press accounts, recollections and memoirs of participants, minutes of decisive meetings and parliamentary debates, government reports, church declarations and chronicles, and ethnographies of national symbols. In establishing the rise of fusion of national and religious

[111] As Rogers Brubaker warns, "the field of nation-talk is vast, heterogenous, and chronically contested; one can't judge the degree to which nation-talk is framed in religious terms simply by giving examples of such religious framing, no matter how numerous or vivid" (Brubaker 2012, 11).

[112] The question was asked again in the 2013 module, but as of mid-2014, that data was not available.

[113] As a result, this account is likely to underestimate the covert and informal institutional access that occurs.

identities, I rely on historical accounts, using a diverse set of scholars and interpretations. Historians have examined the Catholic Church extensively, especially in Poland, Italy, and Ireland. In making their arguments, historians seek nuance and context—political scientists look for broad patterns that hold across countries and issues. This book is not the work of a historian. However, it recasts conventional understandings of national identity and its effects by reinterpreting historical accounts. These are cited as precisely as possible, allowing for replication.[114]

Some of this evidence was amenable to cross-national statistical analysis, which is presented in the Appendix. It relies on an original data set collected for this project, using public opinion data from the recent waves of the World Values Survey (especially the 5th wave, 1999–2004, and the 6th wave, 2010–14) and the International Social Survey Programme (ISSP 1999, 2003, and 2008), as well as measures of religious attendance, belief, and participation; religious affiliation and denominational make-up; state regulation of religion; electoral support for Christian Democratic parties; and control variables such as percentage of the population that is Catholic, gross domestic product per capita, and so on. I include all Christian democracies for which WVS and ISSP data is available. The results are robust to including other European countries such as Islamic Albania, Turkey, and Moldova, as well as to dropping the non-European cases, suggesting the correlations that hold here are not simply limited to Christian and European countries.

Conclusion

In sum, even in the most pious of societies, churches do not command routine or inevitable policy influence, and there is surprisingly little popular demand for church influence in politics. As a result, relying on anxious politicians or religious voters alone is rarely enough. Instead, to influence politics, churches have to breach the walls dividing church from state and either ally with political parties or insinuate themselves into state institutions of administration and policy making.

In these efforts, a powerful resource for the churches is their moral authority—their reputation in society as defenders of the nation and a representative of its interests. This moral authority has given churches a great deal to offer to potential secular partners: it allows them to calm restive societies, mobilize voters, and prevent anti-government opposition from spilling into violence. The political significance of religious nationalism stems from the authority it gives clerical actors—and the need of secular governments and parties for church support at critical points.

---

[114] See Kreuzer 2010 and Lieberman 2010 for best practices in using historical data.

Yet if churches are obviously partisan or politically involved, their moral authority suffers—and for this reason, public and partisan coalitions are both costlier and riskier for the churches institutional access, which is non-partisan even if sometimes not covert.

As we will see, the vicissitudes of history and politics are complicated, and churches have used many tactics over time to get their way. The story is relatively clear in religious monopolies such as Ireland or Italy, where the dominant church could take the credit—or the blame—for its historical role in the building of nation-states (a role that was often considerably more nuanced and controversial than the foundational myths would have it). It is more complex where the church gained its moral authority under an openly hostile autocratic government and then weathered the transition to competitive democracy, as in Poland and Croatia. As Croatia shows, even churches with high levels of moral authority must invest it wisely. The story becomes more complicated still in religiously diverse societies, such as the United States or Canada, where a more abstract, interdenominational fusion of religion with nation substituted for the fusion of nation with any one denomination. And it is to these complexities of history, and how they correspond to the scholarly simplification presented in this chapter, that we now turn.

CHAPTER 3

Catholic Monopolies: Ireland and Italy

> "The bishops and priests of Ireland have spoken," said Dante, "and they must be obeyed."
>
> "Let them leave politics alone," said Mr Casey, "or the people may leave their church alone."
>
> —James Joyce, *A Portrait of the Artist as a Young Man*, 1916

> The Church does not say that morality belongs purely (in the sense of exclusively) to her; but it belongs wholly to her.[1]
>
> —Pius XI, 1929

As THE STEREOTYPES OF THE faithful Irish family praying the rosary and the black-clad Italian widow attending mass daily attest, both Ireland and Italy exist in the public imagination as overwhelmingly Catholic. Churches, shrines, and cathedrals crowd in cities and in rural crossroads, and the ecclesiastical hierarchy has been outspoken on economic, political, and social issues for decades if not centuries. This saturation of the public sphere is deceptive; neither the Italians nor the Irish are attending mass or receiving the holy sacraments as often as they had earlier in the twentieth century. Yet in comparison with avowedly secular France or bitterly divided Spain, Ireland and Italy are imbued with a Catholic culture that is not only visible in architecture, public holidays, and individual identities, but that also allows the Catholic Church to mobilize its faithful to sign petitions, demand referenda, and sometimes to vote (or abstain from voting) as the church wishes.

Despite these superficial similarities, these two Catholic monopolies differ in two ways. First, the Irish Catholic Church has dominated politics and public policy far more consistently than its Italian counterpart. Irish schools, health care, and the welfare state were all the province of the church, which ruled them with unquestioned authority (and state funding) in the independent Irish state. The power of the church extended to censoring films; vocational organization of the country; defeating welfare

---

[1] *Divini Illius Magistri* Encyclical on Christian Education, 1929.

schemes; and blocking divorce, abortion, and access to contraceptives. While its direct influence peaked in the 1960s, the Irish church has remained an active and influential political player. In contrast, the Italian Catholic Church had to settle for less: preschools, crucifixes in the classroom, and voluntary religious instruction.[2] The Italian church was unable to block the legalization of divorce, contraception, or abortion. And while most Irish Catholics obeyed church teachings until the late twentieth century, their Italian counterparts always took a more cavalier approach that distinguished between public displays of faith and private behavior.

Second, the *mechanisms* of influence also differed. The Irish Catholic hierarchy saw itself as an active, equal (and sometimes superior) partner in governance—and the successive governments of both Fianna Fáil and Fine Gael acquiesced. The church influenced politics through a variety of institutional means: consultations among top officials, clerical presence on various commissions, the church's pervasive control of education and welfare, and finally an anticipatory deference by policy makers possessed of a deep individual faith and of a fear of the political consequences of crossing the church. In Italy, in contrast, even as the church emerged as one of the few societal institutions left standing after the Mussolini era and World War II, it did not wield the same influence. Instead, the church formed an overt political alliance with the Christian Democratic Party after the war ended—and did so reluctantly, prompted by an overriding fear of communism rather than by a desire to endorse a party it saw as politically weak and ideologically suspect. In keeping with the model presented in Chapter 2, anxious and needy incumbents offered institutional access to an extremely powerful church—and a partisan coalition to a less authoritative one.

These differences can be traced back to the distinct role the Catholic Church played in the founding of the nation-state. Differences in this role separate not only Ireland from Italy but also both countries from others where Roman Catholicism was the dominant religion. In France, the post-1789 myth of a secular, enlightened, and republican France, and more importantly, the anti-clerical clashes of the late nineteenth century and the church's support for the Vichy regime, branded the church as a reactionary force that could not be allowed to enter politics, whether through coalitions or institutional access.[3] There, the Roman Catholic Church was largely excluded as an institutional actor, even if the state's notion of *laïcité* included state support for religious communities and practices. In Spain, the secular-religious cleavages of first the 1812

---

[2] The Italian church does run *private* health clinics and hospitals.
[3] Weber 1976, 359; Warner 2000, 188.

Constituent Assembly[4] and then the 1936–39 Civil War were durable and deep.[5] Under the dictatorship of General Franco and the "liturgical triumphalism" its policy concessions promoted, the church was identified with the regime, even after it belatedly began to support democracy in the 1970s.[6] The Spanish church objected to the "godlessness" of much of the new democratic Constitution of 1978,[7] but mindful of the Civil War's lessons, it was also "extremely concerned to avoid any revitalisation of the religious-secularist tension that had cost Spain so dear in the 1930s, and joined other political actors in seeking consensual solutions to the constitutional debates."[8] Even as the Spanish church opposed abortion, divorce, or the loss of its educational autonomy, it lost each of these battles.

In contrast, the church in both Ireland and in Italy was in a more favorable position by the twentieth century; it was neither excluded a priori from politics, nor was it party to a deep societal cleavage or fratricidal conflict. In Ireland, after initial ambivalence about the tactics of the Republicans, the Catholic Church threw its support behind the new independent state, pointing to a long history of resistance to English colonial rule. In Italy, the Vatican's very location meant that Catholicism would be central to Italian politics, and that its role would be controversial, thanks to the papal conflict with the secular state and Pius IX's disapproval of a united and independent Italy in the late nineteenth century. Catholicism was an institutional opponent of a united Italy and a common religious thread tenuously tying together a new nation-state of distinct regions.

This chapter examines how religion fused with national identity, and how the Roman Catholic Church exercised policy influence in two democracies that were also Catholic monopolies. In both Ireland and Italy,

---

[4] The 1812 Liberal Constitution and the 1813 abolishing of the Inquisition crystallized the cleavage between a Catholic Hispanic Spain (the Serviles) and a liberal Europeanizing one (the Liberales) (Casanova 1994, 7).

[5] Casanova 2013, 47–48; Balcells forthcoming.

[6] Buchanan and Conway 2002, 121; Davie 1999, 78. In the late years of the Franco regime, many of its otherwise secular opponents found shelter and support in the church: "they wrote for publications sponsored or born in the religious realm, held their meetings in convents, and sponsored assemblies of strikers and sit-ins in churches. Funerals of victims of the struggle and repression became political events, and the church intervened on behalf of those being tried and sentenced by the government for insurrection" (Linz 1991, 171; see also Casanova 1994, 87). In Catalonia, the Roman Catholic Church went from being a target of intense anti-clericalism prior to the Civil War, to collaborating with Franco state efforts to rebuild religious practice in the 1940s and early 1950s to defending Catalan interests in the anti-Franco opposition in the late 1960s. As a result, Catalan society went from an anti-clerical stance to a far more tolerant one, even if the church did not gain the moral authority and religious fervor of its Croatian or Polish counterparts (Dowling 2012).

[7] Hanson 1987, 127.

[8] Anderson 2003, 151.

the church relied on the masses of faithful mobilizing to support its directives. But such mobilization could backfire, as the defeats in the second divorce referendum in Ireland and abortion and divorce referenda in Italy showed. The churches thus generally preferred to rely on more direct instruments of influence. In independent Ireland, in keeping with the model, the first governments' strong need for the support of a church with great moral authority promoted direct institutional access: parliamentary consultations, policy committees, and personal calls on policy makers. In Italy, the Christian Democratic Party was in dire straits after the war and offered a coalition to a church with lower moral authority. In each policy domain, successful influence depended on the level of the church's moral authority, the costs and benefits of potential coalitions and institutional access, and the security in office of the secular incumbent. And in both countries, the choice of tactics to influence policy—and to justify this exercise of moral authority—fed back into the church's standing in society.

Ireland

In Ireland,[9] Catholicism was the core pillar of an Irish, as opposed to an English, identity, and the church promoted the fusion of national and religious identities, especially in the nineteenth century. With the local priest serving numerous roles in the community, religion and its practices in Ireland "were very much embedded in everyday social life and relations."[10] National and religious identities fused not only because the church sponsored and protected national ambitions of Irish Catholics against the rule of Protestant London, but thanks also to a popular "willingness to adhere closely to the Catholic Church . . . located in a desire to be and be perceived as morally equal, if not superior, to their colonisers."[11] In the name of protecting the Irish nation, the Catholic Church was heavily involved in policing the moral and political spheres, and in fact argued successfully that the two were the same.[12] Until the late twentieth century, the church's authority was (literally) unquestioned: "while there were frequent public debates and critical assessments of the State, political parties,

[9] The discussion here does not touch on Northern Ireland, where from the late nineteenth century those who opposed Irish home rule worried about the pernicious influence of the clergy, especially the Jesuits, encapsulated in the slogan "Home Rule Is Rome Rule." The incorporation of so much of the church's theology and institutional role into the 1937 Constitution made the prospect of unification all the more difficult, even as it reassured the Catholic Church and ensured its support. I am grateful to Andrew Muldoon for this point.

[10] Taylor 2007, 153.

[11] Inglis 1998, 98.

[12] Keogh 1986; Smith 2004; Girvin 2002; Whyte 1971.

trade unions and other national organisations, the Catholic Church remained above rigorous criticism and public accountability."[13]

The origins of this close embrace lie in the church's historical relationship to the Irish nation, as opposed to the British state. In the eighteenth century, with the native nobility destroyed in Ireland, "her priests had assumed a leadership role among the peasantry which they never lost."[14] As national aspirations emerged in the 1820s and 1830s, especially among the middle class, their "most pronounced feature . . . was the close identity between Catholics and nationalism. . . . The Catholic Church in Ireland became an explicitly Irish church and acquired nationalist sympathies."[15] In the 1840s, as the Irish Potato Famine decimated the peasants, rather than the middle class, it also eliminated the traditional mainstay of Gaelic culture: "the Famine simultaneously deprived Ireland of a quarter of its population and of its primary source of national identity."[16]

The way opened for the modern fusion of nation and religion, as a centralized and traditionalist church supplanted local, more independent forms of Catholicism. An enthusiastic affirmation of public, uniform piety followed with the introduction of religious societies, rosaries, perpetual adorations, novenas, vespers, jubilees, pilgrimages, and so on.[17] As the middle class began to dominate political and social life in Ireland, so did its puritanical mores, which strengthened further the church's position in society (as did the middle class's generous donations of both money and manpower to the church). As the nineteenth century wore on, the mutual embrace of nationalism and religion became even closer. Catholic religious authorities sponsored a nationalist movement and took an active role in shaping national ambitions; priests, for example, were ex officio members of conventions that selected Nationalist candidates for parliament.[18] At the same time, mass attendance rose from 33% in 1840 to 95% in 1890.[19] Aided by such favorable demographics, the church assumed the mantle of national representative—and fomented a heroic myth. By the early twentieth century, the political voice of the church was decisive, as all sides recognized.[20]

[13] Inglis 1998, 2.
[14] Titley 1983, 3–4.
[15] Girvin 2002, 11.
[16] Hanson 1987, 37. Despite some criticism of church passivity during the Famine, "the enduring theme was the memory of the struggle of ordinary priests to ameliorate the suffering of the poor" (Bew 2007, 209).
[17] Brown 1985, 24.
[18] Whyte 1981, 64.
[19] Larkin 1976, 640.
[20] Keogh 1986, 80.

This is not to say that the Catholic Church consistently or actively resisted British oppression. The church trod a careful line between the (nationalist) faithful and the demands of a conservative Vatican to stay quiet and obey. Even as it fought back against the Penal Laws of the eighteenth century, which limited formal education and attacked Catholic institutions, the church sought Catholic emancipation without challenging the British state, worried about charges of domestic overreach and an anti-clerical backlash.[21] In the early nineteenth century, while the church fought to guarantee the emancipation of Catholics, it would have little to do with national independence movements. The Roman Catholic Church and the British government reached an uneasy understanding after the 1800 Act of the Union, giving the British authority over politics and the church control over moral, educational, and religious life during the nineteenth century.[22] Indeed, "both London and Rome supported the Irish bishops, who fostered a new devotional Catholicism,"[23] with London financing the new national seminary at Maynooth. When nationalist movements seemed to threaten this understanding by forcing open conflict with the British, the church protested vociferously and even backed British repression of these movements. Thus, in 1861, the Ultramontane Archbishop of Dublin Paul Cullen condemned the radical nationalist Fenian Brotherhood—not because of their nationalism, but because of their revolutionary commitments to violence and conspiracy.[24] More broadly, the church hierarchy split over the advisability of pursuing sovereignty and independence directly, the best strategy to follow vis-à-vis the British, and the worry about the radical and violent potential of the IRA.[25] Yet given both the increase in religiosity and the dynamism of the newly centralized and conservative church after the Famine, these incidents were successfully framed as protecting the nation from violent, and self-defeating, radical currents.

Independence meant new venues for church influence and cooperation between the church and state. After gaining independence in 1922, Ireland was increasingly referred to as a confessional state. The church became highly influential, both in shaping policy and in controlling state

[21] Titley 1983, 4.
[22] Hanson 1987, 36.
[23] Hanson 1987, 36–37.
[24] Girvin 2002, 19.
[25] Keogh 1986, 75. During the 1916 Easter Uprising, most Irish did not support the rebels or the insurrection—but the harsh British response (five hundred were killed, three hundred of whom were civilians—and of the fifteen rebels who were executed, some were gravely wounded), renewed the opposition to British rule. The War of Independence began in earnest after 1918 and the landslide victory of Sinn Féin in the illegal assembly (Barker 2009, 57).

institutions.[26] Its representatives helped to write the Constitution, took over and expanded the educational and welfare systems, and above all, set the standards of public morality to which secular politicians deferred. The church gained moral leadership and institutional access as "nationalists defended the prominent role accorded the church in public policy . . . and the forces of military Republicanism and conservative Catholicism, bitterly opposed to each other during the civil war, were reconciled in a church ceremony."[27] Fianna Fáil[28] in particular was assiduous in protecting church interests and Catholic moral values; the "tendency to equate 'Irish' and 'Catholic' seems to have been special to Fianna Fáil, and particularly to Mr [Éamon] de Valera himself."[29] The irony here is that the same Republicans that founded Fianna Fáil had earlier been condemned by the Catholic hierarchy and had often been refused the sacraments. Some remained estranged from the church for years. But "the Irish capacity for opposing the clergy in politics while considering one's self a loyal son of the church reasserted itself, and Fianna Fáil proved just as ready as Cumann na nGaedheal[30] to uphold, by law if necessary, the traditional values of the Catholic Church."[31]

The 1937 Constitution (written with the help of the Archbishop of Dublin John Charles McQuaid) explicitly recognized the role of the Catholic Church in the life of the nation and gave it several rights. The result was that an even "close[r] identification between Irish nationalism and the Catholic religion developed."[32] This close association permeated not only the political sphere but also society itself, where the Catholic worldview "came to be taken for granted."[33] Public opinion polls carried out in the early 1960s showed that "Irish Catholics willingly accepted church authority on faith and morals . . . with few if any reservations . . . most of those interviewed believed that a clash between the state and church could not occur."[34] Similarly, "there was little conflict between

---

[26] Andersen 2010, 17.

[27] Kissane 2003, 75–76.

[28] Fianna Fáil ("Soldiers of Destiny") was founded in 1926 and rapidly became a catchall party of government. By 1932, Fianna Fáil (FF) was the largest party in Ireland, a "democratic party with a national appeal which could challenge Cumann na nGaedheal as a nationalist party. Fianna Fáil's nationalism was more active and inclusive, promising welfare for the disadvantaged and a more vigorous promotion of the state as an agent of nationalism" (Girvin 2002, 73).

[29] Whyte 1971, 49.

[30] The conservative "Party of the Irish" of William Cosgrave, in government of the Irish Free State from 1923 to 1932.

[31] Whyte 1971, 40.

[32] Kissane 2003, 75.

[33] Andersen 2010, 17.

[34] Girvin 2002, 132.

church and state before the 1970s,"[35] and a 1962 survey by the American Jesuit B. F. Biever showed that "almost 90 percent of the sample agree that the Church was the greatest force for good in Ireland" and "when asked what side they would take in the event of a clash between church and state, 87% per cent said that they would back their church."[36]

Critical to maintaining this fusion and subsequent access was the church's active role in, and control over, the educational system, as well as a network of social services, ranging from hospitals to orphanages to the notorious mother and baby homes. Starting in the mid-nineteenth century, well before independence, the church provided much of the personnel in the educational system and determined its curriculum, designed to imbue its students with traditional Catholic values and loyalty to the church.[37] With independence, the state now funded the educational system and handed over formal control over the sector. The educational system, and pastoral work in general, broadcast the same message, since the clergy and the church hierarchy were equally morally rigorous and politically nationalist. These values were inculcated in their shared education at the national seminary in Maynooth, founded in 1795.[38] Nation and faith were publicly celebrated, leading to a resilient public piety, and "same fascination with religious argument and the same involvement with charities, social movements, pilgrimages and books persisted in the Ireland of the secularizing modern world of the late 1960s."[39]

In short, the mechanisms of maintaining the fusion between Catholicism and the Irish nation lay "in the organizational manpower and resources of the Church, its dominance in other social fields, and the role being a good Catholic has played in the struggle for symbolic, cultural, and social capital."[40] For decades, the church set the standards for moral authority. It determined who would best serve the interests of the Irish nation, and taught its faithful to judge the church and others by these standards.

Yet both the institutions and moral criteria that were so critical to the church's moral authority eventually led to disillusionment with the church. As robust and durable as the fusion of Irish national and religious identities has been historically, and even as Ireland remains among the most religious societies in Europe, two developments have chipped away at this monolith. First, the Irish nation no longer needed the church's protection as much as it once may have. By 1961, when Ireland applied

---

[35] Girvin 2002, 126.
[36] Garvin 2004, 200–201.
[37] Inglis 1998, chap. 3 and 122ff.; Garvin 2004, 202.
[38] Larkin 1984, 101.
[39] Garvin 2004, 128.
[40] Inglis 1998, 17.

to join the EEC for fear of economic isolation, "the insular protectionist nationalism was challenged by the process of constructing a more modern Ireland."[41] The very process of application meant institutional change and reform, in keeping with EEC demands, such as removing tariffs and other protectionist measures. Joining the European Union meant enormous economic progress in the 1990s and early 2000s, and the influx of hundreds of thousands of immigrants from Poland and other parts of the EU. At the same time, the relationship with Britain improved as well, fracturing a critical pillar of the fusion of national and religious identities in Ireland: the rejection of British foreign domination.

Second, even more corrosive were the belated revelations of the church's own behavior, which called into question its claim of defending the Irish nation and ensuring its physical and moral survival. A series of scandals rocked Ireland in the 1990s and 2000s. The media reported in 1992 that the popular and charismatic Bishop of Galway, Eamon Casey, had a son in the United States with a divorcée. The disgraced bishop resigned shortly thereafter, but not before the Irish band The Saw Doctors immortalized him in a song lyric: "Mighty, mighty, Lord Almighty, off with the collar, off with the nightie."[42] Similarly, Michael Cleary, Dublin's "singing priest" with his own national radio show, not only fathered two children but also abused his young housekeeper.[43]

Even more seriously, reports of sexual abuse by priests, and the institutionalized mistreatment of vulnerable children and adolescents at the Magdalene Laundries (reformatories for wayward girls), the mother and baby homes for unwed mothers, and the industrial schools (for boys) all became public.[44] Victim after victim came forth, detailing the abuse. After a decade of investigation, the government Commission to Inquire into Child Abuse eventually concluded in 2009 that "endemic" neglect, and emotional and sexual abuse in church-run institutions took place from 1936 onward, with the denial or covering up of the abuse by the church hierarchy, and the complicity of government officials.[45] Victim

[41] Girvin 2002, 201.

[42] The Saw Doctors, 1992. "Howya Julia."

[43] "How Catholicism Fell from Grace in Ireland," *Chicago Tribune*, July 9, 2006, available at http://www.chicagotribune.com/news/nationworld/chi-0607090342jul09,0,3397459. story, accessed May 6, 2014.

[44] Up to thirty thousand women were incarcerated between 1922 and 1996 in the Magdalene Laundries, a total of 170,000 children and adolescents entered the fifty or so industrial schools between 1936 and 1970 (staying an average of seven years), and around two thousand to three thousand children and adolescents spent time in a reformatory during this time. Commission to Inquire into Child Abuse 2009, chap. 3: "Gateways."

[45] The Commission published five volumes of its findings, detailing the abuses at various church-run institutions. Rather than buried in government archives, these can be easily found at http://www.childabusecommission.ie/rpt/pdfs/, accessed December 8, 2013.

organizations and the media condemned the church's abuse and its efforts to cover up these scandals, as did prominent politicians and government ministers.

The bitter irony was that Roman Catholic Church set the moral standards for evaluating its role in society—and subsequently failed them. By the twenty-first century, the church's claim to protect and defend Ireland against a hostile external environment rang hollow in light of its inability to protect the Irish children and adults in its care.

Policy Influence

Given the fusion and mutual reinforcement of nationalism and religion, "the Catholic Church's position in Ireland was hegemonic precisely because coercion was not required and because the church's power and influence was not resisted . . . this type of power and influence is not easy to measure, as in many cases no direct influence is exercised. What occurs is that certain policies simply rule themselves out, before they are even considered."[46] Tom Inglis also paints a portrait of a society where one's standing was a function of public adherence to Catholic Church, despite frequent private doubts and dissent.[47] In countries such as Ireland, where public adherence to a doctrine determined one's livelihood and social standing, public dissent was untenable—even if private disagreement was widespread.[48] The church could thus rely on pervasive, and public, acquiescence.

This moral authority, if not hegemony, translated into policy influence in two intertwined ways. First, the church successfully argued (and often simply assumed) that its mission had always been to ensure the survival of the Irish nation, and to do so by protecting its moral values. As the church's demands expanded and became increasingly adamant, "the justification for such an extension of power and influence on the part of the Church, of course, was rooted in its claim that it was responsible for the moral welfare of the nation."[49] In the decades that followed, the church repeatedly framed education, welfare, abortion, and divorce its purview, and the restrictions on these domains as a matter of the moral health of the nation—and given the moral authority of the church, these arguments were reified by secular laws and the educational system. Politicians picked up and amplified religious language in public debates and policy justifications. As a result, the "episcopal insistence on the Church's right

[46] Girvin 2002, 125.
[47] Inglis 1998, 68–77.
[48] Kuran 1991.
[49] Larkin 1984, 121.

to dictate policy in a broad range of social, cultural, intellectual and marital areas was maintained and successfully enforced among Irish Catholics until well into the late twentieth century."[50]

Second, after independence in 1922, the governments of the fledgling new Irish Free State[51] needed church backing to govern.[52] Without such support, the new state would not be accepted or legitimated by the society. As one analyst put it, the alliance between church and state "was partly founded on the recognition that the state could not govern successfully if it were strongly opposed by the Church."[53] As a result, politicians of various stripes invited the church to play a greater role, as a way of ensuring its support and giving it a greater stake in the new Irish state. The main governing parties all sought the church's support: first the Cumann na nGaedheal, desperate for church buttressing to legitimate its initial rule and the independent state[54] and subsequently both Fianna Fáil, whose politicians demonstrated their religious credentials by reproducing church rhetoric and sustaining its policy preferences, and the socially more moderate Fine Gael, which governed with the center-left Labour Party. This durable elite consensus "effectively drained Irish politics of a clerical–anti-clerical dimension. The social and cultural distinctions between practising and non-practising Catholics, as well as the Protestant minority, remained; but disputes over the role of the Catholic Church largely disappeared from mainstream political debate."[55]

Given the lack of open criticism or political opposition, the church was free to pursue its policy preferences, and "the governments of Liam Cosgrave before 1932 and afterward of de Valera freely acknowledged that it was the duty of the state to help maintain traditional Catholic teaching and values. If Cosgrave, for example, refused to legalize divorce or to allow the dissemination of birth control information and censored films and books, de Valera made divorce unconstitutional, banned the import or sale of contraceptive devices, and regulated dance halls, besides incorporating Catholic teaching on the family, education, and private

---

[50] Garvin 2004, 129.

[51] The Irish Free State arose out of the 1921 Anglo-Irish Treaty, which established both Northern Ireland, a state that was part of Britain, and the independent Irish state (with dominion status). The 1920 Government of Ireland Act divided Ireland into North and South, providing each with an independent parliament. In 1922, the Anglo-Irish Treaty was enacted, creating the Irish Free State. The Irish Free State lasted until the 1937 Constitution, which formed the state called Eire. The Republic came into being only in 1949.

[52] See also Gill and Keshavarzian 1999.

[53] Inglis 1998, 79.

[54] Keogh 1986, 123ff.

[55] Conway 2006, 171.

property in the 1937 constitution."[56] The policy results were remarkable: whole swaths of governance fell under church authority, ceded by the secular state with little discussion or opposition. The church provided, and the state funded, education, health care, and welfare services. Church representatives played a critical role in shaping (and in some cases literally writing and enforcing) policy on censorship, dance halls, abortion, divorce, family law, trade unions, agricultural policy, and foreign policy.[57] The result of the church's claim of moral housekeeping, and the governing parties' need for support, was that "the historically powerful Catholic Church and the fledgling Irish Free State cooperated increasingly throughout the 1920s as the self-appointed guardians of the nation's moral climate."[58]

Much of the church's *direct* influence relied on institutional access, and it was both preemptive and hidden; for decades, the church had "extraordinary political and cultural influence, and could, in many policy areas, effectively veto government policy initiatives. Furthermore, these vetoes were commonly covert and did not impinge on public awareness. The clergy typically used private and secretive channels to get their way."[59] Church opinions were regularly sought both officially and in informal consultations between politicians and clerical officials. In the first decades of independence, the "usual device, in an issue of the kind that would interest Church as well as State, was to set up a committee or hold a conference, at which all interested concerned, including of course the Catholic hierarchy, or Catholic societies approved by the hierarchy could present their views. The government would wait for a consensus to emerge, and legislate accordingly."[60] Fundamentally, the state sought church support, and legislative influence was "not so much the result of pressure by the hierarchy as independent initiatives of successive government to maintain state power by appeasing the Church."[61]

Thus the incidence of actual direct intervention in the legal framework was not inordinate; instead, most of the work was done ahead of time, in the various committees, and in the framing of legislation that anticipated and sought to preempt church criticism. Even as John Whyte compiled only sixteen different instances where bishops had direct input on legislation between 1923 and 1970s, there were three to four dozen other items of significant legislation where the church and state were in "formal

[56] Larkin 1984, 121.
[57] Keogh 1986; Keogh 2007; Smith 2004; Girvin 2002; Whyte 1971; Farren 1995.
[58] Smith 2004, 208.
[59] Garvin 2004, 6.
[60] Whyte 1971, 38.
[61] Inglis 1998, 79.

consultation."[62] There were multiple other occasions where bills never left the desk of legislators, given potential church objections. Finally, as pervasive as the church's policy influence was, its authority over matters of public morality was unquestioned.[63]

In the writing of the 1937 Constitution, church officials and interests were explicitly represented; the future Archbishop of Dublin, John Charles McQuaid, provided advice and relevant excerpts from papal encyclicals.[64] The highly influential McQuaid, a personal friend of de Valera and an outsized personality in Irish politics,[65] pushed for the elimination of divorce and for women's place in the home (reflecting both the *Quadragesimo Anno* and *Rerum Novarum* papal encyclicals), and in some accounts actually drafted the article (44) on religion, church, and state.[66] The result, the 1937 Constitution, identified the common good with religious criteria; blurred governmental and church roles in education, family law, and the welfare state; outlawed divorce; affirmed the role of women in the home; and recognized "the special position of the Holy Catholic and Apostolic and Roman Church as the guardian of the Faith professed by the great majority of the citizens" (Article 44). McQuaid's goal was to "make Ireland a model Catholic state with a model

---

[62] Inglis 1998, 79.

[63] Inglis 1998, 77.

[64] Keogh and McCarthy 2007, 109.

[65] Garvin paints a highly evocative portrait: "McQuaid was an odd mixture of the progressive, the reactionary, the creative, and the authoritarian. He built large, sexually segregated, schools and gargantuan triumphalist churches. He even tried (unsuccessfully) to prevent young women from emigrating to pagan England by denying them passports; civil servants pointed out, quite reasonably, that such a measure would be illegal under the law of the land, quite apart from any other consideration. Dublin Corporation was forbidden by him to build council houses below a certain size, lest small families and contraception be encouraged by lack of bed space. For several years in the late 1940s, McQuaid ensured that vaginal tampons were forbidden, and complained repeatedly to the government about the corset advertisements in the *Irish Independent*. He ensured that education was segregated rigidly by sex and creed, helped to modernise the medical health system, exported illegitimate children, probably illegally to Catholic homes in the United States, and had his spies everywhere. He liked women, enjoyed their company, and wished them to be good housewives and cooks. . . . His contempt for the civil law was extraordinary. His agents sent him reports on every significant public meeting held in the Archdiocese of Dublin between 1940 and 1972" (Garvin 2004, 56–57).

[66] Keogh 2007, 101–02. In the initial draft of Article 44, the Roman Catholic Church was identified as "one true church," but this formulation was deleted and the rest attenuated (Keogh and McCarthy 2007, 156). De Valera himself, and many of his peers, expressed ambivalence about Article 44 but recognized that for the Constitution to pass, the article had to be included. Fianna Fáil's position was best summed up by one of its parliamentarians: "we wouldn't get [the support of the majority] if we gave the Bishops any chance to attack us" (Keogh and McCarthy 2007, 172).

constitution which would condition the development of the country."[67] It was not until 1967 that an informal constitutional committee recommended, in keeping with the ecumenical spirit of the Second Vatican Council, to delete article 44.1.2, which recognized the special role of the Catholic Church in Ireland.[68] The official legal relationship between the church and state was only abolished in a referendum in 1972, and at the New Ireland Forum in 1984[69] "the bishops repeated that they 'are not in any sense seeking to require that the teaching of the Catholic Church be made the criterion of constitutional law in this country.' "[70] In the meantime, however, even if case law did not always follow Catholic doctrine, "for nearly forty years after 1938, the Supreme Court acted to strengthen the Catholic, nationalist, and patriarchal nature of the constitution."[71]

This is not to say that the governments simply did the church's bidding; instead, incumbents considered the potential costs of concessions against the benefit of church support and of future policy preferences. For example, in the early 1930s, the bishops pressed for the regulation of dance halls, since they saw them as hotbeds of licentiousness and blamed them for the rise in illegitimate births. The 1935 Dance Hall Act was very much an answer to their pressure; the President of the Executive Council,[72] Éamon de Valera, agreed and complied. At the same time, "a possible *quid pro quo* could be episcopal support for a new Constitution. De Valera was thinking very much ahead."[73] Similarly, for all the influence of several clerical friends and advisors, such as McQuaid and a group of Jesuit academics, de Valera found that constitutional draft's reference to the "one, true church" was politically untenable.[74] It would immediately split public opinion along confessional and republican lines,

---

[67] Keogh and McCarthy 2007, 121.

[68] Girvin 2008, 77. The change was justified in very diplomatic terms: the article "was not intended to give any privilege to the Roman Catholic Church, and the Church never sought to have itself placed in a privileged position. The deletion of this provision would, in particular, dispel any doubts and suspicions which may linger in the minds of non-Catholics, North and South of the Border, and remove an unnecessary source of mischievous and specious criticism" (Committee on the Constitution 1967, 48).

[69] The Department of the Taoiseach and the Irish Civil Service established the New Ireland Forum in 1983–84. Intended to provide an avenue to discuss potential political solutions to the Troubles in Northern Ireland, it also included an effort by Taoiseach Garret FitzGerald to continue his "crusade" to change the confessional and nationalist aspects of the Irish Constitution. The forum invited church delegations to discuss religious pluralism in Ireland and the status of Protestant minority rights.

[70] Girvin 2008, 86.

[71] Girvin 2002, 83; see also Keogh and McCarthy 2007, 14.

[72] The head of government was not known as Taoiseach until December 1937.

[73] Keogh 1986, 207.

[74] Keogh 1986, 210; Keogh and McCarthy 2007, 156ff.

giving ammunition to the opponents of a new Constitution—and yet without united clerical endorsement, the Constitution would not be enacted.[75] Here, the Irish bishops conceded (even though the Vatican itself refused to endorse the Constitution without the "one, true" reference). De Valera finessed the issue using nationalist arguments—and made it "possible to neutralise Irish Catholic criticism by emphasising the nationalist elements of the constitution and the extent to which it was necessary to compromise on some Catholic demands for the sake of national unity and Northern Ireland."[76]

The power of the church to influence public policy was at its peak in the four decades from independence to the 1960s. Two episodes highlight the church's influence at the peak of its powers: the Carrigan Report (1930) and the Mother and Child Scheme (1950–51). The Carrigan Committee and the report it issued identified a moral problem (the licentiousness of young women) and crafted a solution that reified the church's power as a moral authority and a moral guarantee by creating a vast architecture of church-run industrial and reformatory schools, mother and baby homes, adoption agencies, and Magdalene Laundries/Asylums.[77]

The Carrigan Committee was known originally as the Committee on the Criminal Law Amendment Acts and Juvenile Prostitution. The Cosgrove government convened the committee in 1930 to investigate whether changes in laws relating to sexual offenses were required, including the age of consent and juvenile prostitution. The committee came on the heels of several joint church-state efforts; the censorship of films and the abolishing of divorce in 1925 were followed by a series of official investigative committees such as the Inquiry Regarding Venereal Disease (1925), the Committee on Evil Literature (1927), and the Commission on the Relief of the Sick and Destitute Poor Including the Insane Poor (1928). These were all designed to differentiate Ireland from its former British colonizers; as Father R. S. Devane put in a 1924 article, "an attempt should be made to *codify*, as far as possible, all such laws [relating to morality], and thereby set up a national public standard of morality, in complete harmony with Irish Catholic ideals."[78]

---

[75] Keogh 1986, 211.

[76] Girvin 2002, 82.

[77] Smith 2004, 209. The first baby and mother home, Bessboro, was opened in 1921. After the committee's report, children who were orphaned, homeless, destitute, the daughters of sexual offenders, who lived in houses used for prostitution, or who were under the care of "any reputed thief or of any common or reputed prostitute" could be placed in a church-run institution. Over 170,000 children entered the industrial schools alone from 1936 to 1970. Report of the Commission to Inquire into Child Abuse, vol. I, chap. 3, http://www.childabusecommission.com/rpt/01–03.php.

[78] Maguire 2007, 81.

The Carrigan Committee consisted of both secular and church officials (in total, four men and two women), and six of the twenty-nine witnesses were Catholic clergy.[79] The committee found that immoral practices, including rape, prostitution, and child abuse, were prevalent, emphasizing the culpability of "wild girls" in its minutes.[80] The Department of Justice suppressed these findings as damaging to national reputation.[81] The bill that did emerge from the committee's recommendations substantially incorporated the hierarchy's concerns, focusing on prohibition of contraceptive devices, raising the age of consent to eighteen years, licensing of dance halls, and addressing the moral abuse of motor cars. Differences did arise; the Carrigan Committee report favored a tightening of the law to protect women and children, while the Minister of Justice and the parliamentary committee he chaired felt that such changes would be too severe on men. While the report urged punishment for both prostitutes and their clients, the law that resulted, the Criminal Law Amendment Act of 1935, punished only prostitutes. Moreover, the final law was far more stringent in its outlawing of contraceptives. Both this law and the Dance Hall Act of 1935 passed with minimal debate and no public participation.[82]

What is critical about this episode is twofold: first, the acceptance of the Catholic hierarchy's framing of the problem of child abuse, rape, and prostitution as *moral* failings, and second, the direct influence of the hierarchy in the "solution"—institutionalization and the removal from public eye of "fallen" girls and women to stop the further contamination of Irish society and its moral purity. The secular state handed over authority over the care of these women and girls to the church. In one analysis, the Carrigan episode showed the "state's willing abdication of responsibility for matters of sexuality and sexual education to the Catholic Church."[83] Both church and state cooperated in formally and informally enforcing Catholic teachings as a way of differentiating Ireland from England and reifying a distinct Irish national identity in the new state.[84]

The Mother and Child Scheme controversy served as a further warning to politicians that the church would oppose any legislation that it judged to violate its teachings.[85] It also showed the church was prepared

[79] Kennedy 2000, 354; Smith 2004, 220.
[80] Maguire 2007, 86.
[81] Kennedy 2000.
[82] Smith 2004, 219.
[83] Smith 2004, 211.
[84] Smith 2004, 210.
[85] Farren 1995, 223.

to act strategically to defend its interests.[86] In 1950, Dr. Noel Browne, the Health Minister in the coalition government dominated by Clann na Poblachta (a radical new republican party) and Fine Gael, proposed free universal medical care for women and children. The Mother and Child Scheme proposal included the widespread provision of obstetric and neo-natal medical care and education, the inspection of children in schools to make sure they were not malnourished or ill, and broader arrangements for health authorities to provide health care for children. This free health-care scheme for children would have allowed doctors to advise women on family size, and also would have assigned some Catholic women to non-Catholic doctors.

The outraged church lashed back immediately; such provisions would allow state officials to "walk into any Irishman's home and interfere be-tween man and wife and, indeed, between God and married couple."[87] Church officials further objected to an elimination of a means test, since that would constitute an immoral and an infeasible incursion of the state: "there are certain services which the State should supply free to all but these are relatively few."[88] Condemning the scheme on theological and doctrinal grounds, the church "perceived such incursions into the realm of family values and sexual health as a threat to their domain of moral authority."[89] Archbishop McQuaid sent a "freezing" reply to Browne's proposal,[90] and subsequently the bishops drew up a letter of protest to the Taoiseach (Prime Minister), set up a committee to meet with Browne, and met with the government.[91]

There are two notable aspects to the Mother and Child Scheme epi-sode. First, the bishops and state officials communicated directly, rather than appealing to the public. Second, the consequences of the church's condemnation of the scheme were swift and durable. Browne attempted to respond to each of the criticisms: the state was not taking away par-

[86] An earlier Public Health Bill of 1945 would have also centralized health care and introduced mandatory inspection of children, yet the Catholic hierarchy, including Arch-bishop McQuaid, "appeared ready to accept enactment without protest" (Whyte 1971, 138). When the bill was delayed (the sponsoring minister resigned for unrelated reasons), a new bill introduced in 1947 had much the same provisions: but now the hierarchy moved from neutrality to opposition, and launched its first formal protest against legislation (Whyte 1971, 143).

[87] Coyne 1951, 138.

[88] Coyne 1951, 147.

[89] McDonnell and Allison 2006, 821; see also Girvin 2002, 120.

[90] When Browne initially published details of the scheme and sent pamphlets to the bishops, most bishops acknowledged receipt without disapproval: it was only when Arch-bishop McQuaid made his fury known that the Church machine set into motion (Whyte 1971, 217).

[91] Whyte 1971, 217.

ents' rights, the education of mothers and children would be limited to hygiene and diet, not moral issues, and so on, but he made no headway and eventually resigned.[92] The government fell soon afterward, and the legislation was withdrawn. At the next election Fianna Fáil was returned to power and Clann na Poblachta disintegrated.[93] The new Fianna Fáil government "engaged in extended negotiations with the hierarchy to secure agreement on revised legislation . . . and quickly met most of their objections."[94] Much of the public was puzzled; there was widespread confusion as to why the church hierarchy opposed the Mother and Child Scheme, and many thought the bishops simply wrong.[95] Yet no one, not even Browne himself, "denied the church's right to pass judgment" on the Mother and Child Scheme or other legislation.[96] Observers were shaken by the "abject compliance by government with the church's demands,"[97] but neither the political opposition nor civil society articulated these objections publicly. Not surprisingly, Bishop Lucey of Cork claimed in 1955 that bishops were "final arbiters of right and wrong even in political matters."[98] Above all, the episode solidified the church's hold on the welfare state, and on moral housekeeping: "for a quarter of century after this controversy, none of the political parties were prepared to confront the hierarchy on education, health or moral issues. As late as 1965 [Taoiseach] Lemass immediately withdrew tentative suggestions in respect of marriage and divorce once it became clear that Archbishop McQuaid was opposed."[99]

Throughout this era, the 1920s through 1960s, "what is noticeable is the virtual absence of public criticism of the church and the public expression of views hostile to the church, even at the time of the Mother and Child Controversy in 1951–52."[100] Sociological studies in the 1950s and 1960s suggested that the authority of the church was so great there was a "widespread resistance to the idea that there could be a conflict between church and state in Ireland."[101] The church hierarchy was free to repeatedly frame issues as falling into the church-sanctioned moral domain, and to veto policies it saw as objectionable. This is not to say that the church was omnipotent in its pronouncements; while society accepted

---

[92] Whyte 1971, 222.
[93] Speed 1992; Smyth 2005.
[94] Girvin 2002, 128.
[95] Whyte 1971, 270.
[96] Girvin 2002, 125.
[97] Farren 1995, 223.
[98] Whyte 1971, 312.
[99] Girvin 2002, 129.
[100] Girvin 2002, 124.
[101] Girvin 2008, 76.

the church's *moral* claims on abortion, education, or divorce, stances perceived as anti-nationalist—such as the church's repeated condemnations of the IRA—would meet with far less resonance or approval.[102] Yet here, so long as the church objected to the violence of the methods, rather than to the nationalism of the sentiment, these statements did not undermine the church's overall moral authority.

For its part, even as some ministers attempted to gain greater autonomy, both personal faith and the fear of church reaction meant the state would actively comply and cooperate with the church. Taoiseach John Costello (in office in 1948–51 and 1954–57), openly prioritized his faith over his secular office: "I am a Catholic first."[103] It is thus not entirely surprising that the church had "considerable influence in the formation and acceptance of the Irish Constitution, the type of referenda which have been proposed and voted on, and the type of social and cultural legislation which the Dail has passed."[104]

Catholic doctrine so suffused policy and society that government reports cited church teaching; the Report of the Commission on Vocational Organisation from 1943, for example, openly and frequently referred to *Quadragesimo Anno*, Pope Pius XI's encyclical,[105] as did the Dignan Report on Social Welfare.[106] State ministers argued their positions using references to church doctrine and papal encyclicals, even when answering the church hierarchy's criticisms.[107] Not surprisingly, "the church's Marian Year of 1954, for example, was celebrated with almost the same fervour by the state as it was by the church."[108] Whether all parties complied with church demands equally fervently (the view of Whyte) or Fianna Fáil did relatively more (Girvin's view): the outcome was that under both Fine Gael and Fianna Fáil governments church preferences were anticipated and enacted.[109]

As the initial closeness (and need) of the early independence era gave way, both church and state shifted strategies. It was not until the 1960s

---

[102] Whyte 1971, 375.

[103] Farren 1995, 223.

[104] Inglis 1998, 220.

[105] Commission on Vocational Organisation 1943, 8ff.

[106] Yet Fianna Fáil, victorious in the 1944 elections and sure at the time of its future success, rejected both the plans (Whyte 1971, 113).

[107] Whyte 1971, 182–83 and 189–91, for accounts of Minister of Social Welfare William Norton and Attorney General Charles Casey.

[108] Farren 1995, 222.

[109] Fianna Fáil *voters* reflected church preferences more closely: in 1983, 80% of FF supporters voted for the pro-life amendment, against 61% of Fine Gael. A majority of Labour voters opposed. Similar patterns held in the 1986 divorce referendum, and in the 1990s with abortion. Yet this relationship was not constant; it was Fine Gael that criticized the 1940s health bills, as against church teachings.

that disagreements between individual politicians and individual clergy appeared. By this point, politicians and clergy did not mix in the same social circles, and some of the personal access to politicians had ebbed. Church support was no longer the sine qua non of survival for the secular state. It was then that the Parliament took up changes in education and censorship as well as constitutional reform (allowing divorce to Protestants), with either little protest from the clergy or little consultation.[110] At the same time, the reforms of Vatican II reached Ireland as well, and so the church stated that it did not expect all sins to become criminal offenses, nor did it want "special privilege" from the state.[111] Here, the church made nuanced distinctions; at the 1983–84 New Ireland Forum, the Bishop of Down and Connor, Cahal Daly, argued that the Catholic Church in Ireland rejected the idea of a confessional state, but had the right "to alert the consciences of Catholics to the moral consequences of any proposed piece of legislation . . . while leaving to the legislators and to the electorate their freedom to act in accordance with their consciences."[112]

As a result, in both the 1983 abortion referendum and the 1986 divorce referendum, Catholic civil society organizations mobilized the electorate, with the tacit backing of the church and the complicity of Fianna Fáil elected officials and others, but in its official statements and campaign activities, the church hierarchy did not become involved in politicking or campaigning directly. By this point, then, the church could rely on the values it had inculcated through the educational system and exercise its own demographic dominance in referenda, which further meant the church could amend the Constitution. The moral authority that earlier had allowed it to control one public sector—education—now allowed it to exercise power in others.

One such referendum in 1983 made abortion, already illegal, now unconstitutional as well. The church supported the referendum, rather than relying on access alone, because amendments to the Irish Constitution must be approved by a popular referendum. The amendment was spurred by the *Roe v. Wade* decision in the United States, among others, and anxieties that the High Court, largely autonomous of the church, could also liberalize abortion in Ireland. The Catholic Church and the Pro-Life Amendment Campaign (PLAC) exerted heavy pressure on the electorate, and "the result was clearly a vindication of the Catholic Church's authority and demonstrated the vulnerability of the political process to a campaign orchestrated by well-organized interest groups."[113] A 1992 referendum, on the heels of

---

[110] Whyte 1971, 350.
[111] Inglis 1998; Hogan 2003.
[112] Keogh 2007, 126.
[113] Kissane 2003, 81.

the notorious "X case" (where a raped girl was not allowed to travel to England for an abortion) resulted in the freedom to travel—but with no further provisions for legalizing access to abortion. It was not until 2002 that an attempt to introduce tougher penalties on doctors for abortion failed in a popular referendum. Education and divorce followed similar patterns.

When courts rather than popular legislatures decided policy outcomes, however, the church was less successful. In the 1995 Regulation of Information Bill, which the government passed despite church opposition, the government insisted on superiority of parliament over interest groups. The Supreme Court ruled on the legislation—and here the real bombshell was not that the court upheld the law, but that it insisted on superiority of the Constitution to natural law, to the outrage and condemnation of the Catholic hierarchy.[114] In 2002, high court decisions ended the ban on contraception, the proscriptions on homosexuality were reduced, and no-fault divorce became a possibility. One analyst argued that "the close identification of the nation with the Catholic faith was unraveling."[115] Yet the church could still frame the rhetoric of political debates, forcing all political actors to eventually debate the issues on the church's terms. Public religiosity and opinion had already shifted, but policy debates and outcomes continued to reflect Catholic doctrine, and the church remained a key political participant.

Considerable institutional access persisted well beyond the drop in moral authority that came about in the 1990s as a result of the widespread abuse scandals within the church. For example, the church gained formal authority over education in the 1920s, but it was not until 2010 that it began to concede control, and the motivating factor was a shortage of personnel. Similarly, for all the closings of the reform schools and Magdalene laundries in the 1990s, the church continued to control much of the welfare and health-care sectors. Finally, even if personal ties between clergy and state officials weakened, no serious consideration of changes in abortion policy occurred despite numerous rulings from the Supreme Court and European Court of Human Rights. For example, it took Irish politicians over twenty years (and a highly publicized tragedy) to declare what would constitute the threat to the mother's life that would justify a legal abortion.

Education

Education illustrates church authority and the mechanisms of its replication over time; the state handed over the formal control of the primary

---

[114] Girvin 2008, 91.
[115] Kissane 2003, 85.

and secondary educational system to the church, which then ensured that the curriculum included both daily religious education and the inculcation of Catholic doctrine and ritual practices, such as prayers, retreats, and preparation for holy sacraments. The "control of the education system has been fundamental to the Catholic Church maintaining adherence to its rules and regulations. Within the schools young Irish children have been slowly and consistently instructed in and also imbued with the Church's teachings."[116] In effect, "the vast majority of children, in so far as they got educated at all, got the education the Catholic Church thought they should get."[117]

The primacy of the church in Irish education had its roots in British penal laws, which outlawed Catholic education. An informal system of "hedge schools" was founded instead in the eighteenth century. When the Relief Act of 1782 restored to Catholics the right to teach in schools, the hedge schools formalized and linked to parish systems, under the authority of the local priest, who either ran the schools or hired and supervised teachers.[118] The clergy were already seen as community leaders; the government paid for buildings and salaries, but the schools themselves were "established and managed by prominent individuals in the community, usually clergy."[119] The nineteenth century saw the church now supporting the national project, emphasizing the Irish language and a decrying Anglicization (in which the church had earlier participated), as part of a greater effort to preserve the traditional and rural nature of Catholicism itself.[120] In 1831, the government established a system of primary schools, which were to provide "joint secular and separate religious instruction to children of all faiths." In Brian Titley's account, both Catholic and Protestant authorities quickly set about destroying the secular aspects of the system; restrictions on when and how much religion could be taught disappeared, and schools won the right to exclude clergy from other denominations from their classrooms. Thus by the end of the nineteenth century "the system had become de facto denominational."[121] Subsequent attempts by the British government to introduce a nondenominational educational system in the 1900s were frustrated by "an alliance between the new Sinn Fein party and the Catholic hierarchy"[122] in the name of Irish national identity and values. The enduring result was not only that the church had authority over education, but also that specific orders

---

[116] Inglis 1998, 57.
[117] Garvin 2004, 125.
[118] Inglis 1998, 123.
[119] Titley 1983, 5.
[120] Garvin 2004, 127.
[121] Titley 1983, 5–6. See also Coolahan 2014, 474.
[122] Kissane 2003, 75.

educated entire swaths of the Irish elite: "it is not that [the Christian Brothers] educated every Irish male. It is rather that they, or the priests, educated and trained nearly every male who attained a high position in Irish society."[123]

In the fledgling new state, the Catholic Church was subsequently able to insist on its primacy in education, with little opposition. Nor could there be doubt about "the stand of the Catholic Church on educational matters. Complete church control of the schools and colleges to be attended by Catholics was its persistent demand; anything less than complete control by the church was seen as a reluctant compromise."[124] The government readily agreed, and there was no public protest against the continuation of denominational education.[125] Instead, the cabinet consulted the bishops on the wording of Article 10 of the Constitution concerning education.[126] The Constitution enshrined the Catholic Church's official position on education: that the responsibility for education rests primarily with parents. In practice, this meant that in a Catholic-dominated society, the overwhelming majority of formal education should take place within Catholic schools. Under Article 42.2, the state had the right to establish schools, but until 2008, for example, it had not provided primary schools.[127] The subsequent ministers of education were inevitably observant Catholics, and the prevailing conviction of both secular and religious authorities was that neutrality would translate into bias against belief.

The system of church-run but state-funded primary and secondary education ("patronage") persisted throughout the twentieth century. Of the state's national schools, 95% were Catholic-run, with a Catholic ethos that included sacramental instruction. Roughly half of the voluntary secondary schools were also Catholic.[128] From the 1930s onward, the church controlled primary schooling and the administration of juvenile justice. De Valera, as Minister of Education in 1940, "offered the entire [vocational educational] system to a religious order to remove it from state control."[129] The Council of Education, established in 1950, was an official advisory government to the Department of Education,

---

[123] Inglis 1998, 52.

[124] Farren 1995, 9.

[125] After 1922, the Minister of Education, Eois MacNeill, charged a committee headed by the Jesuit Father Lambert McKenna to examine schooling. Not surprisingly, the Conference Report concluded that schooling should be infused with a "religious spirit" (Coolahan 2014, 475).

[126] Farren 1995, 109.

[127] Coolahan 2014, 476.

[128] Byrne 1999; Inglis 1998, 59.

[129] Girvin 2002, 122.

and a quarter of its members were Catholic clergy, as was its chair.[130] The council produced two reports, on primary and secondary curriculums, which confirmed the primacy of the Catholic Church in education. Among the "Rules for National Schools," published in 1965, Rule 68 stated that "of all parts of a school curriculum Religious Instruction is by far the most important" and that "a religious spirit should inform and vivify the whole work of the school."[131] The government was reluctant to change the educational system; despite some reforms in 1965, a 1995 White Paper on the topic found that century-old current arrangements were effectively protected by the Constitution.[132]

In the decades until the 1990s, the church's hegemony remained largely unquestioned: as Whyte describes it,

> Over most of the period of since independence, the most remarkable feature of educational policy in Ireland has been the reluctance of the State to touch on the entrenched positions of the Church. This is not because the Church's claims have been moderate: on the contrary, it has carved out for itself a more extensive control over education than in any other country in the world. It is because the Church has insisted on its claims with such force that the State has been extremely cautious in entering its domain. This has given Church-State relations in Ireland an unusual characteristic. Taking the world as a whole, one can say that education has caused more trouble between Church and State than any other topic. In self-governing Ireland, it has only rarely been an issue.[133]

---

[130] Coolahan 2003, 139.

[131] The full text of the controversial Rule 68 reads:

> Of all the parts of a school curriculum Religious Instruction is by far the most important, as its subject-matter, God's honour and service, includes the proper use of all man's faculties, and affords the most powerful inducements to their proper use. Religious Instruction is, therefore, a fundamental part of the school course, and a religious spirit should inform and vivify the whole work of the school.

> The teacher should constantly inculcate the practice of charity, justice, truth, purity, patience, temperance, obedience to lawful authority, and all the other moral virtues. In this way he will fulfil the primary duty of an educator, the moulding to perfect form of his pupils' character, habituating them to observe, in their relations with God and with their neighbour, the laws which God, both directly through the dictates of natural reason and through Revelation, and indirectly through the ordinance of lawful authority, imposes on mankind.

[132] Inglis 1998, 224.

[133] Whyte 1971, 21.

The church thus had to agree to—or volunteer—any more fundamental changes. That did not happen until the 2010s, when demographic changes and immigration prompted a new Programme on Patronage and Pluralism to review the church's role in education. The committee included explicitly secular advocates and eventually called for divesting the church of patronage and the removal of Rule 68.[134] By this point, however, the church itself did not object to the divestment; with fewer and fewer monks and nuns, the church had difficulty staffing the schools itself, and had long turned to secular teachers. The numbers were simply unsustainable: by 1998, 660 members of orders were in secondary education, down from 2,300 in 1969. Fewer than 5% were under thirty-five.[135] Given the personnel burdens of administering the educational system, the 2010 review did not overturn church preferences. Minister of Education Ruairí Quinn ordered the forum to take into account "the expressed willingness of the Roman Catholic Church to consider divesting patronage of primary schools."[136]

The scandals surrounding the Irish church in the 1990s, and the changing face of Ireland, which was becoming more multicultural and pluralist, further weakened the church's dominance in education.[137] In 2012, Minister of Education Quinn went as far as to question why so much class time is devoted to Irish language and to religion in primary school: the implication that both are less relevant than other topics to preparing pupils for future study and employment, especially in a challenging and rapidly shifting economic environment.[138] Yet for over a hundred years, the church was able to set the moral standards by which it would be evaluated, and to inculcate these standards, as well as religious practices and rituals, and a favorable view of the church, in generations of Irish men and women. In so doing, the church ensured that "the dominance of the Catholic Church in the educational field has been central to preventing a more rapid decline in its position in Irish society."[139]

Abortion

Abortion in Ireland was not only a moral or an ethical issue; "the control of women's bodies is . . . a familiar issue to Americans, but what

---

[134] Coolahan 2003; Coolahan et al. 2012.

[135] Byrne 1999. From 1970 to 1995, the orders experienced a 58% decrease in brothers, 35% in sisters, 43% in clerical religious orders, and 7% in diocesan clergy, for an average of 35% (Inglis 1998, 212).

[136] Coolahan 2003; Coolahan et al. 2012, 4.

[137] Andersen 2010, 17.

[138] Flynn, Seán. 2012. "Quinn Questions School Emphasis on Irish, Religion." *Irish Times*, April 5.

[139] Inglis 1998, 223.

is different in this case is its role in nationalist discourse: the borders of the woman were the borders of Ireland."[140] The interpretation might seem melodramatic, but the controversies surrounding abortion and its importance to the church are undeniable. Abortion had already been a criminal offense in Ireland since Britain's Offences Against the Person Act passed in 1861. Contraception at this time appears to have been relatively widely available, thanks both to legal changes in Britain and cultural norms among Irish women, where it was commonplace (along with infanticide). However, as part of the broader effort to discipline the Catholic masses in the nineteenth century, and supported by the ascendant middle class, the Roman Catholic hierarchy in Ireland imposed a new sexual morality.[141] The Catholic Church further marshaled nationalist feeling from this point on by portraying sexual liberty as a godless and a British invention and colonial imposition.

Affirming both Catholic social teaching and a patriarchal position on sex, reproduction, and the family, Article 41.2.1 of the Irish Constitution stated in 1937 that "in particular, the State recognizes that by her life within the home, woman gives to the State a support without which the common good cannot be achieved," directly echoing the *Quadragesimo Anno* encyclical of Pope Pius XI. Divorce was banned at this time, along with the sale and advertising of contraceptives (by Section 17 of the 1935 Criminal Law Amendment Act). Married women could not work in the civil service or other state jobs,[142] and motherhood was the one women's role that both the church and the state celebrated. From the very beginning of the Irish Free State, abortion was illegal, and this ban was critical to the new moral and political order where a particular notion of the family was central.

Until the 1970s, the ban on abortion appeared durable. However, events abroad had put contraception and abortion on the agenda for legal reform in Ireland, whose judiciary tended to be affected by developments in Britain and the United States. The repeal of the 1861 Offences Against the Person Act in Britain gave women liberal access to abortion in 1967, while *Roe v. Wade* invalidated American anti-abortion laws in 1973. Ireland's nascent anti-abortion lobby saw these as potentially dangerous precedents foreshadowing liberalization in Ireland.[143] These fears were heightened in December 1973 by an Irish Supreme Court ruling (*McGee v. The Attorney General*) that the ban on contraceptives was

---

[140] Taylor 1995, 248.
[141] Inglis 1998.
[142] Smyth 2005.
[143] O'Reilly 1988; Smyth 2005.

unconstitutional because it violated rights to privacy.[144] Anti-abortion groups began to form, most notably the Society for the Protection of Unborn Children (SPUC) and the Pro-Life Amendment Campaign (PLAC).

Within two weeks of PLAC's formation in April 1981, both Fine Gael and Fianna Fáil leaders (Garret FitzGerald and Charles Haughey respectively) committed to introducing a constitutional amendment banning abortion.[145] Abortion was already illegal; the intention of such a provision would be to ensure it could never become legal. In 1982, Haughey proposed an amendment that would protect the "right to life of the unborn" and thus preclude an Irish *Roe v. Wade* decision. After Haughey's minority government collapsed later that year, FitzGerald proposed a narrower and more negative wording (which would allow parliament to liberalize legislation but preclude courts from interpreting the Constitution as facilitating abortion). The defeat of FitzGerald's wording in the Dáil Éireann led to a referendum on the original wording in 1983. The referendum passed by a 67% majority, enabling Article 40.3.3: "The State acknowledges the right to life of the unborn and, with due regard to the equal right to life of the mother, guarantees in its laws to respect, and as far as practicable, by its laws defend and vindicate that right."[146]

The church's discourse was unambiguously sacral. As the 1983 amendment to the Constitution was being debated, the Irish Episcopal Conference issued a statement that the amendment was a matter of "great moral seriousness" and described "the sacredness of human life, as created by God in his own image."[147] The campaign demonstrated church strength in that it "showed the ability of the Church to limit political practice and discourse, and what was to be regarded as legal and unconstitutional."[148] Nor did the church have to exert direct pressure to obtain its preferred

---

[144] Earlier, "the arrival of the contraceptive pill in the mid-1960s offered an immediate and comic challenge to the blanket ban on contraceptive devices imposed by the law. Irish women were solemnly declared by their doctors to have the most irregular cycles in the world, and the 'Pill' was sold as a cycle regulator but not as a contraceptive" (Garvin 2004, 160). Pope Paul VI's 1968 encyclical forbidding "artificial" contraception was met with quiet resistance among Catholic women.

[145] Inglis 1998, 83.

[146] The opposition took the form of an unorganized coalition of liberal intelligentsia and autonomous women's groups with no effective mainstream political representation. Fine Gael was basically supportive of the amendment, and some of its members even crossed the floor to vote in favor of the stronger wording. One of the opposition group's most effective arguments concerned the increasing numbers of Irish women going to Britain for abortions. Subsequent to the amendment, courts declared that information on abortion was unconstitutional, and a number of clinics providing information and counseling were shut down after prosecutions that were frequently initiated by SPUC (Smyth 2005).

[147] Dillon 1993, 105.

[148] Inglis 1998, 85.

outcomes, relying instead on the electorate's adherence to church teaching. While the church actively supported the constitutional amendment, "it was only toward the end of the campaign that the clerical resources of the Church began to be used fully"[149] when pastoral letters urged a "yes" vote.

The next decade would bring several controversies and public debate—but little policy change. In 1983–84, public discussion over sexual morality erupted—the very discussions the Carrigan Report sought to bury—thanks to the Pro-Life Amendment campaign, the Anne Lovett case (a fifteen-year-old who gave birth in an outdoor grotto and succumbed to hemorrhage and shock), the "Kerry babies" scandal (where a woman pregnant by a married man confessed to murder of a newborn found on a beach, despite evidence the baby was not hers), and the 1983 referendum itself.[150] Yet abortion policy and debates remained unchanged.[151]

It was not until the X case that the law changed. In 1992, the parents of a fourteen-year-old, pregnant, rape victim (referred to as "X") asked the local police for advice on how to provide fetal tissue after an abortion as legal evidence in the rape trial. The police sent the case to court, and the High Court issued an injunction, preventing X from obtaining an abortion or from leaving the country for nine months (cutting off the common option of obtaining an abortion in Britain). The fact that X had been diagnosed as suicidal was not seen as a substantial enough threat to her life to justify an abortion. The Supreme Court reversed the High Court's decision, deeming suicide a health risk that could justify an abortion, and ruled the High Court's decision was an unwarranted interference with the authority of the family.[152]

The Catholic hierarchy and anti-abortion activists immediately demanded another referendum.[153] The result was the second abortion referendum, in November 1992. Unlike 1983, when the anti-abortion movement formed an alliance with Fianna Fáil, this time around the Taoiseach from Fianna Fáil, Albert Reynolds, vowed that there would be no return to the 1983 position. For its part, the church hierarchy in 1992 was divided

[149] Inglis 1998, 84.

[150] Oaks 2002, 321.

[151] Contraceptives were legalized, however. Over a decade after the Irish Supreme Court found that contraceptives could be legalized in 1973, the Health (Family Planning) Bill of 1985 allowed the sale of condoms and spermicide without a prescription to people over eighteen. Fianna Fáil actively opposed the law, and Dublin Archbishop Kevin McNamara "declared that contraception was not an issue that could be left to the individual conscience." He further admonished public officials that "Catholic politicians are strictly bound to take account of what the bishops teach where that touches on faith or morals" (Girvin 2008, 85).

[152] Smyth 2005.

[153] Girvin 2008, 89.

over the referendum, as not doing enough to eliminate abortion. As a result, the Catholic Bishops' Conference issued a statement, to be read at all masses right before the vote, in which abortion was condemned but parishioners were told to vote their conscience.[154] In addition, the bishops sent pamphlets all around the country. The referendum upheld two points: the right to travel abroad for an abortion and to obtain information. A third provision, which proposed a distinction between the "life" and the "health" of the mother (only the former could justify an abortion), allowing abortion on grounds of threat to the mother's life other than suicide, was soundly defeated.

The X case thus established that abortion was permissible in the cases of real and substantial risk to the life of the mother, which could only be avoided by the termination of the pregnancy. Yet what followed were decades of legal limbo. Labour insisted that the Case X provisions be legislated, but no party wanted to introduce legislation. In 1994, when Labour entered the government, legislation for travel and information was introduced and passed the Dáil in face of Fianna Fáil opposition, but the Case X provisions were not included. Two years later, the Constitution Review Group recommended legislation be introduced to carry out the Case X judgment, delineating the circumstances when abortion was permissible, and this was followed by the 1999 Green Paper, which also noted the advantages of such legislation. Yet no laws passed.

The result was that no effective legislation delineating the circumstances under which abortion is permissible was enacted, since "no Irish government . . . wants to be written into history as the one that opened the door to abortion in Ireland."[155] The issue remained so sensitive that the government has published no data on the number of, much less reasons for, legal abortion.[156] The Irish Medical Council adopted new guidelines in 2001, stating that termination is permissible when there is a "real and substantial risk to the life of the mother."[157] Yet doctors were afraid of the legal repercussions, no matter what their professional association might advise, since no laws specified the exact conditions justifying abortion. Instead, risk-averse legislators left the issue to referenda and to the courts. After the scandals in the church erupted in the early 1990s, politicians tried to limit the church's institutional access; when in 1996 the All-Party Oireachtas Committee on the Constitution began a comprehensive review of abortion since 1983, the medical profession was given priority for the first time, rather than church representatives dominating the

[154] Cap 2004, 10.
[155] Oaks 2002, 317.
[156] *Irish Times*, December 22, 2010.
[157] Oaks 2002, 328; Kissane 2003, 85.

witness stand.[158] Indeed, the Irish Bishops' Conference met with the committee on the same day as the representatives of other faiths. For their part, the bishops no longer had the confidence that the voters' preferences would allow the church to obtain its goals through referenda. In 2002, voters narrowly defeated a Fianna Fáil–sponsored (and church-backed) constitutional amendment that would have removed the threat of suicide as grounds for legal abortion (by 50.4% to 49.6%), allowing the Case X provisions to stand, and "suggesting that those in a minority in the 1970s now represented a majority."[159]

Yet referenda were still preferable to court decisions, over which the church had the least power. To compound the 1992 decision, in the 2007 "Miss D" case, the High Court ruled that no woman could be lawfully thwarted from traveling, even when a ward of the state.[160] In 2010 the European Court of Human Rights mandated that Ireland specify when abortion was permissible, after the ABC ruling put up by the Irish Family Planning Association.[161] Ireland now had to legislate when and how abortion is allowed when the woman's life is in danger, including from the risk of suicide, by specifying what was meant by "threat to woman's life." The ruling changed little, in that "hypocrisy has long dominated public discussion about abortion, with frightened legislators preferring to leave hard decisions on hard cases to the courts."[162] The Catholic Primate of All-Ireland, Cardinal Seán Brady, continued to "maintain that the issue is one for the Irish people, not lawmakers."[163]

The Cardinal's words would come back to haunt him. In October 2012, the tragic case of Savita Halappanavar yet again showed the inadequacies created by the legal ambiguity. Halappanavar was admitted to University Galway Hospital, suffering a miscarriage that could not be stopped at nineteen weeks of pregnancy. At this stage of pregnancy, a fetus is not viable, and the miscarriage was inevitable. However, since a

---

[158] Girvin 2008, 94.

[159] Girvin 2008, 97.

[160] The seventeen-year-old girl in question was pregnant with an anencephalic fetus, and the Health Service executive prevented her from traveling to Britain, presumably to obtain an abortion.

[161] The case involved three women: A, living in poverty with children in state care and fearful that another pregnancy would jeopardize her chances of regaining custody of her children; B, who took the morning after pill but was told by doctors she ran the risk of ectopic pregnancy; and C, who had a rare form of cancer and feared a pregnancy would cause her to relapse, but was unable to obtain information whether or not she could get an abortion (*Irish Times*, December 18, 2010). The ECHR found for C, but not for A or B, finding that allowing women to travel abroad, while prohibiting abortion domestically, preserves their human rights.

[162] *Irish Times*, December 18, 2010.

[163] *Irish Times*, December 18, 2010.

fetal heartbeat was detectable, the hospital doctors continued to refuse to perform an abortion. Over the course of the next days in the hospital, Halappanavar developed sepsis and died, along with the fetus. The tragedy catalyzed immediate and widespread public outrage that even the church had to take into account. After the Halappanavar case, the bishops quickly declared that treatment that endangers fetuses is permissible, provided efforts are made to save the fetus, and that the church has never prized fetal life over the mother's.[164]

In July 2013, accordingly, the Oireachtas (Parliament) considered the Protection of Life during Pregnancy Bill, which specified for the first time in thirty years the conditions under which abortion would be allowed, including suicidal intent. The law kept in place most of the restrictions on abortion, but the bishops immediately criticized it and launched a last-minute appeal and round of contacts with parliamentarians to urge them to vote against bill. The governing Fine Gael, however, imposed parliamentary discipline on the vote, and it passed with four parliamentarians expelled from the party for voting against the bill. In discussing the church's opposition to the bill, Archbishop Eamon Martin admitted that "the scandal of child abuse by Catholic priests and how it had been dealt with by senior members of the church had 'in the eyes of many people, eroded our credibility' and admitted that some people were 'less likely to listen' due to this background."[165]

In short, initial church advocacy instilled its preferences on abortion in the legal framework—and a popular referendum enshrined the ban on abortion in the Constitution. The church was on surest ground when working directly to formulate policy and then in advising voters on the referenda. It was on far less certain of success when the courts became involved, and as time wore on and voter preferences no longer reflected a loyalty to the church, referenda became less reliable as well. The erosion of moral authority as a result of the abuse scandals also meant that future legislation was more likely to ease the legal limits on abortion. Even so, abortion in Ireland remains heavily restricted—a direct reflection of the church's moral authority in the *preceding* decades.

Divorce

With the church's avid backing, divorce remained illegal in Ireland until 1997, despite rising popular support for divorce,[166] two referenda, and a lack of political consensus surrounding the prohibition. The ban on

---

[164] *RTE News*, November 20, 2012.

[165] *Irish Times*, July 10, 2013.

[166] Support nearly doubled over 1981–90, from 12% of poll respondents who found divorce justifiable in 1981 to 21% who did so in 1990 (and nearly tripled, to 35%, by 2010). World Values Survey data.

divorce dated back to the 1937 Constitution as part of the differentiation of Ireland from Britain.[167] The Constitution reinforced rather than changed the existing legal practice; in the 1920s, no provision for divorce existed, either, which meant that "now that we have turned our backs on the Imperial Parliament . . . the domiciled citizen of the Free State who desires this form of relief must seek it from the native Legislature."[168]

Unlike the centripetal issue of abortion, where all parties spoke the sacral language of church morality, secular officials publicly worried about the rights of non-Catholic minorities and their implications for the potential reunification with largely Protestant Northern Ireland. Thus Seán Lemass, the Taoiseach from 1959 to 1966, even suggested divorce laws might be liberalized, so that those citizens with religions that allow divorce could pursue it. But Cardinal McQuaid opposed any changes in divorce or contraception laws, and the fear of "violent opposition" from the hierarchy ended the discussion.[169] Similarly, the 1967 Report of the Committee on the Constitution noted that the prohibition on divorce was unfair to those who belonged to religions that allowed it, violating minority rights, yet the church did not respond favorably, not even to the argument that Ireland should allow divorce for those whose religion permits it in the name of Vatican Council II's ecumenical reforms.[170]

As a result, while other countries saw a silent revolution in the 1960s and 1970s, as pragmatic judges, lawyers, and bureaucrats worked to quietly transform divorce legislation and its application, Ireland remained an exception. The "public conflict was such that two referenda were needed before divorce became legal in 1997."[171] In the first of these, in 1986, the coalition government of Fine Gael and Labour proposed a new article in the Constitution that would allow dissolution in certain cases (where marriage had failed for at least five years, where there was no possibility of reconciliation, and where adequate provisions were made for children and dependent spouses). The 1986 referendum was a result of public opinion polls showing shifting opinions and desire for legal regulation, the perennial issue of aligning legislation so as to make reunification with Northern Ireland more feasible, and the mobilization of the Divorce Action Group[172]—and of consultations with the churches, as the Attorney General emphasized.[173] As with abortion, 63% of the voters rejected the proposal.

[167] Burley and Regan 2002, 204.
[168] *Irish Times*, February 23, 1924.
[169] Girvin 2008, 80.
[170] Committee on the Constitution 1967, 43–44.
[171] Burley and Regan 2002, 204.
[172] Prendiville 1988, 358.
[173] *Irish Times*, March 17, 1986.

Even as the Attorney General consulted the hierarchy, the church had altered its main tactics in the abortion and divorce referenda of the 1980s. Rather than relying only on the direct institutional access it had gained in obtaining control over education, health care, and the welfare state in the 1920s–1960s, the church now exploited a vision of Irish society that it had itself influenced and inculcated—one where the rejection of divorce was not simply a function of "unquestioned adherence to Roman Catholic dogma," but of a prevailing self-perception of Irish society where marriage and the family are central.[174] Church disapproval of divorce was unambiguous; the church emphatically stated that "the provision of civil divorce was a moral issue"[175] and officially declared at the end of a five-hour meeting with the Taoiseach in April 1986 that they stood firm in opposition to divorce.[176] A pastoral letter was read out loud that divorce is not permissible because its existence would undermine other marriage bonds.[177]

Nonetheless, despite their fierce opposition, the bishops were careful to state that "the Catholic Church does not ask that the law should enshrine any particular provision because it accords with Church teaching."[178] Unlike in the first abortion referendum in 1983, many bishops emphasized that the ultimate decision rests with the people—and their individual consciences,[179] leaving unsaid that these consciences were shaped by years of church education and social presence. They were also careful to point out that holding the referendum itself was entirely a political matter, and the church would offer no advice—nor did the Taoiseach seek it.[180] Similarly, Fianna Fáil officially took a position of neutrality.

Allied activists were the main actors: the *pro*-divorce lobby had been active since the 1970s, while the *anti*-divorce movement formally organized only in the early 1980s. Family Solidarity, a conservative movement that arose in the wake of the 1983 abortion referendum, was "organized on a national parish basis, has the support of Catholic clergy, and uses parish facilities for its meetings."[181] It was joined by the Anti-Divorce Campaign (ADC), an ad hoc group of Catholic lay people that formed only after announcement of the referendum. These lay groups emphasized church teachings and successfully transformed the central issue from one of civil rights of non-Catholics to "the common good of Irish

[174] Prendiville 1988, 356.
[175] Inglis 1998, 88.
[176] *Irish Times*, April 8, 1986.
[177] Prendiville 1988, 360.
[178] Summary of presentation to Taoiseach, quoted in *Irish Times*, April 8, 1986.
[179] Inglis 1998, 89.
[180] *Irish Times*, April 8, 1986.
[181] Dillon 1993, 32.

society,"[182] making divorce a moral matter, not simply a political issue. "Divorce posed, in these cleverly devised campaigns, a threat to the Irish lifestyle, and, more importantly, the Irish identity."[183]

In contrast, the pro-divorce campaign made the vote a test of Irish "progressiveness," with predictable backlash. Opinion polls consistently showed that a majority of Irish people favored some kind of divorce reform prior to the referendum, and that the same majority was visible in polls shortly after the referendum. The problem, as John Waters argues, was with the way the pro-divorce campaign was presented. Irish voters were receptive to arguments that divorce legislation could be a practical solution to the practical problem of marriage breakdown. But the overall tenor of the pro-divorce campaign placed too much emphasis on progress, modernity, and liberalism, and the rural population especially believed the campaign embodied an urban hostility toward rural life and tradition (of which the Catholic Church was an integral part).[184]

The second divorce referendum in 1995 had a different result, with 50.3% voting in favor of divorce and 49.7% against. The 1995 referendum was partially the result of a new coalition government unanimously supporting divorce reform, led by John Bruton, and a report by the Oireachtas Joint Committee on Marriage Breakdown, created "to consider the protection of marriage and of family life, and to examine the problems which follow the breakdown of marriage." The committee received over seven hundred written submissions and had direct oral consultations with twenty-three groups.[185] These groups included a wide range of religious organizations; only the Catholic Church and the Mormons rejected the necessity of legislating divorce. The Catholic Church framed their arguments in terms of "the common good."[186] The bishops officially condemned divorce but did not demand Catholics vote against the proposed legal changes.[187]

By this point, it was clear that "the official Church position against divorce had very little influence on the way these people voted. One reason

[182] Inglis 1998, 90.
[183] Burley and Regan 2002, 203.
[184] Waters 1997, 122.
[185] Duncan 1988, 64.
[186] Keogh 2007, 130.
[187] Foreign divorces had been recognized since 1986. The 1989 Judicial Separation and Family Law Reform Act introduced grounds for legal separation, very similar to divorce provisions in other countries, but without the possibility of remarriage (Burley and Regan 2002, 205). Even after the 1995 referendum, the divorce process was arduous, since the new laws demanded a very long separation period before divorce was granted and did not allow a "clean break"; changes in the financial circumstances of one or both partners allowed them to renegotiate the settlement.

was that the credibility of bishops, clergy, brothers, and nuns alike had been seriously undermined by the revelations of child abuse, paedophilia, and long-term clerical relationships that had borne children. A number of interviewees talked about how their faith had been 'rocked' by the hypocrisy of the Church authorities who had covered up these behaviours for 40 years . . . even among those voting No, 'only seven percent cited the Church's teachings as the basis of their opposition.' "[188] Over the course of only a few years, the church's moral authority had plummeted—and so had its ability to obtain its preferences through popular acclamation and consent. Nor were matters helped by some of the church's representatives. Archbishop Dermot Clifford argued that "divorcees smoke and drink more than married people, are more prone to psychological problems, and their stepchildren are at great risk of sexual abuse." In addition, he claimed that "divorced couples were three times as likely to cause road accidents."[189]

The trajectory of divorce legislation in Ireland shows how the different levels of moral authority of the church led it to rely on different strategies to influence policy: from directly advising the writers of the Constitution to ban divorce, to reliance on public referenda as expressing values inculcated by the church, to eventually losing the same public consultations after moral authority eroded and the church failed the very standards it had set out for itself and transmitted to the citizens. It also suggests, as does the story of education and abortion, that while institutional access persists despite a decrease in moral authority, voter behavior responds much more quickly. That would prove problematic for the church in the next issues encountered. While the church could still frame stem cell technology as akin to abortion, it was unable to stem the rapidly rising tide of popular support for same-sex marriage.

Stem Cell Research and Assisted Reproduction

Stem cell research and assisted reproduction also became public issues in the 2000s, after the abuse scandals had eroded the church's moral authority. Yet even though the moral authority of the church had waned, its earlier framing of embryos as full-fledged human beings remained a powerful constraint on policy making. The church placed both stem cell research and assisted reproduction in the same category of unacceptable treatment of unborn human beings. Much as with abortion, governments

---

[188] Burley and Regan 2002, 211.
[189] "Ireland-Divorce Legislation." *Boston Irish Reporter*, October 1, 1995.

were consequently loath to legislate when life began or how to protect it. Even though the church now relied on arguments that had less to do with moral authority than with scientific merit, this earlier framing continued to shape policy.

As of 2014, Ireland has not moved to legalize embryonic stem cell research, but there has been substantial debate in Ireland around EU legislation on the subject. In 2003, the European Commission proposed guidelines for the use of EU funds for stem cell research. The guidelines included bans on the use of funds for embryonic research in any country where such research was illegal. The debate, in Ireland and in other European countries, was over whether EU funds, drawn from all member states, should be used at all for purposes that were illegal in some member states.[190]

The Catholic Church had already positioned itself prominently in the debates over assisted reproduction and stem cell research, but with limited success. The Bishops' Committee for Bioethics was established in 1996 to seek a regulatory framework predicated "on the life of the unborn and the unique status of the family founded on marriage."[191] During the EU controversy in 2003, the committee, "assuming its privilege as an institutional actor close to the centre of decisionmaking, addressed the Irish government directly in order to press its case for a uniquely Irish position with regard to EU research proposals for embryonic stem cell research."[192] The bishops proposed that the EU should make more funds available for adult stem cell research as an alternative to funding for embryonic stem cell research.[193] Similarly, the Pro-Life Campaign argued that destroying human embryos was wrong and adult stem cells were superior, and further evoked societal opposition and democratic backlash against scientific technocracy.[194]

Instead of raising the morality of the issue or doctrinal objections to stem cell research, the church concentrated instead on its legal standing and the scientific merits. For example, Father Kevin Doran, secretary of the Irish Bishops' Committee for Bioethics, argued that adult stem cells would be far more available, and useful, than previously realized; embryonic stem cells are more unpredictable, making them riskier for research

---

[190] Staunton, Dennis. 2003. "EU Sets Guide to Embryo Stem Cell Research." *Irish Times*, July 10.

[191] McDonnell and Allison 2006, 828.

[192] McDonnell and Allison 2006, 829.

[193] Gartland, Fiona. 2006. "Bishops Call over Adult Stem Cell Research." *Irish Times*, June 15.

[194] Fianna Fáil backbenchers and some Irish Members of the European Parliament (MEPs) also opposed the EU guidelines, and argued EU funds should not be used for any activity that was illegal in some EU countries.

purposes. Doran further argued that adult stem cells are superior because they can be harvested without loss of life. The rhetorical priority was to establish scientific credibility before making more traditional pro-life arguments. Finally, Doran appealed to science, arguing that science shows us that a human embryo is not "a haphazard cluster of cells," but a genetically distinct being capable of living and developing apart from its mother. Only then did a moral argument enter: "the moral evil is not associated with the fact that embryos die, but with the fact that somebody decides to kill them."[195]

Yet even as they meticulously framed their opposition chiefly in secular terms, the bishops faced a credibility problem. An editorial *against* embryonic research in the *Irish Independent* highlighted how the church could no longer count on its views resonating:

> The Bishops' call is likely to be ignored. In fact, their call could well cause the opposite to the intended effect by driving people into the embryo stem cell camp instead of away from it. The reason is that episcopal statements provoke in us a visceral response that has nothing to do with reason and everything to do with prejudice. For a start, we are still reacting against the excessive authoritarianism bishops displayed in the past. "Rome (or Maynooth) has spoken, the matter is finished" tends not to work on us anymore. Secondly, we fancy we are an independent-minded lot these days and the best way to show this is to defy the church across almost the entire gamut of issues. . . . When it relates to matters of medical research, a third reason hovers into view, namely our presumption that the Bishops are pitting their irrational faith against scientific reason.[196]

Public opinion was divided, and the government cabinet was split. While PLAC claimed in 2005 that 74% of its poll respondents agreed the Dáil should legislate to protect the human embryo, other polls showed over 50% *supporting* embryonic stem cell research.[197] By 2006, 84% of Irish poll respondents would not refuse a treatment derived from human embryo stem cells.[198] Meanwhile, the cabinet disagreed not over the EU proposal but over whether embryonic stem cell research should be allowed at all in Ireland specifically. On the same day in June 2006 when

---

[195] *Irish Times*, November 17, 2003.

[196] "Pulpit Friction," *Irish Independent*, June 16, 2006.

[197] Lyons 2012; *Irish Times*, June 13. 2006. The poll, commissioned by the ICB, also showed that 57% of respondents believe that life begins at conception, 44% stating that supernumerary IVF embryos should be used in medical research, and 54% saying they would use treatments developed using embryonic stem cell research (Lyons 2012, 378).

[198] *Irish Times*, June 13, 2006.

Enterprise, Trade, and Employment Minister Micheál Martin said he might approve of embryonic research in Ireland, the Minister of Foreign Affairs, Dermot Ahern, met with the Pope and assured him that the government would not allow stem cell research.[199]

Against heavy Catholic opposition, the Fianna Fáil/Progressive Democrats government of Bertie Ahern ultimately backed the European Commission plan in the final vote of the Council of Ministers in 2006. In the end, Taoiseach Bertie Ahern and EU Commissioner David Byrne argued that the EU guidelines posed no threat to Ireland because of the "protection of the unborn" clause 40.3.3 in the Constitution. In other words, Fianna Fáil would allow other countries to fund stem cell research without allowing such research or funding in Ireland.[200]

Proponents of embryonic stem cell research described the decision as a "fairly typical Fianna Fáil halfway house decision."[201] On the one hand, the church had lost much of its ability to frame policy debates or to influence policy directly. On the other hand, so long as an embryo was seen as an unborn human being, policy makers were reticent to legislate on abortion, embryonic stem cell research, or assisted reproduction technologies.

Much as with abortion, and as a legacy of the X case, a legislative vacuum resulted. The government never legislated directly on stem cell research or on the legal status of embryos, without which such research was left in a legal limbo. The Green Paper on abortion in 1999 had already pointed out that the ambiguity in the constitutional term "unborn" posed legislative difficulties for whole area of assisted reproduction.[202] In 2000, the government established the Commission on Assisted Human Reproduction (CAHR),[203] and in 2002, the Irish Council for Bioethics (ICB), which functioned until 2010 when the government discontinued its funding.[204] In 2005 and in 2007, respectively, these bodies issued reports backing the limited and regulated use of embryonic stem cells, but successive governments did not act on the issue.

---

[199] *Irish Independent*, June 29, 2006.

[200] *Irish Times*, June 19, 2006.

[201] *Irish Independent*, June 26, 2006.

[202] McDonnell and Allison 2006, 826.

[203] The commission became a key pressure point for the pro-life lobby as it attempted to defeat assisted reproduction technologies and embryonic stem cell research.

[204] The Irish Council for Bioethics was an independent, national body set up by the government in 2002 to consider the ethical questions raised by developments in science and medicine. The council was to provide independent advice to government and policy makers, and to promote public understanding and informed discussion of bioethical issues. Two theologians were among its members, but the church was not explicitly represented (nor were other bodies or professions). The government discontinued funding in December 2010.

Once again, courts ruled where legislators would not. A 2006 High Court decision determined that three frozen embryos were *not* considered unborn under the Constitution, opening the doors to stem cell research.[205] In 2009, the Supreme Court again ruled than an embryo created by IVF is not an unborn, without deciding its precise legal status.[206] Once again, the Court stressed the need for legislation in this area, and once again, the government failed to legislate. Critics chafed that "while many European states were moving towards the institutionalization of bioethics through the formalization of national debates on regulatory issues the Irish state was otherwise preoccupied in securing its 'pro-life' agenda against any external point of reference in European institutions and a rights discourse."[207]

Irish medical practitioners took a conciliatory approach, adopting conservative measures that complied with church teaching as much as possible, despite lack of legislation.[208] They were not willing to define life, either; in May 1999, the Assisted Reproduction Sub-Committee of the Institute of Obstetricians and Gynecologists published a report that advocated freezing of embryos, but without mentioning the word "embryo," for fear of provoking an abortion-style controversy.[209]

Whether or not assisted reproduction technologies (ART) or stem cell procedures took place depended on the religious control of the institution. Generally, throughout the twentieth century, "the Church has been successful delaying or preventing procedures such as sterilization, artificial fertilization and amniocentesis from being introduced not only in Catholic voluntary hospitals, but in public hospitals run by the Regional Health Boards."[210] Even "Catholic voluntary hospitals that came under direct state control in the 1990s retain an overarching Catholic ethos, continuing to require physicians to sign what has become known as the "Bishops' Clause."[211] In contrast, universities had more independence; accordingly, in 2008 the University College of Cork (UCC) recommended that embryonic stem cell research proceed. Yet even here, given the legis-

---

[205] The "R vs. R" case, as it was known, pitted an estranged couple against each other. Mrs. R wanted to transfer three frozen embryos, frozen after a successful previous IVF attempt. Mr. R did not consent to have the embryos frozen, did not want the embryos transferred, and did not want another child with Mrs. R. The High Court ruled that since Article 40.3.3 was concerned with abortion, it referred to transferred embryos, and thus not to frozen ones. The decision meant Mrs. R could not insist on transfer of the embryos, but it also meant that Irish law did not expressly prohibit embryonic stem cell research.

[206] *Irish Times*, December 16, 2009.

[207] *Irish Times*, September 8, 2011.

[208] McDonnell and Allison 2006, 827.

[209] McDonnell and Allison 2006, 825.

[210] Inglis 1998, 226.

[211] McDonnell and Allison 2006, 829.

lative vacuum, researchers could only use established stem cell lines and could not harvest embryos or produce their own stem lines. Nonetheless, Dr. Dermot Clifford, the Archbishop of Cashel and a member of the UCC's governing body, immediately protested the UCC decision.[212]

The arrival of these bioethical questions in the political arena in the 2000s followed the fall of the church's moral authority in Ireland, leading the church to adopt rhetoric and arguments that could not simply refer to or rely on its traditional monopoly on adjudicating moral issues in Ireland. Society was moving on; politicians remained cautious, however, torn between the contested legal and moral status of embryos, and the powerful legacy of church teaching on the status of embryonic life. The result was even though language of morality and the automatic deference this gave to the Catholic Church in Ireland were no longer dominant— and for many, not even relevant—the church's preferences continued to shape policy.

Same-Sex Marriage

By the time that same-sex marriage became a political issue in the 2000s, in Ireland or anywhere else, the Irish Roman Catholic Church no longer commanded the moral authority it wielded earlier. Social and legal acceptance changed dramatically over the course of two decades; homosexuality itself was illegal until 1993 (and delegalized against church opposition), but by 2011, two-thirds of the population was in favor of same-sex marriage. As noted in Chapter 2, acceptance of homosexuality in Ireland quadrupled over 1982–2011—a faster rate of change than in any of the other cases examined here. If no politician wanted to introduce abortion to Ireland, by 2012 the challenge was "to find a prominent politician prepared to oppose gay marriage out loud."[213]

Same-sex marriage first became a public issue in Ireland in 2004, when an Irish lesbian couple who married in Canada in 2003 sought to have their union legally recognized in Ireland. Ann Louise Gilligan and Katherine Zappone (a member of Ireland's government-appointed Human Rights Commission) sought to file taxes as a married couple, arguing that neither the 1937 Constitution nor the tax code defined marriage as solely between a man and a woman. Their lawyer, Gerard Hogan, memorably argued that constitutional law should not be trapped within "the

---

[212] *Irish Times*, October 29, 2008.

[213] In one account, "supporting gay marriage has become a kind of shorthand way of indicating one's superiority over the hordes, particularly those of a religious or redneck persuasion" (Sheridan, Kathy. 2012. "How Gay Marriage Went Mainstream." *Irish Times*, July 14).

permafrost of 1937."[214] In his decision to allow the case a full hearing, High Court Justice Liam McKechnie noted the issue "isn't simply about tax bonds," and could have "profound ethical, cultural and religious implications."[215] The High Court ruled in December 2006 against the couple, interpreting the Constitution as limiting marriage to relations between a man and a woman, and finding that the couple was not suffering discrimination for taxation purposes. Nonetheless, the judge recommended that the Dáil pass legislation granting civil and financial rights to same-sex couples, stopping short of marriage—the approach publicly favored by Taoiseach Bertie Ahern and, as polls suggest, by the Irish public at large.[216]

The Zappone and Gilligan case had two consequences. First, in 2007 Taoiseach Bertie Ahern announced that the government was committed to full equality of opportunity for all. In 2008, Dermot Ahern, the Minister for Justice, Equality, and Law Reform, said that the government had approved a Civil Partnership Bill that proposed "to set up a system for registration of same-sex partnerships and to set out the duties and responsibilities attached to the legal partnership. Under this proposal, same-sex couples will not have the right to be considered for joint adoption and there is no provision for non-biological parents to acquire guardianship."[217] In 2010, President Mary McAleese signed the bill, under which marriage-like benefits were extended to gay and lesbian couples over areas such as property, social welfare, succession, maintenance, pensions, and taxes.

Second, the case, and its plaintiffs, two women of "unthreatening, almost nunlike ordinariness,"[218] made same-sex marriage and civil rights familiar and feasible. Views on gay rights and marriage shifted rapidly across the European Union, and the change was just as dramatic in Ireland. If 41% of the population in 2006 favored same-sex marriage,[219] five years later 67% of poll respondents were in favor.[220] By 2012, "in nearly every county, town, and village, family, friends, and neighbours flaunted their wedding invitations as a badge of pride, or of cool, or of downright

[214] Pogatchnik, Shawn. 2004. "Dublin Approves Lesbian Couple's Challenge to Ireland over Gay Marriage." *Lexis Nexis*. Associated Press, November 9. Web. 2012.

[215] Ibid.

[216] *Boston Globe*. 2006. "Lesbians Lose Marriage Case in Ireland; Judge Says Union Not Recognized under Constitution." December 17.

[217] Kavanagh 2009.

[218] *Irish Times*, July 14, 2012.

[219] *Gay and Lesbian Review Worldwide*. 2007. "EU Countries Divided on Same-Sex Marriage." March. The Irish respondents were slightly below the EU average at this point, suggesting a more secular shift in attitudes across the EU.

[220] *Irish Times*, August 10, 2011.

relief after years of whispers and cover-ups . . . These folk look normal . . . Those couples at community level have changed everything."[221] Gay Pride parades in Dublin now featured representatives of every party, including Fianna Fáil.

It is not that the church did not take a stance on same-sex marriage; it is that by the 2010s its views were increasingly seen as irrelevant in this area. Not surprisingly, Catholic clergy were critical of same-sex marriage. In April 2005, representatives of the Irish Bishops' Conference told the Joint Oireachtas Committee on the Constitution that same-sex marriage would threaten the institution of marriage and the centrality of the family in Irish society. Their arguments focused on national tradition and the upbringing of children, yet neither were convincing. The bishops argued that amending Article 41 of the Constitution "runs the risk of emptying or removing the special position of the family based on marriage," and that marriage had already been "rocked to its foundation" by the divorce referendum. The Archbishop of Armagh, Sean Brady, contended that "this is not the time for Ireland to undermine an institution which has served it so well. I wonder if we will have the courage to go against the trend and to defend what has contributed to our success, or will we simply roll over and give ourselves up to the prevailing trends?"[222] Church representatives also asserted that "the recognition of same-sex unions on the same terms as marriage would suggest to future generations and to society as a whole that marriage as husband and wife, and a same-sex relationship, are equally valid options, and an equally valid context for the bringing up of children. What is at stake here is the natural right of children to the presence normally of a mother and father in their lives."[223]

The church hierarchy was also opposed to same-sex civil unions, but took a more nuanced stance. Civil unions were "contrary to God's plan for sexual love and all Christians are called to holiness and chastity." Nonetheless, the bishops "acknowledged the real issue about how the law should protect those involved in long-term, mutually dependent relationships, such as elderly siblings or a man who shares a house with his wife's sisters after she dies. However, the bishops noted the bill only protects those who are in a sexual relationship. This is real discrimination— choosing to help one vulnerable group over another when they are in similar circumstances, they said."[224] The Irish Bishops' Conference further

---

[221] *Irish Times*, July 14, 2012.

[222] "Brian McFadden Calls for Gay Marriage Legalization in Ireland." *Asian News International*, August 15, 2011. *Infotrac Newsstand*. Web. January 22, 2012.

[223] *Irish Times*, April 22, 2005.

[224] Jones, Kevin J. 2011. "Civil Partnerships Begin in Ireland, but 'Gay Marriage' Still Debated." *Catholic News Agency*. April 6. Accessed February 18, 2012.

argued that the civil partnership legislation was unconstitutional and "is not compatible with seeing the family based on marriage as the necessary basis of the social order."[225]

Yet despite the church's opposition, civil unions were introduced in 2010. In the abortion and the divorce referenda the church could rely on affiliated activists and civil society movements; there was no corresponding force in the case of same-sex marriage. The Iona Institute, "blessed with extremely high-profile members with priceless multimedia platforms"[226] was opposed to same-sex marriage, and several smaller groups mobilized against civil partnerships and same-sex marriage. But in the words of Jim Walsh, a Fianna Fáil senator, "the gay and lesbian lobby groups are far more effective, far more professional in their approach, far better resourced."[227] While same-sex marriage seemed far off (Taoiseach Enda Kenny famously collided with a flowerpot rather than answer a question about same-sex marriage during a 2012 press conference), most Irish elites supported gay rights and civil partnerships. Nearly all major political parties, including Labour (Fine Gael's coalition partner) and the Progressive Democrats, already supported civil union arrangements short of marriage.[228]

The issue of civil partnerships and same-sex marriage was notable in two ways: First, the church had little influence in this domain, as changes in public preferences quickly outpaced whatever arguments the church was making, and the church no longer had the moral authority by this point to convince the population. Second, ironically, this was one issue where politicians and the hierarchy initially did not disagree: in the 2000s, same-sex partnerships were acceptable; full-fledged marriage rights were not.[229] Yet even political elites were caught by the pace of societal change. Bertie Ahern remarked on RTE public television in 2004 that same-sex couples need greater legal equality, even if same-sex marriage was "a long way off in this country." The All-Party Committee on the Constitution reflected the "agreement across the party political and religious spectrum" around Ahern's position.[230] Not a decade later, in 2013, the Fine Gael–Labour government followed the recommendations of the constitutional committee and announced that a referendum would be held in 2015 to amend the Constitution to allow same-sex marriage, among other proposed reforms. The Catholic Church, rather than condemning the oppo-

---

[225] Ibid.

[226] *Irish Times*, July 14, 2012.

[227] *Irish Times*, July 14, 2012.

[228] *Irish Times*, November 20, 2004. Only the Greens, prompted by a petition from their youth section, advocated full marriage rights.

[229] *Sunday Tribune*. 2005. "Trouble and Strife for Gay Unions." July 10.

[230] *Sunday Times*, July 10, 2005.

sition, carefully announced it would "participate fully in the democratic debate leading up to the referendum."[231]

Backlash?

Ireland experienced a broad arc of moral authority, from unquestioned church consultation and vetting of major policy in the first four decades of statehood, to increasing distancing from the church, and eventually the dramatic erosion in the 1990s of the church's moral authority. The perception was that the church's own actions, rather than widespread secularization, were responsible: "the successes of the abortion and divorce referenda in the 1980s, at a time when the Catholic Church would have appeared to have been losing its institutional foothold in the political sphere, suggested that the Church still represented the moral conscience of Irish society. This role has been undermined throughout the 1990s, not so much by secularising influences within Irish society, but by the institutional crisis within the church itself in relation to child sexual abuse and sex scandals."[232] As one commentator acidly put it, "it was not so much that the members of the clergy were shown to be guilty of the sins of promiscuity, adultery, fornication, paedophilia, rape and buggery, but that for centuries they had been castigating these contraventions of the Natural Law not just as intrinsically evil, but as the greatest of sins."[233] The consequence of this perceived hypocrisy was that "one of the strengths of the Catholic Church during the twentieth century has been its close identity with the majority of the Irish people. There was widespread confidence in the church in the 1980s, but by 2000 a majority of respondents reported they had little confidence."[234] The Roman Catholic Church had set the moral standard for decades—and by failing to live up to these standards, lost its standing in society within a few years.[235] What was lost was the key to its earlier influence, the church's "air of being *essential*,

[231] Agence France Presse. 2013. "Ireland's Gay Marriage Referendum to be Held in 2015." November 5.

[232] McDonnell and Allison 2006, 832.

[233] Inglis 1998, 217.

[234] Girvin 2008, 92.

[235] Adding to the complexity of the situation was the hierarchy's earlier decision to assert its noninvolvement in politicking—declaring in the late 1970s that "legislators should legislate" and that the secular laws should not bind non-Catholics to Catholic teachings. These would then be held against the church; for example, when in the 1983 debate over the availability of contraceptives two bishops (Jeremiah Newman of Limerick and Kevin McNamara of Dublin) publicly appealed to Catholic politicians to "follow the guidance of the Church," their involvement drew a direct rebuke from Garret FitzGerald that would have been unlikely two decades earlier (Smith 1985, 434). He went on to argue that "it is of course for them (the Hierarchy) to state what the moral position of the Catholic Church is

that somehow the Irish would never be able to cope with civil life without the good priests and nuns to lead them, advise them (well or idiotically), and provide for them."[236]

As late as the 1980s, the church had undeniable policy accomplishments, largely achieved by allied proxies such as the PLAC, in both the abortion and divorce referenda in 1983 and 1986, respectively. This made the policy retreat on abortion (in 2002 and in 2013) and on divorce (1996) sting all the more. That said, policy shifts on divorce, same-sex marriage, or some forms of contraception were considerably easier to obtain for their proponents than abortion, stem cell research, or assisted reproduction. The church's framing of these issues as involving the killing of unborn babies remained trenchant and powerful for politicians, who did not want to risk censure by legislating, and who in many cases were genuinely worried about the moral implications of such legislation.

In contrast, the attitudes and behaviors of *society* shifted more quickly, by several measures. As noted earlier, Ireland saw the biggest shifts in popular opinion among the countries examined, with acceptance of abortion, divorce, and homosexuality skyrocketing over the last three decades. Church attendance dropped steadily, halving over the last three decades. More than 90% of Catholics attended church weekly in the 1980s, dropping rapidly to 77% in 1994 to 60% in 1998 to 45% in 2010.[237] Between 1966 and 1996, the number of vocations dropped by 92% from 1409 to 111.[238] Finally, if in 1960 the total fertility rate was 3.76, it fell to below replacement rate, 1.98, in 2003.[239] As noted in Chapter 2, the transformation of public opinion on a variety of issues was most pronounced in Ireland—but even here, divorce and homosexuality became relatively more acceptable than abortion.

It is unlikely that these shifts are easily reversible; the changes in religious and spiritual identities were most pronounced among the young (nineteen- to twenty-year-olds), as result of a loosening church grip on education, social welfare, public policy, and the media, and the church's "demise as the sole arbiter of private morality."[240] In inculcating moral standards in generations of Irish men and women, and in asserting a moral standing that made it the representative of the national good, the church would eventually hoist itself on its own petard; its moral authority

---

in relation to the use of contraceptives by people who are members of that Church . . . but it is for the Government and legislators to decide" (Smith 1985, 434–35).

[236] Garvin 2004, 227.
[237] Girvin 2008, 82; Oaks 2002, 321; O'Mahony 2010, 4.
[238] Inglis 1998, 212.
[239] Andersen 2010, 22.
[240] Andersen 2010, 15.

was both its greatest advantage and, when it failed to live up to these standards, its greatest vulnerability.

Italy

Italy appears to be the quintessential Catholic country, with churches at every corner and strong traditional religiosity. The Vatican is located in Rome, and for centuries, Pope after Pope was inevitably Italian (until John Paul II, elected in 1978). Yet beneath the facade of a Catholic nation, the relationship between the church and state has been a complicated one. The Roman Catholic Church (and specifically, the Vatican) was opposed to the unification of Italy in the nineteenth century, banned Catholics from participating in the new state on the pain of excommunication, and vehemently fought any attempts to constrain the power of the Vatican. It could not claim to speak for the "Italian nation"—no such homogenous nation arose, partly thanks to church obstinacy—and never gained the moral authority of its counterparts in Ireland or in Poland.

The church fought both the idea and the reality of a national Italian state. Liberalism and nationalism threatened the church's political power, and the church opposed the 1848 revolutions and the Risorgimento.[241] As a result, the nation-building years of 1861–1924 saw repeated conflict between the church and the newly united Italian state,[242] with the church actively opposing the construction of a unified and secular Italy. Many clergy backed the unification of Italy, but the papacy did not. The unification of Italy meant the loss of large swaths of secular authority for the Vatican, most notably the Papal States, the territories under sovereign rule of the Pope that dated back to the sixth century and at their peak included Romagna, Marche, Umbria, and Lazio. In response to unification, Pius IX (1846–78) forbade Catholics from participating in Italian state politics with a *non expedit* in 1864, a ban that was not relaxed until 1913.[243]

The church's hostility to the Italian nation-state was repaid: state building meant the destruction of the Papal States, and the key state builder, Piedmont, having been rebuffed when it sought church support, reduced the church's privileges. Rome itself was captured in 1870. The Liberals

---

[241] Hanson 1987, 32.

[242] Donovan 2003, 97; Kalyvas 1996.

[243] The ban was not fully lifted until 1919, when suffrage was expanded and the church revoked the ban to thwart a Socialist victory. The *non expedit* itself was technically not a blanket prohibition, even if it was widely assumed to be one. The actual statement was that "considering all circumstances, it is not expedient" for Catholics to vote or participate in elections (Molony 1977, 17).

then actively built the welfare state and the educational system by excluding the church.[244] Catholic civil society blossomed in the 1890s,[245] and Pope Leo XIII's 1891 encyclical against the exploitation of workers, *Rerum Novarum*, helped to ease the tensions (and bring about the lifting of the *non expedit*). Yet it was not until World War I that relations between the church hierarchy and the state improved, further enabled by Catholic participation in wartime efforts and their obvious patriotism.[246]

It was the fascist government of Benito Mussolini that reached an understanding with the church in 1929, after nearly six decades of mutual hostility. The church hierarchy initially cautiously welcomed the March on Rome and the fascist takeover of power[247]—both then and after World War II, its chief concern was the "red atheism" of communism. Both sides had something to gain; the church would help Mussolini eliminate the democratic opposition, and the church could gain greater financial and legal privileges. These benefits for the church were immediate and obvious. In exchange, the Vatican ordered Don Luigi Sturzo, the popular (and committed anti-fascist) priest, to resign from the party he led, the Christian Democratic People's Party of Italy (Partito Popolare Italiano, PPI), and calmly watched as the PPI was dissolved in 1925 along with other non-fascist trade unions and parties.[248]

Such moves by the church did little to promote a fusion of religious and national identities, or to dispel the strong currents of anti-clericalism among the fascists and among their opponents. This is not to say that Italians were not religious, or that there were not close ties between *local* clergy and communities. However, this religiosity was not married to a sense of national destiny, or to a conviction that the church represented national political interests. Instead of exercising the moral authority of the Polish or Irish churches, the Italian church's attempts to influence politics met with more resistance from the political class and from the faithful themselves, cynical about the ostentatious privileging of the church and its hierarchy's acquiescence in the destruction of inconvenient political parties and movements.

---

[244] Lynch 2009.

[245] A vast network of grassroots Catholic civil society organizations emerged in the 1890s, especially in northern Italy, such as peasant leagues, credit unions, cooperatives, and so on. Elite mediators arose, such as the economist Giuseppe Toniolo, the leader of Catholic Action.

[246] Pollard 2008, 69.

[247] It did so despite repeated attacks on priests and Catholic activists by thugs associated with Mussolini. Priests and activists suspected of supporting the Popular Party were beaten, forced to drink castor oil, and threatened with greater violence (Kertzer 2014, 55).

[248] Pollard 2008, 83; see also Scoppola 2005, 78–79, and Molony 1977, 163ff. for an account of Vatican-fascist complicity in destroying the PPI.

National and religious identities did not fuse, not only because of the church's spotty historical record, but also because two other mechanisms were at work to separate individual religiosity from nationalism. First, regional identities in modern Italy have continued to exert a powerful (and primary) hold on political loyalties and individual imaginations. The failure of fascism as a national project may have exacerbated the rise and growth of loyalty to "piccole patrie," or the primacy of local, as opposed to national, patriotism.[249] Many Italians never identified with the postwar state, which they saw as dominated by both the DC (Democrazia Cristiana) and church interests: "well into the 1970s, the state was usually identified by critics as the 'DC-state,' and this state was seen, particularly through the 1950s, as a clerical one."[250] Rather than the church fostering the fusion of national and religious identities, then, its association with two successive corrupt regimes precluded such identification. Strong traditional faith is also internally differentiated among local groups and lay organizations.[251] Italy's history as an archipelago of city-states and principalities, united only in the mid-nineteenth century, was so powerful that the church, among many other actors, was unable to foster a strong and coherent sense of national, or confessional, identity.[252] Subsequent territorial cleavages (notably the "Red Belt" of Emilia-Romagna, Marches, Tuscany, and Umbria that voted for communist local governments), the diversity within the church's lay movements, and strong anti-clerical currents meant there was neither a homogenous Italian nation nor a uniform Catholicism to fuse together.[253] As a result, the church may have had national reach—but not moral authority as a defender and representative of a cohesive nation.

The church itself was historically suspicious of Italian national aspirations, a skepticism that would be unintelligible in Ireland or Poland. Given this lack of national resonance, and given the importance of the papacy to the church's identity in Italy, the church turned outward: the "historical absence of a 'national' Church . . . impressed upon Italian Catholicism a particularly strong universalist perspective."[254] After World War II, as it reached a rapprochement with the Italian state,[255] the church articulated a "collective myth" of Italian national unity to bolster both

---

[249] Gentile 2003, 186; Haddock and Bedani 2000, 178.

[250] Donovan 2003, 98.

[251] Garelli 2007, 28.

[252] Formigoni 1998, 166.

[253] Allum 1990.

[254] Bedani 2000, 215.

[255] In the 1961 jubilee, Catholic hostility toward the state was gone, and instead the church emphasized "the Catholic leadership of the national state and the reappropriation of the nation by the Catholics" (Gentile 2009, 344).

the DC and its own role in society, but could not persuade Italians.[256] It was not until the 1990s, after its coalition partner, the Christian Democrats, collapsed and separatist parties such as Lega Nord arose and began to openly question Italian national integrity, that the church spoke convincingly in the name of a united, national interest.[257]

Second, unlike Ireland, where formal education was fully under the control of the church, or some of the communist countries, where informal education reinforced the importance of religious aspects of national identity, the Italian church was unable to control the socialization and education of the faithful as thoroughly. The church did run its own welfare institutions, such as some hospitals, care for the aged, or aid to the poor—but it did not achieve the power of the curriculum or the formal institutional access to the state of the Irish church. The Lateran Pacts did give the church say over education,[258] and mandated both religion in schools and crucifixes in the classrooms. However, religious education was optional and did not become a part of the regular school curriculum (unlike Ireland or post-1989 Poland, respectively). Nor, given the low levels of national and religious fusion, were notions of national and religious identities inculcated at home, as was the case in communist Poland or Croatia. As a result, while Italy's fragmented territorial organization and the location of the Vatican in Italy meant an enormous proliferation of dioceses, bishops, and clerical institutions,[259] this organizational presence in society translated into neither a cohesive national identity nor unquestioned moral authority in politics.

As a result, the Italian church could support Mussolini's rule and mobilize voters for the Christian Democrats after World War II, but it was unable either to set the terms of the policy debates or to push through its preferences. Instead, the church began to *lose* its moral authority, thanks to its coalition (and public identification) with the Christian Democrats. The coalition and the nature of the DC state itself both cast the church's integrity into doubt.[260] Not surprisingly, popular dissent against church and state grew, culminating in the fierce protests of 1967–71. The Second Vatican Council of the mid-1960s upheld the importance of individual conscience and thus inadvertently led to this foment. Membership in the lay Catholic Action (Azione Cattolica Italiana, ACI) collapsed: halving between 1966 and the 1970s, and then halving again by 1978,[261] even as

---

[256] Formigoni 1998 and Pace 1995.
[257] Formigoni 1998.
[258] Warner 2000, 212.
[259] Garelli 2007.
[260] Scoppola 1985, 20ff.
[261] Pollard 2008, 41.

membership in the communist party and other groups considered radical by the church increased. (ACI and other Catholic lay organizations, with a politically diverse but religiously committed membership, such as Focolare, Opus Dei, Caritas, and Comunitá Sant'Egidio, subsequently maintained a steady presence in the last thirty years or so.[262]) Mass attendance dropped from 69% of adults in 1961 to 35% in 1972.[263]

It was only after the coalition (and the DC itself) collapsed in the mid-1990s that the church *gained* moral authority and became more widely trusted, but its teachings continued to be ignored by private individuals, and religiosity continued to decline. The church was a prominent institution in Italian public life, but for much of the nineteenth and twentieth centuries, it was unable to convince Italians of either a national identity coterminous with their religion or of its role as a representative of that nation's common good.

Policy Influence

Italy between World War II and the 1990s exemplified a coalition between the Catholic Church and a dominant governing party, illustrating the logic of these alliances and their limitations. In comparison with the relationship of the Irish church with its secular government, certainly, the Catholic Church in Italy obtained far fewer policy benefits. The church's involvement in Italian politics is perhaps best summarized by Mark Donovan as having "evolved from one of subversive non-participation in the liberal period through competitive collaboration under Fascism to critical alignment with the hegemonic state party in the Christian Democratic period and, finally [after 1994] to non alignment."[264] Over the course of a century and a half, the church traveled from the 1874 *non expedit* of Pius IX that excommunicated any active participant in the new Italian Republic to the 1929 Lateran Accords that privileged the church, to the 1946–94 coalition with the Christian Democrats to withdrawing from purely partisan politics after the coalition's collapse.

---

[262] Garelli 2007, 27. Nearly 12% of Italians are involved in these organizations, which range from spiritual movements (Focolare, Rinnovamento dello Spirito, Cursillos) to societal engagement (Catholic Action, Christian Youth Workers, ACLI: Christian Association of Italian Workers), to a more political and conservative outlook (Comunione e Liberazione, Opus Dei), peace movements (Communita Sant'Egidio), and charity and welfare volunteers (Caritas, San Vincenze, Abele). All are explicitly Catholic; few are political. One public exception was the conflict between the more orthodox, right wing Comunione e Liberazione and more conciliatory Catholic Action after the latter broke with the Christian Democrats to enter dialogue with all political sides, including the Left (Allen 2005).

[263] Hanson 1987, 137.

[264] Donovan 2003, 114.

The patterns of influence of the Roman Catholic Church in Italy illustrate three more general aspects of church-state relations. First, few churches are monoliths; within the Italian church, as within others, there were personal differences among the clergy and the hierarchy, and more institutional ones between the Vatican and the Pope, the apex of the Catholic hierarchy, on the one hand, and the bishops of the Italian Episcopal Conference (Conferenza Episcopale Italiana, CEI) on the other. Second, as a result of the conflicts and struggles among these factions, church strategies changed over time and according to circumstance. Third, these changes affect moral authority; once the church withdrew from partisan alliances and chose to influence policy by pressuring individual politicians and making public declarations, the moral authority of the church recovered. Italians may disapprove of church influence on policy, but they viewed coalitions with discredited parties even more unfavorably.

The Italian church was well aware that direct access to the state was more effective than working through allied political parties. Pius XI was not alone in his preference to "bypass political parties, even Catholic ones and speak directly to the state."[265] Despite the damage that fascism would bring to Italian society, it achieved for the church "the ideal situation, a direct interlocutory relationship with the Italian state without the complicating presence of a strong Catholic party in politics."[266] Consequently, in 1926 secret negotiations began between the state and the church. Mussolini increased the clergy's stipends, reintroduced religion into schools (replacing the anti-clerical Minister of Education with a devout Catholic), and held secret meetings with Cardinal Gaspari to rescue the failing Banco di Roma, in which the church held considerable shares.[267] In February 1929, these efforts culminated in the *Conciliazione*, the signing of the Lateran Pacts. The Pacts signaled a reconciliation between church and state and a partial restoration of church privilege and influence, offering multiple valuable concessions to the church.[268] They technically made Italy a confessional state.

[265] Fattorini 2011, 37.

[266] Pollard 2008, 85.

[267] Pollard 2008, 87; Warner 2000, 53.

[268] The pacts established Catholicism as the official religion of Italy, made sovereign the Vatican city-state, compensated the church for loss of papal territories, made church marriage legally sufficient, mandated religious instruction in secondary schools, exempted priests from military service, created state stipends for clergy, and guaranteed operation for church-sponsored associations such as Catholic Action while repressing others (Donovan 2003, 97–98; see also Warner 2000). Mussolini's regime further recognized church participation in schools, restored crucifixes to schools and courtrooms, repaired churches, raised clerical salaries, closed down anti-clerical journals, and banned freemasonry. Catholic schools became much more autonomous and better funded (Jemolo 1960, 268).

The partnership was not an easy one. Mussolini's regard for the church was only tactical and superficial, and the Lateran Pacts were a concession to gain the church's acquiescence. Mussolini appreciated the "political utility of religion,"[269] but he had little regard for the church or its theology (he was an avowed *mangiaprete*, or anti-clerical "eater of priests," earlier in his career).[270] He immediately began to downplay the significance of the Pacts, emphasizing both the sovereignty and the supremacy of the state, and the dominance of secular laws over the church.[271] Asserting that the Church is not sovereign nor is it free," Mussolini enraged the Pope by adding that Christianity was a lucky survivor, "one of many sects that flourished in [the] overheated environment" of early Palestine.[272]

For his part, Pius XI initially went as far as to call Mussolini "the man sent to us by Providence,"[273] and was as suspicious about democracy as Mussolini was enthusiastic about destroying it.[274] The Pope finally criticized the fascist regime openly (if with caveats) in his 1931 encyclical, *Non Abbiamo Bisogno*, prompted by Mussolini orders to dissolve Catholic Action and other youth organizations.[275] Even so, the church hierarchy supported the invasion of Ethiopia in 1935–36, a near-genocidal campaign that also marked the peak of fascist support. By the time Pius XI was going to launch a serious critique of Mussolini in early 1939, it was too late; he himself was too feeble, and too many in the hierarchy had benefited from the earlier privileges.[276]

Critically, the church enjoyed substantial independence under Mussolini. By making the church autonomous of the fascist state, the Pacts allowed the church to disavow fascism eventually and thus avoid recriminations after the war.[277] The Vatican officially took up a position of neutrality during the war, and if the local clergy at first supported the war

---

[269] Burleigh 2007, 55.

[270] Kertzer 2014, 52ff.

[271] Fattorini 2011, 37.

[272] Kertzer 2014, 121.

[273] Smith 1997, 379.

[274] Kertzer 2014, 55.

[275] Eventually, Catholic Action was allowed to re-form, with local organizations under the authority of the local bishop, and eventually collaborating with the Fascist police on campaigns for female modesty, for example (Kertzer 2014, 169).

[276] Much of the hierarchy supported Mussolini, but Pius XI began to have doubts and wrote an encyclical against racism and Mussolini's racial laws. Pius XI died in February 1939, before it could be made public. The original was destroyed by Cardinal Eugenio Pacelli, the future Pius XII (Kertzer 2014, xxxiii; Fattorini 2011, 189). The full text was not made public until 2006 (Kertzer 2014, 373).

[277] De Franciscis 1989, 54; Warner 2000, 53.

effort, they also acted to protect the populace as fighting came to Italy.[278] After Mussolini's government fell and Germany occupied Italy in 1943, priests secretly supplied the partisans with food, clothes, weapons, and identity papers, and were imprisoned and killed for doing so.[279] Such participation in the armed resistance "was crucial to the post-war political situation in Italy. It helped wash away the 'sin' of collaboration between the Church and Fascism, gave a patriotic character to the re-emerging Catholic political forces, and guaranteed those forces, the Christian Democrats, representation on the central Comitato di Liberazione Nazionale, the overall governing body of the Resistance movement."[280] Furthermore, the church was now actively glossing over its earlier opposition to the Italian nation-state project: "the Church was not against devotion to one's country. On the contrary, it encouraged this sentiment: it only condemned its degeneration into exaggerated and exclusivist passion or worship of the nation, as had happened during Fascism."[281] The tensions between the Pope and Mussolini in the late 1930s, the role of clergy in protecting the populace in the last two years of the war, the preservation of its organizational structure, and the church's ties to the United States all meant that the church could argue it was "a rock of stability in a sea of uncertainty, and seemed to wipe out all memories of its less palatable early relations with Fascism."[282]

Thus the church was in a relatively strong position after World War II. With the monarchy abolished, democratic parties and forces inchoate, and a fear of communism rapidly spreading, the church emerged as one of the few surviving national institutions. Church backing was seen as critical to the new regime: "The DC [Christian Democratic] leadership viewed the Church's support of democracy as essential to democracy's survival"—and "they also knew of the Church's potential to undermine democracy."[283] Moreover, all actors involved knew that the church would endorse whatever organization would best protect its interests, as it did with fascists in 1920s. The church "made a stand only against regimes that have persecuted her, that have hindered her teaching, that have sought to interpose themselves between her and the Faithful."[284]

---

[278] Mussolini entered the war in June 1940, and Allied troops invaded Italy on July 10, 1943. Popular support for the war plummeted, and Mussolini was removed from office by the end of the month. A secret armistice was signed, but by the first week of August Germany strengthened its military presence in Italy and effectively occupied the country.

[279] Gallo 2003, 159–69; see also Behan 2009.

[280] Pollard 2008, 107; see also Pavone 1991.

[281] Gentile 2009, 262.

[282] Bedani 2000, 220.

[283] Warner 2013, 263.

[284] Jemolo 1960, 276.

The church's chief worry was the specter of communism, and a communist regime taking over Italy, fears made all the more keen by the dominance of the left in postwar Italy by a healthy native communist party (Partito Comunista Italiano, PCI) led by Palmiro Togliatti. Yet Pius XII was not convinced that the DC could stabilize and govern Italy effectively; he had misgivings about the organizational capacity and the electoral chances of the Christian Democrats. It took combined efforts of the party leader, Alcide de Gasperi, and the Vatican Under Secretary of State, Monsignor Giambattista Montini, to convince the Pope to "accept the role of the Christian Democrats as the Church-sponsored party in Italian politics."[285]

The church hierarchy (or, more precisely, the Pope—since the Italian Bishops' Conference did not exist until 1956) began to cautiously nurture the DC, and eventually threw the church's considerable organizational weight behind the Christian Democrats beginning with the 1948 elections.[286] Even if the church had its doubts about the DC, it was clear that its situation would be considerably worse in a communist regime. For lack of alternatives, then, the church saw the DC was "the essential political instrument to defeat the Socio-Communist challenge in Italy."[287] In turn, the DC relied on the church's mobilizational capacity to compensate for the party's meager organizational resources after the war—and to guarantee the church's support for the nascent Italian democracy.

Initially, both coalition partners gained. The DC had "little or no independent mass base at a local level, the membership and electorate being effectively provided by the Church."[288] Meanwhile, the church had great potential to mobilize the voters, with Catholic Action itself claiming 10% of Italians as members. Anxious about the possibility of an anti-clerical communist regime, the church mobilized its auxiliary organizations on behalf of the DC, portrayed the electoral campaigns as a battle of good and evil in the Catholic press in 1948, and excommunicated communist party members and voters in 1949. As a result of these initial efforts, the DC was able to dominate the party system and hold fast onto the state in the first four decades of postwar Italian politics. From 1948 to 1987, their national vote share did not drop below 34%, and the party provided every Prime Minister from December 1945 to June 1981 (and several more thereafter).[289]

[285] Pollard 2008, 111–12.
[286] Pollard 2008, 109–15.
[287] Donovan 2003, 98.
[288] Pollard 2008, 123.
[289] Furlong 1996, 59.

For its part, "the Church wanted guarantees of influence and of anti-Communism, and it was beginning to appear that the DC would be able to offer both."[290] The Lateran Pacts were included in the Constitution (in Article 7), and the rights of other religions were not revised until 1984. Article 7 was enormously controversial, with representatives of the church warning "that unless the new democratic regime sanctioned the Pacts, there would be a 'religious war,' "[291] but the fact that the DC pushed them through, against fierce socialist opposition,[292] convinced the church they "were the sole reliable instrument for the defense of its interests in Italy."[293] The DC sustained Catholic principles by financing Catholic hospitals, seminaries, schools, and Catholic cultural, educational, and social activities.[294] New clerical privileges were established, such as clerical legal immunity and influence over legislation regarding education, divorce, and censorship. The Lateran Pacts had been the result of secret negotiations with the fascist regime, and a source of church access to schooling, state funding, and legal privilege. Now, in an openly partisan act, the DC cemented them into the Constitution as both the price—and the symbol—of its new alliance with the church.

In the era immediately following the 1948 elections, a Catholic triumphalism took over. The church insisted on fascist-era laws to censor papers and books it considered offensive, limited the rights of religious minorities, excommunicated political opponents, and on the local level made clerical approval critical both to getting jobs and to becoming a DC candidate.[295] In short, "the Church exercised a massive, pervasive, deeply rooted, and politically focused institutional presence during the late 1940s and early 1950s."[296] Meanwhile, all political parties, including the left wing, largely accommodated the church during this period, with even the Left agreeing with the church that the family was the "fundamental unit of society."[297] The reasons for this unusual consensus were simple: the survival of the new democracy required the cooperation of all actors, and many parties wanted to prioritize the Constitution and economic issues over church-state conflict.[298] Given the "genuine uncertainty with

---

[290] Warner 2000, 108.

[291] Pollard 2008, 114.

[292] Ironically, even as the Socialists rejected the inclusion of the Lateran Accords in the Constitution, the Communists embraced the accords to preserve the "political and moral unity of the nation" (Palmiro Togliatti, quoted in De Franciscis 1989, 67).

[293] Pollard 2008, 113.

[294] Ignazi and Wellhofer 2013, 38.

[295] Pollard 2008, 122.

[296] Ignazi and Wellhofer 2013, 38.

[297] Seymour 2006, 164.

[298] De Franciscis 1989; Jemolo 1960.

regard to the balance of opposing forces,"[299] it was far better to appease the church.

Yet in retrospect, the 1948 elections were the peak of church influence. The church was initially indispensable in the 1940s, only to become steadily less relevant to the DC's fate by the late 1980s, when the party's anti-communism had spent itself, and its own corruption led to its collapse in 1993–34. Already in 1946, the church was angered by the Christian Democratic government's laxity in failing to include the sanctity of marriage in the Constitution, and allowing labor the right to strike.[300] The DC had to remind the church that if a new government took its place, the Lateran Pacts would very well be removed from the Constitution. And these setbacks were only the beginning; over time, the church was able to achieve less and less through the coalition with DC—yet it had nowhere else to turn.

The Christian Democrats themselves chafed under the alliance; soon after its 1948 electoral victory was assured, the party began to seek mechanisms that would make the DC more independent of the church. The DC sought greater autonomy by diversifying its coalition partners and by building alternative electoral infrastructure—the greater its independence from the Church, the greater its opportunities, both in choosing coalition partners and in demonstrating its strength to the church. Thus, the DC formed an alliance with Marxist parties in 1944–47, "despite the opposition of the Catholic right and the displeasure of Pius XII,"[301] but ended it when the Pope began to openly discuss other partisan allies. The DC forced the communists out of government in May 1947 to reassure the church (and the United States.)

Yet after the 1948 elections, de Gasperi formed the coalition with Socialists (PSDI), Liberals (PLI), and Republicans (PRI), even after achieving an absolute majority, to "reduce the effects of ecclesiastical pressure upon his government."[302] Nor did the DC invite the monarchists and the right-wing MSI into the coalition, as the church would have preferred.[303] The church was unable to prevent the "opening to the Left," and the entry of the Socialists (PSI) into the coalition in 1963 (not least because while the Italian Episcopal Conference, the CEI, opposed it, Pope John XXIII made it clear during a 1961 state visit by DC Prime Minister Amintore Fanfani to the Vatican that he would not support the CEI's objections).[304] Following

[299] Jemolo 1960, 285.

[300] Warner 2000, 119.

[301] Donovan 2003, 101.

[302] Pollard 2008, 119.

[303] Donovan 2003, 101.

[304] Bull and Newell 2005, 89. The Italian church has been dominated historically by the Vatican; while the bishops formed an interregional conference in 1952, the CEI was not

the reforms of the Second Vatican Council, with its turn toward ecumenism and a greater tolerance of heterodoxy, the connection between the church and the party loosened even further, and the public political declarations of the church also shifted to a more ecumenical tone.

Perhaps the most durable change to the power dynamic between the church and the DC came when the party began to rely on patronage, obviating the need for the church's organizational mobilization of the voters.[305] From 1953 onward, the DC created networks of public-sector companies and associations for housing and construction and enmeshed these large state industries into a clientelistic network that included giants such as the Institute for Industrial Reconstruction (Istituto per la Ricostruzione Industriale, IRI) with turnover equal to 4–5% of the GDP in 1989.[306] Pension schemes, public subsidies, and legal exceptions (the *leggine*, or "little laws") all directed funding to build loyalty to the DC. The Cassa per il Mezzogiorno (Development Fund for the South), established in 1950, provided jobs and contracts to a desperately underdeveloped south—and further consolidated the metamorphosis of the DC into a clientelistic party. With these moves, the party asserted a new organizational autonomy from the church.[307] Instead, the DC developed its own mass organizations, such as the Italian Catholic Workers' Association (ACLI) and others. These were loyal to the party, not the church.[308] Soon, it seemed to many Catholics that "the DC was a form of Catholic Action," an omnipresent (if secular and self-interested) organization with multiple local branches, auxiliary organizations, and centrality in Italian society.[309]

The church failed to counter these moves because anti-clerical forces were resilient (especially after 1953 when DC needed coalition partners to govern after losing parliamentary majority), and because massive urbanization and dislocation led to a decline in the number of loyal Catholic voters it could mobilize. The church had to contend with greater political opposition to its policy projects just as its ability to mobilize votes for the DC began to waver. The cleavage in Italy between active, committed Catholics and nominal affiliates to Catholicism was growing more pronounced—and the proportions were shifting in favor of the

---

formally founded until 1972, after the Vatican II reforms. The Vatican not only asserted authority over the CEI but also engaged the DC and politics far more than the bishops wished. An attempt by the CEI to end the partnership with DC was blocked by John Paul II, for fear of a greater role for the PCI (Donovan 2003, 104; Magister 2001, 56).

[305] Warner 2000, 176–77.
[306] Guzzini 1995, 31, 47.
[307] Gundle 1996, 60; see also Furlong 1996, 60; Donovan 2003, 101; and Pollard 2008.
[308] Donovan 2003, 101.
[309] Bedani 2000, 227.

latter.[310] As Italy underwent its economic miracle and its economy grew very rapidly during the 1950s and 1960s,[311] an estimated five million people changed their place of residence between 1945 and 1971, with more than half of Italians living in large urban areas.[312] This decline of agricultural employment and rise of industry, combined with urbanization and rise in formal education, meant that the DC vote declined after the 1960s.[313] These changes only intensified an existing popular skepticism: "the public repeatedly affirms its dislike of the church giving advice on political or even public welfare matters and this distinction, and the more general public disinclination to follow Catholic moral teaching, has led prominent ecclesiastics to fear the reduction of the church to little more than a welfare agency."[314] The church could no longer deliver the vote as it once had, nor command the loyalties it did.

From the 1960s on, both the DC and the coalition with the church wobbled further. Rapid secularization, protest movements (including the Hot Autumn of 1969–70 and the broader period of turmoil—the Years of Lead (*Anni di Piombo*) that lasted from the late 1960s to the early 1980s), increasing corruption, and the prevalence of organized crime all began to undermine the DC.[315] Meanwhile, the Second Vatican Council loosened the connection between Italian Catholic hierarchy and auxiliary organizations, so mobilization was even less effective.[316]

It was after the divorce referendum of 1974 that the close coalition between DC and church irrevocably dissolved.[317] Divorce and abortion laws passed in 1970 and 1978, respectively. The church tried to undo these in successive referenda, but failed. First, the church fiercely backed the 1974 divorce referendum that would have abrogated the permissive legislation of 1970. It obtained the support of only 40% of voters, making the voters' disdain for both church and DC instructions all too clear. The episode was followed by a similar fiasco in the 1981 abortion referendum, with 68% voting against repealing abortion and in favor of the existing laws allowing abortion. And as we will see, prosaic coalition politics and party electoral calculations, far more than the moral edicts or

[310] Bull and Newell 2005, 64; Ignazi and Wellhofer 2013.

[311] Pollard 2008, 129.

[312] Pollard 2008, 132.

[313] Ignazi and Wellhofer 2013, 45. Ignazi and Wellhofer explicitly test whether modernization, as measured by these variables, or secularization, as measured by the rate of civil marriage, explained CD votes, and found that secularization was not responsible.

[314] Donovan 2003, 113.

[315] Bedani 2000, 231.

[316] Bedani 2000, 232.

[317] Ignazi and Wellhofer 2013, 47; Warner 2013, 259.

the political pressure of the church, determined the timing and the course of the referenda.

The abortion and the divorce decisions, and the social shifts they demonstrated, necessitated the revisiting of the church-state agreements. Accordingly, a 1984 revision of the Concordat formally separated church from state, removed Catholicism as a state religion, ended Rome's status as a sacred city, and abolished compulsory religious teaching in schools.[318] A logic of exchange underpinned the revision;[319] on the one hand, the Vatican bank was now legally regulated, church properties were now taxable and state stipends ended. The revision made compulsory religious teaching in schools optional, with a large majority of parents enrolling their children in the optional lessons. On the other hand, the financing of the church was changed to voluntary donations through a 0.8% income tax transfer. Of Italian taxpayers, 56% used their right to assign the 0.8% to religious or charitable organizations, and of those, 41% opted to give it to the Catholic Church.[320] Further, bishops no longer had to pledge loyalty to the Italian state, and the state no longer had a say in naming clergy.[321] The church and the DC continued to hold similar conservative political views, but they were no longer political partners and they did not seek to benefit each other.

Mired in political scandals and investigations of corruption, and having lost its ideological raison d'être by dint of the collapse of communism, the Christian Democrats collapsed over the course of 1993–94. The church did not form a new electoral coalition with any of the new parties that arose from the ruins of the postwar political order. These were not much of an option and could not offer the church either access or a coalition. The Left was ideologically opposed to giving the church inroads into the state, and the Right was too fragmented (and in Silvio Berlusconi's case, too objectionable to the church) to entertain a serious party-church coalition.[322] For all of the PCI's surprising earlier deference to the

---

[318] Hanson 1987, 137.

[319] Pace 1995, 16.

[320] Pollard 2008, 155.

[321] Hanson 1987, 137.

[322] Government commissions have been formed to advise the government on religious liberties, to draft agreements with religious denominations, to implement the 1984 Concordat, review the funding of the church (1992), coordinate relations with other religious communities, and research restitution toward the Jewish community after the Holocaust (2004–09). Several of these were formed at the behest of European Union legal demands, such as the Advisory Committee for Religious Freedom, formed in 1997 to ensure that religious liberty would be observed, or the committee formed to oversee the implementation of the 1984 Concordat and to ensure legal changes harmonized with EU law (Commissione governativa per l'attuazione delle disposizioni dell'Accordo tra Italia e Santa Sede, firmato il 18 febbraio 1984, e ratificato con legge 25 marzo 1985, n. 121 [Government Committee to

church, the communists (and their successors after the party's collapse in 1990) could not serve the role of a coalition partner because of ideological incompatibility. Thus, the 1993–94 collapse of the DC "obliged and enabled the Vatican finally to break its nearly 50-year-long support for Catholic party politics in Italy."[323]

Instead, the church moved explicitly from relying on partisan allies and intermediaries to a new neutrality toward parties and directly addressing politicians and the public.[324] Cardinal Camillo Ruini, general secretary of the CEI since 1986 and its president from 1991 to 2007, developed and implemented the idea of "extra-parliamentary church."[325] The church would now rely on "pulpit" rather than the "party." It emphasized its own autonomy, directly articulated its ethical and moral stances, and relied on its presence in society, through the religious communities, charities, and lay associations. The Bishops' Conference also turned to explicit appeals to the electorate and to individual parliamentarians, regardless of their party affiliation, as a way of influencing policy on key issues such as immigration, the financing of Catholic schools, the Iraq War, bioethics, and same-sex marriage.[326] This approach was especially successful in defeating the stem cell referendum of 2005.

The demise of the DC, and the collapse of the coalition, prompted the church to change tactics, but not its strategic goals. It asserted a new neutrality—but that hardly meant a new indifference. First, the church began to emphasize more national appeals. Thus, from the early 1990s on, it consistently emphasized pro-national and pro-state identity, criticizing both the separatist movements and the pervasiveness of the Mafia as threats to national integrity.[327] Second, in its direct appeals to the electorate and individual legislators, it crystallized and emphasized its traditional views on morality policy, to the point that they were now described as "neo-intransigent."[328]

Ironically, as the church abandoned the partisan coalition, it gained greater authority within society and greater power to influence policy.

Implement the Provisions of the Accord between Italy and the Holy See, signed on February 18, 1984, and ratified into law on March 25, 1985]).

[323] Donovan 2003, 95.

[324] Ceccarini 2010, 177.

[325] Magister 2001; Ceccarini 2010, 180. By this point, the CEI had gained an upper hand in developing domestic Italian political strategies. The Polish-born Pope John Paul II (1978–2005) was not particularly interested in Italian politics but in the global reach of the church. In contrast to John XXIII, who scuppered CEI attempts to gain greater autonomy, John Paul II gave greater leeway to the CEI domestically.

[326] Pollard 2008, 173.

[327] Donovan 2003, 111.

[328] Magister 2001, 71–83.

It became among the most trusted of political institutions, and *gained* moral authority after the coalition ended. Public opinion continued to condemn direct influence on politicians (61% of those polled did not accept church pressure on individual Catholic parliamentarians, as of 2007).[329] Religiosity continued to decline, but the percentage of people who felt that church moral exhortations were important to follow remained the same, at 25%.[330] Pressure on individual politicians was often very successful; after the collapse of the Christian Democrats, Catholic politicians now split between the center-right and center-left coalitions, fracturing old political divides. The result was that church pressure on individual politicians could spoil party discipline, such as it was, and preclude policy reforms that went against church preferences. In short, the church had "a greater capacity to impose its issues and its agenda exactly when . . . it has abandoned direct links with parties, when Catholics are in a minority in society and among the electorate. . . . The moral influence of the Church, therefore, seems to be greater among politicians than Catholics themselves."[331] It helped the church that the individual "politicians [we]re still very insecure in the Second Republic, under the new electoral system."[332]

Yet whether it relied on a partisan coalition or individual lobbying, the church was unable to change much in abortion, divorce, or education, issues that by that point had been decided as far as the electorate and the parliament were concerned. Church efforts did succeed in the area of stem cell research and assisted reproduction—or, more precisely, in persuading enough voters to stay home to invalidate the 2005 referendum that would have liberalized the legislation. It did so through pressuring Catholic politicians, mobilizing its affiliated associations, preaching at masses, and appealing to individuals at demonstrations and meetings, rather through either a political coalition or institutional access. As we will see, the church relied on a fragmented political elite and an apathetic electorate, rather than on moral authority and the ability to speak for the nation.

Nor was institutional access a feasible option, either after the war or after the collapse of the DC in 1993–94; the initial reliance on church support by the DC did not translate into handing over education and the welfare state, as it did in Ireland. While Italian school children had their weekly hour of religious instruction (with the overwhelming support of their parents), and crucifixes hung in public schools, there was no formal

---

[329] Ceccarini 2010, 196.
[330] Ceccarini 2010, 195.
[331] Ilvo Diamanti, cited in Pollard 2008, 174.
[332] Pollard 2008, 175.

control of state-funded education, no effective inculcation of deference to church teachings, or imbuing generations after generations with church moral edicts. Majorities continued to disregard church teachings in their private lives and did not accept the church as a moral or political authority. The church played an important role in the care of drug abusers, the elderly, the infirm, and immigrants—but these *augmented*, rather than substituted for, the mainstays of the secular welfare state and never offered the possibility of full control over either institutions or policy implementation that the church in Ireland enjoyed.[333] The church also did not dominate the health-care sector the way the Irish church did, with the number of church-run hospitals, clinics, and counseling centers well below the European average.[334] The Christian Democrats had little incentive to offer costly institutional access to the church—and their successors had even less, given the erosion of the church's moral authority.

In comparison with the position of the Irish church, then, the church was unable to continue to benefit from its original role in buttressing the new democratic regime, and the policy influence stemming from the DC-church alliance was always fragile. Despite its marriage of convenience, the Italian church achieved far less than it had sought and did not have the moral authority to gain more.

Education

If in Ireland 95% of the postwar school system was run by the church but funded by the state, the opposite applied in Italy: 7% of students attended church-run schools, mostly preschools, which the state did not fund. That said, religious education was compulsory until 1984, the legacy of the Lateran Accords' inclusion in the 1948 Constitution. In Ireland the church's role was inherited from the priest-run "hedge schools" that provided education despite the British ban on it in the nineteenth century; in Italy the prevalent secularism of national education similarly remained true to its origins. Education on a large scale was first introduced by liberal, nationalist reformers—who tended to be anti-clerical. The Italian clergy was historically denied a direct role in secular public schooling, although religious orders themselves still operated many schools, mainly for the well to do.[335] After 1877, the provision of religious education became a choice for local authorities and in many cases a local electoral issue.[336] Even under the Lateran Accords, church influence in education

[333] Donovan 2003, 113.
[334] Garelli 2007, 12.
[335] Thomas 2006, 111.
[336] Weisz 1976, 367.

during the fascist period was mainly curricular (compulsory religious instruction and church approval of textbooks and teachers), not extending to directly running schools or receiving funding for doing so.[337] After World War II, the church retained the curricular privileges with the 1948 Constitution—but while Article 33 allowed the formation of religious schools, it explicitly stated these had to come at "no cost to the state."

This relatively modest role in Italian education survived the changes in church-state relations that occurred in the 1960s and 1970s. Unlike abortion and divorce, the presence of the church in public education has not been subject to the same fundamental renegotiation. After the 1984 revision of the Concordat, compulsory teaching of religion in schools ended, but 90% of parents still volunteered their children for it (rather than inculcating these values at home, some critics charged). What did change was the nature of the religious instruction; rather than catechism (the teaching of religious doctrine and rites), the new classes adopted a more anthropological approach to religion and its various manifestations.[338]

This is not to say that there were no controversies, but these disputes involved more symbolic dimensions than a fundamental restructuring of either the church's influence or the educational system itself. In one example, in 1987, the government planned that the optional religious education would take place either at the beginning or the end of the school day. Church authorities objected, fearing that pupils would simply leave school early or show up late and deliberately miss the religious education. The Vatican objected that the 1984 Concordat revision allowed for the voluntary hour of instruction at any time, and since the government could not resolve the controversy with the Vatican, the issue headed to the parliament, where it could have brought down the government of Prime Minister Giovanni Goria. The issue was resolved not by negotiation with the church, but through concessions made to his coalition partners, the Republicans, Socialists, and Liberals. Students who were not taking religious instruction could either take alternative classes or remain in study hall at school. Goria emphasized that the vote would preserve the "autonomy and sovereignty of the State."[339]

In another example, the "Crucifix controversy" of 2003–9 demonstrates the importance of symbols of *Catholic* identity (as opposed to an Italian-Catholic fusion) at a time of increasing religious and ethnic diversity in Italy. In 2003 Abel Smith, founder of the Union of Muslims in Italy, claimed that a crucifix displayed in his son's kindergarten classroom violated the Italian Constitution's guarantee of respect for all religions. The

---

[337] Thomas 2006, 112.
[338] Giorda 2009, 3.
[339] "Sforiata la Crisi, Intesa in Extremis," *La Repubblica*, October 11, 1987.

display of crucifixes in classrooms had been legally mandated since 1924 and was untouched by either the 1948 or 1984 revisions of the Lateran Accords. The civil affairs court of L'Aquila found in Smith's favor, ruling that the display was "anachronistic" and inappropriate to Italy's "process of cultural transformation."[340] The subsequent debate was somewhat idiosyncratic: Pope John Paul II argued that interreligious dialogue should not lead to the erosion of a nation's distinctive religious traditions; Italian politicians from the left and right denounced the L'Aquila court's decision, including the Education Minister, who reaffirmed the place of crucifixes in schools and, more controversially, the extension of state funding for Catholic preschools; and the most prominent Islamic leader in Italy argued that "this attack against a religious symbol is an attack against all Italian religious symbols." Leaders of the small Jewish community defended the decision, as did a secularist teachers' union. The Italian Constitutional Court overturned the decision in 2004[341]—only to have the European Court of Human Rights in Strasbourg ban crucifixes in Italian schools five years later in 2009.

The government argued that the crucifix was a symbol of culture, history, and identity, a symbol of tolerance and even (idiosyncratically) secularism. Yet the overall emphasis was on the importance of the crucifix as a symbol of a more diffuse *European* and Catholic identity, rather than an Italian one, at a time when Islam and Muslim immigrants were sometimes seen as a threat to European values and its Christian heritage.[342] Foreign Minister Franco Frattini spluttered that "this is a death blow for a Europe of values and rights. Europe's roots lie in its Christian identity. At a time when we're trying to bring religions closer, the Christian religion gets whacked."[343] Similarly, Alessandra Mussolini, whose grandfather legislated the crucifixes in the first place, was furious at this "attempt to erase our Christian roots. They are trying to create a Europe without identity and tradition."[344] (Ironically, the Strasbourg decision was heavily criticized in Poland—where the issue *was* perceived as explicitly national. The Polish Parliament adopted a resolution "in defense of the cross" and clergy argued that "only under the cross, under this sign is Poland Poland and a Pole is a Pole."[345])

---

[340] Thomas 2006, 114.

[341] Thomas 2006, 113–20.

[342] For a brilliant discussion of similar processes in Québec, and the inverse—the celebration of all things Jewish in light of a reasserting Catholic hegemony in Poland—see Zubrzycki 2013.

[343] Pisa 2009.

[344] Pisa 2009.

[345] Archbishop Andrzej Dzięga, quoted in *Gazeta Wyborcza*, December 8, 2009.

In sum, in contrast to Ireland, public education in Italy was neither controlled by the church hierarchy nor delivered by the clergy. As in the rest of Europe, religious education was available in the public school system, but the state neither funded schools run by religious authorities nor ceded the public school system to the control of the church. Instead, education occasionally became a symbolic battleground—the secular content of education was not questioned, but schools themselves became arenas where the cultural pervasiveness of Catholicism clashed with the desire of some political actors for institutional autonomy from the Catholic Church.

Divorce

The introduction, and public approval, of divorce in Italy was a major policy defeat for the church. Not only was the church unable to prevent a deeply undesirable policy from being enacted (in 1970), but also this verdict was decisively legitimated in the 1974 referendum, with 60% of the electorate voting against the repeal of divorce despite extensive church pressure. The referendum revealed an Italian electorate that had quietly come unmoored from church teaching in the intervening decades.

After the unification of Italy in 1870, nine different attempts to introduce divorce into civil law failed to pass due to Catholic opposition, and specifically that of the Opera dei Congressi, an independent Catholic organization with extensive local mobilization.[346] Petitions against divorce did not shy from religious argumentation and emphasized the connection between the family and the nation-state.[347] At the turn of the century, the Pope himself entered the fray, addressing parliament directly against divorce.[348] The 1929 Lateran Accords triumphantly reasserted church dominance over family law, and "handed back to the Church its much-prized jurisdiction over the institution of marriage."[349] Their adoption meant that church marriage now had the force of a civil contract—and that while the state could grant legal separations, only the church could annul a marriage.[350] While no provision for divorce existed, neither did a

---

[346] Pollard 2008, 36. Ironically, the church would shut down the Opera in 1904, because it had split between Christian Democrats and older intransigents.

[347] Seymour 2006, 88.

[348] Seymour 2006, 133.

[349] Seymour 2006, 225.

[350] Clark, Hine, and Irving, 1974. The distinction was an important one; a legal separation did not allow the spouses to remarry. An annulment did, but it did not provide for either alimony or custody/support of any children resulting from the marriage.

ban, stimulating a healthy legal debate but doing little for Italian couples in need of legal redress.

Both clerical and secular forces emphasized the family. The leader of the communist party, Palmiro Togliatti, himself declared that the family is the "center of elemental human solidarity" and explicitly opposed any law allowing divorce and took the position that the Constitution should not mention marriage, arguing it should be left to civil law. Article 34 of the Constitution, passed in 1947 with communist support, made divorce reform difficult: "The Italian State, wishing to reinvest the institution of marriage, which is the basis of the family, with the dignity conformable to the Catholic traditions of its people, recognizes the sacrament of matrimony performed according to canon law as fully effective in civil law."[351] Yet at the same time, by a narrow vote of 194 to 191, the Constituent Assembly in 1947 did not include a formulation about the "indissolubility" of marriage, greatly angering the church.[352]

If the alliance between social conservatism and Catholic principles precluded legal divorce, the 1960s saw both economic growth and the social ruptures that allowed arguments for divorce to circulate more broadly within society. As Italian society urbanized, cut its ties to family and village (over a third of Italians moved from 1951 to 1961 to seek new employment),[353] and became more educated, the momentum for divorce became part of a greater reframing of "modernity." Much as in Ireland, the proponents of legal divorce saw it as a progress toward a more modern country. In 1965 the socialist deputy Loris Fortuna (an ex-communist) proposed a divorce law. It reflected ferment "from below," in a pro-divorce campaign by the popular men's tabloid *ABC*, "a self-appointed agent of modernity in what it decried as a backward nation,"[354] as well as "from above," in the remarks of Egyptian Bishop Elias Zoghby at the Second Vatican Council, who suggested broadening the grounds for annulment. In the same year, Socialist deputies Mauro Ferri and Lelio Basso began to push for a revision of the Lateran Accords. Both the Fortuna and Ferri-Basso efforts were subject to delay; it was not until 1967, with the cautious support of the Christian Democratic leadership (though not all of its deputies), that a motion for revision was passed, and the government appointed an ad hoc committee to study grounds for revision. That same year, Pope Paul VI made several public statements against legalizing divorce in Italy, leading to anti-clerical attacks by secular journals such as *Avanti!* and *ABC*.

[351] De Franciscis 1989, 57.
[352] Clark, Hine, and Irving 1974, 336; Warner 2000, 119.
[353] Clark, Hine, and Irving 1974, 337.
[354] Seymour 2006, 190.

Fortuna's divorce bill resurfaced in 1968 after a two-year delay in the Constitutional Affairs Committee (which eventually found it did not violate the Constitution), and was backed by all the left-wing parties but opposed by the Christian Democrats. The issue was kept alive in the face of church disapproval by the Italian League for Divorce (Lega Italiana per il Divorzio, LID), a movement comprised of journalists, lawyers, and other middle-class professional men with a flair for publicity and organizational ability. It was founded early in 1966 specifically to keep the issue from drowning in a sea of "procrastination and parliamentary obstructionism."[355] Nor did across-the-board left-wing support emerge spontaneously; it had to be carefully constructed and negotiated by Fortuna. Despite *ABC*'s enthusiastic christening of the *fronte laico* between the Communists, Socialists, and Liberals, Fortuna's own Socialists were reluctant to commit because of the potentially destabilizing effect on their coalition with the Christian Democrats, while the Liberals wanted an eight-year (rather than the Fortuna bill's five-year) period of separation before divorce could be granted.[356]

Yet once legislative support coalesced, in no small part thanks to the personal connections, protests, and public pressure of LID,[357] the Parliament passed the Divorce Bill in November 1970, in the face of DC opposition and church interventions. The outraged clerical response was predictable, and prompt. The Catholic Church had already warned the government explicitly in 1968 that the divorce bill could jeopardize bilateral negotiations to revise the Lateran Accords. Accordingly, the pontiff now formally ceased negotiations on the Concordat. Rather than relying on the usual partisan DC channels, the Pope launched a formal complaint.[358] Pope Paul VI sent three diplomatic notes to the Italian government outlining his opposition and arguing that the divorce law was a unilateral renegotiation of the Concordat. He called for a "bilateral" revision instead, suggesting that the Divorce Bill was subject to the Vatican's approval. His speech made on February 2, 1970 (while the bill was being discussed in the Senate) publicized these efforts, and "caused much indignation, since the existence of diplomatic exchanges on this issue had previously been unknown, and because it seemed like a clear case of clerical interference in the proceedings of the Italian parliament."[359] Attempting to preempt the introduction of legal divorce, the church streamlined the procedures at the Sacra Rota, the Vatican tribunal that adjudicated

[355] Clark, Hine, and Irving 1974, 339.
[356] Seymour 2006, 203.
[357] Clark, Hine, and Irving 1974, 340.
[358] Seymour 2006, 197.
[359] Clark, Hine, and Irving 1974, 340.

annulment cases—but this move, too, backfired, prompting a first-ever strike of lawyers who alleged the Vatican was entering into competition with the state by offering cheaper and easier divorces.[360]

The most important church response was the last; banking on its backing among a Catholic electorate, and mindful of public opinion polling that showed the voters opposing divorce, the church began to press for a referendum. The pressure was initially not a sincere effort to hold a referendum, but a signal of church power and displeasure; few thought in 1970 that a referendum could even take place.[361] Referenda in Italy can only abrogate (repeal) laws, serving as an important veto function, but the divorce referendum instigated by the church would be the first since the 1946 referendum on the monarchy. The lack of recent precedent prompted all political parties to delay as much as possible for fear of installing a permanent veto player and making parliamentary policy making forever subject to a plebiscite. Given these incentives to delay and the subsequent exigencies of referendum law (it could not be held in the years preceding or following a general election, the Constitutional Court had to check the signatures, etc.), the referendum did not take place until 1974.

Both the church and the Christian Democrats were sure they would win, a sentiment that was broadly shared: "there was a widespread feeling that in the event of a referendum the Catholic contingent would be the clear winners."[362] Even pro-divorce parties were reluctant to campaign heavily, and the "view of the two main political parties was that the hegemony of the Church had to be accommodated (PCI) or exploited in terms of political advantage (DC)."[363] Catholic lay organizations assisted the Christian Democrats in gathering signatures to petition for the referendum. Yet even here, early warning signs were visible: CISL, the Catholic trade union, freed its members to vote their conscience. Even more damagingly, the prominent Comitato dei Cattolici Democratici per il No, an organization of liberal Catholics, also sharply opposed the DC and argued that since marriage was a sacrament of faith, there was no need to have a civil law banning divorce.[364]

For their part, neither the church nor the DC would accept the divorce law. The church refused to consent despite five separate assertions by the Constitutional Court after 1970 that divorce was constitutional. The Christian Democrats, too, were led by a "profound conviction that the

---

[360] Clark, Hine, and Irving 1974, 341.
[361] Clark, Hine, and Irving 1974, 342.
[362] Andall 1994, 240.
[363] Andall 1994, 240.
[364] Clark, Hine, and Irving 1974, 350.

constitution sanctioned the principle of indissoluble marriage,"[365] even as the parliamentary constitutional affairs committee voted that divorce was compatible with the Constitution. The DC also had more cynical considerations; the DC leadership further pushed for the referendum as a means of decisively defeating the Left, which had backed divorce, and worried about splits within DC parliamentary ranks if it did not.[366] Yet many within the DC were cautious; the divorce bill and the referendum would expose the party to competition and risk losing swaths of its female and more liberal voters. The centrifugal forces within this diverse and fragmented party included multiple, crosscutting currents and factions; on the issue of church-state relations alone, these ranged from ultra-Catholic integralists to secular liberals. A referendum could either fissure these further, or it could unite the DC and avoid outflanking by the neo-fascist MSI, who unreservedly supported the referendum.

The referendum was held on May 13, 1974; 60% of the voters supported legal divorce, and only 40% voted to the repeal divorce in Italy. The result was a surprise given the uncertainty in the period immediately before the vote, and the margin shocked both the supporters and the opponents of divorce.[367] The percentage of Italians opposed to divorce legalization had actually increased throughout the 1950s, and by 1962 was at 69%. This had dropped to 62% by 1968, but this was still no grounds to expect the magnitude of the victory in 1974.[368] Ironically, the delay in the referendum was critical; as thousands of Italians took advantage of the divorce law without an avalanche of divorces or the collapse of Italian society in the three years since divorce was legal, many voters simply became acclimated to the new legal and social context and saw no reason to change it.[369]

The divorce referendum was a defeat for the church and for the DC, acting as "a sort of census of the extent to which the Italian people had become secular."[370] Pope Paul VI spoke of his "grief and amazement" (*dolore e stupore*). For all its threats and its opposition to divorce, by 1974 it was "clear that the Church's position has become, or perhaps has always been, a great deal less strong than has been popularly supposed."[371] A few months after the passage of the referendum, in February 1975, Prime Minister Andreotti invited the Vatican back to negotiations on the Concordat, and "the Pontiff, eager to emphasize more strongly separa-

[365] Seymour 2006, 199.
[366] Pollard 2008, 149; Clark, Hine, and Irving 1974, 347.
[367] Sgritta and Tufari 1977, 261.
[368] Phillips 1988, 573.
[369] Clark, Hine, Irving 1974.
[370] Seymour 2006, 221.
[371] Clark, Hine, Irving 1974, 338.

tion of Church and State, especially in matters of politics and elections, accepted."[372]

The referendum on the divorce law showed that there was little automatic popular deference to the church. It further showed the high cost to its perceived interference in politics (as with the Pope's diplomatic note) and the unreliability of coalitions with political parties (whose own considerations did not neatly map onto the church's). Above all, the referendum showed that for many Italians, pragmatic considerations and their own experiences trumped loyalty to church pronouncements—or deference to the instiutional church. Legislatively, the divorce referendum paved the way for the changes in the family law of 1975, the abortion law of 1978, and the renegotiation of the 1929 Concordat in 1984, exemplifying and accelerating the loss of church influence over policy in Italy. By 1987, the separation period before divorce was shortened to three years—and by 2006, Pope Benedict XVI himself called for speedier resolution of annulment petitions, which still took two to three years to be answered.[373] Italy had moved on, irrevocably.

Abortion

Abortion was regarded as a crime against the family in the prewar period, and during the fascist period it became a crime against the race. The Italian Penal Code of 1930 prohibited abortion, except when the life of the pregnant woman was threatened. The pronatalist legislation also prohibited publications about birth control (condoms were still produced and sold, however, to prevent sexually transmitted diseases, especially among the armed forces) and provided subsidies and tax reductions for large families, higher taxes for bachelors, health care for mothers and children, and better economic opportunities for fathers.[374] Along with an emphasis on the role of women as mothers (in Article 37), the legal prohibition on abortion survived in the postwar Constitution as part of the initial policy concessions to the church. The legal sanctions were very harsh, if rarely enforced.[375]

Given the poor enforcement of the laws, a conservative government, and the belated entry of the feminist movement in Italy, the push for

[372] De Franciscis 1989, 81.

[373] Harrison, David. 2006. "Pope Calls for Speedy Annulments as He Softens Church's Stance on Divorce." *The Telegraph*, January 29.

[374] Wanrooiji, 2004.

[375] The law stipulated one to five years' imprisonment for the mother; two to twelve for the abortionist, or ten to twenty if the mother died. According to Figà-Talamanca (1988) there were fifty-nine convictions for illegal abortion in 1973, out of an estimated 340,000 abortions performed that year.

liberalization of contraception and family planning only began in the 1970s.[376] Various organizations defied the law against supplying or advertising contraceptives, and family planning clinics started operating in major cities, untouched by authorities. Despite church objections that contraceptives and abortion contravened the divine moral order, the Constitutional Court ruled in 1971 that the contraceptive provisions were unconstitutional and in 1975 that abortion was permissible in cases of serious health risk for the woman. Along with the legalization of divorce in 1970, the state established family planning centers, allowing them to provide information about contraceptives and contraceptive health services.

In the 1970s, abortion became a major cause of the feminist movement, which staged numerous protests and established freestanding abortion clinics (again, in contrast with Ireland, where the pro-choice movement was far more circumspect). In Irene Figà-Talamanca's account, this era was "one of the few moments in the history of Italian feminism when all fronts were united."[377] The Radical Party decided to concentrate on abortion rights as well, and their campaign was led by an ad hoc organization called the Lega XIII Maggio (13th of May League, in reference to the date of the divorce referendum). Bolstered by the success of the 1974 divorce referendum and backed by increasing public favor for law reform (even among practicing Catholics, who accounted for 47% of abortions in one 1972 study), the feminist movement and the Radical Party pressed for abortion rights. The Radicals and their allies collected the requisite signatures for a referendum to abrogate the Mussolini-era abortion laws in 1975, and so the referendum was to be held in 1976.

All other political parties opposed the 1975–76 referendum effort. Their reasons were not personal morality or an existing alliance with the church; in general, the debates over abortion were often more of a proxy fight between political parties than a consideration of the moral or demographic implications of abortion. Instead, the parties feared parliamentary fission. Specifically, the Christian Democrats were aware of the consistent pro-abortion majorities in the country (55–60%, same as on divorce).[378] A referendum could not only mean electoral defeat, but also a further split within the party between the Catholic integralists and the secular/lay wing. Meanwhile, the Socialists were very much in favor of abortion rights, with Loris Fortuna as prominent in abortion debates as

[376] Women were not granted the vote until 1945, and the Movimento per la Liberazione della Donna was established in 1969 while Lotta Feminista was founded in 1971. Ironically, Italian women lay the foundations for modern feminism by arguing for women's right to education and greater participation in the Renaissance (Ross 2009).

[377] Figà-Talamanca 1988, 281.

[378] Clark and Irving 1977, 16.

he was in the divorce ones, but a referendum would make a center-left coalition with DC difficult, since it would pit the two parties against each other. Finally, the communists worried that their "historic compromise" with the DC would be in peril, while the more conservative "secular" parties like the Liberals or Social Democrats shuddered at the thought of having to join the communists in the referendum campaign.[379]

The best way to avoid a referendum was to legislate. Accordingly, all parties except the neo-fascist MSI put forth an abortion bill in 1975, but the compromise that emerged, which allowed abortion subject to a doctor's approval, was stillborn. It satisfied neither the conservatives, in that it allowed abortion, nor the liberals, in that doctors rather than women would decide. Predictably, the Catholic Church's reaction was to equate abortion with euthanasia and with the Holocaust—and much as in Poland, wonder whether "will this be a more humane society? Certainly no more than the one built over the bodies of millions of human beings exterminated in the concentration camps."[380] The bill collapsed, a new one could not be passed in time, and so a referendum could not be avoided—unless the parliament collapsed. Accordingly, given the far riskier proposition of a referendum, the parliament dissolved itself, and a new election was held in 1976—with the DC retaining its share of the vote (39%), but with the communists making considerable gains (from 27% to 35% of the vote).

Rather than risk another push for a referendum and election, in 1978 the parliament legalized abortion with Law 194 (technically the "norms for the social protection of maternity and the voluntary termination of pregnancy"). The law, much to the consternation of the church, was formally among the most liberal laws in Europe at the time. Women could now terminate a pregnancy virtually upon request in the first trimester.[381] However, backed by the National Catholic Physicians Association and the Movement for Life (the church hierarchy itself was conspicuously absent from the debate) the DC succeeded in getting a "conscientious objection" amendment. The conscience clause made it difficult to find personnel, especially once the Vatican announced that anyone performing or obtaining an abortion would be excommunicated. Nearly 70% of physicians initially invoked the conscience clause (by 1986, the figure dropped to 59%), "owing to the political pressure exerted by the Catholic Church on members of the Christian Democratic Party and the fear of

[379] Clark and Irving 1977.
[380] Clark and Irving 1977, 17.
[381] There were multiple legal grounds for abortion, including economic or social circumstances, "the circumstances in which conception occurred," and physical or mental danger to the mother.

some physicians that their medical practice would consist largely of the performance of abortions."[382] Thus even though abortion was now legal, church pressure in the form of the conscience clause and its use limited actual access. Abortions had to take place in public hospitals, and since staff was not obliged to cooperate, illegal abortions continued. As late as 1993, the Ministry of Health estimated 50,000 clandestine abortions, 70% of which were in the south.[383]

In response to the 1978 law, both the secular Radical Party and the right-to-life movement immediately began to gather signatures for two contrasting referenda. The Radical Party's referendum asked whether to liberalize the law (by repealing the limits on unconditional rights of minors and abrogating the conscience clause); the pro-life movement's whether to restrict it (to abortion under life-threatening circumstances). The church endorsed the latter referendum, as did the DC and the MSI. Despite grandstanding and delays, these were held in 1981, and both were voted down—by super-majorities of, respectively, 88% and 67%. The church was stung by the results; the two-thirds that voted to retain Italy's abortion law "clearly confirmed the message of the 1974 divorce referendum, that Italian society had become more secularized."[384]

Since the referendum debacle of 1981, abortion has rarely appeared on the political agenda. The most significant incident came with the 1988 case of Giampero Boso, whose wife had an abortion without his knowledge. The Constitutional Court declared that the abortion law was a "clear political and legislative choice regarding women's self-determination, irrevocable by the Court."[385] Afterward, Christian Democrats put forth a motion affirming their anti-abortion stance and intending to modify the legislation, but even this largely symbolic declaration did not pass.

In contrast to other predominantly Catholic countries, church leaders in Italy have also avoided the issue after 1981, even as they have weighed in on many other political issues such as immigration and economic justice.[386] After the referenda, "the Vatican has stayed away from the abortion issue, choosing to fight other battles it is more likely to win."[387] Abortion was a non-issue in the elections in the 1990s and 2000s, and there was no abortion litmus test for politicians. It is not that the Italian church changed its adamant objection to abortion; in 1993, the chairman of the Papal Committee for the Interpretation of Legislative Texts stated

[382] UN 2002; Andall 1994, 245.
[383] Wanrooji 2004.
[384] Pollard 2008, 154
[385] Andall 1994, 247.
[386] Thavis 2004.
[387] DiMarco 2009, 13.

unequivocally that women have no right to abortion[388] and in 1995, Pope John Pope II issued his encyclical, *Evangelium Vitae*, condemning contraception and abortion. Instead, the Italian church was hesitant to get politically involved at all in the issue. In the words of the president of Italy's pro-life movement, Carlo Casini, Italian Catholics "consider [abortion] secondary. It's an issue that divides Catholics politically, so the feeling is that it's better not to talk about it."[389] Political priorities also played a role: "the assisted procreation debate is more urgent. And the conditions for a change in the abortion law do not exist at the moment," summarized Father Michele Simone, assistant director of La Civiltà Cattolica.[390] In the run-up to the stem cell referendum of 2005, the parliament was planning on revisiting the 2003 law on assisted reproduction, and the church stayed quiet lest the two issues became linked.

When the issue was eventually reopened, it was not by the church. In December 2007 the conservative journalist Giuliano Ferraro proposed a global moratorium on abortions following the proposed UN moratorium on the death penalty (strongly backed by Italy). Top church officials immediately backed him up. The front-runner in the 2008 elections, Silvio Berlusconi, endorsed the proposed moratorium, but was careful to specify that his party's parliamentarians could vote their conscience.[391] There is some evidence that, in contrast to Ireland, unequivocal popular support for abortion had decreased—in one set of polls, from 25% in 1981 to 16% by 2010.[392] Yet political parties did not respond to this shift, and tended to avoid the issue. Despite the occasional bluster, legal abortion remained on the books, popular sentiment had little patience for church objections or policy influence, and over 120,000 abortions were performed in 2008, the last year for which data is available.[393]

Where the church had the moral authority to mold public opinion and directly influence policy, as in Poland or in Ireland, abortion became the third rail of electoral politics. Even otherwise liberal and secular parties could not reframe the issue as of a woman's choice, and openly worried about the backlash from the church and its loyalists. In contrast, in Italy, where the church did not command such authority, some political parties were willing to back abortion rights. Church objections were duly noted

---

[388] Andall 1994, 250.

[389] Thavis 2004.

[390] Thavis 2004.

[391] AP 2008.

[392] World Values Surveys.

[393] The pattern in Italy is well over 200,000 abortions annually until 1986, with a steady drop thereafter of about 6,000 per year. See http://www.johnstonsarchive.net/policy/abortion /italy/ab-italyr.html, accessed April 26, 2013.

but did not command the framing of the debates or the substance of the policy.

Stem Cell Research and Assisted Reproduction

While the Roman Catholic Church in Italy suffered defeats in abortion, divorce, and education policy, it had a considerable success with stem cell research and assisted reproduction. Here, the Catholic Episcopate wanted both technologies outlawed, while lay politicians pushed for regulation. The stem cell/assisted reproduction controversies occurred after the collapse of the Christian Democrats in 1993–94. After the breakdown of its partner and its coalition, the Italian Bishops' Conference was now careful to stay away from aligning itself with any political party—and as we saw earlier, gained public trust and confidence at the same time. The church now relied on the direct persuasion of Catholic parliamentarians, who not only promoted the church's agenda on moral grounds, but also, along with all secular colleagues, were worried about their political future at a time when parties and coalitions were collapsing and reinventing themselves constantly. The result was a new set of strict new regulations that survived a referendum to abolish them.

In the 1990s, a veto by Catholic parliamentarians of bioethics legislation "resulted in a legislative vacuum, since regulation itself was seen as state recognition of, and participation in, immoral practice."[394] The church preferred this outcome to lenient legislation. However, the veto backfired; scientists were free to experiment, and Italy became "something of a "Wild West" of artificial procreation. Couples flocked to Italy from abroad to take advantage of the legal vacuum. Notoriety quickly followed. In 1994, Dr. Severino Antinori helped a sixty-three-year-old grandmother get pregnant, and then announced his intention to clone embryos.

As early as March 1997, the Italian parliament subsequently banned all activities "even indirectly" linked to human cloning. In 1999, police confiscated a cloned bull, which Health Minister Rosy Bindi claimed violated a ban on animal cloning and a 1992 legislative decree on animal experimentation.[395] In 2001, the Italian parliament passed a Council of Europe pact forbidding the cloning of human beings by a vote of 385 to 3. In late 2002, Health Minister Girolamo Sirchia extended the 1997 ban in response to claims by the Raelian sect that they had cloned a baby from a woman. The Raelian claim triggered a further sequence of bizarre claims by Antinori that he had successfully cloned human embryos, criticism by other scientists, an investigation of Antinori's activities, and his hunger strike in

[394] Donovan 2003, 112.
[395] "Italians 'Arrest' Cloned Bull." Associated Press, September 27, 1999.

front of Silvio Berlusconi's office.[396] Antinori argued the investigation was a violation of his "scientific freedom . . . like in the Holy Inquisition."[397] Antinori eventually abandoned the hunger strike after fifteen days, when he met with prime ministerial aide Paolo Bonaiuti, who assured him of the government's commitment to "the freedom of science and research."[398]

The return of a center-right government in 2001 led to a more restrictive bill on assisted reproduction, cloning, and embryonic research. The bill received bipartisan cooperation in 2004, thanks to the cooperation of Catholic parliamentarians across the government and the opposition. The broader parliamentary support for the bill reflected parliamentary uncertainty; many parliamentarians were deeply worried about their electoral futures, tied as they were to the volatile parties that emerged after the 1994 collapse of the Christian Democrats, and others were pious Catholics. The new regulations were the fruit not of the church's institutional access, which remained low, but of a healthy dose of manipulation: "politicians who rely on the Catholic Church's guidance on ethical and regulatory issues, together with liberal right-wing politicians who sought an instrumental alliance with the Church, drafted a law that included all of the Vatican's objections to assisted fertilization. They sought the advice of various experts, physicians and researchers, but the final bill ignored the opinion of those doctors and researchers who denounced the standards which were being proposed."[399] In the environment of enormous electoral insecurity, some politicians sought the church's guidance, and others wanted to avoid antagonizing the church, even if it no longer commanded its earlier power to mobilize.

The 2004 legislation (known as Legge 40) passed with a 277 to 222 margin, with Catholic and secular parliamentarians both crossing party lines. It banned the use of donor sperm and eggs, forbade embryo freezing and research, and did not allow surrogate mothers. No more than three eggs could be fertilized, and all had to be transferred to the uterus immediately, in the same cycle rather than frozen for future use.[400] More

---

[396] The Vatican had ferociously denounced Antinori's plans to attempt human cloning in 2001, saying he "was delving into Nazi madness." Barnett, Denis. 2002. "World's First Cloned Baby Only Weeks Away: Italian Doctor." Agence France Presse, November 27.

[397] Ruderman, Anne. 2003. "Rome Fertility Doctor Starts Hunger Strike to Protest Investigations." Associated Press Worldstream, January 21.

[398] "Controversial Italian Embryologist Ends Fifteen-Day Hunger Strike." Agence France Presse, February 5, 2003.

[399] Corbellini 2006.

[400] The 1989 regulations of the Irish Medical Council resembled the new regulations in Italy: no embryo freezing was to be allowed, limit on number of eggs fertilized, and all embryos had to be placed in the uterus, as opposed to placing "spare" embryos in the cervix (McDonnell and Allison 2006, 828).

broadly, the law gave embryos rights similar to those of babies, prompting criticism that "the church's opposition to the referendum was a back-door attack on the law allowing abortion—an allegation denied by Cardinal [Camillo] Ruini," the chair of the Italian Bishops' Conference.[401] Importantly, the law did not specify when an embryo comes into existence, leaving their legal rights open to interpretation.[402]

Here, the personal beliefs of policy makers and advisors mattered, especially since they crossed partisan lines. The National Bioethics Committee (Comitato Nazionale per la Bioetica [CNB]), founded in 1990, was to prepare bills, address legal problems, and formulate opinions and guidelines on questions of bioethics. The Prime Minister nominated the committee members directly, and historically they have been predominantly Catholic. Given the nature of the nomination procedure, the religiosity of the committee has varied by Prime Minister. Thus, in 2000, the committee had a number of secularists and helped to bring about an official opinion favorable toward embryonic stem cell research. This changed in 2002 under Prime Minister Berlusconi, who included more conservative Catholic thinkers in the committee, leading to growing levels of conflict between the Catholic and secular members. It was this committee who formulated the 2004 Legge 40.[403]

Women's groups and the secular and liberal Radical Party immediately mobilized to repeal Legge 40 and to liberalize the laws. Beginning in late 2004, they gathered four million signatures, well above the required half million, and ensured a referendum on the law would be held in 2005. Given this outpouring of support, Italian church officials realized a "yes" vote was likely and the laws would be repealed. They were also acutely aware of its past failures to mobilize and to convince voters in referenda.[404] Therefore, under no illusions about their likely success, the church hierarchy changed its previous tactics and advocated a boycott of the referendum, rather than a "no" vote. This way, the quorum would not be reached and the invalidating referendum itself would be invalidated.

---

[401] Flamini 2005.

[402] DiMarco 2009, 17.

[403] Pasotti and Stafford 2006. In 2006, Romano Prodi appointed Francesco Casavola as the committee's president. Casavola, a devout Catholic, chose members of the influential "Science and Life," which strongly opposes embryonic stem cell research, to represent the CNB at national and international meetings and panels. The Vatican helped to form the "Science and Life" committee of Catholic-affiliated academics, scientists, and jurists who claimed the church's objections had scientific basis, even as a countercommittee of secular scientists and physicians, "Research and Health," argued vehemently for a purely scientific standpoint (Corbellini 2006).

[404] Corbellini 2009; Flamini 2005.

The Bishops' Conference advocated "active abstention" and Pope Benedict XVI announced he personally supported it.

Church-affiliated associations organized a network of local Science and Life Committees. Seminars, meetings, and demonstrations tried to convince the electorate to abstain.[405] The church's media, including 140 diocesan weeklies, specialty journals, and two major national newspapers (*Avvenire* and *L'Osservatore Romano*, representing the CEI and the Vatican, respectively) all spoke out in favor of abstention. Politicians crossed party lines in their stances toward the referendum, outraging their party loyalists (and making it difficult for voters to associate parties with sides in the conflict). Thus Francesco Rutelli, head of the center-left Daisy Party, backed abstention, while Gianfranco Fini, the foreign minister and leader of the center-right National Alliance, said he would vote to repeal the laws, defying the church hierarchy.[406] The Prime Minister, Silvio Berlusconi, and the leader of the opposition, Romano Prodi, supported a "no" vote, to maintain the law.

It was the abstinence campaign that worked. Even though the repeal of the strictures was approved by 90% of those who voted, turnout was only 26%. The 2005 referendum failed, much to the surprise of the very bishops who campaigned for the national boycott. (One dismayed bishop was told of the turnout and was quoted as saying, "what? It's as low as that?"[407]) The complexity of the laws and voter apathy also played a role in defeating the referendum.[408] Yet this was an unanticipated success, the product of political contingency that included the collapse of the old party system, the passivity of many voters, and the complexity of the laws. The church did not rely on a partisan coalition or institutional access, but on the personal faith of individual deputies and the inertia of many voters in the face of complex laws and confusing political signals.

Same-Sex Marriage

Same-sex marriage became a salient political controversy in Italy following the passage of Spain's laws in 2004. The church vociferously criticized any proposals to introduce civil partnerships, much less same-sex marriage. Yet while parliamentarians had rejected such bills in the 1990s, by the 2000s they were seriously entertaining the possibility. And here,

---

[405] The president of the Science and Life committee, who organized many of these, was led by Paola Binetti, a member of Opus Dei and a conservative politician, who was subsequently an MP for the center-left Daisy coalition.

[406] Fisher, Ian. 2005. "Italian Vote to Ease Fertility Law Fails for Want of Voters." *New York Times*, June 14.

[407] Flamini 2005.

[408] DiMarco 2009, 21.

the legislative debates over the issue had once again more to do with the exigencies of fragile government coalitions than the moral stances the church advocated.

Several attempts to legislate civil unions were introduced and rejected in parliament in the 1990s, but it was not until July 2002 that Franco Grillini, a member of the opposition Democratic Left Party who had married his partner in the Netherlands in 2002, successfully introduced a civil union bill. It gained center-left support, but failed nonetheless. Both sides of the debate referenced Spain; the gay rights group Arcigay, backed by Grillini, argued that "the extension of matrimony to gay couples represents an act of great civilization and correctly reaffirms the secular nature of the state. . . . Civil and human rights cannot be subject to religious doctrine."[409] The opponents, such as Italy's Minister without portfolio for Reforms and Devolution Roberto Calderoli, a member of the Northern League, argued that "the Good Lord created man and woman and in doing that he put the family at the center of creation. What has happened today in Spain, with the approval of the law authorizing same-sex marriage, is the latest act against God and nature."[410] Others observed that Spain was now more secular than Italy, and the Catholic Church there was in a comparatively weaker position, with a clear division between religious and secular issues.[411]

The center-left, led by Romano Prodi, stopped short of supporting gay marriage but had backed a civil union measure that would protect homosexual and unmarried heterosexual couples in matters such as health care and inheritance. Prodi promised legal rights to de facto couples if elected during the 2006 electoral campaign, but he had been careful to emphasize that civil unions did not represent the legalization of same-sex marriage and was different from Spain's legislation.[412] The "rights of cohabiting people" or "DICO" bill (DIritti e doveri delle persone stabilmente COnviventi: Rights and duties of stable cohabitants) was approved in a special cabinet session, immediately dividing the coalition government, which included centrist Christian Democrats and communists. Since the church had pressured Catholic parliamentarians across the political spectrum, the bill's sponsors responded in kind. The two ministers presenting DICO, the Catholic Rosy Bindi and the secular leftist Barbara Pollastrini,

[409] ANSA. 2005. "Italian Gay Groups Hail Spain's Same-Sex Marriage Move." April 21.
[410] AFP. 2005. "Spanish Gay Marriage Law 'against God and Nature': Italian Minister." June 30.
[411] ANSA. 2005. "Same-Sex Marriage Becomes Political Football." April 22.
[412] ANSA. 2005. "Prodi Sticks to His Guns in Defense of Unwed Couples." September 13. The civil union provisions in the 2006 Center-Left program did not specify gender. As far as the church was concerned, this meant that civil unions would be a Trojan horse for same-sex marriage.

were chosen as symbols of conciliation between "the two main political cultures which are present in the center-left coalition: reformist left and democratic Catholic."[413] Prodi then moved the bill through parliament but was forced to drop it in 2007 to ensure a vote of confidence he needed from both legislative chambers.[414] When an early election was called in 2008, the bill died along with all others in committee.

The Berlusconi–Lega Nord government elected in 2008 did not promise civil unions, much less same-sex marriage, but several of the coalition parliamentarians submitted legislation to the parliament nonetheless. The bill, DiDoRe (DIritti e DOveri di REciprocità dei conviventi, Mutual Rights and Duties for Cohabiting Partners) would not register couples but would provide health and social welfare benefits as well as inheritance rights. Yet by 2012, with public opinion changing and the Catholic Church's apparent shift in support away from Berlusconi to Mario Monti (who explicitly rejected same-sex marriage), even Berlusconi called for granting civil unions and legal recognition to gay couples. However, despite the numerous proposals, and local initiatives by municipalities and regions, no civil union law passed on the national level—victim of the fragile politics of coalition governments rather than of the moral authority of the church.

For its part, the church remained steadfast in its opposition. Responding to the debates surrounding civil unions, and anticipating the legalization of same-sex marriage, the Vatican formally announced in 2003 that no legal recognition of homosexual unions can be permissible, regardless of how any rights granted would differ from marriage.[415] L'Osservatore Romano further attacked Prodi in 2005, after he supported greater rights for unmarried couples, accusing him of "undermining marriage and the moral framework of society, and sacrificing family values to election considerations."[416] In June 2006, the Vatican's Pontifical Council for the Family also spoke out directly against civil unions. Not surprisingly, in these battles over same-sex marriage, "what has outraged many on the Marxist and non-Marxist left is not so much the essentially homophobic tone of many ecclesiastical utterances as the feeling that once again the Church is 'bullying' and bulldozing Italy with its own moral agenda."[417] In keeping with its strategy of pressuring politicians, the CEI issued a formal

[413] Ceccarini 2010, 189.

[414] Off Our Backs. 2006. "Italy: Government Moves on Rights for Same-Sex Couples, Then Backs Off." April.

[415] "Considerations Regarding Proposals to Give Legal Recognition to Unions between Homosexual Persons," 2003.

[416] ANSA. 2005. "Prodi Sticks to His Guns in Defense of Unwed Couples." September 13.

[417] Pollard 2008, 190.

pastoral note in March 2007, which exhorted "Catholic politicians and legislators, conscious of their grave responsibility before society, must feel particularly bound, on the basis of a properly formed conscience to introduce and support laws inspired by values grounded in human nature. There is an objective connection here with the Eucharist."[418] The church also organized demonstrations, such as Family Day in May 2007, against DICO and other provisions.

Yet for all its public announcements in the 2000s, there were no clear points where the church exercised policy influence: no referenda, no legislative bills, and no coalition votes that turned on church support.[419] The regulation of civil partnerships, whether same-sex or other, was left to political parties that were paying more attention to the electorate than to the moral admonitions of the church. And here, as in Ireland, society was outpacing the church. A Demos-Eurisko poll published in November 2004 found only 32% of Italians favored same-sex marriage.[420] By 2012, however, 44% supported same-sex marriage, and 63% supported recognition for same-sex couples. By 2009, dozens of municipalities and cities in Italy had introduced civil union registries, which formally recognize same-sex couples even if these do not have national legal standing. Even conservative politicians recognized this new reality; Monti himself, after joining forces with a proclerical party, the Unione di Centro (Union of the Center), carefully announced in early 2013 that while he rejected same-sex marriage, he was in favor of civil unions and equal standing for gay couples within such civil partnerships.[421]

Backlash?

The alliance with the Christian Democrats had been a double-edged sword; while that coalition (or rather, its prospect), led to the inclusion of the Lateran Accords into the Constitution and all the privilege that flowed to the church as a result, other gains either never materialized

[418] Quoted in Ceccarini 2010, 191.

[419] The exception that proves the rule was the case of Justice Minister Clemente Mastella, who led the small Catholic Party (UDEUR) that gave the Prodi government a one-seat majority in parliament. A devout Catholic, Mastella boycotted the 2007 cabinet vote on civil partnerships. He ended the party's support for Prodi in 2008, depriving it of its narrow majority, but for a different reason: the fall of the government disrupted a pending referendum on the election law, which, had it passed, would have made it more difficult for small parties like UDEUR to get into parliament. When the government collapsed, so did the plans for the legislation.

[420] Religion News Service. 2004. "Looking to America, Italian Professor Launches Values Movement." November 9.

[421] Gessa, Daniele Guido. 2013. Gay Star News, http://www.gaystarnews.com/article /italys-prime-minister-says-no-gay-marriage170113. January 17.

or proved evanescent. For one, the church never gained the institutional access, or the formal control over state sectors such as education, health-care, or welfare institutions, that its Irish counterpart did. Moreover, the overt political involvement of the church, and its cozy relationship with the Christian Democrats, meant the church was identified, to its detri-ment, with the tangled webs of DC corruption, financial scandals, and questionable political entanglements.

The irony is that in some ways, the Catholic Church in Italy became a more influential national player *after* the collapse of its coalition with the Christian Democrats. First, the rise of secessionist movements of the Northern League and others in the 1990s put the church in the unprec-edented position of credibly defending the principles of Italian national unity and identity.[422] Second, the church achieved important policy objec-tives, such as the defeat of the 2005 stem cell referendum, *after* the coali-tion had collapsed, even if careful strategy or the church's moral author-ity had little to do with the victory. Third, in a bittersweet development, confidence in the church in Italy substantially *increased* after the end of the partisan coalition with the Christian Democrats, when the church no longer could channel that popular trust into policy influence.[423] In short, the partisan coalition with the Christian Democrats backfired in many ways—and the post-coalition successes were a haphazard assemblage rather than a firm foundation for durable policy influence.

Conclusion

Ireland and Italy show the complexities of church influence on politics, which has varied over time, across policy domains, and across countries. At the same time, these two countries show stark differences in whether and how religious and national identities fused—and how churches sub-sequently made use of differing levels of moral authority.

For decades, the Irish church's high moral authority meant it not only had access to policy-making institutions—it often controlled them. In-culcating both faith and loyalty to the church through the educational system, omnipresent in society and in politics, the church could influ-ence policy through referenda as well. Politicians deferred to the church, worried about the very articulation of opinions outside of the range of

---

[422] Donovan 2003, 100–111.

[423] Ceccarini 2010, 183. Most recently, some of the church's privileges, such as tax breaks on real estate holdings and corporation taxes (which saved the church approximately two billion Euro every year), were eliminated thanks not to a zealous anti-clerical party but to the keen attention of EU regulators and competition policy directives.

"acceptable" views. In Italy, a church with lower moral authority relied on a partisan coalition, and occasionally on mobilizing the public; even so, these strategies repeatedly backfired. Popular religiosity did not translate into a loyalty to the institutional church, and politicians were more concerned with coalition politics and the polarized nature of Italian party politics (which hid shambolic consensus-seeking within parliament) than with church preferences or anticipatory anxiety about church disapproval.

Beyond these differences, Ireland and Italy suggest that religious monopolies (and specifically, hierarchical monopolies) have a built-in advantage in that the clergy and their political leaders share the same theological commitments. In mixed Protestant-Catholic countries, as we will see, denominations first had to build alliances, and doctrinal disagreements limited which domains they could address. The cases of Ireland and Italy further show that both politicians and clergy were highly strategic actors, choosing as best as they could what they saw as effective tactics of engagement and mutual support: the Irish church embraced the Free State despite an earlier hostility to Republicans, and the DC and the Italian Episcopate carefully weighed the expected costs and benefits of a coalition. Yet for all their savvy, both churches had difficulty predicting their success in mobilizing the populace; the outcomes of popular referenda surprised the churches more often than not. More generally, anxious politicians deferred to the churches far more than the increasingly cynical voters, and the state was more steadfast than the electorate. Thus even if the Irish church initially held onto education and the welfare state in the wake of the scandals of the 1990s, and some morality issues remained too fraught for politicians to address, the church lost standing in a society disappointed by church hypocrisy and increasingly accepting of abortion, divorce, and homosexuality.

Finally, both the Italian and Irish churches had considerable strategic latitude, in that neither church experienced a consistently and profoundly hostile secular regime. Yet as we will see in the next chapter, enduring such hostility meant the Polish and Croatian churches emerged from the collapse of communism with enormous moral authority and even institutional access—but no guarantee these would survive democracy.

CHAPTER 4

Post-Communist Divergence: Poland and Croatia

> The state is a realm of struggle for power. The church by its nature is a realm of struggle for absolute values; in a visible world it is a giver of invisible goods.[1]
> —Adam Michnik, 2001

> It is not important whether in Poland there is capitalism, freedom of speech, or wealth—what matters the most is that Poland is Catholic.[2]
> —Henryk Goryszewski, 1993

> The Croatian Parliament should follow Christian values.[3]
> —Cardinal Josip Bozanić, 2010

IF IRELAND AND ITALY FIRST diverged during the building of the nation-state and then continued their distinct patterns of church-state relations, Poland and Croatia seemed to follow a similar path under communism, only to dramatically swerve apart once democracy arrived. And here, two puzzles arise. First, the two churches had achieved similar levels of moral authority by the end of the communist era. Both countries remained virtual Catholic monopolies, with high rates of religious participation and loyalty and over 90% of the population in both cases claim a Catholic identity. Yet the Roman Catholic Church has influenced public policy in Poland far more than it did in Croatia. Moreover, while in Poland the church relied chiefly on institutional access, in Croatia it was dragged (more or less willingly) into a public and costly coalition with the ruling party, the Croatian Democratic Union (Hrvatska Demokratska Zajednica, HDZ). Accordingly, the Croatian church's policy influence and its moral authority suffered.

---

[1] Michnik 2001, 908.

[2] "Nie jest ważne, czy w Polsce będzie kapitalizm, wolność słowa, czy będzie dobrobyt—najważniejsze, aby Polska była katolicka." Quoted in http://wyborcza.pl/piatekekstra/1,13 2078,13606668,Rzucilam_ciastkiem_w_glowe_papieza__Nie_przeprosze.html, accessed December 16, 2013.

[3] "Sabor treba slijediti kršćanske vrijednosti," homily at Holy Mass at Ludbreg, September 5, 2010.

Second, the roots of the churches' high moral authority and subsequent policy clout lie in supposedly very inhospitable soil: the communist period. For all the talk of enmity between "godless communism" and popular Catholicism, the Roman Catholic Church was able not only to play an important role in stabilizing communist rule and to obtain policy compromises from the communist regime, but also to achieve the institutional access that would make its influence in *democratic* politics both significant and surprisingly immune to popular disapproval. Roman Catholic clergy and institutions did suffer, especially where they were earlier already marginalized, as in the Czech Lands or in Hungary. But the image of lasting and heartfelt enmity between the Catholic Church and the communist regime belies frequent negotiations, compromises, and shared goals of social stability.

Under communism and under democracy, Roman Catholic churches could obtain policy influence by dint of their moral authority. Communist rule, after all, was hardly stable or unopposed; instead, to (highly) varying degrees, it was subject to popular contestation and protest. Where such conflict threatened to destabilize the system, churches with moral authority could step in to calm down the protest in the name of the nation. In exchange, communist governments provided short-term policy concessions and longer-term institutional access to churches that could ensure social peace and the stability of the communist regime. The church could not hold the communist government hostage, since the balance of formal power always favored the communist regime. Nonetheless, even if the church had no army divisions at its disposal, to paraphrase Stalin,[4] it could still extract significant and enduring concessions at times of regime crises when the incumbents feared they could lose all.

The collapse of the communist regime and the emergence of democracy in 1989–91 opened up even greater opportunities. The new democratic governments were inexperienced, unstable, and often uncertain about their ability to establish durable regimes. Historians, playwrights, and shipyard workers became national leaders overnight. Unlike the communist regimes, the new governments were not ideologically hostile to the church, nor did they have to prove their commitment to atheism and anti-clericalism to a foreign sponsor. If anything, they were beholden to a church that had sheltered them during their years as the anti-communist opposition, by reassuring the communist regime and by covertly supporting the dissidents.

---

[4] Stalin's (in)famous quote was "The Pope? And how many divisions does he have?" when asked to help Russian Catholics to win favor with the Pope. Quoted in Churchill 1948, 105.

These new democratic governments sought church support to build broad popular backing for democracy, since both analysts and policy makers feared massive social unrest due to parliamentary fractioning and conflict, painful economic reforms, and the negotiation of new international relationships. Their present was precarious, and the future was uncertain. In exchange, governments could include clergy in formulating policy, give discretion in naming and vetoing secular officials, and seek out church representatives to secular institutions. Such institutional access gave the churches a direct stake in the new democratic states and rewarded them for advocating public patience. It was also largely covert; neither side called attention to it, and it remained largely under the radar of the media. Churches could thus gain considerable access during times of potential instability—precisely when institutional and policy frameworks could be transformed.

Yet high moral authority did not automatically translate into policy influence. First, as Croatia shows, the challenges of the transition required the church's moral authority as a solution; if the dominant conflict was not between the nation and the communist state, it was that much harder to represent the former. Second, churches had to act quickly and decisively. The attention of the electorate and the media was diverted by the enormity of the economic, political, and social change. Policies had to be passed rapidly, implemented amid the chaos and din of multiple economic, political, and social transformations, giving cover to the passage of unpalatable policies. It helped that the nascent democratic regimes were fragile and new—and in desperate need of all the legitimization they could get. But as crises passed, so did the churches' ability to extract concessions in the name of keeping the social peace.

The breadth of the potential policy influence in these new conditions was enormous. First, given the communist-era policies of nationalizing church property and evicting monasteries and churches in the name of land reform, restitution immediately became an issue. Church land holdings, the status of church charities, pensions for clergy, and financing church activities all now entered policy discussions. Second, there were also the multiple policy domains the church interpreted as spheres of morality: abortion, divorce, education, and subsequently same-sex marriage and embryo research technology. These would become the focus of churches eager to assert their new freedom. Third, democratic elections also offered a new arena for the church, and the opportunity to endorse sympathetic parties and candidates, to ensure governments sympathetic to church interests.

Yet as we will see, the more partisan and public the activities of the church, the greater the popular backlash against them and the more limited their success. When clergy spoke out in public and tried to mobilize voters to support particular parties, the church rapidly lost standing in society. Mobilizing the faithful on purely religious grounds, such as signing petitions against abortion after masses, met with more success. But the greatest policy achievements for the church came when it could push through its proposals and policy preferences with minimal public involvement and with no partisan entanglements, when the church could rely on its direct institutional access to policy making rather than on popular mobilization or parliamentary debates.

These channels of institutional access took several different forms. Church officials actively participated in policy-making discussions (special Episcopal commissions, for example, formulated the abortion law in Poland), took part in national negotiations during regime transitions (such as the Round Table negotiations in Poland), and influenced personnel and organizational decisions within ministries. Vulnerable politicians felt they had no choice but to go along with church demands if they were to preserve the new democratic order—even when the church prioritized its interpretation of natural law over democratic rule.[5] The fusion of national and religious identities empowered churches as national representatives and thus guarantors of social peace. Secular actors were willing to buy church support with policy concessions, and the results, both for the democratic stability and specific policies, were long lasting. In contrast, when church leaders became tainted with partisan politics, as in Croatia, they would have less influence on policy.

This chapter examines how the Roman Catholic Church in Poland and Croatia influenced politics, under communism and after, sometimes through popular mobilization and openly partisan electioneering, but much more successfully through covert and "apolitical" institutional access. Communist-era concessions were hard fought and rarely dramatic. In contrast, churches could win far more once democracy arrived, if they were careful in how they pursued their goals.

Poland

In Poland, a complex historical calculation became a simple equation of "Pole = Catholic." Like Ireland, Poland is a religious monopoly, and just as in Ireland, the fusion of nation and religion has been contingent both on demographics (a relatively homogenous population) and an antagonistic historical relationship to a secular state. The resulting fusion of religious and national identities is so salient that some observers conclude the "tight bond between the Roman Catholic Church and the Polish na-

[5] Gowin 1995.

tion is a widely known fact."[6] Yet for all the close intertwining of Polish and Catholic identities, these lands were multilinguistic, multiethnic, and multidenominational for all but the last fifty years of Polish history, which stretches back to the tenth century. There is little doubt that the "bond between faith and fatherland in Poland was more complicated than it might appear."[7] The fusion of nation and religion in Poland is recent, contingent, and reliant on a reinterpretation (or denial) of many aspects of history. Nonetheless, it became a powerful force behind church influence in Polish politics, in setting the terms of political debates and in directly influencing policy making.

Some analysts have placed the origins of the fusion of Polish national identity and Roman Catholicism in the national partitions that began in the late eighteenth century, when Poland was repeatedly divided among Prussia, Austria, and Russia.[8] Poland lost its statehood, but the church protected expressions of Polish national identity, such as language and literature, and allowed a nation without a state to survive.[9] Catholic clergy repeatedly opposed foreign influence, siding with local notables in resisting Prussian initiatives in education, for example, and subsequently supporting Polish-language instruction with a Catholic curriculum. As a result, "linguistic and educational conflict became part of a national struggle which in this century formed an issue in two succeeding world wars."[10] In addition, the Roman Catholic Church in Poland "devised a specific theology of *nation* . . . which resulted in the sacralization of the term and its values." Poland was a martyr among nations, and a symbolic defender (*antemurale*) of Catholic Europe against Turkish, Tatar, Russian, and communist invaders.[11] To summarize this view, "when the Polish state ceased to exist after the partition of 1795, the Church became the guardian of Polish national identity and a symbol of freedom and opposition to foreign powers . . . Catholicism became equated with Polish patriotism."[12]

Yet these arguments fail to account for the fact that Poland before World War II was a multinational and multidenominational entity. Poland was only two-thirds Polish and Catholic, with around 20% Orthodox Ukrainians and Belorussians (or more precisely, Orthodox and

---

[6] Chrypiński 1990, 15.

[7] Porter-Szücs 2011, 7–8.

[8] Gowin 1995, 16. Barker places the rise of Polish religious nationalism even earlier, with the Swedish invasion and the "Deluge" of 1648. (Barker 2009, 87.)

[9] Froese and Pfaff 2001; Ramet 1998.

[10] Swaan 1988, 78.

[11] Borowik 2002, 240.

[12] Eberts and Török 2001, 129; see also Turowicz 1990, 241–42; and Gowin 1995, 24.

Easter-Rite Catholics), 10% Jews, and 2–3% German Protestants as Polish citizens.[13] Catholicism was only one strand of Polish national identity, and one whose public articulation began in earnest only in the late nineteenth century—one hundred years after the first partitions—through the sustained work of teachers, journalists, and even noblewomen teaching peasant children and transmitting national values.[14] Neither an elite nor a popular consensus existed about the content of "Pole" or its link to Catholicism, despite a strong National Democratic stream of political thought that equated the two.[15] This ethnolinguistic diversity, in fact, led advocates of religious and national fusion to sharply distinguish between the state as an administrative framework that could encompass many nations, and the nation as "undoubtedly a creation of God" that denied such diversity.[16]

For its part, the church often sided with the Prussian or Austrian (though not Russian) imperial administrations rather than with the populace. Church officials, for example, protested Bismarck's *Kulturkampf* policies, affecting as they did the church and its institutional autonomy in the 1870s. However, they responded much more mildly to compulsory Germanization in the 1900s, even admonishing Poles to obey their secular Prussian authorities.[17] Independent interwar Poland saw massive anti-clericalism, and the contestation of the "Pole = Catholic" equation by important political forces, including the man who dominated interwar politics, Marshal Józef Piłsudski. Anti-clerical parties gained in popularity as the church began to side with successive interwar governments.[18] Catholics themselves voted for a variety of parties in the interwar period, backing parties across the ideological spectrum.[19] Given the demographic facts on the ground, and the deep splits within the political elite, the idea that to be Polish was to be Catholic was as endemic as it was contested.

It was the ethnic and religious homogenization of Poland that made possible the full fusion of national and religious identities. As the result of the devastation of World War II and the population transfers that followed, postwar Poland became a homogenous Catholic nation—one where communism was seen as an alien imposition that violated tenets of sovereignty and faith. The communist governments and the Catholic Church repeatedly clashed over who was the real and legitimate representative of the Polish nation—and the communists were widely seen as

[13] Majchrowski 1993, 75.
[14] Zubrzycki 2006, 53–54.
[15] Zubrzycki 2006, 76; Chrypiński 1990, 6.
[16] Porter-Szücs 2011, 333.
[17] Porter-Szücs 2011, 162–63.
[18] Chrypiński 1990, 125; Gowin 1995, 18ff.
[19] Kopstein and Wittenberg 2003, 98.

Soviet stooges and lackeys of the historical enemies of Poland.[20] Despite the best efforts of Polish communist governments to present themselves as "true" Poles, the result was a renewed consensus about a "conflation of the ideas, institutions, and so to speak, behavioral displays of religion with nationality in Poland . . . the Roman Catholic Church has provided the means for the emergence and preservation of a modern national consciousness among the Poles."[21] Further, it was "the only institution which—as after the Second World War and during partition—has retained its institutional structure and identity."[22]

In Stalin's formulation, establishing communism in Poland was like "putting a saddle on a cow"; imposing a set of institutions and structures that were not only new and alien, but made all the more suspect by their association with a historically hostile Russia and the Soviet Union. If the foreign-sponsored and widely distrusted communist party identified the church as its foe and rival, then the church became a de facto ally and representative of the nation.

The church worked assiduously to strengthen these bonds, evangelizing and creating a national identity that would withstand communist assimilation. For example, time and again, the church offered alternative celebrations of secular holidays; the September 15 victory over the Soviets in the 1921 war was celebrated as a religious holiday of Our Divine Lady of the Herbs, and the May 3 anniversary of Poland's 1791 Constitution became a holy day of obligation. These allowed Poles to observe holidays forbidden by the communist regime, such as September 15 or May 3, under the guise of a religious obligation, further underscoring the church's commitment to the "real" Polish nation.

Even more ambitiously, Cardinal Stefan Wyszyński launched the "Great Novena" in 1957. Conceived as a nine-year cycle of prayer and building bonds between the church and society, the Novena was ostensibly a celebration of a thousand years since the baptism of Poland—and thus the obvious alternative to the secular communist celebrations of a thousand years of Polish statehood set for 1966. The Novena was a call to renewed religious commitment, made manifest by repeated pilgrimages to the holy shrine of Our Lady of Częstochowa (the Black Madonna) and subsequently the pilgrimage of the venerated portrait of the Black Madonna across Poland, and into every parish. Millions of Poles participated in

[20] This struggle made for strange fellow travelers; for example, the communist party imprisoned Bolesław Piasecki, a fascist interwar religious nationalist and xenophobe, only to recruit him as the leader of the pro-regime Catholic organization "Pax" to build a Catholic-Marxist alliance. See Kunicki 2012, 3–4.

[21] Morawska 1995, 51.

[22] Borowik 2002, 242.

masses, processions, prayer vigils, and pilgrimages. Based on Wyszyński's "theology of nation," the Novena was a "clear and purposeful statement of collective identity—one that was inherently opposed to the socialist identity promoted by the state."[23] The Novena crystallized the notion that to be authentically Polish was to be Catholic—and that the cleavage within Polish society lay between church and society on the one hand and the communist party and a foreign regime on the other.

In short, the fusion of nation and religion in Poland is in fact a relatively new phenomenon. Yet even this fusion did not become politically salient until the church sided with the nation against the communist state in the 1960s and 1970s. The church repeatedly resisted state incursion into its affairs during the communist era and tried to recast these as resistance to the communist imposition on the Polish nation.[24] But it was only in the 1970s that the church moved beyond self-defense and began to speak out more forcefully in favor of human rights.[25] Its moral authority greatly increased with the rise of public anti-communist mobilization, the second pilgrimage of the Black Madonna around Poland in the late 1970s, and the triumphal return of Pope John Paul II to Poland in 1979. These further reinforced the notion that Polish identity was inextricably linked to Catholicism, and served as a political awakening.

The rise of the independent trade union Solidarity in August 1980 cemented these ties. Strikes began among the shipyard workers of Gdańsk in August 1980, quickly solidifying into the independent (and unprecedented) trade union Solidarity, which eventually grew to ten million members, or nearly half the adult population of Poland. During the opening salvo, the August 1980 strike, the workers immediately affixed a cross, a picture of the Virgin Mary, and a photograph of Pope John Paul II to the gates of the shipyards—as symbols of victory.[26] As a result, the 1981 military crackdown on Solidarity led to "an unprecedented rise in the Church's authority."[27] The church, in fact, became a de facto mediator between the communist party and Solidarity, as the representatives of the Episcopate negotiated and attended meetings between the communist and Solidarity sides at both the national and local level, and continually called for moderation from the opposition, civility from the state, and neutrality by the clergy.[28] The bishops emphasized the need for unity and

[23] Osa 1997, 352.
[24] Morawska 1995, 55.
[25] Anderson 2003, 144.
[26] Osa 1997, 362.
[27] Gowin 1999, 24.
[28] Chrypiński 1990, 12; Królikowska 1993; Waniek 2011, 284. This is not to say all bishops or clergy followed these admonishments; several, such as Bishop Ignacy Tokarczuk of Przemyśl (active throughout the communist and post-communist period from his ordina-

stability, "with great care and feeling of responsibility for the further fate of the Country considered, in keeping with its mission as the shepherds of the Church but also as the sons of the Fatherland, the current situation in which our common Home—Poland—has found itself."[29] Throughout the 1980s, especially after the collapse of Solidarity, the church became a protective umbrella for the anti-communist opposition. Churches offered physical protection for individual dissidents and broader opposition activity, sending food packages to the imprisoned and to their families and hosting dissident meetings in its basements. Attending Mass became a political act.

This is not to say the Catholic Church was always a vociferous critic of the communist regime, or that it never misstepped. The Episcopate's 1965 letter to German bishops, with its famous lines of "we forgive and we ask for forgiveness" met with societal disapproval and mixed feelings, not least because the German response was perceived as cold and official.[30] In 1956–80, the church tended to be cautious in regard to the opposition and suspicious of any alternative movements that had leftist tendencies, such as the 1976 Committee to Defend Workers.[31] Finally, an unanticipated consequence of the church's role as a substitute for the sovereign state during the partitions was a lasting conservatism within the church, and an unwillingness to engage with critics or reform.

For all that, the conflicts between the communist regime and the society, above all the 1980–81 Solidarity episode of independent organization and national reawakening, all reinforced the notion that the church was on the side of the nation. Whenever the "Polish state went through a serious political crisis . . . the significance of the Church rose, and society gathered herself around her."[32] Both the communist party and the opposition recognized the church's power; while Solidarity sought the church's shelter, the communist party repeatedly entered into negotiations with the church, easing restrictions in exchange for the church calming down the political situation. By the late 1980s, 80% of society polled said the church worked in the public interest.[33] The church's moral authority also meant it had become the fulcrum in the political scales, and its mediation and endorsement were critical to the success of the Round Table negotiations between Solidarity and the communist

---

tion in 1942 until his retirement in 1993 and death in 2012), were publicly (and notoriously) anti-communist and pro-opposition.

[29] *PO*, 43/80.

[30] Waniek 2011, 275–76; Wigura 2013.

[31] Gowin 1995, 24.

[32] Daniel 1995, 417.

[33] Borowik 2002, 242.

regime in 1989 and the transition that immediately followed. It was a guarantor of social stability and would extract concessions from the government accordingly.

Policy Influence

One of the more remarkable aspects of the church's influence in Poland was how it survived both the communist collapse and the rise of independent democracy. As one commentator put it, "from the time of the PRL [the communist-era People's Republic of Poland], everyone believes that the Church plays a stabilizing role in politics."[34] It gained much of its institutional access during the communist era—when repeated crises necessitated negotiations with the church to keep social peace and prevent bloodshed, and then used this access to push through its two policy priorities (abortion and education) almost immediately after the collapse of communism, when its backing of the nascent democracy was seen as critical to the new regime's success. In exchange for its support of Polish accession to NATO and the EU, the church obtained new legal and financial privileges in the Constitution and the Concordat. Finally, its opposition to the legal recognition of same-sex partners, and to the availability of contraception, assisted reproductive technologies, and stem cell research, subsequently colored the policy debates of the early twenty-first century. But as we will see, these debates came much later, once the church ceased to play the role of a critical stabilizing force.

The Communist Era

After World War II, the Roman Catholic Church and the ruling communist party were each other's hostages. On the one hand, the party repressed the church, especially in the 1950s; it imprisoned Cardinal Stefan Wyszyński and nine hundred other clergy, limited the church's reach (eliminating religion in schools, not allowing building permits for new churches, conducting propaganda campaigns), and revoked its charity networks and its property rights. Infamous cases of secret police torture and repression also surfaced, as in the 1984 murder of the pro-Solidarity Father Jerzy Popiełuszko. Yet compared to the tactics of communist parties elsewhere, as in Czechoslovakia or Hungary, the Polish communist party was unusually circumspect in the scope and intensity of its repression. Monasteries were not dissolved, priests were not forced to abandon their clerical duties for menial labor, and above all, religious practices were tolerated—even among communist party members.

---

[34] Janicki 2002, 26.

The party trod so carefully because the church was acquiring considerable moral authority under communism, through the communist party's hostility and through its own deliberate strategies of building stronger ritual bonds with the lay society, which ranged from neighborhood processions to national prayer appeals. Policy concessions to the church also began under communism. Despite their ostensible conflict, the party-state and the church constantly engaged with each other throughout the communist era. The church mediated in the conflicts between the communist party and the opposition, largely informally, through letters, meetings, communiqués, sermons, and individual interventions.[35] In what would become a crucial formal innovation, church representatives were also invited to a special joint church-state commission, which acted as a forum for policy consultation and coordination.

In the immediate postwar years, 1945–47, the church and the new communist party worked toward similar goals: the full "polonization" of the new Polish state, including the newly (re)gained German territories in the west.[36] During this brief period, the church was largely left alone; once the communist party felt more certain of its hold on power, several years of communist repression followed in the late 1940s and early 1950s, including the imprisonment of Cardinal Wyszyński.[37] The regime censored church publications, took over its Caritas charitable network, nationalized hospitals, and seized church property. Soon after, a characteristic pattern emerged; the state would grant privileges to the church and try to appease it during times of social instability, such as 1956, 1970, or 1976,[38] only to curb those privileges and concessions when the church's mediating and stabilizing role was no longer deemed necessary.[39]

Yet if such policy concessions could be short-lived, institutional access proved durable. The critical forum of negotiation and access, especially in the 1956 and 1980–81 crises, was the Joint Commission of the Representatives of the Polish People's Republic and the Conference of the Episcopate of Poland (Komisja Wspólna Przedstawicieli Rządu RP i Konferencji Episkopatu Polski). The Commission began meeting in 1949 as the "Mixed Commission" (Komisja Mieszana), at the instigation of the

---

[35] Królikowska 1993, 199–203.

[36] Fleming 2010, 645.

[37] Eberts 1998, 819.

[38] The church hierarchy remained largely silent after the student protests of 1968 and the anti-Semitic campaign that followed, which meant the Communist Party no longer saw the church as its main opponent. The protests did not spread to the rest of society—and the anti-Semitic campaign that followed was largely seen as an internal party conflict. (Dudek 1995, 226.)

[39] Eberts 1998, 819; Eberts and Torok 2001, 129.

church. The government agreed to the request so that it could observe the reaction of the church to increasing restrictions, and moderate these as needed.[40] Subsequently, the communist party formalized the Joint Commission through an official agreement of April 14, 1950.

The Commission stopped meeting during 1953–56 but began again in November 1956, after the mass demonstrations and protests in Poznań shook the communist party leadership. And when worker protest threatened to spiral out of control in 1956, the party turned to the church to calm down the situation. The church acceded and issued a public call for moderation and calm in exchange for policy concessions: the release of Cardinal Wyszyński from house arrest, and a formal agreement that gave back the church authority over its internal affairs and clergy appointments. The government abolished its hugely controversial 1953 decree requiring state approval for clerical positions. Once the situation calmed down, however, the government returned to its usual policies by finalizing the abolishing of religious education in the public schools.

After 1958 the Joint Commission met to discuss clergy appointments, the legal rights of the church, its press, tax status, and charitable activity. It met after the controversial 1965 letter of the Polish bishops to their German counterparts only to stop meeting altogether in 1967 when the church designated Bishop Ignacy Tokarczuk, a highly controversial and vehemently anti-communist bishop, as its representative to the Commission. During this time, there were informal meetings and one-on-one interviews between high-ranking party officials and Episcopate representatives. The Primate of Poland and the First Secretary of the communist party met many times to discuss matters of mutual interest and to coordinate policy, and these discussions took on enormous significance during periods of crisis.[41] These meetings, however, did not have the formal standing and policy-generating capacity of the Commission. Yet even as the Joint Commission stopped meeting, the era of First Secretary Edward Gierek (1970–80) brought a new understanding between church and state, marked by a "new custom of consulting with the Church authorities regarding legal acts that touched the Church before they were issued."[42] Church-state relations in the 1970s and 1980s took on the form of "constant dialogue . . . between the Secretariat of the Episcopal Conference and the Ministry for Denominational Affairs, between the Joint Commission and the state, and the direct dialogue between the Head of the Polish State and the Primate (the most effective level)."[43]

[40] Dudek and Gmyz 2003, 44–45.
[41] Borecki and Janik 2011, 17.
[42] Majchrowski 1993, 80.
[43] Interview with Cardinal Józef Glemp, July 22, 1987; *PO*, 40/87v.

The dramatic rise of Solidarity presented an enormous challenge to communist rule. Within a month of the August 1980 strike, the government revived the Commission, ostensibly to discuss the concession already made by the communist party to air Masses over state radio on Sundays. Already at this meeting, the church laid out thirty different demands, the foremost of which was to recognize the legal personhood of the church.[44] Other topics included the visit of the Pope in 1983 and 1987, and the policy of the government vis-à-vis Solidarity. By December 1980, the two sides decided to form a joint *legislative* commission, which met monthly, even under martial law. Its remit included the Catholic Church in Poland and its structures, the activity of the church and its organizations, financial matters, and the church's legal status.[45] These would form the core of discussions until the collapse of communism. Other subcommittees discussed everything from media access to the paper quotas for Catholic publications. The church received considerable concessions, including a much sought-after increase in building permits; as a result, "despite the worst housing crisis in decades the decay of schools and hospitals, and an appalling lack of day care and nursing home facilities, the Church enjoyed a construction boom."[46]

Throughout the communist era, church-communist state relations "oscillated between mutual confrontation, accommodation, and dialogue rather than stagnating in a state of constant struggle."[47] The "Secret Documents" of the Joint Commission are notable for two things: the constant back and forth between church and state in the form of letters, meetings, and phone calls, and the shift over time in church-state relations. These changed from state monitoring of the church in the 1960s to extensive meetings as equals in the 1980s, meetings that by January 1989 ended in shared dinners between communist officials and bishops.[48] Not surprisingly, the Commission was characterized as an "arena for lobbying by the Polish Episcopate of the government authorities, and especially of the Ministers of the Republic."[49] Its functions went far beyond persuasion, or even the targeting of likely allies with information and support.[50] The Commission also became a channel through which actual policy proposals could be funneled to the legislature and to the government.

As Solidarity resurrected itself over the course of 1988–89, church representatives facilitated the process that would eventually result in the

[44] Borecki and Janik 2011, 13.
[45] Orszulik 2008, 254–55.
[46] Ost 1990, 157.
[47] Kunicki 2012, 5.
[48] Aneks 1993, 576.
[49] Borecki and Janik 2011, 21.
[50] Hall and Deardorff 2006.

collapse of communism. Several bishops participated in the initial meetings between Solidarity and the party that began in July 1988, and in the face-to-face meetings between their leaders, Lech Wałęsa and General Czesław Kiszczak. Both sides wanted church involvement during the "Round Table" regime negotiations that started in January 1989. Solidarity wanted witnesses, while the party did not want to be accused of ill will or deception, and Wałęsa was known to change his mind.[51] Three different bishops, Tadeusz Gocłowski, Bronisław Dembowski, and Alojzy Orszulik, were all official observers during the Round Table. The negotiations ended in April 1989 with agreements to, among other things, hold elections, legalize Solidarity, introduce the office of the President, and to abolish the communist monopoly.

Against this background, by the late 1980s, the communist party was negotiating with the church in earnest over the regulatory and financial issues that the church had long prioritized. The lengthy policy negotiations in the Commission bore their fruit; the church obtained some of the biggest policy concessions *before* the collapse of communism. The 1989 Statute of Freedom of Conscience and Faith ensured freedom of religious belief and participation. Another law ensured that the state would pay the pensions and social insurance of the clergy. Finally, and most importantly for the church, the Statute on the Relations between Church and State defined the legal position of the church in Poland, guaranteeing its autonomy while obtaining a variety of material benefits for the church, such as exemptions from income, property, and community taxes or customs duties and the restitution of church property.[52] In a final burst of policy concessions, the communist parliament passed these important laws shortly before the semifree elections held on June 4, 1989.

The Church in a New Democracy

The Polish church quickly translated the political capital earned under the communist regime into political influence in a sovereign democracy. As it pushed for changes in the laws regarding abortion, divorce, and education, "it also felt morally authorized to insult and scold in public those who dared to contest these provisions," denouncing opponents as "the sons and daughters of Russian officers."[53] The church's authority was so great that few parliamentarians dared to risk its disapproval—across the spectrum. For example, politicians widely adopted the church's language of "protecting the unborn" rather than "abortion rights." Its institutional access meant that even as the church's popularity dropped over

[51] Kai, February 6, 2009.
[52] Eberts 1998, 820; Daniel 1995, 408.
[53] Morawska 1995, 62.

the first three years of democracy, bill after bill legislated the church's preferences into law. Moreover, even when the communist successor Democratic Left Alliance (Sojusz Lewicy Demokratycznej, SLD) won the 1993 elections, partly on the strength of its secular credentials, it did not roll back any of the church's legislative gains in abortion, religion in schools, or material privilege. As a result of the institutional access and the generalized anxiety of many politicians in the 1990s, the church continued to obtain its political preferences despite popular disapproval of such activity; by 1992, 81% of survey respondents opposed the church's political involvement (86% in 1996), and by 1998 only 3% of supported church political activity.[54]

The collapse of communism in 1989 meant the church and the erstwhile opposition now found themselves facing dramatic challenges of rebuilding the economy and the polity, and the need to build support for the nascent democracy. While society overwhelmingly rejected the communist regime (the communists lost every seat they could in the 1989 elections), its support for democracy was feared to be brittle and evanescent. The new democratic governments worried about electoral backlash from the pain of market reforms, and recognized that the church had the moral authority to legitimate the new regime (and thus greatly increase its probability of survival). For its part, "the Episcopate knew perfectly that this government needs daily support, that the Church is the key, and that refusing to support this government condemns it to failure."[55]

As a result, these new governments were more than willing to continue the institutional access of the church, and to make further policy concessions. The initial years after 1989 were so significant not only because of the political stakes, but also because of the continuity in institutional access and in church behavior. The first move of the democratic administration of Tadeusz Mazowiecki—as a symbol of removing the past constraints on the rights of the church—was to get rid of the Department for Religious Affairs (Urząd do Spraw Wyznań), long loathed by the church as a gatekeeper on church involvement in politics. The new media law created a national council to monitor the media, and a quarter of its members were church representatives, "concerned with respecting Christian values." These practices even continued into the 2000s, with one Prime Minister admitting that he handed over some of the competencies of the National Radio and Television Council to a "few bishops," and that the administrators of the board got their jobs after clerical recommendations.[56]

---

[54] Eberts 1998, 330; Borowik 2002, 248.
[55] Torańska 1994, 193.
[56] Jarosław Kaczyński, Prime Minister from 2006 to 2007, quoted in *Gazeta Wyborcza*, February 26, 2008.

The reason for these and other institutional concessions was to retain church support for the new democracy: "the point [of the policy concessions in education, abortion, tax, and fiscal policy] was not to put the Church off the new government that was supposed to implement fundamental reforms that would have to address all areas of life."[57] As one analyst put it, the new governments "conscious from the beginning of the risks of leaving campaign promises unfulfilled, and then conscious of their own repeated mistakes and their decreasing popularity, look for support and defense in the Church. This of course requires the appropriate offerings. The Church accepts these offerings and the role that comes with them all the more so that the alternative is a considerable drop in its own standing in society—also in comparison with the place it occupied in communist Poland."[58]

At the same time, the policy preferences of the church were conservative and showed either little experience with democracy or tolerance for divergent opinions. Criticism was perceived as an attack, and opposition was simply dismissed; for example, pro-abortion voices were denounced as "noise on the street that should be seen as a pathological reaction of a wounded conscience, governed by the logic of evil."[59] The church defended its presence in politics as part of its service—and denounced those who criticized it as "envious."[60] Another legacy of the communist era was that the church had closed itself off from the spirit of the Vatican II reforms and continued to view the faithful in strictly hierarchical terms, with the clergy as the "shepherds of souls." The church viewed its interpretation of natural law as trumping any man-made law or popular preferences, and by 1989, even as the church endorsed economic and political reform, it became "triumphalist, convinced of its own critical role . . . [showing] a total lack of criticism regarding any of its past errors, or the price paid by Polish Catholicism for isolating itself from reformist movements for the past decades."[61] Clergy expected politicians and state representatives to act as Catholics first and as government officials second.[62]

[57] Barbara Labuda, quoted in Waniek 2011, 329.

[58] Stanosz 2004, 12.

[59] Father Jerzy Bajda, PO, 20/91.

[60] Speech by Cardinal Józef Glemp at the inauguration of the 1990–91 academic year, PO, 45/90. As the Cardinal argued, "to be present in public life: that is an evangelical postulate contained in church teaching, there are opponents of the Church, mostly those who are jealous of power and accuse the Church of wanting power, who accuse it of wanting to broaden its influence. They read the stances of the Church only in a political sense. . . . Not true! . . . The Church wants to serve. Even if that service is through transmitting its experience, its thoughts, its teaching, this is a great service which the Church will always provide" (PO, 45/90).

[61] Gowin 1995, 27.

[62] "Ks. Sowa: Nie mieszać ambony z polityką," Gazeta Wyborcza, July 16, 2012.

In these early years of democracy, the Joint Commission not only met, but with renewed vigor. And the importance assigned to the commission, at least by the secular state, actually increased; during the communist era, both the communist and the church side had a parity of 3–4 representatives each, on the level of ministers/vice-ministers and bishops, respectively. In the post-communist era, the Commission gained more members, for a total of 10–11, with the secular state now represented by several high-ranking ministers, including internal affairs, education, treasury, and culture. The secular side thus was represented by some of the highest executive officials in the land.[63] The Commission remained a critical point of access to the secular state, even as the tenor of the debates changed over time; by the 2010s, governments no longer needed church support either for democracy to succeed or for political parties to survive.[64] As a result, as we will see, the church also lost its ability to influence policy as directly, and was unable to decisively redefine policies on same-sex marriage or assisted reproduction.

In the early 1990s, the newly triumphalist church relied not only on the Joint Commission but also on personal interventions. As a former government minister recalled, "highly placed members of the church hierarchy thought it was normal, because apparently for years they were used to recommending different people for positions. . . . They called ministry officials and intervened in the case of letting go this or the other employee or director, even though the reasons for letting them go were self-evident, because they were tied to the Security Police and we had proof . . . these same members of the hierarchy thought it appropriate to call with instructions to eliminate or establish this or the other

---

[63] The same was not the case for the church: the Episcopate is not an executive body in the Polish church, where each bishop is technically the ecclesiastical ruler in his diocese (Borecki and Janik 2011, 22).

[64] The leftist SLD had relatively harmonious and frequent relations with the church in the commission in 2001–05, a pleasant change from their cool meetings of 1993–97. The commission met only once during the 2005–07 government of the right-populist PiS-Samoobrona-LPR government, to discuss the upcoming visit of Pope Benedict XVI, financial matters, and strengthening religious education in schools. This may have been simply because other channels were used; this government did present a report to the Episcopate that detailed the promises made to the Episcopate in March 2006, and how these were fulfilled, ranging from religion in schools to financial matters, property restitution, and most importantly, the Church Fund (Borecki and Janik 2011, 278–80). The 2008–12 center-right PO-PSL government and the church met twice a year to discuss education, financial issues, assisted reproductive technologies, family law, media regulations, and state observation of church holidays. By this point, the open incursions of the church (not to mention the controversies surrounding its response to the 2010 airplane tragedy in Smoleńsk that took the lives of much of Poland's political elite, including the President) lowered its moral authority, and the debates became acrimonious.

department, which stupefied us."[65] Such interventions took place in sensitive ministries responsible for the policies the church most prioritized, such as the Ministry of Education or the Ministry of Health.

The lack of familiarity with democratic procedure meant that church demands sometimes exceeded institutional capacities. For example, in 1994, the church called for a joint parliamentary-church commission—a proposal that was met coolly by the government—to which the archbishops responded that all kinds of "informal structures" are possible.[66] A year later, the church demanded outright that those Commission matters approved by the government be immediately presented to the parliament, to ensure their passage.[67] The government responded that this misunderstood the nature of democracy, and that Joint Commission decisions could not be legally binding. Further, even if the government agreed, "it's unlikely that the parliament will agree to a role of a machine for approval votes."[68]

Critically, the workings of the Joint Commission, the legislative committees of the church, the personal interventions, and institutional proposals were kept quiet by both church and government; as a result, even if the public chafed at the levels of church influence, it remained largely ignorant of the church's institutional access.[69] Access was not publicly discussed. Not even the ostensibly secular, left, and hostile communist successor SLD "ever exposed the mechanisms of Episcopal interventions in political life . . . to expose these mechanisms would be to unmask the Church as a political force, which aims for specific earthly goals, and the SLD knows very well, that the bishops will swallow ideological opposition, that they will swallow confrontation, all that, because they're not all that dangerous to them, but they will not swallow exposure and so SLD, to put it gently, behaves very carefully vis-à-vis the Church."[70] The church reciprocated. The full transcripts of the commission meetings remain secret; state archive holdings are incomplete, and the church refuses to divulge its holdings, since it views the meetings as purely confidential.

That said, the church experimented with other forms of policy influence, most notably electioneering. Here, it quickly found that if anything, involvement in elections backfired. The more the church was perceived to favor particular parties, the more accusations of partisanship and inter-

---

[65] Wiktor Kulerski, quoted in Torańska 1994, 196.
[66] Commission meeting, December 7, 1994; Borecki and Janik 2011, 99.
[67] Commission meeting, April 3, 1995; Borecki and Janik 2011, 103.
[68] Minister Leszek Miller, commission meeting, April 3, 1995; Borecki and Janik 2011, 103.
[69] Borowik 2002, 247.
[70] Interview with Wiktor Kulerski; Torańska 1994, 210.

ference flew, and support for the church wavered. When the church actively endorsed the Solidarity camp in the semifree elections of 1989, "the support of clergy for Solidarity was seen as natural and normal."[71] This was the first open electoral contest between Solidarity and the nation on the one side, and the communist regime and its Soviet sponsors on the other, and church support for Solidarity was seen as an extension of the protective role it had played in the 1980s. Accordingly, parish offices became campaign headquarters for Solidarity candidates, priests played an active role in mobilizing the electorate—printing posters, explaining voting rules, reporting on the campaign back to Solidarity, and so on.[72] The clergy was worried by what it saw as a preponderance of leftists among Solidarity candidates and spoke out against voting for atheists or agnostics, since "only people of a sure conscience can serve the public good."[73] Nonetheless, the few instances where clergy did not back the Solidarity candidates were as rare as they were disappointing, and church efforts on behalf of a united Solidarity were expected and applauded.

In the next electoral contest, in 1991, however, Solidarity had fragmented into multiple parties. The church openly mobilized for its preferred ones; it lobbied against the liberal-left Democratic Union (Unia Demokratyczna, UD), and allowed the conservative right-wing Catholic Electoral Action (Wyborcza Akcja Katolicka, WAK) to assume its name, in likely violation of canon law.[74] Clergy openly commented on which parties Catholics should support, argued that no Catholic can vote for a candidate or party supporting abortion, and denounced parties seen as "atheist." "Protection of the unborn" became a top electoral issue.[75] The Episcopate officially stayed away from endorsing specific parties, merely advocating participating.[76] Episcopal letters, which were read out loud in weekly sermons/homilies, were more specific; among the most important criteria for elected officials was that they "guarantee to retain the identity of the Nation and its Christian values"[77] and "speak clearly in the defense of life from the moment of conception."[78] The Episcopate repeatedly referred to Christian ethics and Catholic social teachings as the only acceptable bases for party platforms.[79]

[71] Kosela 2003, 180.
[72] Gowin 1995, 44; Kosela 2003, 184ff.
[73] Gowin 1995, 45.
[74] Gowin 1995, 49–50.
[75] Eberts and Török, 2001, 136.
[76] *PO*, 36/91.
[77] *PO*, 38/91.
[78] *PO*, 42/91.
[79] Borowik 2002, 243.

The Episcopate's message culminated with an unsigned attachment to a pastoral letter that included a list of approved political parties, also to be read out loud at Mass.[80] Perhaps most notoriously, Bishop Michalik declared that "a Christian ought to vote for a Christian, a Muslim for a Muslim, a Jew for a Jew, a mason for a mason, a communist for a communist, each for whom their conscience tells them to vote," making religion into a political ideology and invoking the specter of ethnic xenophobia.[81] Individual priests openly agitated for certain parties in homilies and during pastoral visits with parishioners.

These public and partisan efforts backfired. The 1991 campaign did enormous damage to the church's image and gave rise to new fears of the church as a political hegemon.[82] After all, in 1991, there was no "national" side to support. Instead, the fully free electoral contest was between democratic parties, all of whom had their own supporters and voters, and so mobilizing on behalf of any one of them meant choosing partisan sides instead of representing "national" interests. Church support plummeted, from over 90% in the first months of 1990 to under 40% by mid-1993. While the rates slowly climbed back up, they never again reached the initial heights, generally staying below 60%.[83] Just as importantly, the actual electoral results were a disappointment: only forty-nine of the heavily church-favored WAK candidates made it to the parliament, against sixty-two of the UD.

The church learned from the 1991 fiasco. It was considerably more circumspect in the 1993 elections (even so, not a single Christian Democrat deputy was returned to the 1993 parliament, despite the party's name), and over the course of 1993–95, the Episcopate distanced itself from direct electoral involvement or conflict.[84] The lesson was repeated in the 1995 presidential elections: the church hierarchy openly pushed for the re-election of the former Solidarity leader Lech Wałęsa, instructed the clergy to hold Masses for his victory, and warned against the consequences of electing the former communist Aleksander Kwaśniewski.[85] The voters, tired of Wałęsa's pompous and conflictual style, instead elected the urbane Kwaśniewski, much to the church's chagrin. In subsequent elections, the church largely limited itself to urging voting and making one's political decisions congruent with one's conscience—while politicians continued to avoid provoking conflict with the church.

[80] Eberts and Török 2001, 136; Gowin 1995, 49.
[81] Gowin 1995, 52.
[82] Gowin 1995, 50.
[83] CBOS BS 78/99.
[84] Gowin 1999, 66.
[85] Polityka, December 2, 1995.

Domains of Policy Influence

To achieve its policy aims, the church reframed policy issues as moral ones, and thus falling within its domain. It relied on the language of not only religion but also nation—and the need to protect the moral health and stable development of the (now) sovereign Polish nation. Using its institutional access, the church not only presented specific versions of bills, but also intervened in ensuring that civil servants and officials favorable to its views would be in charge of sensitive ministries and offices. Critically, its greatest push was in the immediate aftermath of 1989, when its support was most needed to preserve social peace and consolidate democracy, and when society's attention was turned away from the details of policy making. All sides of the political spectrum acceded to these demands for fear of destabilizing Polish democracy and newly found sovereignty, and since the church acted so quickly, it was able to obtain many of its preferences within two years of the communist collapse. At the same time, both church and state were nimble political players who exploited their mutual dependence, a situation that could reach a deadlock. When church support was no longer necessary by the 2010s, the church found itself with less influence in same-sex marriage and IVF, two late-blooming policy areas. The discussion below illustrates these dynamics in the controversies surrounding the Polish Constitution, religious education, abortion, marriage, and the status of embryos.

The Constitution

The Polish Constitution, ratified in 1997, was highly controversial from its inception. As early as 1991, the church stated firmly that "it is necessary to exclude from the Constitution the separation of Church and state. This suggests negative associations from the totalitarian period" and instead the Constitution "needs to accentuate the necessity of collaboration between the state and the Catholic Church."[86] Further, the church argued that both natural and positive law is binding, and that the Constitution ought to "guarantee freedoms, dignity, property rights, private activity, family life . . . and religion in schools."[87]

Within the constitutional debates, these demands became a key point of conflict. The church "took an active stand in the constitution-making process . . . and had a firm position on what it wanted to find."[88] The

---

[86] *PO*, 16/91.
[87] "Catholic Constitutional Postulates," *PO*, 18/91.
[88] Eberts 1998, 834.

Episcopate insisted that the Constitution include an invocation to God in the preamble, protection of life from conception to death, the definition of marriage as between a man and a woman, and a reference to the history and culture of the Polish nation.[89] The final document invoked God, enshrined religious education in schools, and marriage as between a man and a woman. These concessions were "chiefly due to the fear, that bishops and oppositional groups would appeal to society to reject the Constitution in the referendum."[90]

In the run-up to the constitutional referendum, the Episcopate initially indicated it would preserve neutrality. It then did an about-face, speaking out against the Constitution at the 288th Episcopal Conference, because the Constitution failed to protect life from conception, instead "only" guaranteeing a legal protection of life to each person, did not include a preamble that identified God as the creator and judge of all order, and did not assert the supremacy of natural law over man-made.[91]

It quickly became apparent that constitutional ratification was a hostage to the Concordat. The Concordat, or the official diplomatic agreement between the Vatican and the secular state of Poland, was paramount to the Episcopate. If in 1987 Cardinal Glemp stated that the Polish church was not seeking a Concordat, because "conditions were not right," after the collapse of communism the church had no problems asking for one. The lame-duck government of Hanna Suchocka had earlier signed the Concordat in July 1993, after heavy pressure from the Episcopate (and after it had already lost a vote of confidence in parliament). The Concordat enshrined religious education in schools, placing its content and the appointment of teachers exclusively under church control, and expanded the obligations of the state to the church, such as the maintenance of buildings and subsidies for Catholic schools. The document did not call for a separation of church and state, but rather their cooperation. It was criticized for being incompatible with existing Polish law, including family law, and for failing to require the church to respect existing secular law, especially the Constitution.[92]

The interdependence of the Concordat and the Constitution was widely recognized and discussed in the Joint Commission, with frequent mentions of church support for the latter being contingent on the ratification of the former.[93] Despite signing the Concordat, no government had *ratified* it, given both the controversy over the secretive nature of the

[89] Eberts 1998, 834.
[90] Waniek 2011, 339.
[91] Gowin 1999, 242–43.
[92] Daniel 1995, 411.
[93] Commission meeting, September 22, 1995; Borecki and Janik 2011, 115–42.

initial agreement under the Suchocka government and the content itself. The left-centrist (and post-communist) SLD-PSL government announced in 1996 that it would ratify the Concordat once the Constitution was ratified, placing the church in a difficult position of playing political chicken. For their part, bishops had earlier argued that the key to resolving the problem of the Constitution lies in ratifying the Concordat.[94] In April 1997, the SLD government formally (and unilaterally) clarified and interpreted several provisions of the Concordat, signaling to the church that the Concordat would be ratified. On May 25, 1997, the Constitution accordingly passed the referendum—the Concordat was formally approved when the conservative AWS-UW government took office in late 1997.[95]

Education

As early as spring 1989, the Episcopate called for the return of religious education into the public school system, recalling the history of religious education in Poland and the struggles with the communist regime. Surprisingly for committed atheists, the communist state in Poland initially allowed religious education classes in the public school system after 1945, as a continuation of prewar policy. By the 1950s, it allowed a front organization called the Association of Friends of Children (Towarzystwo Przyjaciół Dzieci, TPD) to run public schools without religious education; the state could thus claim that it continued to support religious education, even as an increasing number of schools was run by the TPD. In 1961, once the fallout from the 1956 Poznań revolt had subsided,[96] the communists simply removed religious education from schools with a decree announcing that all schools and educational institutions were secular.

The May 1989 decrees on church-state relations allowed the possibility of religious education. The Episcopate's aim, as stated in a May

---

[94] Joint Commission meeting, April 3 1995; Borecki and Janik 2011, 107.

[95] The AWS (Akcja Wyborcza Solidarność) had a religious problem of its own; specifically, a group of twenty-one AWS religious conservative parliamentarians affiliated with Radio Maryja insisted on submitting bills without prior consultation, further cleaving an already fractious party. The group was known as "Oczko" for the popular card game similar to blackjack. Interview with Wiesław Tchórzewski, caucus director and PiS parliamentarian, June 15, 2011. Nalepa and Carroll 2014.

[96] In June 1956, workers in the Cegielski works in Poznań began the first large-scale protest against the communist government; beginning with a call for better wages and working conditions, the protests spiraled into calls for political and economic freedom. As the protest spread, it met with violent repression, including scores of dead, but it also led to a new government in the autumn, and the promise of reform.

1990 communiqué, was "the full return of religious education to public schools, and for the need to guarantee it in the Constitution and in the law on national education."[97] The church introduced the issue in the Joint Commission in the summer of 1990, and it was quickly ratified into law by decree in August 1990 under the implicit threat of the church withdrawing its support for the compromise government. The church relied on a two-pronged strategy: framing the issue of the return of religion to public schools as a matter of national interest and survival, and working directly through state institutions to obtain access.

First, the church argued for the historical significance of religion and religious education, and its role in the preservation of Polish national identity.[98] The church's unequivocal advocacy of religion in schools was justified by national survival, and "repairing the damage society incurred from the totalitarian regime, which aimed to exclude God from human life and thus to dilute national identity."[99] Here and in other domains, its arguments emphasized that the church "is not a competitor or a partner in politics, but a guardian of the moral order, a critical conscience."[100] Religion in schools would deepen Polish cultural identity and repair the damage inflicted by the totalitarian regime. In a pastoral letter read out loud at Masses across Poland in June 1990 the bishops declared that "we do not have to remind the role that religion played in defending the rights of the nation, as in the times of partitions or in the years of both World Wars, or in the years of struggle with the totalitarian system, whose principles negated God and limited basic human rights . . . it would not be an exaggeration to say that education played a fundamental role in these processes . . . it is therefore hard to believe in the enormity of the damage inflicted on the nation through the despoliation of schools of religious values, which always had a place in them."[101] The Episcopate further argued that it would not be enough to return religion to schools, but that there was "no substitute for the source itself," the church; priests and teachers appointed by the church could be the only possible teachers.[102]

Second, the church turned to its institutional access to cement the legislative gains. The actual legal maneuvers were rapid and never involved a parliamentary vote or public consultation. The May 1990 Episcopate communiqué was followed by an agreement in the Joint Commission a month later. In August 1990, a subcommittee of the Joint Commission

[97] PO, 19/90.
[98] Eberts 1998, 821.
[99] Gowin 1995, 140–41.
[100] Archbishop Jerzy Stroba, "Letter on the War on the Church," PO, 9/93.
[101] PO, 29/90.
[102] PO, 26/90.

simply issued an announcement that religious education would be returning to schools in the upcoming school year. A decree signed by the Minister of Education Henryk Samsonowicz made the declaration legally binding and declared that religion could be taught in all public schools if the parents wished it, as an optional subject whose grade would not count toward a student's grade average.[103] Teachers of religion would have the same status as other teachers, including salary, benefits, and tenure, even though they did not hold the same qualifications. The church retained full control over the content of religious education, with bishops further evaluating classes. The state had no say.[104]

The wide controversy that followed centered on the non-democratic way in which religion was brought back into schools; most Poles agreed with the inclusion of religion in public schooling but objected to the secretive and exclusionary process. The Civic Ombudsman immediately brought the statute to the Constitutional Tribunal, since the implementation of the law did not follow democratic procedure. The Tribunal found that the separation of church and state was preserved because the church determined the content of the religious lessons.

The law had immediate effects. By November 1990, over 95% of children attended religious education.[105] Another law passed in September of 1991 (this time by the Parliament) further formalized religious education in schools and stipulated that Christian values are to be respected in all schools and subjects.[106] Episcopal representatives in the parliamentary commission insisted on "Christian values" in education and objected to the Declaration of Universal Rights as too secular and too tied to the French Revolution.[107] In April 1992, the Ministry of Education increased the number of hours devoted to religious education to two per week and introduced ethics, which could be taught in place of religion. Instead of the previous opt-in proviso, parents were now obliged to declare if they wanted to opt *out* of religious education, and students would now receive a grade on their transcript. In both 1991 and in 1992, the government consulted extensively with the Episcopate, and the church vetted who would represent the state's side.[108] Once again, the Civic Ombudsman brought the law before the Constitutional Tribunal, and once again, its provisions were essentially upheld.

---

[103] Eberts 1998, 821.
[104] Gowin 1995, 149.
[105] *PO*, 2/91.
[106] Eberts 1998, 822.
[107] Torańska 1994, 206–7.
[108] Torańska 1994, 196.

The church's response to the backlash and the criticism about the lack of transparency and democracy showed the church unable, and unwilling, to "distinguish criticism from attack."[109] The church repeatedly insisted that its demands were not up for societal consultation or approval and tried to discredit its opponents: "the loud voices of opposition [that] . . . represented an ideology of a bygone era . . . The proponents of this opinion are convinced of the private character of religious life. It bears emphasis that the model of private religiosity is not a Christian model."[110] When the very popular Minister of Labor Jacek Kuroń objected to the introduction of religion to schools, the bishops' key worry was that he keep his criticism quiet, rather addressing his concerns.[111]

For their part, the representatives of the first democratic government that introduced the law felt they had little choice but to bring back religious education to schools. Their foremost concern was with the stability of the government, and the neutrality of the clergy in the upcoming elections.[112] The Prime Minister, Tadeusz Mazowiecki, was convinced that the government would have fallen if the church's demands were not met; he "realistically evaluated the situation, that he could not enter into conflict with the Church."[113] The government fell anyway.

By 1992, the church declared that religion was not "introduced" to schools but that it had "returned," thanks to Solidarity and the national will. Further, "the tie of school and Church, and Church in school is so tight that attempting to break it would be dangerous not only for the Church, but for Poland."[114] In March 1992, the Episcopate and the Ministry of Education signed an agreement that priests and deacons teaching religion in public schools would not be paid by the state in 1991–92 or 1992–93. When the subject came up again in 1994, the Minister of Education argued that in a situation where the educational budget was highly limited, and nearly thirty thousand teachers would have to be let go, to ask the state to pay over one billion złoty for clerical salaries would be difficult. Church representatives rejected this argument, accusing the state of using taxes of the citizens (most of whom are Catholic) to "fight religion" and claiming that any "talk of paying priests at the expense of existing teachers was dangerous and inappropriate."[115] The Ministry of Education backed down.

---

[109] Gowin 1995, 21.
[110] Archbishop of Poznań, Jerzy Stroba, *PO*, 8/91.
[111] Report from the commission meeting, October 15, 1992; Borecki and Janik 2011, 51.
[112] Gowin 1995, 141.
[113] Torańska 1994, 197.
[114] *PO*, 38/92.
[115] Commission meeting, December 7, 1994; Borecki and Janik 2011, 100–101.

Religion continued to be taught by church-certified teachers and priests across Poland, for two hours weekly, and the grade was included in students' report cards.[116] The (re)introduction of religion into schools in Poland highlights three critical aspects of church influence: the importance of the church's moral authority (and thus its ability to argue its preferences amount to national interest); the perceived importance of church support for government stability; and the rapid, non-democratic dynamic of church influence, which relied on institutional access and the implicit threat of government collapse rather than on coalition building, popular mobilization, or parliamentary procedure.

Abortion

Under a law dating back to 1956, abortion was available freely and on demand under the communist regime. Ending it was a priority of the church, justified on both religious and national grounds. Abortion was discussed in the 1950s, in the run-up to the 1956 law permitting abortion, and again in 1980–81, in negotiations with the communist state during the rise of Solidarity. In 1981, the Ministry of Health issued new restrictions on access to abortion in 1981, but once Solidarity was suppressed, the instructions were not enforced and the debate over abortion again subsided.[117]

It was not until 1989 that the church was able to push through a proposal restricting abortion. Written by lawyers appointed by the Episcopate, and finalized in the Joint Commission, the first bill banning abortion was introduced in the Sejm in the last days of the communist regime. This restrictive proposal framed and constrained all subsequent legislative discussion.[118] The church again pursued a multipronged strategy. As with education in schools, the church argued that restricting abortion would serve the national interest, and that as a matter of natural law, it was not subject to popular approval. At the same time, the church mobilized a petition campaign that gathered signatures from the faithful after Masses (sometimes at the threat of denying sacraments to those who would not join the campaign).[119] The Joint Commission, church lawyers, and sympathetic parliamentarians all worked together to write the legislation.

---

[116] However, the Ministry of Education declared in June 2013 that there would be no religious exam on the *matura* (the capstone exam for high schoolers, equivalent to the French *le bac*). Roman Giertych, the Minister of Education from the conservative PiS-LPR-Samoobrona coalition, promised the exam in 2007, and the church demanded the government keep its promise, but to no avail.

[117] Kulczycki 1995, 481.

[118] Eberts 1998, 823; Kulczycki 1995, 483.

[119] Eberts 1998, 824.

The church moved rapidly, hoping to present a ban on abortion to Pope John Paul II, who was slated to visit Poland in 1991.

The church's opposition to abortion had long been couched in a variety of metaphors of and references to national survival. As early as 1953, the Episcopate sadly noted levels of miscarriages and low natural growth—and was appalled that the law eventually passed in 1956 would lower the sanctions for abortion.[120] Throughout the 1980s, the Episcopate increasingly called to limit abortions, chiefly by asking doctors not to perform them, and for society to increase support for pregnant women. In general, the church viewed abortion as a decision made by fearful women in difficult circumstances, where "often a little aid, an assurance of even minimal feeling of safety, is enough for women to accept her child and decide to give birth."[121]

Yet the language could also take apocalyptic turns. In 1984, the bishops declared "life as the greatest wealth of the Nation,"[122] and the low rates of natural growth a "looming disaster." Democracy was linked to restricting abortion, which was increasingly viewed as "murder that becomes the suicide of democracy," a "mortal threat" to democracy, and a continuation of Auschwitz [sic].[123] The hundreds of thousands of abortions performed annually were seen as "huge biological losses for the Nation. The moral losses are impossible to estimate."[124]

Finally, the church viewed abortion as a matter of natural law, and as such, best left to the interpretation by the church (and certainly not open to public debate). In a communiqué from its Plenary Conference of May 1989, the church framed the issue as one of life in all its forms, and "the Bishops noted with sorrow that there are prominent opinions in Poland that are against not only the law of God, but well-understood national interest."[125] Further, these "basic human rights . . . belong to human essence and are his natural privilege, and not the result of the assent of any societal group."[126]

The church was actively involved in formulating the abortion laws at every step. In 1988, members of the Episcopate were invited to a meeting with government officials and parliamentarians to reconsider the communist state's liberal abortion law, in a move clearly designed to split the opposition.[127] Meanwhile, a team of experts and lawyers appointed

[120] April 1952 Episcopal letter, reprinted in *PO*, 45/90.
[121] Primate's Social Council, *PO*, 22/90.
[122] *PO*, 41/84.
[123] Father Tadeusz Styczeń, "The Unborn: A Chance for Democracy," *PO*, 4/90.
[124] Letter of Episcopal Conference of Poland to the Polish Government, *PO*, 47/90.
[125] *PO*, 19/89.
[126] *PO*, 30/89.
[127] Gowin 1995, 105.

by the Episcopate prepared, and over seventy MPs signed, a new bill on abortion.[128] The Episcopal Commission for Family Affairs put forth this extremely restrictive abortion bill in the communist parliament in May 1989, a month before the semifree elections that brought an end to the communist regime in Poland. The proposal would not only eliminate abortion under any circumstances (including threat to the mother's life) but would also punish the mother and any medical personnel involved with jail terms. Since the church viewed abortion as murder, it wanted a total ban and insisted on punishment for the involved parties. By 1990, in addition to criminalizing abortion in all circumstances, the church openly called for punitive measures as a deterrent and as an educational measure; as one bishop explained, "the law along with painful consequences in the case of breaking it are the only effective factor preventing not only social anarchy, but the easiest way of educating the individual."[129] The Bishops' Conference further sent an open memorandum to the Parliament, and church officials pressed for a full prohibition, arguing that the principle "'Thou Shall not kill' does not allow any exceptions."[130]

This proposal became the basis for all subsequent parliamentary discussion, unchallenged by public dialogue. However, even though the church was fully invested in the proposal, the attention of politicians and voters was focused elsewhere: on the first partially free elections of June 4, 1989, and the feverish electoral campaign that preceded this historic event. Afterward, the issue was immediately brought back by the newly created (and elected) Senate, where the 1988–89 bill quickly resurfaced. The Senate approved the restrictive bill in September 1990, which included the right to life from conception, a two-year prison sentence for parties involved in abortion, and abortion only to save a life. The law also outlawed several contraceptive methods such as IUDs and the Pill. The church continued to rely on its representation in the Joint Commission; even as 1989 brought in a swath of new democratic politicians, the clerical representatives remained unchanged.

Public protest against the new restrictions demanded that "clerics should take care of churches, not women's backsides," while the proponents of the restrictions labeled the pro-choice forces "Eichmann-Mengele-Stalin relics of the communist system,"[131] immoral and anti-Polish by definition. As demonstrations for and against the law continued, so did the incendiary language, with pro-choice supporters labeled

---

[128] Gowin 1999, 105.
[129] Bishop Stanisław Stefanek, *PO*, 38/90.
[130] Morawska 1995, 63.
[131] Morozowski 2012.

"Stalinist whores," and pro-life supporters "medieval."[132] Public opinion polls showed majorities disapproving of the elimination of abortion and supported abortion not only to save a woman's life or health, but also for economic or social reasons.

The pressure for a popular referendum mounted, with public opinion polls showing increasing support for a democratic referendum to settle the matter.[133] Mindful of the reaction to the secretive tactics by which religious education reentered schools, several parliamentarians pushed for societal consultation and a referendum in January 1991, obtaining 1.3 million signatures in a petition for a referendum.[134] The church categorically rejected a referendum from the start, stating in July 1989 that "basic principles of social justice, such as the protection of human life, cannot be made dependent on any societal consultation."[135] Public opinion made a referendum a risky proposition from the church's standpoint: over 58% of those polled in early 1993 opposed the church's views on abortion, and 33% supported them. At the same time, because abortion was such a controversial issue, simply pushing through a decree was not feasible. Therefore, in lieu of a referendum, the church flooded parliamentary offices with thousands of letters and petitions against abortion signed after Masses at local churches.[136] These were the authentic voices of "real" Poles—and according to the church, representative ones.

The liberal Democratic Union (Unia Demokratyczna, UD) proposed a compromise: that no referendum would be held, the number of abortions would be limited through more generous social welfare provisions, and abortion legislation would allow exceptions to save a mother's life or in case of crime, while eliminating punishment for the mother. The lower house, the Sejm, was to take up the bill subsequently, but UD representatives effectively delayed the debate until after the October 1991 elections by appointing a new parliamentary committee to reconsider the legislation. The Episcopate was furious, equating the delay with "political manipulation against, of course, the fundamental interests of the nation"[137] and sending an angry letter to the Democratic Union leadership.[138] Once the issue returned in early 1992, another exception to the ban on abortion was added: severe fetal defects. The Episcopal Commission for Family Affairs immediately sent back a response; it insisted on punishment

---

[132] *Polityka*, February 5, 2013.

[133] Kulczycki 1995, 482.

[134] Waniek 2011, 333.

[135] *PO*, 30/ 89. Note the contrast with the statement of Cardinal Brady in Ireland, that abortion is an issue for the people to decide. See Chapter 3.

[136] Gowin 1995, 108.

[137] Torańska 1994, 255.

[138] Kulczycki 1995, 484.

for the mother (albeit no longer jail time), and on abortion as permissible only if it was a secondary consequence of efforts to save the mother's life (as opposed to performing an abortion to save a mother's life). Neither formulation was included in the final law, largely on technical grounds.

After three years of controversy, not only was abortion finally criminalized in January 1993, but with very little final debate in some legislative quarters; for example, all the Senate representatives simply echoed the church position.[139] However restrictive the compromise law, it was nonetheless more permissive than the initial church version.[140] Abortion was now a crime, unless there was a threat to the life or health of the woman, severe and irreversible damage to the fetus, or criminal circumstances of conception. The church finally acceded to the law in exchange for assurances that abortion law would not be subject to a popular referendum, which the church would likely lose.

Cardinal Józef Glemp referred to the law as a "step in the right direction," rather than satisfactory, since the law still allowed abortion in some circumstances.[141] The church continued to remind society about its fundamental opposition to abortion (and opposing the criminal or fetal defect exceptions in particular), but made no move to replace the law with something more restrictive.[142] Moreover, the church, even as it supported freedom of conscience clauses and the informal practice of doctors and pharmacists refusing contraceptive prescriptions, explicitly avoided attempts to delegalize contraception, since "such a ban simply could not be enforced. For that reason alone it is not worth pursuing."[143]

At no point did legislators propose a return to the liberal communist-era laws, and the church continued to vehemently oppose the possibility of a public referendum on abortion. In 1994, the leftist (communist successor) SLD government amended it to allow for "difficult life circumstances" as a justification for abortion, but the bill was vetoed by President Lech Wałęsa, who cited the thousand years of Christian tradition in Poland as one of his reasons.[144] The SLD government once again liberalized the law

---

[139] Casanova 1994, 111.

[140] Competing abortion legislation ranged from a March 1992 proposal by a parliamentary committee (which included church representatives) that permitted abortion only when a woman's life was endangered, restored punishment for self-induced abortions, and banned in vitro fertilization (Kulczycki 1995, 484), to a bill by the Parliamentary Women's Caucus that allowed abortion if the pregnancy threatened a woman's health, was the result of a crime, if it would cause life difficulties for the woman, and in cases of severe fetal defects.

[141] Eberts 1998, 824.

[142] Gowin 1995, 112.

[143] Franciszek Longchamps de Berier, *Życie i Nauka*, February 10, 2013. Public opinion polls shows 68% disapproving of the church's opposition to contraception in 1993, and 73% by 1996 (Eberts 1998, 236).

[144] Gowin 1995, 114.

in 1996, and a different President, Aleksander Kwaśniewski, signed that law. It allowed for early abortions for hardship reasons (and with the approval of two doctors), and met with enormous criticism from the Polish Episcopate and Pope John Paul II. Bishop Tadeusz Pieronek refused communion to its supporters, while Archbishop Józef Michalik threatened excommunication.[145] More demonstrations followed. The Constitutional Tribunal effectively abolished these amendments, a decision called a "present for the Holy Father," in anticipation of another papal visit to Poland. A new center-right government reinvigorated the 1993 restrictions in December 1997. By this point, it became obvious that "anything to do with the sphere of procreation and sex (contraceptives, education, IVF, abortion) is the domain of the Church."[146]

Abortion again became an issue during Poland's accession to the European Union. The accession, planned for 2004, was a critical moment when church support was badly needed for the government to achieve its aim: "the perspective of a [2003] referendum on EU membership in Poland, and the fear that the Church could call on the faithful to reject the accession, concentrated the minds of the President of Poland Aleksander Kwaśniewski and the SLD politicians." From 2001 to 2002, EU accession was a frequent topic of discussions in the Commission, whose members were initially skeptical. The Episcopate itself was split, with Bishops Pieronek, Życiński, Muszyński, and Gocłowski eventually endorsing accession, and prominent clergy such as Bishop Józef Michalik or Father Tadeusz Rydzyk opposing it.[147]

The church offered to back accession if the abortion law remained unchanged. In the 2001 electoral campaign, the left-liberal SLD earlier promised to liberalize the abortion law. Accordingly, the church demanded in 2003, a few months before the EU referendum, that the accession agreements include guarantees of protection of life from conception and marriage as between man and woman.[148] The bishops relented only when the government demonstrated that these matters would remain a question of domestic policy, rather than international agreement. Instead, state representatives emphasized that the EU accession would mean the church would retain its customs privileges and tax free status, presenting a lengthy document in early 2004 that detailed the ways in which

---

[145] *Polityka*, February 5, 2013.

[146] *Polityka*, February 5, 2013.

[147] Some of these bishops and clergy went along with the anti-EU views of a popular radio station associated with Father Rydzyk, Radio Maryja, until the station began to tie Polish national interest with Russia's, when the bishops decisively broke with such views. The irony is that Radio Maryja's virulently anti-EU views had the effect of the church taking a pro-EU stance in the end (Gowin 1999, 231).

[148] Kai, January 20, 2003.

EU membership would not affect the church's position in Poland.[149] The abortion restrictions remain in effect, and have reduced the rate of legal abortions in Poland from 300,000–400,000 in the 1980s to fewer than 1,000 by the 2010s.[150]

Stem Cell and Reproductive Technologies

The Polish church opposed embryonic stem cell research and most reproductive technologies, including in vitro fertilization (IVF) and other assisted reproduction technologies (ART: ART and IVF were often equated, with "in vitro" as a shorthand for all ART). According to church doctrine, both, along with most contraceptives, led to the destruction of embryos, and therefore to the destruction of human beings. The Episcopate mentioned ART for the first time in 1988, a year after the first in vitro birth in Poland, and condemned it as tantamount to abortion.

The first appearance of the issue in the Joint Commission, however, was not for another two decades, when the government began to seriously consider regulating ART (and providing it through the national health system). In December 2007, the Minister of Health announced that in vitro would be funded by the health system. After twenty years of silence, the bishops reacted immediately, renouncing IVF as a form of "refined abortion," since multiple embryos often die. Further, the bishops argued in an episcopal letter, every child has right to be born of marital love, and "no parent has a right to a child, especially if that child's existence is bought with the death of his brothers and sisters."[151]

A game of political hot potato followed; even as the church renounced IVF and other ART, few politicians embraced its stances publicly. Several parliamentarians responded to the episcopal letter that the best place to discuss these matters instead is in the Joint Commission.[152] The commission

[149] Borecki and Janik 2011, 221–44.

[150] The number of legal and official abortions dropped from over 130,000 (the overall figures are estimated to be twice to four times as much) to 31,000 in 1991 to 777 in 1993 (the first year of the new law) to 641 in 2010 (Kulczycki 1995, 475; *Gazeta Wyborcza*, January 21, 2012). Informal strictures further decreased the incidence of abortion: hospitals, rather than doctors, declared they would not perform abortions; physicians waited for certifications that would inevitably be delayed beyond the twelfth week of pregnancy; and prosecutors, psychologists, judges, and others used various delays. The result was a flourishing abortion underground and abortion tourism, along with several notorious cases when abortion was allowed, but not performed or nearly not performed, as in the case of a vision-impaired woman whose pregnancy would threaten blindness, or a fourteen-year-old girl who was a victim of statutory rape. Despite the new restrictions, the total fertility rate in Poland continued to fall: from 1.9 in 1989 to a low of 1.25 in 2006.

[151] *Tygodnik Powszedni*, November 4, 2008.

[152] *Gazeta Wyborcza*, December 19, 2012.

now became a useful way for parliamentarians to avoid engaging or debating controversial issues directly, and confronting the church in the process. The government's response was to announce in April 2008 the establishment of a bioethics commission, whose fifteen members would comprise lawyers, theologians, and biologists.

In 2009, the church openly endorsed a bill sponsored by a parliamentarian from the conservative-populist Law and Justice Party (Prawo i Sprawedliwość, PiS) that would totally ban in vitro technologies, only to find that a considerable part of the PiS parliamentary representation refused to back the proposal.[153] Nonetheless, the church mobilized on behalf of the PiS bill, with bishops calling individual members of the parliament and arguing that society would "react badly" if the bill fell immediately.[154] Sensing the lack of support for its stance, the church then announced in September 2009 that if the bill did not pass, it would support the alternative proposal of Jarosław Gowin of the conservative wing of the centrist Civic Platform (Platforma Obywatelska, PO), which would allow IVF for married couples only, and would ban the destruction of unused embryos. The church had earlier condemned this proposal in 2008, but now saw it as a viable alternative.[155]

All these efforts were for naught; the restrictive PiS bill fell in May 2010. The church's response was characteristically vehement; the Episcopate sent out a letter to Parliament condemning IVF, arguing that that it is "the younger sister of eugenics," because it allows for the selection of embryos and the "killing" of the weaker ones.[156] One bishop (Archbishop Henryk Hoser) threatened excommunication to any politician advocating a bill allowing in vitro. In November 2010, the church heightened its campaign, calling for three days of prayer for (a) children killed before birth and the conversion of abortionists, (b) for forgiveness of the sins of IVF, and (c) thanksgiving for life.

Even as the church equated IVF with abortion, three critical differences arose in these debates: First, in the case of IVF, politicians openly fought back. This took the form not only of the new anti-clerical Palikot Movement (Ruch Palikota) party protesting in front of Hoser's office, but of the very conservative PO parliamentarian (and future Minister of Justice) Gowin declaring that "if someone is afraid of the Church, they should not engage in politics. The Church has a right and a obligation to remind its teachings, and we politicians have the right and the obligation to be

---

[153] *Gazeta Wyborcza*, June 21, 2009.
[154] *Gazeta Wyborcza*, September 12, 2009.
[155] *Gazeta Wyborcza*, September 12, 2009.
[156] *Gazeta Wyborcza*, October 18, 2010.

led by our own intelligence [rozum] and conscience."[157] Second, church representatives themselves were careful to note that the church "does not want to substitute for the state in pointing to specific regulations, but at the same time sees it as imperative to speak in this question, and its stance is not simply a religious one."[158] Third, the church quickly distanced itself from condemning politicians. Once the bills fell, the church's initial response was to have the Church Council on the Family announce that anyone who uses or supports IVF cannot obtain communion.[159] Soon after, church representatives carefully pointed out this was an "advisory statement," not a doctrinal one. A month later, the Episcopate announced that participating in in vitro was an automatic self-exclusion from communion, but refused to comment on politicians supporting it.[160]

Once the bills were defeated, the legal vacuum continued—and the church's opposition was noted without being decisive. By 2011, even conservative analysts declared that "in vitro is not a question of morality, as the Church tries to convince us, but of medical technology."[161] Even though no formal law was passed after the 2010 fiascoes (and despite increasing criticism from the European Union[162]), IVF became funded by the Polish national health system as of July 2013, with all couples (married or not) eligible. Instead of subjecting it to further parliamentary debate (and possibly again dividing his own party), Prime Minister Donald Tusk relied instead on a Ministry of Health decree to regulate and fund the procedure. Here, the Prime Minister declared that in finalizing the regulation of in vitro, "it is very important that the legislation does not make the procedure difficult or impossible."[163] The contrast to abortion, whose formal provision has often been made impossible by

---

[157] *Gazeta Wyborcza,* October 19, 2010.

[158] Bishop Andrzej Suski, commission meeting, November 1, 2008; Borecki and Janik 2011, 325.

[159] *Gazeta Wyborcza,* May 23, 2010.

[160] *Gazeta Wyborcza,* October 18, 2010. The in vitro debates showed the church continued to have a certain unwillingness or inability to confront the realities of parliamentary life. During Commission meetings, Episcopate representatives insisted that the government speed up the process of parliamentary discussion of in vitro legislation. In response, Minister of Internal Affairs Jerzy Miller noted that the government can ask, but cannot legally hasten, parliamentary proposals or discussions, much to the disappointment of the bishops present (December 9, 2009; Borecki and Janik 2011, 372–73).

[161] *Polityka,* November 5, 2011. Grzegorz Rzeczkowski, the head of the PO think tank.

[162] The European Commission officially demanded that Poland regulate IVF; while the EU does not rule whether or not countries make IVF legal, its use in a given country requires regulation. The IVF bill was finally put forth in 2014 by the Ministry of Health. It would allow IVF for both infertility and to avoid genetically transmitted disease. Embryos could not be destroyed, or created for purposes other than procreation. Patients would not be limited by age or marital status (*Gazeta Wyborcza,* July 18, 2014).

[163] Donald Tusk, PAP, January 28, 2013.

obstructive interpretations of the regulation, was unavoidable—and possibly intended. The church continued to condemn the practice, with the Episcopate claiming that in vitro was the taking of life, that divine law precluded "non-natural" conception, and, most notoriously, that IVF children had "identifiable creases" on their foreheads (in an apparent confusion with the simian crease that some Down's children have on their palms). An official Episcopal declaration denounced in vitro and other assisted reproductive technologies in March 2013,[164] but it did little to change the legal framework, medical practice, or popular behavior.

The debates over IVF revealed a church whose preferences were as intense as those concerning abortion or education in schools, but whose direct influence had declined. Church support was no longer necessary for regime survival, and political elites and society diverged on these issues from the church. In perhaps the most ironic coda to the IVF debates, the first city to subsidize it, in late 2011, was Częstochowa, home of the national shrine of the Black Madonna, long the symbol of Polish Catholicism.[165]

Divorce and Marriage

The church adopted a differentiated strategy toward family law: divorce, civil unions, and same-sex marriage. It saw divorce as a secondary priority, given the greater urgency of curbing abortion as by far the greater evil. In the words of one bishop, "there is no real question of changing the laws on divorce. This is not a question of basic values, like abortion, but of changing mentality rather than changing laws."[166] Yet when civil partnerships and same-sex marriage became publicly discussed in the 2010s, the church began to mobilize with far greater passion and intensity against what it saw as an unacceptable redefinition of an age-old and church-sanctioned institution that served as a founding element of Catholic society.

Under communism and after 1989, the Episcopate half-heartedly pushed for greater constraints on divorce, but these debates were neither particularly controversial nor successful. In the 1990s, the church limited itself to trying to make divorce more difficult by increasing the legal documentation and the courts (from family to district courts) involved.[167]

---

[164] Conference of the Polish Episcopate, 2013. "O wyzwaniach bioetycznych, przed którymi stoi współczesny człowiek." 361 Plenary Meeting of the Conference of the Polish Episcopate, March 5, 2013.

[165] *Gazeta Wyborcza*, December 29, 2011.

[166] Interview with Bishop Wojciech Polak, May 29, 2012.

[167] *Polityka*, August 4, 2011.

Church representatives simply did not view divorce as pressing an issue as abortion, religious education, or bioethical questions. Moreover, the church does not recognize the civil procedure of divorce (or remarriage after divorce), only clerical annulment. Since the vast majority of Poles had (and have) church weddings, the church has a potent tool with which to address divorce: it simply refuses to remarry those who have had a civil divorce.

Under communism, the church couched its criticism in the demographic needs of the Polish nation-state. The bishops criticized divorce as part of a "new moral climate," along with contraceptives, abortion, and women's participation in the labor market, as lowering the population growth rate and promoting "huge biological losses for the Nation."[168] Yet at the same time, the church disavowed legal pressure: "No, we respect the law of the Church, according to which marriage cannot be dissolved. If the state decides otherwise, this is a practice we recognize, but with which we do not agree."[169] After 1989, the church addressed divorce obliquely, as part of a greater push to retain traditional family roles and forms. For example, in 2004, the church demanded the elimination of welfare supplements for single parents, since the bishops felt these were responsible for higher divorce rates.[170]

Instead, the church expended far more energy on what it saw as efforts to undermine marriage as the permanent, and child-minded, union between a man and a woman. As early as 1991, the church made it clear that "the choice of homosexual activity with another person of the same sex [sic] is equivalent to the denounciation of the rich symbolism and meaning, as well as the aims and thoughts of the Creator regarding the reality of sex [płeć]." Above all, since it could not result in procreation, homosexual sex is "contradictory to the idea of giving of oneself."[171] Nonetheless, so long as it was a question simply of *private behavior*, the church did not push for greater legal sanctions. Thus, in the 1990s, when "the Church put its stamp on a wide range of social issues, it apparently saw little need to engage with gay rights. They were not a threat."[172]

Once the *public institution* of marriage was questioned, however, the church lashed out against what it perceived as a threat to family, to Polish society, and to its own teachings. The Polish church further saw proposed laws on civil unions and on gender discrimination as "threatening if not

---

[168] Letter of Episcopal Conference of Poland to Polish Government, January 21, 1977, *PO*, 47/90.
[169] Interview with Cardinal Józef Glemp, July 22, 1987, *PO*, 40/87.
[170] Borecki and Janik 2011, 248.
[171] *PO*, 21/91.
[172] O'Dwyer 2012, 340.

destroying families"[173]—and the Polish nation, which the bishops "sadly" noted had very low natural growth rates.[174] The church opposed civil partnerships as a threat to the traditional model of the family. Several bishops were outspoken in their criticism and opposition to the legislative bills, frequently conflating same-sex marriage with civil partnerships (as did many of the parliamentary opponents of civil partnerships). The chair of the Polish Episcopate, Archbishop Józef Michalik, appealed to the faithful in a 2012 Advent letter to respond to the "undermining of God's natural order," insisting that civil partnerships and genetic manipulation were both attacks, "not only on the Bible and Christians, but on the very basis of our human existence."[175]

The Polish church further opposed the EU Basic Charter of Rights, because Article 21 forbids discrimination on the basis of gender. According to the Episcopate, the Charter would open the way to homosexual marriage.[176] Similarly, the Episcopate opposed a new Program on Women's Rights, since it "imposes a 'feminist' model of marriage and family, undermines the constitutional principles of protection of motherhood, and proposes solutions that threaten the good of women."[177] In its vehemence, the church made statements that sound confusing to non-Polish ears; church representatives claimed that outlawing discrimination on the basis of sexual orientation is prima facie evidence of "a feminist group present in the government and parliament." Since the Constitution outlawed discrimination, furthermore, such laws were unnecessary. Two aspects are worth noting here: (a) the conflation of women's rights and gay rights, and (b) the pejorative use of "feminist" (and subsequently "gender"[178]). In the minds of many Polish bishops, both upset a natural order of heterosexual families where women's primary role is that of mothers and wives.

For all the church's criticism, however, political debates and controversies over civil partnerships and same-sex marriage took place within a framework already constrained by church teachings; at no point was same-sex marriage proposed, nor was adoption by gay couples considered. This reflected public opinion: 50% of respondents supported civil

---

[173] Borecki and Janik 2011, 248.

[174] "Letter of Bishops in Advance of the 12th Papal Day," October 7, 2012.

[175] http://www.tokfm.pl/Tokfm/1,103085,12946963,Zwiazki_partnerskie__Abp _Michalik__Reagujcie_na_naruszanie.html, accessed February 19, 2013.

[176] Kai, November 11, 2007.

[177] Commission meeting, November 14, 2003; Borecki and Janik 2011, 219.

[178] The word *gender* became highly charged in Poland after 2000. With no direct equivalent in Polish, the use of the English word to signify the social construction of acceptable roles and behavior for men and women became an indicator of a particular, liberal, stance. This set of ideas came under heavy fire from conservative religious critics.

partnership, 68% opposed same-sex marriage, and 90% opposed same-sex couples' right to adoption of children. By 2013, 85% of Poles accepted *heterosexual* legal partnerships, but only 33% accepted *homosexual* legal partnerships.[179] These views are not unique to Poland; as noted in Chapter 2, post-communist societies, whether secular, Catholic, or Islamic, share similar attitudes. The Polish Constitution itself declares that "marriage as a union of man and woman . . . is protected by the Republic of Poland" (Article 18),[180] but says nothing about civil partnerships. Political parties were reluctant to address civil partnerships, even as their resolution increasingly became necessary.

A Senate bill in 2004 for the registration of partnerships did not come to a vote. The first government of the center-right Civic Platform (Platforma Obywatelska, PO) (2007–11) declared that it would not concern itself with the matter, not only because it was seen as a second priority to economic and other reforms, but also because it could fragment the party itself, where a socially conservative grouping faced a libertarian wing. Instead, a social movement (The Initiatory Group for Civil Partnerships, Grupa Inicjatywna ds. Związków Partnerskich) began to mobilize support for legislation, and the SLD put forth a proposal in May 2011 that would give civil partners inheritance laws, tax status, and hospital/burial rights on par with married couples. Both homosexual and heterosexual couples would be included. The PO government, however, refused to consider the bill for fear of stirring controversy prior to the fall 2011 elections. It was not until 2012 that three proposals were floated in the parliament: two more expansive ones sponsored by the SLD and the Palikot Movement, and a more restricted one sponsored by Artur Dunin, a PO parliamentarian. An alliance of conservative parties, PiS, PSL, and the conservative fraction of the governing PO, eventually defeated all three proposals in January 2013.

Yet for all its vehement criticism of same-sex marriage and homosexual behavior, and its framing of the issues, the church was not as deeply involved in the formulation of policy. The Episcopate's Commission on the Family did write an official letter thanking those parliamentarians who had "voted in the defense of the value of the institution of marriage and family." Its rhetoric invoked the nation: "the protection of marriage as a union of man and woman is always a fundamental issue for the existence and development of the nation."[181]

---

[179] CBOS News 7/2013.

[180] In one reading, this conditional wording neither excludes same-sex marriage nor defines marriage as heterosexual.

[181] *Gazeta Wyborcza*, January 29, 2013.

Yet the arguments used by the opponents in the parliament, no matter how vehement (one MP notoriously referred to homosexual relationships as "sterile unions with no greater benefit"[182]) did not explicitly refer to the church or its teachings, unlike the debates over abortion. The church did not propose legislation, nor was it consulted during the process. Further, within days of the defeat, the PO conservatives returned to the drawing board, emphasizing the practical need for regulating all non-married relationships.[183] Even as Minister of Justice Jarosław Gowin insisted that he and other conservatives would never accept same-sex marriage with the right to adopt children, he openly declared the need for *a* civil union law.[184]

The issue was not a priority at the meetings of the Joint Commission during 2012–13; these, instead, were preoccupied with church finances. Specifically, the government had publicly floated the possibility of eliminating the Church Fund, a government resource that funded church activities, building maintenance, clerical salaries, and so on. The Church Fund was established to compensate all denominations in Poland for confiscation of their property after 1945. It paid for clergy insurance, building maintenance, and the charitable activities of the church. In late 2012, the PO government proposed replacing it with a voluntary tax write-off, a proposition that met with considerable church alarm. Eventually, however, after lengthy negotiations, both church and state agreed to a 0.5% tax write-off to substitute for the Church Fund in February 2013. The *parliamentary* haggling over church finances was public, and it did not escape the attention of many critics that at this point the church's priority was lobbying for its own financial security, rather than aiding the poor or families and children.

This successful framing of debates without direct influence on policy was partly a question of timing; civil partnerships and same-sex marriage did not become public issues until well into the 2000s. By this point, church support was not necessary for democracy to survive. If elites agreed that democracy itself in the early 1990s, and European accession in the 2000s, depended on church support, no such fundamental need existed afterwards. Moreover, the church's moral authority had been undermined, not only by its earlier politicking and (to a far lesser extent) by the sexual abuse scandals that rocked the Catholic Church worldwide in the 1990s, but also by what was increasingly seen as a pursuit of *material* self-interest, contrary to the church's self-avowed spiritual and moral role. The controversy over the Church Fund highlighted what many saw

[182] Krystyna Pawłowicz, PiS MP, January 24, 2013.
[183] For one thing, 20% of Polish children were born to nonmarried parents by 2012.
[184] *Gazeta Wyborcza*, February 5, 2013; February 18, 2013.

as clerical avarice, but it also showed secular government in a position of strength relative to the church.

Backlash?

Given the spectacular policy successes of the 1990s, it is not surprising that one bitter conclusion was that "the Church has accomplished something spectacular. There are now things that no one talks about. The Concordat is beyond questioning, much like the Constitution . . . Religion in schools, which at the beginning of the nineties prompted political fevers, seems today as natural as geography. The defenders of the right to abortion . . . who organized a national referendum on the question, now work in different domains and have left this controversial subject behind. The Church turned out to be unusually effective in introducing its conceptions to the legal framework of the state."[185]

Yet even as these words were written in 2002, the next decade would bring slow change—and challenges to the church's political primacy. In 2008, the media openly reported accusations of priests collaborating with secret police, of pedophilia and other scandals, and of corruption around the restitution of church property. But for many Poles, 2010, and the aftermath of the Smoleńsk tragedy in April of that year, became the final straw. Nearly a hundred Polish elites died in the airplane crash on April 10, 2010, including the President of Poland, Lech Kaczyński, and the First Lady. The church hierarchy, apparently in consultation with the family of the President, subsequently decided to inter the first couple at Wawel Castle, the historical burial site of the most prominent Polish kings. Critics perceived this as an abuse of church authority, and inappropriately partisan (the President was a founding member of the right-wing PiS, a proponent of conservative church teachings). To make matters worse, a cross was erected outside of the Presidential Palace, and the numerous protesters (dubbing themselves the "defenders of the cross") refused to abide by the decision of Archbishop Kazimerz Nycz to move the cross to the nearby Church of St. Anne.

Another significant political consequence (and a final reminder of the disappearance of the elite consensus that froze church-state cleavages out of politics) of the 2010 incidents was that criticism of church activity was not only openly and frequently discussed, but also that it translated into the electoral success of Palikot Movement, the openly anti-clerical party founded in the summer of 2010. Running on a platform explicitly critical of the church (and with Poland's first openly gay and transsexual parliamentarians on board), the party came in third in the 2011 elections,

[185] Janicki 2002, 26.

with 5% of the votes and 10% of the seats. Similarly, in May 2010, a month after the Smoleńsk tragedy, center-left SLD politicians began work on a "Secular State" project that would end chaplaincies in public institutions, state subsidies for religious education, and church privileges.[186] The project was not taken up in the Sejm, but its very proposal would have been unthinkable only a few years earlier.

While the church could recover from such blows to its prestige and authority (as it did after its popularity plummeted in 1990–93), civil partnerships and in vitro entered the parliamentary arena *after* 2010. The effect was that while the church still had its institutional access, its ability to influence policy had decreased; the government was already more independent of church support for survival, and the events of 2010 did not help to bolster the church's moral authority.

By the end of 2010, the moral authority of the church, its ability to act as *national* representative working for the common good and survival of Poland, was no longer unquestioned. If 39% poll respondents thought the church had great influence in the country in 1988, 62% did two decades later in 2007, and only 4% thought the church had little influence.[187] By this point, even as 48% of respondents thought that politics and social life should be based on religious values, 86% opposed its involvement in politics, including any declarations it might make.[188] In 1988, 14% of poll respondents wanted the church to have less influence; in 2007, 50% did. Not surprisingly, one critic concluded that "society is beginning to judge that the Church has eaten through its 'debt of gratitude' for the fight with communism and elites, including partisan ones, take notice."[189]

To be sure, "this relative decline in the scope of religious authority and the ensuing privatization of religion do not necessarily imply the decline of religion, merely its decline as a carrier of sentiments of national affinity and solidarity."[190] Religiosity itself did not undergo changes that were as significant: over 90% of Poles categorized themselves as "believers," and the same 50% went to church weekly.[191] Younger people who classified themselves as "believing and regularly practicing" declined from 70% in 1992 to 50% in 2009, but 95% of them continued to view themselves as faithful.[192] It was the "political involvement of the church, not its religious authority," that was in question.[193] More broadly, many Catholics make

---

[186] *Gazeta Wyborcza*, August 5, 2010.
[187] CBOS BS 78/99.
[188] CBOS BS/37/2007.
[189] Graff 2010.
[190] Zubrzycki 2006, 222.
[191] CBOS BS/120/2009, 4.
[192] CBOS BS/120/2009.
[193] Zubrzycki 2006, 198.

a distinction between the institutional church and the religious beliefs, viewing the former as flawed while remaining deeply loyal to the latter.

Poles remained pious, and society at large continued to listen to the church—but it also expressed disapproval and disappointment with *how* the church went about enacting its preferences. In 2010, "it was the handling of the cross crisis and the burial of the presidential couple that cost the church support, rather than the in vitro controversy."[194] Earlier, the refusal to compromise during the abortion debate, the naming of opponents as "anti-human" or "Himmlerite," the glaring discrepancy between the concern with the fetus and the indifference to the mother, and the equation of abortion with contraceptives in church rhetoric (but not in public opinion) cost the church support in the early 1990s.[195] And this was not a question of profoundly pro-abortion sentiment; Poles remained split. In a 2009 CBOS survey, 44% respondents agreed that abortion should be illegal, but another 25% agreed that it should be allowed in all circumstances. Two years later, 47% of respondents supported abortion rights—and 46% were against.[196]

Instead, the issue was the church's perceived political arrogance and interference. Thus when Bishop Tadeusz Pieronek announced in 2013 that "pedophilia is present, was and will be. The Pope fought far greater problems" and dismissed criticism of the church's cover-up as "abusive,"[197] hundreds of furious comments followed in the online edition, with no one defending the Bishop.[198] A few months later, public uproar also followed Archbishop Józef Michalik's blame-the-victim explanation of pedophile behavior in the church: "many cases of molestation could be avoided if the relations between parents were healthy . . . a child seeks love, it clings, it seeks. And then the child loses himself and pulls in another person."[199]

In short, the Polish church used its institutional access under communism and under democracy to extract policy concessions from secular incumbents. In moments of crisis, when the regime survival was at stake, whether the rise of Solidarity, the transition to democracy, or accession to the European Union, the church was able to obtain more. As crises subsided and the incumbents consolidated their rule, the state offered fewer policy concessions. While the first democratic governments openly relied on church support and recognized its special status, by 2012 government representatives declared that the church was but one of many civil society

---

[194] Mirosława Grabowska, director of CBOS, *Gazeta Wyborcza*, December 15, 2010.
[195] Gowin 1995, 136–38.
[196] CBOS 2009, 2011.
[197] *Gazeta Wyborcza*, February 11, 2013.
[198] http://wyborcza.pl/1,75478,13386538.html, accessed February 12, 2013.
[199] *Gazeta Wyborcza*, October 8, 2013.

organizations, and "we should listen to the voices of different groups, but decisions should be made autonomously."[200]

Croatia

Croatia represents a case of national myths gained and lost and illustrates the risk of close association with a particular political option. The Catholic Church was identified with the Croatian nation under Yugoslav communist rule, a fusion the church perpetuated through symbolic action and informal education. As it entered the post-communist era in 1990 with great moral authority, the Croatian church was poised to shape Croatian politics, but the complexities of Yugoslav politics limited the church's ability to ensure regime survival. The outcome was not institutional access but an inadvertent partisan coalition: the church allowed the new autocratic government to portray the church as a willing accomplice.

Much as in Poland, Lithuania, Slovakia, or Ireland, the Roman Catholic Church in Croatia was an anti-imperial force in the nineteenth century, on the side of national ambitions of many Croats. Beginning in the second half of the nineteenth century, the Catholic Church actively backed the struggle for national autonomy and fought Magyarization efforts under the Dual Monarchy. As in Poland, this role was more complicated in reality than in myth; much of the church hierarchy was loyal to the Habsburgs, even as local priests and clerics worked on behalf of Croat national ambitions.[201] Until the late nineteenth century, while Serbian identity was bound up with Orthodoxy, Croat identity was not tied nearly as closely to Catholicism. Instead, "the ideologists of Croat nationhood, almost to the last practicing Catholic, resisted the equation of Catholicism and Croatdom . . . the attempts to link Croat nationality with Catholicism were extremely rare, though they occurred intermittently in the second half of the nineteenth century."[202]

Nor was the Catholic Church in Croatia solely nationalist; many of its historical leaders, such as Archbishop Juraj Strossmayer, had far broader and more ecumenical attitudes.[203] Throughout the interwar period, the church was divided between advocates of a more liberal vision of a union with Serbia and the proponents of a more exclusivist and nationalist perspective that "preferred the ecclesiastical security of union with Austria-

---

[200] Minister Michał Boni, *Gazeta Wyborcza*, June 25, 2012.
[201] Cuvalo 1990, 155–56.
[202] Banac 1984, 108.
[203] Banac 1984, 82–85.

Hungary if outright independence could not be secured and . . . were loath to bind Catholic Croatia to Orthodox Serbia."[204] The latter view won, and the church helped to found Croatian-language newspapers, a national organization (Matica Hrvatska), the Croatian National Museum, and even the first Croatian savings bank.[205]

Croat Catholicism became explicitly contrasted with Serbian Orthodoxy or Bosnian Islam in the interwar period. Catholicism became not so much a matter of private conscience as of public identity.[206] And as Catholicism in Croatia was contrasted with Serbian Orthodoxy, conflict between the two churches further reinforced national identification with their respective dominant religion. For example, the Serbian Orthodox Church blocked a Concordat with the Vatican in the interwar Kingdom of Serbs, Croats, and Slovenes, which embittered the Croatian Catholic Church and strengthened its nationalist outlook.[207]

During World War II, much as its counterparts had in Italy or in Slovakia, the church benefited from its endorsement of the fascist Independent State of Croatia (Nezavisna Država Hrvatska, NDH) run by the Ustaša, the Croatian Revolutionary Movement (Ustaša–Hrvatski revolucionarni pokret). The Ustaša itself equated Croats with Catholics, and the church obtained several concessions as a result; abortion, pornography, cursing, and blasphemy became illegal, and disrespect for meatless Fridays or working on Sundays became punishable offenses.[208] Anton Pavelić, the leader of the NDH appointed with German support after the conquest of Yugoslavia in 1941, "declared a constitution based on Catholic principles and the local Church hierarchy, led by Archbishop [Alojzije] Stepinac of Zagreb, lent their enthusiastic support to the new regime."[209] Forced conversions of Orthodox Serbs in Croatia were a joint venture between the church and the NDH. Some high-ranking clergy, such as Archbishop Šarić of Sarajevo, were prominent and vocal members of the Ustaša, while others remained neutral.[210] Stepinac himself was ambivalent; he welcomed the policy concessions and was concerned about the atheism of the Partisans, defending the Ustaša against the Vatican, but condemned the atrocities, violence, and "all injustice, all murder of innocent people, all burning of peaceful villages, all killings."[211] As we will

---

[204] Ramet 1998, 155; see also Banac 1984.
[205] Ramet 1998, 155.
[206] Perica 2002, 5.
[207] Perica 2002, 20.
[208] Perica 2002, 24.
[209] Buchanan and Conway 2002, 27.
[210] Kolstø 2011, 39.
[211] Tomasevich 2001, 557.

see, his successors vacillated in similar ways under the post-communist Tuđman regime.

Such support for the NDH government, and the policy concessions that it gained the church, was controversial. For some, the church collaborated with a fascist quisling. For others, it supported a regime that was not nationalist enough; after all, Pavelić conceded Istria, Dalmatia, and other territory to Italy in exchange for Mussolini's support. As a result, many Croats opposed the NDH and joined the armed communist-led resistance fighting for a Croat republic within a Yugoslav federation.[212] Thus the Croat church did not emerge from World War II as a pristine representative of the nation, but with a more ambiguous reputation. Its participation in the wartime conflict strengthened its nationalist credentials in some ways, but tarnished it in others.[213]

Under communism the church was initially prosecuted in the immediate postwar period for its alliance with the NDH. Archbishop Stepinac met with Tito in June 1945, and defended the role of the church during the war. Tito in turn asked for support in keeping Istria Croatian—which Stepinac refused. Bishops sent letters to the new government, with no response. Tensions took a turn for the worse in June 1945, during the Bishops' Conference. The bishops sent a pastoral letter, read out loud at Mass on September 30, 1945, and sent to the religious affairs commissions, which noted the murder of 243 priests, the arrests of an additional 169, and the disappearance of 89. It further made a host of policy demands, including the return of confiscated property and full freedom of Catholic press and schooling.[214] In the government's eyes, the timing was unfortunate, in a hostile international situation and in the run-up to the Constitutional Parliament elections. Tito acidly responded by questioning why the bishops did not send a similarly public and outraged letter during the Ustaša regime, or against the killing of Serbs in Croatia.[215]

The regime's next step was quick and predictable, with the President of the Croatian republican government, Vladimir Bakarić, announcing the launch of a "campaign against priests" in December of 1945. From 1945 to the end of the 1950s, the church endured considerable repression, beginning with the arrest of Archbishop Stepinac in 1946 and his subsequent imprisonment (he was sentenced to nineteen years of hard

---

[212] Perica 2002, 21.

[213] Thus the church still does not send representatives to the annual commemorations in April at the Jasenovac concentration camp (where anywhere from 70,000 to 700,000 Ustaša victims are remembered), suggesting to some its acknowledgment of its complicity in the NDH and its atrocities (Kolstø 2011). In 2007, the local bishops visited, and in 2009, a clerical pilgrimage to Jasenovac took place.

[214] Akmadža 2006, 92–93.

[215] Akmadža 2006, 94.

labor and five additional years of loss of civil rights). Accused of collaboration with the Ustaša, Stepinac refused to cooperate in court and was found guilty. Eventually, the communist politician (and subsequent dissident) Milovan Đilas admitted that the real issue was not the putative collaboration, but the loyalty of the church to the Vatican: "if he had only proclaimed a Croatian Church, separate from Rome . . . we would have raised him to the clouds!"[216] The communist regime would have welcomed such a move as a legitimation of the new communist Yugoslavia (admittedly, an unlikely scenario either in Croatia or in Poland). As matters stood, however, the regime was unable to co-opt the church or its hierarchy—and the Stepinac trial only hardened the church's reluctance.

Subsequently, church publications disappeared, enormous land holdings were confiscated, Catholic hospitals and charities were seized, seminaries confiscated, secondary schools nationalized, and over six hundred priests jailed.[217] The repression continued, even as state representatives were careful to note that "the goal of our struggle against political abuse of religious feelings is not a destruction of a church or religion."[218]

It was only with the deaths of Pope Pius XII in 1958 and now-Cardinal Stepinac in 1960, officially held responsible by the regime for the hostilities, that relations finally warmed. Unofficially, "the regime realized that a repressive policy against the Church does not strengthen the reputation of the regime, and instead it enhances the reputation of the church in the eyes of the people."[219] With close to 90% of the population as self-declared believers, despite the state campaigns against religious bodies, the communist regime felt compelled to find a modus vivendi with the church.

The church would subsequently point to this era of repression as a sign of its shared fate with the Croatian people, but it was the Croat Spring of 1967–71 that secured moral authority for the Roman Catholic Church in Croatia. The church worked assiduously to protect and foster the fusion of national and religious identities and became closely identified again with national aspirations after the Spring. The Spring began in 1967, with calls by writers and academics for a greater recognition of the Croatian language (official federal policy had insisted on a "Serbo-Croatian language," which differed in accents and the alphabet used, but otherwise comprised a single tongue). The demands then grew to include greater economic autonomy and ending the practice of sending military

[216] Ramet 1990, 189.
[217] Ramet 1990, 192; Akmadža 2006, 97–98.
[218] Edvard Kardelj, 4th Congress of the National Front of Yugoslavia, 1953, quoted in Akmadža 2004a, 125.
[219] Akmadža 2004a, 125.

conscripts to faraway republics. Liberals within the communist party and elsewhere articulated a nationalist but secular vision of greater linguistic and cultural independence, which then spilled into society, spread by Matica Hrvatska. As tens of thousands of university students began to strike in support, Tito finally lost his patience. In December 1971, he rapidly cracked down on the Spring and purged the liberals from the party, along with thousands of other members. Matica Hrvatska was summarily disbanded and its publications ceased. Several representatives of the Spring were arrested, including Franjo Tuđman. Tito reasserted the control of both the Croat communist party and Yugoslav, as opposed to Croatian, authority.

Many clergy supported the Spring and its push for greater recognition and autonomy. The bishops themselves were not involved, in contrast to the support of Polish church authorities for Solidarity in Poland. Some were even openly hostile to the reform movement.[220] Nonetheless, "religious symbols were ubiquitous and churches were crowded."[221] *Local* Catholic clergy enthusiastically championed the Spring and began to revive educational programs for youth, gather data on the nationalities of administrators, and call for the rehabilitation of Stepinac.[222] The church hierarchy pursued a national agenda of its own: commemorating Cardinal Stepinac, launching pilgrimages, and reviving the Marian cult beginning with a theological "Mariological and Marian Congress" in Zagreb in 1971, the first of a series of jubilees and celebrations. Over 150,000 pilgrims came to the conclusion of Congress, and Archbishop Frane Kuharić celebrated that it had "reasserted Croatian Catholic identity and unity."[223] Other pilgrimages sponsored by the church that year brought tens of thousands of pilgrims to Rijeka, Nin, and Sinj, with Archbishop Frane Franić leading a "Prayer for the Croatian People."

The crackdown on the Spring strengthened the church's position as the chief guardian and defender of the Croat national interests and the critical representative of national aspirations.[224] In the Croat Silence (Hrvatska šutnja) that followed the Croat Spring from 1972 to 1989, the church became the main representative of the Croat national idea.[225] As many secular politicians and intellectuals stayed silent, bishops and clergy openly mobilized on behalf of the Croat nation and fused Croat national and religious identities ever closer. In 1971, the church under

[220] Cviic 1976, 8; Perica 2002, 57.
[221] Perica 2002, 58.
[222] Ramet 1990, 193.
[223] Perica 2002, 61.
[224] Ramet 1998, 157, Buchenau 2005, 558.
[225] Perica 2000, 534.

Cardinal Frane Franić reintroduced the cult of Virgin Mary as a major religious and national symbol (much as Cardinal Wyszyński had done in Poland with the Black Madonna). The shrine of Marija Bistrica became a national shrine, a center of Marian worship and national symbolism, much like Częstochowa in Poland. Thus "the Virgin Mary 'Queen of the Croats' had become the central cult of Croatian Catholicism, as well as one of the symbols of Croatian nationalism,"[226] with shrines dotting territories both officially and historically Croatian.

More mass pilgrimages, jubilees, and celebrations followed. Cardinal Franić further explicitly fused nationalism and religion under the Great Novena of 1975–84. An icon of Mary circulated for nine years across every parish in Croatia, much as it had in Poland. Pilgrims sang patriotic songs and religious hymns and wore Croatian colors and ethnic dress during Masses and processions.[227] The church published new history books, presided over numerous jubilee Masses and celebrations, and celebrated the loyalty of historical authorities to the church, such as King Zvonimir and Prince Branimir. During these events, Croatian national flags (without the communist red star) were prominently displayed, and the Croat (not Yugoslav) national anthem was sung.[228] Parishes organized catechism classes, further continuing and developing a program of patriotically infused religious education. From 1981 to 1983, the religious and national reawakening culminated in a series of "massive pilgrimages and festivals" organized by the church. According to a government report, these "sought to flex muscles, deliver a message to enemies, encourage the faithful, revitalize the faith, and mobilize believers."[229] By 1984, when the church held the final ceremony of its National Eucharistic Congress, over a thousand priests and four hundred thousand faithful participated in a show of religious and patriotic commitment, a slow procession that included historical artifacts, religious symbols, and thousands of monks, nuns, priests, and foreign and domestic representatives of Catholic, Protestant, and Islamic denominations.[230] In a nation of 4.5 million citizens, over one million participated in parish congresses from 1981 to 1984, according to the government.[231] The Great Novena of 1975–84 thus fused the idea of a Croat nation ever closer to Catholicism and made the church a formidable player.

Subsequently, Franić's successor, the charismatic and nationalist Cardinal Franjo Kuharić (the Primate until 1997) "worked diligently and

---

[226] Perica 2000, 540.
[227] Perica 2002, 61.
[228] Perica 2000, 548.
[229] Perica 2000, 551–52.
[230] Perica 2000, 559.
[231] Perica 2002, 67.

systematically on strengthening the national identity of the Catholic Church, even though it was formally organized under the wing of the Bishops' Conference of Yugoslavia. . . . To stress and ideologically articulate the national aspect of the church, in the 1970s, Kuharić's church intellectuals and ideologists—gathered around the [journal *Voice of the Council (Glas Koncila)*]—launched the concept known as the Church Among the Croats, which persists to this day, due to the precision and transparency of its eminently nationalist call and content."[232] The Church Among the Croats (Crkva u Hrvata) signified a church united and representative of its people: an assertion of moral authority. In the late 1980s, *Glas Koncila* itself shifted from a discussion of human rights, the struggle against atheism, and abortion, to a nationalist reappraisal (and praise) of Croat history: a "Croatisation of the Church and a Catholisation of the nation."[233]

By the late 1980s the Catholic Church in Croatia had fused national and religious identities and gained enormous moral authority as an independent representative of Croat national interests, thanks to the intellectual articulation of its program and its reaffirmation of national-religious fusion in the daily life of the faithful. During the communist era, and especially its latter years, "the Catholic Church was a symbol of Croatian national identity. It was perceived by nationalists and others as a defining characteristic of national identity."[234] The decades of carefully tending the fusion of Croat and Catholic identities paid off; in the 1990s, after the fall of communism and the wars of Yugoslav secession, public opinion polls found that religiosity (measured as belief) was a strong predictor of adherence to ethnic nationalism. In fact, religion was the strongest predictor, more powerfully correlated than age, economic position, minority status, experiences of the war, education, or other demographic factors.[235] Another, more immediate, consequence was that ever-more emboldened clergy met little official resistance to their calls for a change in the regime, and for calls to mobilize on behalf of an increasingly independent and Catholic Croatia.[236]

Both communism and Yugoslavia collapsed over the course of 1990–91. The church continued to defend Croat national aspirations and individual Croats. In 1990, as Croatia seceded from Yugoslavia, church representatives openly supported the drive to autonomy, and the politicians active in obtaining those goals. Croatia gained its independence in 1991, which meant not only national sovereignty, but also a transforma-

---

[232] Lovrenović 1998; see also Perica 2006, 312–13.
[233] Brkljačić 2001, 9.
[234] Bellamy 2003, 163.
[235] Massey, Hodson, and Sekulic 2000, 29.
[236] Perica 2002, 135.

tion of the Catholic Church from a minority church in the federation to a near-monopolist in independent Croatia. As a result, in the early post-communist era, "the Catholic Church in Croatia enjoyed unlimited confidence of the believers and high authority in public life."[237]

Yet two constraints meant that the church would not capitalize fully on this high moral authority. First, the church could not offer the same guarantees and mediation that the Polish church did during the transition. The collapse of Yugoslavia did not offer opportunities for such church intervention. After the Croat Spring, the Croat communist party (Savez Komunista Hrvatske, SKH), had been purged of its liberal members and was a bastion of communist conservatism. By 1989, however, the SKH had condemned the belligerent Serbian nationalism of Slobodan Milošević—and dramatically left the Congress of the League of Communists of Yugoslavia in January 1990, over Serbian attempts to reorganize and dominate Yugoslavia. The very next month it rebranded and reinvented itself as a social democratic party, in preparation for the multiparty elections in May 1990. While it lost the elections to Tuđman's HDZ, the sequence of events meant that there would be no negotiations or conflict between the communist regime on one side and society and anti-communist opposition on the other. The transition took place through declarations and elections rather than negotiations.

Second, and relatedly, the threat to the new regime was the burgeoning conflict with Serbia—and the critical popular demand was national independence, not democracy.[238] The church could have calmed down *domestic* unrest—given its moral authority—but it could not soothe *Serbian* anxiety or aggression, the chief threat to the newly independent Croatia. Once war broke out with Serbia and the rump Yugoslav People's Army that it controlled in 1991, the church had no power to end it. The church could not mollify the international tension, nor could it mediate between a discredited communist party and the opposition, as its Polish counterpart had done. The best it could offer was a different vision of nationalism, one that more closely married Catholicism to Croat national identity. However, church support was not necessary for either a peaceful end to communist rule or the survival of the new regime.

Instead, while the church continued to claim to represent the Croat nation after 1990, it quickly appeared locked in an embrace (if not always a comfortable one) with one political party, undermining its claims to speak for the entire nation. The church frequently endorsed the policies (if not the person) of Franjo Tuđman, the leader of Croatia and the governing Croatian Democratic Union (Hrvatska Demokratska Zajednica, HDZ)

[237] Gruenfelder 2000.
[238] Brkljačić 2003, 43.

party, and did not directly criticize the government until 1997.[239] Tuđman initially seized upon a vague letter from Cardinal Kuharić to suggest that the HDZ had church support; the church protested but was nonetheless pleased that communists did not win the 1990 elections.[240] And even though it tried to distance itself from the war and disapproved of some of the government's actions, the church was also complicit; for example, its chaplains were given full access in the Croatian Army, "portraying the Croatian and Catholic causes as one and triggering manifestations of mass religious adherence among the soldiers."[241] Church leaders opened the parliamentary meetings, politicians and clergy were frequently portrayed together in the media, church and state promoted the cult of Cardinal Stepinac, and high-ranking clergy continued to bless political and military events. Both sides reinforced the notion that church, nation, and the newly independent Croat state were symbiotically linked.[242]

From the start, the HDZ represented itself as a national force rather than a narrow party.[243] The HDZ government Tuđman led repeatedly emphasized the strong link between the church and the Croatian people, reifying the fusion of religious and national identities. In contrast to World War II, "in the 1990s it was the secular leaders who took the lead in using religion to stir up emotions among the masses and ensure group unity."[244] The HDZ frequently interpreted Croat national history through a lens of overt clericalism that failed to take into account the more liberal views of historical Catholic national heroes such as Archbishop Strossmayer.[245] Tuđman insisted that "the Croatian Catholic Church was the only institution to consistently resist the communist authorities . . . by doing so, the Church was responsible for nurturing Croatian national identity during the dark period of communist rule. Many people within the Church itself shared this view of the relationship between Church and nation."[246] He further "never fail[ed] to bring up another of the church's virtues: its strong link with the Croatian people . . . interlacing the church with the very idea of Croatian statehood and nationhood is not unique to Tuđman but common to the Croatian traditional mentality."[247] Tuđman

---

[239] Gruenfelder 2000.
[240] Ramet 1996, 346.
[241] Loza 2009.
[242] Mojzes 1994, 132.
[243] Mojzes 1994, 132.
[244] Dragojević 2005, 72.
[245] Banac 1984; Bellamy 2003, 74.
[246] Bellamy 2003, 156.
[247] Lovrenović 1998.

rehabilitated Stepinac as a "martyr to the Croatian cause."[248] In 1998, the HDZ went as far as to call itself Christian Democratic, affirm its Catholic roots, and adopt the social teachings of the church as its party platform. To underline these new commitments, the new term for post-communist privatization was "pretvorba," which also means "transubstantiation" in church doctrine.[249]

The HDZ was so closely identified with Croat national aspirations that the church mistook its initial widespread popular support for the expression of a genuinely national political movement, similar to Solidarity in Poland. The Croat church itself had consistently supported an independent Croat state, where Catholicism would be dominant and the church's place secured. Even as *Glas Koncila* supported democracy in 1990,[250] the fundamental concern was with national independence. Thus as early as 1989, the Croatian clergy welcomed the foundation of the HDZ and openly agitated for it, even if it never had the opportunity to offer the movement protection and shelter, as the Polish church had done for Solidarity in the communist era. As Yugoslavia crumbled, the HDZ was increasingly seen as the "church's preferred party" thanks to its proindependence credentials.[251] Prior to the 1990 elections, the Croatian bishops seemingly offered support to the HDZ when they "emphasized their fear that [if] left wing parties won, they would continue to treat the Church as a potential threat."[252] Much as their counterparts in Poland, the Croat bishops also advocated voting for parties who would promote "freedom for the Church" and "Christian values." Some clergy were far more explicit and became party officials, including Tomislav Duka, Ante Baković (who later led the pronatalist Croatia Population Movement), Adalbert Rebić, and Jural Kolarić.[253] These priests and others also raised millions for HDZ via émigré communities, and clerical support had palpable impact on electoral outcomes (unlike in Serbia, where Milošević was independently popular).[254]

As Tuđman led Croatia into the wars of the Yugoslav succession (1991–95), some of the church hierarchy grew more ambivalent about the party, if not its goals. Cardinal Franjo Kuharić attempted to maintain

---

[248] Bellamy 2003, 74. In this view, the 1998 beatification of Stepinac by Pope John Paul II seemed the very culmination of the inextricable embrace of nation and religion in Croatia, and a reminder of the ways in which Croat independence relied on both individuals and ideologies affiliated with the Catholic Church.

[249] Perica 2002, 190–91.

[250] Bellamy 2002, 53.

[251] Bellamy 2003, 158.

[252] Ribić 2009, 198.

[253] Perica 2002, 140–41.

[254] Perica 2002, 143.

a distance from the party beginning with the Bosnian war in 1993. His successor, Josip Bozanić, doctrinally as conservative but politically more moderate than Kuharić, was appointed partly to improve relations with Serbia and to suppress the rampant nationalism within the church.[255] He began his tenure by criticizing Tuđman in his inaugural Christmas address of 1997, speaking of the "sins of the power structures." There were also moments of open conflict between the church hierarchy and the Tuđman government, as in 1993, when Cardinal Kuharić called for ethnic tolerance.[256] Several bishops were openly critical of post-1990 privatization (even though restitution benefited the church) and the corruption that followed; Kuharić, Zvonimir Bono-Šagi, and Ivan Grubišić, among others, called the Tuđman privatization policies immoral.[257] They spoke as individual clergymen, however, without the backing of the official church. And even as the church officially criticized the war in 1992 and the havoc it was wreaking, it "rarely . . . expressed its disapproval [of the government] and not even when the government was accused of crimes against humanity, violation of human rights and war crimes."[258]

At the same time, much of the clergy viewed the war through the prism of Croatian independence and national survival. They often interpreted wartime activity as necessary and justified, denying war crimes. Many bishops saw the 1991–95 war as a just war of liberation, and the bishops "rejected any attempt to give the war a negative interpretation."[259] Local clergy actively championed the HDZ; many priests, especially in Herzegovina, were openly and explicitly nationalist, and in some local communities, parish priests even made speeches at HDZ meetings.[260] Baković declared that the majority of the priests supported the war and the government.[261] Kuharić himself did not curtail priests who advocated the HDZ from the pulpit, nor did he protest Tuđman's deft political use of the Pope's 1994 visit to Zagreb.[262] *Glas Koncila*, the official voice of the

---

[255] *Nacional*, August 15, 2002.

[256] Ramet 1996, 349.

[257] Perica 2006, 313.

[258] Gruenfelder 2000. The ambivalence was well expressed by Igor Markovic, editor of the liberal weekly *Arkzin*: "the Catholic Church in Croatia always wants to be on the side of the winner. But at the same time it doesn't want to be seen as a patron of the state or an apologist for human rights violations" (quoted in *Christian Century*, November 8, 1995).

[259] Bremer 2010, 9.

[260] Ramet 1996, 352; Bellamy 2002, 47.

[261] Bremer 2010, 5–6.

[262] "Obituary: Cardinal Franjo Kuharic." *The Independent* (London), March 18, 2002. When the Pope visited, Tudjman had declared this indicated "his moral support from the supreme international moral authority, for Croatia's demand that it has the right to establish its legal system over its entire territory," and also that it represented "a fulfillment of the party program."

church, frequently expressed nationalist sentiment, "in distancing towards the Serbs, but also in critical position to the international community."[263] Cardinal Kuharić defended the Croatian government when it took back Krajina in 1995 (though he subsequently condemned killing of Serbian civilians).[264] Cardinal Bozanić was more critical, but the majority of bishops did not follow him, insisting first on defending the war and then on condemning the War Crimes Tribunal. When Tuđman died in 1999, *Glas Koncila* issued multiple laudatory remembrances. In short, while some clergy opposed the HDZ and its regime, finding the alliance increasingly stifling, enough priests and bishops advocated hardline support for the Tuđman regime to make the co-optation by the HDZ a willing embrace.

Since the war was widely construed as fighting for *national* independence, the church's moral authority grew. During the armed fighting for Croat independence, the church also provided pastoral care and badly needed social services to refugees arriving from Serb-shelled territories such as Vukovar and Dubrovnik.[265] It provided disaster relief, housing, food, and health care.[266] The church shared the fate of Croat civilians and also became a victim of aggression; by June 1994, 40% of churches in occupied Croatia had been destroyed or damaged.[267] In the mid-1990s, the church and its representatives were among the most trusted political actors in Croatia.[268] Cardinal Kuharić was regarded as the most respected person in Croatia (by 31% of poll respondents, against Tuđman's 22%).[269] Religiosity increased in the aftermath of the 1991–95 war; the share of self-declared Catholics in Croatia went from 70% to 90%. By 2003, 87% of Croats continued to self-identify as Catholic, and 78% as very religious, lending further credibility to the resilience of Croat religiosity.[270]

Yet in the end, the tacit acceptance by many bishops of the clammy overtures of the HDZ and the Tuđman government eventually undermined the church's moral authority. The end of the war meant the HDZ needed

[263] Bremer 2010, 10. *Glas Koncila* became far more nationalist and anti-communist in its rhetoric after 2000: see "Novine Katoličke crkve postale HDZovo glasilo" (Newspaper of the Catholic Church became a HDZ journal"), *Nacional*, January 15, 2002. http://www.nacional.hr/clanak/10135/novine-katolicke-crkve-postale-hdz-ovo-glasilo.

[264] Ramet 1996, 348.

[265] Bremer 2010, 3.

[266] Bellamy 2002, 51.

[267] Ramet 1996, 349.

[268] Perica 2006, 321; Ribić 2009, 201.

[269] Ramet 1996, 347.

[270] Perica 2006, 320; Sakalis 2013. Institute for Social Research. 2004. "Social and Religious Changes in Croatia." In the 2011 census, 86% of Croats described themselves as Catholic. http://www.dzs.hr/Eng/censuses/census2011/results/htm/E01_01_12/E01_01_12.html, accessed March 5, 2013.

the church to bolster its waning support, and the church now obtained several important policy concessions and material benefits. It also meant the church tied itself more closely to the HDZ and became tainted with allegations of corruption, privilege, and self-interest that intensified as the economic and political crises deepened.[271] It was now one of Croatia's five richest corporations, and "becoming a part of the newly rich elite seems to have hurt the church's moral authority more than anything else, especially because society has become dramatically impoverished."[272] Once democratic politics returned with the death of Tuđman in 1999 and new elections in 2000, fewer politicians were willing to listen to the church, and Croatia now joined Poland as a country where the church was seen as far too influential.[273] Many politicians remained deferential, but the church was unable to regain its privileged position and faced unprecedented criticism. In short, the church in Croatia cultivated a great moral authority under communism—but did not fully reap the harvest.

Policy Influence

Among post-communist countries, Croatia closely resembles Poland in the high levels of religiosity, postwar fusion of religious and national identities, and high moral authority. The Croatian Bishops' Conference (Hrvatska biskupska konferencija) had policy preferences that were very similar to the Polish Episcopate. As the parliamentary elections of April–May 1990 were gearing up, the bishops declared that "the Church's presence in politics was a requirement of the Gospel."[274] Yet the Roman Catholic Church in Croatia achieved far fewer of its policy aims, either under communism or subsequently.

To be fair, the Croatian case is more complex than the Polish—complicated, first and foremost, by the simultaneous collapse of the communist regime and the extrication from the Yugoslav federation. Nonetheless, it illustrates how even churches with high initial moral authority may be unable to influence policy, because they are not essential for the secular incumbent's hold on power, and because costly and overt partisan coalitions subsequently erode their moral authority. Without domestic conflict that necessitated church mediation, and faced with the demands and needs of different nationalities, the Yugoslav communist govern-

---

[271] Zrinščak 2001, 186.

[272] Perica 2006, 313. Perica details some of the "examples of the church acquiring material wealth apparently at the expense of common social needs," including the eviction of schools, child abuse in church-run charities, and tax evasion allegations (Perica 2006, 329).

[273] Flere 2001.

[274] Kolstø 2010, 51.

ments offered few real concessions. Their post-communist Croat counterparts were equally circumspect and saw little reason to offer institutional access to the church, despite its high moral authority. The Tuđman regime did not need the support of the church to survive, given the mobilizing effects of the war of 1991–95. Instead of negotiating with the church, the Tuđman government adroitly *volunteered* policy concessions in the early 1990s, placing the church in a position of welcoming these advances even as it attempted to reject the suitor. Steering this course would prove too difficult; the church was widely seen as partisan, and its moral authority turned out to be far less resilient than it had expected. When the HDZ needed church help after the end of the war in 1995, the church's bargaining position strengthened, and it achieved its greatest policy success with the signing of the church-state agreements. Yet because the church-HDZ coalition gained teeth in 1995–99, it further undermined the church's moral authority. After the collapse of HDZ rule in 2000, the church tried to gain access and to exert greater policy pressure, inviting prime ministers and other high officials to episcopal meetings and issuing public declarations, but with little impact; it was unable to change policies it considered unfavorable on abortion, divorce, assisted reproductive technologies, or civil unions.

The Communist Era

As in Poland, church-state relations in the communist era oscillated between open hostility and the desire for a mutual settlement. If it had been divided in its support of the fascist Ustaša, the Catholic Church was uniformly opposed to communism.[275] In the immediate postwar period, the new communist state established in Yugoslavia by Marshal Tito was caught between multiple demands: elections to the Constitutional Parliament, an unfavorable international situation, and Serbian pressure to punish those with Ustaše connections, including Croatian Catholic clergy.[276] The leader of the Catholic hierarchy, Archbishop Alojzije Stepinac, was himself implicated (not always fairly) by his connections to the Ustaša and the wartime independent Croatian state—and frequently appeared insensitive to these multiple challenges faced by the new Tito regime.

Thus it was under Stepinac's leadership that the Bishops' Conference issued the highly demanding pastoral letter in September 1945, critical of state policy and demanding immediate abolishment of civil marriage, expropriation of church property, and state efforts to secularize society.

[275] Ramet 1990, 183.
[276] Alexander 1979, 69; Akmadža 2006, 93.

The letter further asked for religious instruction in elementary schools and respect for Catholic cemeteries. A second letter to Tito called for freedom of the press, tolerance of private schools, and return of church property. Rather than responding with dialogue or concessions, the government not only put multiple clergy on trial for collaboration and war crimes, but also eventually indicted the Archbishop himself; in the eyes of the regime, Stepinac showed himself to be an obdurate impediment to the regime's plans.

The first signs of a thaw came in 1953 after Tito broke with Stalin and the Soviet bloc, with the Law on the Legal Status of Religious Communities. The Catholic Church was now recognized as an institution and given some legal protections—until then, the communist regime tended to negotiate only with favorably disposed individual clergy.[277] Already, and "although both sides were reticent about it, there were persistent rumours of contact between high government officials and the church."[278] Yet these talks produced few results; typical was a meeting in December 1954 between Archbishop Franjo Šeper and the president of the Croatian republican government, Vladimir Bakarić. Bakarić asked, "do we want peace or do we want to argue?" Šeper replied that he wanted peace, but also that the government establish contacts with the Vatican. The outcome was further stalling by the government.[279]

After the death of Cardinal Stepinac in 1960,[280] relations between the church and state entered a new era of negotiation and mutual accommodation. First, the government began negotiating in 1960 with Cardinal Stepinac's successor, Archbishop Šeper, ostensibly to discuss the funeral arrangements. These meetings opened up a number of other questions and began a dialogue that lasted several years.[281] Second, the annual Bishops' Conference in September 1960 requested the return of its property, the return of parish registers, the right to manage church buildings, and equal rights for seminary students.[282] Further, the church invited dialogue with the state. The Commission for Religious Affairs of Croatia approvingly concluded a month later that "concerning the bishops' demands in the letter, the Commission noted that these were issues that had been constantly repeated, but were presented in a modest tone."[283] The letter

---

[277] Dolinar 1995, 28–29.
[278] Alexander 1979, 235.
[279] Akmadža 2004a, 128.
[280] The Archbishop was made Cardinal in 1952.
[281] Specifically, several talks were held between 1960 and 1963, when the President of the Croatian Commission for Religious Matters who began the dialogue, Stjepan Iveković, left office (Akmadža 2004b).
[282] Alexander 1979, 241.
[283] Akmadža 2006, 109.

was as notable for its moderation (no major social policy demands were made, for example) as for the government's response: the government proposed direct negotiations with the bishops.

Yet despite the more liberal attitudes on behalf of the state and the new dialogue that ensued, the Croat church did not obtain extensive institutional access. In fact, Croatian bishops could not negotiate with the state without the Vatican's permission, a license the Holy See was loath to grant, having seen the compromises Cardinal Wyszyński had made in Poland. After the Second Vatican Council, the new ecumenism and accommodation within the church and a new, more liberal Yugoslav Constitution of 1963 meant greater contact—but between the Yugoslav communist party and the Vatican itself, rather than domestic clergy in Croatia.[284] Informal negotiations between Yugoslav and Vatican representatives turned into formal meetings over the course of 1962–64 (with no involvement of Yugoslav bishops), and the government signed an official agreement with the Holy See in 1966, guaranteeing free exercise of religion on the one hand, and the church's promise to not use clerical office for political ends and to condemn political terrorism.[285] In the late 1960s, the church made use of this newly liberalized environment to renew its efforts to spread religious education outside of formal schools, and to found new Catholic newspapers and presses, including the influential *Glas Koncila*.

In contrast to Poland, the secular state was less concerned with bargaining with the church than with controlling and then monitoring it.[286] Federal and state Commissions for Religious Affairs (Komisije za vjerska pitanja) were established in 1945, and the Federal Commission for Religious Affairs (Savezna komisija za vjerska pitanja) coordinated the religious policies of the republics. These bodies, however, served chiefly to monitor and regulate the behavior of religious groups, rather than as a forum for dialogue or consultation. The federal commission, dissatisfied with the results achieved by anti-church campaigns, also founded a publicity department in 1955. For their part, both Archbishops Stepinac and Šeper were far more reticent than their Polish counterparts, and "avoided meeting with government representatives unless it was absolutely necessary."[287]

---

[284] The Catholic Church in Croatia also welcomed those reforms of Vatican II, such as the vernacular Mass, that brought the people closer to the church—and thus helped to fuse nation to religion (Buchenau 2005, 553).

[285] Alexander 1979, 246.

[286] A similar ministry existed in Poland: the Ministry for Religious Affairs, and in other communist countries.

[287] Akmadža 2006, 108.

Their reserve was understandable; both the federal and state commissions, in fact, were closely tied to the secret service, serving as de facto agencies of state security until the 1960s (when Tito purged from office Aleksandar Ranković, the Minister of Interior responsible for the monitoring and infiltration of the commissions).[288] Power subsequently devolved to the state commissions, which were instructed to develop cordial relations with clergy and religious leaders. Yet their status and influence was modest; they served a purely advisory role and operated as small offices in the eighty municipalities that had established them, rarely meeting. From 1974 on, the Federal Commission for Relations with Religious Communities (Komisije za odnose s vjerskim zajednicama) was affiliated with the Federal Executive Council (similar commissions existed on the state level.) It only met once or twice a year for informal consultations with state commissions—but did not engage the church itself.[289]

Even after the bishops sought to avoid bloodshed during the post-Spring crackdown, their efforts were not rewarded by the regime. In contrast to the institutional access won by the Catholic Church in Poland for its role in stabilizing difficult situations, the Croat church gained little. There were three reasons: First, orthodox communists returned to the relevant offices after 1972 and had little interest in fostering a dialogue with the church.[290] Second, the regime was hesitant to negotiate with *any* social partner, no matter how high its moral authority,[291] for fear of provoking further demands from other national groups. Rewarding the Catholic Church would have meant responding to other denominations in Yugoslavia (the Orthodox Church in Serbia, the Muslim community in Bosnia and Herzegovina, and so on; if Croatia was predominantly Catholic, Yugoslavia was religiously diverse), which the federal regime could not afford to do. Third, though such divisions were overcome (or at least publicly papered over) in Poland, the Croat bishops remained divided over tactics, with no dominant representative that could easily assert authority. The costs of offering institutional access to the church were simply too high to be tenable for the communist government, even if it would have welcomed such support otherwise. As a result, even if the church were left with the attitude that "the regime should have been grateful to the church for mitigating conflicts and curbing extremism,"[292] that feeling would remain unrequited—and unrewarded.

[288] Buchenau 2005, 550.
[289] Perica 2002, 134.
[290] Buchenau 2005, 550.
[291] Pickering and Baskin 2008, 532.
[292] Perica 2000, 535.

The church did make some policy gains, but largely as an unintended consequence of particular communist regime difficulties. In the 1980s, after the Great Novena, the communist regime started to liberalize. It did so not out of a great desire to reform, but because after Tito, the republics that constituted Yugoslavia began to assert their demands even as the central government lost the authority and the power to balance their demands and control the situation.[293] The state was leaking power—and the church stood ready to take advantage of this new weakness. Accordingly, in the 1980s, the church received the boon of a wave of building permits, much as in Poland, and the federal state tolerated renewed religious expression as a way of acceding to Croatian demands without altering the formal relations between the center and the republics.

Nor did the regime transition offer new opportunities for the church. In contrast to Poland, no Round Table took place between the communist party and the opposition, and there was no widespread need for a stabilizing force. No new channels of policy influence through institutional access developed, largely because in the eyes of the communists, such concessions cost more than they could benefit the regime. In February 1989, as Franjo Tuđman was establishing what would become the HDZ, high-ranking communist party and church representatives met in secret in Zagreb to negotiate a power-sharing arrangement, but produced little in the way of significant policy concessions. Unlike the negotiations held between the church and the government in Poland, which were fully empowered to make policy proposals and concessions, the Croat state representative (Zdenko Svete, a relatively hardline former ambassador to the Vatican), had limited authority and chiefly stalled for time.[294] When the church issued a slew of demands, including the lifting of all restrictions on church activity, the representatives of the Croatian communist regime balked; they were unable to meet these demands because they were also negotiating with the Orthodox Church, and anxious about the claims of the Serbian minority in Croatia throughout the late communist period.[295] As a result, the communist Croat government could not meet the Catholic Church's demands for fear of provoking similar claims from the Orthodox Serbs living in Croatia (close to 12% of the Croat population at the time)—and the ire of leaders in Serbia, keen to interpret any such slights as acts of nationalist belligerence. Concessions to the Croat church would only exacerbate the political instability and nascent conflict.

[293] Kasapović 1996, 87.
[294] Perica 2002, 138.
[295] Perica 2002, 139; Massey, Hodson, and Sekulic 2000, 9. In contrast, for example, the Slovene government could meet the church's demands since it did not have to contend with competing (and contentious) religious authorities within its borders.

Thus, since the Croatian church could not play the critical stabilizing role for the communist regime that the Polish church did, it did not obtain institutional access under communism. The church had the requisite moral authority, but the costs of institutional access for the state outweighed the benefits. Despite the fusion of Croat and Catholic identities, the church could not represent the "nation" vis-à-vis the communist regime, nor could its demands be met without offending the Serbian Orthodox Church. The communist regime had little need to develop a formalized forum where negotiations with the church could take place, or where the church could exercise its moral authority. And if the government had tried to do so, it would have had to develop similar fora for the Serbian Orthodox Church and Muslim community, given the sensitivities of managing ethnic and religious diversity within Yugoslavia.

The Church in Independent Croatia

After the free elections in April–May 1990, and the 1991 declaration of Croatian independence, the Roman Catholic Church went from being an oppressed minority in communist Yugoslavia to a courted monopolist in independent Croatia. From the viewpoint of the Vatican and the church, Croat sovereignty "was virtually an unmixed blessing,"[296] and not surprisingly, the Vatican was among the first to recognize Croat independence. For its part, the Catholic Church in Croatia entered the era of independent Croatia with considerable moral authority, won by decades of increasing fusion between nation and religion, bolstered by the Croat Spring, the Great Novena, and the active support of local clergy for national mobilization in the 1980s.[297] Accordingly, "both reform minded communists and their ethnic nationalist opponents wooed the Church."[298] Given the clergy's support for Croatian autonomy, the church largely endorsed the pro-independence forces in the 1990 elections and the 1991 referendum.[299]

The Tuđman regime courted the church and welcomed its nationalist legitimation, but it did not call on it to keep societal peace or to survive, given both the nature of the transition and the international nature of the threat to its regime. Accordingly, Tuđman and the HDZ did not offer institutional access. Instead, they simply adapted and renamed existing structures of church-state relations. The communist infrastructure was now named "The Commission for Relations among Religious Commu-

[296] Ramet 1996, 346.
[297] Loza 2009.
[298] Perica 2002, 187.
[299] Ribić 2009, 199.

nities" (Komisija za odnose s vjerskim zajednicama). This commission communicated directly with religious leaders and met directly from time to time with the Croatian Bishops' Conference, but did little to sway policy. The bishops themselves were displeased with this institutional access point, contending that it provided extremely limited influence on politics.[300] The Commission did, however, eventually take up the agreements that would be signed eventually between Croatia and the Holy See.

Nor could the church use *informal* channels of access. Unlike Solidarity, the HDZ arose without active church support or protection, and with an autonomous power base, which meant few personal connections or access. On the local level, there were instances where "candidates for positions in the state bureaucracy had to provide letters of recommendation from parish priests and bishops as well as warrants about holy communion, confirmation, and children's participation in religious training."[301] In 2002, the church pressured the Račan government from appointing an anti-clerical historian as Minister of Science.[302] But the scale of such vetting differed vastly from the Polish episcopal hierarchy meeting with, naming, and replacing high-placed government officials, or determining who would be on the teams representing the government in church-state negotiations. Not surprisingly, the Croatian Episcopate "expressed dissatisfaction with the limited influence they have had on policy and have called for a greater church role in the political sphere."[303]

Instead, the church mostly relied on the HDZ. The church was neither explicitly nor unambiguously allied with the HDZ, but it endorsed the same nationalist goals. The HDZ also offered policies the church supported and wanted, such as restitution and religion in schools. These willy-nilly drew the church into an alliance. While the church remained divided, it de facto accepted the offer, because it afforded the best chance to ensure the church's political interests, and because at least at the outset, the HDZ appeared a national movement, rather than the autocratic party it would become. Further, significant factions within the church supported the war as part of its fostering of the fusion of national and religious identities.

In turn, the war justified HDZ rule. Two consequences followed. First, by a political transitive property, support for the war among both the populace and the church also translated into inadvertent endorsement of its main protagonist, the HDZ. The alliance was cemented further. Second, because that support for the war was not contingent, there was nothing

---

[300] Ribić 2009, 200.
[301] Perica 2002, 190.
[302] Vezic 2002.
[303] Ramet 1996, 348.

for the church to offer to (or threaten to withdraw from) the HDZ. Accordingly, the HDZ made relatively few policy concessions to the church. Tuđman pushed through religious education in schools, and the church obtained favorable restitution of its properties (which eventually helped to make the church the fifth wealthiest entity in Croatia by 2005[304]), but abortion and other church priorities remained unresolved.

The situation changed with the end of the war in 1995. The HDZ would now have to find new sources of electoral support and to address public policies it had earlier neglected. The church's bargaining position suddenly grew, as the incumbent's hold on power grew more tenuous and its own moral authority persisted. The HDZ renewed its embrace of the church, to the point that 75% of poll respondents believed the church had actively supported the HDZ in the 1995 election.[305] Its best electoral returns came from regions hit by the war,[306] but the HDZ could not simply rely on these to continue to survive and to dominate Croatian politics.

The church hierarchy took advantage of these new opportunities. It set up a Post-War Negotiation Team as an ad-hoc committee of Catholic experts and clergy in 1996 to negotiate with the government over the role of the Catholic Church in government policy and affairs. If the government was not going to establish institutional access for the church, the church would try to do so itself. Led by Bishop Bozanić, this team primarily negotiated with the government on issues such as the presence of the church in the army and police forces, freedom of church internal affairs and the possibility to exercise pastoral care within state institutions such as prisons and hospitals, access to state media, the presence of the church in the educational system, and possibilities for church public financing. In anticipation of the 1996–97 elections, the church also publicly raised the issue of corruption, and the Episcopate debated its relationship to the HDZ at the Bishops' Conference in October 1996 in Djakovo.[307]

The signals were clear; church support now had to be won, not just assumed. Tuđman understood, and the church obtained a considerable policy concession: three major agreements in 1996–97 between Croatia and Holy See (On Legal Questions, On Spiritual Care in Military and Police Forces, On Co-Operation in the Field of Education and Culture). The fourth treaty, On Economic Issues, was signed in October 1998. All were arranged in secret, and little was known about them until they were officially signed and officially published in the parliamentary gazette. As a critical former clergyman put it, "these Agreements are primarily a pact

[304] See Sakalis 2013.
[305] Bellamy 2002, 56.
[306] Kasapović 1996.
[307] Perica 2002, 194.

between two people: the Bishop of Zagreb [Kuharić] and the Head of the Croat government at the time [Tuđman]. They did not pass through parliamentary debate or a referendum. This was done behind the nation's back."[308] The HDZ government had the treaties signed without the required parliamentary debates and exerted enormous pressure on the parliament to pass the treaties, despite their lack of popularity among legislators.[309]

The secrecy was warranted; the Agreements soon proved controversial. The Agreement on Legal Questions gave civil status to religious marriage, contradicting the Law on Marriage and Family Relations, which explicitly forbids the recognition of religious marriage. It mandated that the judiciary had to inform ecclesiastical authorities before investigating clergy. Other provisions guaranteed access for the church to hospitals, prisons, and the mass media; catechism in all schools including day-care centers; and a military chaplaincy. The 1998 financial package provided permanent financial assistance to the church, pensions for the clergy, restitution of church property, the state financing of reconstruction of churches destroyed in the war, placed military chaplains and religious teachers on the state payroll, and the guarantees of tax exempt status for the church.[310] The Treaty on Co-Operation in Education and Culture granted the Catholic Church special privileges, with access to radio and television and the right to its own public media.[311]

Accordingly, 1996–99 was a time of a church triumphant: Pope John Paul II visited Croatia for a second time, beatifying Archbishop Stepinac; the church signed the treaties; and it gained financial assistance and religious education in schools in the process. New churches were being built everywhere; by 1999, the church was the biggest construction investor in Croatia.[312] Religiosity increased, and the church's moral authority appeared high and resilient.

Yet because the church-HDZ coalition gained teeth in 1996–99, it began to undermine the church's moral authority. Accordingly, once the

---

[308] Don Ivan Grubišić, quoted in *Nacional*, December 2, 2010, available at http://www .nacional.hr/clanak/96810/don-grubisic-glas-koncila-nalikuje-komunistickm-glasilu-a -crkva-glasuje-za-one-koji-plate, accessed November 20, 2013.

[309] Gruenfelder 2000.

[310] Bremer 2010, 9.

[311] The Croatian Radio and Television Corporation is obligated by the Law on the CRTV of 2001 to include a representative of the Catholic Church and of other religious communities on its board. The board is responsible for overseeing public radio and television in Croatia and is further obligated by law to inform the public of religious events and phenomena. The Croatian Television Program of Religious Culture, started in 1991, was broadcasting over three hours weekly in 2001.

[312] Perica 2002, 190.

HDZ lost power in 2000, the church in a democratic Croatia now faced public criticism and questions over its complicity in the Tuđman regime. Other political parties distanced themselves from the church after 2000 and refused to become directly identified with it.[313] Earlier, "irritation with overly close church-state relations was publicly expressed, [but] these concerns did not provoke serious public debate . . . questioning the role of the church in society only became more serious when the profound economic and social crisis intensified."[314] With the defeat of the HDZ, criticisms of the church's role in the war, its wealth, and its privilege came to the fore, and the church was ill equipped to respond.

The Episcopate now tried to disassociate itself from the excesses of the HDZ and to minimize the costs of its coalition with the party, even as many clergy still supported the party itself. At Tuđman's funeral in 1999, Archbishop Bozanić praised the dead and also asked that he be forgiven for "those things that were less worthy and sinful."[315] The church spoke out against the HDZ government's plans for holding the elections in late December 1999 (when low turnout and the votes of Croatian émigrés back in their home country would be likely to benefit the HDZ) as not up to "European" standards, and indirectly but unmistakably criticized the government by calling voters to elect candidates with "integrity and the capability to answer the needs of the current Croatian state and its citizens in the best possible way."[316] Yet local clergy continued to openly support the HDZ, and the independent media now openly questioned the church's motives.

Moreover, neither the hierarchy nor the clergy could bring itself to trust the communist successor party that won the 2000 elections, the Social Democratic Party (Socijaldemokratska partija, SDP). The SDP's victory prompted renewed clerical support for the HDZ, if only out of animosity toward the socialist government. Many in the church were openly and intensely critical of the 2000–2003 SDP government, worried about losing the privileges granted in the agreements and about the possibility of a return to the communist-era policies. Clergy were made even more anxious by the new 2002 Law on Religious Communities, which ignored church preferences.[317] Not surprisingly, a 2003 poll of the clergy found that less than 1% would vote for the SDP, while a plurality of 36% planned to vote for the HDZ (46% of the clergy

---

[313] Loza 2009.

[314] Zrinščak 2001, 186.

[315] Bellamy 2002, 55.

[316] Bellamy 2002, 56. For their pains, the hierarchy was then criticized from the Right as having been responsible for "the return of the Reds" when the HDZ was defeated. Gruenfelder 2000.

[317] Zrinščak 2004, 307–8.

were undecided).[318] Church representatives went as far as to call the new government "anti-Croatian, traitorous, and communist."[319] Archbishop Bozanić continued to call for moderation, but with little resonance. Ironically, *Glas Koncila* was more critical of the democratic and deeply reformist Račan government and the Social Democrats than of the wartime excesses of the HDZ.[320]

In the 2003 election the Croatian Bishops' Conference issued instructions that the church must not take part in pre-election activities.[321] However, the bishops also issued an election message urging voters not to vote for those "advocating the legalization of abortion, euthanasia and same-sex marriages," which was widely interpreted as an attack on the SDP government.[322] The church's criticism and opposition was so intense that the EU eventually asked the Vatican to moderate the church's behavior.[323]

As a result, President Stipe Mesić (himself a former member of the HDZ) and the first post-2000 coalition government, led by Prime Minister Ivica Račan of the SDP and the Social Liberals (Hrvatska socijalno-liberalna stranka, HSLS), had problematic relations with the church. The hugely popular President Mesić (in office 2000–2010) launched a campaign after 2000 against "clerical interference in politics in general and right-wing nationalist groups in particular."[324] For example, he criticized the church for receiving thirty-seven million euros from the state budget annually, "build[ing] monumental offices, and then proceed[ing] to rent [out] the property."[325] After yet another *Glas Koncila* salvo, Mesić eventually called in 2009 for the removal of crucifixes from public office and for greater autonomy from the church, as befits a secular state.[326] His successor, Ivo Josipović, an avowed agnostic, won office in 2010 despite clerical opposition. The situation was a stark contrast with Poland, where for decades all political parties, former dissidents and communist successors alike, deferred to the church and publicly paid it homage.

For lack of a better ally, the church continued to tacitly support the HDZ after it regained the government in 2003, though relations became

---

[318] "Croatia's Catholic Clergy to Vote for Nationalists: Poll." ONASA News Agency, September 23, 2003.

[319] Hedl 2001.

[320] Marinović and Golberger 2008.

[321] "Croatia: SDP Candidate Chides Bishop for 'Siding' with Opposition Coalition." BBC Worldwide Monitoring (HINA news agency, Zagreb), November 15, 2003.

[322] "Croatian Premier Thinks Voters Will Not Be Influenced by Bishops' Message." BBC Worldwide Monitoring (HINA news agency, Zagreb), November 12, 2003.

[323] Hedl 2001; Dragojević 2005, 73.

[324] Perica 2002, 198–99.

[325] *Balkan Insight*, August 14, 2009.

[326] Loza 2009.

increasingly strained. Even when the HDZ returned to power in 2003, with Ivo Sanader as Prime Minister, and again in 2007, few significant policy concessions were made to the church. A 2003–4 controversy over a trade ban on Sundays pitted the HDZ and the Catholic Church against the Croatian People's Party (Hrvatska Narodna Stranka, HNS) and the Social Democratic Party (SDP), and while the ban passed, the main result of the controversy was to heighten criticism of the church's involvement in politics.[327] A spokesman for the Croatian People's Party remarked that "the Church in Croatia is overtly close to the rightist, conservative, and even nationalist segments of the political spectrum, namely the HDZ, and that the HDZ, both during and after the time of Tudjman had always used the Church as its best lobbying agents in elections. Liberal-leaning parties, on the other hand, are obviously, as far as the Church is concerned, representatives of Satan in this world."[328] As if to prove the point, in the lead-up to the 2007 elections, the chief military chaplain, Juraj Jezerinać, labeled certain parties (understood to be the SDP and its allies) "Satanic." This brought condemnation from President Stipe Mesić, who threatened to ban him from entering military facilities.[329]

Nor did new channels of influence open up. In 2005, the Bishops' Conference attempted yet again to establish access to policy making and "inaugurated a new practice of inviting the premier to sessions of the Conference to brief the bishops about various aspects of the cabinet's work and current problems in state and society. The [new HDZ Prime Minister] and practicing Catholic Ivo Sanader complied. [President] Mesić has publicly protested against the practice, which seems inappropriate to him as a blatant violation of the principle of separation of church and state. Consequently, in spite of the 2004 return of the HDZ to power the church remains frustrated and perceives the nation to be

---

[327] Even after the HDZ government briefly changed the laws to ban trading in 2009, the law was found unconstitutional and abolished in 2011. It came into force at the height of the tourist season and sparked protests from both businessmen and consumers, and there was immediate talk of revoking the law—a move the church was determined to stop, since it would "seriously jeopardize its political influence." Robert Bajruši, "Posljednje biskupsoko upozorenje Ivi Sanaderu" (The final warning of the church to Ivo Sanader), *Nacional*, August 19, 2008, http://www.nacional.hr/clanak/48060/posljednje-biskupsko-upozorenje-ivi-sanaderu.

[328] "Croatian Party Criticizes Church for Excessive Interference in Secular Affairs." BBC Worldwide Monitoring (HINA news agency, Zagreb), August 27, 2007.

[329] "Croatian President Warns Army Bishop." Agence France Presse, November 12, 2007. In 2012, Jezerinać claimed that the Croat civil war was the result of "atheization, godlessness, and rejection of God." *Nacional*, January 17, 2012, http://www.nacional.hr/clanak/print/123476, accessed November 20, 2013.

in crisis."[330] By the 2007 elections, the two main parties running, SDP and HDZ, "broadly agree[d] on a number of hot social issues. Neither would restrict abortion rights, nor does either advocate an outright ban on Sunday work, two frequent demands from the Catholic Church in Croatia. . . . The increasingly vocal clergy, whose social attitudes often verge on extremism, knows very well that neither conservatives nor social democrats will fulfill some of their most deeply held desires."[331] Sanader himself, while accused of giving money to the church to ensure a favorable vote in the 2007 elections,[332] cooled off relations with the church even further afterward and tried to make the HDZ appear more liberal when it became clear church support did not translate into electoral victories.

In short, the Roman Catholic Church in Croatia trod a much more tortuous path than its Polish counterpart. Unable to obtain institutional access under communism, the church then relied on an uneasy and increasingly costly democratic coalition with a dominant party that offered few policy concessions. The Croatian church inadvertently accepted a partisan coalition with the HDZ, convinced that its moral authority would allow it to influence policy. Yet it achieved little, since the HDZ did not need the church's active backing during 1991–95, when the war mobilized popular support. After the war was over and HDZ needed help, the church's bargaining position improved, and it obtained more meaningful concessions and privileges that came with the four agreements of 1996–98. However, the numerous privileges that followed from the agreements also meant its moral authority decreased. Popular politicians openly criticized the church, and no party closely allied with it again.

Without stable institutional access, and with its main political partner in and out of office, the church in Croatia was unable to affect durable policy changes, or achieve its aims in abortion, divorce, civil unions, in vitro fertilization, or stem cell research. A 2013 referendum made same-sex marriage unconstitutional, but it owed its success to the conservatism prevalent in all post-communist societies as much as to church support. After 2000 and the collapse of the HDZ dominance, the church had to contend with new anti-clericalism, public criticism by popular politicians, government ministers participating in gay rights parades, and multiple policies passed despite its public opposition.

[330] Perica 2006, 331.

[331] Loza 2007.

[332] Don Ivan Grubišić, quoted in *Nacional*, December 2, 2010, available at http://www .nacional.hr/clanak/96810/don-grubisic-glas-koncila-nalikuje-komunistickm-glasilu-a -crkva-glasuje-za-one-koji-plate, accessed November 20, 2013.

Domains of Policy Influence

In contrast to the Catholic Church in Poland, the Croat church had far fewer policy successes; it was unable to frame political debates or to succeed in changing policy, even in critical areas such as abortion, where it immediately began to pressure the government. Where it achieved gains, the church depended on the favor of partisan allies and incumbents rather than on long-standing institutional access.

Religious Education

As in Poland, religion was introduced into schools without public consultation, and instead via a government fiat. Here, too, it was officially justified by the importance of Catholicism to the national culture, the communist-era suppression of religion, and the importance of developing an ethical framework.[333] Earlier, the communist regime gradually removed religious education from public schools after 1946, at first raising informal obstacles (religious education was scheduled for the last hour of school, so children would leave and not come back, and other teachers in the school engaged in explicitly anti-religious teaching) and obstructing efforts to teach it in churches.[334] Archbishop Stepinac complained of the "extensive communist propaganda" directed at schoolchildren and that "clergy has no access to youth, and young people are on the road to godlessness."[335] By 1952, religious education in public schools was formally abolished and was left to churches and chapels. Yet despite these obstacles, the church was able to reach a considerable share of schoolchildren; even though the 1966 agreement between the Vatican and the Yugoslav government did not mention religious schooling (to the disappointment of Croatian bishops), well over a half of children nonetheless received religious education outside of school.[336]

In contrast to Poland, however, the initiative to reintroduce religious education in post-communist Croatia came from the secular government. Tuđman *offered* to introduce religion in schools immediately in 1990. The state also retained far more control over the curriculum than in Poland, reserving the right to review and approve all syllabi, and to name the teachers (which would be trained by the religious communities).[337] The HDZ government's eagerness had a twofold motivation. First, precisely at

---

[333] Bobinac and Jerolimov 2006, 52.
[334] Akmadža 2006.
[335] Akmadža 2004a, 95.
[336] Ramet 1990, 185; Alexander 1979, 235.
[337] Bobinac and Jerolimov 2006, 52.

a time when Tuđman was claiming church support, it was a signal of the credibility of his commitment to the church (without the unsightly parliamentary debates this would have normally entailed), and the church's acceptance of this offer meant Tuđman could claim church approval. Second, while religious education in Poland had as its goal the retention of another generation of Polish Catholics, it appears to have had a more explicitly national purpose in Croatia; it deliberately stigmatized Serb Orthodox children.[338] Given the forced conversions of Orthodox Serbs by the Ustaša, this was an especially sensitive charge. Cardinal Kuharić himself wrote a letter to parishes throughout Croatia in late November 1994 asking how many non-Catholic children were attending Catholic classes, and whether Orthodox children were being rebaptized into the Catholic Church—an admission that the problem existed.[339] Religion in schools thus served the ethno-nationalist purposes of the HDZ as much as it did to draw the church into an alliance.

As the program was introduced, some clergy were uncertain, and worried that this move might cost the church the faithful. In contrast, the hierarchy agreed to the proposal, and religious education was fully in place in the fall of 1991.[340] In the first year, 50% of all schoolchildren aged six to fourteen took classes, and within a few years, anywhere from 70% (in urban areas) to close to 100% of rural pupils enrolled.[341] Two years after religious classes started, the state Commission for Relations with Religious Communities declared the program a success.[342] As part of the 1996–97 agreements, the right to religious education in school was further enshrined legally in the Agreement on Cooperation in Education and Culture, with the official requirement that the schooling system "must take into account the deeply rooted Catholic tradition in the Croatian cultural heritage" and "appropriate religious and cultural initiatives and programs."[343] The agreement further mandated the teaching of catechism in preschool through secondary schools and the primacy of Christian ethics in the entire public school system.[344]

This last stipulation would prove especially problematic when competing sex education programs were introduced, a process that began in 2005.[345] The HDZ government introduced the TeenStar pilot program, which relied heavily on Catholic teaching and had the bishops' approval.

[338] Perica 1996.
[339] Ramet 1996, 347.
[340] Ribić 2009, 200.
[341] Zajović and Veljak 2011, 177.
[342] Ramet 1996, 347.
[343] Lovrenović 1998; see also Zrinščak 2004, 305.
[344] Bijelić 2008, 330.
[345] Bijelić 2008, 334.

The Ministry of Health, along with the UN Global Fund, proposed MemoAids, a secular program. The Ombudsman for Children, Ljubica Matijevic Vrsaljko, ruled against TeenStar, calling it "religiously colored" and lacking in factual content related to pregnancy and sexual diseases.[346] The bishops, for their part, criticized MemoAids as unduly focused on contraception and contraceptives. Given the controversy, the government formed two ad hoc committees, with a heavy church representation, to decide the issue.[347] Their compromise favored the church's preferences and immediately became the target of major disputes between the Ombudsmen for Children and for Gender Equality and NGOs on the one hand, and the church and the proponents of the GROZD program (as the compromise was known, for the parents' association that favored it: Glas Roditelja za Djecu, Voice of Parents for Children). Despite charges of gender discrimination, homophobia, scientific inaccuracies, and the violation of constitutional stipulations, the Ministry of Health implemented the GROZD program, not least because its traditional values comported with the fusion of religious and national identities in Croatia.[348]

The law on sexual education was changed, yet again, in 2012, under the liberal-left Kukuriku coalition government; not only was a mandatory, secular sex-education program introduced, tailored to the age of the pupils, but also the administration stood fast in the face of the vehement protests from the church and the GROZD parents' association. The bishops' Christmas sermons focused on denouncing the program, angry church supporters distributed leaflets and collected signatures for petitions, Archbishop Bozanić denounced the "gender ideology" of the program,[349] and another bishop compared the government to the Nazis.[350] The government's response? The Prime Minister, Zoran Milanović, called on the church and opponents of the program to end their manipulations, since sex education "is not a matter of a world view but of hygiene."[351] The government refused to back down, bolstered by public opinion polls that showed only 22% of respondents opposed to the program, and 56% rejecting church meddling in education.[352] The Minister of Education,

---

[346] Stefelic 2005.

[347] Bijelić 2008, 335.

[348] Bijelić 2008, 338.

[349] http://daily.tportal.hr/233894/Archbishop-of-Zagreb-celebrates-Christmas-Mass.html, accessed March 5, 2013.

[350] AFP, February 28, 2013.

[351] http://daily.tportal.hr/233732/Milanovic-Croatia-has-a-chance-to-move-forward.html, accessed March 5, 2013.

[352] http://vijesti.hrt.hr/cak-562-graana-protiv-mijesanja-crkve-u-zdravstveni-odgoj, accessed May 22, 2014.

Zeljko Jovanović, dismissed the church as acting in an "unacceptable, ill-intentioned, and defamatory way . . . outside schools they can say whatever they want, but they cannot decide what will be taught."[353] He added he had no intention of wasting more time on the misinformation spread by GROZD or on the church's "medieval" points of view—statements that would be unthinkable from a Polish politician.[354]

In short, the introduction of religious education in schools was more of an unsolicited favor than a concession to a church demand. It was a gift, however, that kept on giving; subsequently, religious education and especially its legal institutionalization in 1996 provided the justification for continued church involvement in public schooling. As the controversies over sex education also indicate, that became a way for the church to obtain influence even in highly contested related arenas. As the evolution of party stances also shows, however, the church went from being courted to being dismissed as a retrograde nuisance. Church influence waned over time, and its efforts became the target of strident criticism.

Abortion

If religious education in public schools was a gift, restricting abortions became a struggle. In contrast to Poland, where the church could use its institutional access, and the anticipatory anxiety of politicians to push through an abortion bill that avoided public approval, the Croat church did not have the access to policy-making institutions, and its support was never so decisive as to convince politicians that banning abortion would be worth the public uproar.

The church had already begun an anti-abortion campaign in 1987, "noting the decline of the birthrate in the predominantly Catholic republics of Croatia and Slovenia as opposed to the other Yugoslav republics."[355] In the newly independent Croatia, the church began lobbying to end abortion completely in 1992, but its proposals never even reached the legislative stage. An attempt to form an "interfaith anti-abortion front" with the Serbian Orthodox Church and the Islamic community of Croatia failed.[356] Open declarations, letters, and mobilization of public opinion by the church bore little fruit. Abortion and contraceptives remained legal, though both were taken off the list of subsidized health services.[357]

---

[353] AFP, February 28, 2013.

[354] http://daily.tportal.hr/233968/Neither-Church-nor-associations-have-any-business-in-schools.html, accessed March 5, 2013.

[355] Bellamy 2003, 160.

[356] Perica 2006, 322.

[357] Shiffman, Skrabalo, and Subotic 2002, 636.

Legal maneuvers were unsuccessful; neither proposed constitutional amendments nor legislative bills ever even reached a parliamentary vote. After independence, the Croatian Constitution of December 1990 nearly included "the right to life of every unborn child" in Article 63 of the draft Constitution,[358] but the widespread mobilization and vociferous protests of women's groups (including a protest conference in November, a month before the constitutional vote) meant the amendment was dropped before it could be approved.[359] Instead, Article 21 states that "every human being has the right to life," Article 62 reads that "the Republic protects motherhood, children, and youths, and . . . the right to a dignified life," and Article 65 includes the explicit freedom to decide about having children. The entire issue of abortion was left to regulation by law, not the Constitution.

In 1992, Cardinal Kuharić sent an official letter to the parliament, requesting a ban on abortion and birth control. The negative public reaction was so strong that the church withdrew, and the bill never reached parliament—and the church did not advocate its position so publicly for another decade.[360] A 1995 draft law by the Ministry of Health would have abolished health insurance coverage for abortion and mandated counseling, but the draft law once again failed to reach the parliament, after a signature-collecting campaign by the feminist group BABE and the intentional slowing down of legal procedures by Andrija Hebrang, the Minister of Health and a HDZ moderate.[361] Similarly, when a director of a large Zagreb hospital declared his institution would no longer perform abortions in November 1991, the social pressure on the Health Ministry was such that the government overturned the decision as incompatible with national law.[362] Abortion was "apparently the one issue that galvanized women," 80% of whom backed abortion rights in 1990, down to 74% in 1997.[363]

Instead, Tuđman took up a pronatalist campaign and charged the Ministry of Development and Reconstruction with promoting demographic growth and decreasing the number of abortions in Croatia, to prevent "the Croatian people facing extinction."[364] Here, he found supporters in the conservative groups around the State Institute for the Protection of Motherhood, Family, and Children, and in Father Ante Baković's Croatian Population Movement, founded in 1991. The Movement was pronatalist,

---

[358] Drakulić 1993, 125.
[359] Wall et al. 1999, 445.
[360] Shiffman, Skrabalo, and Subotic 2002, 635.
[361] Shiffman, Skrabalo, and Subotic 2002, 637.
[362] Drakulić 1993, 123; Lilly and Irvine 2002, 131.
[363] Lilly and Irvine 2002, 131–32.
[364] Bellamy 2002, 51.

and opposed abortion, childlessness, and immigration by young women of childbearing age.[365] It instead advocated a four-child family.[366] A year later, in 1992, Baković also became the first head of the Department for Demographic Renewal, a special office of the Ministry for Development and Renewal, which published a "Concept of Demographic Renewal" that called for, among others, taxes on unmarried people, reduction of day-care centers, and the introduction of "Mother Child Raiser" as a new paid profession.[367] However, independent journalists and NGO activists, alarmed by the dubious mandate of the office, pressured the government into dissolving the department in June 1995.[368]

As the war was winding down and church support became more valuable, the Ministry of Development convened a committee consisting of eighteen demographers, lawyers, economists, and priests to develop a program to address population demographics in 1995. Yet here, too, the preferences of the church were ignored. The National Demographic Development Program was passed unanimously by the Sabor (Parliament), and focused on repatriation of ethnic Croats, limits on immigration of non-Croats, pronatalist financial incentives, and a "positive spiritual climate."[369] However, the program did not call for criminalizing abortion, despite the stated wishes of the church. Baković himself criticized the program for not specifically addressing abortion and deplored that "gynecologists in Croatia have killed five to six times more little Croats than the *Chetniks* [a derogatory term for Serbian soldiers] have."[370]

Open calls for policy change and electoral mobilization were equally unsuccessful strategies. In the 2003 electoral campaign, the bishops instructed the faithful not to vote for parties supporting abortion[371] and claimed the return of the HDZ as a victory for anti-abortion forces. Yet there was little evidence that abortion, rather than the economy and the prospect of European integration, was the decisive issue in the elections. In 2004, the issue was raised again when the Bishop of Varaždin, Marko Čulej, and the papal nuncio to Croatia, Francisco Javier Lozano, spoke out for an end to abortion and called for the suspension of all laws allowing it. Again, state policy did not change. The HDZ "provided verbal support but, fearful of alienating many voters stopped short of bringing the law before parliament," even if individual HDZ parliamentarians

---

[365] Ramet 1996, 346.
[366] Bellamy 2002, 52.
[367] Shiffman, Skrabalo, and Subotic 2002, 635.
[368] *Transition*, April 19, 1996.
[369] Shiffman, Skrabalo, and Subotic 2002, 636.
[370] *Transition*, April 19, 1996.
[371] Perica 2006, 322–23.

supported the church's stance.[372] Subsequently, no party put abortion on the public agenda, despite the church's continued advocacy.[373] As of 2014, the liberal abortion law of 1978 still applied, unchanged.[374]

Stem Cell and Reproductive Technologies

The legal regulation of ART was first taken up in 1997, as a draft law that never reached parliamentary debate, partly because of the church's opposition to IVF and other assisted reproduction technologies. Instead, a 1978 law continued to govern assisted reproduction technologies—and given the advances in medical technology, rapidly became outdated. Cognizant of the increasing debates in the media, the church launched a public campaign in February 2005 aimed at blocking the legalization and regulation of in vitro fertilization. As in Poland, an official declaration of the bishops called IVF "a crime against human life," and the bishops argued that babies conceived via IVF had "significantly more health problems, disorders and diseases," as well as "a series of psychological and psychiatric disorders."[375] Women's groups and parent organizations immediately responded, as they had earlier when the church lobbied to restrict abortion. The church's campaign was "much-ridiculed,"[376] and the bishops' statements were subject to the same criticism and mockery that the Polish bishops would experience in 2012–13. Nonetheless, the church's views were unambiguous, and its public pressure, through declarations and pastoral letters, continued.

For its part, the HDZ government delayed bringing the law to the parliament when it returned to power in 2007; it was no longer as close to the church as it had been in the 1990s, and it was cognizant of the societal backlash and the political defeats of the abortion battles of the early 1990s. Prime Minister Ivo Sanader distanced himself from the church at this point and had little interest in promoting the church's views on the issue. At the same time, the EU made it clear that countries where IVF was available would have to regulate the procedure—and Croatia's accession negotiations were continuing (Croatia would eventually enter the EU in July 2013).

[372] Perica 2006, 322.

[373] Zajović and Veljak 2011; Ritossa 2010, 273.

[374] This is not to say that it is freely available; abortion is not covered by the national health insurance, and patients have to pay for the procedure, limiting access.

[375] Agence France Presse, February 27, 2005.

[376] Loza 2009.

The turning point came when Ivo Sanader abruptly resigned in 2009 as both Prime Minister and leader of the HDZ.[377] The government crisis that followed led the party's conservative faction to ascend, and for it to seek church support. Less than ten days later, the HDZ Minister of Health, Darko Milinović, proposed a new law, adopted by the HDZ coalition later that summer (with no SDP support), with strict criteria regarding eligibility. According to Milinović, the law was a conservative-liberal compromise; in its conservative aspects, IVF was available only to married couples and those who could prove in court they had been in a committed relationship for at least three years. The law ended the freezing of embryos, which Croatian doctors had done under the legal vacuum of the 1978 regulations (which had not anticipated the technology). As Milinović explained, "an embryo is a living being so we are not allowing embryo-freezing."[378] Only three eggs could be fertilized per attempt (although doctors protested that this made little sense, since it was impossible to predict which eggs would prove viable). In what Milinović called a "liberal" provision, sperm and eggs could be donated, but without anonymity provisions. The law was among the most restrictive in Europe at the time, since it limited access to assisted reproduction and severely limited which technologies could be used.

The backlash was immediate. The law that "was to have passed quietly and under urgent procedure, without public debate"[379] instead faced intense public criticism from human rights and parents' groups over the criteria for eligibility. President Stipe Mesić declared he would bring it to the Constitutional Court, since it did not treat all citizens equally (for example, only couples could use IVF). Faced with the prospect of Constitutional Court review, the HDZ backed down. Some of these strictures were eased later on in 2009 (would-be parents now only had to sign a notarized statement that they were a couple, rather than having to prove their relationship in court, and anonymity provisions returned, but the prohibition on embryo freezing continued). Finally, the center-left SDP coalition in July 2012 passed yet another law, which allowed single women to use IVF and authorized the freezing of embryos despite the objections of the Vatican and the domestic Catholic Church.

Both the HDZ and the Croatian Catholic Church protested that the procedure was a violation of the natural order, and an immoral act.[380]

---

[377] He was subsequently charged with corruption in December 2010, fled to Austria, and was extradited back to Croatia. In 2012, he was found guilty and sentenced to prison.

[378] Agence France Presse, July 9, 2010.

[379] *Nacional*, July 14, 2009.

[380] AFP, July 13, 2012.

The Croatian Bishops' Conference issued a public declaration and called on parliamentarians, especially those of Catholic faith, to vote against the law, and on the faithful to use all legal means to prevent its adoption and to change unacceptable legislation.[381] Bishops devoted homilies on Assumption Day (August 15, 2012) to denouncing the newly liberalized laws, calling July 13, 2012, when the law was passed, a "Black Friday" for Croatia.[382] All the denunciations, however, did not change the legal situation, or the church's inability to obtain its preferred policies.

Divorce and Civil Partnerships

As in Poland, the church decried divorce without actively mobilizing to change the family law surrounding it. In Poland and in Croatia, divorce rates remained relatively low, around 17% and 15% in 2000, respectively.[383] Instead, as in Poland, the church promoted Catholic family teaching and focused on abortion, religion in schools, contraceptives, and assisted reproduction as being more important theologically and more feasible targets for influence. In short, divorce was not a priority for the Catholic Church in either Poland or Croatia, not least because it did not recognize the civil procedure.[384]

In contrast, civil unions and same-sex marriage were considerably more controversial. The Croatian Constitution, unlike the Polish one, does not define marriage as between a man and a woman, and so the legal framework was different from the start. As in Poland, however, the church's defense of marriage took the form of mobilizing on behalf of the traditional, and preferable, model of marriage as between a heterosexual couple with the aim of having children. To that end, as in Poland, the church fought civil unions and the extension of marriage to same-sex couples.

The leftist SDP first proposed same-sex civil unions in 2003, a year after SDP Interior Minister Šime Lučin joined the first Pride march for gay rights in Croatia, along with several parliamentarians and the UN

---

[381] http://daily.tportal.hr/193079/Bishops-conference-against-bill-on-medically-assisted-human-reproduction.html, accessed March 5, 2013.

[382] http://daily.tportal.hr/209442/Bishops-slam-medically-assisted-insemination-law-on-Assumption-holiday.html, accessed March 5, 2013.

[383] EuroStat 2003. http://coe.int/t/e/social_cohesion/population/T33–2003.XLS.

[384] In both Ireland and Italy, divorce was not legal before the foundational moments of Irish independence and Italian unification, respectively, and the legal framework preserved that status quo partly in deference to the church. Communist constitutions explicitly allowed divorce, so that the church would have to overturn this policy, along with the liberal laws on abortion and others, and since divorce was not a theological priority, it made little sense to expend capital on this issue.

Human Rights Commissioner.[385] The SDP bill recognized inheritance and financial support rights for same-sex couples, making their rights similar to those given to opposite-sex unmarried couples. The church denounced the law and urged parliamentarians to ban homosexual marriages and denounce homosexuality,[386] but it passed nonetheless. The law's provisions were relatively minimalist; it did not legalize adoptions, or any other right included in family law, or include favorable tax, joint property, pension, or insurance stipulations. A 2005 bill expanding these rights was rejected in Parliament, despite protests from medical and legal associations who pointed out the Constitution bans discrimination. This is where matters rested until 2011 and the Kukuriku coalition, which announced the expansion of rights for same-sex couples to include all those but adoption.[387]

The greatest controversy came in 2013. Two weeks before Croatia joined the European Union, an organization called In the Name of the Family (U ime obitelji) gathered 700,000 signatures (400,000 were required for a referendum), demanding that the Constitution define marriage as the "life-long union of a man and a woman." The leader of In the Name of the Family, Željka Markić, denied that the Catholic Church backed the organization, though she volunteered that it received support from Catholics and some dioceses.[388] The campaign met with three responses: first, press accusations that many signatories were told they could not have their children baptized or attend church unless they signed; second, a review by the Supreme Court of the legality of holding a referendum on the Constitution; and third, a parliamentary bill that would make referenda inapplicable to constitutional questions and require a two-thirds parliamentary super-majority to ratify any referendum (a law that did not apply retroactively to this referendum).

Despite this counter-mobilization, the referendum was held on December 1, 2013, with both the HDZ and the church expressing support. A letter from Cardinal Bozanić was read out loud in churches, declaring that "marriage is the only union enabling procreation. This the key difference between marriage . . . and other unions."[389] In keeping with the low support for gay rights or acceptance of homosexuality in all post-communist countries (see Chapter 2), close to 66% voters agreed that "marriage is

---

[385] Kozole 2002. *Glas Koncila* immediately criticized it as offending the 93% of Croats who are Catholic, and various groups, including skinheads, protested it.

[386] Perica 2006, 324.

[387] http://daily.tportal.hr/193232/Minister-calls-for-raising-tolerance-towards-LGBT .html, accessed March 5, 2013.

[388] Financial Times, June 10, 2013.

[389] http://www.bbc.co.uk/news/world-europe-25172778, accessed December 2, 2013.

matrimony between a man and a woman,"[390] with the areas most affected
by the war expressing the greatest support. The turnout was a relatively
low 38%, but the results were valid; the year before, to ensure the EU
plebiscite would pass, the Croat parliament removed the stipulation that
a majority of registered voters had to participate in a referendum for
it to be binding. As a result, the faithful played the decisive role. In the
words of one prominent critic, they were able to out-mobilize "the silent
majority—those who think that all this does not concern them."[391]

A critical difference with Poland emerged in the aftermath of the referendum. In both Poland and in Croatia, public opinion is conservative,
and in both countries the church objected to same-sex marriage without
necessarily playing the critical role. But a major divergence here lies in the
response of the Croatian political elites; not only have many advocated
same-sex marriage and marriage equality, but also many were willing
to openly take on these Catholic-sponsored efforts. The day after the
vote, Prime Minister Zoran Milanović announced that the government
would push for new rules on referenda, and for an immediate legislation
of same-sex unions that would give the partners virtually the same rights
as in marriage. Croatia's President, Ivo Josipović, further emphasized that
"defining marriage between a man and a woman does not belong to the
constitution. A nation is judged by its attitude toward minorities."[392]

Backlash?

Even though the HDZ would continue to proclaim a relatively nationalist, and thus religiously tinged, rhetoric, it neither needed the church's
support or legitimation nearly as much it did before or after 1995–99.
Nor was the party willing to expend costly political capital in pushing
through church views on abortion. In an increasingly transparent and
critical atmosphere of the 2000s, when government actions were scruti-
nized not only by the opposition but also by the European Union, government decrees were no longer a viable political tactic. Parliaments passed
laws that reflected partisan preferences—only to have civil society lash
back against those, such as the first IVF regulation, deemed too influenced by the church.

Nor did the Croats' continued (and even increasing) religiosity in the
1990s and 2000s let the church reframe issues as preserving the moral

---

[390] See the official results by the Croatian Election Commission, available at http://www
.izbori.hr/2013Referendum/rezult/rezultati.html, accessed December 3, 2013.

[391] Drakulić 2013.

[392] http://www.theguardian.com/world/2013/dec/01/croatia-vote-ban-gay-marriage
-referendum, accessed December 2, 2013.

health of the nation. This rhetorical weakness showed itself repeatedly during the policy debates outlined above—and in other areas, both great and small. For example, the church sought exemptions from strict drunk driving laws passed in the 2000s that lowered the legal drivers' blood alcohol levels to zero, arguing that the offerings of wine at Mass during Holy Communion meant that clergy and the faithful could not legally drive after services.[393] Yet the argument that convinced the government to change the law came instead from winemakers' associations, who successfully showed that the laws were not only inconsistent but would also badly hurt Croatia's wine industry.[394] More significantly, the relationship between President Stipe Mesić and the church was tense throughout his tenure, yet mutual hostility did not prevent his re-election in 2005, much as the church's initial criticism of Aleksander Kwaśniewski did not preclude his popularity or re-election as President of Poland in 2000.

The church itself grew increasingly disillusioned in the 2000s. By 2008, even the HDZ government refused to support an abortion ban proposed by the church, shot down a church proposal to introduce another hour of religious education per week in schools, introduced anti-discrimination legislation protecting gays, and indicated that it was considering revoking the ban on Sunday trading. The bishops grew increasingly critical, and a disappointed church official remarked that "there were too many strange decisions and even humiliation in the incumbent government's policy towards the church recently. The icing on the cake was the passing of the anti-discrimination law."[395]

After Sanader's departure in 2009, the IVF law favored by the church passed only to be quickly modified in light of popular protest. Finally, the main concession of the 1990s, the Vatican Agreements, came under fire for their costly commitment to support the church materially at a time of economic austerity.[396] In light of these setbacks, it is not surprising that after the more liberal Archbishop Marin Srakić replaced Cardinal

---

[393] AFP, February 27, 2005.

[394] *Southeast European Times*, May 27, 2008.

[395] Robert Bajruši, "Posljednje biskupsoko upozorenje Ivi Sanaderu" (The final warning of the church to Ivo Sanader), *Nacional*, August 19, 2008, http://www.nacional.hr/clanak/48060/posljednje-biskupsko-upozorenje-ivi-sanaderu, accessed November 19, 2013. The bill passed in 2008, against church opposition, with the support of 119 out of 177 deputies (*Balkan Insight*, July 10, 2008).

[396] Mesić proposed that Croatia move to a new system of church funding, a tax write-off similar to Italy and (as of 2012–13) Poland, rather than a lump subsidy. The proposal would have reduced the church's funding tenfold (*Nacional*, September 17, 2009), http://www.nacional.hr/clanak/67095/mesicev-crkveni-porez-bez-tudmanovog-testamenta-kler-bi-dobivao-deset-puta-manje, accessed November 20, 2013. He was careful to state, however, that as legal documents, the Agreements must be formally changed (*Nacional*, November 17, 2009).

Bozanić as the leader of the Croatian church in 2008, the Croatian hierarchy moved away from a priori supporting the HDZ or other rightwing parties. Many in the clergy continued to support the HDZ, but "the relationship no longer remotely resembles the one of the time of Franjo Tuđman and Franjo Kuharić. . . . The Church was angered by the HDZ's two-faced behavior."[397] For both partners, then, the coalition of church and political party eventually proved a costly disappointment.

Conclusion

The communist era solidified the fusion of national and religious identities in Poland and in Croatia—and left the churches in both countries in a position of enormous moral authority as communism collapsed. Yet the two churches invested their moral authority very differently. In Poland, the church could continue to rely on the institutional access it had gained in the communist era as it stabilized societal conflicts. It also quickly learned not to favor particular political parties, given the popular backlash. In Croatia, the church could not play the fundamental role in ensuring regime survival and thus never obtained institutional access. Instead, the HDZ volunteered policy concessions and asserted the church was in a coalition with the party—an ill-fated political alliance that proved increasingly costly. Once the parties in power changed, so did the church's position, while in Poland, even as the church's moral authority wobbled, continued institutional access meant the church would still be heard. Even so, by the 2010s, the Polish church, too, found itself less powerful. No longer as critical to the fate of incumbents, the church eventually lost influence.

In Croatia and Poland, the postwar homogenization of the population robbed the countries of enormous cultural richness and vibrancy—but also made the fusion of nation and religion that much easier. When diverse religions, multiple languages, and ethnic identities coexist, fusion is made that much more difficult, yet churches can still gain moral authority and significantly influence politics. To see how this is possible, we now turn to the United States and Canada.

---

[397] Robert Bajruši, "Marin Srakić postao novi pravi vođa crkve" (Marin Srakić to become the new leader of the church) (*Nacional*, April 21, 2009). http://www.nacional.hr /clanak/56926/marin-srakic-postao-novi-pravi-voda-crkve, accessed November 19, 2013.

CHAPTER 5

Religious Pluralism and Church Influence: United States and Canada

> Religion in America takes no direct part in the government of society, but it must nevertheless be regarded as the foremost of the political institutions of that country.
>
> —Alexis de Tocqueville, *Democracy in America*, 1831

> You can make a successful run for political office in this country without an especially thick résumé, any exceptional talent for expressing yourself, a noteworthy education or, for that matter, a basic grasp of science. But you better have religion. You better be ready to profess your faith in and fealty to God—the Judeo-Christian one, of course. And you better be convincing.
>
> —Frank Bruni, *New York Times* editorial, December 7, 2013

> What is considered sinful in one of the great religions to which citizens belong isn't necessarily sinful in the others. Criminal law therefore cannot be based on the notion of sin; it is crimes that it must define.
>
> —Pierre Trudeau, 1993

IN RELIGIOUSLY DIVERSE COUNTRIES such as the United States and Canada, no one denomination can fuse with national identity, and no one church alone can claim the mantle of national moral authority. Moreover, such diversity means that denominations compete with one another and hold different doctrinal views on policy and politics. Thus if the Roman Catholic Church enjoyed a considerable historical and political advantage in Poland, Croatia, Ireland, and Italy, no church had such a favored position in the "mixed" Protestant-Catholic cases of the United States and Canada. Neither has a dominant religion, and both are religiously diverse (see Table 5.1). Moreover, both countries are relatively young postcolonial nation-states, and as nations of immigrants, have no clear single national identity or history.

TABLE 5.1.
RELIGIOUS DIVERSITY IN UNITED STATES AND CANADA

	United States	Canada
Christian overall	75%	67%
Roman Catholic	25%	39%
Protestant:		
Mainline Protestant	15%	15%
Evangelical Protestant	25%	8%
Unaffiliated	20%	24%

Sources: Kosmin and Keysar 2009, 2012 Yearbook of American and Canadian Churches, 2011 Canada National Household Survey. Pew Research, 2013. "Canada's Changing Religious Landscape," http://www.pewforum. org/2013/06/27/canadas-changing-landscape/ (reports Canadian Protestants as 27% of population without breaking down into mainline and evangelical).

Yet despite these obstacles, religious groups have influenced policy in the United States far more than in contemporary Canada. As we will see, national and religious identities could still meld, even where no one religion was dominant. Religious groups claimed moral authority, if more a diffuse one, and gained public trust. Interdenominational alliances took the place of a single monopoly religion in order to take advantage of this moral authority and used coalitions with political parties to advance a shared policy agenda. These partisan coalitions took on a peculiar form; in lieu of gaining access to the state, some religious groups have tried to take over political parties in the United States. Yet unlike the churches in partisan coalitions in Croatia or in Italy, these interdenominational alliances did not pay as heavy a price for their political involvement. Ironically, religious pluralism is an obstacle to religious influence on politics—and a protective canopy for the churches themselves. Their diffused moral authority suffers less than it would in religious monopolies.

In the United States, religious diversity did not preclude a strong national identification with a religious tradition (even if that "Judeo-Christian tradition" was largely invented). The resulting *fusion without monopoly*, rather than either its high levels of religiosity or church influence, is what makes the United States distinctive.[1] Religion, and specifically Reform Protestantism, has historically pervaded American culture

[1] Arguably, however, the American colonies were *individual* monopolies.

and politics.[2] Well into the interwar period, Protestants were the politically dominant group, despite the waves of Catholic and Jewish immigration. After World War II, however, a "Judeo-Christian ethic" (with an emphasis on the "Christian") became the functional substitute for a religious monopoly.

The strong Christian identity of the country manifests itself in a variety of ways. In 1995, 54% of American survey respondents felt it was important to be Christian to be truly American, and this percentage increased to 66% in 2003.[3] Among religious Christians in the United States, 60% saw their country as a "Christian nation" in the 1990s, and around 70% did so in the 2000s.[4] There is considerable social pressure to be religiously observant; the overreporting of church attendance rates is much higher in the United States and in Canada than in Europe.[5] In 1831, Tocqueville noted that "amongst the Anglo-Americans, there are some who profess the doctrines of Christianity from a sincere belief in them, and others who do the same because they are afraid to be suspected of unbelief. Christianity, therefore, reigns without any obstacle, by universal consent."[6] In the modern era, presidential politics abound with constant references to religion, with political candidates of all stripes attending prayer breakfasts, publicly attesting to their faith, and professing their status as born again in Christ.[7] Politicians further signal religious commitments by addressing religious universities, meeting with religious leaders, and giving speeches in religious settings, whether churches or prayer gatherings.[8]

Calling on this Christian identity and the Judeo-Christian "tradition" (however recent or artificial) allowed conservative Christians to influence contemporary politics. American religious groups have been able to affect the rhetoric and the substance of public policy, often in ways that puzzle and infuriate secular observers. Yet while the United States has long been a religiously vibrant society, the last forty years have been remarkable for the degree to which religious conviction entered politics and translated into

[2] Lipset 1963; Morone 2003; McKenna 2007; Bellah 1967; Kurth 2007.

[3] ISSP 1995, 2003.

[4] Straughn and Feld 2010, 281. Straughn and Feld argue that this shift was produced less by demographic change than by the crystallization of identities, especially among Christians, by elevating religiosity, patriotism, and xenophobia, after the terrorist attacks of September 11, 2001 (Straughn and Feld 2010, 287).

[5] Reported church attendance in the United States and in Canada is far higher in surveys than in more objective measures such as time diaries, with a gap of as much as 18 points, suggesting that any "exceptionality" in American religiosity manifests itself more in belief and self-identification than in behavior (Brenner 2011, 16).

[6] Tocqueville, Alexis de. 1831. *Democracy in America*, vol. 1, chap. XVII, part II.

[7] Fowler et al. 2004, 151; Balmer 2008.

[8] Domke and Coe 2008, 79–81.

policy. Conservative Protestants, and especially conservative Evangelicals, entered the political sphere in the 1970s. Beginning in the 1980s, references to "morality politics" such as abortion, gay rights, or the religious content of education skyrocketed in Republican, and to a lesser degree, Democratic Party platforms.[9] Conservative Protestants then joined with traditional Catholics in the 1990s.[10] Papering over the theological differences (and a long history of mutual hostility) between Roman Catholics and Evangelical Protestants, this newly muscular movement borrowed the language of "the culture of life" from Pope John Paul II and used it to justify incursions into abortion, stem cell research, health care, and education. This interdenominational alliance has become a political force, with numbers (for example, 40% of Americans consider themselves born again Evangelicals[11]), intense doctrinal commitments, a compelling choice of issues (those that explicitly mix personal morality with policy, such as abortion), and popular identity (the assertion of a "Christian nation" as a symbolic boundary of Americanness) on their side.

In Canada, in contrast, no fusion arose between national and religious identities, and no similar religious influence on national politics followed. Canada is distinct from the United States in that it has an explicitly binational identity, with no unifying national myth, flag, or anthem of its own until the 1960s, and in that a durable *local* monopoly existed in the Catholic domination of Québec. Not only was there no one denomination that could monopolize moral authority, there also was no one nation to which religion could fuse. No single civil religion, no belief that a higher morality undergirded the country, no ascription of sacred meaning to secular symbols (in fact, no unifying national symbols) arose in Canada, in clear contrast to the United States, where all three did. Instead of inventing a broader religious tradition, Canadian religiosity was fundamentally tied to particular denominations, and these were more strongly tied to the state than in the United States.[12] In contrast to the United States willfully and self-consciously breaking with established religions in favor of a vibrant individual religiosity and a broad "civil religion," Canada retained "strong imprints of established Churches" whether in

[9] Domke and Coe 2008, 105.

[10] The irony here is that Protestantism, and especially Evangelical Protestantism, has long sought to break the link between the individual and the religious institution—and between religion and the secular political order. The Catholic Church's view that it speaks for society and for natural law is at one end of a spectrum that stretches to mainline Protestant concerns with social justice to Evangelical apoliticalism. The Moral Majority has thus been criticized as a "Catholic perversion" by many Protestants, especially Evangelicals. I am grateful to Bill Clark for pointing this out.

[11] Lambert 2008, 185–86.

[12] Lipset 1989, 16.

the educational system or in regional differences.[13] If the Québécois were overwhelmingly Catholic, the small towns and prairies were loyal to the United Church of Canada, and the halls of power and commerce in urban Ontario were largely Anglican. These denominations jostled and competed throughout the nineteenth and early twentieth centuries[14] without ever inventing a broader Canadian religious identity. The eventual (and very Canadian) solution to these conflicts was a political retrenchment of religious denominations from the national political scene after World War II, with the Roman Catholic Church continuing to dominate Québec until the 1960s, when the Quiet Revolution obliterated Catholic popular practice and political influence over the course of a decade.

These divergent paths of the United States (fusion without monopoly) and Canada (oligopoly without fusion) were nonetheless largely peaceful, since both states were established after the violent political conflict of the Reformation and Counter-Reformation in Europe. In contrast, where religious diversity was the result of political conflict, religion was unable to speak for the nation at all. Thus the Catholicism of the victorious imperial Habsburgs in the Czech Lands, and their (literal) defenestration of Protestant Czech nobles branded the Roman Catholic Church as antithetical to Czech national aspirations. In Germany, Protestants and Catholics simmered in mutual antagonism and developed their own national ideas—with nationalism dividing, rather than uniting, society. Bismarck's heavy-handed repression of Catholicism only fueled the mutual intolerance and reinforced the very Catholic beliefs and practices that their Protestant critics found so objectionable.[15] It took the searing experience of Nazism and World War II for political Catholicism (in the form of the Zentrum Party) and Protestantism to unite in the conservative Christian Democratic Union (CDU/CSU). Canada and the United States managed their religious heterogeneity with far less acrimony, not least because neither the United States nor Canada were subject to the post-1555 Treaty of Augsburg principle of *cuius reigio eius religio*, which subordinated individual religious choice to the geopolitical preferences of the ruling monarch.

The comparison of United States and Canada suggests that in religiously plural and competitive settings, religion can still bind to nation, and that this fusion generates moral authority, albeit diffused among several different religious groups. This religious moral authority can be invested to shape public policy. Religious pluralism, on the one hand, obliges denominations to ally. Such interdenominational coalitions have

---

[13] Kim 1993, 266.
[14] O'Toole 1996.
[15] Smith 1995; Blackbourn 1994.

to find doctrinal consensus on a given issue, mindful of their theological commitments and of the faithful's option to exit.[16] On the other hand, the diffusion of moral authority among many churches means their moral authority is actually more resilient; in terms of the model, the depreciation rate for any individual church in the interdenominational alliance is relatively low. Thus it is not that the US churches do not pay a price for their partisan support; Evangelical churches in particular have acquired a poor image in the eyes of nonadherents. It is that they collectively lose less moral authority than a monopoly church would. Beyond the impact of religious pluralism, federalism and a powerful judiciary[17] further confound and complicate the influence of religion on politics. These factors mean that religious groups in the United States and Canada are more likely to influence policy broadly than they are to secure specific policy outcomes that faithfully reflect a given church's preferences. Yet as we will see, some have succeeded nonetheless in setting the terms of political debates and in achieving policy shifts.

United States

The United States is a case of fusion in the absence of a religious monopoly, resulting in a moral authority diffused among many denominations. In this paramount religious marketplace, it "seems perfectly natural to refer to one's religion as a 'preference' instead of as a fixed characteristic."[18] Yet religious diversity and competition do not preclude a strong national identification with religion. Rather than being bound to a particular denomination, however, American national identity is fused to an invented religious consensus. The contrast with monopolies such as Ireland and Poland, where to be Irish or Polish is to be *Catholic*, is stark. Having *a* religious identity, *any* religious identity within the constraints of denominational respectability, remains critical for personal social capital, and for the legitimation of public officials and governance. As one twentieth-

---

[16] They are also much more attuned to their faithful than the monopolistic moral authorities are, because the faithful can leave a given church for another. Given the diffusion of moral authority, churches will enter into coalitions with political parties rather than obtain institutional access. In the United States, political institutions also preclude formal institutional access.

[17] Unlike Europe, neither the United States nor Canada were subject to the 1555 Treaty of Augsburg principle of *cuius reigio eius religio*, which subordinated individual religious choice to the geopolitical preferences of the secular rulers.

[18] Putnam and Campbell 2010, 4.

century President put it, "our form of government has no sense unless it is founded in a deeply felt religious faith, and I don't care what it is."[19]

The American "identification of religion with the national purpose"[20] runs both ways. The founding of the United States did not translate the political ambitions of an existing nation into a political form; no single national identity existed. In its absence, religious references helped to coalesce a notion of American exceptionalism—beginning with John Winthrop's ideal of the new Massachusetts Bay Colony as a "city on a hill" (an image repeatedly referenced in twentieth-century American politics), through the nineteenth-century notions of Manifest Destiny, and the twentieth century's "Judeo-Christian tradition." Secular symbols of the state (the Constitution, the flag) acquired quasi-sacred status over the course of the nineteenth and twentieth centuries. One result was an American "civil religion," the intertwining of patriotism with the notion that Americans were God's chosen people, and a commitment to the idea of America as pluralist, founded on the principles of religious freedom, and also informed by Puritan and Protestant ideas.[21] This nonsectarian civic faith imbued American history and political symbols with sacred meaning: the veneration of the American flag, the prayer-like aspects of the Pledge of Allegiance, or politicians' invocations that "God bless America." In influencing policy, the historical truth of this national myth mattered less than its wide acceptance and the taken-for-granted quality it lent religious (and primarily Protestant) political activity at various points in American history. In terms of the argument presented here, civil religion is a manifestation of an underlying fusion of national and religious identities—a fusion that is not unique to the United States but that took on a specific American form that included a far more diverse set of denominational identities. While civil religion made secular symbols sacred, moral authority allowed sacred values to be made into secular laws.

To summarize two centuries of history, an initially exclusionary religious identification, Puritanism, ceded to a more inclusive Protestant identity over the course of the nineteenth century and culminated in the invention of the "Judeo-Christian tradition" by World War II. The Puritanism that dominated by the end of the eighteenth century (three out of four Americans professed some version of Puritanism[22]) introduced the rhetoric of the chosen people and divine destiny for the nation—and inadvertently separated church from state, in an effort to protect

[19] Eisenhower 1952.
[20] Herberg 1983 [1960], 264.
[21] Bellah 1967; Gentile 2006; McKenna 2007; Wills 2007.
[22] Morone 2003, 33.

the religion from the corruption of the secular world.[23] At the same time, while Anglicans and others "drifted towards neutrality and loyalism," Calvinist doctrinal preoccupations dominated Revolutionary ideology.[24] An important legacy of this initial political primacy of Puritanism was the continued perception of politics as a "matter of right and wrong, salvation and perdition," and of morality as the personal responsibility of sinners.[25] Meanwhile, the culturally powerful Scots Irish immigration to the United States reinforced this marriage of morality and politics, with the church often serving as the one effective institution in the early nineteenth-century frontier.[26] This particularly Puritan intertwining of the moral and the political, and the religious and the national, helps to set the stage for the prominence and religious framing of "morality" issues that place individuals as responsible for "sin," such as abortion and same-sex marriage. These have also compelled electoral attention more than broader issues that make society responsible for ameliorating systemic challenges, such as social justice and foreign aid advanced by liberal churches.

If the colonial era blended morality and politics, subsequent religious revivals such as the Great Awakenings (in the 1730–40s, 1800–1840, and 1850s–1900) created a common and mutually intelligible language for political opponents and a way to stir passions and mobilize crowds.[27] In the process, the revivals forged an American identity that was profoundly Protestant by the middle of the nineteenth century.[28] This new identity united the nation, but also led to nativist backlash against Catholic, and then Jewish and non-Protestant Asian immigration in the nineteenth and early twentieth century.[29]

Bringing together passionate preachers and increasingly diverse economic classes and denominations, these religious revivals "brought to ordinary people the discovery that they could be more than passive specta-

---

[23] Morone 2003, 32.

[24] Bloch 2007, 49 and 53.

[25] Morone 2003, 11 and 13.

[26] Leyburn 1962, 293; Lieven 2004, 94ff.

[27] In explaining the origins of the Awakenings, Starke and Finke argue that the Great Awakenings were not the result of a sudden new surge in piety, but of a "far more plausible" supply-side innovation (Stark and Finke 2002, 33). It is not clear what the standard for plausibility here is.

[28] Swierenga 2007, 147; see also Jensen 1971.

[29] The other religions fought back; for example, the one example of direct political action by a Catholic bishop in US history occurred when an infuriated Bishop John Hughes competed in a state election in 1841 to demand funding for Catholic schools, costing the Democrats seats in the New York Assembly (Hennessey 2007, 250).

tors; they could be participants in this new drama. All it took was for this realization to migrate from the religious sphere to the political—not a great distance in those days—and people were fully prepared for the fiery language of Thomas Paine in his pamphlets and Patrick Henry in his oratory. Both of them used the language that had already been popularized by the revivals."[30] In the First Great Awakening of the 1730s, the Puritan ancien régime and the "revolutionaries" (the itinerant ministers who fired up the crowds and created this extraordinary religious movement) used biblical arguments to make their case and mobilize supporters. This disruptive and passionate movement gave religion its standing as a witness and catalyst of the American Revolution, as "the first trans-American experience" of popular mobilization,[31] and in the millennial passions it excited among the revival crowds.[32]

The Second Great Awakening of the mid-1830s generated "much of the color and texture of American patriotism—its moralism, its missionary spirit, its commingling of Christian and national brotherhood."[33] This evangelical explosion[34] also helped to make America into a "Christian Nation," with a new commitment to faith as a way of countering the potential dilution of Christian identity through the opening up of the frontier and the migration that followed.[35] This religious revival further created a moral movement: abolition. Supporters of slavery and abolitionists alike used biblical arguments to bolster their cases,[36] as arguments raged within churches. These revivals all emphasized piety and morality, further making religion a prevalent basis for American political discourse.[37] Most popular movements were religious in motivation and character.[38] In other words, religious participation gave rise to an American identity and to a shared political language.

---

[30] McKenna 2007, 65.

[31] Morone 2003, 100.

[32] Millennial thought has changed: in the nineteenth century and earlier, religious millenarians assumed that secular society has to first develop a thousand years of peace and justice—ending slavery, ending colonial rule—before Jesus would come back to reign. By the late twentieth century, millennial thought now predicted that Jesus will come first—and the thousand years of peace and justice will follow. I am grateful to Jim Morone for this point.

[33] McKenna 2007, 80.

[34] Evangelical Methodists were the main force behind the Second Great Awakening, and the main beneficiary, going from around 65,000 adherents in 1800 to 1.75 million in 1860 (Wills 2007, 288; see also Noll 2002).

[35] Hughes 2004, 71.

[36] See Morone 2003, chap. 4.

[37] Thomas 1989, 69–70; see also Swierenga 2007, 155ff.

[38] Hatch 2007, 93.

Subsequently, this dominance of Protestantism gave way to greater pluralism and a narrative of "Judeo-Christian tradition"[39] that precluded (or at least papered over) the pervasive anti-Catholic bias and anti-Semitism of the nineteenth and early twentieth centuries. The Judeo-Christian tradition, the great unifier of American national identity, is a recent invention, largely the creation of the American military experience in World War II and "the spiritual side of the democratic ethos."[40] After the sinking of the USAT *Dorchester*, and its four Protestant, Jewish, and Catholic chaplains drowning while praying together, the military not only promulgated the new ecumenical invention but also developed a standard operating procedure for common worship in the armed forces.[41] This "Judeo-Christian tradition" served to integrate the religious diversity within the fighting forces and to broaden the set of religions that could lay claim to moral authority and enable those claims to resonate more broadly. The National Conference of Christians and Jews, political elites, and theologians further championed the notion.[42] Cultural events such as the Freedom Train promoted the idea of a nation that was inclusive and unified.[43] The result was that "during and after World War II, the long-standing equation in public discourse of 'Americanism' with Protestantism gave way rapidly, if incompletely, to the notion that the US was a Judeo-Christian, 'tri-faith,' or broadly 'God-fearing' nation."[44] By the 1950s, Will Herberg noted that "Americanness today entails religious identification as Protestant, Catholic, or Jew in a way and to a degree unprecedented in our history."[45] Above all, religion once again suffused American identity, this time as an explicit rebuttal of "godless communism," throughout the 1940s and 1950s.[46]

This is not to say acceptable religious categories simply expanded without contestation, either in the nineteenth or the twentieth centuries.

[39] Lipset 1963.

[40] Moore 2004, 123.

[41] Moore 2004, 123.

[42] Silk 1988.

[43] Reminiscent of the peregrinations of the portraits of the Virgin Mary in Poland and Croatia, the train, carrying over one hundred original documents ranging from Jefferson's Draft of the Declaration of Independence to Lincoln's Gettysburg Address traveled to all forty-eight states in 1948–49, to enormous celebrations. An estimated 3.5 million Americans saw the exhibit (Wall 2008, 3).

[44] Wall 2008, 9–10.

[45] Herberg 1983 [1960], 258.

[46] In 1954 a Congressional Resolution included "under God" in the Pledge of Allegiance, first written in 1892, after pressure from the Daughters of the American Revolution and the Knights of Columbus. The first Prayer Breakfast, held annually for political leaders and international delegates in Washington, DC, was held in 1953, and every president since Eisenhower has participated.

In 1960, John F. Kennedy still had to reassure nervous voters and religious leaders that he was an American first and a Catholic second, and his loyalty was not divided between the United States and the Vatican. (At a meeting of Protestant leaders convened to discuss Kennedy's Catholicism, for example, Rev. Norman Vincent Peale worried that "our American culture is at stake . . . I don't say it won't survive, but it won't be what it was."[47]) Religious leaders could be lukewarm; the Catholic hierarchy was especially resistant to the "Judeo-Christian tradition," anxious that such cooperation would imply all religions were equally valid.[48] The "tradition" itself may have been as mythical as it was empirically scarce,[49] but it pervaded the national imagination. Even vehement critics of the concept, and its papering over of historical injustice and real theological differences, acknowledged its ubiquity and importance.[50]

In the absence of a religious monopoly, the Judeo-Christian tradition served as the basis for a broad religious identification with American national identity. Political and religious arguments accordingly invoked this national myth throughout the twentieth century. Protestants and Catholics alike "learned to play the twentieth-century game of appealing to the nation's religious heritage, but in a purely ceremonial way."[51] After World War II, foreign and domestic enemies were denounced as "godless communists" and thus anti-American, fusing political opposition and religious heresy. Its proponents could be brutal; Senator Joseph McCarthy vowed that a communist conspiracy aimed "at the total obliteration of the Judeo-Christian civilization."[52] Ronald Reagan's use of religious rhetoric "evoked a deep sense of nationalism-patriotism."[53] In the 1990s and 2000s, many conservative politicians on the federal level now emphasized, as President George W. Bush did, that "the goal of the nation" should be to build a "culture of life" and the "sanctity of marriage" (concepts first used by Pope John Paul II and the Catholic Church).[54] The

---

[47] *Time*, September 19, 1960, http://www.time.com/time/magazine/article/0,9171,826609 –1,00.html, accessed May 30, 2012. More than one hundred Protestant clergy and lay leaders signed a statement in the fall of 1960 arguing that no Catholic president could ever fully turn away from the Catholic Church or his loyalty to the Vatican (Kosmin and Lachman 1993, 169).

[48] Wall 2008, 79.

[49] Mark Silk and Andrew Walsh argue that the coexistence of Jewish and Christian identities was limited to the mid-Atlantic for most of the twentieth century, largely because the highest concentrations of Jews live in the area (Silk and Walsh 2008, 210).

[50] Cohen 1971, 200.

[51] Marsden 2007, 465.

[52] Silk and Walsh 2008, 210.

[53] Roof 2009, 290.

[54] March 17, 2005, White House press release, cited in http://mediamatters.org/research /2007/09/20/cameron-described-schiavo-case-as-face-off-betw/139876, accessed August 12,

Judeo-Christian tradition continued to justify moral arguments for policies; the Defense of Marriage Act of 1996, for example, which precluded the federal recognition of same-sex marriage, was justified as a protection of "normal" marriage and of the "Judeo-Christian moral tradition" underpinning American society.[55]

These foundational myths amalgamated moral and political rhetorics and further defined the essence of an *American* identity. The boundaries of the Judeo-Christian tradition also help to explain why some religions have found such difficulty gaining acceptance: Islam, for example. It is not just the case that fewer Americans know Muslims, as Robert Putnam and David Campbell argue, and that this lack of contact prevents greater comity.[56] After all, Muslims and Jews each comprise roughly 1–2% of the American population. It is that Muslims, Buddhists, and certainly atheists are not part of the Judeo-Christian tradition, and its identification with Americanness.[57] For similar reasons, Mormonism is controversial, and the crux of the debate in in the United States has been not whether it is a religion (as is the case with Scientology in Germany, for example), but whether it is a *Christian* religion.[58] As one skeptical analyst noted, "the primary effect of the term was exclusion rather than inclusion . . . this newly coined Judeo-Christian tradition sought to exclude all others— practitioners of Asian religious, Mormons, Pentecostals, Jehovah's Witnesses, and the like—from the realm of 'American' religion."[59]

In short, an invented tradition identified who could legitimately assert moral authority in American politics in the twentieth and twenty-first centuries. This is a subtler, and more tenuous, intertwining of nationalism and religion than in the other cases examined here, but a powerful myth nonetheless. Given the pervasiveness of the identification of religion and national identity, and the shared use of religious language by all sides, political parties have not challenged the churches' right to become politically involved, or criticized their positions. Religious authorities were able to influence politics, first by forming interdenominational myths

---

2013. The term *culture of life* featured most prominently in the 2005 case of Terri Schiavo, a brain-dead woman whose husband wanted to take her off life support, against the wishes of the rest of her family.

[55] *New York Times*, July 13, 1996, accessed online February 17, 2010.

[56] Putnam and Campbell 2010, 505ff.

[57] When asked about feelings toward religious groups on a "feeling thermometer," Jews, Catholics, and Evangelicals all scored in the same "warm" range of 61–63, while Muslims received the "coldest" score, of 40 (with atheists receiving 41, Mormons 48, Hindus 50, and Buddhists 53) (Pew Research Center, American Trends Panel, wave 4, May 30–June 30, 2014, available at http://www.pewforum.org/2014/07/16/how-americans-feel-about-religious-groups/, accessed August 4, 2014.)

[58] Givens 2004; Mason 2011.

[59] Balmer 2006, 206.

and coalitions (with the willing assistance of secular actors), and then by forming coalitions with political parties. In the absence of fusion of one nation with one denomination, such efforts were legitimated by a much broader national identification with an invented religious tradition. Yet as we will see, an important difference over time lay in who used religious rhetoric—it had become partisan. While politicians of various stripes spoke the language of religion throughout American history, the Right would eventually capture it in the late twentieth century.

Policy Influence

Fusion allowed American churches to wield moral authority to influence policy. Religious diversity and contestation, however, meant that rather than one denomination asserting itself, several would compete (and eventually ally) to influence politics. Moreover, institutional firewalls constrained the tactics of policy influence. The constitutional separation of church and state has been found to sustain an unregulated religious market with higher rates of religious participation and a flowering of multiple denominations.[60] That same separation of church and state, however, also precluded the kind of national-level institutional access we saw in Poland and Ireland. Instead, interdenominational alliances influenced policy through partisan politics: forming coalitions with, and then coming to power within, political parties—in effect gaining access to political parties rather than to the state. In particular, a coalition of conservative Evangelicals and Catholics has colonized the Republican Party, as partisan activists, authors of party platforms, and vetters of political candidates. Fusion, moral authority, and channels of influence are all evident in the United States—but in distinct forms.

Religious competition further meant that religious leaders could not ignore the wishes of their faithful, and instead had to be more responsive, for fear of losing their followers to other churches. This was especially the case for Protestant denominations, where relatively small doctrinal differences meant that church leaders constantly had to worry about defections and conversions. (Since Catholics face higher conversion costs—Catholic apostates face more theological and community opprobrium for leaving their religion than most Protestants would—their leaders can afford to be less sensitive to the opinions of the faithful, in the United States and elsewhere.) In turn, denominations could not claim political power without a sizeable group of loyal adherents; these were needed for the survival of the denomination, for influence within an interdenominational alliance, and for electoral strength. As a result, churches did not

---

[60] Finke and Stark 1992; Finke and Stark 1998; Clark 2010.

take up some theologically compelling but unpopular issues, such as divorce. Competition also insulated religious groups in general from the costs of overt political activity; those disappointed with their religious leaders' political acts could leave for a different denomination without depressing the overall moral authority of churches.

Religious and political actors in the United States historically entered into coalitions that crusaded for various social and political issues, and political movements from all sides have used religious language. The conservative Christian alliance we see today is just the most recent manifestation—and differs from its predecessors in that only the Right now speaks in a religious register. The Whig Party of the early nineteenth century was a natural political home for pietists seeking to "purge the world of sin."[61] Major reform movements of the nineteenth century, such as the anti-slavery or temperance movements, had an evangelical component[62]—as did the hostility against the influx of Catholic and Jewish immigrants in the second half of the nineteenth century. Prior to the 1920s, conservative theology and *progressive* politics joined in campaigns for abolition, Prohibition, Comstockery, and so on. In the 1920s realignment brought together conservative theology and politics, a "vastly important development that would reach fruition fifty-five years later when conservative evangelicals helped put Ronald Reagan in the White House."[63]

In the postwar period, progressive churches, civil society organizations, and the Democratic Party joined forces to push for civil rights and equality in employment in the 1960s, mobilizing especially around the 1964 Civil Rights Act and the 1965 Voting Rights Act. Umbrella groups such as the Leadership Conference on Civil Rights brought together the NAACP, black labor organizations, and religious groups. Federations of Jewish organizations, such as the American Jewish Congress and the National Jewish Community Relations Advisory Council, and the United States Catholic Conference supported and mobilized for these efforts along with liberal groups like Americans for Democratic Action and labor unions.[64] Protestant and Catholic clergy and nuns led regular rallies near Capitol Hill during a crucial period during the crafting of the 1964 Civil Rights Act. These alliances on the Left successfully pushed for legislation in areas such as civil rights or fair employment "by linking procedure to

---

[61] Swierenga 2009, 75.

[62] The Republican Party that emerged from the joining of a strongly anti-slavery Republican Party with the equally anti-Catholic Know Nothings after 1856 "had a strong Puritan-evangelical component, bent on regulating society according to Christian principles" (Marsden 2007, 462). See also Swierenga 2009, 80ff.

[63] McKenna 2007, 234.

[64] Gillon 1987; Plotke 1996.

the interests of burgeoning social movements and by placing the issue on the national agenda."[65] These groups used the moral authority of religion to appeal to the better angels of public opinion, and to lobby individual members of Congress (sometimes on the steps of the Capitol), rather than by threatening to withhold partisan votes or public support.

Yet two decades later, in the 1980s, similar mainline Protestant-Catholic-Jewish alliances were unable to prevent welfare state retrenchment under Reagan, shape US policy in Central America, or preclude further nuclear armament. Part of the reason was a new partisan alliance on the Right between conservative Christian groups and the Republican Party. This new partisan alliance helped to capture the language of religion for the Right. Conservative religious groups allied with the Republicans—and then subsequently went on to transform the Republican Party itself.

There was nothing preordained about this coalition; even very religious working-class people, Catholics and Protestants, were mostly Democrats, given economic interests, the power of trade unions, and the mobilization of machine politics in some cities. However, the anti-communism of conservative Christians and the Republican Party had meant they long held elective affinities for each other.[66] The secularism and liberalism of the Democratic Party in the 1970s did make Republicans "a more attractive political option for religious conservatives, particularly the traditionally Democratic evangelical Protestants."[67] Yet Jimmy Carter himself was an evangelical,[68] and the evangelical movement had long-standing apolitical tendencies, with a doctrine skeptical of secular politics.[69] For decades many Evangelical Christians insulated themselves from formal politics as corrupt and too removed from the sacred. Jerry Falwell proclaimed in

[65] Zelizer 2004, 7.

[66] Williams 2010.

[67] Layman 2001, 43.

[68] I follow Randall Balmer's definition of Evangelicals as subscribing to three core tenets: the importance of individual conversion experience, the emphasis on the authority of the Biblical scripture, and the importance of evangelization, or sharing one's faith (Balmer 2006, xviii–xix). "Conservative Christians" refers to politically and theologically conservative Evangelicals and others: Southern Baptists, other Baptists, Missouri Synod Lutherans, Assemblies of God, Pentecostals, LDS, Church of Christ, and the traditional Roman Catholics. Critically, evangelical Christians are diverse in their religious convictions and their political views; they are more likely than other Protestants *on average* to vote Republican and to oppose abortion, homosexuality, or pornography. However, the majority of evangelical Christians are not consistently pro-life (14% oppose abortion in all circumstances, but 22% are consistently pro-choice), and the percentage convinced that homosexuality was wrong has been falling rapidly since the 1990s (Greeley and Hout 2006, 3 and 69).

[69] Layman 2001, 43; Guth 1983; Shupe and Stacey 1983; Guth et al. 1997.

1965 that he "would find it impossible to stop preaching the pure saving gospel of Jesus Christ, and begin doing anything else—including fighting communism, or participating in civil-rights reforms" (a statement that conveniently ignored his earlier defense of segregation and denunciations of *Brown v. Board of Education* as against God's will).[70] Pat Robertson similarly refused to campaign (for his father) in 1966, and denounced partisan politics.[71] Finally, Evangelicals themselves were, and remain, quite pluralist in experience and belief. In the 1970s, for example, politically progressive and theologically conservative Evangelicals emphasized "anti-war, civil rights, anti-consumer, communal, New Left, and third-world principles, even as they stressed doctrinal and sexual fidelity,"[72] and a strong liberal strand is resurgent in the twenty-first century. Evangelicalism was and is as diverse as it is prominent in modern American culture.[73] And conservative Christians differ greatly among themselves in theology and in practice; it was considerably more difficult for fundamentalists, for example, to ally themselves with Catholics than for many Evangelicals.[74] As a result, while Evangelicals and conservative Christians more broadly were frequently involved in *local* morality policy, such as the sale of alcohol or the content of education, they historically shied away from *national* politics.

Yet the profound disappointment with the liberalism of the 1960s, the 1971 *Green v. Connally* decision (which rescinded tax-exempt status for segregationist institutions such as Bob Jones University and was perceived as unwarranted government interference in religious affairs) and the alarm over the 1973 *Roe v. Wade* decision legalizing abortion all mobilized conservative Christians. Many Evangelicals had also grown wealthier and ascended into the middle class. They now had the material resources to make political mobilization more feasible, just as they came in unwelcome contact with the pervasive sinfulness of their new neighbors in middle America. Meanwhile, Democrats were becoming more explicitly secular in their political appeals, and Catholics had already shown themselves to be politically diverse, giving Eisenhower 50%

---

[70] Quoted in Marsden 1982, 155.

[71] Wills 2007, 481.

[72] Swartz 2012, 3.

[73] See Miller 2014.

[74] Mainstream Evangelicals led by Billy Graham were more affiliated with the Republican Party than the fundamentalists led by Jerry Falwell, who became active politically later, and alienated many northern evangelicals and Southern Baptists. Finally, it took Pat Robertson to bring many Charismatics and Pentecostals into the conservative Christian Coalition (see Williams 2010, 5–6).

of their vote.[75] The confluence meant new opportunities for conservative politicians seeking religious allies.[76]

At the same time in the 1970s, the Republican Party faced a crisis. On the one hand, there was opportunity; demographic shifts meant that "after decades of dormancy, the one-party Democratic South was fragmenting and becoming a competitive two-party place."[77] On the other, the Republican Party saw Nixon forced out of office in 1974, and a new dominance in the House and Senate, as the Democrats had solidified control of Congress after the Watergate scandals. Within the Republican Party itself, new conflicts compounded the crisis. In short, the Republicans were a minority party in need of a new support base that would make them more competitive—and victorious.

Accordingly, it was not Evangelical clergy who formed the coalition between conservative Christians and the Republican Party, but secular conservative political operatives such as Richard Viguerie, Paul Weyrich (themselves both Catholics), and Howard Phillips. They convinced evangelical and conservative Protestant leaders such as Jerry Falwell, Pat Robertson, and Ed McAteer to enter politics, having met many of them and learned of their political anxieties through the Heritage Foundation and other gatherings.[78] In the 1970s, these secular "New Right" entrepreneurs aimed to make the Republican Party reliably conservative rather than to evangelize it or make it more religious. To gain control of the party, "conservatives needed to bring a new constituency into Republican politics that would provide consistent support for conservative candidates and policies. Evangelical Christians were a large, unattached constituency, and cultural conservatism provided a way to draw them into the GOP."[79] Republican Party operatives thus sought out Evangelical support, giving rise eventually to a partisan coalition that would also transform the party from within—and give rise to an unintended access to party institutions.

By 1979, three key organizations were in place: Moral Majority, Christian Voice, and the Religious Round Table, led by Jerry Falwell, Robert

[75] Steinfels 2007, 357.

[76] Balmer 2008 emphasizes *Green v. Connally*, while others such as Layman 2001 see *Roe v. Wade* as critical to mobilizing conservative Christians.

[77] Dochuk 2011, 329. Kevin Phillips, in *The Emerging Republican Majority* (1969), identified the Sunbelt as a key potential base for the Republican Party and argued for a racially, socially, and fiscally conservative set of policies to capture southern and southwestern voters.

[78] Dochuk 2011, 384.

[79] Layman 2001, 45.

Grant, and Ed McAteer, respectively.[80] Conservative evangelicals and fundamentalists became the mainstay of Moral Majority, Christian Voice, Concerned Women for America, the Freedom Council, and the American Coalition for Traditional Values, all of whom emerged after the 1970s to fight elite secularization, including the Equal Rights Amendment (ERA), access to contraceptives, and abortion.[81] These organizations began to engage in a full range of political activities, ranging from newsletters and seminars to voter registration to lobbying.[82] They shared strategies of indirect lobbying: rallying preachers around moral issues and counting on clergy to mobilize their flocks to flood congressional offices with letters and phone calls.[83]

It was a long way from the historical Evangelical denunciation of politics and political activity, and the 1942 founding of the National Association of Evangelicals (NAE) to "vigorously oppose modernity."[84] "The year of the Evangelical" was 1976, and by the late 1970s, the Evangelical ascension was thriving. With the presidency of Ronald Reagan, himself "more an evangelical's president than an evangelical president,"[85] politicians invoked religious values (and their own faith as a badge of suitability for office), religious leaders regularly appeared at meetings and demonstrations organized by political parties, and "piety and politics became almost passionate bedfellows."[86]

The emergence of a conservative Catholic-Protestant alliance, for its part, was more cautious and gradual, hindered as it was by mutual doctrinal antipathies and suspicions. Reagan himself had earlier helped to bring together conservative Catholics and Protestants, if inadvertently. Reagan's signature of the abortion law in California in 1967 prompted an outpouring of Catholic criticism and brought about a rapprochement with conservative Protestants, who admired the intense commitment of

---

[80] Casanova 1994, 147. Each of these appealed to a different audience: Moral Majority was a personal instrument of political activism of Jerry Falwell. Christian Voice was initially an extension of anti-gay and anti-pornography groups that united laymen and ministers, including some Catholics and Mormons, and relied heavily on Pat Robertson's TV program, the *700 Club*, to reach a broader audience. The Religious Roundtable was designed to appeal to conservative clergymen and train them to enter politics. See Guth in Green et al. 1996, 16–17.

[81] Hertzke 1988, 33 and 40; Williams 2010, 106ff.

[82] Marty and Appleby 1992, 71.

[83] These organizations' direct lobbying was far less effective, as was their support for the "Family Protection Act," "a compendium of virtually every New Rights social policy objective that has languished in Congress since 1979." Such efforts launched massive (and mainline Protestant) opposition, as was the case with the school prayer bill (Guth 1996, 18).

[84] Kosmin and Lachman 1993, 186.

[85] Miller 2014, 64.

[86] Demerath 1991, 28; Domke and Coe 2008.

the Catholics, even if they did not necessarily share the same views on abortion.[87] Evangelicals and Catholics also worked together on anti-obscenity campaigns and anti-pornography campaigns on the *state* level in the 1970s.[88]

As Evangelicals were becoming more active politically in the 1976, the Catholic Church began to pursue a more direct strategy of lobbying politicians and reframing issues as moral, after years of watching politics from the sidelines.[89] (Ironically, American Catholics themselves, increasingly unmoored from their ethnic identities as Italian American or Irish American Catholics, began to leave their church.[90]) Increasingly emphasizing cultural issues at the expense of social or economic justice from the 1970s onward, Catholic bishops in the United States launched a right-to-life movement that vetted political candidates starting with the 1976 campaign, and then entered the electoral fray "shamelessly" in 1984,[91] screening candidates and issuing proscriptions against voting for pro-choice candidates. In 2004 and 2008, some bishops stood ready to deny church sacraments to pro-choice Catholic candidates.

By the 1990s, traditional Catholics joined their Protestant brethren in a *conservative Christian coalition*, "drawn by the same blending of morality, faith, and nation that Reagan offered."[92] Evangelicals and Catholics joined forces at the national level in the early 1990s after discovering they had liberal enemies in common: advocates of multiculturalism, secular humanism, and sexual liberation (including abortion). In 1994, after a series of meetings, religious leaders and theologians such as Charles Colson, Pat Robertson, and Richard John Neuhaus, several bishops and philosophers, and the leaders of Campus Crusade for Christ, Wheaton College, Assemblies of God, and others signed "Evangelicals and Catholics Together," a statement of spiritual ecumenism and doctrinal agreement, largely devoted to abortion.

The alliance had its roots in the 1973 *Roe v. Wade* decision, not because Evangelicals were necessarily as consistently and intensely against abortion as the Catholics had been, but because they eventually viewed *Roe* as "an assault on the family and the nation's Christian identity."[93] Thus Christian Family Renewal, led by the Catholic journalist Murray Norris, already gathered Catholics and Evangelicals to attack the ERA and *Roe v. Wade* as threatening families, while Baptist fundamentalists

[87] Dochuk 2011, 346.
[88] Dochuk 2011, 340.
[89] Steinfels 2007, 350.
[90] Putnam and Campbell 2010, 297.
[91] Casanova 1994, 199.
[92] Domke and Coe 2008, 4.
[93] Williams 2010, 119.

and neo-Pentecostals began to reconcile.[94] Similarly, individual mediators, such as Father Richard John Neuhaus,[95] helped to midwife the interdenominational cooperation that had its roots in aligned political and moral interests.[96] The interdenominational coalition was also fostered by an ecumenical rapprochement within the Catholic Church hierarchy after Vatican II.[97]

Conservative Protestants and Catholics worked hand in hand on several morality policy targets of the Republican Party—abortion, stem cell research, and gay rights—through the joint efforts of their proxy and allied lay organizations. They articulated a new set of demands centered on the "culture of life" and pushed for more restrictive policies on abortion, access to contraceptives, same-sex marriage, and stem cell research largely through a coalition with (and the takeover of) the Republican Party—but frequently with the acquiescence of the Democrats, who, too, had to contend with a religious electorate (especially the Latino Roman Catholic vote, perceived as critical to the party's future and conservative on these issues).[98] Their growing power meant that if Bill Clinton's presidential campaign, rich with religious imagery, featured a very Protestant "New Covenant,"[99] George H. W. Bush, himself a mainline Protestant, opened his re-election campaign in 1992 with a speech peppered with references to the "sanctity of life," a phrasing distinctively used by the Catholic Church.[100]

The electoral ramifications were quickly apparent. The alignment of conservative Christian (Catholic and Protestant) opinion over moral issues, and the polarization between Republican and Democratic parties already meant that by the 1990s, many Catholics shifted their support to the Republican Party. The conservative Christian coalition transformed

[94] Dochuk 2011, 340.

[95] Neuhaus traveled from Lutheranism to Catholicism, and from a progressive civil rights supporter and anti-Vietnam activist to a neoconservative. He authored *The Naked Public Square* (1984), which argued for a greater role for religious values in public debates.

[96] Miller 2014, 126–27.

[97] In one interpretation, the collapse of the Soviet Union in 1991, and with it the disappearance of the threat of communism, also spurred a rethinking within the Republican Party, and the focus on morality politics was an attractive substitute for the anti-communism of the postwar era (Sullivan 1998).

[98] Although unexamined here, the conservative Christian Coalition also played an important role in transforming foreign policy beginning in the early 1990s: making religious freedom a "core aim of American foreign policy, to be monitored and promoted by the State Department" (Croft 2007, 696), funding faith-based organizations and transforming rules on their participation in foreign aid (Hurd 2012, 950), and developing its own norm entrepreneurs and critiques of foreign policy, including Bush's War on Terror (Croft 2007, 692).

[99] Domke and Coe 2008.

[100] Kosmin and Lachman 1993, 158.

the landscape of religious-partisan loyalties, drawing Catholics into the Republican Party and undermining their support for the Democrats.[101] Both Evangelical and Catholic voters shifted: "predominantly Democratic during the 1960s, committed evangelicals began to abandon the Democrats in the 1970s, became increasingly loyal to the Republican Party during the 1980s and 1990s, and now heavily identify with the GOP in the 2000s." Meanwhile, "overwhelmingly Democratic during the 1960s, committed Catholics as now as likely to identify with the Republicans as with the Democrats."[102] Among Christians, a "traditionalist/ modernist" cleavage pitting traditional morality against more liberal interpretations began to supplant Protestant-Catholic differences.[103]

This interdenominational, conservative Christian coalition was a sign of how far the Catholic and conservative Protestant activists had come; the latter's suspicion of the national loyalties of the former began with late nineteenth-century immigration of Irish, Italian, and Polish Catholics and continued through the presidential campaigns of Al Smith and John F. Kennedy. Yet if Kennedy had to prove his independence from the Vatican in 1960, John Kerry in 2004 had to defend his pro-choice views after the US Conference of Bishops threatened to withdraw communion to Kerry and to any other politician who did not promise to outlaw abortion, and further instructed the faithful that "politicians have an obligation in conscience to work toward correcting morally defective laws," abortion especially.[104]

However, because of its diverse nature, the conservative Christian coalition was never a tightly coherent movement, and it was "uneasy, a pragmatic marriage born of overlapping interests rather than genuine ardor."[105] As we will see, at several points theological disagreements and differing priorities gave rise to conflict between member denominations. Catholics and Protestants disagreed over the death penalty, assisted reproduction technologies, and contraception. Catholic bishops protested cuts in social services and the nuclear arms buildup, rather than focusing

---

[101] From the 1930s to 1950s, the chairman of the DNC was an Irish Catholic from the Midwest or Northeast, an emissary to the Irish-run Democratic urban machines. Both parties have had sections that do outreach, mobilization, and constituency service work for various ethnicities and religions, to demonstrate their commitment to these constituencies, or as in the case of the early Colored Division of the DNC in the 1930s, a party's aspirations to lock in a group. I am grateful to Rob Mickey for pointing this out.

[102] McTague and Layman 2009, 336.

[103] This division began to take place among Evangelicals in the 1980s. For Catholics and mainline Protestants, it emerged in the 1990s (Kellstedt et al. 2007).

[104] Domke and Coe 2008, 7; Balmer 2008, 151.

[105] Balmer 2006, xxvii.

on abortion or other "moral issues" alone.[106] Moreover, many individual Protestants and Catholics were mutually suspicious and skeptical of working together, despite concerted efforts such as Ralph Reed's Catholic Alliance to reassure them.[107]

These two nested alliances, an interdenominational partnership of conservative Christians and a coalition of these Christians and the Republican Party, were the critical element of religious influence on policy in the United States in the late twentieth century. They did not rely on institutional access per se; while religious representatives gave testimony before congressional committees, and politicians and clergy consulted through back channels, we rarely see the clerical writing of legislature, direct vetting of high-ranking officials, or other legislative input, other than through political party allies. The strictures of separation of church and state in the United States made such institutional access far less feasible— although the 2000–2008 administrations of President George W. Bush came close. They consulted Evangelical organizations affiliated with the Republican Party on morality policy and legislative bills.[108] Religious conservatives also staffed sensitive posts such as the White House Office of Personnel, Centers for Disease Control, Health and Human Services, and so on: "the White House was alive with piety."[109] Similarly, Patrick Henry College, an evangelical college drawing on the homeschool movement, "was able to secure 100 places for their evangelical students in the Bush Administration. Its purpose . . . is 'Grooming Politicians for Christ.' "[110] Yet even as the White House Office of Faith-Based and Community Initiatives, established by President George W. Bush in 2001, sought to finance faith-based social service delivery, it did not allow formal channels of feedback from religious groups to policy.[111]

---

[106] Williams 2010, 197.

[107] Williams 2010, 234. The founding of the Catholic Alliance, without a prior consultation with the US Bishops' Conference, was controversial; several bishops charged it would split "Catholics from their bishops" and undermine Catholic political efforts ("Truths and Untruths about the Catholic Alliance," *First Things*, February 1996, available at http://www .firstthings.com/article/2007/09/001-truths-and-untruths-about-the-catholic-alliance-33).

[108] Wills 2007, 498.

[109] Wills 2007, 499.

[110] Croft 2007, 698.

[111] Other Centers for Faith-Based and Community Initiatives (CFBCI) were founded in the Departments of Justice, Labor, Health and Human Services, Housing and Urban Development, Education, and Agriculture, as well as USAID. Federal funds could not be used to support religious activities such as prayer or worship and agencies could not discriminate on the basis of religion when providing services, even after the 2004 policy change that funded organizations that combined development or foreign aid with inherently religious activities and allowed them to engage in discriminatory hiring (Hurd 2012, 950). After repeated criticisms about the office's funding of various ministry efforts, and conflict with the

The power of this Republican-conservative Christian coalition derived instead from delivering a solid vote—and a subsequent colonization of the Republican Party by conservative Christians. Conservative religious groupings obtained the promise of policy concessions; the Republican Party welcomed a group of voters committed to the party. The share of Evangelicals in the population had increased, from 17% to 22% of US adults from 1972 to 2004.[112] Since 26% of American voters are self-described conservative Christians, and 40–45% are born again (1993–2000 GSS data), the largest religious group in the American electorate, they were well worth the attention.[113] And over time, Evangelicals and committed Catholics have become more conservative on moral issues.[114]

The Republican Party began to rely on these voters. Prior to the late 1960s, religiosity and politics were barely correlated with religious liberals and unchurched conservatives.[115] This was no longer the case by the end of the century; if until 1988 there was little difference in the voting patterns of religious attendees and nonattendees, by 1992 George H. W. Bush had won the vote of the churchgoers by a 20% margin.[116] Evangelicals accounted for a third of the Republican congressional vote in 1992, and close to 40% in 1996.[117] And these voters became a solid voting block: 80% of white Evangelicals voted for Ronald Reagan in 1984 and for George H. W. Bush in 1988.[118]

Thus "the Republicans have come to depend on Religious Right voters as their most reliable constituency."[119] And conservative religious leaders were fully aware they could withhold this resource from the party; in 1996, when Christian Action Network leader Martin Mawyer saw Bob Dole as inadequately attentive to cultural matters, he warned that "all we have to do on Election Day is stay home, and that's what an increasing number of pro-family, born-again voters plan to do this November."[120] Jerry Falwell issued similar threats: he would mobilize

---

doctrinal and proselytizing priorities of many of the religious groups involved, the Office was renamed the Office of Faith-Based and Neighborhood Partnerships under the Obama administration, and its focus shifted to foreign aid rather than domestic initiatives.

[112] Domke and Coe 2008, 22.

[113] Greeley and Hout 2006, 43; Kohut et al. 2000, 18.

[114] Kohut et al. 2000, 68.

[115] Putnam and Campbell 2010, 82.

[116] Gelman 2010, 84.

[117] Williams 2010, 8.

[118] Williams 2010, 206; Domke and Coe 2008, 30. Partly as a result of the coalition's concerted efforts, 30% of Republican voters were evangelical by the 2000s, and 15% were unaffiliated, while only 14% of Democratic voters were evangelical, and 16% were unaffiliated by 2004 (Domke and Coe 2008, 26).

[119] Balmer 2006, 169.

[120] Quoted in Layman 2001, 322.

voters and rally support for Ronald Reagan—but only if sufficient attention was paid to this electorate and its policy demands. Otherwise, the religious conservatives would "sit on their hands as they've been doing for the last 30 or 40 years."[121]

If the Republican Party has come to depend more on conservative Christians, those Christians have also become more Republican. By 2004, 56% of Evangelicals identified with the Republican Party, and 35% with the Democrats—a turnaround from the early 1970s, when the opposite held.[122] Similarly, the share of Catholics identifying with the Republican Party increased, to 39% by 2004. Churchgoers are more likely to vote for the Republican Party, a relationship that grows stronger with the level of income (and thus of potential political donations). Nonattendees (both rich and poor) are more likely to vote for Democrats.[123] An examination of voting preferences in the American National Election Studies from 1980 to 1994 shows that conservative Evangelicals in particular are more likely to vote Republican, even as moral issues were not decisive for other voters.[124] On morality issues, religious voters support Republicans, even though class and economics override the importance of abortion and homosexuality in actual voting.[125] Conversely, on issues raised by mainline denominations, such as immigration, the death penalty, foreign aid spending, there is virtually no difference between religious and nonreligious voters.[126]

Yet the *mechanisms* of this mobilization did not include overt politicking in America's churches; churches are the least common channels for direct political and partisan mobilization.[127] Very few ministers, even the most committed, tried to convince their parishioners from the pulpit—and when they did, the faithful did not listen.[128] The opposition to direct political mobilization by religious groups runs deep and wide in the United States: across various denominations, over 75% of respondents object to being told how to vote by their religious leaders.[129] Churches themselves were careful in their political activity, so as not to run afoul of tax regulations. Their activities had to be non-partisan: general voter registrations after Sunday services, hosting the signing of petitions for policies but not political candidates, public declarations support for policies but not candidates, and so on. Of course, such efforts could serve

---

[121] Falwell, quoted in Domke and Coe 2008, 17.
[122] Domke and Coe 2008, 22.
[123] Gelman 2010, 88–89; see also Greeley and Hout 2006, 40ff.
[124] Layman 1997.
[125] Gelman 2010; Greeley and Hout 2006; Kellstedt et al. 2007.
[126] Putnam and Campbell 2010, 386–88.
[127] Putnam and Campbell 2010, 430.
[128] Guth 1996, 21.
[129] Putnam and Campbell 2010, 421.

partisan purposes. Here, Jerry Falwell was instrumental in registering Evangelical voters in in the 1970s. When he found out only half had been registered, his response was to adopt a new mantra: "Get them saved, baptized, and registered."[130]

Proxy organizations, such as the United States Catholic Conference, tightly linked to the churches and espousing faithfully their views, had more leeway to mobilize petition-signing campaigns and to raise funds. Allied organizations such as umbrella coalitions (Americans for Life, Christian Coalition, Moral Majority, National Right to Life Committee) provided fund-raising and voter lists, and an extensive media presence that made clear their preferred candidates and policies. Various political action committees could engage in more explicit politicking; for example, the Red White and Blue Fund raised money from Evangelicals and conservative Catholics to fund candidates such as Rick Santorum in 2008, the Campaign for American Values mobilized these voters in 2012 with ads claiming President Obama would "force gay marriage," and so on.

Religious conservatives, and the concerted efforts of the conservative Christian alliance of the 1990s onward, have also been able to provide a critical informational subsidy to their legislators.[131] They offered a clear and coherent set of electoral demands to policy makers, resolving considerable uncertainty for many (and further concentrating the minds of politicians with the sheer numbers of religious conservatives). In general, legislators do not know their constituency preferences very clearly, and the median voter only loosely and conditionally influences legislative votes.[132] Not surprisingly, politicians are therefore biased toward a conservative status quo.[133] Legislators are more certain, and more likely to respond, in small, homogenous districts and over highly salient issues.[134] Further, legislators perceive resource-rich and well-organized constituencies far more clearly and accurately.[135] Legislators tend to respond to interest groups when they expect issues to recur, and when given interest groups "serve their information and propaganda needs better than the other informants, that is, they need evidence of lobbies' competitive advantage."[136]

Given these conditions, the conservative Christian coalition—resource rich, well organized, and with numerous and committed members—could

---

[130] Domke and Coe 2008, 17.
[131] Hall and Deardorff 2006.
[132] Miller and Stokes 1963; Fenno 1978; Miler 2007; Gerber and Lewis 2004.
[133] Lax and Phillips 2009.
[134] Fiorina 1974; Bartels 1991; Burstein 2003; Gerber and Lewis 2004; Miller 2007; Lax and Phillips 2009.
[135] Hansen 1991; Miller 2007.
[136] Hansen 1991, 13.

be highly effective. Given the growing importance of religion in American political life, the number of religious lobbies grew from sixteen in 1950 to over eighty by 1985.[137] But unlike mainline Protestant lobbying, the conservative religious efforts were clear and focused. For example, while the religious conservatives in the 1980s had a coherent and limited set of attainable objectives (abortion, school prayer, the Equal Rights Amendment), the mainline efforts of the time included food stamp cuts, aid to the Contras, civil rights, South African sanctions, foreign aid, international trade, nuclear strategy, military budgets, tax reform, social security, day-care funding, environmental protection, labor legislation, farm bills, and such.[138] If in the 2000s the main issues for the conservatives were abortion and gay marriage, the 2004 agenda of the mainline National Council of Churches included urban initiatives, racial justice, justice for women, economic and environmental justice, public funding of religious social services, migrant labor, international peace, and the battle against religious persecution.[139] This was not always the case; in the 1960s and thereafter, Catholic bishops and clergy had also spoken out on the war in Vietnam, social injustice, cuts in welfare—but found they had almost no effect.[140] In short, the conservative religious lobbies offered a cohesive and salient message, and they focused on issues on which their adherents had homogenous and intense preferences, backed up with considerable resources.

Beyond voting for the Republican Party, conservative Christians also transformed it by taking part in (and often dominating) Republican primaries, shaping the party platforms, and in directly creating pools of potential officeholders themselves. Such influence is critical; politicians frequently reflect the activists' preferences and do not need convincing to enact them.[141] The conservative Christian alliance has influenced party platforms on both the state and national level.[142] It has transformed party conventions, becoming the numerically dominant group at Republican Party Conventions.[143] If in 1984 they were 10% of the Republican Party Convention delegates, two decades later conservative Evangelicals were over 25%. Conservative Christian leaders vetted political candidates for high office. For example, in the fall of 2013, would-be presidential candidates such as Rand Paul and Ted Cruz met with such religious leaders, who were concerned chiefly with the candidates' religious credentials and

---

[137] Hertzke 1988, 5.
[138] Hertzke 1988, 5.
[139] Fowler et al. 2004, 113.
[140] Balmer 2008, 57–58.
[141] See Aldrich 1995; Cohen et al. 2008, Bawn et al. 2012.
[142] Conger 2010, 651.
[143] McTague and Layman 2009, 345.

their born-again status.[144] In short, conservative Christian groups have formed a coalition with the Republican Party and have gained access to and transformed the party from within.

As a result, conservative Christians exert considerable influence within the Republican Party and can claim credit for ballot initiatives and legislative measures limiting access to abortion, stem cell research, and same-sex marriage. To prove that the conservative Christian stances were a matter of principle and not simply political gain, the Republican Party further adopted religious and moral language in official party platforms and prioritized the very issues of concern to the conservative Christians: opposition to abortion, same-sex rights, and stem cell research in the name of natural law and of American values.[145] It further committed itself to a remolding of the Supreme Court and the judiciary to reflect conservative religious and political values.

Yet these efforts were of limited appeal to the electorate at large. Even during controversial elections, such as the 2004 presidential elections, which saw same-sex marriage initiatives on ballots in many states, same-sex marriage and abortion had no effect on voter decisions among Independents, in battleground states, or in states with gay marriage ballots. Only in the Sun Belt was there an effect, and even there, this impact of moral issues was minimal compared to the economy, the Iraq war, and terrorism.[146] As a result, the conservative Christian coalition, after years of providing electoral support to increasingly conservative politicians, failed to obtain many of its key policy aims at the *federal* level, even as states restricted abortion and banned same-sex marriage.

Moreover, many of the legal achievements were subject to judicial review, where the coalition had far less direct influence. As we will see, the judiciary proved an important obstacle; in a series of decisions from 1961 to 1971, the Supreme Court removed religion from schools and precluded public funding for it. *Roe v. Wade* invalidated state prohibitions on abortion. Finally, the Court struck down provisions of the Defense of Marriage Act in June 2013. Not surprisingly, religious conservatives "blamed the Court for many of their troubles, indeed for all the many things wrong with the country."[147] They saw control of the Supreme Court as a critical issue and a main motivation for the partisan coalition; Republican electoral victories would be key to ensuring that control.

This kind of a partisan coalition has hurt Catholic churches in Italy and Croatia. Yet in the United States, the moral authority of religion

---

[144] *New York Times*, November 1, 2013.
[145] Domke and Coe 2008, 103.
[146] Hillygus and Shields 2005.
[147] Wills 2007, 533.

remains. Why did the conservative Christian churches not pay the reputational costs of political coalitions? After all, Evangelical churches had historically rejected politics and should have thus paid the steepest price for betraying this earlier stance. Yet this is exactly where the religious diversity of the United States comes in; because moral authority is diffused, so is the cost to individual church reputations. There was no single church hierarchy to speak for religious interests; instead, diverse groups of churches chose to ally with the broader conservative movement, without central guidance (or responsibility). Anyone dissatisfied with their church's political activity could simply move to a different, more politically and spiritually sympathetic church—or found a new one, in a spirit of religious innovation that is impossible in the Roman Catholic Church or the mainline Protestant denominations. This is another reason why, even as mainline Protestants have declined in religious observance, Evangelicals have remained religiously observant and Evangelical churches have proliferated since the 1980s.[148] Political coalitions thus posed fewer costs.[149] In terms of the model, the depreciation rate of the churches' moral authority is not as high as it is for a monopoly church. The diffusion of moral authority means that the individual responsibility of churches is blurred—and their collective moral authority endures.

The churches in the religious coalition with the Republican Party did pay a price for their partisan coalition; they acquired a poor reputation with *nonadherents*. The image of conservative Christians was hurt, since "evangelical and fundamentalist Christians are linked by voters not only to staunch conservatism, but also to the Republican Party, with negative views of fundamentalists growing more connected to negative evaluations of the GOP and its candidates."[150] The percentage of Americans with no religious preferences doubled from 7% to 14% in the 1990s, becoming "unchurched" in the process, apparently reflecting disappointment with church participation in domestic politics.[151] Yet religious conservatives were unlikely to leave the Republican Party because they had no other political alternative, and because their considerable investments in the party have paid off, with influence over party nominations, the party platform, and the party machinery.[152] The result was a disaffected

---

[148] Putnam and Campbell 2010, 103–13.

[149] For a different reason, historically black churches have not paid a price for their political involvement; their adherents saw them as representing a minority's interest against the repression of the majority and provided the material support, physical space, and spiritual sustenance for an oppressed group, much as the Catholic Church had done in Poland or in Ireland.

[150] Campbell et al. 2011, 44.

[151] Hout and Fischer 2002.

[152] Layman 2001, 340.

and increasingly unchurched Left, and a committed and conservative religious presence in the Republican Party—and a conservative Christian coalition that has largely retained its moral authority.

Below, I examine how the conservative Christian alliance, and its coalition with the Republican Party, played out in the five issue domains. In each, religious competition, powerful courts, and the importance of the states in the American federal system complicate the story—but also show the importance of religious moral authority and the limitations of partisan coalitions.

Abortion

Opposition to abortion is at the core of contemporary conservative Christian policy demands. Its abolition is a key aim itself and a symbol of a broader set of values, "a bundle of beliefs that, grouped together, can be called moral traditionalism."[153] The profound differences in worldviews on fetal life, family, and gender roles Kristin Luker described[154] between the pro-life and the pro-choice camp persist. Yet the opposition to abortion—and its politicization—is relatively new in American politics, dating to the liberalization of state laws in the 1960s and the *Roe v. Wade* decision of 1973. Even Roman Catholic leaders, who consistently opposed abortion, were not vocal until the 1960s: "as long as conservative religious leaders believed that most Americans shared their opposition to abortion, they saw little need to address the subject."[155]

Historically, prior to 1845 abortions before the "quickening" (detectable fetal movement) were widely permitted, but by the turn of the century nearly all states had passed laws restricting the procedure. The campaign to restrict abortion was led by orthodox physicians seeking to professionalize medicine, and targeted the "irregular" physicians (especially midwives) who generally performed abortions.[156] There was little political opposition to the restrictions, which in most cases limited abortions to life-threatening circumstances. As a result, illegal abortions were widespread during the early and mid-twentieth century. In the 1960s, estimates of illegal abortions ranged between 200,000 and 1.2 million annually and were believed to account for 20% of deaths related to pregnancy and childbirth.[157]

[153] Putnam and Campbell 2010, 390.
[154] Luker 1986.
[155] Williams 2010, 112.
[156] Tietze, Forrest, and Henshaw 1988; Luker 1986.
[157] Tietze, Forrest, and Henshaw 1988, 473.

Yet in contrast to the other cases discussed in this book, the major policy actors in liberalizing abortion laws were not national legislatures. Instead, the courts and *state* legislatures shaped access to abortion, drawing the contempt of evangelical leaders (in the words of Jerry Falwell, "nine men, by majority vote, said it was ok to kill unborn children").[158] A major impetus for law reform in some states was the Supreme Court's 1965 *Griswold v. Connecticut* decision, which ruled that a state law prohibiting the sale of contraceptives was unconstitutional because it violated rights to privacy. Between 1965 and 1973, fourteen states liberalized their laws to allow abortion in the case of rape, incest, or threat to the mother's health, while four (New York, Alaska, Hawai'i and Washington) allowed abortions on demand. One state, Pennsylvania, became more restrictive during this period and continued to lead the nation in restrictions after *Roe*. Rosemary Nossiff attributes this to the unusual strength of the Pennsylvania Catholic Conference, which enjoyed substantial informal influence through the unreformed municipal party machines in that state.[159]

In 1973 *Roe* invalidated all state anti-abortion laws, a decision reaffirmed by the courts on several occasions. The ruling left substantial room for state regulation, especially in the second trimester when abortion is often more dangerous to the woman than childbirth. Two additional Supreme Court decisions would grant states more autonomy: *Webster v. Reproductive Health Services* (1989) and *Planned Parenthood of Southeastern Pennsylvania v. Casey* (1992). These allowed states to restrict access to abortion so long as such legislation did not pose an "undue burden" on women. A set of legal decisions defined the legal and institutional space within which abortion would be debated; religion would provide much of the *content* of this debate.

Initially, religious opinion remained mixed after *Roe*. The Roman Catholic Church mobilized in opposition—but many Protestant churches did not. The Catholic hierarchy had long objected to abortion but became politically active on this issue only in the 1960s, pressuring state legislatures to delegalize or constrict abortion.[160] These efforts intensified after the 1968 *Humanae Vitae* papal encyclical, which "absolutely excluded" abortions and led the bishops to declare that opposition to abortion was a "defining aspect of the Catholic identity."[161] Accordingly,

---

[158] Quoted in Domke and Coe 2008, 102.

[159] Nossiff 1995.

[160] Williams 2010, 113.

[161] "Human Life in Our Day: A Statement Issued by the National Conference of Catholic Bishops." *Priests for Life*. November 15, 1968. http://www.priestsforlife.org/magisterium /bishops/68–11–15humanlifeinourdaynccb.htm.

the Roman Catholic Church opposed the movement to liberalize abortion laws from its outset.[162]

Most conservative Protestant churches delayed. First, many denominations, such as the Southern Baptists, lacked a clear theological position on abortion, and so many pastors remained silent. In 1970, 80% of Southern Baptist preachers opposed abortion on demand, but 70% favored abortion to protect the physical or mental health of the woman—and 64% allowed abortion in the case of fetal defects.[163] The Southern Baptist Convention even approved a resolution in 1971 that called for the legalization of abortion in some circumstances.[164] *Mainline* Protestant clergy, for their part, supported the *liberalization* of abortion laws. Second, and relatedly, many Protestants viewed abortion as a "Catholic issue"[165]—and many fundamentalists refused to join Catholics in the pro-life movement, founding their own isolated organizations instead.

Yet *Roe v. Wade* eventually galvanized conservative Christians by distilling the dissatisfaction with women's liberation, the Equal Rights Amendment, and government interference in schooling into one clear target. By 1974, Robert Holbrook had founded Baptists for Life and joined four Catholic cardinals in testifying against abortion before Congress.[166] In 1979, as part of their effort to mobilize conservative Christian voters, Paul Weyrich and Richard Viguerie organized several pro-life political action committees—the Right to Life PAC, the Life Amendment PAC, and the American Life League—to support Jerry Falwell's Moral Majority, and thus the coalition with the Republican Party. By the late 1980s, the Southern Baptist Convention founded the Christian Life Commission and publicly joined the fight against abortion. With the formation of the conservative Christian coalition, abortion became one of the clearest targets, and one to which conservative Christians remained passionately committed.

The national *partisan* politicization of abortion is just as recent a phenomenon. The Republican Party (much like their future evangelical allies) had not always opposed abortion; several Republican politicians headed the efforts to liberalize abortion laws in California, Colorado, and New York. Republican women were the stalwarts of pro-choice activism before *Roe*.[167] If anything, Republicans were *more* supportive than Democrats of abortion. In 1972, 68% of Republicans supported the

---

[162] Greenhouse and Siegel 2011, 2068.
[163] Williams 2010, 115.
[164] Putnam and Campbell 2010, 392.
[165] Dillon 1995; Southern Baptist Convention n.d.
[166] Williams 2010, 119.
[167] Williams 2010, 111.

statement "the decision to have an abortion should be made solely by a woman and her physician," compared with 58% of Democrats (at a time when a record high of 64% of Americans supported the full liberalization of abortion laws).[168] As late as 1976, three years after *Roe v. Wade*, the Republican national party platform was neutral on abortion. In an early attempt to gain the conservative religious vote, Richard Nixon reversed his pro-abortion stance in 1971, declaring that abortion on demand was incompatible with his "personal belief in the sanctity of human life— including the life of the yet unborn."[169] As part of a conscious effort to reframe himself as a cultural conservative, and to split a chunk of Catholic voters from the Democratic Party, Nixon sent a letter to the Archbishop of New York, Terence Cook, in May 1972 in full support of efforts to criminalize abortion in the state. He followed an advisor's suggestion that "favoritism toward things Catholic is good politics; there is a trade-off but it leaves us with the larger share of the pie."[170]

But it was only in 1980, during the presidential campaign that resulted in the election of Ronald Reagan, that both the Democratic and Republican Parties took a firmer side in their party platforms and in their election campaigns, and voters began to have a choice.[171] In hammer-

---

[168] See Greehouse and Siegel 2011, 2068. George Gallup, "Abortion Seen up to Woman, Doctor." *Washington Post*, August 25, 1972, A2.

[169] Nixon, Richard. 1971. "Statement about Policy on Abortions at Military Base Hospitals in the United States." *American Presidency Project*. April 3. http://nyti.ms/z0clgg.

[170] Memorandum from "Research" to the Attorney General H. R. Haldeman (October 5, 1971), in Hearings before the S. Select Comm. on Presidential Campaign Activities, 93d Cong. 4197, 4201 (1973).

[171] Putnam and Campbell 2010, 391. The 1980 Republican Party platform stated, "There can be no doubt that the question of abortion, despite the complex nature of its various issues, is ultimately concerned with equality of rights under the law. While we recognize differing views on this question among Americans in general—and in our own Party—we affirm our support of a constitutional amendment to restore protection of the right to life for unborn children." In contrast, its 1976 statement had simply noted, "The question of abortion is one of the most difficult and controversial of our time. It is undoubtedly a moral and personal issue but it also involves complex questions relating to medical science and criminal justice. There are those in our Party who favor complete support for the Supreme Court decision which permits abortion on demand. There are others who share sincere convictions that the Supreme Court's decision must be changed by a constitutional amendment prohibiting all abortions. Others have yet to take a position, or they have assumed a stance somewhere in between polar positions."

By the same token, in 1980 the Democratic Party platform stated that "the Democratic Party supports the 1973 Supreme Court decision on abortion rights as the law of the land and opposes any constitutional amendment to restrict or overturn that decision," a firmer statement than in 1976: "we fully recognize the religious and ethical nature of the concerns which many Americans have on the subject of abortion. We feel, however, that it is undesirable to attempt to amend the U.S. Constitution to overturn the Supreme Court decision in this area." http://www .presidency.ucsb.edu/ws/?pid=25843#ixzz2glAhuLkl,http://www.presidency.ucsb.edu/ws/?pid

ing out the nascent coalition between conservative Christians and the Republican Party, both sides informally agreed that the coalition would focus on abortion, rather than on divorce. Ironically, while Evangelicals did not have a clear position on abortion, "the prohibitions on divorce had been close to absolute."[172] However, given Ronald Reagan's personal history and the rising rates of divorce among Evangelicals, such strictures were also highly politically inconvenient. These partisan lines quickly congealed; by the mid-1980s, attitudes on abortion correlated to partisanship, as did church attendance.[173] Republicans began to vote against abortion at a higher rate than Democrats in Congress, and abortion became a politically polarized issue.[174] Abortion had become the glue holding together the coalition between conservative Christians and the Republican Party.

Yet abortion was simply not the priority for most American voters. Popular views on abortion were also considerably more nuanced than either a strict prohibition or abortion on demand. The opinion of secular and religious voters split: 71% of white Evangelicals, 34% of white mainline Protestants, 42% of black Protestants, 45% of Catholics, and 63% of Americans who attend church weekly or more believe abortion should be illegal in all or most cases, against 28% of Americans with no religious affiliation. Conversely, 23% of white Evangelicals, 55% of white mainline Protestants, 48% of black Protestants, and 45% of Catholics currently believe abortion should be legal in all or most cases, as do 68% of Americans with no religious affiliation and 64% of those who never or rarely attend services.[175] Ironically, given their historical stances, white Evangelicals now tilt heavily toward banning abortion, while Catholics and black Protestants are evenly split.

In the years since *Roe v. Wade*, the conservative religious coalition has influenced abortion policy on both the federal and state level. First, the movement has framed the issue to reflect its own moral premises regarding the "intrinsic humanity of unborn children," that fetal life is morally equivalent to a child or an adult human being, and deserves the same legal protections. In this framing, fetuses are "unborn children," and women are "mothers." And religious language suffused the political

---

=25844#ixzz2glBX4Uy8http://www.presidency.ucsb.edu/ws/?pid=29607#ixzz2glBFp5cl, http://www.presidency.ucsb.edu/ws/?pid=29606#ixzz2glAw73c7, accessed October 4, 2013.

[172] Balmer, 2008 112.

[173] Putnam and Campbell 2010, 394.

[174] Greenhouse and Siegel 2011, 2069.

[175] Pew Forum on Religion and Public Life 2009b. Current Catholic support for abortion is actually higher than Evangelical—perhaps not that surprising if we consider that in the 1980s, Catholic women had abortions at a rate 30% higher than Protestant or Jewish women (*Washington Post*, October 8, 1988).

debates; for example, in overturning President Clinton's veto of the partial-birth abortion ban in 1996, members of Congress "on both sides spoke loudly of God and motherhood."[176] Religious pro-life groups have also yoked their biblical (in the case of conservative Protestants) and natural law (in the case of Catholics) arguments about the "fundamental right to life" to constitutional language that invokes central tenets held to be American. These include speaking of the "inalienable rights of the unborn" (evoking the Declaration of Independence) and the "freedom of conscience" of medical personnel to refuse to perform abortions and pharmacists not to dispense contraceptives (paralleling the five freedoms enumerated in the First Amendment). Such language even justified legislation: "all persons are endowed by their Creator with certain inalienable rights," in the words of the sweeping anti-abortion bill introduced in 2012 by Florida state representative Charles Van Zant.

Second, pro-life groups were reliable allies for the churches because their membership overlapped with conservative Christian churches, and because they offered an additional channel of lobbying and policy pressure. Among the several religiously affiliated anti-abortion groups, the oldest and largest is the National Right to Life Committee (NRLC), formed in 1973 by representatives of thirty state groups. Less noted by the group itself is the fact it grew out of an effort by the National Conference of Catholic Bishops, who authorized its Family Life Bureau (FLB) in 1967 to mobilize against abortion legislation—and subsequently to channel funding in support of the NRLC. The NRLC has since grown to a political action committee, a general counsel office, and an educational trust fund. These serve to develop and disseminate the group's views through the media and its grassroots organizations, support pro-life candidates, wage legal action, and formulate legal bills on both the state and federal level. The NRLC opposes not only abortion but also human cloning, embryonic stem cell research, and euthanasia. Its literature attacks Planned Parenthood (a third of its "factsheets" are devoted to criticism of Planned Parenthood),[177] purported health-care rationing and the "Obama Abortion Agenda," and the resurrection of the Equal Rights Amendment. Critically, while not a proxy, it is a close ally to several pro-life churches and distributes its materials through grassroots church organizations.

Pro-life groups have also repeatedly demonstrated their numerical strength publicly; protests and demonstrations also articulated preferences, even if they did not directly influence policy. The annual March for Life in Washington, DC, begun in 1974 on the first anniversary of *Roe v. Wade*, consistently draws upwards of 300,000 participants who are bused in by

---

[176] *New York Times*, September 20, 1996.
[177] www.nrlc.org/factsheets, accessed June 7, 2013.

churches from across the nation. The rhetoric and strategies of the allied groups go well beyond what most politicians could say or do; at the first March for Life, John C. Wilke of National Right to Life Committee compared knowledge that abortion existed to "smelling smoke of the burning Jews from Dachau."[178] Explicitly Christian anti-abortion groups such as Operation Rescue have also staged aggressive sit-ins and demonstrations in front of abortion clinics.[179]

Third, a critical form of influence on abortion legislation has been electoral support for the Republican Party in general and for specific candidates in particular. Christian pro-life groups rallied their members in support for the party, and abortion became a critical clarion call in mobilizing this electorate. For example, the National Conference of Catholic Bishops repeatedly issued voters' guides (such as "Forming Consciences for Faithful Citizenship" in 2007 and 2011) that called on Catholics to make abortion the central point in evaluating presidential candidates (and urged non-partisan voter registration drives in parishes).[180] Catholic bishops also threatened to excommunicate supporters of abortion rights, and especially political candidates who advocated abortion rights; in 1984, Catholic bishops criticized vice presidential candidate Geraldine Ferraro's pro-abortion stance, and in 1990 John Cardinal O'Connor of New York suggested that pro-choice politicians risked excommunication. In 1996, less than a week before the US elections, retired New Orleans Bishop Philip Hannan told Louisiana Catholics that they could not vote for President Clinton or pro-choice Catholic Senate candidate Mary Landrieu.[181] In the 2012 GOP primaries, the National Presidential Pro-Life Forum (sponsored by the Christian ministry Personhood USA) invited Republican candidates to sign a pro-life pledge. Candidates who did not attend were disparaged at the event.[182] Finally, conservative churches and proxy organizations issued public statements regarding state legislative bills.

The political response to the groups' efforts was robust. In 1984, Ronald Reagan proclaimed a National Sanctity of Life day to coincide with

---

[178] Johnson, Janis. 1976. "50,000 Protest Abortion." *Washington Post Metro*, January 23.

[179] The huge backlash that followed after the murder of Dr. George Tiller, the target of Operation Rescue's "Summer of Mercy" demonstrations, led Operation Rescue to change its name to National Operation to Save America.

[180] The National Conference of Catholic Bishops also sent some eight million postcards to members of Congress before the 1996 congressional vote upholding the ban on "partial-birth" abortion (*New York Times*, September 20, 1996).

[181] The US Bishops' Political Activism against Abortion; A CHRONOLOGY. *Conscience*. Washington, DC, Summer 2004, XXV, 2.

[182] Bohon, David. 2011. "GOP Candidates Pledge to Pursue a Pro-Life 'Personhood' Agenda." *New American*, December 30. http://bit.ly/rE5Wjy.

the *Roe v. Wade* anniversary and met with thirty anti-abortion leaders prior to the March for Life. In response, the leadership of the NRLC publicly declared that Reagan was the first pro-life president and had the movement's full backing in the upcoming November 1984 elections. George H. W. Bush followed in Reagan's footsteps, with four such National Sanctity of Life Day declarations—and though Bill Clinton omitted the commemorations, George W. Bush reinstituted them.[183] For its part, the NRLC claimed credit for the 1994 pro-life and Republican majority in the House of Representatives, for derailing the Clinton-era Health Care Act, and for propelling George W. Bush to his 2000 victory over Al Gore.[184] The prominence of these claims in the publicity materials of the NRLC suggests their importance in the movement's self-perception.

A fourth form of religious influence on policy involved legislative communication: testimony in front of congressional committees, filing of amici curiae briefs in front of the Supreme Court, and more personal contact with congressional representatives and senators.[185] Roman Catholic bishops in particular testified on numerous congressional committees and openly supported legislation limiting access to abortion (and to contraception) such as the 1976 Hyde Amendment, sponsored by the (devoutly Catholic) Representative Henry Hyde (R-IL), which eliminated Medicaid funding for abortion and proposals for the Human Life Amendment to the Constitution in 1974, which would have made abortion unconstitutional.[186] Cardinals and bishops testified before Congress in the 1970s in favor of the Human Life Amendment, in the 1990s against late-term abortions, and in the 2000s during the debates over the Obama administration's health-care proposals. The National Conference of Catholic Bishops and the Southern Baptist Convention jointly filed an amicus curiae brief in the 1992 Supreme Court *Planned Parenthood v. Casey* case. Federal lobbyists for the National Right to Life Committee and affiliated groups also testified on so-called "partial abortion" congressional hearings in the 1990s, and on the 2010 "Obamacare" Patient Protection and Affordable Care Act.[187] Here, while Republicans were the main sup-

---

[183] Domke and Coe 2008, 85–86.

[184] www.nrlc.org/factsheets/fs01_NRLCToday.pdf, accessed June 7, 2013.

[185] In a notable example, Francis Schaeffer, an evangelical activist, showed "Whatever Happened to the Human Race?" an anti-abortion film, to a meeting of more than fifty congressmen and twenty senators, ranging from Henry Hyde to Bob Dole. For more on Schaeffer, his Swiss retreat L'Abri, and how the film helped to align conservative Protestants with conservative Catholics, see Miller 2014, 51–53; and Wills 2007, 522. Schaeffer long argued that abortion would be the issue to bring together conservative Catholics and Evangelicals.

[186] Efforts to amend the US Constitution to overturn the decision have been unsuccessful, partly because the anti-abortion movement was divided (Tietze, Forrest, and Henshaw 1988, 474).

[187] Catholic bishops also entered the debates over the Affordable Care Act by vociferously arguing against universal birth control coverage and demanding exemptions for any

porters of the conservative religious coalition, Democrats still could not afford to alienate the Catholic Church, and so the bishops frequently met with both sides. According to members of the congressional pro-choice caucus, it was the pro-life Democrats' insistence on the "Stupak amendment" (which would forbid subsidies for insurance that covered abortions) that nearly derailed the Obama health-care act.[188] In one of the few instances of direct legislative access, there are indications that the bishops may even have helped to write the Stupak Amendment.[189] They also relied on pastoral letters read out loud at Masses, and a campaign of phone calls and letters by parishioners to congresspeople.[190]

Yet in the absence of direct institutional access to the judiciary, where the biggest abortion decisions were made, and without an authoritative religious monopoly that would discipline politicians at the federal level, the conservative Christian-Republican coalition was unable to overturn legal abortion. Much as in the Irish case, several legislative victories could be laid at the feet of religion—but the judiciary proved far more autonomous, and decisive. The policy outcomes at the *national* level consisted of the 1976 Hyde Amendment (technically a rider), which eliminated Medicaid funding for abortion, and its subsequent versions, which eliminated federal funding for abortion on military bases. After years of debates, and a two-time veto by President Bill Clinton in 1996 and 1997, the Partial Birth Abortion Ban Act of 2003 passed by the Republican-majority Congress banned intact dilation and extraction, a rare late-term abortion procedure.

Yet these did not entirely fulfill the desired aim (and Republican party promise) of delegalizing abortion. On the one hand, the Republican Party has repeatedly delayed or not followed through on campaign promises; for example, the Human Life Statute in 1981 or the Family Protection Act of 1981, both of which would have outlawed abortion but were put on the back burner given the more urgent economic recession.[191] On the other hand, the problem is a lack of political control, not simply a lack of commitment. The coalition formed by the party with conservative

---

employers whose religious beliefs oppose such funding. The Catholic hierarchy's opposition to any potential for funding abortion or contraception was so intense that some bishops declared that "no health care reform is better than the wrong sort of health care reform," as Bishop R. Walker Nickless of Iowa argued (*New York Times*, August 28, 2009).

[188] *New York Times*, November 9, 2009. Accessed November 10, 2009. In the end, pro-life Democrats agreed to a compromise that excluded the Stupak language from the bill in exchange for an executive order that would ban health-care funds from being used for abortion.

[189] http://www.huffingtonpost.com/2011/11/01/the-men-behind-the-war-on-women, accessed January 20, 2012.

[190] *New York Times*, November 9, 2009. Accessed November 10, 2009.

[191] Balmer 2006, 121.

Christians is still subject to review by a broader (and more diverse) electorate and by the judiciary, both of whom dilute its influence (even if they increasingly uphold restrictive legislation).[192]

On the *state* level, however, the coalition could claim more success. With the 1989 *Webster v. Reproductive Health Services* decision, which upheld restrictions on state funding for abortion services, the states assumed a new prominence, and over four hundred bills were introduced in the first year after *Webster*.[193] There are suggestions that interest groups mattered in subsequent policy decisions: abortion restrictions were considerably lower in states with greater membership in the National Abortion Rights Action League (NARAL), female legislators, and Democratic female legislators. In contrast, the percentage of Catholics within a state (as a proxy for NRLC membership, for which data was unavailable) significantly increased abortion restrictions.[194] Similarly, interest group activity and percentage of conservative Protestants and Catholics were correlated to local initiatives limiting abortion access.[195] More broadly, local public opinion on abortion influenced state abortion policies, suggesting that in conservative states, the coalition would have more influence.[196]

Given the relatively moderate (and complex) views of most Americans on abortion, restrictions on abortion are seen as acceptable; abolishing abortion entirely is not. Accordingly, state laws *eliminating* abortion were either found unconstitutional by courts or were repealed by voters; for example, South Dakota's 2006 statue made abortion a felony but was repealed in a popular referendum later that year. Personhood USA was responsible for getting anti-abortion amendments to state constitutions on the ballot in three different states (Colorado, Montana, and Oregon), but to date none have passed. Laws *limiting* abortion, on the other hand, are prevalent. These include laws restricting insurance coverage (eight states), invoking freedom of conscience clauses for medical personnel (forty-six states), regulating ultrasounds (twenty-two states), parental consent for minors (thirty-eight states), waiting periods (twenty-six states), or anti-abortion counseling (seventeen states).[197]

In short, abortion illustrates the conservative Christian coalition's power to shape the public debate and influence the policy outcomes. The interdenominational coalition and its Republican partisan allies have succeeded in restricting abortion, but not as comprehensively as they had

[192] For example, the ban on intact dilation and extraction was subsequently upheld in *Gonzalez v. Carhart* in 2007 by the Supreme Court.
[193] NARAL 1991.
[194] Medoff 2002, 487.
[195] Roh and Haider-Markel 2003.
[196] Arceneaux 2002; Cohen and Barilleux 1993; Goggin and Wlezien 1993; Norrander and Wilcox 1999; Wetstein and Albritton 1995.
[197] Guttmacher Institute 2013.

hoped, failing to fully enshrine the "culture of life" in law. The reliance on a partisan coalition meant an attenuated influence, limited to the more conservative states. On the federal level, the judiciary remained a powerful actor, opening up the floodgates with *Roe v. Wade* and subsequently allowing states to restrict access to abortion.

Education

In the United States, provisions for religion in public schools (such as morning prayers) have been ruled to violate the Constitution because they amount to "aiding religion." In a series of decisions in the early 1960s and 1970s, including *Engel v. Vitale* (1962), *Abington School District v. Schempp* (1963), and *Lemon v. Kurtzman* (1971), the Supreme Court established that any state-sponsored activity must have a secular purpose, neither advance nor inhibit religion, and not result in an excessive entanglement of state and religion. Even the very few forms of indirect aid that have been allowed to stand (such as providing busing or textbooks to religious schools) have attracted much controversy.[198] This doctrine of "a wall of separation" between church and state in the schoolhouse is unique to the United States; other democracies with a commitment to religious neutrality have provided funding in order to maintain an equal footing between religious and secular organizations.[199]

Prayer in schools, as controversial as it was in the 1960s through 1980s, has the support of of the majority of Americans, numerous churches and many politicians—but a slew of Supreme Court decisions has repeatedly struck it down. Even if deeply unpopular, these decisions meant there was little point in expending political effort to reintroduce prayer.[200] Instead, "moments of silence" became a popular way to provide a moment for prayer (without forcing it) in the 1970s and 1980s, with over fifteen states mandating such moments, and over twenty others allowing them during the school day by the 2000s.[201] Further, there are doctrinal differences over the details. Catholic leaders fulminated against the 1962 *Engel v. Vitale*

---

[198] See Doerr and Menendez 1991.

[199] It has also only ever applied to elementary and secondary education, and only after 1947 (the Supreme Court's *Everson v. Board of Education* decision), see Monsma and Soper 1997.

[200] If anything, this is the one area where the secularist efforts tend to be successful, given the relatively clear legal rulings. Organizations such as Americans United, the Secular Coalition for America, and the Freedom from Religion Foundation issued letters and statements reminding local authorities of the unconstitutionality of school-sponsored prayer, and even opening meetings of school boards with prayer. See http://www.secularnewsdaily .com/2012/10/school-board-prayer-out-silence-in/, accessed June 10, 2013.

[201] These were held as legal, so long as their primary purpose was not to offer a substitute for school prayer. Thus in 1985 the Supreme Court *Wallace v. Jaffree* decision struck down an Alabama statute providing a moment of silence for "meditation or voluntary prayer."

ruling, which banned state-composed or -endorsed prayers ruling. In contrast, Evangelicals and fundamentalists had little use for state-composed prayer and were uncomfortable with the idea of schoolchildren reciting rote prayers composed by ecumenical authors, as opposed to spontaneous prayer and devotions.[202]

As a result, if the teaching of religion in public schools is the main bone of contention in religious influence on European educational policy, in the United States the main debates surround proxy issues, such as the teaching of evolution, abstinence-only sex education, or "released time." If state-mandated religious observance was banished resolutely from public education, biblical teaching was not. First, major controversies surround the teaching of evolution, creationism, and intelligent design. Creationists hold that "the creation story in the Old Testament or Hebrew Bible book of Genesis is literally true and is akin to scientific explanation for the creation of the Earth and the development of life," while intelligent design holds that "life is too complex to have evolved entirely through natural processes and that an outside, possibly divine force must have played a role in the origin and development of life."[203] Several denominations, including the Roman Catholic Church, see evolution as compatible with their doctrine, or hold no official views (these include the Evangelical Lutheran Church, American Jewish Congress, Episcopal Church, LDS, United Methodist Church). Some conservative Christians, however, such as the Southern Baptist Convention and the Lutheran Church (Missouri Synod), reject evolution and advocate intelligent design or creationism.

Much as it supports prayer in schools, public opinion favors the teaching of creationism alongside evolution, with 64% of Americans in a 2005 Pew poll supporting it.[204] There is little opposition to the teaching of some form of creationism, with only Jews and the religiously unaffiliated as the opponents. Nearly all conservative Christians (90%) and majorities of both mainline Protestants and Catholics support the teaching of creationism or intelligent design.[205] This result is robust to different framings and phrasings of the question, suggesting that it is not the result of biased public opinion surveys.[206] These numbers further reflect the general acceptance of creationist views, which has remained largely unaltered since the early 1980s: the plurality of Americans (44% in 1982 to 46% in 2013) say that God created humans in their present form, with a smaller minority allowing for humans evolving with God's guidance (38%–32%). Only

---

[202] Williams 2010, 63; Balmer 2006, 89.
[203] Pew Forum on Religion and Public Life 2009a.
[204] Pew Forum on Religion and Public Life 2009a.
[205] Berkman and Plutzer 2010, 71.
[206] Berkman and Plutzer 2010, 33.

9% to 16% of Americans viewed evolution as taking place without God involved.[207] As with abortion, public opinion and interest groups influence *state*-level policies; anti-evolution forces succeed the most in states with large numbers of conservative Protestants, while evolution is supported in states with large numbers of scientists and professionals.[208]

The controversies over the teaching of evolution in the United States reach back to the 1920s. In 1922, Tennessee Governor Austin Peay signed into law the Butler Act, which prohibited the teaching of the theory of evolution in any Tennessee school or university receiving public funds. This led to the notorious Scopes Trial of 1925 in which John Scopes, a substitute biology teacher, was convicted of breaking the law by teaching evolution. In light of subsequent historical developments, however, this marked the beginning of defeats for anti-evolutionist education. The massive negative publicity attracted by the trial, according to R. Murray Thomas, "was instrumental in the defeat of anti-evolution teaching laws in all but two (Arkansas, Mississippi) of the fifteen states that had such bills before legislatures in 1925."[209] By midcentury, Darwinism was taught in American public schools by consensus, reinforced later by court cases in the 1960s and 1980s that overturned some southern states' attempts to introduce "creation science" into schools.

The aggressive contemporary push for creationism is relatively recent, reaching its apex in 2005, when George W. Bush and Bill Frist made comments supporting the teaching of intelligent design along with evolution—and a federal judge dismissed the inclusion of "intelligent design" as a religiously motivated and thus unacceptable addition to the school curriculum.[210] Churches have at times been directly involved; clergy and church spokespeople have often directly commented on or otherwise intervened in debates, but nearly always at a strictly local level and rarely attracting

---

[207] Gallup 2013a.

[208] Berkman and Plutzer 2010, 91.

[209] Thomas 2007, 59.

[210] In August 2005, President Bush commented that "both sides" of the evolution controversy should be taught in schools, "so people can understand what the debate is about." In support of President Bush, Dr. Richard Land of the Southern Baptist Convention argued: "It's what I've been pushing, it's what a lot of us have been pushing . . . if you're going to teach the Darwinian theory as evolution, teach it as a theory." Land himself was identified as having "close ties to the White House" (*New York Times*, August 3. 2005). A second, quite different controversy arose over Catholic teachings on evolution. In July 2005, Vienna Archbishop Christoph Schönborn claimed in a *New York Times* editorial that Darwinian evolution was "not true" and that Pope John Paul II's writings on the compatibility of Darwinian evolution and church teachings have been misinterpreted. However, Bishop Francis X. DiLorenzo, chair of the US Conference of Catholic Bishops' Committee on Science and Human Values, emphasized that "Catholic schools should continue teaching evolution as a theory backed by convincing evidence" (*Philadelphia Inquirer*, August 3, 2005).

national attention. There have been some exceptions: Barrett Duke, Vice President for Public Policy of the Southern Baptist Convention, was quoted as saying, "I think it's appropriate for students to understand that evolution is a theory, not a fact. . . . There's no question that many Christian young people are going out to public school and they're coming out much different than their parents expected them to come out!"[211] In Oklahoma, the Southern Baptist Convention (SBC) supported textbook disclaimers stating that "evolution is a theory, not a fact, regarding the origin of living things. This material should be approached with an open mind, studied carefully, and critically considered."[212] More recently, the SBC has advocating withdrawing children from public schools and homeschooling them. Roger Moran, a member of the SBC's executive committee, told NPR in 2006 that "it is time for responsible Southern Baptists to develop an exit strategy out of the public schools, because the public schools are no longer allowed to train our children in the ways that the Scriptures commands that we train them. And that is in the ways of the Lord, not in the ways of the world."[213]

For the most part, however, allied conservative Christian interest groups rather than church representatives were at the forefront of the lobbying and legislative efforts in advocating alternatives to evolution. The decentralized organization of most American denominations and the policy level at which these debates occur (even more locally than with abortion), made national-level church campaigns difficult. Instead, a number of allied groups and think tanks provided experts who testified at school board hearings regarding the teaching of evolution. The "new wave" of anti-evolution pressure began in 1963 with the founding of the Creation Research Society.[214] Two other prominent organizations were the Discovery Institute (founded 1990), and the Institute for Creation Research (founded in 1970). All were religious allies rather than proxies, maintaining no direct ties with individual churches but explicitly aligning themselves with Christian and biblical teaching.[215]

In their advocacy efforts, these organizations argued for the inclusion of creationism and intelligent design as the "other side of the story," a

[211] Sweeney, Kate. 2004. "Evolution Challenged in Georgia School Debate." *Voice of America News*, August 29.
[212] "Profs Stand Up Keating, Textbook Crew Rapped." *Tulsa World*, December 18, 1999.
[213] Elliott, Debbie. 2006. "Baptists Bypassing Public Schools over Evolution." National Public Radio, *Weekend All Things Considered*, May 27.
[214] Marty and Appleby 1992, 76.
[215] Creation Research Society, "CRS Statement of Belief, http://www.creationresearch .org/belief_wndw.htm. The Discovery Institute. 1999. "The Wedge Document," and Institute for Creation Research, "Image of God." http://www.icr.org/image-of-God/, accessed June 10, 2013.

valid and scientifically equivalent alternative to the evolutionary consensus. Mindful of legal precedent and constitutional constraints, their arguments emphasize academic freedom rather than including a religious perspective in schooling. Here, the Discovery Institute, which houses nearly all prominent creationists with scientific credentials,[216] changed the face of creationism in two important ways. First, it made a decisive break with the easily ridiculed "young earth" creationism. Instead, the Institute has advocated Intelligent Design (ID), which accepts the idea of a very old earth and gradual change within species, but argues that Darwinian "macroevolution" is a seriously flawed theory that can be disputed on scientific grounds. It does not make biblical references in making this case. Second, the Discovery Institute articulated a clear and ambitious political strategy, authored by Berkeley law professor Philip E. Johnson. Labeled the "Wedge Strategy," it emphasized (1) research and publication, (2) publicity and opinion making, and (3) cultural confrontation that would have as its short-term aim a full legitimation of intelligent design as an alternative—and its dominance in the long term.[217] The Institute established the Center for Science and Culture in Washington, DC, to lobby policy makers to embrace its "Teach the Controversy" campaign and held special congressional briefings to promote this position. Rick Santorum (R-PA) cited this research in his amendment to the No Child Left Behind Act, emphasizing "alternative theories" to evolution.[218]

Once again, however, the courts proved decisive and struck down a number of state laws that include "creation science" and intelligent design. In the 1987 *Edwards v. Aguillard* decision, the Supreme Court found that since creationism lacked a secular purpose, its teaching was unconstitutional. After this ruling, some proponents of creationism began to advocate the teaching of intelligent design, which makes no biblical references. However, in *Kitzmiller v. Dover Area School District* (2005) a federal judge ruled that it was also unconstitutional for a school district to present intelligent design as an alternative to evolution in high school biology courses because it was a religious viewpoint that advanced "a particular version of Christianity" and it was "creationism relabeled."[219]

---

[216] Comfort 2007.

[217] Discovery Institute 1999.

[218] "Statement by Senator Santorum upon the Passage of the Education Act 2001." *Congressional Record*, December 18, 2001 (Senate) Page S13365–S13422. http://bit.ly/H2YzWV.

[219] *New York Times*, December 21, 2005. The Thomas More Law Center (TMLC), a conservative Catholic law institute, represented the school district. The center, based in Ann Arbor, was founded in 1999 by Domino's Pizza magnate Tom Monaghan and former Michigan prosecutor Richard Thompson (who gained prominence in the prosecution of Jack Kevorkian). The center's advisory board has included Rick Santorum and Alan Keyes.

After the *Kitzmiller* ruling, Republican (and Southern Baptist) representatives in Mississippi and Florida (Gary Chism and Stephen Wise, respectively) introduced bills to authorize the teaching of intelligent design, but these did not pass. As with abortion, judicial rulings preempted legislative efforts.

Another controversy surrounded the teaching of abstinence. Federally funded programs emphasizing abstinence began with the Adolescent Family Life Act (AFLA) of 1981, in response to the conservative Christian coalition's demands. AFLA's main goal was "to promote chastity and self-discipline" by allocating funds to organizations that would promote abstinence-based school sex education. These organizations were largely church groups, who flocked to the program and its largesse.[220] The Act's sponsors saw it as a necessary counter to federal funding to Planned Parenthood and other organizations promoting contraception. Luker quotes an article from the *Conservative Digest* celebrating that "the Adolescent Family Life Act was written expressly for the 'noble purpose' of diverting (federal) money that would otherwise go to Planned Parenthood into groups with traditional values."[221] Yet the Act itself was a compromise; to win the support of Ted Kennedy in the Labor and Human Resources Committee, two-thirds of its funding would go to programs for pregnant and parenting adolescents, and only one-third to promoting abstinence.[222]

The ACLU soon challenged the program in 1983, arguing it violated the separation of church and state. It was found unconstitutional in 1985's *Kendrick v. Sullivan* by the US District Court. The decision was then reversed by the Supreme Court in 1988, but subsequent litigation led to a 1993 settlement in which AFLA grantees were required to submit curricula to the Department of Health and Human Services for review, which would certify that materials were not promoting religion and were "medically accurate."[223] Federal funding for abstinence-only education was substantially increased in 1996 as part of the Personal Responsibility and Work Opportunity Reconciliation Act, best known as the welfare reform act produced by the Clinton presidency and the Republican-

---

Since at least 2000, representatives from the TMLC had been searching for a school board willing to face a lawsuit in order to introduce creationist material into the curriculum; in 2005, the *New York Times* reported that Robert Muise, a TMLC lawyer, had traveled to Charleston, West Virginia, to persuade the school board to use the intelligent design textbook *Of Pandas and People*. In any resulting lawsuit, TMLC would provide a legal defense free of charge. The Charleston school board declined to act as a test case, as did school districts in Michigan and Wisconsin (Goodstein 2005).

[220] Thomas 2007, 221.
[221] Luker 2006, 222.
[222] Saul 1998.
[223] Saul 1998.

controlled Congress. Commonly referred to as Title V (the section of the Social Security Act it amended), it provided $250 million over five years to the states for abstinence-only programs for teens and young adults.[224] These programs not only resulted from the conservative Christian coalition's efforts, but then also served to strengthen that coalition: "federal money was available for producing abstinence-only curricula because traditional sex education programs offended conservatives, who were now getting mobilized under the banner of the pro-family movement. And bringing together like-minded sexual conservatives meant that networking and coalition building among various groups could take place."[225]

Finally, the issue of "released time" (schools setting aside a portion of the day for religious instruction *not* provided by the school itself) was the converse of school prayer, in that it garnered far less attention, yet "released time" was found to be constitutional. It was first introduced in Gary, Indiana, in 1914 to deal with growing disquiet from non-Protestant minorities over Bible reading and other Protestant-oriented religious education in public schools. Under the released-time program, students would be able to receive religious instruction from an outside instructor in their chosen faith. Instead of teaching religion as part of the school curriculum, as is the case in Europe, released-time programs allow students to attend religious instruction off the school premises. By 1947, nearly two million children in 2,200 communities received instruction in released-time programs.[226] There were two legal challenges to released-time programs; in *McCollum v. Board of Education* (1948), the Supreme Court established that such programs could not be held in public school classrooms or use public school teachers to monitor attendance; and in *Zorach v. Clauson* (1952), the Supreme Court decision upheld New York City's released-time program. In his majority ruling, William O. Douglas relied on national tradition to support his case: "we are a religious people whose institutions

[224] The program's effects are unclear: according to a 1999 survey of secondary school principals, 58% of schools taught "comprehensive" sex education, 34% taught "abstinence only," and 8% taught something else (Henry J. Kaiser Family Foundation 2002). When asked who influenced the development of their curricula, 88% reported local governments and school districts had some influence, 70% reported state directives had some influence, and 31% reported federal funding had some influence. In 2004, California congressman Henry A. Waxman released a report stating that two-thirds of federally funded abstinence-only programs contained inaccurate information about abortion, contraception, genetics, and STDs. The Heritage Foundation contested his findings in a counterreport (Thomas 2007, 222–23). A 2007 report commissioned by Congress questioned the effectiveness of abstinence only, arguing that middle school students who took part in these programs were just as likely to engage in sex in their teens as those who did not. http://www.mathematica-mpr.com/publications/PDFs/impactabstinence.pdf.

[225] Luker 2006, 223.

[226] Thomas 2007, 190.

presuppose a Supreme Being. When the state encourages religious instruction or cooperates with religious authorities by adjusting the schedule of public events to sectarian needs, it follows the best of our traditions . . . To hold that it may not would be to find in the Constitution a requirement that the government show a callous indifference to religious groups."[227] As a result, released-time programs are allowed today in twenty largely northern and midwestern states. While released-time programs are usually initiated directly by local churches, they have faced little or no secular opposition, largely because they have been successfully framed as keeping religious activity *out* of the classroom.

In repeatedly upholding the firewall between church and state, courts have stymied the efforts of the advocates of prayer in schools, creationism, and abstinence-only sex education. The influence of religion on education was repeatedly curbed not by public opinion, which favored prayer in schools and the teaching of creationism or intelligent design, but by the judicial system. At the same time, given doctrinal divisions over prayer and evolution, these efforts were conducted less by the coalition than by individual churches and allied organizations. Their successes came at the local level, in keeping with the diffusion of church moral authority and the centrality of local school boards and officials to these decisions.

Divorce

Restrictions on divorce are the dog that did not bark of religious influence on politics; churches did not try to limit divorce, despite multiple compelling factors to mobilize against it. Americans share a widespread worry about high divorce rates and the breakdown of the family; for example, 88% of Americans agree that the divorce rate is too high.[228] A doctrinal consensus within the conservative Christian coalition opposes divorce. Evangelicals have long seen divorce as sin, "citing Jesus' teaching that anyone who leaves his wife causes her to commit adultery and whoever marries a divorced woman also commits adultery."[229] For its part, the Roman Catholic Church refuses to recognize divorce. And the issue had legal urgency; by the time Evangelicals entered politics, no-fault divorce was becoming legal, beginning with California in 1970. By 1985, it was legal in all states.

Yet this doctrinal opposition has not translated into policy demands. While conservative Christian organizations repeatedly emphasize their commitment to family, and to family values, these priorities are not al-

---

[227] Thomas 2007, 191.
[228] Pew Forum on Religion and Public Life 2008; Hawkins et al. 2002.
[229] Lambert 2010, 267.

ways reflected in political activity. If on abortion Evangelicals had to be convinced of the pro-life political position, with divorce they remained peculiarly quiet, despite their existing (and intense) convictions. The silence prompted some critics to charge they are guilty of "selective literalism," choosing to emphasize those biblical proscriptions that are politically useful.[230] The various allied organizations of conservative religion also did not emphasize restricting divorce: "abstract support has not been matched by a sustained commitment to spending time or resources on the issue."[231] The Moral Majority in the 1980s, the Christian Coalition in the 1990s, and the Family Research Council in the 2000s prioritized abortion, gay rights, school prayer, school choice, and other issues, but even in their formal statements of priorities, divorce is missing.[232]

Part of the reason is simple; divorce is prevalent among conservative Christians. While Catholics have a lower-than-average divorce rate (30%, against the mean of 38%), Evangelical Protestants have a 43% divorce rate.[233] Further, religious commitment does not inoculate marriages from breaking down; levels of religiosity are not associated with incidence of divorce.[234] Indeed, the Bible Belt states have the highest divorce rates. Given the religious competition that exists, especially among American Protestants, a church that condemned divorce could find its pews emptier[235]—and the faithful deserting the church for one that better understands their life experience. Where religious competition exists and the targeted "sinners" comprise a major constituency, there is little political benefit to attempting to abolish divorce (or IVF, as we will see). Conversely, focusing on abortion or gay rights rather than on divorce or in vitro fertilization "allows them to locate sin *outside* of the evangelical subculture (or so they think) by designation as especially egregious those dispositions and behaviors, homosexuality and abortion, that they believe characteristic of others, not themselves."[236]

Indeed, several Protestant denominations have relaxed their stances on divorce, increasingly viewing "inviolable marriage as an ideal rather than a biblical command."[237] Some conservative Christian groups have

[230] Balmer 2006, 9.

[231] Smith 2010, 77.

[232] Smith 2010, 75.

[233] Smith 2010, 83.

[234] Department of Health and Human Services 2002; National Center for Policy Analysis 1999.

[235] Despite the overwhelming anxiety about high divorce rates, only 47% of Americans agreed that the divorce laws should be changed to make a divorce more difficult to get (2001 Gallup poll, cited in Hawkins et al. 2002).

[236] Balmer 2006, 10.

[237] Smith 2010, 71.

turned to incentives rather than punishment to preserve traditional forms of family and marriage, convincing legislatures to institute "covenant marriage"—an optional legal commitment that would make subsequent divorce more difficult for the married couple. Covenant marriage allows the marrying couple to add extra legal requirements to govern their marriage and restrict the possibility of divorce. The central difference with standard civil marriage is that both parties must accept limited, fault-based grounds for divorce: abuse, adultery, addiction, felony imprisonment, or separation for two years.[238] Three states adopted the legislation in the 1990s: Louisiana, Arizona, and Arkansas, making covenant marriage an available option (and not changing the legislation surrounding non-covenant marriage). Around 2% of subsequent marriages were drawn up as covenant marriages.[239]

Covenant marriage bills were authored and promoted in the late 1990s by a small policy group, including Louisiana representative Tony Perkins, who identifies as a devout Mormon (and who would go on to become the President of the Family Research Council), and law professor Katherine Spaht, who stated she "promised God" she would support covenant marriage. Spaht attempted to draft covenant marriage laws in a way that was neutral to religion. But when discussing the efforts of covenant marriage proponents, she referred to them as doing "intensive missionary work . . . winning converts one couple at a time."[240] While proponents of the law claimed it was a civil measure, religious officials were granted explicit abilities to fulfill the premarital counseling requirement of the law. In the Arizona covenant marriage law, both parties entering into this marriage had to demonstrate that they "received premarital counseling from a member of the clergy or from a marriage counselor" before entering into a civil marriage contract.[241]

A number of religious organizations worked to promote the covenant marriage legislation in the late 1990s when the laws first appeared in state legislatures. The Covenant Marriage Movement, an initiative headed by a Baptist minister Phil Waugh, stated that it is "a movement of God to initiate revival within the lives of couples and families in this nation and around the world."[242] This initiative was supported by the 50,000 mem-

[238] Hawkins et al. 2002.

[239] Allman, K. 2009. "Covenant Marriage Laws in Louisiana." *Gambit*, March 2. http://bit.ly/z4Q72q. Accessed March 26, 2013.

[240] Spaht 1998.

[241] "Covenant Marriage in Arizona." *Administrative Office of the Arizona Supreme Court*. 2006. http://bit.ly/wizqrd. Accessed March 12, 2013.

[242] Waugh, Phillip. 2006. "About Us." Covenant Marriage Movement Website. http://bit.ly/ABzprZ. Accessed March 23, 2013.

ber American Association of Christian Counselors, with its president, Tim Clinton (a Baptist minister and theologian), declaring that "God is rallying His people to join Him in upholding marriage as He has always purposed it to be, a covenant relationship . . . over and beyond an understanding of marriage as a contractual relationship or simply an institution."[243]

Yet once again doctrinal differences precluded a consensus position. Some evangelical Christian groups "embraced the movement," and some even announced that they would *only* be solemnizing covenant marriages. The Catholic Church, however, was skeptical of the initiative, praising the intent to "strengthen the institution of marriage" while criticizing the requirement that couples must discuss the limited grounds for divorce, for fear that this would obscure the church's teaching that the *only* grounds for dissolution is an invalid marriage.[244] In short, despite a shared concern for divorce rates, conservative Christian denominations differed over the severity of the problem and the possibilities for a solution, even as their faithful continued to divorce. And without a consensus position, or their members' assent, the conservative Christian coalition would not enter the political fray to limit divorce in the national political arena.

In Vitro Fertilization and Stem Cell Research

Moral apprehensions, rather than scientific concerns, were at the forefront of the embryonic stem cell research debates, for two reasons. First, in the 1970s and 1980s theologically conservative government advisors feared such research would promote abortion by undercutting the contention that human life begins at conception. Second, in the 2000s the conservative Christian-Republican coalition successfully reframed their opposition to embryonic stem cell research as another way of "protecting the unborn." Yet embryonic stem cell research also shows the *limits* of coalitional influence on politics. National policy decisions revolved around funding at the federal level rather than the legality of the research. And related procedures, such as in vitro fertilization (IVF), remained untouched, despite the theological opposition of a key member of the coalition, the Roman Catholic Church.

In contrast to the European cases discussed earlier, even as embryonic stem cell research and many assisted reproduction technologies have in common the creation of embryos in a lab by fertilizing an egg extracted from a woman (and the subsequent destruction of many of these embryos),

---

[243] Clinton, Tim. 2006. "A Word from Our Chairman." Covenant Marriage Movement Website. http://bit.ly/ABzprZ. Accessed March 26, 2013.
[244] Feld 2002.

they remain politically distinct issues in the United States. After its intro-duction in the United States, IVF became an accepted technology, while stem cell research became linked to cloning and to human experimenta-tion and remained far more controversial. Further, as a legacy of the abor-tion debates, Congress has refused to fund embryo research for fear of encouraging abortions, while leaving IVF and stem cell research in the un-regulated private sector and under the authority of states.[245] Federal rules restrict stem cell research; they leave IVF unregulated.

Why have IVF and stem cell research (or abortion, for that matter) evoked such different political responses from the conservative Chris-tian coalition and its political allies? Here, both doctrine and electoral calculations dictate a more muted stance on IVF than on abortion or even stem cell research. First, as with divorce, the official Catholic stances on IVF do not reflect a broader consensus among conservative Chris-tians. The Catholic Church in the United States and elsewhere has un-equivocally condemned in vitro fertilization—in addition to leading to the destruction of "spare" embryos, the procedure is viewed as immoral in that it separates the act of intercourse from procreation.[246] However, this last point is unique to Catholic doctrine and has not resonated more broadly among other denominations. The Southern Baptist Convention has stopped short of condemning IVF, arguing instead that parents are responsible for unused embryos left behind.[247] Most Evangelical churches have either not espoused a stance on IVF or hold conflicting views on the procedures: "Evangelicals are generally not opposed to contracep-tion, as are Catholic elites, and lack the Catholic concept of a unitive purpose of sexual relations."[248] In the absence of a religious monopoly that represents the national moral interest in the United States, a broader interdenominational agreement is critical, but there was no theological basis for one here.

Second, for politically minded religious organizations, there is a rather cynical calculus at hand. Women undergoing abortion tend to be young, single, and poor,[249] and thus politically marginal. Similarly, the benefits of embryonic stem cell research are largely far off and uncertain, making its potential constituency relatively weak and its expected utility to politi-

---

[245] Wertz 2002.

[246] http://old.usccb.org/prolife/programs/rlp/98rlphaa.shtml, accessed June 11, 2013.

[247] http://www.abpnews.com/culture/social-issues/item/8414-sbc-leader-says-life-begins-in-vitro#.UbdvhLbPE98, accessed June 11, 2013.

[248] Evans 2010, 51. As Evans notes, however, the acceptance of IVF is coming under greater scrutiny, given an emerging concern originally articulated by the Catholic Church with the discarding of "excess embryos."

[249] Davis 2006, 289.

cians low. In contrast, the more well-off, married population likely to make use of IVF has more political clout and is more likely to overlap with the membership of conservative religious denominations.[250] In sum, as one critic pointed out, embryonic stem cell research and IVF both destroy embryos, but the opponents of stem cell research do not pursue banning IVF: "they're not doing that because it's politically suicidal and self-contradictory: fertility treatment, after all, is just a latter-day means to be fruitful and multiply; what could be more 'pro-life'?"[251]

As a result, the *political* mobilization by religious organizations against IVF is nearly nonexistent. Cognizant of the cleavage within the conservative Christian coalition and of the political realities faced by the Republican Party, even the Catholic Church's mobilization and political opposition to IVF and to the development of the infertility industry has been muted in the United States.[252] According to their proponents, even "personhood" amendments proposed in Colorado and elsewhere would eliminate abortion and end stem cell research—but allow IVF.[253] For its part, the federal response has been to leave the matter largely unregulated; unfunded by the federal government, most of the research and procedures have been developed in the private sector. In 1978, the first Ethical Advisory Board (EAB) was appointed to approve IVF research, and the EAB recommended in 1979 that the federal government fund IVF research. The government, however, let the EAB simply expire without funding the research rather than to engage the IVF further.[254]

Stem cell research has proven far more controversial, invoking the specter of chimera monsters and the cloning of human beings. Here, the Lutheran Church–Missouri Synod and the Southern Baptist Convention joined the Roman Catholic Church in opposing such research.[255] These and other religious organizations cast embryonic stem cell research as *equivalent* to abortion, and thus, to murder. Critics ranging from the Christian Coalition of America to the Traditional Values Coalition to the National Conference of Bishops spoke of the need to preserve the rights of the unborn and human dignity by banning embryonic stem cell research.[256] Southern Baptists argued that "the Bible teaches that human beings are made in the image and likeness of God (Gen. 1:27; 9:6) and

[250] Davis 2006, 288.
[251] Rosenberg 2001.
[252] Davis 2006, 275; Dolgin 2000.
[253] Personhood Colorado Director Gualberto Garcia Jones, quoted in http://colorado independent.com/57321/personhoods-jones-says-amendments-effects-exaggerated-but-real.
[254] Belew 2003, 479.
[255] Wertz 2002, 676.
[256] *New York Times*, August 21, 2001.

protectable human life begins at fertilization."[257] The language verged on the apocalyptic: Arianna Grumbine of Survivors, a pro-life youth group, declared that "we as the survivors of abortion holocaust, we are a pro-life youth group, and we take a stand for all human life, because we do believe it's sacred. . . . We are not against stem cell research, we are definitely pro-technology, pro-science. We believe in the advancement of all sciences, except for those that destroy human life."[258] The Conference of Catholic Bishops made references to the national interest, expressing concern with "mak[ing] taxpayers complicit in such killing through use of public funds" and arguing that the Declaration of Independence "declared that members of the human race . . . are created equal in their fundamental rights, beginning with the right to life."[259]

Religious views are an important factor in the opposition to stem cell research as well; more than half (52%) of those opposing stem cell research cited religion as their main influence, compared to only 7% of supporters.[260] Even though less than 10% of these opponents participated in the debate (by contacting representatives, attending meetings, donating to organizations), nearly all received requests from church organizations to do so. Not surprisingly, church recruitment was the one significant predictor of individuals becoming politically active in the stem cell debate.[261]

Reframed as protecting the unborn, opposition to embryonic stem cell research found numerous allies within the Republican Party and resonated with religious views.[262] Federal regulations had already prevented the use of federal funds for experimentation on human embryos since 1974, when Congress applied a temporary moratorium on federal funding after the *Roe v. Wade* decision (the fear was that aborted fetuses and embryos would be exploited).[263] The moratorium was extended indefinitely in 1989 by the Department of Health and Human Services Secretary Louis Sullivan, accepting arguments from theologically conservative members of the Human Fetal Tissue Transplantation Research Panel that such research would increase

[257] "Resolution on Human Embryonic and Stem Cell Research." Southern Baptist Convention, June 1999, SBC website, retrieved October 3, 2011. http://www.sbc.net/resolutions /amResolution.asp?ID=620.

[258] Hunter, Melanie. 2008. "Pro-Life Group Protests Embryonic Stem Cell Research." *CNS News*. July 7. http://www.cnsnews.com/news/article/pro-life-groups-protest-embryonic -stem-cell-research.

[259] "On Embryonic Stem Cell Research." USCCB Publishing, Washington DC, 2008.

[260] Pew Forum on Religion and Public Life 2006.

[261] Goidel and Nisbet 2006, 187–89.

[262] Banchoff 2012, 3 and 231.

[263] Wertz 2002, 674.

abortions by legitimating the use of fetal tissue from abortion.[264] When the Clinton administration authorized the use of federal funds for research on leftover embryos in 1995,[265] Congress intervened to pass the Dickey Amendment, a rider to the Labor, Health and Human Services and Education appropriations bill, prohibiting the Department of Human Health and Services from using appropriated funds for any research involving specifically created research embryos or the destruction of any embryos. A Dickey Amendment has been added to every one of these appropriations bills since 1995.

The situation changed with the isolation of human embryonic stem cells in 1998. The Clinton administration decided that these cells could be harvested without directly causing the destruction of embryos—and thus the Dickey Amendment no longer applied. It was left to President Bush in 2001 to authorize the use of federal funds for embryonic stem cell research. He was heavily pressured by the Catholic Church and pro-life organizations, which equated stem cell research with abortion and demanded its end. Bush received numerous letters from the US Conference of Bishops and met privately with Pope John Paul II, who further urged him to end the funding. Bush's public address in 2001, explaining his decision to allow federal funding for research on sixty *existing* embryonic lines, explicitly referred to the "culture of life":

> My position on these issues is shaped by deeply held beliefs. I'm a strong supporter of science and technology, and believe they have the potential for incredible good—to improve lives, to save life, to conquer disease. Research offers hope that millions of our loved ones may be cured of a disease and rid of their suffering. . . . I also believe human life is a sacred gift from our Creator. I worry about *a culture that devalues life*, and believe as your President I have an important obligation to foster and encourage respect for life in America and throughout the world.[266]

---

[264] Wertz 2002, 647. The panel recommended that such research be regulated and funded by the federal government, but Sullivan chose to extend the moratorium. Report of the Advisory Committee to the Director, National Institutes of Health, "Human Fetal Tissue Transplantation Research," Bethesda, Maryland, December 14, 1988, available at http://bioethics.georgetown.edu/pcbe/reports/past_commissions/fetal_tissue_report.pdf, accessed June 12, 2013. The panel included several physicians as well as lawyers and representatives of minority organizations. Several theologians and religious representatives were present.

[265] http://clinton6.nara.gov/1994/12/1994–12–02-president-on-nih-and-human-embryo-research.html.

[266] http://www.whitehouse.gov/news/releases/2001/08/20010809–2.html. Emphasis added.

Bush here did not shy away from sacral language, which after all was a major component of his 2000 campaign and featured prominently and consistently in his rhetoric as President. By limiting research to existing stem cell lines, he avoided the "life and death decision" altogether and attempted to preserve his pro-life credentials. The decision profoundly disappointed religious moderates.[267] It also temporarily split the conservative Christian coalition. The rhetorical connection between embryonic stem cell research and abortion was a double-edged sword: the pragmatists within the coalition approved Bush's decision, but the purists saw the limits as inadequate. Thus Pat Robertson praised the Bush decision as "firmly protecting the rights of the unborn," while other groups, including the National Bishops' Conference, decried the decision to allow research as furthering "killing."[268] This cleavage within the conservative coalition over Bush's decision did not follow denominational lines— Evangelicals and Catholics could be found on both sides—but ran between pragmatists and purists. Yet even the purists were not willing to oppose the President further, in hopes of future legislative action. They were not disappointed; in 2006 and 2007 Bush further vetoed legislation to expand stem cell research to donated embryos left over from IVF treatment.

On the state level, where the legality of embryonic stem cell research was decided, six states prohibited the creation or destruction of human embryos for medical research (Arkansas, Indiana, Louisiana, Michigan, North Dakota, and South Dakota).[269] By 2013, four states amended their constitutions by popular referendum to *allow* stem cell research, joining several others that had legalized such research earlier (Connecticut, Illinois, Maryland, New York, Iowa, Massachusetts, and Missouri). In all cases, the opposition included right to life and religious organizations. Yet on the state level, the campaigns rarely included references to the right to life of the unborn or the culture of life, much less religious symbols or language. Even religious allies, such as the state Right to Life groups, made little use of religious language. Once again, doctrinal differences made Catholic opposition more intense—and unlike abortion, there was no easily identifiable set of politically vulnerable "perpetrators" (scientists and the very ill hardly qualified). Instead, to paper over the theological differences and lack of easy political targets, the campaigns on the state

---

[267] Domke and Coe 2008, 136.
[268] *New York Times*, August 12, 2001.
[269] See Pew Forum on Religion and Public Life 2008.

level revolved around the scientific promise and public expense of stem cell research.[270]

In short, both embryonic stem cell research and in vitro fertilization result in the destruction of embryos that abortion opponents find so objectionable. Yet the response to these two issues differed greatly from each other—and from abortion, where the religious-partisan coalition saw enormous electoral gains to be made. Further, religious organizations took very different tacks addressing the two issues. IVF was largely left

---

[270] In California, Proposition 71 in 2004 was a constitutional amendment that made conducting stem cell research a state constitutional right. It allocated three billion dollars in state funds to stem cell research over ten years, with priority given to embryonic stem cell research. The campaign for Proposition 71 was led by the Coalition for Stem Cell Research and Cures, which included numerous celebrities, California state officials and legislators, various disease and patient advocacy groups, twenty-two Nobel Laureates, and several minority advocacy groups including the NAACP. Opponents included the Catholic Church (the United States Conference of Catholic Bishops donated tens of thousands of dollars), the California Pro-Life Council, the California Nurses Association, and the Green Party. http://ballotpedia.org/wiki/index.php/California_Proposition_71_ (2004). Despite the general opposition of the Republican Party, Governor Arnold Schwarzenegger endorsed the Proposition on October 18. In Missouri, Amendment 2 in 2006 legalized embryonic stem cell research within the limits of federal law. The campaign for the amendment was led by the Missouri Coalition for Lifesaving Cures, in response to a move by the legislature to ban research within the state. The main coalition against the measure was Missourians against Human Cloning, who emphasized scientific reasons for preferring adult stem cells, and also highlighted the concern that poor and vulnerable women could be exploited for their eggs. New Jersey authorized all forms of stem cell research in 2003 and was the first to devote public money, but a 2007 Bond Act to raise funding for the research failed. Several Democratic legislators supported it, along with Michael J. Fox (who has appeared in support of nearly every ballot initiative on the issue) and Governor Jon Corzine, who contributed $150,000 toward a PAC running ads. The measure was opposed by the New Jersey Right to Life (NJRL) and by Americans for Prosperity (AFP), a pro-business, small-government organization founded by David Koch, the billionaire libertarian. AFP argued that the private sector had not invested in stem cell research, and government funding "amounts to corporate welfare for the biochemical industry." http://ballotpedia.org/wiki/index.php/New_Jersey_Public_Question_Two_ (2007). Neither NJRL nor AFP made religious appeals in their campaign. Finally, in 2008 Michigan voters approved Proposal 2 as an amendment that would allow embryonic stem cell research on discarded embryos donated by IVF clinics. Several patient/disease advocacy organizations, and prominent politicians such as Bill Clinton, Carl Levin, and Jennifer Granholm all endorsed the amendment. The opposition was led by Michigan Citizens against Unrestricted Science & Experimentation (MiCAUSE). Allied organizations included the American Academy of Medical Ethics, Archdiocesan Advisory Committee on Health Care Ethics (Detroit), Assemblies of God, Baptists for Life, Democrats for Life, Knights of Columbus, Lutherans for Life, Michigan Catholic Conference, and Right to Life Michigan. The language of the campaign, however, was entirely secular, arguing that tissue rejection and tumor formation were the major problems with embryonic stem cell trials, while adult stem cells were scientifically appropriate substitutes. Other arguments included references to Tuskegee syphilis experiments, and the potential tax burden, but there were no references to religious symbols or "culture of life."

alone, given the diverging religious views and political costs (and, perhaps its high profitability in the private sector). Stem cell research, in contrast, was likened by its opponents to abortion, and once this rhetorical move was made, groups opposing abortion would pounce to eliminate it.

Same-Sex Marriage

If divorce was acceptable in the "family values" framework, same-sex marriage was not. If anything, same-sex marriage became the "new abortion," in the words of Gary Bauer, president of American Values.[271] It was the "new enemy," not only a grave aberration and a threat to the American family, but also a political lightning rod, an issue on which the members of conservative Christian coalition readily agreed and easily mobilized.[272] It is therefore all the more worrying to opponents of same-sex marriage that popular support for it has soared: from 25% of poll respondents in the mid-1990s to 50% by 2010 to 63% by 2013.[273]

The issue of gay rights could be ignored as long as most gays remained silent and concealed. Once the National Gay Task Force began to lobby for legislative protection in the early 1970s, however, conservative Christians reacted much as they had to abortion. By the mid-1970s, they began to sign petitions against Gay Pride celebrations and anti-discrimination ordinances.[274] In 1976, the Southern Baptist Convention passed its first resolution against homosexuality and began to endorse the campaigns of gospel singer Anita Bryant and others to exclude gays from education and other arenas.

In their national legal strategy for the defense of the family, the conservative Christian coalition has focused on preventing or eliminating same-sex marriage rather than banning divorce. The logic is electoral and coalitional; reliant as they are on the support of their members, to remain within a given church and to provide the votes necessary for the coalition to remain a political force, conservative Christian churches have considerably more to gain by pursuing a minority outside of the churches than the "sins" of its own faithful. Further, without a monopoly or dominant religion that claims the moral authority in the United States, stances on political issues have to be reconciled within the religious coalition and

---

[271] Domke and Coe, 117.

[272] Balmer 2006, 22, 24.

[273] Gelman, Lax, and Phillips 2010. Reuters/Ipsos poll, 2013, http://www.reuters.com/article/2013/03/25/us-usa-gaymarriage-idUSBRE92O05G20130325. Accessed October 14, 2013.

[274] Williams 2010, 146–47.

its doctrinal least common denominator. Here, theological opposition to same-sex marriage unites both Catholics and conservative Protestants.[275]

As with abortion and stem cell research, the conservative Christian coalition captured the *national framing* of the issue and policy at the federal levels, but local electorates, and the opinion differences among them, drove much of the variation in *state policy*. If "frequent reference to Judeo-Christian scripture"[276] drove the opposition, it played out in distinct ways in the states. Same-sex marriage took on national importance in the 1996 electoral campaign, once a Hawai'i court ruled in 1993 that denying marriage licenses to same-sex couples violated the Equal Protection Clause of the Constitution. The ruling was immediately denounced as "judicial tyranny" by the Traditional Values Coalition and mobilized religious opponents in the run-up to the presidential election.[277] The National Campaign to Protect Marriage, a group affiliated with the Christian Right, responded by insisting that all Republican presidential candidates sign the Protect Marriage Resolution before the Iowa caucuses.[278]

In a decisive move at the federal level, Representative Bob Barr (R-GA) authored the 1996 Defense of Marriage Act (DOMA) to exempt all states from recognizing same-sex marriages performed in other states. Echoing the rhetoric of religious groups, he argued that the bill was needed because "the flames of hedonism, the flames of narcissism, the flames of self-centered morality are licking at the very foundation of our society, the family unit."[279] Another supporter of DOMA, the head of the House Judiciary Subcommittee on the Constitution, Charles Canady (R-FL) declared that "the traditional family structure—centered on a lawful union between one man and one woman—comports with our Judeo-Christian

---

[275] That said, the doctrinal consensus belied differences of opinion among the faithful: 55% of Catholics opposed same-sex marriage while 35% favored it, making the membership substanti-ally more liberal than evangelical Protestants, where the numbers are 80% to 13%. There were also differences within denominations: in 2005, the general synod of the 1.3-million-member United Church of Christ passed a resolution affirming same-sex marriage; this caused a split in the church, with some southern congregations breaking away despite pleas from other southern dissidents to stay (*Winston-Salem Journal*. 2005. "Same-Sex Marriage Vote Assailed; Group of Regional Churches Shows Its Dissent with United Church of Christ's position." July 8). Divides also occurred among the United Methodists, which officially forbids same sex unions, but whose Northern California clergy had openly defied church authority on the issue (*San Francisco Chronicle*. 2004. "Even in S.F., Religion Still Divided over Gay Marriage; Catholics, Muslims Steadfast over Ban on Same-Sex Unions." February 14).

[276] Segura 2005, 190.

[277] *New York Times*, December 4, 1996.

[278] Lewis and Oh 2008, 45.

[279] *New York Times*, July 13, 1996.

tradition."[280] The law passed both houses by large majorities, and (Democratic) President Bill Clinton quickly signed it into law in September 1996, in the hopes of avoiding electoral controversy in the upcoming November elections. Section 3 of the bill explicitly prohibited federal recognition of same-sex marriage, including filing of joint tax returns, obtaining Social Security survivors' benefits, immigration status, and insurance benefits for federal employees.

At the same time, however, efforts to push through a Federal Marriage Amendment (FMA), which would have defined marriage in the United States as "the union of a man and a woman," ran aground. The proposal was put forth in 2002 by an allied organization, the Alliance for Marriage, and the influential Christian commentator James Dobson spoke out in its favor. A year later, the Supreme Court reached the *Lawrence and Garner v. Texas* decision, which struck down a state anti-sodomy law and grounded the decision in the same right to privacy that so many found objectionable with *Roe v. Wade*. Shocked by the decision, and the rapidity with which Massachusetts declared same-sex marriage legal just a few months later, Dobson approached the 2004 re-election campaign of George W. Bush with an ultimatum: to win the support of the conservative Christian coalition, Bush would have to endorse the FMA.[281] The chief of Bush's electoral campaign, Karl Rove, readily agreed, largely because the issue had huge potential to mobilize conservative Christian voters.[282] Bush himself eventually supported the measure—but again compromised by stating that he did not "support attempts to prevent states from offering civil unions to gay couples."[283] In Congress, FMA bills failed repeatedly, on at least six different occasions.

In campaigning against same-sex marriage, the conservative Christian coalition, now joined by the Church of Jesus Christ of Latter-Day Saints (LDS, the Mormons), collected petition signatures, filed amici curiae briefs, heavily donated to referendum campaigns, established political action committees (Yes on 8, Hawai'i's Future Today, Hana Pano), and reminded their faithful to vote and to contact their representatives.[284] Affiliated religious groups (National Organization for Marriage, Focus on the Family, American Family Association, Citizens for Community Values) also played a major role in advancing anti-same-sex marriage amendments in the 2000 and 2004 election years, mobilizing voters to support ballot initiatives and

[280] *New York Times*, July 13, 1996.
[281] Williams 2010, 256.
[282] Oldmixon and Calfano 2007 found that the percentage of conservative Christians in a given constituency already affected their representatives' voting in Congress.
[283] Williams 2010, 259.
[284] Crapo 2008.

conservative candidates through voter guides, rallies, sample sermons, petitions, and television advertisements.[285] A notable mobilization technique was the Shubert Flint strategy, named after the firm responsible for the successful "Yes on 8" campaign in California, in which marketing firms produced professional campaigning materials for use by church volunteers.[286] The strategy called for conservative Christians to have "priests in every parish . . . identify a 'church captain' in order to create an 'ad hoc committee' " to oppose same-sex marriage.[287]

The religious rhetoric blended appeals to historical tradition, threats of church-state conflict, and appeals to the nation: "marriage and religious freedom are both deeply woven into the fabric of this nation," as an open letter signed by evangelical, Catholic, and LDS leaders declared in an "Open Letter to all Americans."[288] The Family Research Council declared that it "promotes the Judeo-Christian worldview as the basis for a just, free, and stable society . . . FRC champions marriage and family as the foundation of civilization, the seedbed of virtue, and the wellspring of society."[289] These local mobilization efforts appeared successful: Gregory Lewis and Seong Soo Oh find that the strength of *local* evangelical communities and local public opposition were significant predictors of same-sex marriage policy outcomes, as with abortion.[290] Same-sex marriage may have also stimulated electoral turnout (if not which vote would be cast) in 2004. Evangelicals turned out in greater numbers, as did all other religious groups save mainline Protestants.[291]

Thirty-six states passed laws prohibiting same-sex marriage between 1996 and 1997. Another twelve states did so between 1997 and 2008.[292] In 1998, Hawai'i itself voted by over a two-thirds majority to define marriage as a compact between a man and a woman (a similar measure

---

[285] Duncan 2007, 55–56.

[286] Duncan 2007, 56. Religious same-sex marriage opponents used similar tactics in 2006 and 2008, but their initiatives passed by lower margins (about 60%) and were even defeated by same-sex marriage proponents in Arizona.

[287] "Minn. Archdiocese Plans Anti-Gay Marriage Committees in Every State Catholic Church." *Washington Independent*. October 17, 2011. http://bit.ly/pSnqHx. Accessed October 16, 2013.

[288] Anderson et al., "Marriage and Religious Freedom: Fundamental Goods That Stand or Fall Together. An Open Letter from Religious Leaders in the United States to All Americans." *United States Conference of Catholic Bishops*. January 12, 2012. http://bit.ly/wPiEwl. Letter signed by Rev. Leith Anderson, President, National Association of Evangelicals; New York Archbishop Timothy M. Dolan, president of the U.S. Conference of Catholic Bishops; H. David Burton, presiding bishop of the Church of Jesus Christ of Latter-Day Saints.

[289] "Mission Statement." *Family Research Council*. Press release. n.d. http://bit.ly /ywHqzC. Accessed October 16, 2013.

[290] Lewis and Oh 2008.

[291] Claassen and Povtak 2010.

[292] Lewis and Oh 2008, 45.

passed the same year in Alaska). The Mormon Church was heavily involved financially in both campaigns. Opponents of same-sex marriage gathered in Hawai'i in an organization called Hawai'i's Future Today, backed by the Catholic and Mormon Churches as well as major conservative groups from the mainland. The organization campaigned for an amendment banning same-sex marriage in Hawai'i, with funding from the political action committee Hana Pano, which had been organized by the Mormon Church. Additionally, the Mormon Church contracted the marketing agency Hill and Knowlton to develop a lobbying and public opinion campaign for Hawai'i's Future Today.[293] The amendment passed in 1998 by a margin of 69% to 29%.

The Roman Catholic Church's strategy focused on bishops addressing both the faithful and local politicians, reminding them that on this issue as on others, "there is to be no separation between one's faith and life in either public or private realms. All Catholics should act on their beliefs with a well-formed conscience based on Sacred Scripture and Tradition."[294] It did so most controversially in Massachusetts, both a Roman Catholic stronghold and the epicenter of clergy sexual abuse scandals. In May 2003, the four Catholic bishops of Massachusetts told clergy to remind their members of the church's opposition to same-sex marriage, and to encourage them to contact legislators. In the words of Bishop Daniel P. Reilly of Worcester, bishops had "a right and a duty" to remind parishioners that the church defines marriage as a relationship between one man and one woman. This prompted an angry response from gay and lesbian groups (including Catholic members), who put forth an argument that would become very familiar: because of its failure to respond adequately to child sexual abuse within its ranks, the church had forfeited its authority on moral issues and was looking for a way to distract attention from its own problems. As David Breen, a Catholic member of the Gay and Lesbian Political Caucus, argued: "so much for 'He who is without sin should cast the first stone.' . . . The bishops have as much credibility to speak out on marriage as Jack Kevorkian has to speak out on elder care."[295] Some gay members protested the statement by walking out of Mass when it was announced.[296] The Supreme Court of Massachusetts would ultimately rule in late 2003 that obstacles to same-sex marriage were unconstitutional. Legislative opponents of same-sex marriage subsequently began a cam-

[293] Crapo 2008.

[294] "Between Man and Woman: Questions and Answers about Marriage and Same-Sex Unions." *United States Conference of Catholic Bishops*. 2003. http://bit.ly/yd28jx.

[295] *Boston Globe*. 2003. "Gays, Lesbians Lash Out at Church Same-Sex Marriage Opposition Blasted." May 31.

[296] AP. 2003. "Gay Groups Protest Church's Opposition to Gay Marriage." June 1.

paign to overturn it in the legislature; in 2006, the Catholic Church again urged parishioners to contact lawmakers and to pray for the success of an anti-same-sex marriage bill. Lay Catholic supporters of same-sex marriage responded by signing a series of newspaper ads declaring Cardinal O'Malley of Boston did not speak for them and by distributing thousands of copies of a brochure called "Why we don't vote on civil rights."[297]

Two religious groupings that were normally outside of the conservative Christian coalition became embroiled in the issue. First, traditionally black churches vehemently opposed same-sex marriage. A Gallup poll found that 72% of blacks were opposed to equal recognition of same-sex relationships (compared to 59% of the general population). The 5.5 million member Church of God in Christ (the country's largest black church) issued a public proclamation against same-sex marriage, and the African Methodist Episcopal Church banned its ministers from officiating in any same-sex unions.[298] Leading African American clergy such as Jesse Jackson almost unanimously opposed same-sex marriage, and the Black Ministerial Alliance rejected it.[299] Some individual black clergy have endorsed same-sex marriage, but the most prominent black advocates have been two secular figures, Coretta Scott King and NAACP chairman Julian Bond. When Bond (not speaking for the NAACP) called the issue one of civil rights, other black leaders angrily rejected the comparison. A spokesman for a coalition of black churches in Southern California stated that "gays have never gone through slavery nor been put down and abused like blacks . . . it's an insult to use that parallel."[300] One North Carolina minister commented that "I feel that it's my calling to make sure people realize there are no connections between the homosexual agenda and the civil rights movement. . . . We want to make it overwhelmingly clear that [homosexuality] is nothing like being black. Blackness is not deviant."[301]

The Church of Jesus Christ of Latter-Day Saints (LDS) was also involved very early in the campaign against same-sex marriage, with the First Presidency (the top LDS church leadership) issuing a statement in 1994 (as same-sex marriage was becoming an issue in Hawai'i) urging Mormons "to appeal to legislators, judges and other government officials to . . . reject all efforts to give legal authorization or other official

---

[297] *Boston Globe.* 2006. "Bishops Vote for a Ban on Marriage." October 31.

[298] *Houston Chronicle.* 2004. "Issue Helps Bush with Blacks: Churchgoers Taking Second Look Due to His Stance on Gay Marriage." August 8.

[299] *Boston Globe.* 2007. "A Black Church to Host Gay Service Event Is a Victory for Advocates." July 9.

[300] *San Francisco Chronicle.* 2004. "Black Clergy Gather to Fight Gay Matrimony." May 14.

[301] *News and Observer* (Raleigh). 2004. "Rights Parallel Disputed: Black Clergy Split on Gay Marriage." April 6.

approval or support to marriages between persons of the same gender."[302] Anti-same-sex-marriage coalitions in the early battlegrounds of Alaska and Hawai'i received hundreds of thousands of dollars from the LDS. In Nebraska and Nevada, the church is believed to have played a large grassroots role in ballot measures that made same-sex marriage unconstitutional.[303] In Utah, the issue has been seen as a "litmus test" for politicians running for national office, much as the ERA (which the church also opposed) was in the 1970s.[304] This church involvement in the politics of the issue has generated backlash. When the church raised funds across the country, and mobilized thousands of California members in favor of Proposition 8 in 2008, a member of the San Francisco Board of Supervisors, among others, attacked the church's tax-exempt status and political activism. Critics repeatedly accused the church of trying to influence the outcome of the ballot through large donations (an estimated $20 million in the case of Proposition 8). The public backlash was so severe that in the 2012 national elections, the LDS remained largely silent on the issue. It quietly filed amicus curiae briefs with the US Supreme Court but no longer campaigned openly against same-sex marriage—and no longer funded campaigns against same-sex marriage.[305]

Once again, as with abortion, the Supreme Court would cast the decisive vote, this time with a 5–4 majority in June 2013. In *United States v. Windsor*, the Court ruled DOMA, and specifically Section 3, violated the equal protection amendment of the Constitution by not giving same-sex couples the same tax standing, federal benefits, inheritance status, and other legal recognition and benefits that heterosexual couples received. At the same time, the Court ruled that the defendants in *Hollingsworth v. Perry* had no standing in court, which meant that Proposition 8 in California was struck down, enabling same-sex marriages to resume.

The Court's rulings were an immediate defeat, and the issue also illustrated a quandary for the conservative Christian coalition. Because the opinion of the faithful matters so much to denominational survival in the United States and to the ability of the conservative Christian-partisan coalition to deliver the votes (and thus affect policy), churches and their po-

---

[302] *Deseret News* (Salt Lake City). 1996. "Stance on Same-Sex Marriage Is Likely to Handicap Anderson." July 5.

[303] *Deseret News* (Salt Lake City). 2000. "Church Backing Helps Measures in 2 States." November 8.

[304] *Deseret News* (Salt Lake City). 1996. "Stance on Same-Sex Marriage Is Likely to Handicap Anderson." July 5.

[305] http://www.reuters.com/article/2013/03/25/us-usa-gaymarriage-idUSBRE92O05G 20130325. The church launched a website that encouraged greater understanding of "same sex attraction" at http://mormonsandgays.org/. The LDS doctrinal stance now resembles the Catholic Church: condemning homosexual activity but not the sexual preference itself.

litical allies are likely to face a dilemma. On the one hand, unlike abortion, or other aspects of sexuality such as pornography, adultery, or premarital sex, *popular attitudes* regarding gay rights and same-sex marriage have shifted considerably since the early 2000s. As Chapter 2 noted, Americans increasingly accept homosexuality as well as same-sex marriage, protection from unemployment discrimination, and the right to serve openly in the military.[306] Younger cohorts are notably more in favor: if 8% of those born before 1924 agree that same sex couples ought to be allowed to marry, 50% of those born after 1974 do.[307] Public support has gone from a quarter of respondents in 1994 to nearly two-thirds in 2013. It was partly in recognition of these changing demographics that the Obama administration declined to defend DOMA in *United States v. Windsor*. On the other hand, the *religious* opposition to same-sex marriage remains constant; the conservative denominations that form the conservative Christian coalition have not altered their doctrine or changed their public commitments. The likely result is that conservative religious groups will continue to be the mainstay of the opposition to same-sex marriage— but they will have an increasingly difficult time convincing the broader populace.

Backlash?

For all its success in mobilizing mass constituencies and reframing policy issues, the conservative Christian coalition did not succeed uniformly. First, powerful courts stymied its aims, whether with prayer in schools or abortion. Second, Republican politicians—and more importantly, the broader electorate—often had other priorities, the chief of these being economic growth and pocketbook issues. As a result, beginning with the presidency of Ronald Reagan, when the alliance made its political debut, the electoral power of the conservative religious coalition did not necessarily translate into securing policy outcomes.

Reagan himself appointed Evangelicals to cabinet posts in the Department of Health and Human Services and the Department of Education, the very government sectors he hoped to abolish.[308] He delayed action on the moral issues important to the conservative coalition, justifying these delays with the need to resolve economic problems first. Neither the school prayer amendment nor an anti-abortion amendment materialized, and not just because of a Democratic congressional majority or presidential lethargy, but because the broader electorate simply did not support these

---

[306] Gallup 2011; Egan, Persily, and Wallsten 2008.
[307] Egan, Persily, and Wallsten 2008.
[308] Williams 2010, 195.

aims.[309] Even George W. Bush, who enacted several measures that could be seen as policy victories for the conservative Christian coalition, did not fulfill his electoral promises. He signed the Partial-Birth Abortion Act of 2003, the first federal statute to prohibit an abortion procedure, and the Unborn Victims of Violence Act of 2004, which increased the penalties for harming pregnant victims of violence if their fetus was injured. He also founded the White House Office of Faith-Based and Community Initiatives, issuing an executive order prohibiting discrimination against religious organizations applying for federal funding. Yet on issues such as gay rights or abortion, the President expended little political capital, and his stem cell research compromise disappointed many conservative Christian leaders. Not even the policy gains in abortion, education, and stem cell research were enough to preclude a bitter suspicion that "this has been an unholy alliance in which the evangelicals have given everything and gotten nothing in return."[310]

The persistence of this pattern through several Republican administrations led some conservative Christian leaders to threaten to abandon their coalition with the Republican Party; the conservative Christians had delivered the votes but did not receive the promised policy concessions. These threats were highly strategic, coming when the religious strength had been greatest and the partisan partner most vulnerable. For example, in 1998, Focus on the Family chair James Dobson threatened to leave the Republican Party, "saying that in the sixteen months following the November 1996 elections, Republicans failed to deliver on socially conservative issues."[311] At the same time, both sides realized that so long as "moral issues" were at the center of the conservative Christian commitment to the Republican Party, neither side had anywhere else to go, especially given the growing divergence with the Democratic stances on these same issues.

In the end, the conservative Christian coalition was not fully satisfied but had no other potential partner. It succeeded in a takeover of the Republican Party platform, but institutional access was formally prohibited. Any other influence would continue to rely on its partisan alliance with the Republican Party on both the federal and state levels. Yet many American churches overcame their doctrinal differences and a history of mutual suspicion to form the conservative Christian coalition in the first place, and to capitalize on a long history of a religiously tinted national identity. Nor did they suffer a collapse of their moral authority, given its

---

[309] Williams 2010, 203.

[310] Richard Cizik, quoted in Feder, Lester. 2008. "Explaining McCain's Success among Evangelicals," available at http://www.huffingtonpost.com/lester-feder/explaining-mccains-succes_b_82378.html, accessed June 14, 2013.

[311] Williams 2010, 242.

diffusion among different churches and denominations. Their counterparts in Canada could claim no such successes.

Canada

The fusion of religious and national identities flourished in the United States, yet it never blossomed in Canada, with neither an invented religious tradition nor a national religious monopoly. Clear subnational divisions between the Francophone and Anglophone communities meant that while Catholicism and a French-Canadian identity fused for decades, no *national* fusion of religion and national identity took place. There was no American-style religious infusion of political rhetoric, no "promised land" and no civil religion—and, in fact, no national flag until 1965 and no official national anthem until 1980.

If anything, Canadian observers defined their national identity in *opposition* to the United States. As early as 1880, *Canadian Methodist Magazine* summarized some of the differences between the two countries: "we are free from many of the social cancers which are empoisoning the national life of our neighbors. We have no polygamous Mormondom; no Ku-Klux terrorism; no Oneida communism; no Illinois divorce system; no cruel Indian massacres."[312] Progressive and conservative critiques were combined under a flag of Canadian moral rectitude and social stability, in contrast to America's libertinism and social chaos. Canadian institutions such as a parliament and a constitutional monarchy were also widely seen as superior to American arrangements. Even a French-Canadian Prime Minister such as Wilfrid Laurier (in office 1896–1911) declared Canada a "self-governing British kingdom" and enthusiastically participated in the Queen's Jubilee celebrations.[313]

A single nationalism did not arise, much less fuse with religious sentiment. The state arose and encompassed distinct Francophone and Anglophone populations, which dominated Lower and Upper Canada, respectively. In the religious sphere, Catholicism and Protestantism coexisted without either dominating. These two competing religious traditions persisted within Canada, overlapping with durable linguistic and cultural differences.[314] The history of this "protracted religious oligopoly . . . is, in large part, the story of conflict, competition and accommodation among

[312] Quoted in Phillips 1988, 465.
[313] Levitt 1993, 95.
[314] The 1840–41 Act of Union, which united the Anglophone Upper Canada and the far more populous (and primarily Francophone) Lower Canada, effectively gave the Anglophones greater representation and cemented their hold on political authority.

Anglicans, Roman Catholics, and the groups that formed what is now the United Church (notably Methodists and Presbyterians)."[315]

It is not that there was no opportunity for fusion. In the early nineteenth century, religious questions dominated the political life of the colony, and worship was a public act.[316] Nor was there a want of effort: the Catholic Church assiduously worked to bolster Francophone identity, while the Anglican Church (the established church until the mid-nineteenth century[317]) saw as its goal "to make the church coterminous with the nation, to bring the Anglican message of salvation to every subject in the Crown."[318] However, without favorable national and linguistic demographics or a dominant denominational tradition, religion could not help to build a Canadian identity, and "this was less a result of consensus Protestantism's fragility or conflicts with Roman Catholics than a consequence of Canada's fragmented national identity. In the United States a more coherent civil religion evolved."[319] The result was that no one national religious identity perpetuated an overarching Canadian myth, and national heterogeneity meant no fusion was possible.

Instead, religion and *subnational* identities were more tightly linked, and religion became a source of informal regional identity: "British North America's political architects bolstered the colonial Anglican Church as a bulwark against further revolution. This effort failed, as evangelicals and other dissenters effectively challenged the Anglican quasi-establishment for the souls of the people in the colonies and then disestablished Anglicanism . . . Nonetheless, religion became a powerful source of legitimation, as an informal Protestant cultural establishment coalesced in English Canada and a Roman Catholic one in Québec."[320]

The most powerful example, and a case unto itself, was Québec, where for most of the nineteenth and twentieth centuries "the Catholic Church was the only major institution under the control of the French Canadians, and, paralleling to some extent the Irish Catholic experience, Catholics bonded to, and appropriated, the Church in their creation of a distinct French Canadian Catholic identity."[321] The church extended a protective canopy over Québec, an island of Francophone Catholics in an at best indifferent and frequently hostile sea of Anglophones. Much as in

[315] O'Toole 2000, 45.

[316] Westfall 2001, 26.

[317] The disestablishment itself, in the wake of the 1837–38 uprisings, was a way of accommodating the two religious monopolies (Noll 2007, 425).

[318] Westfall 2001, 27.

[319] Katerberg 2000, 286.

[320] Katerberg 2000, 285; see also Murphy and Perin 1996 and Stacey 1983 on culturally Protestant Ontario.

[321] Dillon 2007, 241.

Ireland, the Québécois church became a dominant political and societal force, influencing the moral and economic life of the province: mandating large families; operating hospitals, schools, and welfare institutions; and reigning as a local political hegemon. In both cases, the church's high moral authority translated into institutional access.

The church received institutional access from the Crown after the 1840 Act of Union eliminated French as an official language and suspended French-Canadian educational and legal institutions,[322] in exchange for pacifying the population and quelling the opposition to these moves.[323] The defeat of the governing liberal bourgeoisie led to an ideological and administrative vacuum that the church filled, with the full acquiescence of British colonial authorities, slowly taking over education, health, and welfare and becoming a "crypto-state" within Québec.[324] Further, these domains were given to the provinces under the first constitution, the 1867 British North America Act, which thus "sanctioned a preexisting arrangement in which the church largely delimited a French-Canadian public space. The Québec government would later exercise its autonomy indirectly and by proxy, relegating public powers to a private institution for the benefit of the majority of its population."[325]

Aided by the rise of a robust Ultramontanism among its clergy, the church set out to build its influence in society and its moral authority.[326] The church's institutional power was bolstered by the religious zeal that gripped the post-1840 years: "conversion was not simply a private matter, but a social even involving masses of people. The thirst for religious

[322] After the Rebellions of 1837, the Act of Union merged Upper Canada, with a British and Protestant majority, with Lower Canada, with a French and Canadian majority. Since Lower Canada was growing more slowly, the hope was to assimilate it into an Anglophone and Protestant domain. In effect, French Canadians were deprived of access to the state apparatus: high-ranking Québec ministers were invariably English speaking, for example, and the Québec provincial autonomy was limited by the new powers of the federal authorities and by the guarantees wrested by the Anglo-Protestant minority in Québec (Perin 2001, 90).

[323] Baum 1986, 437; Zubrzycki 2013, 432–33.

[324] Zubrzycki 2013, 433; Ferretti 1999.

[325] Perin 2001, 92.

[326] The Catholic Church in Canada had been monopolized since the Conquest by the Séminaire de Saint-Sulpice, which encouraged a discreet form of Catholic practice for fear of offending the British (Perin 2001, 91). Ignace Bourget, the bishop from 1840 to 1876, broke this monopoly and promoted public piety and the flowering of religious practice as well as the creation of public services and welfare institutions by religious communities. The church used the doctrine of Ultramontanism, which asserts the power of the papacy over local prerogatives, to assert its autonomy and to frame the church as the mainstay of the *Église nation*. The church in the 1960s rejected Ultramontanism in favor a church that served Québec society (Seljak 1996, 121).

renewal was so great that the local clergy could not keep pace with it."[327] Enormous processions, liturgies, devotional literature, Eucharistic Congresses (the 1910 Eucharistic Congress drew half a million estimated participants[328]), and celebrations both within Québec and outside of it, in French-Canadian communities like those in Manitoba and Alberta, all produced a religious fervor that would be familiar to Irish and Polish Catholics decades later. Such religiosity gave public testimony not only to the intensity of the faith but also to the regard in which the church was held.

As a result, Québec subsequently had no ministries of education, public health, or social assistance under Premier Maurice Duplessis (1936–39, 1944–59). His administrations conceded these state sectors to the Catholic Church, "producing a unique instance of ecclesiastical power."[329] The church's dominance went unchallenged, and its moral authority appeared unquestioned, reinforced and transmitted through the educational system and the steady presence of the church in the welfare state serving the society. This moral authority rested on a fusion of religious and national identities: "the cultural power of the Church was enormous. It defined Quebec's cultural identity in opposition to the Protestant and secular culture of North America."[330] This cultural power and moral authority translated into political influence: "no provincial government prior to 1960 would have introduced legislation of any significance without first seeking the approval of the Québec hierarchy."[331]

Yet this seemingly invincible domination gradually dissipated after World War II. Political and social critics began to question the agrarian and church-controlled status quo,[332] eventually culminating in the "Quiet Revolution" (*Révolution tranquille*) that took place over the course of the 1960s. The Revolution transformed Québec into a secular, extremely liberal province where the relevant cleavages were territorial and linguistic, submerging ethno-religious identities as parochial and outdated. A slew of new state policies promoted a territorial identity, economic modernity, and political autonomy for the Québec *nation* (a term first

---

[327] Perin 2001, 93.

[328] See Perin 2001, 99.

[329] Baum 2007, 270.

[330] Baum 2000, 150.

[331] Tentler 2007, 4.

[332] The two main currents of political thought were the neo-nationalists, centered on the journal *Le Devoir*, who sought a secular, urban-industrial state of Québec, and the Keynesian liberals, centered on organized labor and the journal *Cité Libre*, who sought to reduce the church's influence on the state and advance economic growth and income equality. These eventually became the kernels of the Parti Québécois and the Québec Liberal Party (see Behiels 1985).

used in the 1960s)—and the church, associated with the old order, lost its place.

The Quiet Revolution itself began *within* lay Catholic circles,[333] among mid-level state elites who found themselves unable to advance in the immense bureaucracy created by the church, since the best positions were reserved for clerics.[334] These lay Catholic elites were imbued with traditional Catholic teaching and yet nurtured "modern, rational and democratic values." Their frustration with the ossified Duplessis regime, and the complicity of the church in this conservatism, led them to demand greater transparency, rationalization of the bureaucracy, and a modernizing nationalism that was "defined as much against the Catholic Church as [against] the anglophone business elites."[335]

Once they ascended into power with the Liberal Party government of Jean Lesage, elected in 1960, these elites began to develop the state bureaucracy (which grew by over 40% during 1960–65[336]), nationalized the utilities, and handed over public services to the state, increasing the presence and influence of secular French-Canadian elites. The aim was to modernize Québec and to advance its economy, rather than anti-clericalism per se: "l'etat, c'est nous" was the rallying cry, and the aim was to build up bureaucratic competence, enlarge the domain of the state, and promote Francophone managers and enterprise. The state now took over education, health care, and welfare—and the sphere for church activity accordingly shriveled.[337]

The church no longer commanded moral authority as the representative of society's interests—not only because it was blamed for its complicity in Québec's underdevelopment, but also because the very identity of society had changed from ethnic and religious ("French-Canadian") to an explicitly territorial and linguistic one ("Québécois"). As part of the Quiet Revolution and the secularization of the welfare state and educational systems, "language partly replaced religion at the heart of Québecois self-consciousness."[338] In other words, "Quebeckers ceased to think of themselves in ethnic terms as part of the entire French-Canadian nation. They now thought of Québec as their own nation, defined in terms of citizenship rather than ethnicity."[339] Once identities shifted from ethno-religious to territorial-linguistic, these newly emboldened citizens

[333] Specifically, according to Gauvreau, within the younger cohorts of Catholic Action of the 1930s, who criticized their elders as elitist and hidebound (Gauvreau 2005, 355).

[334] Gauvreau 2005; Baum 1980.

[335] Seljak 1996, 113.

[336] Seljak 1996, 114.

[337] Gauvreau 2007.

[338] Martin 2005, 69; Oakes 2004.

[339] Baum 2000, 151.

moved to claim what was theirs to rule. Two consequences followed: national independence became a dominant political cleavage and aim, and the church's political influence greatly diminished. Schools and other services were placed in the hands of secular authorities.[340] By 1980, no nationalist group sought to promote a Catholic political culture or church teachings.[341]

Popular religiosity plummeted as the institutional church fell from grace. The public enthusiasm for the Liberal reforms went hand in hand with an increasing rejection of the old forms of public piety and loyalty to the church.[342] This rejection was spurred by the criticism of the lay Catholic reformists, who successfully derided existing religious practices as too "soft" and "traditional," unsuitable for the new and modern Québec[343]— and by the timing of the Vatican II ecumenical reforms, which meant further dislocation, as the familiar Latin Mass, incense and ceremony were replaced by vernacular services, guitars, and new informality. As a result, religious belief and observance fell, victims to the forces of a backlash against the church's role in keeping Québec "backward" and its families impoverished,[344] the shifts of Vatican II, and a new rhetoric of modernity. Within a decade, religious influence and religious practice were a shadow of their pre-1960 selves; not only did the newly muscular state assume control over welfare, education, and other sectors, but attendance at Mass also collapsed from 88% in 1965 to 46% by 1975.[345]

As a result of the Quiet Revolution, Roman Catholicism in Québec became a historical curiosity instead of a powerful institutional player, national representative, and spiritual master of Québec. The twin processes

[340] Christiano 2007, 22.

[341] Seljak 1996, 123.

[342] Zubrzycki 2013, 429.

[343] These were the same Catholic Action elites who launched the Quiet Revolution, including the future Prime Minister, Pierre Trudeau. As this group moved into more prominent positions in the state, media, and church, it not only depicted traditional Catholicism as too conformist and ritualistic, but also "turned the language of Catholic Action into an aggressive, male-centred spiritual elitism that was profoundly contemptuous of popular religious practice in Québec" (Gauvreau 2005, 355).

[344] The sexual revolution, and new access to contraceptives, was an additional force against the church, which had traditionally encouraged high birthrates, enormous families, and relegated women to the role of mothers. I am grateful to Geneviève Zubrzycki for this point.

[345] Christiano 2007, 30. The church accepted the Quiet Revolution with "relative serenity" (Seljak 1996, 110), partly because it had some roots in the church, and partly because the Vatican II reforms of the 1960s within the broader church led it to affirm the autonomy of civil society and the freedom of individual conscience (Seljak 1996, 111). The church-commissioned Dumont Report concluded in 1971 that the Quiet Revolution was an irreversible break with the past (Baum 2000, 152). Subsequently, the church focused on issues of social justice through the 1980s before reentering the debates over same-sex marriage and stem cell research.

of the political and economic expansion of the role of the state on the one hand and of the cultural redefinition of Québec identity as territorial and linguistic on the other relegated the institutional church to the margin.

The Quiet Revolution also rapidly transformed the church into a more left-leaning critic of government policy that repeatedly called out for greater social justice, poverty relief, and indigenous rights.[346] The reforming spirit of Vatican II also undermined conservative opposition within the church to the modernization of Québec. Yet by the 1990s, conservative elements within the church that were more concerned with morality policy grew more prominent. When policy controversies over abortion, same-sex marriage, assisted reproductive technologies, and stem cell research arose, the Roman Catholic Church in Québec and elsewhere in Canada spoke out in opposition—but could not, by then, change the debate. The church had lost not only its access to policy, but its hold over society as well. Today, even as most Québécois continue to identify themselves as nominally Catholic, Québec has among the most liberal abortion, reproductive technology, and embryonic research laws in the country.

As a result of the Quiet Revolution's transformation of religious and national identity, the Roman Catholic Church's political influence is minimal in Canada, even though its theological commitments are formally identical to those in Ireland or Poland. Similarly, even though Evangelical Protestants are flourishing, their theological similarities to their American brethren have not translated into political influence. Without a clear historical religious identity (invented or otherwise), churches cannot claim moral authority. No religion or interdenominational alliance can claim to influence Canadian politics, at either the provincial or federal level, whether through a partisan coalition or institutional access.

Policy Influence

Today, just over half (54%) of Canadians believe it is important to be Christian to be Canadian, compared to two-thirds of Americans (65%). However, without either a single dominant religion or a coalition of politically minded denominations, these convictions do not translate into moral authority for churches, or a potential to represent national interests. While the Catholic Church did play a historical role in defending French-Canadian identity (as in the Manitoba Schools Question) and gained enormous institutional access in Québec, it was never able to gain such authority on the *national* level. After the Quiet Revolution, the Catholic Church joined the Protestant churches in speaking out—but no longer expected to be listened to.

[346] Stackhouse 2000, 115.

Accordingly, while Roman Catholic bishops in the United States felt it was their duty to threaten excommunication to politicians supportive of abortion in the 1990s and 2000s, their counterparts in contemporary Canada took a much more discreet position—and even criticized the vehement stances of the pro-life organizations dominated by Catholics.[347] At the height of the abortion debates in 1988–90, Catholic bishops testified that while they opposed abortion, their views were one of many to be taken into account and "no one group has the right to impose its particular point of view," given the pluralism of Canadian society.[348] The bishops' willingness to enter the fray in the United States, and their caution in Canada, exemplifies the distinctive role played by organized religion in the two countries. In contemporary Canada, the churches' moral authority is relatively low, and incumbents do not rely on churches to enter or to stay in office. As a result, neither institutional access nor a coalition is an attractive option for secular actors, and few policy concessions are made to the churches.

Unlike the United States, moreover, there is no vibrant religious marketplace that would allow religions to compete—or to form coalitions—to influence politics. Instead, the establishment traditions of Europe and England followed into Canada: the state recognized and privileged particular religions, through the educational system, registration requirements, and so on.[349] Numerous privileges for religions (as social groups, not as individual rights to worship) were written into successive constitutional documents, in contrast to the formal separation of church and state in the United States.[350] This led to a dampening of religious observance and religious competition; the setting up of new churches was more difficult than in the United States, and the options for new converts and seekers more limited. Even newly resurgent evangelical communities counted on birthrates, rather than conversions, as the main engine of religious growth.[351] After the marginalization of the Catholic Church in Québec, and the rapid emptying of Anglican and United Church of Canada pews, Canadian churches chose to bear witness and even defer to the state rather than make demands or attempt to influence government policies. Thus, if the Roman Catholic Church in Ireland embraced and endorsed *Humanae Vitae*, the 1968 papal encyclical banning contraception, Canadian bishops responded to the encyclical "with barely concealed dismay, speaking

---

[347] Dillon 2007, 255.
[348] Tatalovich 1997, 133–34.
[349] Kim 1993.
[350] Christiano 2000, 76; Egerton 2000, 90.
[351] Bibby 1987.

pointedly of the rights of conscience."[352] Nor have the bishops condemned or disciplined politicians who support abortion or same-sex marriage, unlike their counterparts in the United States, Poland, and Italy.

Attempts to form an interdenominational coalition have also largely foundered; on the one hand, conservative Protestants and Catholics formed the Centre for Renewal of Public Policy in Ottawa in the 1990s,[353] a think tank that articulated a conservative Christian position on a variety of political, economic, and moral issues. Ad hoc coalitions have formed "to meet particular challenges and to advance particular agendas—and particularly to respond to unwelcome government initiatives."[354] Several more informal alliances also formed among liberal denominations, such as the Interfaith Social Assistance Review Committee, which as its name suggests was to review the Ontario government's social assistance policies. Others in the 1970s included the Coalition for Development, Interchurch Consultative Committee on Development and Relief, the Interchurch Committee for the Promotion of Justice in Canada, Taskforce on the Churches and Corporate Responsibility, and so on. The late 1980s and 1990s saw the emergence of transdenominational networks of evangelical Protestantism, which issued a steady stream of briefs and declarations, mostly at the federal level, on abortion, euthanasia, homosexuality, Christian education, but also on Aboriginal rights and constitutional revision.[355] Critically, however, these never reached either the cohesion of the conservative American interdenominational coalition or its explicitly political ambitions. Many, such as Citizens for Public Justice, straddled the liberal-conservative and mainline-evangelical divides, far more blurred in Canada than in the United States. Canadian coalitions focused on articulating concerns publicly rather than explicitly pressuring for policy change, but had no concerted efforts or successes of their southern neighbors.

A loose conservative alliance of mostly Protestant denominations did emerge in the early 1980s around the proposed Charter of Rights and Freedoms. Their allied organizations (the Evangelical Fellowship of Canada, Renaissance Canada, and the TV program *700 Huntley Street*, hosted by David Mainse, a Pentecostal leader) attempted to mobilize their constituencies to protect what they saw as the rights of religious organizations and enshrine in the Charter protections for the traditional family and

---

[352] Tentler 2007, 17.
[353] Stackhouse 2000, 119.
[354] Stackhouse 2000, 114.
[355] Stackhouse 2000, 117.

the unborn.[356] Conservative members of the parliamentary Hays-Joyal Committee, set up by Prime Minister Pierre Trudeau in 1980 to examine the draft of the Charter, "were happy to champion the items desired by evangelical Christians" and include references to God in the Charter,[357] only to have the amendment defeated. Mindful of the evangelical backlash, and the dynamism of Evangelicals in Canada,[358] Trudeau and the Liberals (many of whom had ties to the Evangelicals) reinserted a reference to God, even though Trudeau himself did not think "God gives a damn whether he was in the constitution or not."[359] Expedience, and a tactical concession, won the day.

At no point, however, did a coalition form between political parties and churches. Instead, "the history of most of these groups is of freely criticizing, and suggesting positive change to, the party in power, whatever its label and orientation."[360] The result is that conservative Christians have obtained symbolic concessions in lieu of substantively changing policy. For example, Stephen Harper, the conservative Prime Minister in office since 2006, has refused to fund abortion as part of international initiatives, cut off funding for Gay Pride events, and appointed prominent conservative Christians to his own staff. Yet when it came to actually restricting abortion in Canada, this same Prime Minister announced he would force his MPs to vote against any bill recriminalizing abortion.[361]

Compared to the United States, there is simply less basis for an effective coalition between party and church(es); not only have denominations failed to present a united front, but they have little to offer political parties. Conservative Canadian Christians do plump for conservative politicians; for example, an estimated 75% of the religious right voted for Conservatives in 2008.[362] Yet such support, however loyal, has not resulted in the kind of political clout that the conservative Christians had

[356] Egerton 2000, 101–2. The Evangelical Fellowship of Canada would go on to become a main political voice of Evangelicals in Canada, making their case in front of the media and the courts.

[357] Egerton 2000, 101.

[358] Several Liberals with ties to Evangelicals assembled a brief for Trudeau, which "summarized polling and political reporting on the moral majority phenomenon in the United States, and demographic data on recent Canadian religious trends that held political salience," including the numerical advantage of Evangelical training schools over mainline seminaries and "the remarkable new convergence of evangelical Protestantism and charismatic and traditional Catholicism in many points of theology, as well as political attitudes on such issues as abortion, drugs, homosexuality, and capital punishment" (Egerton 2000, 105).

[359] Quoted in Egerton 2000, 106.

[360] Stackhouse 2000, 123.

[361] Gagnon 2010.

[362] Hepburn 2011.

in the United States. Despite their rapid growth, the numbers of Evangelical Christians in Canada are low (7% of the population[363]), and while they share theological commitments with American Evangelicals, they are considerably less politically vociferous.[364] They are also more diverse in their political views than their American counterparts and have been so throughout Canadian history.[365] For instance, while the Evangelical Fellowship of Canada prioritizes abortion, euthanasia, homosexuality, and Christian education, it is also a prominent advocate of Aboriginal rights and social justice.[366]

More generally, secularization in Canada is pronounced and has accelerated over the course of the twentieth century.[367] Although more religious than Europe in broad spiritual belief, Canada is more secular than the United States; for example, 35% of Europeans claimed God was important in their lives in 1990, against 51% of Canadians and 70% of Americans. Two-thirds of Canadians continue to identify themselves as affiliated with the Roman Catholic Church, the United Church of Canada, or the Anglican Church. Yet this sentimental identity is not borne out in religious observance (measured as either attendance or adherence to religious tenets): while over 60% of Americans report attending church at least once a month, only 36% of Canadians do.[368] Another poll found that the percentage of Canadians attending religious services weekly dropped from 67% in 1946 to 20% by the 1996.[369] In the former Catholic bastion of Québec, the rates of church attendance collapsed from 88% in 1965 to 46% by 1975 to 28% by 1998.[370]

The lower rates of adherence and attendance also mean that many of the channels of indirect religious political mobilization available in the United States—voter registration drives in churches, affiliated political organizations, and so on—are simply not as effective in Canada.[371] And

---

[363] O'Toole 1996.

[364] Reimer 2000.

[365] Gauvreau 1990, 86–92.

[366] Stackhouse 2000, 117–18.

[367] For example, from 1957 to 1991, the share of Canadians with religious identity dropped from 99% to 87%. In 1990, 85% of Canadians claimed to believe in god, in 1995, 80% did (Eisgruber and Zeisberg 2006).

[368] WVS; ISSP.

[369] Christiano 2007, 30.

[370] Gauvreau 2007, 85.

[371] This argument differs from Wald, who argues that with a smaller state in the United States, there is more space for religious organizations to fill in the gaps left behind (Wald 1997). But if a small state is the sole driver of religious organizations, then pro-abortion groups should enjoy the advantage as much as anti-abortion organizations in the United States. That they do not suggests that the content and form of organization matter as much as the opportunities for creating them in the first place.

"there is no organized religious right in Canada that wields significant and obvious political power in the electoral process—nor any religious left or centre for that matter. None of these groups has attempted to marshal votes through direct mail and 'voter's guides'; none has organized Christian candidates through the formal political system; none has seriously claimed to 'deliver' support for this or that leader or party."[372]

Moreover, Canadian popular attitudes on issues dear to Christian churches are considerably more liberal than in the United States. Even in 1990, Canadians were as tolerant of homosexuality as Europeans (24% and 28%, respectively, against 13% for Americans), divorce (49% European average, 52% Canadian, 37% American), and euthanasia (32% European average, 40% Canada, 24% Americans). And in contrast to their American brethren, "regardless of whether one looks at racial, political, religious, or moral tolerance, Canadian evangelicals are more tolerant."[373]

For its part, political conservatism in Canada did not invoke religious ideas, or even rely on religious voters or ideas. The Evangelical support for the conservative Reform Party was spottier and far less numerous than the Evangelical support for the Republican Party in the United States, even though every leader thus far of the Reform Party has been a devout Evangelical.[374] These conservative leaders, in a critical difference to the United States, have been reluctant to raise religious or moral issues in public.[375] Nor is there evidence of institutional ties between religious groups and parties: "not one of these Canadian Christian groups is aligned with a political party.[376] On the one hand, political parties did not seek out these constituencies, and on the other, churches did not command religious voting blocs that would have made partisan coalitions attractive.

As a result of these popular attitudes and lower religious observance, and debates among and within the churches themselves,[377] there is little organized religious push for particular policies. Instead, secular considerations, even if they accorded with traditional morality, were far more likely to drive policy outcomes, whether in inculcating morality in nineteenth-century public education, or limiting divorce until the mid-twentieth century. And where religious groups actively pushed for policy influence, they largely did so on their own, without either religious or secular partners.

[372] Stackhouse 2000, 123.
[373] Baum 2000, 235.
[374] Guenther 2008.
[375] Katerberg 2000, 296.
[376] Stackhouse 2000, 123.
[377] After the Quiet Revolution, for example, "on every important issue, from the debate on education reform to abortion, there was a Catholic presence on both sides of the issue," making it impossible to simply identify Catholicism with conservatism (Seljak 1996, 118).

Education

While in the United States controversies raged about the introduction of religious elements into a secular school system, in Canada the political issue was how to get religion *out* of schools. Religion had infused Canadian schooling to a degree that would have been unthinkable to an American observer—and familiar to an Irish one. Yet the presence of religion in Canadian schools resulted chiefly from a secular concern for morality and managing denominational competition, rather than an Irish-style church takeover of the educational system.

For most of the nineteenth and twentieth centuries, schooling and textbooks "underlined the centrality of Christianity in the school," with mandatory school prayers, scripture study, and clerical oversight of the inculcation of Christian values.[378] Irish or Polish Catholic bishops could have written the government manual for teachers, valid from 1937 to the 1960s, which stated that "religious teaching cannot be confined to separate periods on the timetable . . . It will affect the teaching of all subjects."[379] Yet the concern was chiefly with the morality of the Canadian citizenry, not the inculcation of a religious identity. The Drew regulations of 1944, which made religious instruction compulsory in elementary schools, were introduced during wartime to counter perceived moral decline, rather than to bolster religious adherence. The Minister of Education himself, George Drew, "was not directed by a strong and influential church, but rather, he gave to the public school those duties which he felt that the churches were no longer capable of fulfilling" by dint of low attendance.[380]

Prior to the 1960s, the public school system was also split between formally confessional Roman Catholic schools and informally Protestant schools. For most of the nineteenth and twentieth centuries, most provinces maintained a system of "separate" schooling, in which children went to either Protestant or Catholic schools that were equally funded by the state[381] as an accommodation to the Francophone-Anglophone division. In the 1840s, Ontario first established its system of general (public) schools and particular (separate, or religious) schools. In Québec and Newfoundland all public schools were confessional, Catholic or Protestant, until 2001.[382] In Manitoba, Nova Scotia, New Brunswick, and

---

[378] Gidney and Millar 2001, 280.

[379] Quoted in Gidney and Millar 2001, 280. This was the Programme of Studies for Grades 1 to 6, originally introduced in 1937 and in force until the 1960s.

[380] Michel 2003, 88.

[381] Benabarre 1959, 104–9.

[382] Choquette 2004, 291. In Québec, the post-1840 educational system, intended to assimilate French Canadians, created nondenominational schools where English would be the

Prince Edward Island, the school systems were officially neutral, but each government struck a deal with Catholics and quietly funded their schools. Only British Columbia had an exclusively secular school system from the start—even there, in 1977 it was decided that religious schools would be funded. The prevailing dual system of Catholic and Protestant education underlined denominational differences between Canadians: "Canadian Catholic children in most provinces grow up taking for granted that their society recognizes two kinds of children, Catholic and non-Catholic, and takes responsibility for providing each kind with appropriate educational resources. Thousands of Catholic teachers, moreover, had the experience of being public employees *as* Catholics, subject to church authority as a condition of employment in the public sector."[383]

Episodes of conflict over education showed the primacy of secular alliances and political calculations, rather than religious influence through electoral mobilization, partisan coalitions, institutional access, or the anticipatory anxiety of politicians. The primacy of purely secular thinking is exemplified even in the "Manitoba Schools Question," described as "Canadian history's most extensive and concerted effort on the part of church authorities to influence the national political process."[384] Following a wave of anti-Catholic and anti-French sentiment precipitated by the Métis rebellions of the 1870s and 1880s,[385] the Liberal government of Manitoba revoked Roman Catholic school privileges in 1890, and thus French language education. The Conservative federal government of John MacDonald tried to force Manitoba to reinstate public funding for Catholic schools. The Manitoba issue gained national significance and was the central issue of the election of 1896, which established the Liberals as a natural party of government in Canada.[386] During the campaign, Wilfrid Laurier and the Liberals backed the Manitoba government against the Conservatives, encountering resistance from some Catholic clergy.

Extensive debate among Catholic bishops over whether to officially back the Conservatives eventually led to a pronouncement issued by

---

language of instruction. In response, the church created an alternative educational system of French language and Catholic instruction, a move that required massive recruitment of nuns and monks—and thus a strengthening of the church's role in society. These religious communities then also created the convents, hospitals, and welfare societies that substituted for secular welfare provision until the 1960s.

[383] Westhues 1978, 254.

[384] Crunican 1973, 322.

[385] Louis Riel, a deeply religious Catholic, tried to found independent governments in Manitoba for the Métis (of mixed French-Canadian and Indian parentage). He was executed, but a bitter conflict ensued between "British Protestants eager to assert that Protestant dominance prevailed in the new western provinces and French Catholics who felt Riel had been wronged" (Noll 2007, 429).

[386] Blake 1979; Crunican 1973, 316.

Archbishop Langevin, which urged Catholic voters to support the reinstatement of Catholic education in Manitoba (remedialism) but nonetheless refrained from endorsing either side. This was far too mild for Trois-Rivières Bishop Louis-François Laflèche, who insisted in a homily that "Catholics, under pain of grave sin, could not vote for Laurier or his followers until they had publicly disavowed this position."[387] Laflèche seems to have had the support of a number of other bishops, and most of the Québec clergy. Once in office, Laurier orchestrated a policy compromise; Catholic (and thus French) education would return to Manitoba, but only in those schools with at least ten French-speaking pupils. The episode strengthened French-Canadian nationalism but also set a precedent that even religious leaders could not easily frame political debates or obtain their desired ends.

Similarly, the opposition to the secularization of education also came not from religious leaders, but from secular politicians when educational reform began in Ontario in the late 1960s. Responding to the Mackay Report of 1969,[388] Ontario began to replace long-standing imperatives for "Christian education" with "moral" and "ethical" education in official documents, although frequently "Judeo-Christian morality" (the term was used to denote an ecumenical set of values, rather than a national tradition) was a compromise term. The policy change reflected the practice within the Ministry of Education, which was at best spotty in enforcing religious education in public schools.[389] Major political protests broke out over symbolic features; the removal of "Christian" from "Christian morality" led to thousands of angry letters, and acerbic criticisms such as "Hitler, Idi Amin, Pol Pot, and Stalin all developed values related to personal religious and ethical systems: they would have met Ontario's values criterion."[390] When the Toronto Board of Education proposed in 1979 to replace the morning recitation of the Lord's Prayer with a "moment of silence," provincial politicians, not clergy, reacted angrily and partly in response to public opinion. Premier William Davis, for example, argued that "the Lord's Prayer establishes a common respect for a society where morality, humility and faith in God are important pillars of stability and the social norm."[391]

For its part, Québec created a Ministry of Education in 1964, wresting control of education from the Catholic Church during the Quiet

---

[387] Crunican 1973, 276.
[388] The Report on Religious Information and Moral Development of the Mackay Commission was the result of a three-year study of religious education in public schools in Ontario.
[389] Gidney and Millar 2001, 281–82.
[390] Quoted in Gidney and Millar 2001, 285.
[391] Quoted in Gidney and Millar 2001, 286.

Revolution.[392] The most withering critique of the church-controlled education system first came from a Marist brother, Jean-Paul Desbiens. Writing as Frère Untel, he scathingly denounced the "solemn mediocrity" of the educational system.[393] His 1960 pamphlet, *Les insolences du Frère Untel*, was an opening salvo of the Quiet Revolution and catalyzed many of the changes that followed. The Liberals set up the Parent Commission (named for Monsignor Alphonse-Marie Parent, who headed the commission in deference to the Catholic Church), which recommended a slew of modernizing reforms that would eventually secularize education. The move appalled conservative Catholics and split Catholic opinion. It prompted public debates and soul searching and became the lightning rod for both supporters and critics of the Quiet Revolution. On the one hand, the curriculum was archaic, and nearly half of Québec pupils left school by fifteen. The situation was even more desperate in rural areas. On the other, as Archbishop Maurice Roy, the leader of the Canadian Catholic Church argued, "there are, in this great enterprise established a hundred years ago, guiding principles that cannot be changed without endangering its solidity."[394] Nonetheless, reform was pushed through by the Liberal Lesage government as part of a broader effort to build up the secular state.[395] Québec accordingly raised the age of compulsory education, standardized the curriculum, and promoted access to higher education, making the new (and secular) Ministry of Education the arbiter and executor of educational standards.

In general, although Canada was becoming increasingly secular and pluralistic, public opinion was divided on these issues; many "believed that the schools should continue to exhibit distinctly Christian affinities, and that the symbolic links between the state and the Christian faith should not be abandoned."[396] Yet the anxiety was less about retaining specifically religious values than it was about continuing to imbue young Canadians with a set of moral standards. With the passage of the Canadian Charter of Rights and Freedoms (1982), Christian privileges in the public school system were further pared back, lest they violate the religious freedom clauses. Most provinces abolished the denominational system of separate schooling.[397] The major impetus to reform was top-down

[392] The Ministry of Public Instruction had been abolished in Québec in 1875, in keeping with Ultramontane notion that education belongs to the family and its religious choices.

[393] Quoted in http://www.cbc.ca/history/EPISCONTENTSE1EP16CH1PA1LE.html, accessed August 13, 2013.

[394] Ibid.

[395] Seljak 2001.

[396] Gidney and Millar 2001, 286.

[397] Ontario, Alberta, and Saskatchewan retained separate school boards for Catholic schools.

and institutional, and even the defenders of the old system were less concerned with keeping churches happy than with ensuring Canadian moral rectitude. The Roman Catholic Church and other denominations were less the authors of policy than its addressees.

Divorce

Prior to 1968, divorce was available through the tedious, costly process of petitioning the provincial legislatures. Divorce policy followed English law, and the Matrimonial Causes Act of 1857 required that the petition for divorce be fault-based and provide evidence of wrongdoing such as adultery or desertion. This "diverse, complex legal framework accompanied by often cumbersome procedures was used to settle private marital problems. Divorce in Canada was squarely founded on a belief in innocence and guilt, which meshed nicely with the moral pathology of divorce."[398] For Canadians wishing to obtain a divorce in the late nineteenth or early twentieth century, the best option was to seek divorce in the United States, especially in the states with lighter residency requirements: Massachusetts, Michigan, Illinois, California, Nevada, Washington, and Oregon.[399] This relatively easy availability of divorce had an unintended consequence of limiting policy pressure in Canada; it sapped Canadian advocates of liberalizing divorce laws of political will by providing an alternative abroad.

In the Canadian debates over divorce, the rhetoric was often moral, but rarely sacral, and differences with the United States were repeatedly emphasized. On the divorce question, the anti-American trope was also prominent. Prior to the Second World War, divorce reform bills were introduced in parliament on several occasions, usually by sole, crusading Liberal members, and were invariably defeated by large majorities that included other Liberals. Of these, a bill introduced in 1901 by a Member of Parliament representing Kingston was probably the most widely debated. Laurier's argument against this bill is telling: "for my part I would rather belong to the country of Canada where divorces are few, than belong to the neighbouring republic where divorces are many. I think it argues a good moral condition of a country where you have few divorces, even though they are made difficult—a better moral condition than prevails in a country where divorces are numerous and made easy by law."[400] Secular and religious leaders policed public morality and respectability, helping to

---

[398] Snell 1991, 51.
[399] Snell 1991, 228.
[400] Quoted in Snell 1991, 52.

ensure Canada had one of the lowest divorce rates prior to World War II, but without invoking natural law or divine mandate.

Churches largely stayed out of these debates—not that they needed to get involved, given the near consensus against divorce that existed in parliament. Lay movements (the Catholic Women's League of Canada and la Fédération des Femmes Canadiennes-Françaises) stood ready to support the status quo, but this capacity was rarely used because would-be divorce reformers were just as weak and isolated outside parliament as they were within it. The United Church of Canada, which was influenced by social democracy and the liberal theology of the Social Gospel, came out in favor of divorce (on the grounds of adultery) in 1932. Other churches, however, remained opposed: "there was a fundamental and unshaken belief that marriage was an institution ordained and sanctified by God."[401] If anything, the division of Canadian Christianity along ethnic lines made divorce such a sensitive issue that politicians had to avoid it, preserving the anti-divorce status quo; with "Roman Catholics forming 46 per cent of the total population and adherents of the Church of England a further 13 per cent, the Federal government was more than willing to ignore such a political 'hot potato.' "[402]

How, then, did divorce become an accepted legal institution? It was legalized, along with homosexuality, in 1969 as part of an Omnibus Bill Pierre Trudeau introduced while he was still Minister of Justice (he became Prime Minister in 1968, and served until 1984 with a brief interlude in 1979–80). In fostering the Bill, Trudeau explicitly and publicly strived to separate crime from sin, to replace "theology" with "intelligence," and to get the state out of the bedroom. He "not only struck a sympathetic chord with public opinion, he also received the eager support of the mainline Protestant church leaders for liberalization of laws governing birth control and abortion (Commons 1966–8), as well as divorce (Parliament 1966–7; see also Commons 1967–9, Omnibus Bill)."[403]

The Divorce Act of 1968 standardized divorce policy at the federal level, introducing "permanent breakdown of marriage" as the legal grounds for divorce, but to prove such breakdown, one of the parties needed to demonstrate wrongdoing such as adultery, desertion, or abuse. No-fault divorce only became available with the Divorce Act of 1985, which made a one-year separation of spouses sufficient to prove marital breakdown. In 1990, the Divorce Act was further amended to accommodate religious differences in more multicultural Canada; specifically, a spouse now had

---

[401] Snell 1991, 42.
[402] Holden 1971, 63.
[403] Egerton 2000, 97.

to demonstrate "genuine grounds of a religious or conscientious nature for refusing to remove the barriers" to remarriage.[404]

Religious groups found little purchase, no matter what their views, given the key secular actors involved, and especially Pierre Trudeau, who led the charge for reform and successfully preempted religious opposition. Trudeau's Canadian nationalism was defined in terms of liberal, universal, individual rights against sectarian and communal claims, which Trudeau saw manifested in Québec nationalism even after the Quiet Revolution.[405] His core philosophy can be summarized as a commitment to liberal universalism, particularly the protection of individual rights, and hostility to *ethnic* nationalism, for which the obvious referent was Québécois nationalism.[406] Thus Trudeau consistently opposed Québec separatism (sometimes with armed force) and special privileges accorded to the French language. The divorce and criminal code reforms were part of Trudeau's vision of liberal universal rights, and the sweeping away of an archaic, sacral, and communal edifice represented by Québécois nationalism for Trudeau. He repudiated what he perceived as narrow ethnic claims, and the fusion of religious and secular identities, in favor of a Canadian nationalism defined by liberal rights, and a mild anti-Americanism that boiled "down to a simple formula: Canadians are more compassionate and sharing than their American counterparts and they expect their governments to defend policies that reflect this cultural difference."[407]

On assuming the Justice Ministry in 1967, Trudeau set out to tackle problems that various predecessors had deliberately neglected—the legal status of homosexuality, abortion, and divorce. There seemed to be a political consensus that something "needed to be done" about these issues, but there was little political will, as successive minority governments and other politicians avoided sensitive issues that could provoke controversy. Trudeau himself introduced religious language before launching the divorce and homosexuality reform bills in the autumn of 1967. As he reminisced, "it was necessary first to prepare public opinion by drawing a very clear distinction between sin and crime. . . . Criminal law therefore

---

[404] Viklund 2007.

[405] Critics charge that Trudeau's understanding of Québec was outdated, caricatured, and deficient. Couture, for example, argues that Trudeau "ended up repeating the grossest prejudices about the non Anglo-American world current in certain parts of French Canadian society—in particular the idea that French Canada was an ideologically monolithic society until the Quiet Revolution" (Couture 1998, xv).

[406] Bickerton, Brooks, and Gagnon 2006, 119–20; Couture 1998.

[407] Bickerton, Brooks, and Gagnon 2006, 136. Note the change in emphasis from the early twentieth century: morality and order is supplanted by sharing and compassion. Anti-Americanism would no longer be a weapon in the arsenal of those who opposed reforms; if anything, it worked in favor of reformers.

cannot be based on the notion of sin; it is crimes that must define it. But I also had to make it understood that in decriminalizing a given action, the law was in no way challenging the moral beliefs of any given religion."[408] While the term *sin* did not appear in the Criminal Code, and was not used in defense of the status quo in the political discourse, Trudeau used the word very effectively to paint the status quo as an inappropriate intrusion into secular life. As he argued more abstractly in the Commons: "people are beginning to realize, perhaps for the first time in the history of this country, that we are not entitled to impose the concepts which belong to a sacred society upon a civil or profane society."[409] This, in essence, was the articulation of a specifically secular and liberal Canadian identity; just as Québécois nationalist ideology "no longer corresponded" to modern reality so the divorce law was "archaic" and the Criminal Code needed to "be brought up to date."[410]

The timing of the bills took advantage of three developments. First, by 1967 there was no commonplace, coherent anti-reform argument, and opponents were unprepared for Trudeau's onslaught, having for years hidden behind the sensitivity of the status quo. Second, the greatest potential opponent of reform, the Catholic Church, was reeling from the Quiet Revolution, which by now had its greatest popular impact. By publicly using the word *sin* Trudeau could implicitly preempt the arguments of the Catholic Church—and the bishops themselves accepted the difference between crime and sin, and law and morality in the case of divorce (though not, as we will see, for abortion).[411] Mainline Canadian Protestant churches supported Trudeau's legislation.[412] Finally, as a result of the Quiet Revolution in Québec and broader societal change in the 1960s in Canada and elsewhere, the public acceptance for divorce had grown. Within Québec itself, while intellectuals were frequently hostile to Trudeau and his repudiation of Québec identity, Québec *voters* were consistently loyal to him for sixteen years.[413]

Trudeau's liberal vision continued to exert a powerful influence on Canadian national identity, largely because of the implementation in 1982 of his Canadian Charter of Rights and Freedoms. Divorce reform was the specific result of a sustained push by particular policy actors and also a demonstration of a moral and national identity that did not invoke

---

[408] Trudeau 1993, 82–83.
[409] Trudeau 1993, 96.
[410] Quoted in Couture 1998, 6.
[411] Dillon 2007, 254.
[412] Sachdev 1988, 67.
[413] Nemni and Nemni 2006, chap. 1.

the sacred. The concern with morality historically came from primarily secular politicians rather than from convincing campaigns by religious groups—which further meant that once the politicians had changed, so could the law, with relatively little resistance from religious actors.

Abortion

Abortion policy in Canada followed a similar trajectory to the United States, swinging from permissiveness to stricture and back to greater access. The difference lay in the role and influence of religious actors, especially from the 1960s onward when the debates began in earnest. As in the United States, in the eighteenth century, women were not considered truly pregnant prior to "quickening" (first recognizable movement of the fetus) and could take measures to restore menstruation (herbal remedies, hot baths, and such). Legislation gradually changed this in the nineteenth century; New Brunswick criminalized all abortions in 1810, followed by Prince Edward Island (1836) and Upper Canada (1840). When the Dominion assumed jurisdiction over criminal law in 1869, federal law enshrined the abolition of the "quickening" distinction. Abortion and contraception were banned in 1892 by the Criminal Code, with an exception made in Section 271.2 for saving the life of the mother. A key motivation was the declining birthrate of the upper and middle classes, who were the main clients of professional abortionists. Another was the fear that the prodigious birthrates of Irish and French-descended Catholics would swamp English-descended Protestants.[414]

This status quo, tacitly supported by the Roman Catholic Church in Québec and by a conservative English-descended elite, remained in place until the 1960s, when both the English Parliament and some American states began to liberalize abortion law. In Canada, the debates over abortion split the main denominations. Liberalization was supported by the United and Anglican Churches, who approved abortion first as an emergency measure and then on broader grounds. The Catholic Church and initially the Canadian Medical Association (CMA) opposed it, though the CMA dropped its opposition to emergency abortions in 1965, and then endorsed a far more liberal abortion provision in 1971. The same religious division occurred over the 1969 laws that broadened grounds for divorce and legalized the sale of contraceptives.[415]

---

[414] Backhouse 1991. As in the United States, there was also a conflict between orthodox male doctors who refused to perform abortions and heterodox "irregulars" who included women and people of color and were willing to perform them.

[415] Sachdev 1988, 67.

In 1967 Parliament set up a standing committee to review existing abortion laws, which heard from a variety of groups, including professional organizations and religious denominations. Two years later, in 1969, the Commons passed a bill permitting therapeutic abortion in accredited hospitals when the continuation of pregnancy "would or would be likely to endanger the woman's life or health." The debate over the bill was bitter, but it passed by a margin of 149 to 55. Catholic and Evangelical leaders, and some parliamentarians, had publicly and vociferously opposed the abortion laws; critically, however, this opposition was weak in parliament, with few partisan allies.

Nonetheless, the Catholic Church had something of a quiet victory on abortion because of the eventual terms under which the bill was passed. Abortions would have to be approved by committees of no fewer than three qualified medical practitioners. Hospital committees enjoyed a certain leeway on the definition of "health" (some broadened it to mental and emotional states; others restricted it to life-threatening conditions). Most importantly, hospitals were not compelled to establish the therapeutic committees that would review requests for abortion. As a result, the nearly three hundred Catholic-affiliated hospitals still did not perform abortions, and in 1985 15% of hospitals accounted for nearly three-quarters of abortions.[416] While the Catholic Church could not influence policy outcomes through parliament, it retained power over social outcomes by means of its broader institutional power within society—a power that, in some spheres, has persisted even as church attendance has declined. Much as in the United States, Catholic hospitals could simply refuse to perform procedures they found objectionable. Even in 2003, fewer than 18% of hospitals performed abortions in Canada.[417]

Ultimately, abortion was liberalized, and the practice of committee accreditation dissolved, in the wake of an unusual campaign of civil disobedience led by Montreal doctor Henry Morgentaler. Morgentaler testified in 1967 on behalf of the Humanist Fellowship that any pregnant woman should have the right to a safe, legal abortion (very little testimony to the 1967 standing committee had supported a position this broad). In 1969 he began openly performing illegal abortions (without the approval of hospital therapeutic committees) and was first arrested for it in 1970. He announced he had performed five thousand illegal abortions, even performing one on television for an investigative program.[418] Juries acquitted Morgentaler three times on charges of performing illegal abortions, and in 1975 the new Justice Minister of the Parti Québécois announced that Québec's

[416] Sachdev 1988, 68.
[417] Sharpe and Carter 2006, 206.
[418] Mallick 2003.

abortion law would no longer be enforced.[419] In 1983, Morgentaler and two colleagues were charged in Ontario with procuring illegal abortions. After a Toronto jury acquitted them the same year, the case made its way to the Supreme Court, eventually being heard in 1988. The 5–2 decision in Morgentaler's favor rendered existing Canadian abortion law constitutionally invalid for violating a woman's right to security of the person under the Canadian Charter of Rights and Freedoms (*R. v. Morgentaler* [1988]). As a result, rather than affirming a right to abortion, the court nullified all restrictions, leaving its regulation undecided. The next year, in *Tremblay v. Daigle*, the court unanimously found that a fetus has no status as a person, and that it would not enter into theological or philosophical debates, explicitly excluding religious arguments from personhood jurisprudence. Since the Morgentaler decision no Canadian government has successfully attempted to regulate abortion; the Mulroney government introduced Bill C-43 in 1989, which would have made abortion a criminal offense except when a pregnant woman wished to have one for reasons of physical, mental, or psychological health.[420] The proposed bill split the pro-life movement; some, such as the Evangelical Fellowship of Canada, argued that it was better to have a faulty law rather than no restrictions, but others opposed it on the grounds it would enshrine abortion legally.[421]

A new pro-life movement denounced the Morgentaler decisions. Throughout the 1970s and 1980s—as the Morgentaler saga played itself out in the courts—conservative Christians, and especially Catholics, mobilized. In 1973 the Alliance for Life, headed by Dr. Heather Morris, gathered a petition of over 350,000 signatures requesting a stricter abortion law. On the local level, pro-life activists were able to get elected to local hospital boards and shut down the therapeutic abortion committees, preventing hospitals from performing abortions. This was an especially effective tactic in the more conservative Maritime provinces.[422] Other groups allied with religious organizations, such as Toronto Right to Life (established in 1971), and Campaign Life Coalition (CLC, established in 1978), not only mobilized mass marches and demonstrations but also published guides on legal political activities for pastors and on electoral choices for voters. The CLC organized an annual "Life Chain" across Canada, in which participants "stand on the side walk with others who are not ashamed to be a public witness, and pray for an end to the

---

[419] Sachdev 1988; Mallick 2003.

[420] The bill, which would have penalized doctors for performing abortions in the absence of a health threat, was defeated by a tied vote in the senate.

[421] Wagner 2007.

[422] Wagner 2007.

infanticidal practice of abortion."[423] In response to the 1988 court decision, Christians for Life Toronto organized the largest anti-abortion rally in Canada, which drew 25,000 and featured Mother Teresa. (In general, Canadian Marches for Life gather around 20,000 participants annually.) An extensive pro-life letter-writing campaign urged Parliament to restrict abortion, but to no avail.[424] Evangelical leaders also raised funds and mobilized their own faithful to delegalize abortion.

Similarly, if Catholic bishops could accept divorce, they rallied against abortion, viewing it as murder; in both the 1960s and in subsequent debates, "Catholic spokesmen were willing to make the distinction between the morality that would be required of the faithful and legislation 'for the common good' on such issues as birth control and divorce. When it came to abortion, however, the bishops refused to make this distinction and opposed any legislation that did not protect human life from conception onward."[425]

Yet even as the bishops condemned abortion and helped to sponsor anti-abortion marches,[426] their *political* rhetoric has been more conciliatory, without the public threats of excommunication that Irish or American bishops made. At several points, Canadian Roman Catholic bishops demurred from entering the political debates, while their Anglican and United Church of Canada brethren simply broadened their support for abortion rights. When a delegation from the Canadian Bishops' Conference gave testimony before a parliamentary committee in 1966 and 1968, it was careful to point out that while abortion is against the central teachings of Catholic doctrine, this does not justify the imposition of the doctrine on the land.[427] Similarly, during the debates over the restrictive C-43 law in 1988, the bishops emphasized both that they opposed abortion and also that their view was one of many in a pluralist society where no group can impose its views.[428]

Catholic proxy groups were also more moderate in their political statements. The Canadian Conference of Catholic Bishops, along with the Knights of Columbus, also created proxy groups, such as Priests for Life and the Catholic Organization for Life and Family (COLF), which denounced abortion through public statements and press releases. In con-

---

[423] "Annual day of public witness for children killed by abortion." Campaign Life Coalition. n.d. http://bit.ly/ni6gAc.

[424] Wagner 2007.

[425] Egerton 2000, 97.

[426] The Canadian Conference of Catholic Bishops jointly, and the Archbishops of Ottawa and Toronto individually, helped to financially sponsor the National March for Life organized by the Campaign Life Coalition. http://www.campaignlifecoalition.com/index.php?p=Sponsors, accessed October 24, 2013.

[427] Tatalovich 1997, 133ff.

[428] Tatalovich 1997, 134.

trast to the more radical and conservative CLC, the COLF and the other Catholic proxy groups the church founded were more likely to support more moderate political activity and use the language of (secular) national protection. While the Campaign Life Coalition explicitly calls for political activity, the web sites of COLF and Priests for Life make no reference to clerical political activity at the pulpit or in guiding voter decisions.[429] Instead, they called for supporters to maintain their efforts and sign petitions.

Nor did the Catholic official efforts rely only on the characteristic language of protecting the unborn and the dignity of all life from conception onward. Instead, COLF called for an end to abortion partly on secular and practical grounds, arguing that Canada's birth rate (1.68 total fertility rate [TFR]), "cannot retain current population levels and jeopardizes the nation's future socio-economic health."[430] Similarly, the Canadian Conference of Catholic Bishops declared that "abortion is killing Canada's future."[431] These arguments about the nation's health are less about morality than about demographics (and in the absence of a fusion of national and religious identities, did not resonate widely). More recently, in an attempt to broaden support, these pleas have also turned to gender rights, and against sex-selective abortions,[432] which are widely condemned in Canada but have yet to turn public opinion or legislative elites against abortion rights.

For all the diversity and intensity of these efforts, religious opponents of abortion could not rely on institutional access, partisan coalitions, or support from major parties. Instead, "in these seminal political debates, the voice of traditional Christian morality and jurisprudence no longer was expressed by the elites of the major national parties. From the conservative side it was left to Walter Dinsdale, Salvation Army officer and MP from Brandon-Souris, Manitoba, to articulate the minority views of evangelical Protestantism, while traditional Québec Catholicism could no longer speak through the Liberal party, having to rely for expression on the Creditistes. It was Leonel Beaudoin, Creditiste member from Richmond, Québec, who spelled out the opposition of the Catholic bishops on the abortion legislation before parliament."[433]

Thus even as Archbishop Richard Smith declared that abortion is the "most outrageous injustice today . . . the heart of justice is recognizing

[429] See   www.colf.ca/mamboshop/,   http://www.priestsforlifecanada.com/English/index .php, *and* www.campaignlifecoalition.com/. Accessed June 28, 2013.

[430] "COLF Calls for Reopening of Abortion Debate." *Catholic Register*, May 22, 2012.

[431] "Canada's Greatest Treasure—Its People." *Catholic Organization for Life and Family*. May 11, 2006. http://bit.ly/zuhwZD. Accessed September 28, 2013.

[432] Priests for Life 2013.

[433] Egerton, 2000, 98.

the inherent dignity of every human person,"[434] the efforts of pro-life activists have not succeeded in changing the legal framework. When Cardinal Marc Ouellet denounced abortion in 2010 as a moral crime, even in cases of rape, his speech prompted enormous backlash, with one survey showing 94% of Quebeckers opposed to his position, and widespread media condemnation of the Cardinal's speech.[435] As a pro-life commentator concluded, Canada "is a basically pro-abortion culture, and there will need to be a change at the cultural level before the law is changed. Canada and the other Western countries need to be re-Christianized."[436] In the far less poetic terms of the explanation advanced here, there was no religious monopoly (or interdenominational alliance) that could claim the mantle of national moral authority, gain policy influence through either institutions or coalitions, and effectively change the laws to reflect its preferences in the name of national salvation. Instead, C-43's quick demise in 1989 led many conservative Christians to withdraw from politics—a silence that was only broken when same-sex marriage entered politics in the 2000s.[437]

In Vitro and Stem Cell Research

Unlike their American counterparts, religious denominations in Canada were unable to frame the issue of stem cell research or in vitro fertilization as one of religious morality and the protection of unborn life—and religious interests were neither consulted nor weighed as heavily by legislators as in the United States. Controversies in the United States, however, did catalyze the debates over stem cell research in Canada, which had been unregulated until parliament passed the Assisted Human Reproduction Act in March 2004. The policy itself was formulated not by an executive whose platform explicitly included a pro-life stance, as with President George W. Bush, but by a non-partisan committee called the Working Group on Stem Cell Research.[438]

The Act criminalized therapeutic and reproductive cloning (somatic-cell nuclear transfer, SCNT), along with commercial surrogacy, germ-line alteration, and sex selection. In contrast to the new policy in the United States, however, the Canadian law allowed not only assisted reproduction technologies but also research on surplus embryos from IVF treatments.

---

[434] Craine, Patrick B. 2011. "New Head of Canada's Bishops: 'Abortion Is the Most Outrageous Injustice Today.'" *Life Site News*. October 27. http://bit.ly/x4uerX. Accessed June 27, 2013.

[435] Gagnon 2010.

[436] Wagner 2007.

[437] Mason 2006.

[438] "Report of the Ad Hoc Working Group on Stem Cell Research." *Canadian Institutes of Health Research*. January 2002. http://www.cihr-irsc.gc.ca/e/1489.html. Accessed June 22, 2013.

The legislation was the final culmination of a series of attempts by parliament to construct a regulatory framework for reproductive technologies, a process begun in 1993 with the publication of a Royal Commission Report on New Reproductive Technologies. Previous bills had died, or stalled, at the end of parliamentary sessions due to their low priority in the order of parliamentary business.[439]

Pragmatic and partisan considerations trumped moral ones in parliament. The opposition Canadian Alliance called for "respect for human life," which would require the protection of embryos and a moratorium on stem cell research. However, when the same Canadian Alliance became the Conservative Party of Canada after a merger with the Progressive Conservative Party in 2003, and then led the government in 2006, it did not reopen the issue. The final legislative justifications for the act, moreover, were not moral; there are no references to the moral status of the embryo, in contrast to President Bush's pronouncements in 2004. The opposition generally focused on concerns about commodifying (and therefore exploiting) reproduction, safety issues, and a presumed social consensus—even though the last was "rarely based on polling information or other evidence."[440] For their part, researchers were willing to concede cloning for the sake of a permissive research environment in other areas—and duly got it.

In public opinion polls, Canadians largely accepted embryonic stem cell research, as did Americans; by 2004, 54% of Americans, and 61% of Canadian poll respondents saw stem cell research as acceptable (by 2013, 60% Americans accepted stem cell research[441]). Few people made references to their religious beliefs when discussing the issue.[442] That said, religious respondents were more concerned; those who attended church weekly or nearly weekly were the least likely to agree that stem cell research was acceptable: 35%. Similarly, 43% of Canadians for whom religion was very important felt embryonic stem cell research was acceptable, against 75% of those who say religion was not important in their lives.[443] (The US numbers were comparable: 40% and 81%, respectively.) These similarities in public opinion make the policy difference with the United States all the more striking.

In contrast to the United States, the issues of stem cell research and assisted reproduction in Canada were framed chiefly in secular terms throughout the debates. The main policy actors were secular as well. As early as 1998, the Panel on Research Ethics received no input from

---

[439] Caulfield and Bubela 2007, 53.
[440] Caulfield and Bubela 2007, 56.
[441] See Gallup 2004.
[442] Downey and Geransar 2008, 70.
[443] Gallup 2004.

religious bodies.[444] In 2001, the Canadian Institutes of Health Research (CIHR) asked for public input regarding embryonic stem cell research, but its Ad Hoc Working Group on Stem Cell Research refused to consider the moral status of the embryo,[445] prompting protests from the Canadian Conference of Catholic Bishops. The Catholic Organization for Life and the Family and the Canadian Catholic Bishops' Conference made statements to the Working Group, along with other representatives of civil society and politics, but to little avail. The official release stated that "no attempt was made to articulate an argument regarding the moral status of the embryo, as this was not the mandate of the Working Group."[446] In 2002, when the CIHR (in keeping with the recommendation of the Working Group) established the Stem Cell Oversight Committee, it was composed of philosophers, doctors, and bioethicists—but unlike its counterparts in the United States, Poland, or elsewhere, did not include religious perspectives.[447]

Subsequently, in December 2006, the conservative Harper government appointed the board of Assisted Human Reproduction Canada (AHRC), a new regulatory agency whose formation was recommended back in 1993 by the Royal Commission on New Reproductive Technologies (the "Baird Commission"). The appointment of four (out of thirteen) apparently conservative and religious members to the board was heavily criticized; appointees included the director of research for the Roman Catholic Archdiocese of Toronto, a professor of Jewish studies who openly opposed abortion unless a mother's life was threatened, an oncologist who had previously addressed an anti-abortion conference, and a bioethicist who opposed the use of embryonic stem cells in research.[448] The Commission's powers, however, were curtailed when the Supreme Court found several of the AHRC powers and directives exceeding the constitutional limits on government power. Politically fraught and now limited in its capacity, the board was eliminated as part of budget cuts in 2012.

Apart from formal submissions during parliamentary inquiries, churches and clergy rarely entered the debate directly. In September 2005, representatives from the annual meeting of Canadian Catholic bishops called for stem cell research to be limited to adult stem cells, and for

---

[444] "Tri-Council Policy Statement: Ethical Conduct for Research Involving Humans." *Panel on Research Ethics*. 1998. http://www.pre.ethics.gc.ca/eng/archives/tcps-eptc/Default/.

[445] "Report of the Ad Hoc Working Group on Stem Cell Research." *Canadian Institutes of Health Research*. January 2002. http://www.cihr-irsc.gc.ca/e/1489.html.

[446] Ibid.

[447] Cohen et al. 2008, 86.

[448] "Regulatory Board Lacks Balance." *The Gazette* (Montreal). January 8, 2007. Gloria Galloway, "Ottawa Rejects Concerns over Fertility Panel; Board Appointments Reflect 'Wide Range' of Viewpoints, Health Official Insists." *Globe and Mail*. December 28, 2006.

embryonic research to cease altogether. The bishops' arguments, however, were framed in relatively secular and pragmatic terms: "given the centrality which human dignity and rights occupies within the Canadian Constitution and within our political and cultural consensus, this strikes us as being of particular concern."[449] Ronald Fabbro, Bishop of London, Ontario, emphasized the superiority of research from adult cells: "We are in favour of stem cell research. The scientific results have benefitted tens of thousands of people. . . . All the publicity is for embryonic stem cells, but the progress is in the adult tissue." There was no reason, then, for researchers to prefer embryonic stem cells, which cause the death of embryos when they are removed.[450] Bishops have also made this argument in the United States after 2001 (after Pope John Paul II denounced embryonic stem cell research to President George W. Bush), though Canada's National Institutes of Health argued that adult stem cells do not have the same capabilities as embryonic cells.[451]

Even more importantly, the Catholic Church refused to directly pressure politicians, even Catholic ones. Despite calls from pro-life groups for censure of Catholic politicians such as Dalton McGuinty, who sponsored a bill for a Cancer Stem Cell Consortium, no such measures followed. Pressure on the church to initiate "Church Canon law discipline for all professing Catholics who refuse to make their consciences correct with Magisterial teaching, starting with Premier Dalton McGuinty" went unanswered.[452] Pro-life advocates were further disappointed after the Bishops' Conference did not muster a stronger stand and confined itself to commenting after the act passed the Commons in the fall of 2003 that "it is . . . not our intention to tell Catholic Senators how to vote because it is their responsibility to discern the best way to protect human life and dignity after reflecting on all of the resources available to them."[453] Instead,

[449] "Response to Health Canada's Workbook on Reproductive and Genetic Technologies." *Catholic Organization for Life and Family*. Press release. May 23, 2001. http://tinyurl.com/6fvadwk.

[450] Jackson, Jenny. 2005. "Bishops Call for Cell Research Curbs." *National Post*. September 22, 2005.

[451] Jacobs, Mindelle. 2001. "Tempest in a Test Tube." *Toronto Sun*, June 30, 2001.

[452] Erick Alcock, president *Vote Life Canada*, quoted in Eterlt, Steve. 2007. "Canada Pro-Life Group Attacks Embryonic Stem Cell Research Deal." *Life News*. June 3. http://www.lifenews.com/2007/06/03/bio-2119/. Accessed December 13, 2013.

[453] Canadian Conference of Catholic Bishops. 2003. "Statement by the President of the Canadian Conference of Catholic Bishops on the Passage by the House of Commons of Bill C-13, an Act Respecting Assisted Human Reproduction," available at http://www.cccb.ca/site/eng/bishops/annual-plenary-assemblies/68-plenary-assembly-2003/1917-statement-by-the-president-of-the-canadian-conference-of-catholic-bishops-on-the-passage-by-the-house-of-commons-of-bill-c-13-an-act-respecting-assisted-human-reproduction, accessed December 18, 2013.

the bishops called for Parliament, rather than the Working Group, to be the key agenda setter, and for a full and open discussion of all aspects of the issue, including its moral ones.[454]

A more vociferous opponent of all embryonic stem cell research was the Campaign Life Coalition, which further supported pro-life candidates from both major parties. Other allied groups that officially opposed stem cell research included Lutheran Church Canada, Vote Life Canada, Priests for Life Canada, and COLF. Campaign Life Canada made more visceral arguments against embryonic research than other churches and groups. When in 2002 the Canadian Institutes of Health Research issued guidelines for how clinic-donated embryos would be used in publicly funded scientific research, national Campaign Life organizer Mary Ellen Douglas argued: "these guidelines are saying you can experiment on human beings. It's repugnant. They try to rationalize it by saying these embryos are going to be destroyed. . . . Nazi doctors said we are going to experiment on this block of people because we are sending them to the gas ovens anyway."[455] The Campaign also referred to stem cell research and IVF as "experimentation which kills a human being.[456] Yet here the CLC did not have the support or endorsement of any of the major denominations in Canada, not even the Roman Catholic Church. Once again, largely secular considerations drove public policy, and while religious groups contributed their voices to the debate, they neither framed the rhetoric nor shaped the final policies that followed.

Same-Sex Marriage

Much as in the United States, public opinion in Canada has shifted dramatically on the issue of same-sex marriage, even as the doctrinal commitments of churches resisted change, or split the churches internally. In Canada, acceptance of homosexuality has quadrupled over 1982–2012, and approval of same-sex marriage increased from 37% in 1993 to 54% just a decade later.[457] As in the United States, the issue of same-sex marriage revived a religious conservative movement that had lost momentum and spirit once the campaign against abortion ground on without achieving its main aims.

[454] "Letter to the Federal Minister of Health Anne McLellan Regarding the Final Report of the Canadian Institutes of Health Research on Stem Cell Research." *Canadian Conference of Catholic Bishops*. Open letter. March 6, 2002. http://tinyurl.com/434xaqg.

[455] Abraham. Carolyn. 2002. "Researchers Weigh Personal Risks; Canadian Scientists Who Work with Embryos Fear Being Targeted by Radical Abortion Foes." *Globe and Mail*. March 5.

[456] "Adult Stem Cell Research." *Campaign Life Coalition*. Press release. March 14, 2002. http://www.campaignlifecoalition.com/press/2002/020314.html.

[457] Matthews 2005, 841.

However, in contrast to the United States, the Canadian Supreme Court framed the issue as one of equal rights—a resonant and credible framing that was echoed by *both* religious opponents and supporters of same-sex marriage.[458] Religious mobilization in opposition to same-sex marriage was more limited than in the United States and gained far less traction in either legislatures or public response.

Moves toward the full legality of same-sex marriage at the federal level began in Canada with several legal cases. The Supreme Court gradually established equal rights for homosexual couples over the 1990s, and in 1999, with the *M. v. H.* decision, gave same-sex couples equality in many financial and legal benefits short of marriage. The decision set aside an earlier precedent (in the 1995 *Egan* decision, which found that same-sex equal rights were not a pressing legislative matter), and prompted a "frenzy of legislative activity to implement the decision . . . federally and in Ontario, British Columbia, Québec and Nova Scotia in the lead up to the federal election in November 2000, with changes in Saskatchewan, Manitoba, and Alberta not far behind."[459]

At the time, the Court had not ruled explicitly on same-sex *marriage*. In the House of Commons, a motion by the Canadian Alliance in 2003 to reaffirm the definition of marriage as "the union between one man and on woman" failed by a narrow margin of 137 to 132. As the provinces moved ahead to legalize same sex-marriage in the early 2000s, the government of Jean Chrétien accepted the provinces' redefinition; in 2004 Chrétien presented proposed legislation to the Supreme Court that would bring the federal government's definition of marriage into conformity with the provinces (as a union of two people). The resulting Civil Marriage Act was approved by the Supreme Court and passed in parliament in July 2005. The legislation extended the right to same-sex marriage to Prince Edward Island and Alberta, which had argued against the legislation in Supreme Court hearings.[460] In the 2006 elections, the Conservative Party leader (and himself an Evangelical) Stephen Harper campaigned heavily on the issue, promising to reopen it for a free vote if elected. Despite misgivings from his own party, Harper's government put forward a motion in 2006 calling for a restoration of the traditional definition of marriage. The motion was defeated 175 to 123, and Harper (apparently with some relief) declared the issue permanently closed.[461]

---

[458] Matthews 2005, 849.

[459] Matthews 2008, 249.

[460] *Hamilton Spectator*. 2004. "Same-Sex Marriage Decision Put on Hold." October 8.

[461] *Globe and Mail* (Toronto). 2006. "Same-Sex Marriage File Closed for Good, PM Says." December 8.

While major denominations in the United States opposed same-sex marriage, this was not the case in Canada. The United Church of Canada (Canada's largest Protestant denomination) backed same-sex marriage from the outset of the debate and actively involved itself in a number of ways. In early 2004 it gained intervener status (recognition as an "interested party") in the Supreme Court hearing on same-sex marriage in October. It applied for this status on the grounds that as one of three Christian churches to perform same-sex marriages, it had a direct interest in the hearings and would also offer a valuable perspective in a debate that too often was framed in religious versus secular terms. The church argued that "Christian morality and religious principles require that same-sex couples have access to the same marriage rights as opposite-sex couples."[462] Reverend Peter Short, the church's National Moderator, wrote in a letter to parliamentarians during the 2005 parliamentary debate over same-sex marriage that "some will protest that we must have faith in the Bible, and that the Bible takes an unfavourable view of intimate same-sex relationships. But I would answer that Christian faith is not an uncritical repetition of a received text. It is a mindful commitment to the power of love, to which the text seeks to give witness."[463] In 2006, as Harper and the Conservatives moved to reopen the debate over same-sex marriage, Moderator David Giuliano publicly urged parliamentarians to vote against doing so in the House of Commons.[464]

Canada's Anglican Church, in which individual dioceses enjoy great autonomy, did not take an official position on same-sex marriage. Its Primate, Archbishop Andrew Hutchinson, stated that he personally opposed redefining marriage to include same-sex couples, but could not articulate that as the church's official position when it had not been discussed in any of the church's councils.[465] However, the church was widely seen as in favor of same-sex marriage because of the actions taken by two dioceses. In 2002 the Westminster Diocese of British Columbia allowed its churches to bless same-sex unions, and the Diocese of Niagara in Ontario adopted a similar motion until the Diocese of Toronto overturned it. At the same time, however, the Anglicans remained divided: Ottawa Bishop Peter Coffin banned the blessing of same-sex unions, even as others were willing to participate. The Canadian Anglican Church did not make any official statement until May 2007 when (following a visit from

[462] Canada NewsWire. 2004. "United Church to Appear before Supreme Court of Canada in Same-Sex Marriage Hearing." April 23.

[463] *Anglican Journal*. 2005. "Anglican Church Stays out of Marriage Debate." March 1.

[464] Canada NewsWire. 2006. "United Church Says No to Reopening Debate over Same-Sex Marriage in the House of Commons." October 24.

[465] *Anglican Journal*. 2005. "Anglican Church Stays out of Marriage Debate." March 1.

the Anglican Church leader, the Archbishop of Canterbury Rowan Williams, who openly worried that the liberal stances taken by the American and Canadian churches would split the worldwide Anglican Communion) the bishops issued a pastoral letter stating that an Anglican priest could celebrate the Eucharist with a married same-sex couple (with the approval of the local bishop) but could not bless their union: "the doctrine and discipline of our church clearly does not permit any further action."[466]

In general, Evangelical churches consistently opposed any moves toward legalizing same-sex marriage, and the Supreme Court's rulings galvanized conservative Christians into political action. Much as with abortion in the 1980s, Evangelicals mobilized by forming groups, raising money, and publicly championing their deeply held moral conviction that same-sex marriage was wrong. After the 1999 *M. v. H.* decision, Christian political action groups like the Family Action Coalition and Focus on the Family Canada responded by releasing press statements condemning the verdict as "outrageous . . . to redefine the term spouse . . . [ignoring] biology, reasons, and the natural law."[467] Yet their subsequent rhetoric invoked democratic procedures and the goal of equal rights as much as it did moral concerns. In 2003 Michel Habib, general secretary of Québec's l'Association d'Église Baptistes Évangéliques, stated that "we have to have a national debate over this issue to allow the people to understand the consequences of changing the marriage definition . . . If we start by legalizing same-sex marriage, we will soon see polygamy and other forms of marriages recognized in our society."[468] The Evangelical Fellowship of Canada argued in the Supreme Court hearings that the issue should be decided by parliament, but that legalizing same-sex marriage could infringe on the rights of religious groups who did not wish to perform same-sex marriages. This was disputed in the hearings by the gay rights group Egale, which argued that "the rights for (religious) ministers to follow their religious beliefs and not perform wedding ceremonies will remain unchanged." The United and Universalist Unitarian churches publicly supported Egale during the Supreme Court hearings,[469] and the liberal churches emphasized that the legalization of same-sex marriage would not infringe the rights of those groups who did not wish to perform them.[470]

[466] *Toronto Star*. 2007. "Anglicans Balk at Gay Blessings." May 2.

[467] "Gay and Lesbian Couples Win Equal Spousal Rights in Ontario, Canada." *Religious Tolerance*. http://www.religioustolerance.org/hom_0069.htm#, accessed January 9, 2013.

[468] *The Gazette* (Montreal). 2003. "Three Churches Bless Gay Marriages." July 19.

[469] AFP. 2004. "Battle over Same-Sex Marriage Rights Heats Up in Canada." October 5.

[470] *Leader-Post* (Regina). 2003. "Churches Divided on Same-Sex Marriages." July 19.

In support of their beliefs, the Evangelical Fellowship of Canada, headed by Bruce Clemenger, began a full-time lobbying effort against same-sex marriage in 2003.[471] Dozens of rallies were held, with thousands of participants, and a "Defend Marriage" bus traveled across Ontario and Québec. After the election of the Conservative Stephen Harper in 2006, conservative Christians began to mobilize further in the hopes of a decisive parliamentary vote (as promised by Harper in the election) to delegalize same-sex marriage. In an effort to encourage church activism, the Evangelical Fellowship of Canada released a "tool kit" outlining what churches can do to affect same-sex marriage policy without breaking laws.[472] However, after a final motion to repeal same-sex marriage was defeated in 2007 (parliament voted against reopening the issue), the conservative Christian groupings began to limit their public activity. Disappointed by the failure of Harper and the Conservatives to deliver, they began to focus on the grassroots level, working to elect like-minded candidates who would oppose same-sex marriage along with abortion, stem cell research, euthanasia, and pornography, but doing so without public rallies and bus tours.[473] In an evaluation of candidates held by the Campaign Life Coalition, along with the Fs given to liberal politicians, Harper himself now rated a C+.[474]

In contrast to the United States, and the dramatic references to the moral and societal catastrophe that would follow, Canadian opponents of same-sex marriage were more circumspect. Other opposed religious groups (including Mormons, Muslims, and Seventh-Day Adventists) argued more broadly that legislation would leave them open to lawsuits, as religious groups preaching that same-sex unions are wrong would be sued over their tax-exempt status and have Canada's hate laws used against them.[475] Religious groups opposed to same-sex marriage argued that legalizing it was a threat to religious freedom, or at the very least posed serious legal problems for religious groups. While some groups made arguments about the destruction of the family, these were secondary to the religious rights argument.

In approving same-sex marriage, the Supreme Court ruled that it posed no danger to religious freedom: "the Court is of the opinion that, absent unique circumstances with respect to which we will not speculate, the guarantee of religious freedom in the Charter is broad enough to protect religious officials from being compelled by the state to perform

---

[471] Mason 2006.
[472] *Toronto Star*, April 13, 2011.
[473] Mason 2006; Hepburn 2011.
[474] Hepburn 2011.
[475] *Hamilton Spectator*. 2004. "Same-Sex Marriage Decision Put on Hold." October 8.

civil or religious same-sex marriages that are contrary to their religious beliefs."[476] The language of equal rights, and of equal consideration to religious and secular considerations used by all sides in the debates, echoed the courts' own view of the issue as one of equal rights rather than divine morality—and the liberal value of equality that especially resonated in Canadian society.[477]

This perspective made the rhetoric of the Catholic Church in Canada all the less effective in reframing the issue and producing policy results. The Roman Catholic Church argued that same-sex marriage was contrary to natural law and to a divine moral order—and insisted on enforcing this tenet among its faithful. In 2003, after Prime Minister Jean Chrétien announced the government would accept Ontario's new definition of marriage as a union between two persons, Calgary Bishop Fred Henry notoriously warned Chrétien that he was risking his soul. Chrétien responded, "I am the Prime Minister of Canada. When I am Prime Minister of Canada, I am acting as a person responsible for the nation. The problem of my religion, I deal with it in other circumstances." He was supported by the former Conservative Prime Minister Joe Clark, who said: "churches should not be telling members of parliament what to do . . . I am a Roman Catholic. I was not elected as a Roman Catholic. . . . My constituency and the dictates of democracy require that I vote as an individual who considers these questions carefully, rather than vote on the basis of my faith."[478] In 2005, Bishop Henry further announced at a rally that "the time has come for the government of Canada to use its coercive power to legislate that a couple being married must be a man and a woman . . . it is the Christian teaching on the primordial status of marriage and family life."[479] Although at least one Québec Catholic leader had previously stated that Catholic churches would not mobilize their members against same-sex marriage (saying that the church "is a faith community, not a pressure group"),[480] Canadian bishops urged their

---

[476] *Brockville Recorder and Times* (Ontario). 2005. "Same-Sex Marriage Debate Takes Attention from More Serious Matters." February 5. In an equally prominent inversion of this argument, both religious and secular supporters of same-sex marriage tended to claim that it would have no effect on groups who did not believe in it. National Democratic Party MP Pat Martin triggered protests outside the Manitoba legislature after he declared, "If you're opposed to same sex marriage, don't marry someone of the same sex. Marry somebody of the opposite sex and everybody will be happy" (*Winnipeg Sun.* 2003. "'Hear Our Prayer': Rally; Nix Same-Sex Marriage, Believers Beseech MPs." September 8).

[477] Matthews 2008, 842.

[478] IPS. 2003. "Politics: Same-Sex Marriage Divides Canadians." September 8.

[479] Or 2005.

[480] *Star Phoenix* (Saskatoon). 2003. "Legalizing Gay Unions 'Immoral': Vatican." August 1.

parishioners to lobby their MPs and Prime Minister Paul Martin to oppose same-sex marriage legislation in January 2005.

Yet despite these efforts, arguments based on morality and natural law, and in particular the Catholic Church's, did not resonate. First, as elsewhere, same-sex marriage was becoming more widely accepted, with youth, rather than religion, education, or region, as a key predictor of acceptance. For their part, 57% of Canadian Catholics expressed support for gay marriage at a time when 54% of Canadians in general supported it.[481] Second, the timing of same-sex marriage controversies, occurring as they did after the sexual abuse scandals within the church, made the hierarchy seem hypocritical both in the United States and in Canada. One Catholic dissident, Newfoundland priest Paul Lundigran, gained substantial media attention when he argued that there was no evidence that same-sex marriages would cause moral harm to society, and he would not try to discourage the government from allowing them: "The church should have spoken out on so many other tragic issues and didn't. . . . The church, in recent years, has had thousands of children paraded across the same television screens telling horror stories of how their lives have been shattered by the abuse they suffered in Catholic-run orphanages and residential schools. I think that the hierarchy of our church has lost the moral ground to make judgment on how best to raise children."[482]

Nor did an ad hoc interdenominational coalition succeed. As same-sex marriage proponents won clear victories in the Supreme Court on the basis of equal rights, religious groups mobilized against this action by forming interfaith lobbying coalitions. The Interfaith Coalition on Marriage and Family (composed of the Catholic Civil Rights League, Evangelical Fellowship of Canada, Ontario Conference of Catholic Bishops, and the Islamic Society of North America), and the Association for Marriage and the Family (composed of Canada Family Action Coalition, Focus on the Family Canada, and REAL Women of Canada) acted as interveners before the Ontario Appeals Court during its consideration of the 2003 *Halpern v. Canada* case.[483] The case established the right to same-sex marriage. The group disbanded after Prime Minister Jean Chrétien announced the federal government would not appeal the decision and instead prepared a bill on same-sex partnerships that would eventually become the Civil Marriage Act. When the Canadian parliament moved forward with legislation to comply with the Supreme Court's decision in 2005, these opponents of same-sex marriage also organized a large-scale rally on Par-

---

[481] Matthews 2005; and *National Post*, July 8, 2003.

[482] *Hamilton Spectator*. 2003. "Priest against Church's Stand: No Evidence Same-Sex Marriages Cause Moral Harm to Society." August 14.

[483] Tuns 2003.

liament Hill. Conservative religious mobilization actually increased after the 2005 passing of the Civil Marriage Act; four organizations identifying with the Christian right were established in 2006 in Ottawa, with the explicit goal of repealing same-sex marriage.[484] Yet these alliances did not expand their purview beyond same-sex marriage, and there was little to indicate they could become durable interdenominational coalitions. Moreover, despite both Catholic and Evangelical support for the Conservative Party's stances here, no US-style alliance between denominations and political parties arose over same-sex marriage or other issues.

Conclusion

Religious diversity in the United States and Canada had very different implications for religious influence on policy. In the United States, the myth of a unifying religious tradition fused with national identity and afforded religious groups the authority to shape policy. In Canada, an uneasy stalemate between two religions (and their close association with ethno-linguistic groups) meant no coherent national identity could emerge under a protective denominational umbrella, and no church or religious tradition could assume moral authority on a national scale.

The United States demonstrates that religious myths and traditions can become fused with nation, even if one denomination will not. "Civil religion" and the "Judeo-Christian ethic" are manifestations of a more general, and more ubiquitous, phenomenon of religious nationalism, or the fusion of religious and national identities. The resulting moral authority is diffused among many churches that can speak in the name of the nation, so long as they are part of the tradition, even if no church reigns supreme. Religious groups can influence politics by forming coalitions— with each other, and then with political parties. As the conservative Christian coalition and its alliance with the Republican Party illustrates, religious groups can then gain power *within* the parties, naming candidates, serving as delegates, and shaping party platforms.

Canada in the nineteenth century shows that an overriding concern with morality and moral rectitude need not privilege religious authorities. The twentieth and twenty-first centuries in Canada show churches that wield little political moral authority: representing their doctrines and adherents, but not a broader national common good. Further, as Québec demonstrates, when the definition of the nation changes and encompasses popular rejection of traditional forms of faith and piety, fusion of national and religious identities can collapse. Here, the Roman Catholic

---

[484] Mason 2006.

Church went from quasi-sovereign status—an institution with enormous cultural, political, and even economic power—to a sentimental repository of historical symbols. The cross still hangs in the Canadian parliament, but as a symbol of historical heritage rather than worldly power.

Above all, the United States and Canada show that the political influence of religious groups is contingent not only on the churches' own moral authority, but on the complex calculations of secular politicians. Churches and parties also have powerful judiciaries, the broader electorate, and subnational governments to contend with. The best laid plans of religious groups are overturned by courts, rejected by the electorate, and transformed beyond recognition by provincial and state governments with preferences (and voters) of their own. Influence on public policy is not easy—but then, neither is faith.

Where Churches Matter

> Religion is the sigh of the oppressed creature, the heart of a
> heartless world, and the soul of soulless conditions. It is the
> opium of the people.[1]
> —Karl Marx, 1844

RELIGION IS NOT SIMPLY the "opium of the people." It does not only
provide comfort or moral certainty; it also molds individual and national
identities, mobilizes votes and protests, and as we have seen in this book,
transforms the very policies and institutions believers and nonbelievers
live by. Yet such influence is neither inevitable nor a simple result of popular piety. Instead, some churches can translate popular faith into political feats, if they have been able to carefully nurture historical narratives
and reap moral authority. Religion then (re-)enters the political sphere
in defense of a traditional set of values, against the claims of state and
market, and to maintain a vision of a "common good."[2]

Across the cases examined in the book, this influence and its roots took
on different forms. In Ireland, Croatia, Poland, and the United States, the
historical defense and support of the nation by religious authorities bonded
together national and religious identities. The result was that to be Polish,
Croat, or Irish was to be Catholic—and to be American, to be Christian.
In contrast, the opposition to Italian unification (and to the subsequent
Italian state) by the Catholic Church perpetuated the primacy of regional
identities in Italy—and a greater disconnect between an Italian *national*
identity and religion. Catholicism remained the predominant religion, and
its symbols hung in public buildings, but there was no conflation of national and religious identities. In Canada, the fusion of language, ethnicity,
and religion in Québec lasted for as long as a French-Canadian identity
prevailed; when an explicitly territorial and national one supplanted it,
the power of the church rapidly waned. And it was then, and only then,
that Canada itself acquired national symbols, such as an anthem or a flag;

---

[1] Marx, Karl. 1844. "A Contribution to the Critique of Hegel's Philosophy of Right."
Deutsch-Französische Jahrbücher, February 7 and 10, text available at http://www.marxists
.org/archive/marx/works/1843/critique-hpr/intro.htm.

[2] Casanova 2001, 1048–49; see also Karpov 2010, 240.

previously, the binational and bireligious nature of the country made that kind of symbolic coherence too problematic.

Religion and nation fused when churches played a favorable role in national history and its myths, and when those narratives were repeatedly buttressed and reproduced by favorable demographics and continued religiosity—when these conditions were absent, fusion waned. If it could be sustained, fusion strengthened and transformed the familiar authority of churches from comforting ritual to a potent political asset. Churches with this kind of political moral authority could speak out on behalf of the nation and popular interest. This was the case in Ireland, Poland, and Croatia (as well as Lithuania, Québec, or Walloon Belgium),[3] where the church stood on the side of the "nation" in its quest to free itself from foreign domination. We see a similar, if more diffuse moral authority in the United States, where religious rhetoric pervaded political debates on both the Left and the Right until thirty to forty years ago, when it became monopolized by the Right. The Polish and Croatian cases illustrate that such moral authority can arise relatively quickly, over the course of a few (communist) decades—as do examples from Latin America[4] and Southeast Asia. For example, the Catholic Church gained enormous authority in Chile, where it opposed the repressive military junta that lasted from 1973 to 1990.[5] Over three-quarters of poll respondents subsequently showed trust in the church, and the church capitalized on this moral authority to influence public policy.[6] Similarly, the Catholic Church in the Philippines under Cardinal Jaime Sin moved from acquiescing and supporting the autocracy, to supporting the opposition and helping to overthrow the Marcos regime in 1986.[7] Accordingly, 94% of public opinion

[3] Madeley 2003, 38.

[4] The fusion of nation and religion served as a rhetorical device in Latin America. There, the Catholic Church faced competition from Protestant Evangelicals; it often played up their American origin and insinuated that these competitors represent undue foreign influence, in contrast to the "native" Catholic traditions. I am grateful to Susan Stokes for this point.

[5] Gill 1998 argues that the stances of the Catholic Church toward the junta were determined by religious competition from Protestant churches; Goldfrank and Rowell 2012, in contrast, argue that the historical separation of church and state made the churches autonomous and able to oppose the state (Chile), while the failure to separate church from state made the churches dependent and compliant on the state (Argentina).

[6] WVS data, question E069_01: Confidence: Churches. In 1990, 76% of the respondents expressed either "a great deal" or "quite a lot" of confidence in the church, rising to nearly 80% by 1996, and then 67% in 2006.

[7] The church "provided the most effective leadership for mass discontent against the martial law regime" (Wurfel 1977, 17). Marcos threatened to legalize divorce in 1975, with the unintended consequence of shaking the conservatives in the hierarchy from their torpor and leading them to strengthen Catholic lay organizations. Criticism of military abuses by the religious orders and younger bishops led Cardinal Sin to change in 1979 his stance from

respondents in 1996, and 91% in 2001, expressed either a "great deal" or "quite a lot" of confidence in the church.[8]

The fusion of national and religious identities is not the only way, of course, in which religion mattered. Doctrine was vital in two ways. First, it governed the decision to enter politics. Some churches were much more likely to try to influence politics than others. The Roman Catholic Church has viewed natural law as overriding man-made legislation—and has repeatedly acted to defend this primacy. In contrast, Lutherans tended to see the political and the sacred as two distinct domains of mutual non-interference, while Evangelical Protestants were historically reluctant to enter the worldly and tainted sphere of secular politics. Second, doctrine led churches to pursue and to prioritize specific targets, such as Evangelical objections to pornography or Catholic concerns about contraception.[9]

Religious doctrine also influenced *secular* thinking about policy. Political actors accepted the conceptual categories and normative claims of religious authorities. For example, abortion, stem cell research, and IVF were all considered equally abominable, and for the same reasons, in Catholic countries; they all involve the destruction of embryos, which the Catholic Church now views as human beings with the same right to dignity and to life. As a result, even in secular European countries, stem cell and assisted reproductive technologies are often governed by the same laws. In contrast, in both Canada and the United States the admixture of Protestant theology led to a different categorization of IVF as distinct from abortion and far more acceptable. IVF, after all, was the creation of life. The interdenominational coalition in the United States thus needed to reach doctrinal consensus, first convincing conservative Protestants to oppose abortion despite the absence of clear doctrinal guidelines, and then "compromising" on IVF and assisted reproduction technologies more broadly.

How do churches translate religious nationalism and doctrinal convictions into policy? All religious groups can *indirectly* influence policy

---

"accommodation" to calls for the end of martial law in the Philippines. The more liberal bishops and religious order leaders criticized the eviction of squatters, the lengthy detention of prisoners, the fraudulent referenda, and the torture and execution of opposition members by the Marcos regime—as well as government raids on church institutions and arrests of nuns and priests, much as in Poland (Youngblood 1978). After the assassination of Benigno Aquino, Marcos's strongest opponent, Sin called for the faithful to "join the parliament of the streets." During the revolution itself, Cory Aquino received refuge in a Carmelite convent, and the Catholic station Radio Veritas was the main popular source of information. For an incisive analysis, see Slater 2009, 329–34.

[8] WVS data, question E069_01: Confidence: Churches.

[9] For especially compelling historical expositions of how religious doctrine mattered in the founding of the state and welfare state institutions, see Gorski 2003 and especially Kahl 2005 and Kahl 2014.

by openly declaring their convictions, contacting public officials, or organizing protest. This book examined how churches *directly* engage secular political actors and state institutions by investing their moral authority to influence policy. Where churches had lower or more diffuse moral authority, they could enter partisan coalitions, as the Italian and American churches did. Those churches with high moral authority, on the other hand, could obtain institutional access—a far more powerful way of influencing politics than either partisan coalitions or relying on diffuse voter demand. Institutional access was largely covert and viewed as non-partisan, in stark contrast to openly politicking on behalf of specific parties. It was also far more direct than either coalitions or (frequently unreliable) electorates—many churches preferred to avoid referenda if possible, for example, because they were costly and because they were unreliable, as the Irish, Polish, and Italian churches would agree. Institutional access also offered greater control over policy at a lower cost than partisan coalitions. Because these churches function within secular democracies that separated religion from politics, public scrutiny could be very costly, and because churches rely on moral authority as their key political asset, they needed to protect it. The irony is that for churches to influence politics, they have to appear to be above them.

Yet even churches with high moral authority could squander it by behaving immorally, or by speaking on behalf of only a part of the nation, such as geographical regions or partisan electorates. The Irish church's standing as the defender of national interests and morals was damaged by the abuse scandals that emerged in the 1990s. The Croat church lost its high standing in society over the course of the 1990s, when an autocratic governing party appropriated its support. Similarly, faced with a repressive autocratic regime from 1976 to 1983, the Catholic Church in Argentina was often complicit in autocratic rule—and lost its moral authority as a result, as did the church in Uruguay and Honduras. Subsequent popular trust and confidence in these churches was far lower than the levels found in Chile or the Philippines.[10] For all their political savvy, clerical wise men did not always make the shrewdest of decisions.

---

[10] In Argentina, at most 58% of respondents expressed a great deal or quite a bit of confidence in the church (1999, while in 1984 it was 46.5% and in 2006 it was 50%), while in Uruguay the numbers hovered around 55% (1996) and 50% (2006). WVS data, question E069_01: Confidence: Churches. Policy outcomes were not so clear: abortion remains illegal in Chile and Argentina; although divorce was legalized quite quickly after the downfall of the junta in Argentina, it remained illegal in Chile until 2004. Argentina legalized same-sex marriage in 2010, the only Latin American country to do so. One explanation argues that the differences between the church and policy advocates in economic resources and political access explain these patterns (Blofield 2006).

The importance of moral authority is further underscored by "established" national churches, such as the Church of England, or many of the Scandinavian national churches. By dint of establishment, they have a "seat at the table"—institutional access in the form of representation in the UK House of Lords, where ecclesiastical representatives sit as the Lords Spiritual, for example—but without moral authority, they wield less policy influence than their historically privileged status would lead us to expect.[11] In turn, their low levels of political moral authority stem from a very different relationship to the nation and to the state. Rather than defending the nation against a hostile state, these churches were privileged by secular states and were given "national" status by legal fiat.[12]

Much of the discussion in this book has focused on Catholic religious monopolies, but these established *Protestant* monopolies, such as Sweden, Denmark, Norway, or Finland show further that doctrine matters for church influence on policy, as does the relationship between nation, state, and church. First, the "two realms" doctrine of the Lutheran Church in these Scandinavian cases makes a clear distinction between the spiritual and secular realms, and was increasingly interpreted to imply that "neither shall political authorities interfere with question of faith . . . nor shall the church use its privileges to influence politics."[13] This stands in contrast to the historical Roman Catholic interpretations of natural law as superior to secular law, and to the implied need for the Catholic Church to influence secular policy to comply. Here also, the doctrinal emphasis on the direct relationship between individuals and the scripture, as opposed to an ecclesiastical hierarchy as the mediator between the people and God, hindered Lutheran clergy from representing the nation.

Second, the formal establishment of the Lutheran Church after the Reformation would eventually (and ironically) limit its influence on policy. Establishment as the official state church meant that the *state* and the church were intertwined, rather than the *nation* and the church. Rather than defending the nation against an external challenge, these confessional monopolies arose through limits on competition and legal privileges by the sponsor states. Thus throughout the seventeenth through nineteenth centuries, the Lutheran Church in Sweden had official status as a state religion, and even parliamentary representation. Religious dissent was criminalized.[14] The Lutheran Church became the "national church" in Denmark in 1849, and the state church in newly independent Norway in 1814. These churches were financially and legally dependent

---

[11] The Lords Spiritual may not openly favor, nor belong to, any political party.
[12] Madeley 2003, 37.
[13] Haugen 2011, 484.
[14] Jänterä-Jareborg 2010, 4–5.

on secular states. The government funded the church, reviewed church policy and organization, and appointed its clergy, who as state employees were governed by the civil service acts. Such dependence reduced the possibility that the church could act independently of the state, whether to defend the nation against secular aggression (admittedly an unlikely possibility) or to influence policy.[15]

The pietist revivals of nineteenth-century Denmark and Norway, attempts to use Lutheranism as a marker of a Finnish national identity during the postwar period of political deference to the Soviet Union, and the Norwegian Lutheran Church's emphasis on its organizational independence during the union with Sweden (1814–1905) did not amount to the fusion of national and religious identities in the face of state establishment of churches. The development of the postwar welfare state further diminished the church's role in society. Already low rates of religious participation further dropped, and the Lutheran Church became disestablished in 2000 in Sweden, and 2009–12 in Norway.[16]

As a result, these are national churches, trusted to "give a religious gloss to significant personal and community events and to maintain national heritage by preserving historic church buildings,"[17] but not national moral authorities. The most recent World Values Surveys show that less than a half of Swedes, Finns, and Norwegians have confidence in the churches.[18] The bond between religious and national identities is tenuous: only 17% of Swedes, 20% of Norwegians, 23% of Finns, and 33% of Danes agree that it is important to be Lutheran for their respective national identities.[19] Low rates of religiosity dispel the idea of a fusion of national and religious identities; fewer than 14% attend church services once a month or more, on par with France and the Czech Republic, the

---

[15] Similar dependence on the state, with similar effects, occurred in Orthodox monopolies; Orthodox churches are institutionally dependent on the state for material resources, in return for loyal and active support of the state by the church. They are accordingly less likely to seek shifts in public policy in domains other than those that favor its immediate status, like laws precluding religious competition, guaranteeing the church's financial support, or establishing chaplaincies in the military (Makarkin 2011, 8; Warner 2002).

[16] The 2012 constitutional amendment in Norway changed the status of the Lutheran Church from "the public religion of the state" into a "national church."

[17] Bruce 2000b, 38.

[18] WVS 6th wave, 2010–14. Forty-seven percent of Swedes, 47% of Finns, 43% of Norwegians, and 63% of Danes have confidence in the church in the 2010–14 surveys, a drop from the 56% of Swedes, 64% of Finns, and 51% of Norwegians with confidence in the church in the 5th wave (2005–08) surveys (Denmark was not included in the 5th wave).

[19] The sample mean is 43%, and the standard deviation is 19.6, so all except Denmark lie outside the range where two-thirds of the countries are located.

most secular European countries.[20] Few politicians or political parties make references to God, much less justify public policy with religious arguments.[21]

Accordingly, church influence on politics in these Protestant monopolies is limited; the churches *follow* rather than initiate policy changes, and secular actors explicitly and formally influence church policy. For example, after the parliament voted to change church policy, the Danish Lutheran Church began to perform same-sex marriages in 2012 despite theological reservations.[22] The church "is to a large extent run by the Danish political authorities,"[23] with government ministers vetting not only clerical appointments but also individual sermons. In short, these Protestant monopolies highlight the conditions for church influence on politics: these churches did not have the doctrinal motives, institutional opportunity (ironically, by dint of establishment), or political means (the fusion of national and religious identities and the moral political authority it produced) to decisively shape public policy.

In short, churches influence politics and policy the most when they hold high stocks of moral authority—and that moral authority is conserved when churches appear apolitical, non-partisan, and genuinely working on behalf of the national common good. Church moral authority is bolstered and made into a *political* resource by the historical fusion of nation and religion (which the churches themselves catalyzed), and it is best preserved if the churches appear to stay out of partisan conflicts.

The stories of the individual churches are often more complicated, of course, as the preceding comparisons of the six countries over time shows. Church influence always depended on politicians perceiving a benefit to making concessions, but this simple relationship played out very differently. For example, while divorce remained illegal in Ireland and in Italy after independence, in post-communist Poland and Croatia a ban on divorce was never seriously questioned—not because doctrine had changed, but because the political costs of making divorce illegal in societies with over four decades of liberal communist-era divorce laws would have been extraordinary. Neither churches nor politicians seriously pursued it.

---

[20] As Steve Bruce points out, the deregulation of these religious markets has not resulted in a flowering of either religiosity or other religions, contrary to the predictions of the religious markets literature (Bruce 2000b). Around 70% of citizens are nonetheless formally church members, largely thanks to automatic enrollment at birth.

[21] Jänterä-Jareborg 2010, 2.

[22] The Swedish parliament had voted earlier, in 2009, to allow church weddings for same-sex couples, with the church supporting the law. "Sweden Passes New Gay Marriage Law," *The Local*, April 2, 2009, available at http://www.thelocal.se/20090402/18608.

[23] Haugen 2011, 486.

Modes of access and influence also changed over time. While Archbishop McQuaid could draft paragraphs of the Irish Constitution in 1937 and exchange comments on the text with de Valera, the Polish Episcopate did not have the same opportunity sixty years later, during the writing of Poland's 1997 Constitution. What was widely seen as apposite in the 1930s was simply inappropriate at the close of the twentieth century, and secular and religious actors involved were acutely aware of these differences. Similarly, the new and relatively weak incumbents in nineteenth-century Ireland and Québec conceded education to the church, ensuring that the Catholic Church could for generations inculcate the fusion of nation and religion. Yet in very Catholic Poland and Croatia after 1989, while religious education returned, schools remained resolutely in the hands of the secular state. In the intervening century, the reforms of Vatican II and its recognition of ecumenism and secular authority, global cultural shifts that relegated religion to the private sphere, and a well-established secular educational system meant that the churches did not seek to control education in its entirety—and the state would be unwilling to hand it over.

Religious groups also have a wider choice of tactics at their disposal than simply institutional access or partisan coalitions, as the case studies show. They can mobilize voters directly (though at great cost, as the Polish church found out in the early 1990s), they can instigate and mobilize voters in referenda (as the Irish, Italian, and Croatian churches did), and they can issue public pronouncements and declarations regarding the advisability and theological value of given policies. In religious societies, churches can organize marches, protests, letter-writing campaigns, and votes—even if they cannot count on either popular compliance or on the policy impact of this mobilization. Such mobilization does not require national moral authority as much as the loyalty of the faithful. More broadly, political parties and churches are opportunistic and will use a mix of tactics at various institutional levels. They can even combine elements of institutional access with partisan coalitions, as the Italian church did with the inclusion of the Lateran Pacts in the 1947 Constitution, or the Croatian church did with the secret negotiations around the 1996–98 agreements.[24] At the same time, churches face institutional limits on their action; religious groups in the United States come up against the firewalls of separation of church and state, and Canadian and American churches have to contend with federalism and the fragmentation (and multiplication) of political authorities.

---

[24] Critically, however, even if churches gain aspects of institutional access under partisan alliances, they still pay the price in moral authority for a coalition.

As a final caveat, even if these arguments about fusion, moral authority, and institutional channels of access are convincing, they do not apply everywhere. Instead, this analysis applies to competitive and secular regimes—competitive in that religious groups are one of many competing for state favor and policy influence, and secular in that the law and society recognize the distinctions between the sacred and the secular spheres. For these reasons, it is less likely to apply in autocracies that do not allow churches to compete for hearts and minds, with each other and with secular actors (or pay the costs for doing so), or in regimes where the historical processes of state formation and religious development did not separate church and state as two distinct institutional spheres. Currently, many interpretations of Islam do not make this distinction explicit, for example, and this argument does not apply to theocracies such as Iran.[25] That said, this book sheds light on how the historical relationship between church, state, and nation more broadly shapes religious influence on policy.

Implications

Several implications follow from these arguments: for our understanding of how religious groups influence policy, the role of churches as interest groups, the question of why religions (and religious monopolies) flourish, and even perhaps the uniqueness of American national character.

First, religious coalitions with political parties are far from an ideal arrangement for either partner. They are not the most effective or certain channel of influence, given the possibility of coalition partners reneging on the deal, and the very real risk that a political party would not be re-elected into government. But even when parties are repeatedly re-elected, as the Italian DC was, coalitions tend to be costly to religious groups, undermining their moral authority and tainting them with charges of partisanship and self-interest. They are also costly for political parties in that they limit the strategic electoral and platform options for parties. Not surprisingly, the DC tried to free itself from its reliance on church mobilization as soon as it could and was willing to develop a network of patronage and clientelism as a substitute. For its part, the church gained greater popular approval once the coalition ended. In short, rather than producing gains from political trade, coalitions between churches and political parties can undermine both partners.

[25] Of course, Catholicism was long seen as anti-modern and absolutist religion, incompatible with modernity or democracy. It was "the central focus of the Enlightenment critique of religion," as José Casanova points out (Casanova 2001, 1054).

The churches' obtaining their preferences through covert access rather than public debate is not unique, as an extensive literature on "quiet politics" shows. [26] Business groups have also relied on working quietly behind the scenes, building influence over policy and setting the agenda through their superior political organization and expertise on particularly complicated economic issues.[27] Politicians defer to business and economic experts, especially on complicated issues that are hard to explain to voters who do not particularly concern themselves with these issues in the first place. Such "weapons of quiet politics work best in the shadows, not under the bright spotlight of sustained public attention."[28] When voters care and policy suggestions become hotly contested cleavages, it is much more difficult for organized interests to use back channels to obtain their preferences.

The story of church influence here supports and refines these accounts. First, the limited success of referenda shows that even in religious societies, churches cannot count on a religious public to enact religious policies. Public piety and religious nationalism often conceal a diversity of private political views and decisions at odds with religious teachings. As a result, such "public politics" are far more risky for churches and politicians than legislative bills passed quietly across negotiation tables in legislative back rooms. Second, institutional access is also effective even when the policy issues are controversial. This is because churches can claim a special sort of policy expertise: their moral authority, which serves as an informational shortcut in evaluating which policies are desirable. Much as business leaders can supply simple and convincing metaphors for complexities of corporate governance,[29] so can church leaders frame intricate ethical and societal metaphors in compelling and convincing moral terms. Further, institutional access allows churches to set the agenda and make the first legislative proposals away from public scrutiny, effectively limiting the set of policies and solutions, even on issues that are highly publicized and controversial.

Rather than thinking of churches as political partners, then, we can also consider them as another interest group, as Carolyn Warner has.[30] An interest groups is a set of non-elected actors that represent constituencies interested in specific policies, such as business groups, trade unions, or sectoral interests. This literature has often focused on the historical origins of interest groups, if not on the historical reasons why their claims

---

[26] See Culpepper 2010 for a review.
[27] Jones and Baumgartner 2005; Culpepper 2010; Hacker and Pierson 2010.
[28] Culpepper 2010, 146.
[29] Culpepper 2010, 178.
[30] Warner 2000.

might resonate with the broader public, such as the fusion of identities discussed in this book.[31] If we do think of churches as interest groups, one of the ironies is that their own members frequently do not wish the churches to influence policy, voting, or governments. Many church adherents, unlike trade unionists or businessmen, do not want or even expect their leaders to take political action. As a result, churches involved in politics stand to lose far more authority among their constituents than other interest groups. In fact, churches can suffer backlash from their own adherents even if (and in some cases *because*) they achieve their policy aims.

Yet if churches pursue controversial policies, would we see continuing elite deference to churches? After all, part of the churches' power is their ability to address society, to act in its name, and to threaten to withdraw popular support (including electoral) from secular political projects. If churches do not (or no longer) represent public opinion, why would politicians listen to them? Part of the answer is sociological, and lies not only in the churches' moral authority and divine sanctions, but also in the risk aversion of politicians. Politicians tend to be an older cohort, socialized at a different time and invested in keeping up their reputations. As a result, even if they are privately sympathetic to positions opposed by the churches, it may be difficult for them to confront religious groups. Further, these same politicians, faced with mixed signals from popular opinion polls, would rather err on the side of a conservative status quo and the churches' preferred option—not least because the churches pose a potentially potent electoral threat. Consider an electorate where 40% of the voters go to church, and 30% of these follow the political instructions of churches—representing a 12% religious voting block. Such a group, depending on the electoral system and the distribution of voters across districts, can easily make or break elections.

Institutional access reifies this anticipatory anxiety and diffidence, reminding politicians and society of the churches' presence and witness—and making the churches' implicit threats direct and potent. For politicians, institutional access is an insurance policy, giving the churches a stake in the survival of the regime and its incumbents. But it is also an agreement that is often difficult to renegotiate unilaterally, given the stickiness of historical policy choices, the resistance of secular officials who owe their jobs to vetting by the churches, and durable popular constituencies for church welfare and other provisions. Recall that in Ireland, the church began to hand over education to the state nearly two decades after its moral authority collapsed—and only once its own inability to recruit clergy made staffing schools increasingly infeasible. As a result, it

[31] Clemens 1997; Skocpol, Ganz, and Munson 2000; Hojnacki et al. 2012.

may sometimes take massive exogeneous shifts in popular opinion or in the understanding of fundamental political rights (as in the case of same-sex marriage) for politicians to follow voters rather than their conservative instincts, and the pressure of dominant religious groups. Until such reframing occurs, politicians continue to defer to churches.

Moving beyond the politics of policy influence, two other implications follow for the study of religion and national identity. First, the role of national fusion helps to explain why some religious monopolies remain so lively. Such vibrancy runs counter to the expectations of a set of scholarly approaches labeled the "political economy of religion."[32] In a quest to provide individual-level and finely grained explanations for religious behavior, this approach focuses on how states favor a particular religion over others, and the impact that such regulation has on religions' ability to meet the different preferences of religious "consumers."

Scholars working in this tradition have argued that vibrant religious marketplaces are the sources of religious vigor and influence, and religious monopolies are inherently weak. They have found that where the religious market can freely offer diverse alternatives to meet the demand for diverse religious beliefs and preferences, rates of religious participation and denominational affiliation increase.[33] Competition among religions leads to better meeting consumer "demand," and subsequently to innovation and efficiency. Religious pluralism thus breeds religious fervor. In contrast, where the state regulates religious markets (by financially or politically supporting a state religion), the levels of religious pluralism and participation decrease.[34] Religious monopolies, such as those found in Poland, Ireland, or Italy, are cast in a harsh light, artificially propped up by states—and their use of coercive force.[35] Thus religious monopolies cannot occur "naturally," in the absence of state mandate, and "the only means of enforcing a religious monopoly is by government fiat."[36]

---

[32] See Clark 2010 and Gill 2001 for stimulating and concise overviews. Notable theoretical and empirical criticisms of this approach include Bruce 2000a; Chaves and Gorski 2001; Montgomery 2003; Olson 2002; and Voas, Olson, and Crocket 2002.

[33] Finke and Stark 1992; Chaves and Cann 1992; Stark and Iannaccone 1994; Iannaccone 1998; Gill 2001; Clark 2010.

[34] For example, Chaves and Cann find that for every additional item of state regulation, weekly church attendance drops by 5.3% (Chaves and Cann 1992, 283). Regulation of religious markets is said to depress participation since consumers have no control over the quantity or quality of the religious goods provided; state interests are unlikely to converge with consumer preferences; one publicly sponsored religion can never provide the variety of religious choices demanded by diverse individuals; and finally, even if religious alternatives arise, individuals are already bound to the inefficient state religion (Iannaccone 1991; Chaves and Cann 1992).

[35] Stark and Finke 2002, 37.

[36] Gill 2001; see also Gill 2008; Stark 1992.

Yet as we have seen, religious monopolies can thrive—but thanks to the historical fusion of national and religious identities, rather than to the careful tending and preferential regulation by secular states. The relevant processes are historical and societal rather than economic and legal. Moreover, Catholic monopolies have greater influence than the more competitive Protestant-Catholic markets (and in turn, there is considerable variation in influence among the Catholic churches themselves). Rather than state support resulting in torpid monopolies, then, religious monopolies can arise for historical reasons, flourish, and influence policy and politics. As one scholar warns, "perhaps the religious monopoly just means that people have not felt the need to set up rival religious bodies."[37]

More broadly, the political economy of religion has a curious relationship to history, in two ways. First, in arguing for why some religious monopolies may flourish, it allows that historical societal conflict can act as a substitute for competition in fostering religious vibrancy, since "religious firms can generate high levels of participation to the extent that the firms serve as primary organizational vehicles for social conflict."[38] This proposition has been used to explain the high levels of observance in Catholic Poland. Yet why would societal conflict establish a thriving monopoly in some cases and not in others? Why should such monopolies endure once the conflict ends?

Second, the political economy of religion has difficulty explaining why *removing* regulation does not result in greater observance. Low rates of religiosity in states continue with no state support for a particular religion, such as France, the Czech Republic, or Estonia. In these free markets, we should see high rates of observance, yet religious entrepreneurs have not moved in and the rates of religious observance have not gone up. Instead, "the public resurgence of religion took place in places such as Poland, the United States, Brazil, Nicaragua, and Iran, all places which can hardly be characterized as secularized wastelands."[39] The answer given by the political economy of religion is that historical state support for a given religion precludes current conversions to other religions.[40] Yet if believers are said to freely move between religions, why would past state support for a religious monopoly prevent them from doing so?

We are thus left looking for an account of why some societies might be more *receptive* to religious mobilization or church attempts to influence politics—an explanation that takes into account why religious claims

---

[37] Jenkins 2007, 50.
[38] Stark and Finke 2000, 202; Stark and Finke 2002, 40.
[39] Casanova 1994, 224–25.
[40] Iannaccone, 1994; Starke and Finke 2002, 38.

resonate in some societies but not others,[41] and the ways in which religious choice is embedded socially and historically.[42] Here, the fusion of national and religious identities provides one such answer; it can buttress vibrant religious marketplaces, as in the United States, and keep religious monopolies vibrant, as it did for decades in Ireland, Poland, Lithuania, and Croatia. Conversely, some scholars have emphasized the role of hostile neighbors or religious frontiers in fostering the demand for religious nationalism.[43] Such threats are an important part of the story, but a *supply* of religious identity is also needed. Churches provide these religious idioms and symbols. They not only deliver spiritual sustenance, but also actively fuse religious and national identities and reproduce that fusion over time through popular education, consistent actions, and deliberate rhetoric. In short, churches both consciously nurture and benefit from religious nationalism.

A second implication for the study of national identity is closer to home, where the "uniqueness" of the United States and American identity itself has long fascinated domestic and foreign observers ranging from Alexis de Tocqueville (whose famous *Democracy in America* noted that "Americans combine the notions of Christianity and of liberty so intimately in their minds, that it is impossible to make them conceive the one without the other"[44]) to Jean Baudrillard (who more infamously quipped that "Americans may have no identity, but they do have wonderful teeth"[45]). I argue here that rather than being unique as (one) "nation under God," the United States has in common with other countries a fusion of national and religious identities, one that arose as religion helped to define the nation and give it a coherent identity in the absence of a common history among diverse immigrants and believers. This fusion helps to legitimate the political claims of religious groups, and to suffuse both the language and actions of both Left and Right with religious justification and symbolism.

[41] Rogers Brubaker argues that the intertwining of religious and nationalist language should be studied not only on the "supply" side but also on the "reception" side: the resonance it receives within society (Brubaker 2012).

[42] Edgell 2005; Ellison 1995.

[43] Barker 2009, 35; Rieffer 2003, 226. Threats to group identity from other religions often mask ethnic or other group grievance; for example, Rieffer cites the hostilities incited between Orthodox Serbs and Albanian Kosovars. Yet most analysts agree that it was political entrepreneurship, rather than religious enmity, that ignited the Yugoslav conflict.

[44] Tocqueville, however, also argued that "I am so much alive to the almost inevitable dangers which beset religious belief whenever the clergy take part in public affairs, and I am so convinced that Christianity must be maintained at any cost in the bosom of modern democracies, that I had rather shut up the priesthood within the sanctuary than allow them to step beyond it" (Tocqueville, *Democracy in America*, 1835 [1945], 156).

[45] Baudrillard 2010 [1990], 34.

The case of the United States also illustrates that if nation and religion fuse, ethnicity and religion can reinforce each other as well. For example, American respondents in public opinion polls responded that they feel "warmest" toward Jews, Catholics, and mainline Protestants, less so toward Evangelical Protestants, and less and less toward the non-religious, Mormons, Buddhists, and Muslims.[46] One interpretation of these differences is that these last few are very small groups, and few Americans know them.[47] Yet as we noted in Chapter 5, there are as few Jews in the United States (less than an estimated 2% of the population) as there are Muslims. The framework presented here, on the other hand, suggests a different (testable) interpretation: that those groups that are part of the invented religious Judeo-Christian consensus in the United States are in turn tolerated. It is their degree of their belonging to that consensus, rather than their sheer numbers, that influence popular dispositions.

For all the importance of national identities, underlying religiosity, and public opinion, churches are the critical actors—the organizations that are the agents of influence in morality politics. Without their involvement, several policies that fly in the face of heterogeneous popular opinion, whether abortion in post-communist Poland or stem cell research in Italy, are inexplicable. Churches are critical to the policy process in three ways. First, in the absence of pressure from organized religious groups, many policy items would simply not appear on the legislative program. Second, churches with high moral authority gain concessions from the state, and generate an anticipatory anxiety among politicians that sometimes means churches get more than they even requested. As a result, even when public opinion is either mixed, or opposes, church initiatives, religious preferences are legislated into law—an outcome inexplicable without church involvement. Finally, given the fusion of national and religious identities, and its reinforcement of church moral authority, the demands of churches are simply not another demand; to disregard their religious preferences is to court charges of behaving against the national interest.

The struggle of churches to enact divine values is thus not confined to pews, pulpits, or fellowship meetings. It readily spills over into the political arena. Here, some religious groups and leaders have proven themselves to be savvy political actors, able to translate piety into power, and doctrinal concerns and theological strictures into formal legislation that is enforced by a secular judicial and executive system, and by a more general deference to a powerful moral authority.

---

[46] Putnam and Campbell 2010, 505.
[47] Putnam and Campbell 2010, 534.

Further Tests of the Argument

TO FURTHER ASSESS THE ARGUMENTS advanced in this book, I provide a simple formal model and a broader empirical analysis.

I have argued that the fusion of national and religious identities gives churches moral authority that allows them to act as non-partisan, apolitical, and credible representatives of national interest. In exchange for their support, secular incumbents can offer the churches institutional access or partisan coalitions. Where they hold high moral authority and can ensure the survival of the regime by appealing to the entire nation to support the regime in the name of national interest, churches can gain direct institutional access to policy making. Where they do not wield such broad moral authority, they can still form partisan coalitions that reward individual parties and represent narrower constituencies—but then they depend on the political parties' probability of winning office, and they lose moral authority as a result of their relatively narrow politicking.

The rest of this chapter evaluates this argument in two ways: by checking its internal coherence and logic mathematically and by providing a broader set of comparisons outside of the paired country studies. The simple model strips away the richness of the descriptions for the sake of examining a few key moving parts and how they interact. The broader comparisons allow us to see which factors correlate to policy influence in a larger and more diverse sample of countries.

A Simple Model of Church-State Interactions

The core argument of this book is that in influencing policy, churches have a powerful resource: their moral authority as representatives of national interest. They can invest that authority on behalf of secular governments and political parties, which I denote here as the "incumbent."[1] In exchange for

---

[1] For simplicity's sake, this shorthand includes secular governing actors that include democratically elected governing parties and coalitions, as well as states, regimes, and autocratic rulers and governments. While there are clear conceptual differences between states, regimes, and governments, this formulation has the advantage of applying to democratically elected governing parties and to authoritarian rulers that blur the distinction between government, party, and state.

their support, the incumbent can offer the churches a share of policy-making authority. This share can take the form of institutional access or partisan co-alitions. The former is covert and shares sovereignty between the church and the state—the latter is visible, more uncertain (since parties lose elections) and associates the church with a specific partisan option, which undermines the church's moral authority. Both sides have something the other wants: the church wants to change policies and the incumbent needs church support. The trade-off is that institutional access is costly for the state (because it shares policy-making authority), but highly desirable for the church. Coali-tions are less costly for the incumbent, but far less desirable for the church.

A simple model distills the conditions under which churches obtain coalitions or institutional access. The purpose of this model is to test the logic of the argument rather than to generate hypotheses deductively. It distills the strategic interactions between church and state into a simple sequence where the state offers either coalitions or institutional access, depending on how much it needs church support, and the church either accepts or rejects these offers, depending on its stock of moral authority and how eroded it would be by accepting the offer.

Of course, the starkness of the model does not capture the messiness and complexity of informal personal ties, historical entanglements, and sub rosa deals. It does not directly address the diffuse influence that reli-gious groups can have, such as the anticipation of church preferences by anxious politicians worried about church criticism or electoral backlash. The model also does not capture some of the alternatives available to the churches; for example, the Irish church also relied on referenda, and the Italian one on personal pressure on religious politicians. Further, coali-tions and institutional access may not always be mutually exclusive; for example, the Italian Roman Catholic Church insisted on certain provi-sions within the postwar Italian constitution, even as it entered into a partisan coalition with the Christian Democrats.[2] Nonetheless, it offers an important check of the logic of the argument and shows the universe of possible outcomes that need to be explored.

Order of Play and Payoffs

A potential crisis occurs in the prehistory of the game. This can be an exogenous economic or security shock, massive popular demonstrations

---

[2] There is an empirical asymmetry here: partisan coalitions may involve an element of institutional access, but institutional access rarely leads to partisan coalitions, since it sub-sumes the influence available under partisan coalitions. That said, if a church is in a coali-tion with elements of institutional access, it will still pay the price in moral authority for the coalition.

against the regime, the rise of a new and popular opposition party, and such. The threat prompts the incumbent to turn to the church.

The church has M, moral authority, which we can think of as its ability to mobilize social support on behalf of its goals or other actors. Moral authority is a function of the church's past actions, and its reputation for representing broad, non-partisan interests. Thus overt partisanship will cost it moral authority. M is inherited from the past at some value $M_{t-1} \in [0,1)$.

The incumbent is the secular governing actor, which we can think of as the ruling regime or an individual governing party.[3] The incumbent enjoys the benefits of office.[4] Without church support, it remains in office with probability p. With church support, the incumbent remains in office with probability $p + (1-p)\ \delta_A\ M_{t-1}$, where δ_A is the rate at which the church retains its moral authority M_{t-1} (the subscript $_A$ refers to the retention rate when the church has institutional access, and $_X$ refers to the retention rate when the church is in a coalition). If the historical patterns of fusion determine where the initial levels of moral authority lie (i.e., the intercept), further church actions and political interactions determine both whether moral authority is retained or lost, and the rate of that loss (i.e., the slope.)

This formulation means that:

1. the probability of staying in office increases with the moral authority of the church; in other words, powerful churches contribute more to the incumbent's political survival.
2. church support does not *guarantee* the survival of the incumbent.

In times of crisis, the incumbent turns to the church for support to stay in office. It offers either institutional access A or an overt coalition X to the church. Because the incumbent moves first, and cannot offer voter support to the church, the church cannot choose to rely on voter demand to produce its preferred outcome.[5] The church either accepts the offer or rejects it. The entire sequence is shown in Figure A.1.

---

[3] The incumbent is assumed to be a unitary actor. Regimes and governments, whether democratic or autocratic, are internally diverse. Well-documented conflicts of interest exist between bureaucrats and political parties, for example. However, both bureaucrats and political parties prize regime survival above all else, and neither would want to share power further with a third party—the churches.

[4] Typically, the incumbent prizes both policy and office holding: rather than disaggregating these into two separate parameters, I collapse them here into one and normalize to 1. The central concern is with the authority over policy making and the willingness to make concessions to hold onto it.

[5] If the church was the first mover, and if the goal was policy rather than sharing authority, the church could (a) mobilize voters, (b) initiate a partisan coalition, or (c) demand institutional access.

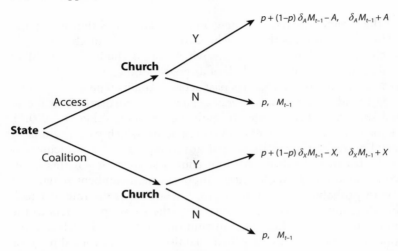

Figure A.1. Model of Church-State Interactions
M: moral authority of church.
X: coalition offer made by secular state to church, concession made by state.
A: institutional access given by a secular state to church, concession made by state.
p: probability of secular actor remaining in office *without* church support.
M_{t-1}: church moral authority inherited from the past.
δ_X and δ_A: retention rate of M for church if it enters into coalition or obtains institutional access, respectively.

If the church refuses to cooperate, it retains its level of moral authority, such that $M_t = M_{t-1}$. The incumbent then remains in power with probability p.

Accepting X, or a coalition with secular actor, is costly for the church; because it signals that the church is allied to a particular political option, and because it ties the church's future to a partisan actor who may or may not be around for much longer. Therefore, when the church accepts X, or a coalition, it loses moral authority, M_{t-1}, such that it obtains $X + \delta_X M_{t-1}$, where $\delta_X \in (0,1)$. δ_X measures how much moral authority the church retains after accepting X. This formulation implies that a coalition with the incumbent reduces a church's moral authority, but churches with initially greater levels of moral authority retain more of it after entering a coalition. The church will always reject an offer of $X = 0$, so that we can interpret that offer as the incumbent not approaching the church (W). The incumbent, in turn, gives up X, but it obtains the church's support, so that it gets a payoff of $p + (1 - p) \delta_X M_{t-} - X$, where $(1 - p) \delta_X M_{t-}$ reflects the church's contribution to the incumbent's survival.

If the church accepts A, or institutional access, it gains authority over policy without publicly becoming involved in politics. It obtains the payoff $\delta_A M_{t-1} + A$, where $\delta_A \in (0,1)$. Because it does not involve explicit politicking, the church retains its existing moral authority M_{t-1} at a higher rate than it would in a coalition: $\delta_A > \delta_X$. (This retention rate captures the imperfections in keeping covert influence secret—in the era of constant media surveillance and leakage of state information, institutional access is unlikely to remain fully hidden.) The incumbent again obtains the church's support, which is now more valuable, because the church retains more of its moral authority, but it has to give up A, so that its payoff is $p + (1 - p) \delta_A M_{t-} - A$. In this model, A is an exogenously fixed amount, since the amount of institutional access tended to be similar across the empirical cases.

The incumbent makes an offer to the church, the church accepts or rejects, and the payoffs are realized. Allowing the incumbent to not approach the church $(X = 0)$, the **church** receives the following payoffs:

- {A, Y}: $\delta_A M_{t-1} + A$
- {A, N}: M_{t-1}
- {X, Y}: $\delta_X M_{t-1} + X$
- {X, N}: M_{t-1}
- {W}: M_{t-1}

The **incumbent** receives the following payoffs:

- {A, Y}: $p + (1-p) \delta_A M_{t-1} - A$
- {A, N}: p
- {X, Y}: $p + (1-p) \delta_X M_{t-1} - X$
- {X, N}: p
- {W}: p

Equilibria

To solve for the subgame perfect Nash equilibrium of the game, we proceed by backwards induction. The specification of an equilibrium requires a move by the incumbent, what the church would do if offered a coalition, and what the church would do if offered institutional access.

The church will accept an offer $X > 0$ if and only if the offer is sufficient to offset the church's loss of moral authority, such that $X \geq (1 - \delta_X) M_{t-1.} \equiv X'$.

The incumbent, in turn, prefers offering X' and having the church accept to offering $X = 0$ and having the church reject if:

(CONDITION 1)

$p + (1-p)\,\delta_X M_{t-1} - X' \geq p$ (the coalition will increase the likelihood of survival for the incumbent).

Substituting $X' = (1 - \delta_X)\,M_{t-1}$ yields

$(1-p)\,\delta_X M_{t-1} - (1 - \delta_X)\,M_{t-1} \geq 0$ (the church's contribution to incumbent survival is greater than the loss of moral authority it suffers), which reduces to

$(2-p)\,\delta_X \geq 1$

In contrast, if $(2-p)\,\delta_X < 1$, the incumbent would rather offer the church $X = 0$ and live without church support, rather than making an offer sufficiently large to gain the church's acceptance. Thus, we have two scenarios:

I. If $(2-p)\,\delta_X \geq 1$, the incumbent has the choice between offering A (which the church accepts) and X' (which the church also accepts).

II. If $(2-p)\,\delta_X < 1$, the incumbent has the choice between offering A (which the church always accepts) and $X = 0$, which the church rejects.

I. In scenario I, $(2-p)\,\delta_X \geq 1$, the probability of incumbent survival p without church support is sufficiently small, and δ_X (the church's retention of its moral authority in a coalition) is sufficiently large. In this scenario, the incumbent prefers offering A to X' (and in turn offering X' to no church support) iff:

(CONDITION 2)

$p + (1-p)\,\delta_A M_{t-1} - A \geq p + (1-p)\,\delta_X M_{t-1} - X'$ (the payoff for the incumbent for the church accepting access is greater than for the church accepting a coalition)

and

(1 − p) $(\delta_A - \delta_X) M_{t-1} + (1 - \delta_X) M_{t-1} \geq A$ (the difference in the church's retention of moral authority between access and coalitions *and* the loss of the church's moral authority under a coalition are equal or greater than the size of the institutional access),

or, put differently:

$$M_{t-1} \geq \frac{A}{(1-p)(\delta A - \delta_X) + (1 - \delta_X)}$$

If both conditions (1) and (2) hold, the incumbent offers institutional access to the church in the subgame perfect Nash equilibrium; the church accepts institutional access.[6]

If condition (1) holds and (2) fails, the incumbent offers a coalition X' to the church in the subgame perfect Nash equilibrium; the church accepts any offer $X \geq X'$ and would accept institutional access if offered (which does not happen).

Therefore, churches with larger levels of moral authority will be offered institutional access; while churches with lower levels of moral authority will be offered a coalition, as condition (2) shows, and as long as (1) holds. The size of the coalition benefit X' increases as the moral authority of the church does.

II. If condition (1) fails, so that *(2 − p)* $\delta_X < 1$, the incumbent would be better off offering $X = 0$ than offering X' and have the church accept. The incumbent thus has to weigh the option of offering institutional access against living without church support. The incumbent prefers offering institutional access iff:

(CONDITION 3)

p + (1−p) $\delta_A M_{t-1} - A > p$ (the value of church institutional access to the incumbent is higher than its probability of survival without church support)

or, put differently:

$$M_{t-1} \geq \frac{A}{(1-p)\delta_A}$$

The incumbent offers institutional access to the church, and the church accepts, so that the equilibrium outcome in this case is the same as above.

---

[6] And the church would accept any offer $X \geq X'$, which does not happen.

When condition (1) fails and condition (3) holds, the incumbent offers institutional access to the church; the church accepts and rejects any offer $X < X'$ (which in equilibrium does not happen). If the church's moral authority is particularly compromised by forming a coalition with the incumbent (in other words, when condition [1] fails, condition [2] is easier to satisfy than [3]), then relatively low levels of moral authority are sufficient for a church to gain institutional access. Finally, when both condition (1) and (3) fail, the incumbent offers $X = 0$, the church rejects any offer $X < X'$, and would accept any offer of institutional access, which does not happen in this equilibrium. In this case, the incumbent is neither sufficiently threatened to seek church support nor is the church's moral authority sufficiently large or resilient to make a coalition attractive.

We can summarize the discussion so far as follows:

Claim 1. The following is a unique subgame perfect Nash equilibrium when $A \geq (1 - \delta_A) M_{t-1}$ (when the size of institutional access exceeds the church's loss of moral authority by obtaining such access).

A. If $(2 - p) \delta_X \geq 1$:

If $M_{t-1} \geq \dfrac{A}{(1-p)(\delta_A - \delta_X) + (1 - \delta_X)}$, the incumbent offers A. The church accepts A, as well as any offer $X \geq (1 - \delta_X) M_{t-1}$, and rejects any other X. The outcome is that the incumbent offers A and the church accepts.

If $M_{t-1} < \dfrac{A}{(1-p)(\delta_A - \delta_X) + (1 - \delta_X)}$, the incumbent offers $X' = (1 - \delta_X) M_{t-1}$. The church accepts A as well as any offer $X \geq (1 - \delta_X) M_{t-1}$, and rejects any other X. The outcome is that the incumbent offers X' and the church accepts.

B. If $(2 - p) \delta_X < 1$:

If $M_{t-1} \geq \dfrac{A}{(1 - p)\delta A}$, the incumbent offers A. The church accepts A as well as any offer $X \geq (1 - \delta_X) M_{t-1}$, and rejects any other X. The outcome is that the incumbent offers A and the church accepts.

If $M_{t-1} < \dfrac{A}{(1 - p)\delta A}$, the incumbent offers $X = 0$. The church accepts A as well as any offer $X \geq (1 - \delta_X) M_{t-1}$, and rejects any other X. The outcome is that the incumbent offers nothing to the church and the church rejects.

It can also be shown that all of these combinations of conditions are feasible, in that there are parameter values satisfying all relevant combinations of conditions.

The equilibrium has a number of implications. First, churches with sufficiently high moral authority,

$$M_{t-1} \geq \frac{A}{(1-p)\delta A},$$

will be offered institutional access. If the church's loss of moral authority after accepting a coalition offer (X) is sufficiently large, the incumbent never offers a coalition. If the church's loss of moral authority after accepting the offer of a coalition is not too large, the incumbent will offer a coalition to churches with relatively low levels of moral authority. Churches with higher levels of moral authority will obtain larger concessions from coalitions.

If the church loses a great deal of moral authority after accepting a coalition, churches with relatively modest levels of moral authority will be offered institutional access as well: the condition on M_{t-1} for the incumbent to offer institutional access in the first scenario, $(2-p)\ \delta_X \geq 1$, is more restrictive than in the second, $(2-p)\ \delta_X < 1$. In this case, since a coalition comes at a very high cost to the church, and compensating for this loss would be too costly for the incumbent, the incumbent can effectively only offer institutional access. For the churches, therefore, it can be beneficial if their moral authority would be compromised severely by accepting a coalition, since it may help them secure institutional access. For instance, if moral authority rests on non-interference with day-to-day politics, coalitions would be especially costly and parties more likely to gain institutional access. Churches whose moral authority would not suffer from a coalition, in contrast, may not be able to obtain institutional access. One implication is that the roots of a church's moral authority may affect whether the church can enter a coalition or gain institutional access.

If the incumbent is highly vulnerable (p is low), it will offer institutional access to churches with sufficiently high levels of moral authority and a coalition to churches with lower levels of moral authority (provided that the church retains enough moral authority). In contrast, if the incumbent's survival does not depend on support by the church (p is large, and in particular approaches 1), it will offer neither a coalition nor institutional access.

If the incumbent values institutional access highly, only churches with high levels of moral authority will be offered institutional access. Moreover, the larger the loss of moral authority from accepting X and the lower the loss of moral authority from accepting A, the more likely it is that the church is offered institutional access. The threshold of moral authority above which a church gains institutional access increases along with the value of the access to the incumbent (A and in δ_X) but decreases in δ_A. The threshold is largest when δ_X and δ_A approach each other.

In sum, the game has three possible equilibrium outcomes: the church accepts an offer of institutional access, the church accepts a coalition, and the incumbent does not seek the support of the church. Institutional access is most likely to be offered to churches with high levels of moral authority, when accepting a coalition is very damaging to the moral authority of a church, or when the incumbent is in a deep crisis.

Thus far, institutional access has been assumed to be sufficiently valuable for the church to accept it if offered: this implied that $A \geq (1 - \delta_A) M_{t-1}$. While this is a reasonable assumption—institutional access is valuable and does not compromise greatly the moral authority of the churches—for the sake of completeness the following describes the subgame perfect Nash equilibrium if $A < (1 - \delta_A) M_{t-1}$.

Claim 2. When $A < (1 - \delta_A) M_{t-1}$, the unique subgame perfect Nash equilibrium is the following: if $(2-p) \delta_X \geq 1$, the incumbent offers $X' = (1 - \delta_A) M_{t-1}$. The church accepts any offer $X \geq X'$, and rejects any offer $X < X'$ as well as A. If $(2-p) \delta_X < 1$, the incumbent offers $X = 0$. The church rejects any offer $X < X'$ as well as A.

Thus if institutional access is sufficiently unattractive to the church, the incumbent will offer a coalition only if the incumbent is highly vulnerable (p is small) and the church retains sufficiently high levels of moral authority after accepting a coalition.

A Graphical Representation

Figures A.2a and A.2b demonstrate the different equilibrium outcomes of the game for various combinations of the parameters. These figures show how the outcomes change depending on different probabilities of survival for the incumbent, and different rates of the church's retention of moral authority.[7] Both figures demonstrate three key points. First, churches with higher levels of moral authority are more likely to be offered institutional access than a coalition. Second, when the incumbent can survive more easily without the aid of the church, and/or when the moral authority of the church is less compromised by accepting a coalition, only churches with the highest levels of moral authority are approached with an offer of institutional access. Third, coalitions are most likely to be offered to

[7] The other parameters are set at 0.99 for delta A, 0.2 for p, and 0.3 for A.

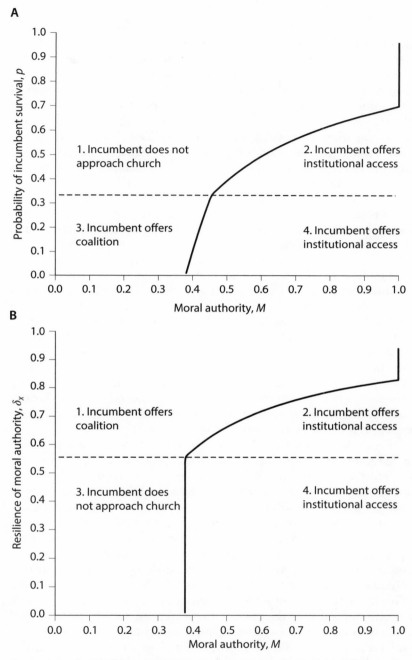

Figure A.2. (A) Equilibrium Outcomes as Function of Moral Authority and Probability of Incumbent Survival without Church Support; (B) Equilibrium Outcomes as Function of Moral Authority and Its Retention by the Church

churches with intermediate levels of moral authority in times of political crises and/or when the moral authority of the church is not going to be compromised too much from accepting a coalition.

Figure A.2a shows the different equilibria for various combinations of moral authority and the probability of the incumbent's political survival without church support. The dotted horizontal line demarcates again the cases in condition 1: above the dotted line, the incumbent would be better off staying without church support than offering a coalition, while below the incumbent would be better off with a coalition. The solid line represents condition 2: to the right of the solid line, the incumbent would prefer offering institutional access.

As a result, in area 1, the incumbent does not approach the church, since the church lacks sufficiently high moral authority and the incumbent is sufficiently safe without the church's support. In area 2, the incumbent would still prefer offering institutional access, but here a coalition is even worse than no support by the church. The area is relatively small and does not exist once p reaches a value of about 0.7. This makes sense intuitively: at high levels of p, the incumbent is independent of the church in terms of its political survival and hence is not willing to give up its authority; only churches with very high levels of moral authority are approached by the incumbent. In area 3 the church does not have sufficiently high levels of moral authority to make an offer of institutional access worthwhile to the incumbent; however, the incumbent is sufficiently insecure in its political survival to offer a coalition to the church. Finally, in area 4, the incumbent prefers offering institutional access to a coalition, which is better than no support by the church.

In Figure A.2b, two lines delineate the relevant conditions. The solid line delineates where the incumbent would prefer offering institutional access; to the right of the solid line, the incumbent would be better off granting institutional access than offering a coalition or living without church support. The area above the dotted line shows where the incumbent would prefer offering a coalition to the church, such that the church accepts the offer, to offering nothing to the church and foregoing church support. Below the dotted line, by contrast, the incumbent would be better off staying without church support than making a coalition offer that is sufficiently large for the church to accept. As the graph indicates, if the moral authority of accepting an offered coalition would severely erode the moral authority of the church, the incumbent would be better off staying without church support. Compensating the church for its lost moral authority would be too costly, and a church with little remaining moral authority would be less useful in securing political survival.

Together, these two lines create four areas in the graph. In area 1, the incumbent prefers offering a coalition to institutional access, and both are better for the incumbent than not having the support of the church. In area 2, the equilibrium outcome will be an offer of institutional access, but while offering institutional access would be the best option to the incumbent, the second-best option would be offering a coalition. In area 3, the incumbent is best off staying without church support. As in area 4, it prefers staying without church support to offering a coalition, but in contrast to area 4, the moral authority of the church is not large enough to make an offer of institutional access worthwhile to the incumbent. Thus the incumbent will not approach the church. In area 4, the incumbent prefers offering institutional access to living without church support to offering a (sufficiently generous) coalition. Consequently, the incumbent will offer institutional access in equilibrium.

A Broader Empirical Test

The formal model shows why churches and secular governments would choose one tactic over another. But do these choices matter? How much does moral authority count? Is institutional access a more powerful channel of policy influence than partisan coalitions? To further test the propositions about the impact of moral authority on religious influence on policy, I constructed the Church Influence in Democracies (CID) data set, which includes data on religiosity, economic development, policy influence, and public opinion regarding church activity and authority, and comprises twenty-nine countries for which survey data on moral authority was available. These countries, along with a summary of the religious influence on policy and a measure of the demand for church influence are presented in Table A.1.

To summarize the results: in nearly every specification where they are included, the fusion of national and religious identities and the institutional access obtained by the churches are closely tied to church influence on policy. Critically, institutional access is far more strongly correlated to policy influence than partisan coalitions or popular demand.

The data is a snapshot of one point in time, the 2000s. Since no comparable and systematic measures of fusion or moral authority over time are available, the best we can do is a cross-sectional analysis. The very small sample size (observations range from 24 to 29) means these relationships are very much suggestive rather than definitive: they may simply not hold up in a larger sample or over time. Despite this uncertainty, the relationship between moral authority, institutional access, and policy influence appears to hold up across a variety of specifications, including simple tests that compare the mean influence on public policy in groups of countries with high and low moral authority, OLS regressions with both additive

TABLE A.1.

VARIATION IN CHURCH INFLUENCE IN PREDOMINANTLY CHRISTIAN DEMOCRACIES[1] ON POLICY 1945–2014.

Country	Influence	% rejecting religious influence on policy	% confirming fusion
Philippines	9	76	84
Ireland	8	72	58
Chile	8	68	54
Austria	7	80	53
Poland	7	81	75
United States	7	51	66
Italy	5	68	52
Slovakia	5	71	50
Croatia	4	79	n/a
Spain	4	73	44
W. Germany	4	71	37
Australia	3	74	37
Bulgaria	3	79	76
Hungary	3	70	43
Portugal	3	89	66
Switzerland	3	69	39
Latvia	2	72	23
Canada	1	67	54
Denmark	1	84	33
Finland	1	58	23
New Zealand	1	73	38
Slovenia	1	73	32
UK	1	65	35
Czech Rep.	0	74	29
E. Germany	0	73	13

(*Continued*)

TABLE A.1. (CON'T)

Country	Influence	% rejecting religious influence on policy	% confirming fusion
France	0	82	17
Netherlands	0	60	13
Norway	0	64	20
Sweden	0	52	17

Influence: 1 for each policy domain in which the churches either set the terms of the policy debate or explicitly obtained their preferred outcome since 1945. Range: 0 to 10. Mean: 3.40. Standard deviation: 2.97.

% Rejecting Influence: World Values Survey, 5th wave, 2005–8, % responding that "religious organizations should NOT influence politics." ISSP data for Australia, New Zealand, and Switzerland: % responding that "religious organizations should NOT influence government."

% Confirming fusion: % responding that it is "Important to be [Dominant Religion] to be [National Identity]." 2003 ISSP data.

[1] *Countries for which public opinion poll data is available in the International Social Science Survey Program. Other European countries that were not included in the surveys: Belgium, Estonia, Greece, Iceland, Lithuania, Luxembourg, Malta, and Romania.*

and interactive terms, and two-stage least squares (2SLS) regressions that use instrumental variables to more cleanly identify causal factors.

To measure the outcome of interest, *policy influence*, I use an index of church influence on policy outcomes and debates across five domains (education, divorce, abortion, stem cell research, and same sex marriage), as introduced in Chapters 1 and 2. In each of the five policy domains, organized religions can obtain 1 point for influencing policy debates or *framing*, and 1 for influencing policy *outcomes*, for a possible total of 10. Only major national policies and debates were included, with statements by national legislators, newspaper editorials, and mentions in party manifestoes. *Framing* is coded as 1 if (a) the churches were the protagonists in the national public debate over the issue, (b) if churches first framed the issue on the national level in religious terms, using phrasing such as "sanctity of marriage," "the culture of life," appeals to the "Christian character" of the nation, or to "natural law," *and* (c) if secular national-level legislators then adopted the same language on the national level, and 0 otherwise. *Outcomes* are coded as 1 if changes to policy were (a) compatible with church teachings, *and* (b) justified by the national legislators passing them as having a Christian character or compatible with church teachings, and 0 otherwise.[8] The *policy influence* variable is cumulative; it represents the situation in 2014 as a snapshot of church efforts up to that point from 1945. Each domain was traced using press and historical accounts to determine whether the conditions above held.[9] Cronbach's alpha for the two components of the index is 0.863, suggesting the index is internally consistent.

We do not have reliable direct indicators of *church moral authority* available. There are two imperfect proxies: a general "confidence in churches" and an indicator of the fusion of national and religious identities, from the 5th wave of the World Values Survey (WVS) and the 2003 International Social Survey Programme (ISSP), respectively. The regression results presented here are robust to using both specifications, and the two variables are correlated at 0.60, $p = 0.007$.[10] However, since moral authority is a political manifestation of the fusion of national and religious identities, fusion is more closely linked to the concept of political moral authority than a general confidence in churches. I therefore use fusion.

Fusion is measured with the percentage of respondents who consider the dominant religion in their country to be important or very important to national identity in the 2003 International Social Survey Programme surveys.[11] Two further caveats about using fusion as a proxy for moral authority apply. First, as we already noted, churches have to make use of the moral authority that fusion generates—and as the Croatian case shows, they can also simply fritter it away. Second, this relatively direct measure is also fairly narrow and static; rather than measuring the accumulated store of moral authority, and how it changes over time, we instead measure the prevailing feeling about the importance of religion to national identity at one point in time. These caveats, however, also mean

---

[8] Churches also use nongovernmental organizations to make their case. If these NGOs are proxies, sponsored and vetted by the churches, they count toward a 1. If they are allies, sharing members and goals with churches but not necessarily strategies, their influence is coded as 0.

[9] Sources: press accounts (e.g., *Anglican Journal, Canada NewsWire, Gazeta Wyborcza, Irish Times, La Repubblica, Osservatore Romano, Nacional, New York Times, Keesings' World News Archive, Pismo Okólne, Vjesti*) and scholarly publications (e.g., Akmadža 2004; Christiano 2007; Gowin 1999; Inglis 1998; Sachdev 1988).

[10] Full results and data set are available from the author.

[11] The ISSP collected this data for Australia, Austria, Bulgaria, Canada, Chile, Czech Republic, Denmark, Finland, France, Germany (East and West), Hungary, Ireland, Italy, Latvia, Netherlands, New Zealand, Norway, Poland, Philippines, Portugal, Russia, Slovakia, Slovenia, Spain, Sweden, Switzerland, United Kingdom, and United States. The specific question is V15. The question was to be repeated in the 2013 ISSP survey, which was not released at the time of writing.

that we are likely to *underestimate*, rather than overestimate, the impact of moral authority.

I examine the direct access of churches to state policy making with binary indicators of institutional access and coalitions, which summarize the presence of access and coalitions in the postwar period. *Institutional access* was coded 1 if an organized religion gained formal representation in national legislative bodies or joint episcopal-parliamentary commissions, ran a ministry or a ministerial sector funded from the state budget, was consulted formally during policymaking, or exercised vetting powers over national appointments in the postwar era (1945–2014), and 0 otherwise. To ensure that there is no overlap between measures of institutional access and policy influence, especially in education, where control over the state sector was a church goal, I differentiate between the *content* of policies and the *control* of sectors: the former is an indicator of influence (or lack thereof); the latter is an indicator of institutional access.

Party-church coalitions are captured in a binary variable that is coded 1 if an explicit, national-level electoral coalition existed between a political party and an organized religion in the postwar era (1945–2014.) Party manifestoes and electoral appeals included positive references to churches and/ or phrasings such as "sanctity of marriage," "the culture of life," appeals to the "Christian character" of the nation, or to "natural law," *and* a church openly mobilized on behalf of a particular political party in elections, engaging in official pronouncements, canvassing, or widespread mobilization from the pulpit on behalf of particular parties that formally affiliated themselves with the church. Both "coalitions" and "institutional access" were coded using contemporary press and scholarly historical accounts, and both compress decades of state-church relationships into a shorthand measure. Neither fusion nor institutional access correlate particularly strongly with coalitions: at –0.07 and –0.039, and with very high p values (0.72 and 0.84, respectively) that suggest we cannot reject the null hypothesis that fusion, institutional access, and coalitions are simply related by chance. Fusion and institutional access correlate strongly at 0.54 (0.003 p value), a substantively and statistically much stronger relationship.

Finally, I include three variables (*economic development, popular religiosity,* and *the prevalence of Catholicism*) as control variables. Economic development is captured with logged GPD per capita in 2000 purchasing power parity.[12] I measure religiosity by using self-reported frequency of church attendance (a more demanding measure than either belief in God or denominational affiliation, though still subject to positive reporting bias): specifically, the percentage of respondents attending services

---

[12] Source: 2000 Penn World Tables.

more than once a month.[13] Since most of the comparisons focus on the Catholic Church, it may also be the case that what we observe is simply an artifact of powerful Catholic monopolies that have the organization and popularity to get their way. I therefore include the percentage of the population that is Catholic as a measure of *Catholicism*.[14] (To account for the possible effects of religious diversity, I reran each specification with an index of religious fractionalization from Alesina et al. 2003,[15] instead of the percentage of the population that is Catholic. The results did not change.) Each of these variables is empirically distinct from fusion, and none can be easily traced back to the fusion of national and religious identities.[16] If anything, both religiosity and Catholicism are historical and theoretical *precursors* to fusion, rather than its consequences.

To model these relationships, I used ordinary least squares (OLS) regression. Since the dependent variable is an additive index that is bounded (values span from 0 to 10), there is a strong argument for using ordered probit, which would allow us to model the latent continuous metric underlying the ordinal responses. Specifically, ordered probit allows us to partition the numeric metric into thresholds that correspond to the ordinal categories and to model how the independent variables affect the probability of moving from one ordinal category to the next. However, ordered probit also uses up additional parameters and has coefficients that are considerably more difficult to interpret, requiring the comparison of probabilities or odds ratios. The construction of the index also explicitly maps the thresholds onto numerical results: each point on the 0–10 scale represents a specific domain of rhetorical or actual policy influence, and contributes equally to the value of the index. I thus ran both OLS and ordered probit regressions, and found that they generate nearly identical results. The predicted values correlate at 0.99 (0.000 p value). For ease of interpretation, and to impose some structure on what is rather thin data, I therefore use OLS.

Institutional Access

First, what is the impact of institutional access and its relationship to policy influence? The core argument of the book and the formal model suggests that institutional access should be a powerful channel of policy influence, and the regression results are consistent with this proposition.

---

[13] Sources: World Values 5th wave, 2005–8, and World Values 6th wave, 2008–11.
[14] Source: 2010 CIA Factbook.
[15] Alesina et al. 2003.
[16] Angerist and Pischke 2009.

The "institutional access" variable is a strong correlate of policy influence across the different specifications. Recall that the theory posits that two different effects: first, institutional access is the critical channel through which moral authority influences policy, so it should explain a large part of the relationship between moral authority and policy influence. Second, institutional access should be more powerful at higher levels of moral authority. I test both these mediating and moderating effects, respectively.

I test the *mediating* effect by comparing the impact of fusion (the proxy for moral authority) alone, and in the presence of institutional access or coalitions.[17] Since moral authority has both a direct effect, through institutional access or coalitions, and a more diffuse, indirect effect through establishing norms and politician anxiety, we should observe a partial mediation effect. Here, the coefficient on fusion (the proxy for moral authority) drops when institutional access is included, as shown by Models 1 and 2 in Table A.2. This is consistent with moral authority generating institutional access, and institutional access then producing policy influence. The impact of institutional access remains even after controlling for numerous likely confounders, such as religiosity, economic development, popular demand for church influence, and denominational monopoly, as Model 2 shows.

In a *moderating* effect, institutional access should be more effective at higher levels of fusion than at lower levels (and conversely, coalitions would be more effective at lower levels of fusion.) Here, I estimate the impact of institutional access conditional on levels of fusion in Model 3. Since interaction coefficients are difficult to interpret, I graph the marginal impact in figure A.3.

As predicted by the formal model, the greater the churches' moral authority, the more powerful institutional access in influencing policy. The institutional access obtained by churches, such as legislative consultations, membership in joint parliamentary commissions, vetting of public officials, lobbying channels, and so on, has a positive impact on the churches' ability to obtain their policy preferences—and increasingly so. The 95% confidence interval crosses 0 when roughly 30% of poll respondents state that the dominant religious tradition is an important part of national identity. A caveat here is that since there are relatively few observations at the very lowest and very highest levels of national-religious fusion, the larger confidence interval in those areas may reflect lack of observations rather than a substantively weaker relationship.

To further evaluate the impact of institutional access, I also compare groups of cases with very high and very low levels of fusion and then

[17] I follow the procedure outlined in Baron and Kenny 1986. See Hayes 2013; and Zhao, Lynch, and Chen 2010, among others, for refinements and critique.

TABLE A.2.
THE IMPACT OF MORAL AUTHORITY AND INSTITUTIONAL ACCESS ON POLICY
INFLUENCE, OLS REGRESSIONS

	Model 1: Unmediated	Model 2: Mediated by Institutions	Model 3: Institutional Access|Fusion
Fusion	0.053*	0.035	0.047*
	(0.03)	(0.02)	(0.02)
	[0.06]	[0.16]	[0.05]
Attendance	0.065**	0.042	0.044
	(0.03)	(0.03)	(0.03)
	[0.04]	[0.12]	[0.11]
Log GDP	−0.543	−0.708	−0.241
	(0.67)	(0.58)	(0.60)
	[0.42]	[0.24]	[0.69]
% Catholic	0.008	0.009	0.010
	(0.01)	(0.01)	(0.01)
	[0.57]	[0.46]	[0.36]
Demand	−0.035	−0.011	
	(0.04)	(0.04)	
	[0.40]	[0.76]	
Institutions		2.235**	0.675
		(0.77)	(1.09)
		[0.01]	[0.54]
Institution*fusion			0.016
			(0.02)
			[0.45]
Constant	6.307	6.943	1.313
	(7.67)	(6.94)	(6.27)
	[0.42]	[0.33]	[0.84]
Obs	25	24	28
R-sqr	0.80	0.87	0.84

*p < 0.10, ** p < 0.05, *** p < 0.01*
(standard errors)
[p levels]

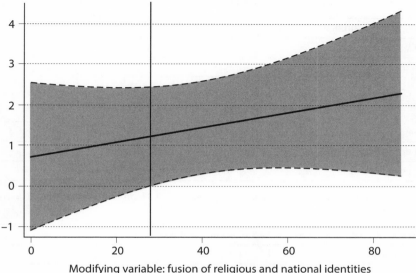

Figure A.3. Marginal Impact of Institutional Access on Policy Influence

again within the very high levels of fusion. What is the role of institutional access, and how does it vary in countries with very high and very low moral authority? Where churches gain institutional access, they obtain an average of 6.6, which translates into affecting both rhetoric and policy in over three out of the five policy domains (or similar combinations: affecting policy in four areas and rhetoric in three, for example). Where churches do not have institutional access, they gain influence equivalent to affecting rhetoric or policy in only one domain. The difference in policy influence between the top and bottom quartiles of religious and national fusion is considerable. In countries with very low levels of fusion of religious and national identities, levels of church influence average 0.50 (out of a possible 10), which translates into affecting neither rhetoric nor policy in any of the five policy domains. In contrast, where fusion levels are high, churches obtained an average of 5.88. Within the group of countries with high fusion of religious and national identities, churches obtained an average of 7.17 if they had institutional access—and where institutional access was absent, churches obtained far less, or 1.33. The difference of means tests suggest we can reject the null hypothesis that there is no difference between groups of countries with high and low church moral authority, and with high and low institutional access within these.

TABLE A.3.
POLICY INFLUENCE AT DIFFERENT LEVELS OF FUSION[1]

Impact of institutional access on policy influence:

IA present:	IA absent:
6.6	0.56

Two group difference of means test (H_0 difference is 0, H_a difference ≠ 0 Pr |T| > |t| = 0.000), t = −6.45

Impact of fusion of national and religious identities on policy influence:

High (top quartile):	Low (bottom quartile):
5.88	0.50

Two group difference of means test (H_0 difference is 0, H_a difference ≠ 0 Pr |T| > |t| = 0.0004), t = 4.65

Within the high fusion cases, impact of institutional access:

IA present:	IA absent:
7.17	1.33

Two group difference of means test (H_0 difference is 0, H_a difference ≠ 0 Pr |T| > |t| = 0.005), t = −4.02
1. *"Fusion" variable: Percentage respondents agreeing that to be [national identity], one has to be [dominant religion]. Minimum = 7.3%, maximum = 84.4%. Mean 42.6, standard deviation 19.9, top quartile: 54.1–84%, bottom quartile: 7.3–29.3%.*

Finally, to help establish a causal relationship between institutional access of the churches and their policy influence, I use a two-stage least squares regression with an instrumental variable. To satisfy the exclusion restriction, the instrumental variable must be orthogonal to the outcome, but related to the variable of interest. Here, the instrument for institutional access is "population shocks," defined as civilian casualties and losses (in percentages of the population) in the nineteenth and first half of the twentieth centuries, which correlate to institutional access at 0.48 (0.016 p value). In most cases, these are civilian deaths in World War II, but the Irish Potato Famine (1845–52) and the Spanish Civil War (1936–39) are also included. Such population shocks are correlated to institutional access but have no clear theoretical influence on policy; for example, the connection between nineteenth-century civilian losses and same sex marriage legislation in the twenty-first century is extremely tenuous. Perhaps the most controversial case might be abortion policy, where population losses might translate into subsequent pronatalist policies, but the same countries with the greatest World War II losses (Poland, Russia, Latvia, and East Germany) also adopted the most permissive abortion policies after the war under the communist regimes, driven by secular ideology rather than by demographic need. If population shocks could only influence policy through institutional access, then we could use fusion as an instrumental variable for institutional access and roughly approximate a randomized trial. The results reported in Table A.4 are suggestive but not conclusive: institutional access has a coefficient of 2.7 at $p = 0.17$.[18]

In nearly all of these specifications, moral authority and the institutional access it produces are consistently associated with policy influence, even taking into account economic development, prevalence of Catholicism, church-party coalitions, and popular demand for church influence. Further, it is unlikely that we have the causation reversed, and that influence on politics promotes fusion: both because fusion precedes influence on politics, by decades and sometimes by centuries, and because if vast popular majorities object to church influence on politics, it is unlikely that it would strengthen the church's standing in society, or increase its popular moral authority.

How do the competing explanations hold up? *Coalitions* between churches and political parties do not appear to correlate to church policy influence. The fusion coefficient does not drop in the presence of partisan coalitions in Model 4 in Table A.5, suggesting that there is no mediating effect: moral authority does not influence policy through coalitions. Even a stripped-down model that only includes coalitions and the controls (not shown) similarly fails to show correlation between coalitions and policy influence. Further, the impact of coalitions does not appear to be conditional on fusion, as Model 5 suggests (the same results hold if coalitions are interacted with religiosity). Once again, for greater ease of interpretation, I graph the results in Figure A.4. There is no discernible impact of coalitions at any level of religiosity: the confidence interval always includes 0.

The *demand for religious influence on government* does not appear to be a determinant of church influence. These results are robust to using both WVS survey questions and ISSP survey questions that explicitly ask respondents to agree that organized religions should influence votes and incumbents. Even in bare-bones models (not presented here) that included popular demand for influence and the controls, demand is not associated with policy influence. If all independent variables are included,

[18] T-statistics rather than Z-statistics are reported, given the small sample size. Limited Information Maximum Likelihood estimator (LIML) results are identical to 2SLS. I use covariates because the assignment of the instrumental variable (population shocks) may not have been random and may have been correlated to religiosity and other covariates. Correlation between casualty and institutional access: 0.48 @ 0.016 p; and between casualty and policy influence: 0.64 @ 0.0004 p.

TABLE A.4.
THE IMPACT OF INSTITUTIONAL ACCESS ON POLICY INFLUENCE,
INSTRUMENTAL VARIABLE TWO-STAGE LEAST SQUARES REGRESSION

Institutions	2.677
	(1.88)
	[0.17]
Coalitions	−0.559
	(0.75)
	[0.47]
Demand	0.009
	(0.04)
	[0.83]
Attendance	0.065
	(0.04)
	[0.12]
Log GDP	−0.000
	(0.00)
	[0.15]
% Catholic	0.001
	(0.02)
	[0.95]
Constant	1.175
	(3.65)
	[0.75]
Obs	22
R-sqr	0.85
F (6, 15):	13.26
Prob > F	= 0.0000

*$p < 0.10$, ** $p < 0.05$, *** $p < 0.01$
(standard errors)
[p values]
Dependent variable: policy influence. Institutional access instrumented
by population shocks: civilian casualties in the nineteenth and twentieth
centuries.

TABLE A.5.
THE IMPACT OF COALITIONS ON POLICY INFLUENCE, OLS REGRESSIONS

	Model 4: Mediated by Coalitions	Model 5: Coalition|Fusion	Model 6: All IV
Fusion	0.052*	0.057**	0.030
	(0.03)	(0.03)	(0.02)
	[0.07]	[0.05]	[0.23]
Attendance	0.064**	0.070**	0.038
	(0.03)	(0.03)	(0.03)
	[0.05]	[0.01]	[0.16]
Log GDP	−0.584	−0.253	−0.943
	(0.75)	(0.66)	(0.65)
	[0.44]	[0.71]	[0.16]
% Catholic	0.009	0.003	0.012
	(0.02)	(0.01)	(0.01)
	[0.57]	[0.82]	[0.33]
Demand	−0.036		−0.017
	(0.04)		(0.04)
	[0.40]		[0.66]
Coalitions	−0.097	0.886	−0.527
	(0.71)	(1.43)	(0.60)
	[0.89]	[0.54]	[0.40]
Coalitions*fusion		−0.019	
		(0.03)	
		[0.54]	
Institutions			2.376***
			(0.79)
			[0.01]
Constant	6.856	0.894	9.964
	(8.85)	(7.08)	(7.80)
	[0.45]	[0.90]	[0.22]
Obs	25	29	24
R-sqr	0.80	0.79	0.88

* $p < 0.10$, ** $p < 0.05$, *** $p < 0.01$
(standard errors)
[p values]

Marginal Effect of Party Coalitions on Policy Influence

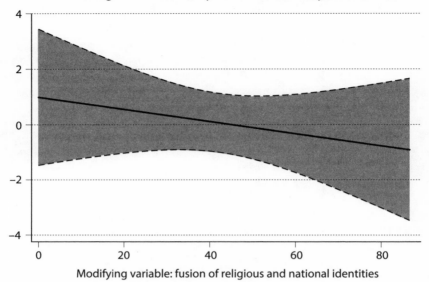

Modifying variable: fusion of religious and national identities

Figure A.4. Marginal Impact of Coalitions on Policy Influence

as in Model 6, demand continues to be very poorly correlated to church influence.

Religiosity, or more precisely, frequent attendance at religious services is associated with policy influence in several models. This makes sense since moral authority is predicated on religiosity: a church cannot claim to represent the nation if few people are its members or faithful. Churches cannot have moral authority or potential in mobilizing voters (coalitions) or ensuring support for regime (access) without committed and numerous adherents. However, religiosity is far less consequential once we include institutional access in the models, and even more so once other independent variables are included. Surprisingly, since the Catholic Church is such a powerful player, and since so many of the countries where Christian religions influence politics are predominantly Catholic, *Catholicism* has no impact on policy influence. Even in a bare-bones model (not reported here) that only included the % Catholic with the control variables, there was no correlation between *Catholicism* and policy influence. This conclusion confirms to other findings that Catholic states do not differ from Protestant countries as far as policy outputs are concerned.[19] Finally, *economic development* does not appear to correlate to church influence on policy in any of the specifications.

[19] Knill, Preidel, and Nebel 2014.

Conclusion

In short, institutional access works. Legislative back rooms, rather than ballot boxes, offer a powerful channel of influence for churches that wish to influence public policy. This chapter shows that the logic of state-church interactions means that the higher the moral authority of the churches, and the bigger the crisis facing the secular regime, the more likely that states will share sovereignty with churches in order to survive. The broader empirical analysis similarly demonstrates that moral authority is a potent determinant of church influence on politics—and that institutional access offers a much more powerful tool of policy influence than partisan coalitions.

References

Abramowitz, Alan. 1995. "It's Abortion Stupid: Policy Voting in the 1992 Presidential Election." *Journal of Politics* 57: 176–86.

Akenson, Donald Harman. 1992. *God's Peoples*. Ithaca, NY: Cornell University Press.

Akmadža, Miroslav. 2004a. *Katolička crkva u Hrvatskoj i komunistički režim, 1945–1996*. Rijeka: Otokar Keršovani.

———. 2004b. "Razgovori zagrebačkog nadbiskupa dr. Franje Šepera sa predsjednikom Komisije za vjerska pitanja NR Hrvatske Stjepanom Ivekovićem (1960–1963)." *Radovi-Zavod za hrvatsku povijest* 34–35–36: 245–81.

———. 2006. "The Position of the Catholic Church in Croatia, 1945–1970." *Review of Croatian History* 1: 89–115.

Aldrich, John. 1995. *Why Parties?* Chicago: University of Chicago Press.

Alesina, Alberto, Arnaud Devleeschauwer, William Easterly, Sergio Kurlat, and Romain Wacziarg. 2003. "Fractionalization." *Journal of Economic Growth* 8 (2): 155–94.

Alexander, Stella. 1979. *Church and State in Yugoslavia since 1945*. Cambridge: Cambridge University Press.

Allen, John. 2005. "The Word from Rome." *National Catholic Reporter*, August 26, 2005.

Allum, Percy. 1990. "Uniformity Undone: Aspects of Catholic Culture in Postwar Italy." In *Culture and Conflict in Postwar Italy*, edited by Zygmunt Barański and Robert Lumley, 79–96. Basingstoke: Macmillan.

Andall, Jacqueline. 1994. "Abortion, Politics, and Gender in Italy." *Parliamentary Affairs* 47 (2): 238–51.

Anderson, Benedict. 1991. *Imagined Communities*. London: Verso.

Anderson, John. 2003. "Catholicism and Democratic Consolidation in Spain and Poland." In *Church and State in Contemporary Europe: The Chimera of Neutrality*, edited by John T. S. Madeley and Zsolt Enyedi, 137–56. London: Frank Cass.

Andersen, Karen. 2010. "Irish Secularization and Religious Identities: Evidence of an Emerging New Catholic Habitus." *Social Compass* 57 (1): 15–39.

Aneks. 1993. *Tajne Dokumenty Państwo-Kościół, 1980–1989*. London: Aneks Publishers.

———. 1996. *Tajne Dokumenty Państwo-Kościół, 1960–1980*. London: Aneks Publishers.

Angrist, Joshua, and Jörn-Steffen Pischke. *Mostly Harmless Econometrics*. Princeton, NJ: Princeton University Press.

Appleby, R. Scott. 2007. "Decline or Relocation? The Catholic Presence in Church and Society, 1950–2000." In *The Church Confronts Modernity*, edited by Leslie Woodcock Tentler, 208–35. Washington, DC: Catholic University Press.

Arceneaux, Kevin. 2002. "Direct Democracy and the Link between Public Opinion and State Abortion Policy." *State Politics and Policy Quarterly* 2 (4): 372–87.

Atran, Scott. 2002. *In Gods We Trust*. New York: Oxford University Press.

Balcells, Laia. 2014. *Rivalry and Revenge: The Politics of Violence in Civil War*. Book manuscript, Duke University.

Balmer, Randall. 2006. *Thy Kingdom Come*. New York: Basic Books.

———. 2008. *God in the White House: A History*. New York: Harper.

Banac, Ivo. 1984. *The National Question in Yugoslavia*. Ithaca, NY: Cornell University Press.

Banchoff, Thomas. 2012. *Embryo Politics; Ethics and Policy in Atlantic Democracies*. Ithaca, NY: Cornell University Press.

Barker, Philip. 2009. *Religious Nationalism in Modern Europe*. Abingdon: Routledge.

Barro, Robert, and Rachel McCleary. 2003. "Religion and Economic Growth across Countries." *American Sociological Review* 68: 760–81.

———. 2005. "Which Countries Have State Religions?" *Quarterly Journal of Economics* (November): 1331–70.

Baron, Reuben, and David Kenny. 1986. "The Moderator-Mediator Variable Distinction in Social Psychological Research: Conceptual, Strategic and Statistical Considerations." *Journal of Personality and Social Psychology* 51: 1173–82.

Bartels, Larry. 1991. "Constituency Opinion and Congressional Policy Making: The Reagan Defense Buildup." *American Political Science Review* 85 (2): 457–74.

———. 2006. "What's the Matter with What's the Matter with Kansas?" *Quarterly Journal of Political Science* 1 (2): 201–26.

———. 2008. *Unequal Democracy: The Political Economy of the New Gilded Age*. New York: Russell Sage Foundation; Princeton, NJ: Princeton University Press.

Baudrillard, Jean. 2010 [1990]. *America*. London: Verso.

Baum, Gregory. 1980. *Catholics and Canadian Socialism*. Toronto: James Lorimer.

———. 1986. "Catholicism and Secularization in Québec." *Cross Currents* 36 (4): 436–58.

Baum, Gregory. 2000. "Catholicism and Secularization in Quebec." In *Rethinking Church, State, and Modernity: Canada between Europe and America*, edited by David Lyon and Marguerite Van Die, 149–65. Toronto: University of Toronto Press.

———. 2007. "Comparing Post–World War II Catholicism in Québec, Ireland, and the United States." In *The Church Confronts Modernity*, edited by Leslie Woodcock Tentler, 268–95. Washington, DC: Catholic University Press.

Bawn, Kathleen, Martin Cohen, David Karol, Seth Masket, Hans Noel, and John Zaller. 2012. "A Theory of Political Parties: Groups, Policy Demands and Nominations in American Politics." *Perspectives on Politics* 10 (3): 571–97.

Beatty, Kathleen, and Oliver Walter. 1984. "Religious Preference and Practice: Reevaluating Their Impact on Political Tolerance," *Public Opinion Quarterly* 48 (1): 318–29.

Bedani, Gino. 2000. "The Christian Democrats and National Identity." In *The Politics of Italian National Identity*, edited by Bruce Haddock and Gino Bedani, 214–38. Cardiff: University of Wales Press.

Behan, Tom. 2009. *The Italian Resistance: Fascists, Guerrillas, and the Allies*. New York: Palgrave Macmillan.

Behiels, Michael. 1985. *Prelude to Québec's Quiet Revolution*. Montreal: McGill-Queen's University Press.

Belew, Kara. 2003. "Stem Cell Division: Abortion Law and Its Influence on the Adoption of Radically Different Embryonic Stem Cell Legislation in the United States, the United Kingdom, and Germany." *Texas International Law Journal* 39: 479–520.

Bell, Daniel. 1977. "The Return of the Sacred? The Argument on the Future of Religion." *British Journal of Sociology* 28 (4): 419–49.

Bellah, Robert. 1967. "Civil Religion in America." *Journal of the American Academy of Arts and Sciences* 96 (1): 1–21.

Bellamy, Alex. 2002. "The Catholic Church and Croatia's Two Transitions." *Religion, State, and Society* 30 (1): 45–61.

———. 2003. *The Formation of Croatian National Identity*. Manchester: Manchester University Press.

Benabarre, Benigno, 1959. *Public Funds for Private Schools in a Democracy: Theory and Practice in Fifty-One Countries*. Manila: M.C.S. Enterprises.

Berger, Peter. 1977. *Facing Up to Modernity*. New York: Basic Books.

———. 1967. *The Sacred Canopy*. Garden City, NY: Doubleday.

———, ed. 1999. *The Desecularization of the World*. Washington, DC: Ethics and Public Policy Center.

Berger, Suzanne. 1985. "Religious Transformation and the Future of Politics." *European Sociological Review* 1 (1): 23–45.

Berkman, Michael, and Eric Plutzer. 2010. *Evolution, Creationism, and the Battle to Control America's Classrooms*. Cambridge: Cambridge University Press.

Berman, Eli. 2009. *Radical, Religious, and Violent*. Cambridge, MA: MIT Press.

Berry, Jeffrey. 1977. *Lobbying for the People: The Political Behavior of Public Interest Groups*. Princeton, NJ: Princeton University Press.

Bew, Paul. 2007. *Ireland: The Politics of Enmity, 1789–2006*. New York: Oxford University Press.

Bibby, Reginald. 1987. *Fragmented Gods: The Poverty and Potential of Religion in Canada*. Toronto: Irwin Publishing.

Bickerton, James, Stephen Brooks, and Alain-G. Gagnon. 2006. *Freedom, Equality, Community: The Political Philosophy of Six Influential Canadians*. Montreal: McGill-Queen's University Press.

Bijelić, Nataša. 2008. "Sex Education in Croatia: Tensions between Secular and Religious Discourses." *European Journal of Women's Studies* 15: 329–43.

Blackbourn, David. 1994. *Marpingen: Apparitions of the Virgin Mary in Bismarckian Germany*. New York: Oxford University Press.

Blake, Donald E. 1979. "1896 and All That: Critical Elections in Canada." *Canadian Journal of Political Science* 12 (2): 259–79.

Bloch, Ruth. 2007. "Religion and Ideological Change in the American Revolution." In *Religion and American Politics*, edited by Mark Noll and Luke Harlow, 47–64. New York: Oxford University Press.

Blofield, Merike. 2006. *The Politics of Moral Sin*. New York: Routledge.

Bobinac, Ankica, and Dinka Jerolimov. 2006. "Religious Education in Croatia." In *Religion and Pluralism in Education*, edited by Zorica Kuburić and Christian Moe. Novi Sad: Centre for Researches on Religion.

Borecki, Paweł, and Czesław Janik, eds. 2011. *Komisja Wspólna Przedstawicieli Rządu Rzeczypospolitej Polskiej i Konferencji Episkopatu Polski W Archiwaliach z Lat 1989–2010*. Warsaw: Wydawnictwo Sejmowe.

Borowik, Irena. 2002. "The Roman Catholic Church in the Process of Democratic Transformation: The Case of Poland." *Social Compass* 49 (2): 239–52.

Borowik, Irena, and Miklós Tomka, eds. 2001. *Religion and Social Change in Post-Communist Europe*. Kraków: NOMOS.

Bremer, Thomas. 2010. "Croatian Catholic Church and Its Role in Politics and Society." *Religion in Eastern Europe* 30 (3): 1–15.

Brenner, Philip. 2011. "Exceptional Behavior or Exceptional Identity? Overreporting of Church Attendance in the US." *Public Opinion Quarterly* 75 (1): 19–41.

Breuilly, John. 1983. *Nationalism and the State*. Manchester: Manchester University Press.

Brkljačić, Maja. 2001. "Croatian Catholic Church Imagines the Nation." *Balkanologie* 5 (1–2), available at http://balkanologie.revues.org/668.

———. 2003. "What Past Is Present?" *International Journal of Politics, Culture, and Society* 17 (1): 41–52.

Broockman, David, and Chris Skovron. 2013. "What Politicians Believe about Their Constituents: Asymmetric Misperceptions and Prospects for Constituency Control." Working Paper, http://www.ocf.berkeley.edu/~broockma/broockman_skovron_asymmetric_misperceptions.pdf, accessed August 8, 2013.

Brooks, Clem, and Jeff Manza. "A Great Divide? Religion and Political Change in US National Elections 1972–2000." *Sociological Quarterly* 45 (3): 421–50.

Brown, Terence. 1985. *Ireland: A Social and Cultural History, 1922 to the Present*. Ithaca, NY: Cornell University Press.

Brubaker, Rogers. 1992. *Citizenship and Nationhood in France and Germany*. Cambridge, MA: Harvard University Press.

———. 2004. *Ethnicity without Groups*. Cambridge, MA: Harvard University Press.

———. 2012. "Religion and Nationalism: Four Approaches." *Nations and Nationalism* 18 (1): 2–20.

Bruce, Steve. 2000a. *Choice and Religion: A Critique of Rational Choice Theory*. New York: Oxford University Press.

———. 2000b. "The Supply-Side Model of Religion: The Nordic and Baltic States." *Journal for the Scientific Study of Religion* 39 (1): 32–46.

———. 2002. "The Poverty of Economism." In *Sacred Markets, Sacred Canopies*, edited by Ted Jelen, 167–85. Lanham, MD: Rowman and Littlefield.

Buchanan, Tom, and Martin Conway. 2002. *Political Catholicism in Europe, 1918–1965*. Oxford: Oxford University Press.

Buchenau, Klaus. 2005. "What Went Wrong? Church-State Relations in Socialist Yugoslavia." *Nationalities Papers* 33 (4): 547–67.

Bull, Martin, and James Newell. 2005. *Italian Politics: Adjustment under Duress.* Cambridge: Polity Press.

Bumpass, Larry. 1995. "Abortion and Public Opinion: Demographic and Measurement Contexts." CDE Working Paper 95–14, Center for Demography and Ecology, University of Wisconsin, Madison.

Bunce, Valerie. 2005. "The National Idea: Imperial Legacies and Postcommunist Pathways in Eastern Europe." *East European Politics and Society* 19 (3): 406–42.

Burden, Barry. 2004. "An Alternative Account of the 2004 Presidential Election." *The Forum* 94, http://www.bepress.com/forum, accessed October 30, 2012.

Burleigh, Michael. 2007. *Sacred Causes.* New York: Macmillan.

Burley, Jenny, and Francis Regan. 2002. "Divorce in Ireland: The Fear, the Floodgates, and the Reality." *International Journal of Law, Policy, and the Family* 16: 202–22.

Burstein, Paul. 2003. "The Impact of Public Opinion on Public Policy." *Political Research Quarterly* 56: 29–40.

Byrne, Anne. 1999. "Church or State at the Top of the Class?" *Irish Times*, September 21.

Byrnes, Timothy, and Peter Katzenstein, eds. 2006. *Religion in an Expanding Europe.* Cambridge: Cambridge University Press.

Campbell, David, John Green, and Geoffrey Layman. 2011. "The Party Faithful: Partisan Images, Candidate Religion, and the Electoral Impact of Party Identification," *American Journal of Political Science* 55 (1): 42–58.

Campbell, David, and Carin Larson. 2007. "Religious Coalitions For and Against Gay Marriage: The Culture War Rages On." In *The Politics of Same-Sex Marriage*, edited by Craig Rimmerman and Clyde Wilcox. Chicago: University of Chicago Press.

Campos, Nauro, Ahmad Saleh, and Vitaliy Kuzeyev. 2009. "Dynamic Ethnic Fractionalization and Economic Growth in the Transition Economies from 1989 to 2007." IZA Discussion Papers, 4597, Institute for the Study of Labor (IZA).

Cap, Krystyna. 2004. "The Roman Catholic Church and the Democratic Process." *Critique* (Fall): 1–18.

Capoccia, Giovanni. 2010. "Normative Frameworks, Electoral Interests, and the Boundaries of Legitimate Participation in Post-Fascist Democracies: The Case of Italy." Paper presented at the American Association of Political Science Annual Meeting, Washington, DC.

Carmines, Edward C., and Geoffrey C. Layman. 1998. "When Prejudice Matters: The Impact of Racial Stereotypes on the Racial Policy Preferences of Democrats and Republicans." In *Perception and Prejudice*, edited by Jon Hurwitz and Mark Peffley. New Haven, CT: Yale University Press.

Carmines, Edward, and James Stimson. 1986. "On the Structure and Sequence of Issue Evolution." *American Political Science Review* 80 (3): 901–20.

Carwardine, Richard. 2007. "Methodists, Politics, and the Coming of the American Civil War." In *Religion and American Politics*, edited by Mark Noll and Luke Harlow, 169–200. New York: Oxford University Press.

Casanova, José. 1994. *Public Religions in the Modern World*. Chicago: University of Chicago Press.

———. 1996. "Global Catholicism and the Politics of Civil Society." *Sociological Inquiry* 66 (3): 356–73.

———. 2001. "Civil Society and Religion: Retrospective Reflections on Catholicism and Prospective Reflections on Islam." *Social Research* 64 (4): 1041–80.

———. 2006. "Religion, European Secular Identities, and European Integration." In *Religion in an Expanding Europe*, edited by Timothy Byrnes and Peter Katzenstein, 65–92. Cambridge: Cambridge University Press.

Casanova, Julián. 2013. *A Short History of the Spanish Civil War*. London: I. B. Tauris.

Castles, Francis 1994. "On Religion and Public Policy: Does Catholicism Make a Difference?" *European Journal of Political Research* 25 (1): 19–40.

Caulfield, Timothy, and Tania Bubela. 2007. "Why a Criminal Ban? Analyzing Arguments against Somatic Cell Nuclear Transfer in the Canadian Parliamentary Debate." *American Journal of Bioethics* 7 (2): 51–61.

CBOS. 2007. "Opinie o działalności Kościoła." Warsaw. March.

Ceccarini, Luigi. 2010. "The Church in Opposition: Religious Actors, Lobbying, and Catholic Voters in Italy." In *Religion and Politics in Europe, the Middle East, and Africa*, edited by Jeffrey Haynes, 177–201. London: Routledge.

Chaves, Mark, and David Cann. 1992. "Regulation, Pluralism, and Religious Market Structure." *Rationality and Society* 4 (3): 272–90.

Chaves, Mark, and Philip Gorski. 2001. "Religious Pluralism and Religious Participation." *Annual Review of Sociology* 27: 261–81.

Chong, Dennis, and James Druckman. 2007. "Framing Theory." *Annual Review of Political Science* 10: 103–26.

Choquette, Robert. 2004. *Canada's Religions*. Ottawa: University of Ottawa Press.

Christiano, Kevin. 2000. "Church and State in Institutional Flux." In *Rethinking Church, State, and Modernity: Canada between Europe and America*, edited by David Lyon and Marguerite Van Die, 69–89. Toronto: University of Toronto Press.

———. 2007. "The Trajectory of Catholicism in Twentieth-Century Québec." In *The Church Confronts Modernity*, edited by Leslie Woodcock Tentler, 30–61. Washington, DC: Catholic University Press.

Chrypiński, Vincent. 1990. "The Catholic Church in Poland, 1944–1989." In *Catholicism and Politics in Communist Societies*, edited by Pedro Ramet, 117–41. Durham, NC: Duke University Press.

Churchill, Winston. 1948. *The Second World War*. Vol. 1, *The Gathering Storm*. London: Cassell.

Claassen, Ryan, and Andrew Povtak. 2010. "The Christian Right Thesis: Explaining Longitudinal Change in Participation among Evangelical Christians." *Journal of Politics* 72 (1): 2–15.

Clark, Martin, David Hine, and R.E.M Irving. 1974. "Divorce—Italian Style." *Parliamentary Affairs* 27 (June): 333–58.

Clark, Martin, and R.E.M. Irving. 1977. "The Italian General Election of June 1976: Toward a 'Historic Compromise'?" *Parliamentary Affairs* 30 (1): 7–34.

Clark, William R. 2010. "Towards a Political Economy of Religion." *Political Economist* (Spring): 2–10.

Clemens, Elisabeth. 1997. *The People's Lobby: Organizational Innovation and the Rise of Interest Group Politics in the United States, 1890–1925*. Chicago: University of Chicago Press.

Coffey, Daniel. 2007. "State Party Activists and State Party Polarization." In *The State of the Parties*, edited by John Green and Daniel Coffey, 75–91. Lanham, MD: Rowman and Littlefield.

Cohen, Arthur. 1971. *The Myth of the Judeo-Christian Tradition*. New York: Harper and Row.

Cohen, Cynthia, Michael Enzle, Bernard Dickens, Bruce Brandhorst, Teren Clark, Catherine Clute, Diana Dunstan, Donald Evans, Raymond Lambert, Sylvie Langlois, Arthur Leader, and Cheryl Robertson. 2008. "Oversight of Stem Cell Research in Canada: Protecting the Rights, Health, and Safety of Embryo Donors." *Health Law Review* 16 (2): 86–102.

Cohen, Jeffrey, and Charles Barilleaux. 1993. "Public Opinion, Interest Groups, and Public Policy Making: Abortion Policy in the American States." In *Understanding the New Politics of Abortion*, edited by Malcolm Goggin. Newbury Park, CA: Sage.

Cohen, Marty, David Karol, Hans Noel, and John Zaller. 2008. *The Party Decides*. Chicago: University of Chicago Press.

Cohen, Shari J. 1999. *Politics without a Past*. Durham, NC: Duke University Press.

Comfort, Nathaniel C., 2007. *The Panda's Black Box*. Baltimore: Johns Hopkins University Press.

Commission on Vocational Organisation. 1943. *Report on Vocational Organisation*. Dublin: Government Stationery Office.

Committee on the Constitution. 1967. *Report of the Committee on the Constitution*. Dublin: Government Stationery Office.

Conger, Kimberly. 2010. "Party Platforms and Party Coalitions: The Christian Right and State-Level Republicans." *Party Politics* 16: 651–68.

Conger, Kimberly, and Green, John. (2002). Spreading Out and Digging In: Christian Conservatives and State Republican Parties. *Campaigns and Elections* 23 (1): 58–60.

Conway, M. 2006. "The Christian Churches in Europe 1914–1939." In *World Christianities c. 1914–2000*, edited by Hugh McLeod. Cambridge: Cambridge University Press.

Coolahan, John. 2003. "Church-State Relations in Primary and Secondary Education." In *Religion and Politics in Ireland at the Turn of the Millennium*, edited by J. P. Mackey and E. McDonagh. Dublin: Columba Press.

———. 2014. "The Shaping of Ireland's Faith-Based School System and the Contemporary Challenge to It." In *International Handbook of Learning, Teaching, and Leading in Faith-Based Schools*, edited by J. D. Chapman et al., 473–87. Dordrecht: Springer Science.

———, et al. 2012. *The Forum on Patronage and Pluralism in the Primary Sector*. Forum Advisory Group. Dublin.

Corbellini, Gilberto. 2006. "Reproductive Medicine, Politics, and Religion in Italy: Reflections on the 2005 Referendum." *Ogmius Newsletter* 15 (Spring), available at http://sciencepolicy.colorado.edu/ogmius/archives/issue_15/reproductive_medicine.html, accessed March 18, 2013.

Couture, Claude, 1998. *Paddling with the Current: Pierre Elliot Trudeau, Étienne Parent, Liberalism, and Nationalism in Canada.* Edmonton: University of Alberta Press.

Cowley, Philip. 2001. "Morality Policy without Politics? The Case of Britain." In *The Public Clash of Private Values,* edited by Christopher Mooney, 213–26. New York: Seven Bridges Press.

Coyne, Edward, S.J. 1951. "Mother and Child Service." *Studies: An Irish Quarterly Review* 40 (158): 129–49.

Crapo, Richley H. "Chronology of Mormon/LDS Involvement in Same-Sex Marriage Politics." *Mormon Social Science Association.* Web. January 4, 2008. http://bit.ly/xynQqm.

Cristi, Marcela. 2001. *From Civil to Political Religion: The Intersection of Culture, Religion, and Politics.* Waterloo, ON: Wilfrid Laurier University Press.

Croft, Stuart. 2007. "'Thy Will Be Done': The New Foreign Policy of America's Christian Right." *International Politics* 44: 692–710.

Črpič, Gordan, and Siniša Zrinščak. 2010. "Dynamism in Stability: Religiosity in Croatia in 1999 and 2008. *Društvena istraživanja,* 19 (1–2): 3–27. Available at hrcak.srce.hr/index.php?show=clanak&id_clanak_jezik=79777.

Crunican, Paul. 1973. *Priests and Politicians: Manitoba Schools and the Election of 1896.* Toronto: University of Toronto Press.

Culpepper, Pepper. 2010. *Quiet Politics and Business Power.* New York: Cambridge University Press.

Cuvalo, Ante. 1990. *The Croatian National Movement, 1966–1972.* New York: East European Monographs.

Cviic, Chistopher. 1976. "Recent Developments in Church-State Relations in Yugoslavia." *Religion, State and Society* 1–2: 6–8.

Daniel, Krystyna. 1995. "The Church-State Situation in Poland after the Collapse of Communism." *Brigham Young University Law Review* 2: 401–19.

Darden, Keith. Forthcoming. *Resisting Occupation in Eurasia: Mass Schooling and the Formation of Durable National Loyalties.* Book manuscript, American University.

Darden, Keith, and Anna Grzymala-Busse. 2006. "The Great Divide: Precommunist Schooling and Postcommunist Trajectories." *World Politics* 59: 83–115.

Davidson, James. 2007. "The Catholic Church in the United States: 1950 to the Present." In *The Church Confronts Modernity,* edited by Leslie Woodcock Tentler, 177–207. Washington, DC: Catholic University Press.

Davie, Grace. 1990. "Believing without Belonging: Is This The Future of Religion in Britain?" *Social Compass* 37 (4): 455–69.

———. 1999. "Europe: The Exception That Proves the Rule? In *The Desecularization of the World,* edited by Peter Berger. Washington, DC: Ethics and Public Policy Center.

Davis, Dena. 2006. "The Puzzle of IVF." *Houston Journal of Health Law and Policy* 275: 275–97.

De Franciscis, Maria, 1989. *Italy and the Vatican: The 1984 Concordat between Church and State*. New York: Peter Lang.

De La O, Ana, and Jonathan Rodden. 2008. "Does Religion Distract the Poor?" *Comparative Political Studies* 41 (4/5): 437–76.

Demerath, N. J., III. 1991. "Religious Capital and Capital Religions: Cross-Cultural and Non-Legal Factors in the Separation of Church and State." *Daedalus* 120 (3): 21–40.

Department of Health and Human Services. 2002. "Cohabitation, Marriage, Divorce, and Remarriage in the United States." *Vital and Health Statistics* 23 (22). July 2002. http://1.usa.gov/WdS8e.

Dillon, Michele. 1993. *Debating Divorce: Moral Conflict in Ireland*. Lexington: University Press of Kentucky.

———. 1995. "Religion and Culture in Tension: The Abortion Discourses of the US Catholic Bishops and the Southern Baptist Convention." *Religion and American Culture*: 159–80.

———. 2007. "Decline and Continuity: Catholicism since 1950 in the United States, Ireland, and Québec." In *The Church Confronts Modernity*, edited by Leslie Woodcock Tentler, 239–67. Washington, DC: Catholic University Press.

DiMarco, Erica. 2009. "The Tides of Vatican Influence in Italian Reproductive Matters: From Abortion to Assisted Reproduction." *Rutgers Journal of Law and Religion* 10: 1–30.

Discovery Institute. 1999. "The Wedge," available at http://www.scribd.com/doc/20872000/The-Discovery-Institute-s-Wedge-Document. Accessed July 18, 2009.

Dochuk, Darren. 2011. *Bible Belt to Sun Belt: Plain-Folk Religion, Grassroots Politics, and the Rise of Evangelical Conservatism*. New York: Norton.

Doerr, Edd, and Albert J. Menendez. 1991. *Church Schools and Public Money: The Politics of Parochiaid*. Amherst, NY: Prometheus Books.

Dolgin, Janet. 2000. "Choice, Tradition, and the New Genetics: The Fragmentation of the Ideology of Family." *Connecticut Law Review* 32 (2): 523–66.

Dolinar, France. 1995. "Normalization of Church-State Relations in Yugoslavia, 1945." *Slovene Studies* 17 (1–2): 25–36.

Domke, David, and Kevin Coe. 2008. *The God Strategy: How Religion Became a Political Weapon in America*. New York: Oxford University Press.

Donovan, Mark. 2003. "The Italian State: No Longer Catholic, No Longer Christian." In *Church and State in Contemporary Europe: The Chimera of Neutrality*, edited by John T. S. Madeley and Zsolt Enyedi, 95–116. London: Frank Cass.

Dowling, Andrew. 2012. "For Christ and Catalonia: Catholic Catalanism and Nationalist Revival in Late Francoism," *Journal of Contemporary History* 47 (3): 594–610.

Downey, Robin, and Rose Geransar. 2008. "Stem Cell Research, Public and Stakeholder Views." *Health Law Review* 16 (2): 69–85.

Dragojević, Mila. 2005. "Competing Institutions in National Identity Construction: The Croatian Case." *Nationalism and Ethnic Politics* 11: 61–87.

Drakulić, Slavenka. 1993. "Women and the New Democracy in Yugoslavia." In *Gender Politics and Post-Communism*, edited by Nanette Funk and Magda Mueller, 123–30. London: Routledge.

Drakulić, Slavenka. 2013. "A Neoconservative Revolution." *VoxEurop*, November 29, available at http://www.voxeurop.eu/en/content/article/4364401-neo conservative-revolution, accessed January 20, 2014.

Druckman, James. 2001. "On the Limits of Framing Effects: Who Can Frame?" *Journal of Politics* 63 (4): 1041–66.

Dubow, Sara. 2011. *Ourselves Unborn: A History of the Fetus in Modern America*. New York: Oxford University Press.

Dudek, Antoni. 1995. *Państwo i Kościół w Polsce 1945–1970*. Kraków: PiT.

Dudek, Antoni, and Ryszard Gmyz. 2003. *Komuniści i Kościół w Polsce*. Kraków: Znak.

Duncan, Ann, and Steven Jones, eds. 2007. *Church-State Issues in America Today*. Westport, CT: Praeger.

Duncan, William. 1988. "The Divorce Referendum in the Republic of Ireland: Resisting the Tide." *International Journal of Law, Policy and the Family* 2 (1): 62–75.

Eastwood, Jonathan, and Nikolas Prevalakis. 2010. "Nationalism, Religion, and Secularization: An Opportune Moment for Research." *Review of Religious Research* 52 (1): 90–111.

Eberts, Mirella. 1998. "The Roman Catholic Church and Democracy in Poland." *Europe-Asia Studies* 50 (5): 817–42.

Eberts, Mirella, and Peter Török. 2001. "The Catholic Church and Post-Communist Elections: Hungary and Poland Compared." In *Religion and Social Change in Post-Communist Europe*, edited by Irena Borowik and Miklós Tomka, 125–47. Kraków: NOMOS.

Edgell, Penny. 2005. *Religion and Family in a Changing Society*. Princeton, NJ: Princeton University Press.

Egan, Patrick J., Nathaniel Persily, and Kevin Wallsten. 2008. "Gay Rights." In *Public Opinion and Constitutional Controversy*, edited by Nathaniel Persily, Jack Citrin, and Patrick J. Egan. Oxford: Oxford University Press.

Egerton, George, 2000. "Trudeau, God, and the Canadian Constitution: Religion, Human Rights, and Government Authority in the Making of the 1982 Constitution." In *Rethinking Church, State, and Modernity: Canada between Europe and America*, edited by David Lyon and Marguerite Van Die, 90–112. Toronto: University of Toronto Press.

Eisenhower, Dwight. 1952. Address at the Freedoms Foundation, Waldorf Astoria, New York City. http://www.eisenhower.archives.gov/all_about_ike/quotes .html.

Eisenstein, Marie. 2006. "Rethinking the Relationship between Religion and Political Tolerance in the US." *Political Behavior* 28 (4): 327–48.

Eisgruber, Christopher L., and Mariah Zeisberg. 2006. "Religious Freedom in Canada and the United States." *International Journal of Constitutional Law* 4 (2): 244–68.

Ekelund, Robert, Robert Tollison, Gary Anderson, Robert Hébert, and Audrey Davidson. 1996. *Sacred Trust: The Medieval Church as an Economic Firm.* New York: Oxford University Press.

Ellison, Christopher. 1995. "Rational Choice Explanations of Individual Religious Behavior." *Journal for the Scientific Study of Religion* 34: 89–97.

Enloe, Cynthia H. 1980. *Ethnic Soldiers: State Security in Divided Societies.* Athens: University of Georgia Press.

Enyedi, Zsolt. 2003. "The Contested Politics of Positive Neutrality in Hungary." In *Church and State in Contemporary Europe: The Chimera of Neutrality,* edited by John T. S. Madeley and Zsolt Enyedi, 157–76. London: Frank Cass.

Evans, John. 2010. *Contested Reproduction: Genetic Technologies, Religion, and Public Debate.* Chicago: University of Chicago Press.

Farren, Sean. 1995. *The Politics of Irish Education, 1920–1965.* Belfast: Queen's University Institute of Irish Studies.

Fattorini, Emma. 2011. *Hitler, Mussolini, and the Vatican.* Malden, MA: Polity.

Fearon, James, and David Laitin. 2008. "Integrating Qualitative and Quantitative Methods." In *Oxford Handbook of Political Methodology,* edited by Janet Box-Steffensmeier, Henry Brady, and David Collier, 756–76. New York: Oxford University Press.

Feld, Scott, Katherine Brown Rosier, and Amy Manning. 2002. "Christian Right as Civil Right: Covenant Marriage and a Kinder, Gentler, Moral Conservatism." *Review of Religious Research* 44 (2): 173–83.

Fenno, Richard. 1978. *Home Style: House Members in Their Districts.* Boston: Little, Brown.

Ferretti, Lucia. 1999. *Brève histoire de l'Eglise catholique au Québec.* Montreal: Boréal.

Figà-Talamanca, Irene. 1988. "Italy." In *International Handbook on Abortion,* edited by Paul Sachdev, 279–92. New York: Greenwood Press.

Fink, Simon. 2008. "Politics as Usual or Bringing Religion Back In?" *Comparative Political Studies* 41 (1631): 1645–46.

Finke, Roger, and Rodney Stark. 1992. *The Churching of America: Winners and Losers in Our Religious Economy.* New Brunswick, NJ: Rutgers University Press.

———. 1998. "Religious Choice and Competition." *American Sociological Review* 63 (5): 761–66.

Finke, Roger, and Patricia Wittberg. 2000. "Organizational Revival from Within: Explaining Revivalism and Reform in the Roman Catholic Church." *Journal for the Scientific Study of Religion* 39 (2): 154–70.

Fiorina, Morris. 1974. *Representatives, Roll Calls, and Constituencies.* Lexington, MA: Lexington Books.

FitzGerald, Garret. 1972. *Towards a New Ireland.* London: Charles Knight.

———. 2003. *Reflections on the Irish State.* Dublin: Irish Academic Press.

Flamini, Roland. 2005. "Church Blocks Italian Referendum." UPI, June 15, 2005. http://www.upi.com/Business_News/Security-Industry/2005/06/15/Analysis-Church-blocks-Italian-referendum/UPI-11131118811157/, accessed October 24, 2013.

Fleming, Michael. 2010. "The Ethno-Religious Ambitions of the Roman Catholic Church and the Ascendancy of Communism in Post-War Poland (1945–50)." *Nations and Nationalism* 16 (4): 637–56.

Flere, Sergej. 2001. "The Impact of Religiosity on Political Stances." In *Religion and Social Change in Post-Communist Europe*, edited by Irena Borowik and Miklós Tomka, 29–41. Kraków: NOMOS.

Formigoni, Guido. 1998. *L'Italia dei cattolici: Fede e nazione dal Risorgimento alla repubblica*. Bologna: Il Mulino.

Fowler, Robert Booth, Allen Hertzke, Laura Olson, and Kevin Den Dulk. 2004. *Religion and Politics in America*. Boulder, CO: Westview Press.

Fox, Jonathan. 2006. "World Separation of Religion and State into the 21st Century." *Comparative Political Studies* 39 (5): 537–69.

———. 2008. *A World Survey of Religion and State*. Cambridge: Cambridge University Press.

Fox, Jonathan, and Ephraim Tabory. 2008. "Contemporary Evidence Regarding the Impact of State Regulation of Religion on Religious Participation and Belief." MS, Bar Ilan University.

Freedman, David. 2008. "Do the N's Justify the Means?" *Qualitative Methods* (Fall): 3–15.

Froese, Paul, and Steven Pfaff. 2001. "Replete and Desolate Markets: Poland, East Germany, and the New Religious Paradigm." *Social Forces* 80 (2): 481–507.

Furlong, Paul. 1996. "Political Catholicism and the Strange Death of the Christian Democrats." In *The New Italian Republic: From the Fall of the Berlin Wall to Berlusconi*, edited by Stephen Gundle and Simon Parker, 59–71. New York: Routledge.

Gagnon, Lysiane. 2010. "A Distinctly Quebec View on Abortion." *Globe and Mail*, May 31, updated September 6, 2012.

Gallo, Patrick. 2003. *For Love and Country: The Italian Resistance*. Lanham, MD: University Press of America.

Gallup. 2004. "Stem Cell Research Morally OK in Britain, Canada, and U.S." October 19. Available at http://www.gallup.com/poll/13681/stem-cell-research-morally-britain-canada-us.aspx, accessed October 25, 2013.

———. 2011. "Support for Legal Gay Relations Hits New High." http://www.gallup.com/poll/147785/support-legal-gay-relations-hits-new-high.aspx, accessed August 27, 2014.

———. 2013a. "Evolution, Creationism, Intelligent Design." http://www.gallup.com/poll/21814/Evolution-Creationism-Intelligent-Design.aspx, accessed December 18, 2013.

———. 2013b. "In US, Record-High Say Gay, Lesbian Relations Morally OK." http://www.gallup.com/poll/162689/record-high-say-gay-lesbian-relations-morally.aspx, accessed October 25, 2013.

Garelli, Franco. 2007. "The Public Relevance of the Church and Catholicism in Italy." *Journal of Modern Italian Studies* 12 (1): 8–36.

Garvin, Tom. 2004. *Preventing the Future: Why Was Ireland So Poor for So Long?* Dublin: Gill and Macmillan.

Gates, Gary. 2011. "How Many People are Lesbian, Gay, Bisexual, and Transgender?" Williams Institute, UCLA Law School, available at http://williams institute.law.ucla.edu/research/census-lgbt-demographics-studies/how-many -people-are-lesbian-gay-bisexual-and-transgender/.

Gauthier, Mary. 1997. "Church Attendance and Religious Belief in Postcommunist Societies." *Journal for the Scientific Study of Religion* 36 (2): 289–96.

Gauvreau, Michael. 1990. "Protestantism Transformed: Personal Piety and the Evangelical Social Vision, 1815–1867." In *The Canadian Protestant Experience*, edited by George Rawlyk, 48–97. Montreal: McGill Queen's University Press.

———. 2005 *The Catholic Origins of Québec's Quiet Revolution, 1931–1970*. Montreal: McGill-Queen's University Press.

———. 2007. "'They Are Not Our Generation': Youth, Gender, Catholicism, and Québec's Dechristianization, 1950–1970." In *The Church Confronts Modernity*, edited by Leslie Woodcock Tentler, 62–90. Washington, DC: Catholic University Press.

Gellner, Ernest. 1983. *Nations and Nationalism*. Ithaca, NY: Cornell University Press.

Gelman, Andrew, David Park, Boris Shor, Joseph Bafumi, and Jeronima Cortina. 2010. *Red State, Blue State, Rich State, Poor State: Why Americans Vote the Way They Do*. Princeton, NJ: Princeton University Press.

Gelman, Andrew, Jeffrey Lax, and Justin Phillips. 2010. "Over Time, a Gay Marriage Groundswell." Editorial, *New York Times*, August 22, 2010.

Gentile, Emilio. 2003. *The Struggle For Modernity: Nationalism, Futurism and Fascism*. Westport, CT: Praeger.

———. 2006. *Politics as Religion*. Princeton, NJ: Princeton University Press.

———. 2009. *La Grand Italia: Myth of the Nation in the 20th Century*. Madison: University of Wisconsin Press.

Gerber, Elisabeth R., and Jeffrey B. Lewis. 2004. "Beyond the Median: Voter Preferences, District Heterogeneity, and Political Representation." *Journal of Political Economy* 112 (6): 1364–83.

Gidney, Robert, and Wyn Millar. 2001. "The Christian Recessional in Ontario's Public Schools." In *Religion and Public Life in Canada*, edited by Marguerite Van Die. Toronto: University of Toronto Press.

Gill, Anthony. 1998. *Rendering unto Caesar: The Catholic Church and the State in Latin America*. Chicago: University of Chicago Press.

———. 2001. "Religion and Comparative Politics." *Annual Review of Political Science* 4: 117–38.

———. 2008. *The Political Origins of Religious Liberty*. Cambridge: Cambridge University Press.

Gill, Anthony, and Arang Keshavarzian. 1999. "State Building and Religious Resources: An Institutional Theory of Church-State Relations in Iran and Mexico." *Politics and Society* 27: 431–65.

Gill, Anthony, and Erik Lundsgaarde. 2004. "State Welfare Spending and Religiosity: A Cross-National Analysis." *Rationality and Society* 16 (4): 399–436.

Gillon, Stephen. 1987. *Politics and Vision: The ADA and American Liberalism, 1947–1985*. New York: Oxford University Press.

Giorda, Mariachiara. 2010. "Religious Education in Italy: Themes and Problems." Paper presented at CESNUR Annual Conference, Turin, Italy, September 9–11.

Girnius, Kestutis. 1989. "Catholicism and Nationalism in Lithuania." In *Religion and Nationalism in Soviet and East European Politics*, edited by Pedro Ramet, 109–37. Durham, NC: Duke University Press.

Girvin, Brian. 1994 "Moral Politics and the Irish Abortion Referendums, 1992." *Parliamentary Affairs* 47 (2): 203–21.

———. 2002. *From Union to Union*. Dublin: Gill and Macmillan.

———. 2008. "Church, State, and Society in Ireland since 1960." *Éire-Ireland* 43 (1 and 2): 74–98.

Givens, Terryl. 2004. *The Latter-Day Experience in America*. Westport, CT: Greenwood Press.

Goggin, Malcolm, and Christopher Wlezien. 1993. "Abortion Opinion and Policy in the American States," in *Understanding the New Politics of Abortion*, ed. Malcolm Goggin. Newbury Park, CA: Sage.

Goidel, Robert, and Matthew Nisbet. 2006. "Exploring the Roots of Public Participation in the Controversy over Embryonic Stem Cell Research and Cloning." *Political Behavior* 28 (2): 175–92.

Goldfrank, Benjamin, and Nick Rowell. 2012. "Church, State, and Human Rights in Latin America." *Politics, Religion, and Ideology* 13 (1): 25–51.

Goodstein, Laurie, 2005. "In Intelligent Design Case, a Cause in Search of a Lawsuit." *New York Times*, November 4, 2005.

Gorski, Philip. 2003. *The Disciplinary Revolution: Calvinism and the Rise of the State in Early Modern Europe*. Chicago: University of Chicago Press.

Gorski, Philip, and Gülay Türkmen-Dervişoğlu. 2013. "Religion, Nationalism, and Violence: An Integrated Approach," *Annual Review of Sociology* 39: 193–210.

Gowin, Jarosław. 1995. *Kościół po Komunizmie*. Kraków: Znak.

———. 1999. *Kościół w czasach wolności, 1989–1999*. Kraków: Znak.

Graff, Agnieszka. 2010. "Wojna pseudolewic." *Krytyka Polityczna*, August 29, http://www.krytykapolityczna.pl/Wywiady/GraffWojnapseudolewic/menuid -431.html, accessed August 29, 2014.

Greeley, Andrew, and Michael Hout. 2006. *The Truth about Conservative Christians*. Chicago: University of Chicago Press.

Green, John, James Guth, Corwin Smidt, and Lyman Kellstedt. 1996. *Religion and the Culture Wars*. Lanham, MD: Rowman and Littlefield.

Greenfeld, Liah. 1996. "The Modern Religion?" *Critical Review* 10 (2): 169–91.

Greenhouse, Linda, and Reva B. Siegel. 2011. "Before (and After) *Roe v. Wade*: New Questions about Backlash." Yale Law School, Public Law Working Paper 228.

Gruenfelder, Anna Maria. 2000. "The Church and Croats." *Central European Review* (May 15).

Grzymala-Busse, Anna. 2013. "Why There Is (Almost) No Christian Democracy in Post-Communist Europe." *Party Politics* 19 (2): 319–42.

Grzymala-Busse, Anna, and Pauline Jones Luong. 2002. "Reconceptualizing the State: Lessons from Post-Communism." *Politics and Society* 30 (4): 529–54.

Guenther, Bruce. 2008. "Ethnicity and Evangelical Protestants in Canada." In *Christianity and Ethnicity in Canada,* edited by Paul Barmadat and David Seljak, 365–414. Toronto: University of Toronto Press.

Gundle, Stephen, and Simon Parker. 1996. *The New Italian Republic: From the Fall of the Berlin Wall to Berlusconi.* New York: Routledge.

Guth, James. 1983. "Southern Baptist Clergy: Vanguard of the Christian Right?" In *The New Christian Right: Mobilization and Legitimation,* edited by Robert Liebman and Robert Wuthnow, 117–30. New Brunswick, NJ: Transaction Publishers.

———. 1996. "The Politics of the Christian Right." In *Religion and the Culture Wars,* edited by John Green, James Guth, Corwin Smidt, and Lyman Kellstedt, 7–29. Lanham, MD: Rowman and Littlefield.

Guth, James, John Green, Corwin Smidt, Lyman Kellstedt, and Margaret Poloma. 1997. *The Bully Pulpit: The Politics of Protestant Preachers.* Lawrence: University Press of Kansas.

Guttmacher Institute. 2008. "State Policies in Brief: An Overview of Abortion Laws." Memo.

———. 2014. "Induced Abortion in the United States," available at http://www.guttmacher.org/pubs/fb_induced_abortion.html, accessed August 27, 2014.

Guzzini, Stefano. 1995. "The 'Long Night of the First Republic': Year of Clientelistic Implosion in Italy. *Review of International Political Economy* 2 (1): 27–61.

Hacker, Jacob, and Paul Pierson. 2010. *Winner-Take-All Politics.* New York: Simon and Schuster.

Haddock, Bruce. 2000. "State, Nation, and Risorgimento." In *The Politics of Italian National Identity,* edited by Bruce Haddock and Gino Bedani, 11–40. Cardiff: University of Wales Press.

Hall, Peter, and Michele Lamont. 2013. "Why Social Relations Matter for Politics and Successful Societies." *Annual Review of Political Science* 16: 49–71.

Hall, Richard, and Alan Deardorff. 2006. "Lobbying as Legislative Subsidy." *American Political Science Review* 100 (1): 69–84.

Hanley, David, ed. 1994. *Christian Democracy in Europe: A Comparative Perspective.* London: Pinter.

Hansen, John Mark. 1991. *Gaining Access: Congress and the Farm Lobby, 1919–1981.* Chicago: University of Chicago Press.

Hanson, Eric. 1987. *The Catholic Church in World Politics.* Princeton, NJ: Princeton University Press.

Harris, Frederick. 1999. *Something Within: Religion in African-American Political Activism.* New York: Oxford University Press.

Hasselmann, Chris. 2006. *Policy Reform and the Development of Democracy in Eastern Europe.* Aldershot: Ashgate.

Hastings, Adrian. 1997. *The Construction of Nationhood.* Cambridge: Cambridge University Press.

Hatch, Nathan. 2007. "The Democratization of Christianity and the Character of American Politics." In *Religion and American Politics,* edited by Mark Noll and Luke Harlow, 93–120. New York: Oxford University Press.

Haugen, Hans Morten. 2011. "The Evangelical Lutheran Church of Denmark and the Multicultural Challenges." *Politics and Religion* 4: 476–502.

Haughton, Timothy. 2005. *Constraints and Opportunities of Leadership in Post-Communist Europe*. Aldershot: Ashgate.

Hawkins, Alan, et al. 2002. "Attitudes about Covenant Marriage and Divorce: Policy Implications from a Three-State Comparison." *Family Relations* 51 (2): 166–75.

Hayes, Andrew. 2013. *Introduction to Mediation, Moderation, and Conditional Process Analysis: A Regression-Based Approach*. New York: Guilford Press.

Hedl, Dragutin. 2001. "Croatia: Clerics Attack Government Institute for Women's Policy Research (IWPR), The Centre for Peace in the Balkans." Available at http://www.balkanpeace.org/index.php, accessed May 15, 2013.

Hehir, Bryan. 2006. "The Old Church and the New Europe: Charting the Changes." In *Religion in an Expanding Europe*, edited by Timothy Byrnes and Peter Katzenstein, 93–116. Cambridge: Cambridge University Press.

Hennessey, James. 2007. "Roman Catholics and American Politics, 1900–1960." In *Religion and American Politics*, edited by Mark Noll and Luke Harlow, 247–65. New York: Oxford University Press.

The Henry J. Kaiser Family Foundation. 2002. "Sex Education in the U.S.: Politics and Policy." *Issue Update*, October 2002. Available at http://kaiserfamily foundation.files.wordpress.com/2013/01/sex-education-in-the-u-s-policy-and -politics.pdf, accessed August 30, 2014.

Hepburn, Bob. 2011. "Religious Right a Force for Harper." *The Star*, April 13, 2011, http://bit.ly/emvWkR, accessed January 9, 2013.

Herberg, Will. 1983 [1960]. *Protestant-Catholic-Jew*. Chicago: University of Chicago Press.

Hertzke. Allen. 1988. *Representing God in Washington*. Knoxville: University of Tennessee Press.

Heston, Allen, Robert Summers, and Bettina Aten. 2006. Penn World Table Version 6.2, Center for International Comparisons of Production, Income and Prices at the University of Pennsylvania.

Hillygus, D. Sunshine, and Todd Shields. 2005. "Moral Issues and Voter Decision Making in the 2004 Presidential Election." *PS: Political Science and Politics* (April): 201–9.

Hobsbawm, E. J. 1990. *Nations and Nationalism since 1780*. Cambridge: Cambridge University Press.

Hogan, L. 2003. "Interpreting the Divorce Debates: Church and State in Transition." In *Religion and Politics in Ireland at the Turn of the Millennium*, edited by J. P. Mackey and E. McDonagh. Dublin: Columbia Press.

Hojnacki, Marie, David Kimball, Frank Baumgartner, Jeffrey Berry, and Beth Leech. 2012. "Studying Organizational Advocacy and Influence: Reexamining Interest Group Research." *Annual Review of Political Science* 15: 379–99.

Holden, A. C. 1971. "Divorce in the Commonwealth: A Comparative Study." *International and Comparative Law Quarterly* 20 (1): 58–74.

Hout, Michael, and Claude Fischer. 2002. "Why More Americans Have No Religious Preference: Politics and Generations." *American Sociological Review* 67 (2): 165–90.

Htun, Mala. 2003. *Sex and the State*. Cambridge: Cambridge University Press.

Huber, John. 2005. "Religious Belief, Religious Participation, and Social Policy Attitudes across Countries." MS, Columbia University.

Hughes, Richard. T. 2004. *Myths America Lives By*. Urbana: University of Illinois Press.

Hurd, Elizabeth Shakman. 2007. "Theorizing Religious Resurgence." *International Politics* 44: 647–65.

———. 2012. "International Politics after Secularism." *Review of International Studies* 38 (5): 943–61.

Hurrelman, Achim, Stephan Leibfried, Kerstin Martens, and Peter Mayer. 2007. *Transforming the Golden-Age Nation State*. Houndmills: Palgrave Macmillan.

Iannaccone, Laurence R. 1988. "A Formal Model of Church and Sect." *American Journal of Sociology* 94: S241–S268.

———. 1991. "The Consequences of Religious Market Structure: Adam Smith and the Economics of Religion." *Rationality and Society* 3 (2): 156–77.

———. 1992. "Sacrifice and Stigma: Reducing Free-Riding in Cults, Communes, and Other Collectives." *Journal of Political Economy* 100 (2): 271–91.

———. 1994. "Why Strict Churches Are Strong." *American Journal of Sociology* 99 (5): 1180–211.

———. 1998. "Introduction to the Economics of Religion." *Journal of Economic Literature* 36: 1465–96.

Ignazi, Piero, and E. Spencer Wellhofer. 2013. "Votes and Votive Candles: Modernization, Secularization, Vatican II, and the Decline of Religious Voting in Italy: 1953–1992." *Comparative Political Studies* 46 (1): 31–62.

Inglis, Tom. 1998. *Moral Authority: The Rise and Fall of the Catholic Church in Modern Ireland*. Dublin: University College Dublin Press.

Janicki, Mariusz. 2002. "Czerwone i czarne." *Polityka* 7 (16): 24–26.

Jänterä-Jareborg, Maarit. 2010. "Religion and the Secular State: The National Report of Sweden." 18th International Congress on Comparative Law, Washington, DC, July–August 2010, available at http://www.crs.uu.se/digitalAssets /55/55502_Religion_in_the_Secular_State.pdf.

Jelen, Ted. 2006. "Religion and Politics in the United States: Persistence, Limitations, and the Prophetic Voice." *Social Compass* 53 (3): 329–43.

———, ed. 2002. *Sacred Markets, Sacred Canopies*. Lanham, MD: Rowman and Littlefield.

Jelen, Ted, and Clyde Wilcox. 2002. *Religion and Politics in Comparative Perspective*. New York: Cambridge University Press.

Jemolo, Arturo Carlo. 1960. *Church and State in Italy: 1850–1950*. Oxford: Basil Blackwell.

Jenkins, Philip. 2007. *God's Continent*. New York: Oxford University Press.

Jensen, Richard. 1971. *Winning the Midwest: Social and Political Conflict, 1888–96*. Chicago: University of Chicago Press.

Jerolimov, Dinka Marinović, and Siniša Zrinščak. 2006. "Religion within and beyond Borders: The Case of Croatia." *Social Compass* 53 (2): 279–90.

Johnson, James. 2002. "How Conceptual Problems Migrate: Rational Choice, Interpretation, and the Hazards of Pluralism." *Annual Reviews of Political Science* 5 (June): 223–48.

Jones, Bryan, and Frank Baumgartner. 2005. *The Politics of Attention: How Government Prioritizes Problems*. Chicago: University of Chicago Press.

Jordan, Jason. 2014. "Religion and Redistribution in 13 Countries." *West European Politics* 37 (1): 19–41.

Juergensmeyer, Mark. 1993. *The New Cold War? Religious Nationalism Confronts the Secular State*. Berkeley: University of California Press.

———. 2008. *Global Rebellion: Religious Challenges to the Secular State*. Berkeley: University of California Press.

Kahl, Sigrun. 2005. "The Religious Roots of Modern Poverty Policy: Catholic, Lutheran, and Reformed Protestant Traditions Compared." *European Journal of Sociology* 46 (1): 91–126.

———. 2014. *Poverty and Eternity: How Religion Shapes Assistance to the Poor, from Early Church to Modern Welfare State*. Book manuscript, Yale University.

Kalyvas, Stathis. 1996. *The Rise of Christian Democracy in Europe*. Ithaca, NY: Cornell University Press.

Karpov, Vyacheslav. 2010. "Desecularization: A Conceptual Framework." *Journal of Church and State* 52 (2): 232–70.

Kasapović, Mijrana. 1996a. "1995 Parliamentary Elections in Croatia." *Electoral Studies* 15 (2): 269–82.

———. 1996b. "Demokratska tranzicija i političke institucije u Hrvatskoj." *Politicka Misao* 33 (2–3): 84–99.

Katerberg, William. 2000. "Consumers and Citizens: Religion, Identity, and Politics in Canada and the United States." In *Rethinking Church, State, and Modernity: Canada between Europe and America*, edited by David Lyon and Marguerite Van Die, 283–301. Toronto: University of Toronto Press.

Kavanagh, Eimear. 2009. "Same-Sex Marriage or Partnership and Adoption: Debate for Ireland." *Critical Social Thinking*, available at http://www.ucc.ie/en/appsoc/researchconference/conf/cstj/v1toc/gender/EimearKavanagh.pdf.

Kellstedt, Lyman, Corwin Smidt, John Green, and James Guth. 2007. "Faith Transformed: Religion and American Politics from FDR to GW Bush." In *Religion and American Politics*, edited by Mark Noll and Luke Harlow, 270–95. New York: Oxford University Press.

Kennedy, Finola. 2000. "The Suppression of the Carrigan Report: A Historical Perspective on Child Abuse." *Studies: An Irish Quarterly Review* 89 (356): 354–63.

Keogh, Dermot. 1986. *The Vatican, The Bishops, and Irish Politics, 1919–1939*. Cambridge: Cambridge University Press.

Keogh, Dermot. 2007. "The Catholic Church in Ireland since the 1950s." In *The Church Confronts Modernity*, edited by Leslie Woodcock Tentler, 93–149. Washington, DC: Catholic University Press.

Keogh, Dermot, and Andrew McCarthy. 2007. *The Making of the Irish Constitution, 1937*. Douglas Village, Cork: Mercier Press.

Kepel, Gilles. 1995. *The Revenge of God*. University Park: Pennsylvania State University Press.

Kertzer, David. 2014. *The Pope and Mussolini*. New York: Random House.

Kilp, Alar. 2005. "Catholicism and Democracy in Post-Communist Europe." Paper prepared for the 3rd ECPR Conference, September 2005, Budapest.

Kim, Andrew. 1993. "The Absence of Pan-Canadian Civil Religion: Plurality, Duality, and Conflict in Symbols of Canadian Culture." *Sociology of Religion* 54 (3): 257–75.

Kissane, Bill. 2003. "The Illusion of State Neutrality in a Secularising Ireland." In *Church and State in Contemporary Europe: The Chimera of Neutrality*, edited by John T. S. Madeley and Zsolt Enyedi, 73–94. London: Frank Cass.

Kitschelt, Herbert, Kirk Hawkins, Juan Pablo Luna, Guillermo Rosas, and Elizabeth Zechmeister. 2010. *Latin American Party Systems*. New York: Cambridge University Press.

Knill, Christoph, Caroline Preidel, and Kerstin Nebel. 2014. "Brake Rather Than Barrier: The Impact of the Catholic Church on Morality Policies in Western Europe." *West European Politics* 37 (5): 845–66.

Kohut, Andrew, John Green, Scott Keeter, and Robert Toth. 2000. *The Diminishing Divide: Religion's Changing Role in American Politics*. Washington, DC: Brookings Institution Press.

Kolstø, Pål. 2011. "The Croatian Catholic Church and the Long Road to Jasenovac." *Nordic Journal of Religion and Society* 24 (1): 37–56.

Kopstein, Jeffrey, and Jason Wittenberg. 2003. "Who Voted Communist? Reconsidering the Social Bases of Radicalism in Interwar Poland." *Slavic Review* 62 (1): 87–109.

Koseła, Krzysztof. 2003. *Polak i katolik: Splątana tożsamość*. Warsaw: IFiS PAN.

Kosmin, Barry, and Seymour Lachman. 1993. *One Nation under God: Religion in Contemporary American Society*. New York: Crown.

Kosmin, Barry, et al. 2009. "American Nones: The Profile of the No Religion Population." Hartford, CT: Institute for the Study of Secularism in Society and Culture.

Kozole, Lovorka. 2002. "Croatia's Coming Out." *Transitions Online* (July 12).

Kreuzer, Marcus. 2010. "Historical Knowledge and Quantitative Analysis: The Case of the Origins of Proportional Representation." *American Political Science Review* 104 (2): 369–92.

Kreider, Rose, and Renee Ellis. 2011. "Number, Timing, and Duration of Marriages and Divorces: 2009." US Census Bureau, Washington, DC.

Królikowska, Jadwiga. 1993. "Socjologiczne Problemy Obecnosci Kościoła Rzymskokatolickiego w Konflikcie Społecznym w Polsce w latach 1980–1982." In *Religie I Kościoły w Społeczenstwach Postkomunistycznych*, edited by Irena Borowik and Andrzej Szyjewski, 199–203. Kraków: NOMOS.

Kubik, Jan. 1994. *The Power of Symbols against the Symbols of Power*. University Park: Pennsylvania State University Press.

Kulczycki, Andrzej. 1995. "Abortion Policy in Post-Communist Europe: The Conflict in Poland." *Population and Development Review* 21 (3): 471–505.

Kunicki, Mikołaj Stanisław. 2012. *Between the Brown and the Red: Nationalism, Catholicism, and Communism in Twentieth-Century Poland—The Politics of Bolesław Piasecki*. Athens: Ohio University Press.

Kunovich, Robert. 2006. "An Exploration of the Salience of Christianity for National Identity in Europe." *Sociological Perspectives* 49 (4): 435–60.

Kuran, Timur. 1991. "Now Out of Never: The Element of Surprise in the East European Revolution of 1989." *World Politics* 44 (1): 7–48.

Kurth, James. 2007. "Religion and National Identity in America and Europe." *Society* 44: 120–25.

Lambert, Frank. 2008. *Religion in American Politics*. Princeton, NJ: Princeton University Press. *Journal of Church and State* 50 (4): 733–34.

———. 2010. "Religion and the American Presidency." *Religion and American Culture*, 20 (2): 259–69.

Larkin, Emmet. 1976. *The Historical Dimensions of Irish Catholicism*. New York: Arno Press.

———. 1984. *The Historical Dimensions of Irish Catholicism*. Washington, DC: Catholic University of America Press.

Lax, Jeffrey, and Justin Phillips. 2009. "Gay Rights in the States: Public Opinion and Policy Responsiveness." *American Political Science Review* 103 (3): 367–85.

Layman, Geoffrey C. 1997. "Religion and Political Behavior in the United States: The Impact of Beliefs, Affiliations, and Commitment from 1980 to 1994." *Public Opinion Quarterly* 61: 288–316.

———. 2001. *The Great Divide: Religious and Cultural Conflict in American Party Politics*. New York: Columbia University Press.

Layman, Geoffrey C., and Edward G. Carmines. 1997. "Cultural Conflict in American Politics: Religious Traditionalism, Postmaterialism, and U.S. Political Behavior." *Journal of Politics* 59 (3): 751–77.

Leege, David, and Lyman Kellstedt. 1993. *Rediscovering the Religious Factor in American Politics*. Armonk, NY: M. E. Sharpe.

Leff, Carol Skalnik. 1988. *National Conflict in Czechoslovakia: The Making and Remaking of a State, 1918–1987*. Princeton, NJ: Princeton University Press.

Levitt, Joseph, 1993. "English-Speaking Intellectual Defense of Canadian Nationhood." In *Unequal Partners: A Comparative Analysis of Relations between Austria and the Federal Republic of Germany and between Canada and the United States*, edited by Harald von Riekhoff and Hanspeter Neuhold. Boulder, CO: Westview Press.

Lewis, Gregory, and Seong Soo Oh. 2008. "Public Opinion and State Action on Same-Sex Marriage." *State and Local Government Review* 40 (1): 42–53.

Leyburn, James. 1962. *The Scotch-Irish*. Chapel Hill: University of North Carolina Press.

Lieberman, Evan. 2010. "Bridging the Qualitative-Quantitative Divide: Best Practices in the Development of Historically Oriented Replication Databases." *Annual Review of Political Science* 13: 37–59.

Lieven, Anatol. 2004. *America Right or Wrong: An Anatomy of American Nationalism*. New York: Oxford University Press.

Lilly, Carol, and Jill Irvine. 2002. "Negotiating Interests: Women and Nationalism in Serbia and Croatia, 1990–1997." *East European Politics and Societies* 16: 109–44.

Linz, Juan. 1991. "Church and State in Spain from the Civil War to the Return of Democracy." *Daedalus* 120 (3): 159–78.

Lipset, Seymour Martin. 1963. *The First New Nation*. New York: Basic Books.

———. 1989. *Continental Divide*. New York: Routledge.

————. 2003. *The First New Nation.* New Brunswick, NJ: Transaction Publishers.

Lipset, Seymour, and Stein Rokkan, eds. 1967. *Party Systems and Voter Alignments: Cross National Perspectives.* New York: Free Press.

Lovrenović, Ivan. 1998. "Sympathy for the Devil." *Transitions Online* (December 15).

Loza, Tihomir. 2007. "Strange Bedfellows." *Transitions Online* (November 20).

————. 2009. "Croatia: Cross References." *Transitions Online* (August 27).

Luker, Kristin. 1986. *Abortion and the Politics of Motherhood.* Durham, NC: Duke University Press.

Lupia, Arthur, and Matthew McCubbins. 1998. *The Democratic Dilemma: Can Citizens Learn What They Need to Know?* New York: Cambridge University Press.

Luxmoore, Jonathan, and Jolanta Babiuch. 1999. *The Vatican and the Red Flag.* London: Geoffrey Chapman.

Lynch, Julia. 2009. "Italy: A Christian Democratic or Clientelist Welfare State?" In *Religion, Class Coalitions, and Welfare States,* edited by Kees van Kersbergen and Philip Manow, 91–118. Cambridge: Cambridge University Press.

Lyons, Barry. 2012. "The Irish Council for Bioethics: An Unaffordable Luxury?" *Cambridge Quarterly of Healthcare Ethics* 21 (3): 375–83.

Madeley, John T. S. 2003. "A Framework for the Comparative Analysis of Church-State Relations in Europe." *West European Politics* 26 (1): 23–50.

Madeley, John T. S., and Zsolt Enyedi, eds. 2003. *Church and State in Contemporary Europe: The Chimera of Neutrality.* London: Frank Cass.

Magister, Sandro. 2001. *Chiesa extraparlamentare.* Naples: L'ancora del mediterraneo.

Maguire, Moira. 2007 "The Carrigan Committee and Child Sexual Abuse in Twentieth-Century Ireland." *New Hibernia Review* 11 (2): 79–100.

Majchrowski, Jacek. 1993. "Uwagi o Praktyce Legislacyjnej Dotyczacej Stosunków Państwowo-Koscielnych." In *Religie i Kościoły w Społeczeństwach Postkomunistycznych,* edited by Irena Borowik and Andrzej Szyjewski, 75–82. Kraków: NOMOS.

Makarkin, Aleksei. 2011. "The Russian Orthodox Church: Competing Choices." *Russian Politics and Law* 49 (1): 8–23.

Mallick, Heather, 2003. "Why Doesn't This Man Have the Order of Canada?" *Globe and Mail,* January 18, 2003. Available at http://www.theglobeandmail.com/series/morgentaler/, accessed February 14, 2009.

Marinović, Ankica, and Goran Golberger. 2008. "*Glas Koncila*: A True Mission or Simply a Name?" *Sociologija i prostor* 45 (3–4): 269–300.

Marsden, George. 1982. "Preachers of Paradox: The Religious New Right in Historical Perspective," In *Religion in America: Spirituality in a Secular Age,* edited by Mary Douglas and Steven Tipton, 150–68. Boston: Beacon Press.

————. 2007. "Religion, Politics, and the Search for an American Consensus." In *Religion and American Politics,* edited by Mark Noll and Luke Harlow, 459–69. New York: Oxford University Press.

Martin, David. 1991. "The Secularization Issue: Prospect and Retrospect." *British Journal of Sociology* 42 (3): 465–74.

———. 1999. "The Evangelical Protestant Upsurge and Its Political Implications." in *The Desecularization of the World*, edited by Peter Berger. Washington, DC: Ethics and Public Policy Center.

———. 2005. *On Secularization: Towards a Revised General Theory*. Aldershot: Ashgate.

Marty, Martin, and Scott Appleby. 1992. *The Glory and the Power*. Boston: Beacon Press.

Mason, Christopher. 2006. "Gay Marriage Galvanizes Canada's Religious Right." *New York Times*, October 18, 2006. http://nyti.ms/pK2U3R, accessed September 20, 2014.

Mason, Patrick. 2011. *The Mormon Menace*. New York: Oxford University Press.

Massey, Garth, Randy Hodson, and Dusko Sekulic. 2000. "Ethnic Nationalism and Liberalism in Post-War Croatia." NCEEER Research Report, Washington, DC.

Matthews, J. Scott. 2005. "The Political Foundations of Support for Same-Sex Marriage in Canada." *Canadian Journal of Political Science* 38 (4): 841–66.

McCleary, Rachel, and Robert Barro. 2006. "Religion and Economy." *Journal of Economic Perspectives* 20 (2): 49–72.

McDonnell, Oral, and Jill Allison. 2006. "From Biopolitics to Bioethics: Church, State, Medicine, and Assisted Reproductive Technology in Ireland." *Sociology of Health and Illness* 28 (6): 817–37.

McKenna, George. 2007. *The Puritan Origins of American Patriotism*. New Haven, CT: Yale University Press.

McManus, Seumas. 2005 [1921]. *The Story of the Irish Race*. New York: Cosimo.

McTague, John Michael, and Geoffrey Layman. 2009. "Religion, Parties, and Voting Behavior: A Political Explanation of Religious Influence." In *The Oxford Handbook of Religion and American Politics*, edited by James L. Guth, Lyman A. Kellstedt, and Corwin E. Smidt, 330–70. New York: Oxford University Press.

Medoff, Marshall. 2002. "The Determinants and Impact of State Abortion Restrictions." *American Journal of Economics and Sociology* 61 (2): 481–93.

Meier, Kenneth. 2001. "Drugs, Sex, and Rock and Roll: A Theory of Morality Politics." In *The Public Clash of Private Values*, edited by Christopher Mooney, 21–36. New York: Seven Bridges Press.

Michel, Anthony. 2003. "Building a Christian Democracy: George Drew, the Protestant Churches, and the Origins of Religious Education in Ontario's Public Schools, 1944–45." Historical Papers, Canadian Society of Church History.

Michnik, Adam. 2001. "The Montesinos Virus." *Social Research* 68 (4): 905–16, 908.

Miler, Kristina. 2007. "The View from the Hill: Legislative Perceptions of the District." *Legislative Studies Quarterly* 32 (4): 597–628.

Miller, Steven. 2014. *The Age of Evangelicalism: America's Born Again Years*. New York: Oxford University Press.

Miller, Warren, and Donald Stokes. 1963. "Constituency Influence in Congress." *APSR* 57 (1): 45–56.

Minkenberg, Michael. 2002. "Religion and Public Policy: Institutional, Cultural, and Political Impact on the Shaping of Abortion Policies in Western Democracies." *Comparative Political Studies* 35 (2): 221–47.

———. 2003. "The Policy Impact of Church-State Relations: Family Policy and Abortion in Britain, France, and Germany." *West European Politics* 26 (1): 195–217.

———. 2013. "Religious Path Dependency? A Comparative Analysis of Patterns of Religion and Democracy and of Policies of Integration in Western Societies." Paper presented at the Annual Meeting of the American Political Science Association, Chicago, August 29–September 1.

Mitchell, Clare. 2006. "The Religious Content of Ethnic Identities." *Sociology* 40: 1135–52.

Mojzes, Paul. 1994. *The Yugoslavian Inferno*. New York: Continuum.

Molony, John. 1977. *The Emergence of Political Catholicism in Italy*. London: Croon Helm.

Monsma, Stephen, and Christopher Soper. 1997. *The Challenge of Pluralism*. Lanham, MD: Rowman and Littlefield.

Montalvo, José G., and Marta Reynal-Querol. 2005. "Ethnic Polarization, Potential Conflict, and Civil Wars." *American Economic Review*: 796–816.

Montgomery, James. 2003. "A Formalization and Test of the Religious Economies Model." *American Sociological Review* 68 (5): 783–809.

Mooney, Christopher, ed. 2001. *The Public Clash of Private Values*. New York: Seven Bridges Press.

Moore, Deborah Dash. 2004. *GI Jews: How World War II Changed a Generation*. Cambridge, MA: Harvard University Press.

Moorehead, James. 1994. "The American Israel: Protestant Tribalism and Universal Mission." In *Many Are Chosen: Divine Election and Western Nationalism*, edited by William Hutchinson and Hartmut Lehmann. Harvard Theological Studies 38. Minneapolis: Fortress Press.

Morawska, Ewa. 1995. "The Polish Roman Catholic Church Unbound." In *Can Europe Work?*, edited by Stephen Hanson and Willfried Spohn. Seattle: University of Washington Press.

Morone, James. 2003. *Hellfire Nation: The Politics of Sin in American History*. New Haven, CT: Yale University Press.

Morozowski, Andrzej. 2012. "Aborcja w Polsce: (Nie)moralny kompromis." http://historia.focus.pl/polska/aborcja-w-polsce-niemoralny-kompromis-1142, September 24, accessed October 25, 2013.

Murphy, Gary, 2003. "Pluralism and the Politics of Morality." In *Public Administration and Public Policy in Ireland: Theory and Methods*, edited by Maura Adshead and Michelle Millar. London: Routledge.

Murphy, Terence, and Roberto Perin. 1996. *A Concise History of Christianity in Canada*. Oxford: Oxford University Press.

Nalepa, Monika, and Royce Carroll. 2014. *Parties Ascendant: Representing Voters and Organizing Legislatures in Post Communist Europe*. MS, University of Chicago.

NARAL Foundation. 1991 and other years. "Who Decides? A State-By-State Review of Abortion Rights." Washington, DC: National Abortion Rights Action League.

National Center for Policy Analysis Website. 1999. "Bible Belt Leads U.S. in Divorces." November 19. http://bit.ly/wn0zd.

Nemni, Max, and Monique Nemni. 2006. *Young Trudeau: Son of Québec, Father of Canada, 1919–1944*. Toronto: McLelland and Stewart.

Noll, Mark. 2002. *America's God: From Jonathan Edwards to Abraham Lincoln*. New York: Oxford University Press.

———. 2007. "Canadian Counterpoint." In *Religion and American Politics*, edited by Mark Noll and Luke Harlow, 423–40. New York: Oxford University Press.

Norrand, Barbara, and Clyde Wilcox. 1999. "Public Opinion and Policymaking in the States: The Case of Post-*Roe* Abortion Policy." *Policy Studies Journal* 27: 707–22.

Norris, Pippa, and Ronald Inglehart. 2004. *Sacred and Secular: Religion and Politics Worldwide*. Cambridge: Cambridge University Press.

Nossiff, Rosemary, 1995. "Pennsylvania: The Impact of Party Organization and Lobbying." In *Abortion Politics in American States*, edited by Mary Segers and Timothy Byrnes. Armonk, NY: M. E. Sharpe.

Oakes, Leigh. 2004. "French: A Language for Everyone in Québec?" *Nations and Nationalism* 10 (4): 539–58.

Oaks, Laury. 2002. "Abortion Is Part of the Irish Experience, It Is Part of What We Are: The Transformation of Public Discourses on Irish Abortion Policy." *Women's Studies International Forum* 25 (3): 315–33.

O'Dwyer, Connor. 2012. "Does the EU Help or Hinder Gay-Rights Movements in Post-Communist Europe? The Case of Poland." *East European Politics* 28 (4): 332–52.

Oldmixon, Elizabeth, and Brian Calfano. 2007. "The Religious Dynamics of Decision Making on Gay Rights Issues in the U.S. House of Representatives, 1993–2002." *Journal for the Scientific Study of Religion* 46 (1): 55–70.

Olson, Daniel. 2002. "Competing Notions of Religious Competition." In *Sacred Markets, Sacred Canopies*, edited by Ted Jelen, 133–66. Lanham, MD: Rowman and Littlefield.

O'Mahony, Eoin. 2010. *Religious Practice and Values in Ireland*. Maynooth: Irish Catholic Bishops' Conference.

Or, Eunice. 2005. "Canada Goes Ahead with Same-Sex Marriage Bill Despite Christian Protest." May 6, *Christian Today*, http://bit.ly/wJwbbQ, accessed January 9, 2013.

O'Reilly, Emily, 1992. *Masterminds of the Right*. Dublin: Attic Press.

Orszulik, Alojzy. 2008. "Droga do pełnej normalizacji stosunków między państwem i Kościołem oraz między PRL a Stolicą Apostolską." *Studia Loviciencsia* 10: 253–66.

Osa, Maryjane. 1989. "Resistance, Persistence, and Change: The Roman Catholic Church in Poland." *East European Politics and Societies* 3 (2): 268–99.

———. 1997. "Creating Solidarity: The Religious Foundations of the Polish Social Movement." *East European Politics and Societies* 11 (2): 339–65.

Ost, David. 1990. *Solidarity and the Politics of Anti-Politics*. Philadelphia: Temple University Press.

O'Toole, Roger. 1996. "Religion in Canada: Its Development and Contemporary Situation." *Social Compass* 43: 119–34.

———. 2000. "Canadian Religion: Heritage and Project." In *Rethinking Church, State, and Modernity: Canada between Europe and America*, edited by David Lyon and Marguerite Van Die, 34–51. Toronto: University of Toronto Press.

Pace, Enzo. 1995. *L'Unita dei cattolici in Italia: Origine e decadenze di un mito collettivo*. Milan: Guerrini e Associati.

Parsons, Talcott. 1977. *The Evolution of Societies*. Englewood Cliffs, NJ: Prentice-Hall.

Pasotti, Jacopo, and Ned Stafford. 2006. "It's Legal: Italian Researchers Defend Their Work with Embryonic Stem Cells." *Nature* 442 (7100): 229.

Pavone, Claudio. 1991. *Una guerra civile: Saggio storico sulla moralità della Resistenza*. Turin: Bollati Boringhieri.

Perica, Vjekoslav. 2000. "The Catholic Church and the Making of the Croatian Nation, 1970–1984." *East European Politics and Societies* 14: 532–64.

———. 2002. *Balkan Idols: Religion and Nationalism in Yugoslav States*. New York: Oxford University Press.

———. 2006. "The Most Catholic Country on Earth? Church, State, and Society in Contemporary Croatia." *Religion, State, and Society* 34 (4): 311–46.

Perin, Roberto. 2001. "Elaborating a Public Culture: The Catholic Church in Nineteenth-Century Québec." In *Religion and Public Life in Canada*, edited by Marguerite Van Die, 87–105. Toronto: University of Toronto Press.

Perrin, Robin, Paul Kennedy, and Donald Miller. 1997. "Examining the Sources of Conservative Religious Growth: Where Are the New Evangelical Movements Getting Their Numbers?" *Journal for the Scientific Study of Religion* 36 (1): 71–80.

Pew Forum on Religion and Public Life. 2000. "Religion and Politics: The Ambivalent Majority." Available at http://people-press.org/reports/pdf/32.pdf, accessed August 7, 2008.

———. 2002. "Americans Struggle with Religion's Role at Home and Abroad." Available at http://people-press.org/reports/pdf/150.pdf, accessed August 7, 2012.

———. 2006. "Religion and Stem Cell Research." Pew Forum Fact Sheet, July 18, 2006. Accessed November 4, 2012.

———. 2008. "Stem Cell Research at the Crossroads of Religion and Politics." Available at http://pewforum.org/docs/?DocID=316, accessed March 19, 2009.

———. 2009a. "Overview: the Conflict between Religion and Evolution." Available at http://www.pewforum.org/Science-and-Bioethics/Overview-The-Conflict-Between-Religion-and-Evolution.aspx, accessed June 10, 2013.

———. 2009b. "Support for Abortion Slips." Available at http://www.pewforum.org/Abortion/Support-for-Abortion-Slips.aspx, accessed May 22, 2013.

Phillips, Roderick. 1988. *Putting Asunder: A History of Divorce in Western Society*. Cambridge: Cambridge University Press.

Philpott, Daniel, and Timothy Samuel Shah. 2006. "Faith, Freedom, and Federation: The Role of Religious Ideas and Institutions in European Political Convergence." In *Religion in an Expanding Europe*, edited by Timothy Byrnes and Peter Katzenstein, 34–64. Cambridge: Cambridge University Press.

Pickering, Paula, and Mark Baskin. 2008. "What Is to Be Done? Succession from the League of Communists in Croatia." *Communist and Post-Communist Studies* 41: 521–40.

Pisa, Nick. 2009. "Vatican's Fury as Court Bans Crucifixes in Italian Classrooms Because They 'Breach Religious Rights of Children.'" *Daily Mail*, November 3. http://www.dailymail.co.uk/news/article-1224954/Vaticans-fury-court-bans-crucifixes-Italian-classroom-breach-religious-rights-children.html, accessed November 15, 2013.

Plotke, David. 1996. *Building a Democratic Political Order: Reshaping American Liberalism in the 1930s and 1940s*. Cambridge: Cambridge University Press.

Pollard, John. 2008. *Catholicism in Modern Italy: Religion, Society, and Politics since 1861*. New York: Routledge.

Porter-Szücs, Brian. 2011. *Faith and Fatherland*. New York: Oxford University Press.

Potočnik, Dunja. 2007. "Religious Socialization and Youth Issues in Croatia." In *The Future of Religion: Toward a Reconciled Society*, edited by Michael Ott, 365–84. Leiden: Brill.

Powell, Bingham. 2000. *Elections as Instruments of Democracy*. New Haven, CT: Yale University Press.

Powell, Bingham, and Guy Whitten. 1993. "A Cross-National Analysis of Economic Voting: Taking Account of the Political Context." *American Journal of Political Science* 37: 391–414.

Prendiville, Patricia. 1988. "Divorce in Ireland: An Analysis of the Referendum to Amend the Constitution, June 1986." *Women's Studies International Forum* 11 (4): 355–63.

Priests for Life Canada. 2013. "A New Pro-Life Legislative Effort: Motion 408." Available at http://www.priestsforlifecanada.com/English/News_Events/Sex_Selection_Motion/index.php, accessed June 28, 2013.

Putnam, Robert, and David Campbell. 2010. *American Grace: How Religion Divides and Unites Us*. New York: Simon and Shuster.

Ramet, Sabrina. 1996. "The Croatian Catholic Church since 1990." *Religion, State, and Society: The Keston Journal* 24 (4): 345–55.

———. 1998. *Nihil Obstat: Religion, Politics, and Social Change in East-Central Europe and Russia*. Durham, NC: Duke University Press.

———. 2002. *Balkan Babel*. Boulder, CO: Westview Press.

———. 2006. "Thy Will Be Done: The Catholic Church and Politics in Poland since 1989." In *Religion in an Expanding Europe*, edited by Timothy Byrnes and Peter Katzenstein, 117–47. Cambridge: Cambridge University Press.

———, ed. 1990. *Catholicism and Politics in Communist Societies*. Durham, NC: Duke University Press.

Reimer, Sam. 2000. "A Generic Evangelicalism? Comparing Evangelical Subcultures in Canada and the United States." In *Rethinking Church, State, and Modernity: Canada between Europe and America*, edited by David Lyon and Marguerite Van Die, 228–46. Toronto: University of Toronto Press.

Rémond, René. 1999. *Religion and Society in Modern Europe*. Oxford: Blackwell Publishers.

Ribić, Biljana. 2009. "Relations between Church and State in Republic of Croatia." *Politics and Religion* 3 (2): 197–206.

Rieffer, Barbara-Ann. 2003. "Religion and Nationalism." *Ethnicities* 3 (2): 215–42, 225.

Riker, William. 1996. *The Strategy of Rhetoric: Campaigning for the American Constitution*. New Haven, CT: Yale University Press.

Ritossa, Dalida. 2010. "Taking the Right to Abortion in Croatia Seriously." *Cardozo Journal of Law and Gender* 13 (2): 273–303.

Roemer, John. 1998. "Why the Poor Do Not Expropriate the Rich: An Old Argument in New Garb." *Journal of Public Economics* 70: 399–424.

———. 2001. *Political Competition*. Cambridge: Cambridge University Press.

Roh, Johngo, and Donald P. Haider-Markel. 2003. "All Politics Is Not Local: National Forces in State Abortion Initiatives." *Social Science Quarterly* 84 (1): 15–31.

Rokkan, Stein. 1970. *Citizens, Elections, Parties*. Oslo: Universitetsforlaget.

Roof, Wade Clark. 2009. "American Presidential Rhetoric from Ronald Reagan to George W. Bush: Another Look at Civil Religion." *Social Compass* 56 (2): 286–301.

Roof, Wade, and William McKinney. 1987. *American Mainline Religion*. New Brunswick, NJ: Rutgers University Press.

Rosenberg, Scott. 2001. "Bush's Stem-Cell Fumble." salon.com, August 10. Available at http://www.salon.com/2001/08/10/stem_cell_5/, accessed June 12, 2013.

Ross, Sarah Gwyneth. 2009. *The Birth of Feminism: Woman as Intellect in Renaissance Italy and England*. Cambridge, MA: Harvard University Press.

Sachdev, Paul, 1988. "Canada." In *International Handbook on Abortion*, edited by Paul Sachdev, 66–97. New York: Greenwood Press.

Sahliyeh, Emile, ed. 1990. *Religious Resurgence and Politics in the Contemporary World*. Albany: State University of New York Press.

Sakalis, Alex. 2013. "The Most Catholic Country in Europe? Croatia and the Catholic Church." Open Democracy, http://www.opendemocracy.net/70943, accessed February 27.

Salvadori, Massimo. 2001. *Storia d'Italia e crisi di regime*. Milan: il Mulino.

Saul, Rebekah. 1998. "Whatever Happened to the Adolescent Family Life Act?" *Guttmacher Report on Public Policy* 1 (2).

Schanda, Balázs. 2003. "Religion and State in the Candidate Countries to the European Union: Issues concerning Religion and State in Hungary." *Sociology of Religion* 64 (3): 333–48.

Scheufele, Dietram. 2000. "Agenda-Setting, Priming, and Framing Revisited: Another Look at Cognitive Effects of Political Communication." *Mass Communication and Society* 3 (2 and 3): 297–316.

Scheve, Kenneth, and John Stasavage. 2006. "Religion and Preferences for Social Insurance." *Quarterly Journal of Political Science* 1: 255–86.

Schildkraut, Deborah. 2011. *Americanism in the Twenty-First Century*. New York: Cambridge University Press.

Scoppola, Pietro. 1985. *La "Nuova cristianitá" perduta*. Rome: Studium.

———. 2005. *La Democrazia dei Cristiani*. Rome-Bari: Editori Laterza.

Scott, James C. 1985. *Weapons of the Weak: Everyday Forms of Peasant Resistance*. New Haven, CT: Yale University Press.

Segura, Gary. 2005. "An Introduction and Commentary—A Symposium on the Politics of Same-Sex Marriage." *Political Science and Politics* (April): 189–93.

Seljak, David. 1996. "Why the Quiet Revolution was 'Quiet': The Catholic Church's Reaction to the Secularization of Nationalism in Québec after 1960." *Historical Studies* (62): 109–24.

———. 2001. "Catholicism's Quiet Revolution: *Maintenant* and the New Public Catholicism in Québec after 1960." In *Religion and Public Life in Canada*, edited by Marguerite Van Die, 257–74. Toronto: University of Toronto Press.

Seymour, Mark. 2006. *Debating Divorce in Italy: Marriage and the Making of Modern Italians, 1860–1974*. New York: Palgrave Macmillan.

Sgritta, Giovanni, and Paolo Tufari. 1977. "Italy." In *Divorce in Europe*, edited by Robert Chester. Leiden: Martinus Nijhoff Social Sciences Division.

Sharpe, Neil F., and Ronald F. Carter. 2006. *Genetic Testing: Care, Consent, and Liability*. Hoboken, NJ: John Wiley and Sons.

Shiffman, Jeremy, Marina Skrabalo, and Jelena Subotic. 2002. "Reproductive Rights and the State in Serbia and Croatia." *Social Science and Medicine* 54 (4): 625–42.

Shupe, Anson, and William Stacey. 1983. "The Moral Majority Constituency." In *The New Christian Right*, edited by Robert Liebman and Robert Wuthnow, 104–16. New York: Aldine.

Silk, Mark. 1988. *Spiritual Politics: Religion and America since World War II*. New York: Simon and Schuster.

Silk, Mark, and Andrew Walsh. 2008. *One Nation, Divisible*. Lanham, MD: Rowman and Littlefield.

Skocpol, Theda. 1995. *Protecting Soldiers and Mothers*. Cambridge, MA: Harvard University Press.

Skocpol, Theda, Marshall Ganz, and Ziad Munson. 2000. "A Nation of Organizers." *American Political Science Review* 94: 527–46.

Skocpol, Theda, et al. 1993. "Women's Associations and the Enactment of Mothers' Pensions in the United States." *American Political Science Review*, 87 (3): 686–701.

Slater, Dan. 2009. "Revolutions, Crackdowns and Quiescence: Communal Elites and Democratic Mobilization in Southeast Asia," *American Journal of Sociology*, 115, 1: 203–54.

Smith, Anthony. 1998. *Nationalism and Modernism*. New York: Routledge.

———. 2003. *Chosen Peoples: Sacred Sources of National Identity*. Oxford: Oxford University Press.

———. 2008. *The Cultural Foundations of Nations: Hierarchy, Covenant, and Republic*. Malden, MA: Blackwell Publishing.

Smith, Dennis Mack. 1997. *Modern Italy: A Political History*. Ann Arbor: University of Michigan Press.

Smith, Helmut. 1995. *German Nationalism and Religious Conflict*. Princeton, NJ: Princeton University Press.

Smith, James. 2004. "The Politics of Sexual Knowledge: The Origins of Ireland's Containment Culture and the Carrigan Report (1931)." *Journal of the History of Sexuality* 13 (2): 208–33.

Smith, Raymond. 1985. *Garret: The Enigma*. Dublin: Aherlow Publishers.

Smyth, Lisa, 2005: *Abortion and Nation: The Politics of Reproduction in Contemporary Ireland*. Aldershot: Ashgate.

Snell, James, 1991. *In the Shadow of the Law: Divorce in Canada, 1900–1939*. Toronto: University of Toronto Press.

Sommerville, John. 1998. "Secular Society, Religious Population: Our Tacit Rules for Using the Term Secularization." *Journal for the Scientific Study of Religion* 37 (2): 249–53.

Soper, J. Christopher, and Joel Fetzer. 2011. "The Last Refuge of the Scoundrel: Religion and Nationalism in Global Perspective." Paper presented at the 2011 Annual Meeting of the American Political Science Association, Seattle, Washington.

Southern Baptist Convention. n.d. "Resolutions on Abortion and the Sanctity of Life." http://bit.ly/A4qF7b.

Spaht, Katherine. 1998. "Why Covenant Marriage? A Change in Culture for the Sake of the Children." *Louisiana Bar Journal* 46: 116–11.

Speed, Anne, 1992. "The Struggle for Reproductive Rights: A Brief History in Its Political Context." In *The Abortion Papers, Ireland*, edited by Ailbhe Smyth, 138–48. Dublin: Attic Press.

Stacey, Charles P. 1983. *A Date with History: Memoirs of a Canadian Historian*. Ottawa: Deneau.

Stackhouse, John, Jr. 2000. "Bearing Witness: Christian Groups Engage Canadian Politics since the 1960s." In *Rethinking Church, State, and Modernity: Canada between Europe and America*, edited by David Lyon and Marguerite Van Die, 113–28. Toronto: University of Toronto Press.

Stanosz, Barbara. 2004. *W Cieniu Kościoła, czyli Demokracja po Polsku*. Warsaw: Książka i Wiedza.

Stark, Rodney. 1992. "Do Catholic Societies Really Exist?" *Rationality and Society* 4 (3): 261–71.

———. 1996. *The Rise of Christianity*. San Francisco: Harper.

———. 1999. "Secularization, RIP." *Sociology of Religion* 60 (3): 249–73.

Stark, Rodney, and William Sims Bainbridge. 1985. *The Future of Religion: Secularization, Revival, and Cult Formation*. Berkeley: University of California Press.

———. 1986. *A Theory of Religion*. New Brunswick, NJ: Rutgers University Press.

Stark, Rodney, and Roger Finke. 2000. *Acts of Faith: Explaining the Human Side of Religion.* Berkeley: University of California Press.

———. 2002. "Beyond Church and Sect: Dynamics and Stability in Religious Economics." In *Sacred Markets, Sacred Canopies,* edited by Ted Jelen, 31–62. Lanham, MD: Rowman and Littlefield.

Stark, Rodney, and Laurence R. Iannaccone. 1994. "A Supply-Side Reinterpretation of the 'Secularization' of Europe." *Journal for the Scientific Study of Religion* 33 (3): 230–52.

Staton, Jeffrey. 2010. *Judicial Power and Strategic Communication in Mexico.* Cambridge: Cambridge University Press.

Stefelic, Marko. 2005. "Learning Curves." *Transitions Online* (March 24).

Steinfels, Peter. 2007. "Roman Catholics and American Politics, 1960–2004." In *Religion and American Politics,* edited by Mark Noll and Luke Harlow, 345–66. New York: Oxford University Press.

Straughn, Jeremy Brooke, and Scott Feld. 2010. "America as a Christian Nation? Understanding Religious Boundaries of National Identity in the United States." *Sociology of Religion* 71 (3): 280–306.

Strøm, Kaare, Wolfgang C. Müller, and Daniel Markham Smith. 2010. "Parliamentary Control of Coalition Governments," *Annual Review of Political Science* 13: 517–35.

Sullivan, Andrew. 1998. "Going Down Screaming." Editorial, *New York Times,* October 11, 1998.

Swaan, Abram de. 1988. *In Care of the State: Health Care, Education, and Welfare in Europe and the USA in the Modern Era.* New York: Oxford University Press.

Swartz, David. 2012. *Moral Minority: The Evangelical Left in an Age of Conservatism.* Philadelphia: University of Pennsylvania Press.

Swatos, William, and Kevin Christiano. 1999. "Introduction—Secularization Theory: The Course of a Concept." *Sociology of Religion* 60 (3): 209–28.

Swierenga, Robert. 2007. "Ethnoreligious Political Behavior in the Mid-Nineteenth Century." In *Religion and American Politics,* edited by Mark Noll and Luke Harlow, 145–68. New York: Oxford University Press.

———. 2009. "Religion and American Voting Behavior." In *Oxford Handbook of Religion and American Politics,* 69–94. New York: Oxford University Press.

Tancerova, Barbora. 2002. "State vs. Church?" *Transitions Online* (September 20).

———. 2003. "Catholic Yet Liberal?" *Transitions Online* (September 11).

Tatalovich, Raymond. 1997. *The Politics of Abortion in the United States and Canada.* Armonk, NY: M. E. Sharpe.

Taylor, Charles. 2007. *A Secular Age.* Cambridge, MA: Belknap Press of Harvard University Press.

Taylor, Lawrence. 1995. *Occasions of Faith: An Anthropology of Irish Catholics.* Philadelphia: University of Pennsylvania Press.

———. 2007. "Crisis of Faith or Collapse of Empire?" In *The Church Confronts Modernity,* edited by Leslie Woodcock Tentler, 150–73. Washington, DC: Catholic University Press.

Tentler, Leslie Woodcock, ed. 2007. *The Church Confronts Modernity*. Washington, DC: Catholic University Press.

Thavis, John. 2004. "Political Priorities: In Catholic Italy, Abortion Is Not a Big Issue." Catholic News Service, October 15. Available at http://www.catholic news.com/data/stories/cns/0405680.htm.

Thomas, George M. 1989. *Revivalism and Cultural Change*. Chicago: University of Chicago Press.

Thomas, R. Murray. 2006. *Religion in Schools: Controversies around the World*. Westport, CT: Praeger.

———. 2007. *God in the Classroom*. Westport, CT: Praeger.

Thomas, Scott. 2005. *Global Resurgence of Religion and the Transformation of International Relations*. New York: Palgrave Macmillan.

Tietze, Christopher, Jacqueline Darroch Forrest, and Stanley Henshaw. 1988. "United States." In *International Handbook on Abortion*, edited by Paul Sachdev, 473–94. New York: Greenwood Press.

Titley, E. Brian. 1983. *Church, State, and the Control of Schooling in Ireland, 1900–1944*. Kingston and Montreal: McGill-Queen's University Press.

Tomasevich, Jozo. 2001. *War and Revolution in Yugoslavia: 1941–1945*. Stanford, CA: Stanford University Press.

Torańska, Teresa. 1994. *My*. Warsaw: MOST.

Trejo, Guillermo. "Religious Competition and Ethnic Mobilization in Latin America: Why the Catholic Church Promotes Indigenous Movements in Mexico." *American Political Science Review* 103 (3): 323–42.

Trudeau, Pierre Elliott. 1993. *Memoirs*. Toronto: McLelland and Stewart.

Tuns, Paul. 2003. "Religious, Pro-Family Groups Launch Legal Battle against Same-Sex 'Marriage.'" The Interim, August 4. http://bit.ly/xAMuez, accessed January 9, 2013.

Turowicz, Jerzy. 1990. *Kościół nie jest łodzią podwodną: (wybór publicystyki z lat 1964–1987)*. Kraków: Znak.

United Nations Population Division, Department of Economic and Social Affairs. 2002. *Abortion Policies: A Global Review*. Available at http://www.un.org/esa /population/publications/abortion/profiles.htm, accessed March 6, 2013.

Vardys, Stanley, and Judith B. Sedaitis. 1997. *Lithuania: The Rebel Nation*. Boulder, CO: Westview Press.

Vedantam, Shankar. 2010. "Walking Santa, Talking Christ." slate.com, December 22. http://www.slate.com/id/2278923/, accessed January 5, 2011.

Vezic, Goran. 2002. "Croatia: Priests Flex Their Muscles." Institute for War and Peace Reporting. http://iwpr.net/report-news/croatia-priests-flex-their-muscles, accessed May 22, 2014.

Viklund, Andrea. 2007 "Canada Divorce Act Section 21.1: Removal of Barriers to Religious Remarriage." *Ottawa Divorce*. http://bit.ly/ydPDbs, accessed 5 April 2012.

Voas, David, Daniel Olson, and Alasdair Crocket. 2002. "Religious Pluralism and Participation: Why Previous Research Is Wrong." *American Sociological Review* 67: 212–30.

Voicu, Malina. 2011. "Effect of Nationalism on Religiosity in 30 European Countries." *European Sociological Review* 28 (3): 1–11.

Wagner, Michael. 2007. "Not without a Fight: The History of the Pro-Life Movement in Canada." *Reformed Perspective*. November 12. http://reformed perspective.ca/index.php/resources/53-canadian-pro-life-history?catid=43%3Aall -you-need-to-know-to-stand-up-for-the-unborn-and-elderly, accessed March 12, 2013.

Wald, Kenneth, Adam Silverman, and Kevin Fridy. 2005. "Making Sense of Religion in Political Life." *Annual Reviews of Political Science* 8: 121–43.

Wall, Sally, Irene Hanson Frieze, Anuska Ferligoj, Eva Jarosova, Daniela Pauknerova, Jasna Horvat, and Natasa Sarlij. 1999. "Gender Role and Religion as Predictors of Attitude towards Abortion in Croatia, Slovenia, the Czech Republic, and the United States." *Journal of Cross-Cultural Psychology* 30: 443–65.

Wall, Wendy. 2008. *Inventing the "American Way": The Politics of Consensus from the New Deal to the Civil Rights Movement*. New York: Oxford University Press.

Waniek, Danuta. 2011. *Orzeł i krucyfiks: Eseje o podziałach politycznych w Polsce*. Warsaw: Wydawnictwo Adam Marszałek.

Wanrooiji, B.P.F. 2004. "The Italian Republic." The Continuum Complete International Encyclopedia of Sexuality. The Kinsey Institute: 620–35. December 20, 2011. http://www.iub.edu/~kinsey/ccies/it.php#unconvent.

Warner, Carolyn. 2000. *Confessions of an Interest Group*. Princeton, NJ: Princeton University Press.

Warner, Stephen. 2002. "More Progress on the New Paradigm." In *Sacred Markets, Sacred Canopies*, edited by Ted Jelen, 1–29. Lanham, MD: Rowman and Littlefield.

Warner, Carolyn. 2013. "Christian Democracy in Italy: An Alternative Path to Religious Party Moderation." *Party Politics* 19 (2): 256–76.

Waters, John. 1997. *An Intelligent Person's Guide to Modern Ireland*. London: Duckworth.

Weber, Eugen. 1976. *Peasants into Frenchmen*. Palo Alto, CA: Stanford University Press.

Weigel, George. 1999. "Roman Catholicism in the Age of John Paul II." In *The Desecularization of the World*, edited by Peter Berger. Washington, DC: Ethics and Public Policy Center.

Weisz, Howard R. 1976. *Irish-American and Italian-American Educational Views and Activities, 1870–1900*. New York: Arno Press.

Wertz, Dorothy. 2002. "Embryo and Stem Cell Research in the United States: History and Politics." *Gene Therapy* 9: 674–78.

Westfall, William. 2001. "Constructing Public Religion at Private Sites: the Anglican Church in the Shadow of Disestablishment." In *Religion and Public Life in Canada*, edited by Marguerite Van Die, 23–49. Toronto: University of Toronto Press.

Westhues, Kenneth, 1978. "Stars and Stripes, the Maple Leaf, and the Papal Coat of Arms." *Canadian Journal of Sociology* 3 (2): 245–61.

Wetstein, Matthew, and Robert Albritton. 1995, "Effects of Public Opinion on Abortion Policies and Use in the American States." *Publius: Journal of Federalism* 25 (4): 91–105.

Whyte, John. 1971. *Church and State in Modern Ireland, 1923–1970*. Dublin: Gill and Macmillan.

———. 1981. *Catholics in Western Democracies*. New York: St. Martin's Press.

Wigura, Karolina. 2013. "Alternative Historical Narrative: 'Polish Bishops' Appeal to Their German Colleagues' of 18 November 1965." *East European Politics and Societies* 27: 400–412.

Wildavsky, Aaron. 1987. "Choosing Preferences by Constructing Institutions: A Cultural Theory of Preference Formation." *American Political Science Review* 81 (1): 4–21.

Williams, Daniel K. 2010. *God's Own Party*. New York: Oxford University Press.

Wills, Garry. 2007. *Head and Heart: American Christianities*. New York: Penguin.

Wilson, James Q. 1995. *Political Organization*. Princeton, NJ: Princeton University Press.

Wittenberg, Jason. 2006. *Crucibles of Political Loyalty*. Cambridge: Cambridge University Press.

Woodberry, Robert. 2011. "Religion and the Spread of Human Capital and Political Institutions." In *The Oxford Handbook of the Economics of Religion*, edited by Rachel McCleary. New York: Oxford University Press.

Woodberry, Robert, and Timothy Shah. 2004. "The Pioneering Protestants." *Journal of Democracy* 15 (2): 47–61.

Wurfel, David. 1977. "Martial Law in the Philippines: The Methods of Regime Survival." *Pacific Affairs* 50 (1): 5–30.

Youngblood, Robert L. 1978. "Church Opposition to Martial Law in the Philippines." *Asian Survey* 18 (5): 505–20.

Zajović, Staša, and Lino Veljak. 2011. "Tendencies of De-Secularisation in Serbia and Croatia." *Women Living under Muslim Laws*. Dossier 30–31, July.

Zampaglione, Gerardo. 1956. *Italy*. New York: Praeger.

Zrinščak, Siniša. 2001. "Religion and Social Justice in Post-Communist Croatia." In *Religion and Social Change in Post-Communist Europe*, edited by Irena Borowik and Miklós Tomka, 181–94. Kraków: NOMOS.

Zelizer, Julian. 2004. *On Capitol Hill: The Struggle for Reform Congress and Its Consequences, 1948–2000*. New York: Cambridge University Press.

Zhao, Xinshu, John G. Lynch Jr., and Qimei Chen. 2010. "Reconsidering Baron and Kenny: Myths and Truths about Mediation Analysis." *Journal of Consumer Research* 37 (2): 197–206.

Zubrzycki, Geneviève. 2006. *The Crosses of Auschwitz*. Chicago: University of Chicago Press.

———. 2013. "Aesthetic Revolt and the Remaking of National Identity in Québec, 1960–1969." *Theory and Society* 42: 423–75.

Index

Abele, 111n263
Abington School District v. Schempp, 265
abortion: 1, 3–4, 44–45, 55–57, 63–64, 332n10; Catholic church views on, 19n19, 32, 56–7, 80, 147, 163, 172, 256, 259–61, 314, 331; in Canada, 2, 297–98, 300, 308, 311–16; in Croatia, 3, 187, 194, 201, 208, 213, 217–20, 225; Evangelical Protestant views on, 56–57, 241n69, 256–57, 260, 273, 301, 315, 323, 331; illegal, 131, 134, 255, 312–13; in Ireland, 44, 65, 71, 73, 81–82, 86–92, 99–100; in Italy, 44, 63, 119–20, 131–36; laws regarding 8, 73, 81–82, 87–88, 90, 119, 131, 133–35, 148, 171–72, 175–76, 217–18, 222n384, 244, 262–64, 277, 312–13, 375; late-term 261–62; public opinion regarding, 41, 44–45, 132, 174, 187, 218, 241n69, 258–59, 289; rates of, 1, 56n103, 131, 132, 134, 136n294, 172, 177, 255, 259n176, 260n178, 276; in Poland, 1–2, 32, 148, 154, 159, 171–77, 178–79, 180, 85, 187; referenda on, 44, 65, 80n109, 81–83, 89, 91, 94, 104, 105–6, 119, 132, 174; and stem cell research, 279–81; in the United States, 45, 242, 244–46, 252, 255–65, 270n225, 276. *See also* contraception; *Griswold v Connecticut*; Halappanavar, Savita; *Humanae Vitae*; Morgentaler, Henry; *Planned Parenthood of Southeastern Pennsylvania v. Casey*; *Roe v. Wade*; *Tremblay v. Daigle*; *Webster v. Reproductive Health Services*; "X case"
Act of the Union (Ireland), 67

Ad Hoc Working Group on Stem Cell Research, 318
Adolescent Family Life Act (AFLA), 270
adultery, 105, 272, 274, 289, 307–8
Advisory Committee for Religious Freedom, 120n323
affiliation, religious, 18, 24, 45, 60, 340; in Canada, 259; as a measure of religiosity, 361; in United States, 259. *See also* monopoly, religious
Affordable Care Act, 262
Ahern, Bertie, 99, 102, 104
Ahern, Dermot, 99
Akcja Wyborcza Solidarność (AWS), 167
All-Party Oireachtas Committee on the Constitution, 90
Americans for Prosperity (AFP), 281n271
Anglo-Irish Treaty, 1921, 72n51
Anni di Piombo (Years of Lead), 119
Anti-Divorce Campaign (ADC), 94
Antinori, Dr. Severino, 136–37
anti-slavery movement, 240
Aquino, Benigno, 331n7
Aquino, Cory (Corazon), 331n7
Arcigay, 140
Argentina, 48, 330n5, 332
Assisted Human Reproduction Canada (AHRC), 318
assisted reproduction technologies (ART), 99–100, 165, 175, 177–80, 186, 213, 220–21, 247, 273, 275–76, 281–83, 316, 320, 331
l'Association d'Église Baptistes Évangéliques, 323
Associazioni Cristiane Lavoratori Italiani (ACLI), 111n263, 118
attendance, religious, 34n50, 340; in Canada, 3, 301; in Ireland, 66, 106;

420 • Index